Perspectives on Modern South Asia

Global Perspectives

In a time of ever increasing global phenomena, the series *Global Perspectives* offers regionally focused volumes that attempt to move beyond the standard regional studies model. Each volume includes a selection of previously published articles and an extensive introduction by the volume editor, providing an overview of the history and cultures of the region under discussion. The articles are chosen to illustrate the dynamic processes by and through which scholars have described and understood regional history and culture, and to show how profoundly the ethnography of each region has influenced the direction and development of anthropological and social theory. The *Global Perspectives* series thus furnishes readers with both an introduction to the cultures of a vast array of world regions, and a history of how those cultures have been perceived and interpreted. The contributors include anthropologists, historians, philosophers, and critics. Collectively they show the multiplicities of voice in regional studies, and reveal the interpenetration of ideas and concepts within and across disciplines, regions, and historical periods.

Published

1. *Perspectives on Africa: A Reader in Culture, History, and Representation, 2ⁿᵈ Edition*, edited and introduced by Roy Richard Grinker, Stephen C. Lubkemann, and Christopher B. Steiner

2. *Perspectives on Las Américas: A Reader in Culture, History, and Representation*, edited and introduced by Matthew C. Gutmann, Félix V. Matos Rodríguez, Lynn Stephen, and Patricia Zavella

3. *Perspectives on the Caribbean: A Reader in Culture, History, and Representation*, edited and introduced by Philip Scher

4. *Perspectives on Modern South Asia: A Reader in Culture, History, and Representation*, edited by Kamala Visweswaran

EDITED AND INTRODUCED BY KAMALA VISWESWARAN

perspectives on
Modern
South Asia

A Reader in Culture, History, and Representation

WILEY-BLACKWELL

A John Wiley & Sons, Inc. Publications

This edition first published 2011
Editorial material and organization © 2011 Blackwell Publishing Ltd.

Blackwell Publishing was acquired by John Wiley & Sons in February 2007. Blackwell's publishing program has been merged with Wiley's global Scientific, Technical, and Medical business to form Wiley-Blackwell.

Registered Office: John Wiley & Sons Ltd, The Atrium, Southern Gate, Chichester, West Sussex, PO19 8SQ, United Kingdom

Editorial Offices: 350 Main Street, Malden, MA 02148-5020, USA
9600 Garsington Road, Oxford, OX4 2DQ, UK
The Atrium, Southern Gate, Chichester, West Sussex, PO19 8SQ, UK

For details of our global editorial offices, for customer services, and for information about how to apply for permission to reuse the copyright material in this book please see our website at www.wiley.com/wiley-blackwell.

The right of Kamala Visweswaran to be identified as the author of the editorial material in this work has been asserted in accordance with the UK Copyright, Designs and Patents Act 1988.

Wiley also publishes its books in a variety of electronic formats. Some content that appears in print may not be available in electronic books.

Designations used by companies to distinguish their products are often claimed as trademarks. All brand names and product names used in this book are trade names, service marks, trademarks or registered trademarks of their respective owners. The publisher is not associated with any product or vendor mentioned in this book. This publication is designed to provide accurate and authoritative information in regard to the subject matter covered. It is sold on the understanding that the publisher is not engaged in rendering professional services. If professional advice or other expert assistance is required, the services of a competent professional should be sought.

Library of Congress Cataloging-in-Publication Data

Perspectives on modern South Asia : a reader in culture, history, and representation / edited and introduced by Kamala Visweswaran.
p. cm. – (Global perspectives ; 6)
Includes bibliographical references and index.
ISBN 978-1-4051-0062-5 (hardback) – ISBN 978-1-4051-0063-2 (pbk.)
1. South Asia – Civilization. 2. South Asia – Social conditions. 3. Group identity – South Asia.
4. Ethnicity – South Asia. I. Visweswaran, Kamala.
DS339P48 2011
954 – dc22
2011001517

A catalogue record for this book is available from the British Library.

Set in 9.5/11.5pt Times by Laserwords Private Limited, Chennai, India.
Printed in Singapore by Ho Printing Singapore Pte Ltd

1 2011

Contents

Acknowledgments

I would like to thank Akbar Hyder and Zia Mian for their suggestions and contributions to this volume; also Linda Hess and the anonymous Blackwell's reviewers of the volume for their ideas and recommendations. I am indebted to Leela Tanikella who assembled many of the materials for the reader, and to Raja Visweswaran for editorial suggestions. I am grateful for permission to reprint excerpted versions of the essays. I also thank Dhanya Ramesh and her team at Laserwords, Chennai for their meticulous shepherding of the volume through press.

Acknowledgment of Sources

Figure 1: "Languages of South Asia by Numbers of Speakers," from *Cambridge Encyclopedia of India*, p. 403. Cambridge University Press, 1989.

Map 1: "Principle Languages of South Asia," from *Cambridge Encyclopedia of India*, p. 404. Cambridge University Press, 1989.

Maps 2 and 3: "Village Endogamy Norms/Close Kin Marriage Norms" and "Purdah Practices," from Bina Aggarwal, *A Field of One's Own: Gender and Land Rights in South Asia,* pp. 372–3. Cambridge University Press, 1996.

Map 4: "Partition of India," from Karl Schmidt, *An Atlas and Survey of South Asian History,* p. 83. Armonk, NY: M.E. Sharpe, 1995.

Rizwan A. Ahmed, "The State and National Foundation in the Maldives," *Cultural Dynamics,* 13(3): pp. 294–6, 298–9, 299–301, 313–14, 2001.

Hamza Alavi, "The Politics of Ethnicity in India and Pakistan" from *South Asia.* Hamza Alavi and John Harriss (eds), pp. 222–4, 225–35, 238–45, last para 246. New York: Monthly Review Press, 1989.

Tashi Choden. "Indo-Bhutan Relations: Recent Trends," *Journal of Bhutan Studies,* pp. 112–19, 122–3, 126–7, 2002.

Bernard Cohn. "Notes on the History of the Study of Indian Society and Culture," from *An Anthropologist Among the Historians,* pp. 137–62, 164–71. Delhi: Oxford University Press, 1987.

Shobha Gautam, Amrita Banskota and Rita Manchanda, "Where There are no Men: Women in the Maoist Insurgency in Nepal" from *Women, War and Peace in South Asia,* pp. 214–24, 238–43, 248–51. Delhi: Sage, 2001.

Arjun Guneratne, "What's in a Name? Aryans and Dravidians in the Making of Sri Lankan Identities" from *In The Hybrid Island.* Neluka Silva (ed.), pp. 20–35, 37–40. New York: Zed, 2002.

Gopal Guru and Anuradha Chakravarty, "Who Are the Country's Poor? Social Movement Politics and Dalit Poverty" from *Social Movements in India.* Raka Ray and Mary Katzenstein (eds), pp. 135–42, 145–53. 2004.

Sandya Hewamanne, "City of Whores': Nationalism, Development, and Global Garment Workers in Sri Lanka,' *Social Text,* 26(295): pp. 35–8, 39–44, 48–9, 56–9. 2008.

Syed Akbar Hyder, "Towards a Composite Reading of South Asian Religious Cultures: The Case of Islam" revised version of "Contemplating the Divine" from *Speaking Truth to Power Religion Caste, and the Subaltern Question in India,* Manu Bhagavan and Anne Feldhaus (eds). Delhi: Oxford University Press, 2008.

Kancha Iliah. 1996. "Hindu Gods and Us: Our Goddesses and the Hindus" from *Why I am Not Hindu.* Calcutta: Samya, pp. 71–81, 87–96. 1996.

Naila Kabeer, "The Quest for National Identity: Women, Islam, and the State in Bangladesh" from *Women, State and Islam,* Deniz Kadyoti (ed.), pp. 116–28, 131–8, 140–3. Temple University Press, 1987.

Lamia Karim, "Politics of the Poor? NGOs and Grass-roots Political Mobilization in Bangladesh,' *Polar.* 24(1): pp. 94–104, 106–7. 2001.

Nighat Said Khan, "Identity, Violence, and Women: A Reflection on the Partition of India 1947" from *Perspectives on Women and Multiple Identities,* N. Khan, Rubina Saighol and Afiya Sherbano Zia (eds), pp. 157–65. Lahore: ASR Publications, 1994.

Radha Kumar, "From Chipko to Sati: The Contemporary Women's Movement in India" from *Gender and Politics in India,* Nivedita Menon (ed.), pp. 60–86. Delhi, Oxford University Press, 1999.

David Ludden, "Development Regimes in South Asia," *Economic and Political Weekly.* September 10, pp. 2–23, 29–30. 2005.

Shail Mayaram, "Beyond Ethnicity: Being Hindu and Muslim in South Asia" from *Lived Islam in South Asia: Adaptation, Accommodation and Conflict,* Imtiaz Ahmad and Helmut Reifeld (eds), pp. 19–25, 30–3, 37–9. Delhi: Social Science Press, 2004.

Ritu Menon and Kamla Bhasin, "Abducted Women, the State, and Questions of Honour: Three Perspectives on the Recovery Operation in Post-Partition India" from *Embodied Violence,* Kumari Jayawardene and Malathi de Alwis (eds), pp. 1–22, 30–1. Delhi: Kali for Women Press, 1997.

Zia Mian, "Pakistan's Fateful Nuclear Option" from *Out of the Nuclear Shadow,* Smithu Kothari and Zia Mian (eds), pp. 101, 103–15. 2001.

Pankaj Mishra, "Ayodhya: the Modernity of Hinduism" from *Temptations of the West. How to be Modern in India, Pakistan, Tibet, and Beyond,* pp. 80–96, 105–6, 108–12. New York: Farrar, Straus & Giroux.

Valentine M. Moghadam, "Nationalist Agendas and Women's Rights: Conflicts in Afghanistan in the Twentieth Century" from *Feminist Nationalism.* Lois West (ed.), pp. 75–7, 81–90, 97–9. New York: Routledge, 1997.

Vasudha Narayanan, "Tolerant Hinduism: Shared Ritual Spaces – Hindus and Muslims at the Shrine of Shahul Hamid" from *The Life of Hinduism,* John Hawley and Vasudha Narayanan (eds), pp. 266–70. Berkeley: University of California Press, 2006.

Chitraroopa Palit, "Monsoon Risings: Mega-Dam Resistance in the Narmada Valley," *New Left Review.* no. 21, pp. 82–100. 2003.

Rajendra Pradhan, "Ethnicity, Caste, and a Pluralist Society" from *The State of Nepal,* Kanak Mani Dixit and Shastri Ramachandran (eds), pp. 1–21. Kathmandu: Himal Books, 2002.

Darini Rajasingham-Senanayake, "Identity on the Borderline: Modernity, New Ethnicities, and the Unmaking of Multiculturalism in Sri Lanka" from *The Hybrid Island,* Neluka Silva (ed.), pp. 46–53, 55–62, 68–70. New York: Zed, 2002.

Shahnaz Rouse, "Women's Movement in Pakistan: State, Class and Gender," *South Asia Bulletin.* VI(1): pp. 32–35, 37. 1986.

Amartya Sen, "Radical Needs and Moderate Reforms" from *Indian Development: Selected Regional Perspectives,* pp. 1–11, 13–25, 27–32. Delhi: Oxford University Press, 1996.

Nazif M. Shahrani, "War, Factionalism, and the State in Afghanistan," *American Anthropologist.* 104(3): pp. 715–20. 2002.

M.N. Srinivas, "A Note on Sanskritization and Westernization" from *Caste in Modern India,* pp. 42–52, 54–5. Bombay; MPP, 1962.

Seira Tamang, "The Politics of 'Developing Nepali Women'" from *The State of Nepal,* Kanak Mani Dixit and Shastri Ramachandran (eds), pp. 161–75. Kathmandu: Himal Books, 2002.

Stanley J. Tambiah, Presidential address. "Reflections on Communal Violence in South Asia," *Journal of Asian Studies.* Nov 1990, 49(4): pp. 741–9, 752, 757–9. 1990.

Achin Vanaik, "Developing the Anti-Nuclear Movement," *Economic and Political Weekly.* May 5–11, pp. 1–3, 4. 2001.

Introduction

Reconceptualizing Nation and Region in Modern South Asia

Kamala Visweswaran

I. Histories, Areas, Politics

'Modern' South Asia refers to the emergence of the modern nation states of India (1947), Pakistan (1947), Sri Lanka (1948), Bangladesh (1971), and of the transformations of the monarchies of Afghanistan, Bhutan, Maldives, and Nepal into modern republics. These eight countries share common cultures, languages, and religions, in spite of national differences.

This is an interdisciplinary reader that draws from literary/cultural studies, history, anthropology/sociology, economics, and political science to introduce students to the major themes and concepts that aid in understanding the complexity of modern South Asia. As such, it can neither cover any of the countries of South Asia in full detail, nor can it attend to the depth of *pre-modern* South Asia – a central part of the Indian Ocean trade with shared historic connections to the Middle East, Africa, China, and Southeast Asia. In recent years, debates about pre-modern South Asia have been contentious, often influencing and impacting our understanding of modern South Asia, even as the notion of 'modernity' itself demarcates what we take to be the 'past' and is the only lens we have available to study it. Two of the central debates about pre-colonial South Asia concern plurality and the mutability of pre-modern social and religious formations, and the impact colonialism has had upon social structure and identity – themes addressed in Parts I and II of the reader.

In one sense, 'culture' in all its resilient and multiple guises is the greatest strength of the South Asian region: it is flexible, inclusive, hybrid, and ever-changing. In another sense, 'culture' is its biggest problem: it is mobilized by interest groups, from the smallest local level of the village to the largest level of the nation-state, to divide and differentiate between people,

Perspectives on Modern South Asia: A Reader in Culture, History, and Representation, First Edition.
Edited by Kamala Visweswaran.
© 2011 Blackwell Publishing Ltd. Published 2011 by Blackwell Publishing Ltd.

sometimes with devastating results. From an anthropological perspective, there are no 'pure' cultures. The history of the South Asian region (and indeed, of the world) is one of cultural mixing and change. It is the work of nationalism – ethnic, racial, linguistic, or religious – to transform the creative and accommodative flow of cultures into static or rigid ideas of cultural purity and exclusion. In South Asia (and elsewhere), these forms of nationalism are frequently violent and seek to expunge from the social record the evidence of simple neighborliness. Parts II–IV of this reader explore the tension between the lived experience of cultural (or religious) tolerance (as not only *respect for*, but *interest in* difference), and the deployment of culture or religion for nationalist purposes. While the emergence of different kinds of nationalism in South Asia has led to reification or hardening of identities, social and religious practices throughout the region transcend narrow community, regional, or political identities, becoming reservoirs of shared humanity and peaceful coexistence.

For historians, the emergence of 'modernity' in South Asia is contested, alternately seen to emerge with the consolidation of British territorial control after the Battle of Plassey in 1757, or in 1857, the year of the 'Sepoy Mutiny,' the first expression of Indian nationalist resistance to British colonization. Yet Afghanistan fought and won three wars against Britian – the last in 1919 – and was never formally colonized. Until recently, Nepal and Bhutan were also kingdoms. Thus, if our conception of modern South Asia was only of those countries that experienced direct British colonial rule, we would have to include Burma (a province of British-administered India until 1937; independent in 1948) and exclude Afghanistan, Nepal, and Bhutan, as well as the princely states. We would also miss the forms of colonial modernity that were shaped by Portuguese, Dutch, and French trade and intervention in South Asia.

We should better understand the shape and arrival of colonial modernity in South Asia as uneven, and as sometimes affected by developments outside either Europe or South Asia, or as traversing continents. For example, one trajectory of what is called 'Islamic modernity' – a coupling of reformist ideas within Islam with Western notions of progress – can be traced to the circulation of Jamal al-Din al-Afghani's writings through Iran, Afghanistan, India, Turkey, Egypt, and France. In a like vein, the presumption that India is a 'Hindu' country, might be seen more as an expression of something called 'Hindu modernity,' than as an outgrowth of ancient organically rooted Hindu communities. As Romila Thapar points out, the presumption of a strong 'inside' and 'outside' for the region did not exist in pre-modern times.[1] 'Hind' or 'Al-Hind' was simply the term Persians and Arabs used to describe the inhabitants of the land beyond the Sindhu/Indus River. There is some evidence of use of the term Hindu to designate religious identity in 15th century Shaiva and 16th century Vaishnava texts, but use of the term 'Hinduism' to designate a religious community was not widespread until the 19th century (under British colonialism).[2] The question of the nature and onset of modernity in South Asia – is it merely a reflection of European modernity, or are there 'alternate modernities' – has been an area of much recent debate and critique.[3]

As an analytic field, South Asian area studies first emerges as part of the legacy of European colonialism, whereby the study of 'Oriental' languages such as Sanskrit and Persian was undertaken to provide translations of religious, political, or legal texts for aiding in the administration of colonial rule. Perhaps the most important Orientalist legacy was the discovery of the Indo-European or Indo-Aryan language family in the 18th century. As early as the 15th century, European travelers to India had noticed similarities between Indian and European languages. In 1786, Sir William Jones, an official with the East India Company, and President of the Asiatic Society, theorized a relationship between Sanskrit, Latin, Greek, and English. Faced with the contradiction of a sophisticated language coupled with an apparently debased Hindu society, but also ancestrally linked to a self-evidently superior Western culture, Europeans developed an 'Aryan' racial theory to explain the decline of 'Aryan civilization' in India. It posited the period of composition of Sanskrit texts as a 'Golden age of Hinduism'[4] which had been destroyed by Muslim incursions into India, and which would be restored by British colonialism. The resulting division of South Asian history into ancient 'Hindu,' medieval 'Islamic,' and modern 'British' periods is thus a product of British colonialism, and points to the need to rethink current historical frames.

The discovery of the Dravidian family of languages by the missionary Robert Caldwell in 1856 also fueled notions of a Dravidian racial theory, whereby the Dravidians were seen as the original inhabitants of the Indus Valley civilization who were pushed south by invading Aryans. Although Aryan racial theory was widely discredited after World War II, and repudiated by anthropological scholarship, ideas of Aryan supremacy and of Dravidian oppression at the hands of Aryan invaders still inform contemporary Indian and Sri Lankan politics in the guise of Hindu and Buddhist nationalism (discussed in Parts II and IV) and Dravidian nationalism (discussed in Parts I and II).

In its more recent form in post-war Europe and North America, area studies are a product of the Cold War between the (Soviet) East and the West. Between 1945 and 1968 alone, sixty-six countries achieved independence, and were expected to align with one of the great powers. The idea that these newly independent nations, many of them influenced by socialism throughout the course of their anti-colonial struggles, would tilt the world balance of power in favor of the Soviet Union and communism, precipitated forms of US interventionism whose legacy of division and strife is all too present today.

Yet, shared political processes have also forged links and solidarities between the countries of South Asia, as we will see in Parts V and VI. Among these forged links, the history of socialism in the region is perhaps the most important. Like many Indian nationalists, India's first Prime Minister, Jawaharlal Nehru, was favorably impressed by the Russian revolution of 1917. India's emergence as the region's first electoral democracy was also accompanied by the development of communist and socialist parties during the era of anti-colonial nationalism in the region. In India there have been stable, long-term, elected communist governments in Kerala and West Bengal. As a result, as Jean Dréze and Amartya Sen suggest, there is a much higher quality of life and educational achievement in these two states.[5]

The 1970s were particularly important for the consolidation of state socialism in South Asia. Zulfikar Bhutto, as Prime Minister of Pakistan from 1970 to 1977 and leader of the Pakistan People's Party, propounded a form of 'Islamic Socialism' that declared 'Islam is our faith, democracy our politics, socialism our economy, power to the people.' In 1972, Sheikh Mujibur Rehman, leader of the Awami League and first Prime Minister of Bangladesh, declared 'Nationalism, Socialism, Democracy, and Secularism' to be the four pillars of the new state's constitution. The period of 1973 until 1979 when the Soviets intervened was also a period of independent but politically turbulent socialist governance in Afghanistan. A 1976 amendment to the Indian Constitution declared it to be a 'Sovereign, Socialist, Secular, and Democratic Republic.'[6] Similarly, the 1978 Sri Lankan Constitution declares that Sri Lanka shall be known as 'a free, Sovereign, Independent and Democratic Socialist Republic.'[7] The recent (2008) electoral victory of the Maoists in Nepal will likely also see socialist principles embedded in Nepal's new constitution.

India attempted to forge a third way through the first and second world blocs of the Cold War by helping to form a Non-Aligned Movement of mostly third world countries with meetings in Bandung (Indonesia) in 1955 and in Belgrade (Yugoslavia) in 1961. The United States, however, reacted strongly to India's friendship with the Soviet Union, sending its first military aid package to Pakistan in the guise of a 'mutual defense assistance agreement' a year after martial law was declared (in the Punjab) in 1953. Over the succeeding decades, it supported a series of military coups in the country as a bulwark against Soviet-leaning India. The United States thus sought to extend its sphere of influence in South Asia by installing pro-US governments in Pakistan and Bangladesh as part of an Indian containment strategy. It supported the coup of General Zia ul-Huq in 1977 which resulted in the death of Bhutto in Pakistan; it was also implicated in the CIA-backed military coup in Bangladesh that brought General Zia ur-Rehman to power in 1975, and resulted in the assassination of Sheikh Mujib.[8] Later, the United States would use Pakistan as a base to launch CIA-backed incursions of so-called 'freedom-fighters' or 'mujahideen' into Afghanistan to provoke a Soviet invasion and occupation of the country.[9]

The 'blowback' effects of the Cold War in South Asia have in turn contributed to the emergence of forms of militant Islam that have emerged in Afghanistan, Pakistan, Bangladesh, and the Middle East.[10] These extremist forms of Islam, however, may be more directly tied to the history of US intervention in South Asia than to dynamics internal to Islam itself. The history of Cold War politics in South Asia has also had the effect of relocating Afghanistan in South Asian Studies.

Thus, even a cursory examination of recent geopolitical alignments reveals the relative arbitrariness with which region and state have been studied in South Asia. Afghanistan is often studied with Central Asia or the Middle-East, yet the Indus valley civilization and its trading centers may have reached as far north as parts of modern day Afghanistan and as far south as Bombay, India. By one route, Buddhism travelled out of South Asia through Afghanistan's Hind Kush; centuries later Islam travelled in through the same route. Trade through the Khyber Pass also brought Greeks and Central Asian peoples to South Asia, contributing to its unique cultural, linguistic, and religious heritage.

Similarly, Nepal is more often included in Himalayan Studies along with Ladakh (in Kashmir), Tibet, Bhutan, and the Indian states of Sikkim and Arunachal Pradesh. Yet Nepali is also recognized as an Indian official language in the Eighth Schedule of the Indian constitution, and many of the ethnic groups of Nepal's *terai* (or plains region) are contiguous with the ethnic and caste groupings in the Indian states of Uttar Pradesh and Bihar. Shared languages and ethnic groups, as well as a great deal of cross-border migration between Burma, Bangladesh, and India's northeastern states of Assam, Meghalaya, Tripura, Mizoram, Manipur, and Nagaland denote another sub-field of study. South India and Sri Lanka share common languages and kinship structures, constituting yet another sub-region.

II. Language, Kinship, Religion

Nearly half the population of South Asia speaks Hindi or Bengali (see Figure 1), yet the region is marked by extensive linguistic and cultural diversity. As a consequence, cultural practices and languages often transcend national borders. In India alone, there are twenty-two officially recognized languages included in the eighth schedule of the Indian constitution and several hundred dialects. Shared languages also cut across religious and national identification (See Map 1). While Dari is one of the official languages of Afghanistan, its second official language, Pashto, is also an Indo-Iranian language spoken in Pakistan. Urdu is the national language of Pakistan and Hindi is the national language of India, yet Hindustani, Urdu, Punjabi, Sindhi, Dogri, and Kashmiri are some of the Indo-Aryan languages[11] shared in common between Pakistan and India. Nepali, the national language of Nepal, is also the official language of the Indian State of Sikkim, and is widely spoken in Northeast India and Bhutan. Dzongka, the national language of Bhutan, and Tamang, one of the official languages of Nepal, are Tibetan languages, as are Bodo (an official language of Assam), Garo (an official language of Meghalaya), the various Naga languages of Nagaland, and Methei (the official language of the State of Manipur) – all of which are spoken in Northeast India. Khasi, the other official language of Meghalaya, and Santali, spoken by adivasi (or tribal) peoples in India, Nepal, and Bangladesh are Austro-Asiatic Languages. Bengali, or Bangla, which is spoken throughout North/Eastern India, is the official

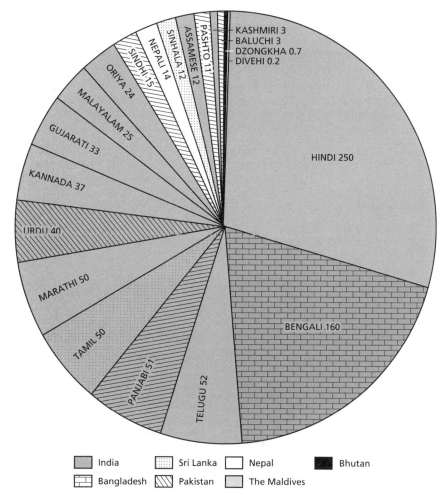

Figure 1 Languages of South Asia by numbers of speakers.
(Redrawn with permission)

language of West Bengal and Tripura and the national language of Bangladesh. Divehi, the State language of the Maldives is related to the Sinhala language, one of the official languages of Sri Lanka. Tamil, the other national language of Sri Lanka, is a Dravidian language also spoken in South India. Though Sinhala is an Indo-Aryan language related to Bengali, the Sinhala people share much more in common with Tamils who have lived in Sri Lanka for centuries, than with Bengalis in either India or Bangladesh. Geographic proximity has thus made South Asia a region of intense plurality as well as of composite cultures.

The languages of South Asia fall into four major language groups: Indo-European, Dravidian, Tibeto-Burmese, and Austro-Asiatic. Irwati Karve, one of the founders of social anthropology in India has pointed to distinct regional kinship systems that overlap with Indo-Aryan, Dravidian, and Mundari (or Austro-Asiatic) language families in the Northern, Southern and Eastern parts of South Asia respectively. She argues that South Asian kinship systems roughly fall into four different zones, Northern (including the Sindh, Punjab, and Kashmir in India/Pakistan,

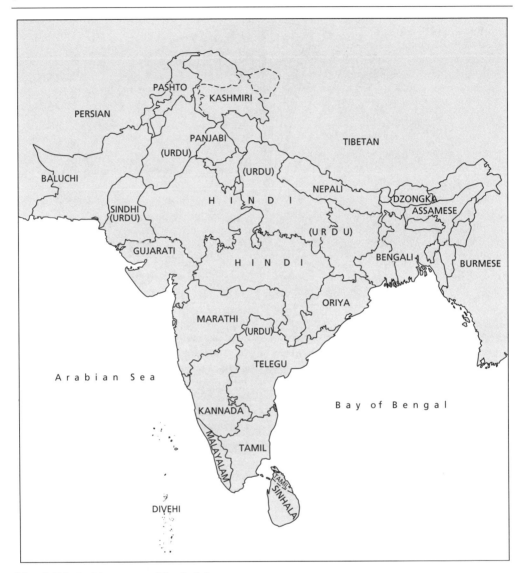

Map 1 Principal languages of South Asia.
(Redrawn with permission)

Uttar Pradesh, Madhya Pradesh, Bihar, Bengal, Assam in India, and Nepal), Central (including Maharasthra, Gujarat, Rajasthan, Madhya Pradesh, Orissa), Southern (including Andhra Pradesh, Karnataka, Kerala, and Tamil Nadu; as well as much of Sri Lanka) and Eastern (including Austro-Asiatic and Tibeto-Burmese language communities predominantly found along the Himalayan spine of the subcontinent).

Patrilineal descent, patrilocality, and dowry marriage are the norm throughout much of South Asia; however, matrilineal communities also exist in Sri Lanka, South and Northeast India, and the Himalayan region. Brideprice forms of marriage, which have historically been associated with the higher status of women, predominate among Muslim communities, lower caste and dalit (former untouchable) communities, and in the Eastern zone. While a high premium is placed on village exogamy for most communities in the Northern kinship zone, South Asian Muslims who follow a preference for parallel (or other) cousin marriage share something in common with Hindu communities of the Southern zone (and Sri Lanka) which practice forms of cross cousin marriage, because the preference is to marry the daughter within the family or village. These marriage patterns, which may also be linked to women's higher status and inheritance rights, can also be summarized by noting a tendency for village endogamy and close-kin marriages in Pakistan, Nepal, Sri Lanka, and in Southern and Northeast India (see Map 2). Purdah is common in Hindu communities of North India as well as in Afghanistan, Pakistan, and Bangladesh (see Map 3), but as M.N. Srinivas notes in his essay in this volume, the social process of Sanskritization, whereby low-ranked communities take on the beliefs and practices of high-ranked communities, can also result in the seclusion of Hindu women elsewhere.

Four of the countries of modern South Asia (Pakistan, Afghanistan, Bangladesh, and the Maldives) have Muslim majorities. The minority Indian Muslim population, combined with the populations of Pakistan and Bangladesh, makes South Asian Muslims the largest population of Muslims in the world.[12] Understanding this fact requires that we revisit the analytic frameworks that have been devised to describe normative Islamic thought and practice. How does our understanding of Islam change when we locate it in the hybrid and composite mixing of South Asian languages, cultures, and religions? West Bengalis who are predominately Hindu and Bangladeshis who are predominantly Muslim have shared culture, language, literary, and musical traditions. Muslim, Sikh, and Hindu Punjabis in India and Pakistan share a common language and religious practices, despite also having distinct religious traditions. While Islam is the state religion of Pakistan, Afghanistan, Bangladesh, and the Maldives, Islamic practices in these countries include Sunni, Shia, and several heterodox forms of Sufism or Amhadism that echo or draw from other religious practices of the subcontinent. Though Islam as a religion posits equality among believers, its proximity to Hinduism throughout many parts of South Asia has also led to incorporation of aspects of social ranking and status differentiation found in the caste system. The same is true of the relationship of Christianity to Hinduism in South Asia.

There are small Christian communities scattered throughout South Asia (in India they are less than 3% of the population), but the largest populations are found in Sri Lanka and in concentrated areas of Northeast India (where they are a majority population), as well as West, and South India (where the Syrian Christians of Kerala are the oldest community). In addition, historic Jewish communities are found in Cochin, Bombay, and Calcutta, while the Parsis or Zoroastrians are mostly found in Bombay and Gujarat. The Sikh religion, founded by Guru Nanak, is centered in the Punjab region of India and Pakistan, though after Partition, most Sikhs left West Punjab (Pakistan) to settle in East Punjab (India). Travel, migration, and displacement have led to the presence of these diasporic groups all over South Asia (as well as other parts of the world).

India and Nepal are predominantly Hindu countries, yet Hindus in India commonly visit Sufi shrines, and the dominant form of Hinduism practiced in Nepal is more influenced by (Tibetan) Buddhism. Nevertheless, substantial Hindu minorities also exist in Sri Lanka, Bhutan, and Bangladesh, while a much smaller number of Hindus remain in Pakistan. Buddhism, while it originated in India and spread throughout Southeast and East Asia, is today a majority religion of South Asia only in Bhutan and Sri Lanka. However, the notion of *ahmisa*, or non-violence,

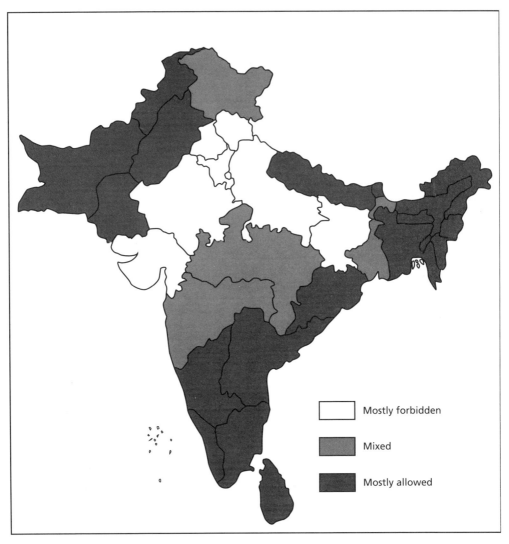

Map 2 Village endogamy norms/close kin marriage Norms: A comparative perspective.
(Redrawn with permission)

which originated in the Buddhist and Jain traditions, is a component of many forms of Hinduism. There are substantial Buddhist minorities in Ladakh (Kashmir) and along the Himalayan spine into the Northeastern India, as well as in Western India as a result of dalits following their leader B.R. Ambedkar's conversion to the faith.

When we study the history of nationalist movements in South Asia, we can see both that ethnic or linguistic separatism has marked post-independence politics in India, Pakistan, Bangladesh, and Sri Lanka, and that Hindu, Muslim, and Buddhist religious nationalism have been

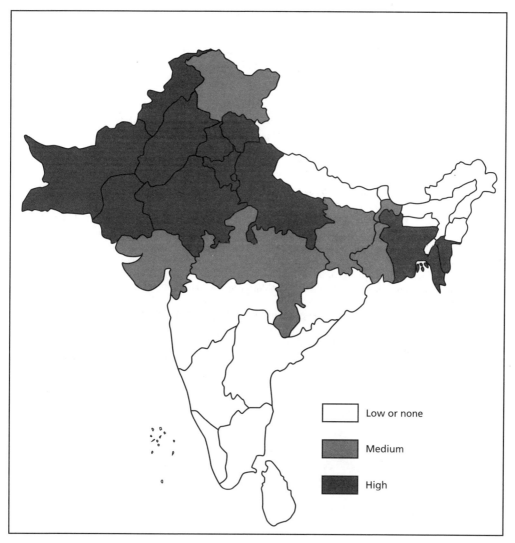

Map 3 Purdah practices: Tracing cross-regional diversities.
(Redrawn with permission)

particularly important in those countries. Class conflict also works its way through separatist and nationalist movements. Yet, when we understand the way gender has been deployed in such movements, we find many more similarities than differences. This volume thus attempts to integrate a feminist analysis into its understanding of the central dynamics that comprise South Asia as a cultural, political, and economic region.

Notes

1   Romila Thapar, *Early India: From the Origins to* AD *1300*. Berkeley: University of California Press, 2002.

2   See Gavin Flood (Ed.), *The Blackwell Companion to Hinduism*, p. 3. Malden, MA: Blackwell, 2005.

3   See for example, Dipesh Chakrabarty, "Postcoloniality and the Artifice of History," from *Provincializing Europe*, pp. 26–46. Chicago: University of Chicago Press, 2000.

4   Not all Sanskrit texts were religious in nature, for example Panini's grammar, composed in the 4th century, BCE.

5   See Jean Dréze and Amartya Sen, *India: Development and Participation*. Delhi: Oxford, 2001.

6   http://indiacode.nic.in/coiweb/coifiles/preamble.htm.

7   http://www.priu.gov.lk/Cons/1978Constitution/Chapter_01_Amd.html.

8   See Christopher Hitchens, "Bangladesh: One Genocide, One Coup, and One Assassination," from *The Trial of Henry Kissinger*, Chapter 4. London: Verso, 2001; also Lawrence Lifschultz, *Bangladesh: The Unfinished Revolution*. London: Zed Press, 1979; and Lawrence Lifschultz and Kai Bird, "Bangladesh: Anatomy of a Coup," *Economic and Political Weekly* 14(49) 1979, pp. 1999–2001, 2003–2014.

9   "The CIA's Intervention in Afghanistan, Interview with Zbigniew Brzezinski, President Jimmy Carter's National Security Adviser," *Le Nouvel Observateur,* Paris, 15–21 January 1998; published in English, Centre for Research on Globalisation, 5 October 2001, http://www.globalresearch.ca/articles/BRZ110A.html.

10 See Chalmers Johnson, *Blowback, the Costs and Consequences of American Empire*. Holt, 2004; and Ahmed Rashid, *Taliban: Militant Islam, Oil and Fundamentalism in Central Asia,* Yale University Press, 2000.

11 Many linguists still use the term 'Indo-Aryan' to designate this sub-family of the Indo-European languages; 'Indic' is also used to designate the sub-family.

12 Indonesia is the world's largest Muslim country, followed by Pakistan, and Bangladesh.

Part I

Debates about Origins: Pre/Modern Religious Pluralities in South Asia

Introduction

The central debates concerning the study of pre-modern South Asia are about plurality and the nature of social formation in pre-modern times, and the nature and significance of Vedic society for an understanding of contemporary South Asia. The impact colonialism has upon the analytic tools developed for understanding South Asia is also a major subject of debate. Two historic periods in particular have shaped debates about modern South Asian history.

The first and perhaps most contentious debate centers around the Indus Valley civilization and its decline, initially thought to be around 1500 BCE. Colonial scholarship first propounded the notion of an 'Aryan Invasion' that led to the end of Indus Valley civilization and emergence of 'Aryan civilization' described in the Rg Veda (dated to 1500 BCE or to the period of 1200 and 1000 BCE). While the more established dates now in use for the Indus Valley civilization are (2600–1900 BCE), early dating put the end of the Indus Valley civilization close to the date of the earliest known text, the Rg Veda, suggesting a connection between the decline of the Indus Valley civilization and coming of the Aryans. The existence of a Dravidian language, Brahui, still spoken by about two million people in modern Pakistan, has led Dravidian nationalists to theorize that Aryan 'invaders' pushed the true indigenous peoples, the Dravidian remnants of the Indus Valley, to the southern region of the subcontinent. While the current consensus is that there was probably a gradual migration of Central Asian or Aryan peoples into the Indian subcontinent over the centuries, Hindu nationalists (described in Part IV) have tried to argue that the Aryan society described in the Rg Veda is contemporaneous with the Indus Valley civilization, thus claiming that Aryans are 'indigenous' to the subcontinent. It should be noted here, that while both Hindu and Dravidian nationalists may lay claim to 19th century racial theories, Hindu nationalism is a hegemonic political force, and frequently uses violence to attain

Perspectives on Modern South Asia: A Reader in Culture, History, and Representation, First Edition.
Edited by Kamala Visweswaran.
© 2011 Blackwell Publishing Ltd. Published 2011 by Blackwell Publishing Ltd.

its goals; Dravidian nationalism, of the kind elaborated by Kancha Iliah in his essay, is neither hegemonic nor violent in its manifestation.

The second debate of importance about pre-modern history concerns the nature of Muslim rule in India. After the Crusades, the Christian west viewed Muslims as either invaders or despoilers of the peoples over whom they ruled. In the Orientalist view, Muslims had destroyed Hindu temples, and pushed Hinduism into decline by imposing conversion. As Syed Akbar Hyder points out in his essay, this view ignores the fact that Hindu rulers also sacked Hindu temples for wealth, and since there was no unified group of Muslims in India, but rather Turks, Persians, Arabs, and Afghans, there was as much conflict between groups of Muslims as between Muslims and others. It also ignores the collaborative and plural forms of governance under Mughal rule. Under Emperor Akbar's reign in particular, the jizya, or tax on non-Muslims was lifted, non-Muslims held high rank in government, subjects had the right to be held to the religious or customary laws of their own communities, intermarriage between Mughal rulers and Rajput kings was encouraged, and composite forms of Hindustani music, painting, architecture, and the Urdu language itself developed. While colonial historiography emphasized Mughal despotism – no doubt due to the British policy of putting Muslim rulers on retainer in exchange for their cooperation – the Raj also continued the Mughal policy of legal pluralism, while radically transforming its system of land tenure.

The scenarios of 'Aryan invasion' and 'Muslim invasion' (or 'Mughal despotism') have been challenged by current scholarship, but persist in popular and national imaginaries as a means of demonstrating that what seem to be hardened and exclusivist identities today were also present in the past. In fact, social and religious practices throughout contemporary South Asia (and much of the world) are expansive, inclusive, and heterogeneous, frequently transcending narrow community, regional, or political identities, as Shail Mayuram points out in her essay. People may identify simultaneously with more than one community or religious tradition. For example, the Sufi poet-saint Kabir eludes easy categorization: he was born a Muslim, revered Lord Ram, and his verses comprise part of the Sikh Guru Granth. Kabir Panthis (disciples) are found throughout South Asia; they practice a form of *bhakti* devotionalism that seeks a personal relationship with God, and refuse to recognize social differences between believers. It is no accident that that bhakti and the qawwali tradition of Sufi devotionalism also challenge the idioms of sexual and gender inequality,[1] as Akbar Hyder explains. The bhakti tradition is both open and diverse – South Asians may be orthodox members of any religion and partake of it; bhakti devotionalism both exists alongside and permeates the major religious traditions of South Asia. It remains one of the most popular and vibrant forms of religious expression in South Asia today. The bhakti tradition began in pre-modern South India, and then traveled North, illustrating how religious practices may renew themselves by working their way into the vernacular languages of the region to form new kinds of composite culture. A verse of the Bhagyat Mahatmya (I, 48–50) proclaims 'Bhakti was born in Dravida (Tamil country), grew to womanhood in Maharasthra and Karnataka, and became old in Gujarat. On reaching Vrindavan[2] she again became a young and beautiful woman.'

As we can see, both travel and proximity have resulted in shared religious practices or culture. Hinduism, as one of the oldest world religions, carries within it many different strains of thought and practice, but these have shifted over time and also developed through interactions with other traditions. This has led, as Vasudha Narayanan points out, to Hindu patronage of Sufi Muslim shrines, and as Shail Mayuram explains, to shared or syncretic religious practices within groups like the Meos who can identify as both Hindu and Muslim. The justification for the caste system can be found in one of the oldest (and most sacred) Sanskrit texts, the Rg Veda. Yet, bhakti devotionalism, Buddhism, Jainism, and Sikhism emphasize social equality among believers, emerging in dialogue with the broader Hindu tradition but also producing critiques of Brahminical Hinduism, which codified caste hierarchy and exclusion. Kancha Iliah's article is one example of a Dalit-Bahujan (majority) critique of the upper-caste nature of some forms of Hinduism that also relies on a political appropriation of the categories 'Aryan' and 'Dravidian' discussed in Part II.

Notes

1 For a more extended discussion of alternate forms of sexuality in the pre-modern period, see Ruth Vanita and Saleem Kidwai, *Same Sex Love in India*. New York: Palgrave, 2001.
2 See Meenakshi, "Andal: She Who Rules," from "Women Bhakta Poets," *Manushi* 50–52, 1989, p. 35. Vrindavan is both the abode of Krishna, and a city located in the State of Uttar Pradesh (North India). The verse thus traces bhakti devotionalism (often focused on Radha's love for Lord Krishna) through Tamil, Kannada, Marathi, Gujarati, and Hindi, and uses the metaphor of a woman's life cycle to speak of her spiritual renewal through love for Krishna (upon arrival in Vrindavan).

1

Beyond Ethnicity? Being Hindu *and* Muslim in South Asia

Shail Mayaram

Introduction

This paper addresses a question I have visited before in my work which is, as the title suggests, what does it mean to be simultaneously Hindu and Muslim? The partners of the combine can easily be substituted by other combinations involving being simultaneously Hindu *and* Christian or Muslim *and* Sikh/Christian *and* Buddhist/Jewish and Christian. The early part of the paper will appraise some of this complex ethnic universe in South Asia and elsewhere. The second part of the paper will review the conceptual vocabulary used to describe this universe. I regard this section, to use a Sufi metaphor, as a further *maqam* (station, halting place) in a journey that has time and again negotiated with and interrogated the idea of the syncretic and also attempted to contend with the question of an alternative that will describe states of identity that are seen as mixed, impure, even heretic and most certainly, confused and a source of contamination. I conclude with a more contemporary case from our times of a person

whose self-description was of a Hindu-Christian monk. The larger issue I have lived with for some time is, how do these states of living, feeling and being, destabilize boundaries of religion, sect and denomination? In terms of numbers this refers to the cultures of a fairly substantial population since the South Asian population comprises one-fifth of the world's population (Stein 2001). The region is home to the largest concentration of Muslim population in the world.

Three significant themes need to be foreground in the contemporary discussion of religious identities: the consequences of cultural encounter for the histories of castes and communities; the possibility of dual or triple religious affiliation expressed openly or unconsciously; and, dimensions of liminality articulated through varied registers. These manifest as a series of identities that are seen as 'border line Muslims', 'half Hindus' or 'half Muslims', or 'half Christian' (whatever the components of the 'half' may be).

Perspectives on Modern South Asia: A Reader in Culture, History, and Representation, First Edition.
Edited by Kamala Visweswaran.
© 2011 Blackwell Publishing Ltd. Published 2011 by Blackwell Publishing Ltd.

How does one approach the theme of cultural encounter? One obvious way in the subcontinent is to narrate a history of conquest, iconoclasm, conflict and underwrite a politics of writing historical wrong. But there are other ways. The political theorist, Rajeev Bhargava, uses the metaphor of the palimpsest, the idea that something is altered yet bears traces of its original form.[1] One visualizes here a stone that is constantly written over or an artist's palette, witness to the magical play of colours, the emergence of endless new shades through flow and combination. We know of Tibetan civilization that became Buddhist but could not quite overwrite its past of the Bon religion (Snellgrove 1967). The pilgrimage site of Mount Kailash is resonant with the overlapping symbolism that is Hindu and Jain, Buddhist and Bon and is what draws the inveterate Himalayan trekker, philosopher-psychoanalyst Madhu Sarin season after season. Fisher's recent ethnography of the Thakali of Nepal who inhabit the borderlands of central Nepal wryly comments that scholars have seen Hinduism, Buddhism and shamanism together intensifying their influence on the Thakali (Fisher 2001). Sylvain Levi commented in 1905, that the traditions of Hinduism and Buddhism are so closely interwoven in Nepal that it made no sense to see Nepalese gods as either Hindu or Buddhist.

The Indian subcontinent is not unique in this respect. From Indonesia to the Maghreb a range of scholarships have described the fascinating negotiation between Islamic textual models and pre-Islamic worlds. Even as the contemporary Afghan has been frozen into the Taliban terrorist, we know the long tradition in Afghanistan of adaptation to both Islam and Pakhtunwali/Pushtunwali, the legal and moral code that frames the social order and might even be in opposition to the shariah. Ethnographers have described Afghan identity with its blood feud and own interpretation (some would call distortion!) of Islam. The good violent Pathan in Tagore's *Kabuli wallah* (1916), is a case in point.

The coming of Islam and Christianity to the Indian subcontinent resulted in a phenomenal cultural encounter. India's encounter with Islam opened up new connections with West Asia, just as Buddhism linked India with East Asia (Kulke 1990). 'Conversion' intensified the available plurality that had already seen the efflorescence of the *vaidika* and non-*vaidika* religions, the challenge of the *sramana* traditions of Buddhism and Jainism, the many *adivasi* cosmologies, the atheist Carvaka and the *agamika-tantrika* schools as also the wave of devotional traditions that would become such a prominent theme through the medieval period. Friedhelm Hardy refers, in addition, to the somewhat autonomous world of *gramya* or village religion that involved, from the point of view of the *vaidika* Brahman, heterodox vulgarities of village cults involving the consumption of alcohol, smoking opium, shedding blood, killing animals, eating meat, states of possession (Hardy 1995). South Asia has had more complex identities than any other region of the world.

The idea that peoples, regions and cultures have had more than one religious affiliation, however unacknowledged and silenced, has gained some currency. Ashis Nandy reminds us that for a Japanese it is possible to be simultaneously both Shinto and Buddhist. Shintoism, the original religion of Japan, involved the worship of local deities called *kami* that were later introduced into Buddhism so that Buddha and Bodhisattvas were identified with local deities.[2] Similarly in China no absolute boundary demarcated Buddhism from Confucianism (the cult of the ancestors). A community in Vietnam continues to incorporate both Hindu Ahier Cham and Muslim Awal Cham sections, representing the yang (male) and yin (female) principles, respectively.

In South Asia, some enumerations relating to India mention 600 odd bi-religious communities and there are even thirty-eight tri-religious communities according to K. Suresh Singh (Singh 1992, cited in Nandy 1995). Describing these groups in terms of bi-religiosity and tri-religiosity, however, presents problems as these categories elude the rather high levels of internal differentiation within these communities, Further, the phenomenon of overlapping and blurring of identities is far more pervasive than has hitherto been suspected and I will merely indicate the range in the subcontinent which requires far greater attention from researchers.

We know today of a large number of identities that have at a historical juncture occupied an interstitial space, straddling two or more religious traditions. My own familiarity is with the Muslim Meos of India and Pakistan, who are today one of the largest Muslim communities of the subcontinent and with the Merat of north-western India. The Rawat–Chita–Merat comprise a complex group formerly called the Mer and were divided into Hindu–Muslim–Christian sections. Significantly the Hinduism of the Hindu Rawat was described as hardly recognizable and the Muslimness of the Merat was viewed as similarly evanescent! They not only intermarried but their cosmologies inhabited by gods, goddesses, spirits, pirs, and ancestors were shared. The psychologist, Morris Carstairs, describes secret cults called *kunda* or *kachli panth* whose practices challenged the dominant discourse with respect to caste, gender and sexuality so that even what is called incest is redescribed as a mode of worship (Carstairs 1961).

Across the subcontinent there are many groups whose cultures suggest that it is possible to be simultaneously Hindu and Muslim. Castes and communities associated with storytelling and the performing art traditions in South Asia have had particularly nubile identities. In western India the Langas, the Manganiyars and the Mirasis also defy categorial classification.[3] In eastern India the role of the Baul singers is particularly illustrative. These singers are classified as Muslim but their identity transcends our simplistic classifications, 'Hindu' and 'Muslim' and is expressed in one of the world's most profound traditions of mystical music. I have a lurking suspicion that Jayadeva's poetry that carries Krishna bhakti to new heights might have absorbed the theme of love that is sensual and adulterous from Baul songs. It is no coincidence that the annual congregation of some 10,000 Bauls takes place where Jayadeva, the author of *Gita Govinda* was born. This twelfth century lyrical masterpiece

became crucial to the making of a new literary culture in India as it inspired music, painting, sculpture and drama. Gayatri Spivak writes of the 'poetic counter theology' of the famous Baul singer, Lallan Shah fakir (1774–1890) in which *advaita* becomes the abstract God of Islam. The *nirakar*, the formless, combines with the dualist urge to *rupa* (manifestation or form) so that Khadija, Mohammad's eldest wife is Allah (*je khodija a sher to khobai*) but also the chief goddess (Spivak 1999).

Like the cultures of performing artists, those of peasant and pastoral tribe-castes have hitherto been 'mixed'. I deliberately use the hyphenated tribe-caste to highlight that these were also not walled-off social formations. The data is telling. The 1921 Census records that there were 47.3 per cent Hindu and 33.4 per cent Muslim Jats (besides others who were Sikh). In this respect they were similar to the Rajputs (27.7 per cent Muslim and 70.7 per cent Hindu) and Gujars (25.3 per cent and 74.2 per cent Muslim) (Edye and Tennant 1923). Wink points out that the culture of Jats and Gujars had a significant Persian component (1990:138). The Ahirs likewise had Muslim branches even as the Mewatis and Mirasis had Hindu populations.

Ruling and warrior castes and the so-called Sudra castes of the subcontinent also suggest significant religious complexity. In the region of Rajasthan, with which I am more familiar, the category 'Muslim' includes the Musalman Rajputs, Khanzadas, Desi Musalman, Kayamkhanis and Sindhi Sipahis (Kothari 1984). In Uttar Pradesh we know of the Malkanas who claimed to be neither Hindus nor Muslims and preferred to be called Mian Thakur. Helena Basu points out that the Jadeja Rajputs of Gujarat who were described as 'half Muslim' employed African (Muslim) Sidi slaves as cooks.[4]

Some of this description comes from the early censuses of the twentieth century, that one can see as a dialectic between the imposition of homogeneity by the state and a mirroring of ethnic complexity that emerges from the interstices. Regrettably research on the Census, as Peterson points out, has ignored mixed identities with the exception of the Anglo-Indians (Peterson 1997). The world of scholarship, in general, has not given much cognizance to the phenomenon of overlapping identities, interpenetrating cultures and religions, and the transgression of boundaries. Only now as ethnicity, nationalism, militarization overtake the worlds we inhabit and boundaries are etched in blood and genocidal violence have we woken up to the realization that possibly the world itself, its past and present, needs to be described differently. There is some very significant recent work on South Asia that challenges ethnic faultlines (see, for instance, Silva 2002; Gilmartin and Lawrence 2000; Gottschalk 2001). The importance of these cultures for both the writing of history and ethnography and the larger understanding of religion and cultural encounter can hardly be overemphasized.

This is not to deny that the boundary making enterprise is not also a constant for the worlds these cultures inhabit as also within themselves. State Shintoism is quick to decry the mixing of popular Japanese practice. Official recognition of the Bon religion from Tibetan Buddhism dates only to the current Dalai Lama who has recognized it as a living tradition. Reformist and purist trends in state and civil society have frequently sought to purge the popular of 'corrupt' and 'depraved' practices. Performing artists have been recruited by nationalist ideologues, Hindu, Muslim, Sikh.

Challenges of Conceptualizing This Universe: Liminality

When I first began my work on the Meos of India and Pakistan there was hardly any vocabulary that would capture the complexity of a culture that was simultaneously Hindu and Muslim. The search for a language to describe the phenomenon of blurring and interaction has taken scholars in varying directions advocating varied concepts such as ambiguity, fuzziness, the idea of the border and frontier, the hybrid, and, of course, the age-old syncretic. Some of this work marks a shift of interest from

boundary to borderlands, borders being conceived as frontiers that are zones of interaction. This reverses the erstwhile conception of the frontier as a space to be mastered and conquered by an imperial/racial project.[5] Anzaldua asserts, 'To survive the Borderlands you must live *sin fronteras* (without frontiers) be a crossroads' (Anzaldua 1987). Border zones are seen as arenas of partially realized identities, manifest contradictions and deliberate ambiguity. Uberoi (1999) elaborates on this using the metaphor of a revolving door for Afghanistan. Islam comes in through one door and Buddhism goes out through another.

Liminality and Syncretism

A range of new research has brought out the syncretisms of world religions. There are the hypothesized beginnings of Christianity from the dissenting Jewish sect of the Essenes; the Jewishness of Jesus; and the derivation of aspects of Christian and Judaic belief such as the worship of the Madonna or the celebration of feasts and festivals from pagan traditions. Hence, Gunkel's description of Christianity as syncretic. The view of the Christian community as separate and distinct from Judaism. Van der Veer has highlighted that the very term syncretism is associated with the rise of Protestantism and the decline of the absolute authority of Catholicism that had pronounced on the syncretic as the heretical (Van der Veer 1994).

The association of Mecca with the pagan ritual involving priestesses of three goddesses has frequently been written about. The Egyptian feminist writer, Nawal El-Saadawi, pointed out that the practice of kissing the black stone housed in the Ka'ba shrine derives from pre-Islamic practice. She has since been accused of heresy and almost forced to divorce her husband in accordance with a law that requires Muslims not to remain married to apostates. Ismailism draws upon Pythagoras and Aristotle, Christianity and the Manicheans and upon Judaism. Sufism grew in Mesopotamia, Eastern Iran, and Khorasan where it was influenced by Buddhist monastic ideals. Later period influences included those of neo-Platonism, Christianity and Central Asian and Indian asceticism (For a discussion, see Schimmel 1992).

In South Asia, Dumont viewed orthodox Brahmanism as syncretic contrasted with a sect. Puranic syncretism has been pointed out frequently (Chakrabarti 2001). Sikh holy scripture incorporated the verses of Kabir and Farid I or Farid II and Bhikan the Sufi (Uberoi 1999). That syncretism is strategically deployed in the history of religions has been demonstrated again and again. Eaton shows in relation to Bengal how syncretism was actually used to further conversion. Distancing himself from the use of orthodox and unorthodox, fundamentalist and syncretic as unproductive terms, Eaton argues that Islam in Bengal absorbed an enormous amount of local culture so that it was never regarded as foreign. Eaton maintains that it is inappropriate to speak of 'conversion' of Hindus to Islam, instead what occurred in the Bengal context was an expanding agrarian civilization whose cultural counterpart was the growth of the cult of Allah. A simultaneous syncretism and anti-syncretism is manifest in movements of social and religious reform such as the Brahmo and Arya Samaj and more recently in the Vishva Hindu Parishad.

In the west the so-called New Age Religion has produced new sycretic combinations. One version combines *tantra, wicca*, spirit possession and Christianity. There is in existence a highly syncretic post modern Christianity. Wilson mentions that nearly a quarter of the west's Christian population now believes in reincarnation rather than a realizable Heaven. There is also a new emphasis on Christ's humanity, his role as an ethical teacher rather than merely on divinity. Ideas of the Original Sin (of children having been born of sin) and of damnation have similarly been given up (Wilson 1999). Feminist theologians have been emphasizing the idea of a gender-neutral God who ought to substitute the idea of God as exclusively male. Black cults are similarly syncretic variants of Islam and the Baptist religion. Further, syncretisms

have married western ideas of individualism and liberalism with Christianity and socialism with Islam.

The question is how does one theorize these identities? For one thing Asian religions did not stress singularization that was associated with the institutional framework of Christianity and the idea of heresy. For people embedded in a traditional world religious view, liminality followed from a quest for the power of the transcendental. It meant, what has been called, a policy of double insurance: if one's own gods were not powerful enough, others might provide a better guarantee of the fulfilment of desire. For persons located in modernist contexts liminality derives from the quest for a moral life, in which inherited traditions might be drawn upon but are also subject to scrutiny and other spiritualities might become potential sources of insight and guides to living.

Lest it be concluded that liminality relates to only premodern, folk theologies one might mention two particularly well-known contemporary persons of our times. Ramakrishna Paramhans (1836−86), one of the greatest Indian sages and mystics, said to have experienced *moksha* in his lifetime, and who actually lived for brief durations as a practicing Muslim and Christian. *The Gospel of Ramakrishna* brings out how in his state of ecstatic illumination he experienced himself as a woman, Jew, Muslim, Jain and Buddhist as he beheld the varied manifestations of God, as Christ, Mohammad and also as the Divine Mother, as Sita and Rama and Krishna.

Gandhi's life and work illustrates the point. Ramachandra Gandhi points out Gandhi's rejection of exclusivist identities. 'He was a Hindu, but insisted that he was simultaneously also a Muslim, Christian, Jew, Buddhist, Jaina, etc.: a believer in the truth of all faiths' (Gandhi 1994: 9). Madan points out that his Ram Raj recalled no mythic Hindu past, but the Asokan vision of Dhamma (Madan 1998:230−1). Gandhi also acknowledged the enormous influence of the moral teaching of Christianity on his thoughts particularly the Sermon on the Mount and declared, 'Jesus has given a definition of perfect *dharma*.'[6] Nandy has similarly pointed out that

Gandhi's idiom cut across the boundaries of Christian, Hindu and Buddhist world views (Nandy 1992: 35). Saxena demonstrates the influence on Gandhi of the Jain notions of *syadvada* and *anekantada* that theorize the multiplicity of viewpoints (1988).

Notes

1 Presentation, at, International Conference on Living Together Separately: Cultural India in History and Politics, organized by Academy of Third World Studies, Jamia Millia Islamia, New Delhi, 19–21 December 2002.
2 A Japanese has been known to respond to the question, are you Buddhist or Shinto? with the mocking answer, Shinto is our religion for times of happiness and Buddhism for times of sorrow!
3 See Kothari in conversation with Bharucha (Bharucha 2003).
4 Presentation, International Conference on Lived Islam, Goa, 5–7 December 2002.
5 Elsewhere, I have critiqued the syncretic and the hybrid as inadequately theorized formulations of the subject under discussion (Mayaram 1998).
6 Indeed, Gandhi's first biographer commented, 'I question whether any system of religion can absolutely hold him. His views are too closely allied to Christianity to be entirely Hindu; and too deeply saturated with Hinduism to be called Christian, and his sympathies are so wide and catholic that one would imagine he has reached a point where the formulae of sects are meaningless' (cited in Madan 1998: 230n).

References

Anzaldua, Gloria. 1987. *Borderlands la frontera: The new Mestiza*, Aunt Lute, San Francisco.

Bharucha, Rustom. 2003. *Rajasthan: An Oral History*, Komal Kothari in conversation with Rustam Bharucha. Penguin.

Carstairs, G. Morris. 1961. *The Twice Born*, Hogarth Press, London.

Chakrabarti, Kunal. 2001. *Religious Process: The Puranas and the Making of a Regional Tradition*, Oxford University Press, Delhi.

Edye, E.H.H. and W.R. Tennant. 1923. *Census of India*, 1921, Government Press, Allahabad.

Fisher, William. F. 2001. *Fluid Boundaries: Forming and Transforming Identity in Nepal*, Columbia University Press, New York.

Gandhi, Ramachandra. 1994. *Sita's Kitchen*, Wiley Eastern, New Delhi.

Gilmartin, David and Bruce Lawrence (eds). 2000. *Beyond Hindu and Turk: Rethinking Religious Identities in Islamicate South Asia*, University Press of Florida.

Gottschalk, Peter S. 2001. *Beyond Hindu and Muslim: Multiple Identity Narratives from Village India*, Oxford University Press, New Delhi.

Hardy, Friedhelm. 1995. *The Religious Culture of India*, Cambridge University Press.

Kothari, Komal. 1984. Introduction, *The Castes of Marwar*, compiled by Munshi Hardyal Singh, Jodhpur Printing House, Jodhpur.

Kulke, Hermann and Dietmar Rothermund. 1990. *A History of India*, Routledge, London.

Madan, Triloki Nath. 1998. *Modern Myths, Locked Minds: Secularism and Fundamentalism in India*, Oxford University Press, Delhi.

Nandy, Ashis. 1992. *Traditions, Tyranny and Utopias: Essays on the Politics of Awareness*, Oxford University Pres, Delhi.

———. 1995. *Coping with the Politics of Faiths and Cultures: Between Secular State and Ecumenical Traditions in India*. Culture and Identity Project, International Centre for Ethnic Studies, Colombo.

Peterson, William. 1997. *Ethnicity Counts*, Transaction Publishers, New Brunswick, NJ.

Saxena, Sushil. K. 1988. *Ever unto God: Essays on Gandhi and Religion*, Indian Council for Philosophical Research, New Delhi.

Schimmel, Annemarie. 1992. *Islam: An Introduction*, SUNY, New York.

Silva, Neluka. (ed.) 2002. *The Hybrid Island: Culture Crossings and the Invention of Identity in Sri Lanka*. Social Scientists' Association, Colombo.

Singh, Kunwar, Suresh. (ed.) 1992. *People of India: An Introduction*. Anthropological Survey of India, Calcutta.

Snellgrove, David. 1967. *Nine Ways of Bon: Excerpts from Gzi-Brjid*, London Oriental Series, London, 18.

Spivak, Gayatri, Chakarbarti. (ed.) 1999. Moving devi, in Vidya Dehejia and R. Shaw (ed.), *Devi: The Great Goddess, Female Divinity in South Asian Art*, Mapin, Ahmedabad.

Stein, Burton. 2001. *A History of India*, Oxford University Press, New Delhi.

Uberoi, Jit Pal Singh. 1999. *Religion, Civil Society and the State*, Oxford University Press, Delhi.

van der Veer, Peter. 1994. Syncretism, Multiculturalism, and the Discussion of Tolerance, in C. Stewart and R. Shaw (eds), *Syncretism/Anti-Syncretism: The Politics of Religious Synthesis*, Routledge, London and New York.

Wilson, B. 1999. *Christianity*, Routledge, London and New York.

Wink, Andre. 1990. *Al-Hind*, vol 1., Oxford University Press, Delhi.

2

Towards a Composite Reading of South Asian Religious Cultures: The Case of Islam

Syed Akbar Hyder

In short, my heart is also inclined towards piety, but –
The shameful practices of the pious have forced me into infidelity

Ghalib

Mirza Asadullah Khan "Ghalib" (1797–1869), the acclaimed Urdu and Persian poet of the last Mughal court in Delhi, was arrested in 1857 on charges of gambling and thereby contributing to disorder in the city. When confronted by the British colonial official about his religious identity, Ghalib riposted: "I am half Muslim; drink wine but refrain from swine." In this essay, I draw upon Ghalib's tongue-in-cheek statement in order to make two points about religious identity in South Asia: it is often playfully (and at times painfully) composite and it is constituted by silences as much as it is vocalized. While Ghalib tells the colonial official he is half Muslim, the other half is not indebted to exclusivist religious identity. Even though the purview of Islamic dietary laws extends beyond the consumption of alcohol and pork, Ghalib reminds us that sometimes, points such as these must be deliberately constrained.

It is impossible for this or any other single essay to draw attention to all aspects of the composite religious traditions of South Asia. I thus focus on particular themes that highlight the manner in which Muslim religious traditions dynamically borrowed from and contributed to other traditions that inhabited their milieu. The first part of this work sketches a socio-political overview of issues necessary to guide any discussion of Islam in South Asia, and the second part discusses the literary–musical qawwali tradition that aesthetically draws on the values and symbols of the South Asian composite cultures.

When speaking of composite religious culture, I do not wish to imply that exclusivist "Muslimness" or "Hinduness" have never been privileged as such. Nor do I presume that South Asian religions have been fused together indistinguishably or inextricably. I simply state that religious identities and definitions have often

Perspectives on Modern South Asia: A Reader in Culture, History, and Representation, First Edition.
Edited by Kamala Visweswaran.
© 2011 Blackwell Publishing Ltd. Published 2011 by Blackwell Publishing Ltd.

been mutually inclusive and flexible, varying across intersecting temporal, regional, linguistic, economic, and sectarian vectors. Unfortunately, while a documentation of the variegated spaces of composite religious culture might seem self-evident and simplistic to some, such documentation has been violently suppressed by political and religious authorities throughout South Asia.

One instance of this reality is, of course, the 2002 violence in Gujarat, when the shrine of Vali Dakhni-Gujarati was razed in the aftermath of the Indian state's anti-Muslim pogroms. For more than two hundred years the shrine had stood as the convergence site for people of all stripes of spirituality. Vali's Urdu poetry celebrated the cosmopolitan ethos of eighteenth-century Gujarat, especially the city of Surat:

'ajab shahran men hai pur nur yak shahr
bila shak voh hai jag men maqsad-i dahr
ahe mashhur us ka nam surat
keh jave jis ke dekhe son kadurat
...
sharafat men yeh hai jiyun bab-i makka
to hai sab mulk par us ka jo sikka
...
vahan sakin ite hain ahl-i mazhab,
ke ginti men na aven unke mashrab
agarche sab hain voh abna-i adam,
vale binash men rangarang-i 'alam
bhari hai sirat o surat
sun surat, har ek surat hai van anmol murat
khatam hai amradan upar safa'i
vale hai beshtar husn-i nisa'i
sabha indar ki hai har ek qadam men,
chupa indar, sabha kon le 'adam men
Kishan ki gopiyan ki nain hai yeh nasl,
rahin sab gopiyan voh naql, yeh a
* * *

Among all cities, wondrous is one city:
Without doubt, in the world, it is the raison
    d'être of time!
Famous is its name, Surat,
From its gaze, malice vanishes
...
In nobility [Surat] is like the gate of Mecca,
Exercising its authority over the entire region
...
So many people of so many religions live there,
Their sects cannot possibly be counted.
Even though they are all children of Adam,

In their appearance, however, they are a
    multicolored spectrum.
Surat [the city] is filled with numerous ways
    and surats [forms],
Each one of these, a priceless image.
Fairness reaches its perfections in the boys [of
    Surat]
But the beauty of [its] girls is even superior.
At every step, stands the court of Indra,
Even though Indra hides himself, with his court,
    in non-existence.
This generation is not of Krishna's gopis,
For those gopis were imperfect imitations – this,
    the real

As Sunil Sharma so eloquently points out, Vali's "amorous sweep of the demography of the city results in a catalogue of beautiful and industrious beloveds among whom are Hindus, Muslims, Parsis, and also Europeans, each contributing to the city's overall prosperity."[1] Notwithstanding the narratives of composite culture, whether generated by the pens of Vali or Ghalib, we must also remember the disruptions within these narratives.

Eminent historians like Romila Thapar have shown that the most obvious protracted effort to undermine the discourse of mutually-inclusive composite traditions manifests itself in colonial history writing of the South Asian subcontinent that is self-servingly appropriated by the religious nationalists of Hindu and Muslim traditions. James Mill, when writing the *History of British India* during the dawn hours of colonialism in the 1820s, marked the history of this region with three distinctive phases: the Hindu, the Muslim, and the British.[2] Several fallacies follow from this periodization: (1) the religious identity of the populace is determined by the religious identity of the rulers; (2) India as imagined by the British colonizers of the late-eighteenth and early-nineteenth century is the same India that has seamlessly survived from ancient times; (3) Hindu and Muslim are monolithic categories that remain unchanging (somewhat internally united) over time; (4) "India" can be easily distinguished by internal and external boundaries; (5) the internal domain of India encountered violent infringements with the arrival of Islam.

The land of India that extends from the Indus river region to the Himalayan mountains has never been a singular political or cultural unit. There is no evidence before the nineteenth century, that people living on the banks of the Ganges felt more connected to people in Kanyakumari, on the southern tip of India, than to people living in the cities of Central Asia. The idea of what constituted "inside" India and "outside" India frequently changed depending on who ruled and who wrote. Thus, the notion that religion of Islam (and by extension Christianity, Judaism, or Zoroastrianism) came to India from "outside" only makes sense if we want to freeze the historical "inside." Moreover, we must also beware of presuming that sectarian and ideological identities within the Muslim community (Shii Ismaili, Shii Ithna ashari, Sunni Deobandi, Sunni Barelve, Mahdavi and Ahmedi, among others) are irrelevant when the issue of Muslims and their "others" is raised.

Ambition for a larger territory and hence a more substantial revenue base was a desire common to both Muslims and non-Muslims. In pursuit of wealth and territory, Muslim rulers attacked each other's territories and in this process mosques, treasuries, and military camps were wrecked. Even the most sacred site of Islamic devotion in Mecca, the Kaaba, was not spared when Muslims girded for war against each other. Such intra-religious discord is not alien to any tradition, be it Islamic, Hindu, Buddhist or Christian. The political and military trajectory followed by non-Muslims in India has hardly been different: Hindu rulers plundered Hindu temples, while Buddhist sanctuaries of worship have been attacked by non-Buddhists and vice versa. What is surprising is that in segments of today's India, the destruction of particularly wealthy temples (like the one located in the Somnath of eleventh-century India) generates astonishment, implying that these temples would have been spared if an army led by non-Muslims had attacked the city.

Notwithstanding frictions between Muslims and others (including conflict between Muslims of different ideological orientations), any discussion of South Asian religion must point to the aesthetic realm in which inter-religious practices and ideals have been produced collaboratively despite differences of perspective on particular issues at certain moments. Oft times these productions have been acts of resistance in the face of text-centric orthodoxies and hegemonies. The very inception of Buddhist, Jain, Sufi, bhakti, and Sikh traditions testify to a diminution of ritualistic religiosity. When speaking of South Asian composite religiosity, how can one not remember Kabirdas, the weaver-saint of sixteenth-century Banaras, whose poetry inexorably reveals the exultant aspects of self-realization above all other human aspects. Kabir's verses, revered within the Islamic mystical traditions of Sufism as well as within the traditions of bhakti and Sikhism, usurp the privilege of particularly exclusivist texts and rituals and represent devotional aspirations towards a higher spirituality that sustain their reign by celebrating an intensely personal but shared spirituality.[3] Issues of religious urgency within Kabir's writings are not informed by an emphasis on ritualistic pilgrimages to Mathura (city celebrated as Krishna's birthplace), Kashi (another name for Banaras, the city known as the abode of Shiva), or Kaba (pivot of Muslim devotion in Mecca), but are spurred forward by an introspective lyricism. Even in death, we are told through a popular legend, Kabir united his followers, one group that wanted to cremate him and the other group that wanted to bury him; his corpse was transformed into a heap of flowers, some of which basked in the fire of cremation and others resting peacefully under the earth's cover.

For many Muslims, disagreement within their own community has constituted a divine blessing and the diversity within the larger creation is a feature of God's plan to enhance the knowledge of all: "We have created you into nations and tribes so that you may get to know each other and compete with each other in good deeds," is a verse from the Qur'an (49:13) that has been read as divine reasoning, encouraging one community of people to gain knowledge about the other and for communities to compete with each other in good deeds. As Muzaffar Alam points out in his important work on medieval India, Muslim scholars and poets like

Mirza Mazhar Jan-i Janan of Delhi (d. 1764) had a sophisticated breadth of vision when it came to Islam's relationship with other faiths:

> According to the Qur'an, each community had a prophet, God has not left India without Prophets... Since the Qur'an is silent about many Prophets, it is good that we adopt a liberal view of the Prophets and religions of India. The same should be our attitude with regard to the people of ancient Persia, and for that matter of all other countries.[4]

Muslim political authorities like the Mughal emperor Akbar (d. 1605), prince Dara Shikoh (d. 1659), and the Nizam of Hyderabad (d. 1967), not only patronized temples but also funded translation of texts that held spiritual authority among non-Muslims. Dara Shikoh went so far as to say that the profound secrets of the Koran are concealed in the ancient Indian texts of the Upanishads. When reciting solemn elegies for their seventh-century martyrs, or panegyrics for their contemporary religious authorities, Muslims of Lucknow and Bhuj have relied on classical Indian melodies that are named after gods and goddesses not present in the devotional lore of Persian or Arab worlds. The poet Iqbal (d. 1938), often (mis?)identified as the intellectual father of Pakistan, sang praises of Ram, Guru Nanak, and Gautam Buddha in the same tone that he used to celebrate the splendor of Arabian and Persian heroes. While he claimed to belong to the Sunni Hanafi school of religious thought, a sense of fractured religious and ethnic identity resonates in his poems, one of which identifies him as a craftsman of verse who "does not think of Hindus as unbelievers, has a bit of Shiism in his disposition, believes the classical Indian melodies to have a role in devotion, does not begrudge the sellers of beauty (prostitutes)... is an accumulation of pardoxes."[5]

Likewise, the Bengali poet Rabindranath Tagore, the Hindi-Urdu writer Munshi Premchand, and one of the leading icons of India's anti-colonial struggle, Mohandas Gandhi, saw kindred spirits in the heroes of Islam's early history, especially in the grandson of the Prophet Muhammad, Husain ibn Ali, who confronted the supreme political authority of his time in Karbala, Iraq. The story of Husain, to Gandhi, Tagore, and Premchand was readily assimilable to a broader vision of a just struggle. Gandhi actually invoked Karbala when he embarked on his first salt march which, like Husain's band at Karbala, had approximately seventy-two people in it. Gandhi claimed that the seventh-century incident of Karbala had "arrested" him, while he was still young. He claimed to have studied the life of the "hero of Karbala" and came to the conclusion that the people of India must act on the principles of Husain in order to attain true liberation. The historical progress of Islam, according to Gandhi, is not the legacy of the Muslim sword but a result of the sacrifices of Muslim saints like Husain.[6]

Contemplating the Divine in the Qawwali Tradition

Within South Asian popular culture, the qawwali tradition, which covers the varied linguistic and regional swathe of this region, stands as a repository of the composite cultural and religious values; it is therefore critical in understanding South Asian religious matrices. The word *qawwali* derives from the Arabic word *qawl*, which in general means "saying," but more specifically refers to the sayings of the Prophet Muhammad – though the *qawwali* texts take stock of works of literature beyond those ascribed to the Prophet. In fact, it is through the *qawwali* tradition that many classic mystical texts are routed for mass consumption in South Asia. *Qawwalis* are instructional as well as entertaining. They frequently provide a significant counterweight to discourses generated from other sites of religious knowledge production, such as mosques and temples, thereby leading their audiences into an alternative world with a less rigid gender divide where ideological differences pertaining to an understanding of God and religion are accommodated, and where a circumvention of a hyper-theological and scholastic discourse is possible through the enunciation of simple, heartfelt sentiments. The *qawwali* tradition deploys the "composite" idea in much the same manner as Vali's poetry or the legends surrounding Kabir's burial–cremation.

The poetic strands that tie together many *qawwali* narratives through the technique of *girah bandi* (knot-tying) range from classical works of Sufism, such as the *Masnavi* of Jalaluddin Rumi and the *ghazals* of Amir Khusro, to verses composed by local poets, Muslim as well as non-Muslim. *Girah bandi* allows *qawwals* (qawwali singers) to embed invigorating variations on a single theme by interpolating poetry from disparate sources in order to create a coherent narrative.

The three *qawwalis* that are translated here were made popular by the acclaimed Hyderabadi *qawwal*, Aziz Ahmad Khan Warsi.

Qawwali 1

The first stanza of the *qawwali* is a quatrain composed by Hyderabad's most renowned Sufi poet, Amjad Hyderabadi (d. 1961), and the second stanza is a quatrain of the greatest Urdu elegist, Mir Anis (d. 1872). This *qawwali* impresses complex ideals on its audience by adopting finely wrought parables: the first (stanza 3) is a translation of a section of Rumi's *Masnavi*, and the second and third (stanzas 5 and 6) are the exegeses of the ideas of *wahdat al-wujud* (unity of being), closely tied to Muhiuddin Ibn al-'Arabi, the grand master of theosophical Sufism. The translators of these parables, Bedam Warsi (d. 1936) and Zamin Ali (d. 1855), are Urdu poets known for their lucid expressions of complex Sufi ideas.

The main locus of the first parable valorizes devotion as an intimately personal experience that is beyond even a prophet's comprehension. Also threaded into this parable is a devotional allusion to Lord Krishna, a manifestation of the divine who at times appears as an adorable youth in his cradle. The second and third parables help the audience understand the ideal that all appearances are a manifestation of the One Real Being. The pivot of Muslim devotional life, the Kaba in Mecca, is itself invoked in the symbolic language of Laila's veil, as God compares Himself to this dark-skinned, moon-like sweetheart of Islamicate literature who drove mad her lover Qais (Majnun). The mystical cadences that lace this qawwali come to life most notably through the tension-laden elision and reinforcement of differences in the relationship between God and His creation: Moses must recognize that his devotional path is different from that of the shepherd and Majnun must come to terms with his Laila by accepting her as God's splendorous manifestation, a variation of Himself.

God, Just He (Allah Hu)

Stanza 1

Pukara khana-e tan se yahan par kaun hai ghar
    men
Sada a'i dar-e dil se yahan allah hi Allah hai
Allah hu Allah hu Allah hu Allah hu

Tu hai ke hamesha karam fermata hai
Amjad hai ke rah par nahin ata hai
Main khugar-e jurm tu hai karam ka 'adi
Ham donon men dekhen kaun barh jata hai

From within my body's abode I called,
"Who dwells within this house?"
From the heart's threshold was heard a cry,
"God, there is none else but God!"
God, just He
God, just He
God, just He
God, just He

You, the One, ever lavishing mercy
Amjad, the one adrift on the path
habituated to transgressions
You, accustomed to clemency
Let us see who can exceed the other

Stanza 2

Gulshan men saba ko justaju teri hai
Bulbul ki zaban pe guftagu teri hai
Har rang men jalva hai teri qudrat ka
Jis phul ko sunghta hun b uteri
Na gul chaman men rahenge na gul men bu baqi
Yeh sab tujhi pe mitenge rahega tu baqi
Allah hu, Allah hu, Allah hu, Allah hu

In the rose garden the zephyr yearns for You
From the nightingale's lips Your talk springs
In every hue Your majesty shines
From every flower, Your fragrance emanates
Neither will the roses last in the garden

Nor their perfumes dwell there
All these will perish for Your sake
You alone will stay

God, just He
God, just He
God, just He
God, just He

Stanza 3

Ek charvaha kisi jangal men tha
Ya mah-e kamil kisi badal men tha
Yad-e maula men hamesha mast tha
Asman us ki zamin pe past tha
Yad karte karte thak jata tha jab
Chikh uthta dard se ba sakta lab
Tu meri kutya men kyun ata nahin
Kya mera jangal tujhe bhata nahin
A, utar a 'arsh se ghar men mere
Pa'on dho dho kar piyunga main tere
Subha uth kar munh dhula'unga tera
Rat din jhula jhulaunga tera
Bhik dar dar mang kar main launga
Pahle main tujh ko khila ke khaunga
Kar raha tha voh yunhi shor o fughan
Hazrat-e Musa bhi a nikle vahan
Dant kar bole are bakta hai kya
Nur-e mutlaq ko muqayyad kar diya
kis qadar kam bakht tu nadan hai
kya khuda teri tarah insane hai
tu zarur is kufr ka phal payega
ghairat-e haqq se yanhi jal jayega
kar chuke Musa jo us ko dil hazing
vahi a'i hazrat-e haqq se vahin
kya kiya Musa yeh tum ne kya kiya
kar diya bande ko maula se juda
tujh ko bheja jorne ke vaste
tu nahin tha torn ke vaste
are hoshiyaron ka tariqa aur hai
dil jalon ka aur hi kuch taur hai
Allah hu, Allah hu, Allah hu, Allah hu

Once upon a time, a shepherd lived in a forest
Like a full moon, eclipsed by clouds
Always drunk with the memory of his master
The canopy of heaven, lying low on his earth
Entangled in His remembrance, he grew weary
      one day
In agony he cried out in dismay:
"Why do You not come to my small hut?
Does not my wilderness hold some charm?

Come, come down from Your heavenly throne
      to my home
I'll quench my thirst by washing Your feet
Waking up in the morning, I'll cleanse Your face
Night and day I'll rock Your cradle
Begging door to door, I'll gather goods for You
Only after feeding You will I eat my fill"
Such were his cries and rants
When the honorable Moses passed his home
That with an anger-ridden voice roared this
      God's Prophet:
"Watch the words you recklessly utter
Imprisoned you hold this limitless light
How wretched you are, O silly fool!
Is God a mere human just like you?
Certainly, you'll reap the wrath of this breach
By the rage of the Truth, you'll turn to ashes"
Just when Moses racked his heart through
God's revelation echoed:
"What have you done Moses, what have you
      done
From the master you have sundered his slave
You were sent to mend hearts
You exist not to break hearts
O you! Prescribed for the clever is their own
      path,
A different way designed for the smoldering
      hearts

God, just He
God, just He
God, just He
God, just He

Stanza 4

'arz ki majnun ne haqq se ek rat
Aye mere malik khuda-e shish jihat
Rahm ke qabil hai mere hal-e zar
Rahm kar mujh par mere parvardigar
Jama-e dil shirk se maila hua
Tera banda 'ashiq-e laila hua
'ashiq-e laila banaya kyun mujhe
Apni nazron se giraya kyun mujhe
Nagahan hatif se a'i yeh nida
Mere majnun bas na kar itna gilah
'ishq-e laila se tujhe gar yas hai
Gham na kar rabb tera tere pas hai
Are 'ishq ka majnun banana kam hai
Mere hi jalvon ka laila nam hai
Allah hu, Allah hu, Allah hu, Allah hu

One night, turning to the Truth, Majnun said:
"My Master, Lord of all directions
My pitiful state deserves clemency
Have mercy on me, my Sustainer
The cloak of my heart is sullied by infidelity
Your slave has become Laila's lover
Why did You make me Laila's lover
Why did You disgrace me in Your eyes"
Suddenly, a voice from the invisible issued:
"My Majnun, do not bewail with such hurt
If Laila's love fills you with anguish,
Grieve not, for your Lord is with you
It is love's calling to make Majnuns,
It is my disclosure named Laila"
Hidden behind that curtain is the Laila of both
    worlds
Oh Bedam, there is a reason the Kaba dons the
    black cloak

God, just He
God, just He
God, just He
God, just He

Stanza 5

Ek din Qais se laila-e mah ru
Boli mere siva kis ki hai justagu
Vajd men a ke ki Qais ne guftagu
Raz ki bat hai khair sun mah ru
Na to majnun hun main aur na laila hai tu
Allah hu, Allah hu, Allah hu, Allah hu

The moon-faced Laila asked Qais one day:
"Whom do you pursue besides this dark one?"
Enraptured, Qais rendered into words:
"'T'is but a secret, listen O Moon-lit one
I am not Majnun, neither are you Laila
I am not mad, neither are you black

God, just He
God, just He
God, just He
God, just He

Stanza 6

Main ka jhagra hi kya is men kya guftagu
Jo mita tujh pe us ko mili abru
Tere jalve nigahon men hain char su
Ghair koi nahin hai faqat tu hi tu
Allah hu, Allah hu, Allah hu, Allah hu

There is no quarrel over the "I" –
This matter, free of qualms
Those vanished in You alone gain honor
Your presence looms at every turn
No Other subsists, You and only You

God, just He
God, just He
God, just He
God, just He

Zamin Ali, annihilated in remembering
God, just He
God, just He

Qawwali 2
According to the lore of the Hyderabadi *qawwali* tradition, Amjad wrote "A Three-Colored Picture" after the death of his young daughter, as a cathartic consolation for the young girl's mother. In the first stanza, Amjad celebrates the arrival of his daughter. He invokes the tradition attributed to the Prophet Muhammad that the salutations of God, Muhammad, and the archangel Gabriel will be sent upon whichever house is blessed by a daughter. Amjad speaks of his daughter's arrival as though it were surreal and dream-like.

Amjad speaks in a feminine voice while praising his child in a masculine langue. This discourse is intertextually bound to the discourse of the bhakti tradition in which the lover speaks in a feminine Radha-like voice. John Stratton Hawley clarifies this:

> But when they [Hindu devotional/bhakti poets] speak of lovesickness, they project themselves almost exclusively into the voice of one of the women who wait for Krishna – before love-making or, even more likely, afterward. And although there is plenty of humor, there is a deep sense of longing and lament. This lament is echoed in the narrative line, for according to most versions, this love story has no happy ending: Krishna never really returns to the women he leaves behind. Whether one conceived it in the secular or religious sense (and these are not entirely separable), longing has a definite gender: it is feminine.[7]

There is also a tradition of Urdu poetry known as *rekhti* in which male poets speak in a female voice. But as Carla Petievich and others have pointed out, much of this literature is a parody-laden, wishful male imagination, with no charge of a serious discourse.[8] In Urdu literary circles of the late nineteenth-century, shaped very much by colonial aesthetics, a discourse in the feminine voice was not seen as legitimate in terms of its literary merits, or in terms of its Sufi stature. So these *qawwalis* are very much a reflection of how Urdu poets like Amjad cast their devotion, not only in a transcommunal language, but also in a transmasculine idiom, hence resisting the hegemony of the Urdu canon-guardians. Again, we can see clearly why *qawwalis* have not been studied as serious literary artefacts: they never met the standards of male literary or religious sentries.

In the second stanza, the daughter is spoken of as the beloved, jealously guarded by her lover. The lover hopes that she will never depart from his sight. But, alas, fate has decreed something else: in the third stanza, as the lover/father blinks in his dream-like state, his beloved vanishes. The poet, without risking neat celebratory or elegiac effects, employs the bhakti/Sufi language of eros to relay a state of mind for which he has no name at all, attesting to the mysteries of debuts and departures, meditating on the transience of joy and the open-endedness of grief. It is perhaps the likeness of this state of mind that occasions the double-bindedness of Jacques Derrida's idea of mourning:

One should not develop a taste for mourning, and yet mourn we *must*. We *must*, but we must not like it – mourning, that is, mourning *itself*, if such a thing exists: not to like or love through one's own tear but only through the other, and every tear is from the other, the friend, the living, as long as we ourselves are living, reminding us, in holding life, to hold on to it.[9]

A Three-Colored Picture (*Sah Rangi Tasvir*)

Sun katha meri achchi saheli
Rat main so rahi thi akeli
A'i khushbu mujhe 'atr ki si
Chu ga'i sans mujh ko kisi ki

Cha ga'i dil peh karam ki
Band ankhon men bijli si chamki
Ho gaya fazl-e bari ta'ala
Aya ghar men mere 'arsh vala

Hear my tale, dear [girl] friend,
Last night I slumbered, alone
A perfume scent wafted down to me
Someone's breath touched my soul
A cloud of mercy covered my mind
With eyes closed, a lightning force glimmered
Favors rained from the highest lord
The heavenly-one descended to my place

Mahv-e did-e rukh-e yar hun main
Khwab men hunk e bedar hun main
Ab jale ag men meri sautan
Main to bandhungi daman se daman
Ab kahin us ko jane na dungi
Ghair ko munh dikhane na dungi
Ghamkade men mere 'id hogi
Ab to athon pahar did hogi

Struck by the vision – my beloved's cheeks
Do I dream, do I wake?
Envy-ridden rival, may she burn in fire
While I cling to my sweetheart's garb, tight
Never to grant his leave
Never to grant his vision of my other
In sorrow's abode, spreads splendid joy
Day and night I hold him in sight

Main isi vajd men jhumti thi
Apni qismat ka munh chumti thi
Yak ba yak ankh meri jo chamki
Kar kara kar giri gham ki bijli
Hai qismat ne phir rang badla
Phir yeh dekha ke us ko na dekha
Us ne jalva dikhaya hi kyun tha
Jane vala phir aya hi kyun tha
Baithe baithe mera ji jalaya
Chupne vale ne munh kyun dikhaya
Ab voh ham hain na voh hamnashin hai
Hae sab ho ke kuch bhi nahin hai

In this very rapture, I swayed
Kissing passion, my fate's lips
In the instant my eye blinked
lightning sorrow struck, a roaring sound
Alas, fate changed its colors
I saw then: I'll never see him again

Why display his splendor to me
Why come to depart
Without reason he burnt my heart
Why alight then vanish
I am not the same, nor my mate
Alas, in so much, there's nothing left

Qawwali 3

This next *qawwali*, "Where's my Ram," is an
extrapolation of the idea of *hama ust* (Everything is He), which is tied to Ibn al-'Arabi
and Muhammad Ashraf Simnani. Amjad uses
the image of a female lover-devotee in the
process of discovering her beloved; when she
does, she realizes that he's within herself. The
beloved of this *qawwali* is Ram, who like
Krishna is an *avtara* (manifestation) of Lord
Vishnu. The geographical motifs (the Ganges,
the rain clouds) of this poem are clearly meant
to engage theosophical ideas of Sufi and bhakti
traditions that valorize the "Oneness of Being."
Not only is the lover in this poem thirsting for
her beloved just like the devotees of Krishna do,
but she also identifies with the Biblical–Koranic
Prophet Jacob, who loses his vision because of
his incessant searching and weeping for his son
Joseph. Amjad, writing in the early twentieth
century, is exerting a hermeneutics closely
tied to Kabir and Guru Nanak as well as to
the Arabic and Persian Sufi discourses that
often speak of the lover-seeker as Jacob and
the object of their search as Joseph, frequently
referred to as the "Moon of Canaan." Apart
from the Hindu/bhakti traditions, the supreme
lord is identified as Parameshwar even in the
Sikh devotional literature. Toward the end,
the *qawwali* also contains a wordplay quite
frequently employed in bhakti poetry: Har,
from Sanskrit, is an epithet of Lord Shiva; and
har in Persian and several Indian linguistic
traditions means "every."

Where's my Ram? (*Mera Ram kahan hai*)

Rat jab log sote the sare
Chup kahri thi main ganga kinare
Lahren leta tha darya ka pani
Josh par thi nadi ki javani
Chand pani men tha aksafgan

Ma'i Ganga ka pur nur joban
Dekh kar aisa dilkash nazara
Shiddat-e gham se main ne pukara
Ruh bismil hai jan nim jan hai
Main yahan ram mera kahan hai

At night while all slumbered
Silently, I stood on the shores of Ganga
The river's water churned waves
The stream's youth flowing full with passion
Fallen reflection, the moon in water –
Mother Ganga's bosomy youth
I laid eyes on this alluring sight
and with a pang of pain so sharp, I cried out:
Injured is my soul, half-dead my life
I am here, but where's my Ram?

Charkh par ghumne vale badal
Mah ka munh chumne vale badal
Asman tak hai teri rasa'i
Khak uftada main na saza'i
'arsh-e a'la pe teri nazar hai
Farsh-e khaki pe dukhya ka sar hai
Yusuf-e gum shuda ka pata de
Dhund kar mujh ko itna bata de
Chand kis burj men voh nehan hai
Main yahan ram mera kahan hai

Those clouds that roam the spheres,
Those clouds that kiss the moon,
Your reach, to the sky
My worth, only dust
Your glances land on a heavenly throne
My pained head, on the spread of dust
Point me towards the long-lost Joseph
Seek him for me, and tell me this:
Oh moon, in which sphere does he hide?
I am here, but where's my Ram?

Aye lo kis zor se bijli karki
Ruh qalib men ghabrake pharki
Bunden parti hain jhim jhim zamin par
Asman ho gaya kham zamin par
Cha'i hai kya ghata kali kali
Chand ne dark e surat chupa li
Khauf se mera dil bhi hai muztar
Main chupun kis ke daman me jakar
Ah kis ja mera jan-e jan hai
Main yahan ram mera kahan hai

Watch how lightning roars
Terrified, my soul flutters in my heart

Drops pour down on the mouth of this
    parched soil
The sky has bowed to earth's presence
How the black clouds spread themselves
fearful moon in hiding
My heart, too, restless with fear
In whose protection shall I seek my shelter
Alas, where is my darling mate
I am here, but where's my Ram?

Koi bekas ka rahbar nahin hai
Mehrban mujh pe ko'i nahin hai
Lak ro ro ke main ne pukara
Mahv-e ghaflat hai sansar sara
Yas ki os barsi jo dil par
Di sada ra'd ne yeh garaj kar
Dekh hai parmeshvar mujh men tujh men
Ram tujh men hai ram mujh men
Ram hai jan men ram tan me
Ram jal thal men hai ram ban men
Ram ka zikr har nam men hai
Ram sab men hai sab ram men hai
Jalva us ka bad o nek men hai
Shan us har ki har ek men hai
Kis liye phir yeh shor o fughan hai,
main yahan ram mera kahan hai

Nowhere does the destitute find his guide
Not a single soul favors me

A thousand times I cried out
to the whole world, lost in utter stupor
When the dew of despair rained on my heart
Thunder, roaring, replied, a cry:
Look, the Parameshwar is in me, and in you
Ram is, in you and in me
Ram is, in soul and in body
Ram in flowing streams, Ram in forests
Ram's remembrance graces every name
All is in Ram and Ram is in all
His splendour, in the good and in the bad
Har's majesty shines from every single (*har*)
    form
Why then are these cries and tumults raised:
"I am here, but where's my Ram?"

These *qawwalis*, texts par excellence of South Asian shared cultural milieu, foreground the devotees intimate relationship with the divine and rework rigid gender, nationalist, and communal hierarchies; they make those who wish to safeguard neat and text-centric cultural and religious divides more inured to alternative existential modes: the primary (and most legitimate) epistemic basis of devotion in these textual traditions is the sincere heart and not any written text.

Notes

1   Sunil Sharma, "The City of Beauties in Indo-Persian Poetic Landscape," *Comparative Studies of South Asia, Africa and the Middle East* 24(2), p. 77, 2004.

2   See Romila Thapar, *Early India: From the Origins to AD 1300*. Berkeley: University of California Press, 2002, p. 5.

3   See John Stratton Hawley and Mark Juergensmeyer, *Songs of the Saints of India*, New Delhi: Oxford University Press, 2004, pp. 35–61.

4   See Muzaffar Alam, *The Languages of Political Islam: 1200–1800*, Chicago: The University of Chicago Press, 2004.

5   See Muhammad Iqbal, *Kulliyat-e Iqbal Urdu*, New Delhi: Maktaba-e Islami Publishers, 1997, p. 51.

6   See Syed Akbar Hyder, *Reliving Karbala: Martyrdom in South Asian Memory*, New York: Oxford University Press, 2006, p. 170.

7   John Stratton Hawley, "Krishna and the Gender of Longing," from *Love, Sex and Gender in the World Religions*, Joseph Runzo and Nancy Martin (eds), p. 240. Oxford: Oneworld, 2000.

8   See Carla Petievich, "*Rekhti*: Impersonating the Feminine in Urdu Poetry," *South Asia* 24, 2001, pp. 75–90.

9   Jacques Derrida, *The Work of Mourning*, Pascale-Anne Brault and Michael Naas (eds), p. 110. Chicago: University of Chicago Press, 2001.

3

Tolerant Hinduism

Shared Ritual Spaces – Hindus and Muslims at the Shrine of Shahul Hamid

Vasudha Narayanan

In contrast to what is commonly perceived as Hindu–Muslim conflict in the Indian Subcontinent, the sharing of a metaphoric world and the mutual adaptation of religious vocabulary and ritual among Hindus and Muslims may be found in the Tamil-speaking region of South India. A striking example of this mutual adaptation can be found at the *dargah* (shrine) of Shahul Hamid (ca. 1513–1579) in the city of Nagore.

Nagore is on the eastern coast of South India, and the dargah is right on the Bay of Bengal. This is where Shahul Hamid lived in the later part of his life, and where he is buried. Shahul Hamid was apparently a thirteenth-generation descendant of Muhiyudin Abd al-Qadir (Katiru) al-Jilani, a renowned Sufi saint. When just a child, he was visited by the prophet Kiliru (Khazir) and blessed by him. Kiliru spit into Shahul Hamid's mouth, thus transmitting divine grace (a common motif in Tamil Islamic poetry). Shahul Hamid did not get married but is said to have spiritually fathered a son. (This son, Yusuf, and a daughter-in-law are also buried at Nagore.) At the age of 44, after extensive travels all over the Middle East, Shahul Hamid reached the city of Nagore. He was received with honor by Achutappa

Nayakar, the Hindu ruler of Thanjavur, who is said to have donated two hundred acres of land to his entourage. Later, another Hindu ruler – Raja Pratap Singh (1739–1763) – paid for the dargah's fifth minaret (the tallest of the five), after he was blessed with a son through the grace of Shahul Hamid. Yet another Hindu king, Tulasi, is said to have bestowed fifteen villages on the dargah.

When one visits the Nagore shrine today, one is struck by the number of Hindus offering worship to the saint. According to the managing trustee of the dargah, about 60 percent of the premises has been built by Hindus, and about 50 to 75 percent of pilgrims on any given day are Hindu.

Some patterns of worship at the shrine parallel Hindu worship in temples. Hindus as well as Muslims come here, for example, to shave the head of a child for a first tonsure. While this is also a Muslim custom, most of the Hindu participants in the ritual are not aware of the Islamic precedent. Hindus and Muslims also buy tin- or silver-plated facsimiles of body parts, houses, sailboats, motorcycles, and the like to offer to the saint, just as they would make an offering to a deity in a Hindu temple. The image of a

Perspectives on Modern South Asia: A Reader in Culture, History, and Representation, First Edition.
Edited by Kamala Visweswaran.
© 2011 Blackwell Publishing Ltd. Published 2011 by Blackwell Publishing Ltd.

particular body part is offered when one requests a cure in that part of the body. Similarly, tiny models or etchings of houses or motorcycles are offered when devotees petition to procure the real thing. When a cure is effected or when one obtains what one wants, a return pilgrimage is made to offer a thanks-giving donation.

There are other symbols of worship that suggest the Hindu cultural context. Shahul Hamid's footprint is preserved in the dargah. Veneration of footprints or the feet of a guru is typical of many Hindu traditions, but not as common in an Islamic context. Generally in Tamil Islamic literature, the motif of spitting into a disciple's mouth is seen as a spiritual and "biological" conductor of right lineage, functioning like the feet and their imprint in Hindu circles. What we find in the case of Shahul Hamid is the image of saliva in literature and the foot in ritual, bringing together two cultural markers of veneration.

While the trappings of worship sometimes reflect the Hindu cultural context, the architecture does not. It may not be possible to speak of "Hindu" or "Muslim" architecture in northern India, but in the south the architecture of a mosque is clearly different from that of a temple. The dargah of Shahul Hamid is more Muslim minaret and dome than Hindu tower and pillar.

The central part of the dargah is the tomb of Shahul Hamid. It is set like a Hindu inner shrine (*garbha grha*), which one approaches through seven thresholds. Four of these doorways are made of silver, and three of gold. To the left (as one faces the tomb) are two other shrines – those of Shahul Hamid's son Yusuf and daughter-in-law Ceytu Cultan (Sayid Sultan) Bibi. The doors to the tombs (called *samadhi*, using a Sanskrit word) are usually closed; they are open only very early in the morning and late in the evening. Hindu and Muslim men and women mingle freely and go up to the doorways to offer their prayers. The dargah, therefore, becomes a negotiated space for Hindus, Muslims, men, and women to come together and worship a common source of power, a power that is called *barkath* or *shakti* by followers.

Behind the shrines is a well. According to one of the hereditary trustees of the dargah, the waters of this well and the waters of *zam zam* (the spring at Mecca) have the same source. Beyond the well is a large "tank" – similar to the temple tanks found all over South India. Pilgrims wash their feet or take a dip in the water before going in to worship. The waters serve as markers for the two emphases of this dargah – the connection with the Middle East and the connection with the local Tamil Hindu culture. The activities near the dargah tank are similar to those that take place near any Hindu temple of Tamilnadu; and yet the waters of the well nearby are considered to be miraculously connected to the *zam zam*, near Mecca. The figure of Shahul Hamid has the same dual connection; while he is uniquely part of the Tamil landscape, he is inextricably linked with al-Jilani and parts of the Middle East.

While terms like "Hindu" and 'Muslim' are often used today to compartmentalize people and to articulate politically rigid categories, a nuanced understanding of the relationship between Hinduism and Islam must take into account the political, social, and intellectual contexts of the two traditions. There are, of course, some strict caste and community boundaries within the many Hindu traditions (marking, in particular, issues of diet and marriage), but there are also many permeable boundaries between the Hindu communities and Islam. A visit to the dargah of Shahul Hamid in Nagore reminds us of this permeability and helps us to understand just how frequently religious "boundary crossings" can and do happen in India.

Notes

This essay was previously published as "Shared Ritual Spaces: Hindus and Muslims at the Shrine of Shahul Hamid in South India," *Religious Studies News*, February 1998, 15, 30, 41.

4

Hindu Gods and Us: Our Goddesses and the Hindus

Kancha Iliah

What is the relationship between the Hindu Gods and ourselves? Did the Hindu brahminical Gods treat us as part of their people, or even as legitimate devotees? Why did Hinduism create the images of many Gods as against the universal ethic of monotheism? Did brahminical polytheism work in the interest of Dalitbahujan masses or did it work in the interest of brahminical forces who are a small minority? Further, what is the relationship between the Dailtbahujan Goddesses and Gods and the Hindus? Did the Hindus respect these deities or worship them? What are the socioeconomic and cultural forms of the Dalitbahujan Goddesses and Gods? Since the majority of the people relate to the Dalitbahujan Goddesses and Gods, isn't there a need to present their narratives? I shall discuss all these aspects in this chapter.

Hinduism has a socioeconomic and cultural design that manipulates the consciousness of the Dalitbahujans systematically. It has created several institutions to sustain the hegemony of the brahminical forces. Through the ages it has done this by two methods: *(i)* creating a consent system which it maintains through various images of Gods and Goddesses, some of whom have been co-opted from the social base that it wanted to exploit; and *(ii)* when such a consent failed or lost its grip on the masses, it took recourse to violence. In fact, violence has been Hinduism's principal mechanism of control. That is the reason why many of the Hindu Gods were weapon-wielders in distinct contrast to the Gods of all other religions. No religion in the world has created such a variety of Gods who use both consent and violence to force the masses into submission. Thus, the relationship between the Hindu Gods and the Dalitbahujans has been that of the oppressor and oppressed, the manipulator and the manipulated. Of course, one of the 'merits' of Hinduism has been that it addressed both the mind and the body of the oppressed.

Brahminical theoreticians have constructed their own theory of consciousness with a specific notion that the majority (bahujan) consciousness is confined to one specific activity

Perspectives on Modern South Asia: A Reader in Culture, History, and Representation, First Edition.
Edited by Kamala Visweswaran.
© 2011 Blackwell Publishing Ltd. Published 2011 by Blackwell Publishing Ltd.

and that that consciousness has to be constantly monitored in order to arrest its further growth. If a consciousness is manipulated to become and remain the slave of another consciousness, some day or the other it will rebel. These revolts are mostly suppressed. All religions have worked out strategies to manipulate and contain such revolts by teaching the slaves a so-called divine morality. But no religion has succeeded in suppressing the slaves for ever.

Other religions admitted slaves into their fold, although they suppressed them in the political and economic domains. But the Dalitbahujans never became part of Hinduism.

Hinduism differs from other religions even in terms of the way it has structured its Gods and Goddesses. All the Gods and Goddesses are institutionalized, modified and contextualized in a most brazen anti-Dalitbahujan mode. Hinduism has been claiming that the Dalitbahujans are Hindus, but at the same time their very Gods are openly against them. As a result, this religion, from its very inception, has a fascist nature, which can be experienced and understood only by the Dalitbahujans, not by Brahmins who regard the manipulation and exploitation as systemic and not as part of their own individual consciousness. But the reality is that every 'upper' caste person takes part in that exploitation and manipulation and contributes towards the creation and perpetuation of such cultures in the Indian context. The creation and perpetuation of Hindu Gods is a major achievement of this culture.

In the face of the Dalitbahujan revolts, the brahminical forces of India invoked their Gods to suppress the consciousness of the revolt. The most obvious and immediate example in the all-India context, is that of the Hindu response to the implementation of the Mandal report in 1990. The 'upper' castes opposed the reservations to OBCs with all the strength at their command, and the Hindutva movement was organized mainly to oppose the pro-reservation movement. Hence, unless one examines in detail how all the main Hindu Gods are only killers and oppressors of the Dalitbahujans, and how the Dalitbahujan castes have built a cultural tradition of their own, and Gods and Goddesses of their own (who have never been respected by the brahminical castes), one cannot open up the minds of the Dalitbahujans to reality.

The Brahminical Gods and Goddesses

The head of the brahminical Gods, Indra, is known as the *Deevatideeva*. He is the original Aryan leader who led the mass extermination of the Indus valley based Adi-Dravidians, who were also Adi-Dalitbahujans. Brahmins consider him a hero because he killed hundreds and thousands of Dalitbahujans at that time. After conquering the Dalitbahujans, he established a pastoral Aryan kingdom. In this kingdom, he did not organize people into production, he merely established a big harem. Enjoying the pleasures of that harem and dancing and drinking were his main tasks. Ramba, Urvashi, Tilothama who are again and again symbolized as representing Hindu beauty and Hindu ideals of service were part of his harem. He might have also been a seducer of many Dalitbahujan women which is probably why brahminical literature constructs him as a powerful *Kaamaabhimaani* (one who enjoys sex) hero. But the most important aspect is that he was the main political leader of the Aryans. It was he who led them to political victory. This leader was first and foremost a killer and an exploiter of Dalitbahujans.

Brahma and Saraswathi

The most important Hindu God – the first of the three murthies – is Brahma. Physically Brahma is represented as a light brown-skinned Aryan. He bears the name of Brahma, which means wisdom. Sometimes he is shown as a person who has four hands, sometimes as one who has only two hands. This God of wisdom is armed with weapons to attack his enemies – the Dalitbahujans. He was the one who worked out the entire strategy of war designed to defeat the Adi-Dalitbahujans. It was he who was responsible for the reconstruction of brahminical society. The Brahmins have worked out the social divisions of caste by claiming that they were born from his head, Kshatriyas from his chest, Vaisyas from his thighs and Sudras from his feet. Such an explanation gave a divine justification for the four classes – which have come to be known as the four *varnas*. Subsequently these classes – particularly the Sudra-slave class – were divided into further castes so that class revolt could be curbed once and for all. Brahminical theoreticians – Kautilya, Manu, Vedavyasa and Valmiki – all worked out mechanisms that structured these castes/classes basically in the interest of the brahminical forces. As we have seen in earlier chapters, it is because of this ideological hegemony that the brahminical order – in philosophy, economy and politics – could be maintained from ancient times to the present age of post-colonial capitalism.

Brahma's wife is known as Saraswathi, which also means learning. The construction of the Brahma–Saraswathi relationship takes place strictly within the philosophical bounds of patriarchy. Brahma himself is shown as the source of wisdom in the Vedas, the early Brahmin writings, which were designed to subordinate the native masses of India. The Vedas themselves express the mixed feelings of crude Brahminism. But since they were written by the Brahmins (i.e. by the early literate Aryans), the texts go against Dalitbahujans. In fact, they are anti-Dalitbahujan texts. The absurdity of Brahmin patriarchy is clear in these texts. The source of education, Saraswathi, did not write any book as the Brahmins never allowed women to write their texts. Nowhere does she speak even about the need to give education to women. How is it that the source of education is herself an illiterate woman? This is diabolism of the highest order. Brahminism never allowed women to be educated. The first woman who worked to provide education for all women is Savithribai Phule, wife of Mahatma Phule, in the mid-nineteenth century. To our Dalitbahujan mind, there is no way in which Saraswathi can be compared to Savithribai Phule. In Savithribai Phule one finds real feminist assertion. She took up independent positions and even rejected several suggestions made by

Jyotirao Phule. Saraswathi, the Goddess, never did that. Her husband, Brahma, is a Brahmin in all respects – in colour, in costumes – and also in the alienation from all productive work. He was responsible for manipulating the producers – the Dalitbahujans – into becoming slaves of his caste/class. Whenever the need arose he never hesitated to initiate a bloody war against the Dalitbahujan masses.

Leave alone the ancient and medieval periods, even in the twentieth century, Hindutva attempts to seduce us into accepting this first enemy of Dalitbahujans as our prime deity. The manipulator of knowledge is being projected as knowledge itself. But there are two kinds of knowledge: *(i)* the oppressor's knowledge and *(ii)* the knowledge of the oppressed. Brahma's knowledge is the oppressor's knowledge. The Dalitbahujans have their own knowledge, reflected in several of the ideas of the Charvakas (Dalitbahujan materialists) of the ancient period. The ancient Brahmins hegemonized their knowledge and marginalized the knowledge of the Dalitbahujan Charvakas, using the image of Brahma. Brahma, thus represented the Brahmin patriarchs, and Saraswathi represented the Brahmin women who had been turned into sexual objects.

Saraswathi is also a contradictory figure. Though she was said to be the source of education, she never represented the case of Brahmin women who had themselves been denied education, and of course she never thought of the Dalitbahujan women. She herself remains a tool in the hands of Brahma. She becomes delicate because Brahma wants her to be delicate. She is portrayed as an expert in the strictly defined female activities of serving Brahma or playing the veena – always to amuse Brahma. Brahma is never said to have looked after cattle, or driven a plough; similarly, Saraswathi never tends the crops, plants the seed or weeds the fields. She is said to have become so delicate that she could stand on a lotus flower. She could travel on a *hamsa* (a swan, a delicate bird). This kind of delicateness is a negative delicateness. It only shows that her alienation from nature is total. In order to live this alienated but luxurious life, the Brahmins have built up an oppressive culture. That oppressive culture was sought to be made universally acceptable.

Vishnu and Lakshmi

The second God who is said to have played a predominant brahminical role, yuga after yuga, is Vishnu. Why is Vishnu said to have been a blue-skinned God? The reason is quite obvious. He is the projection of an association between the Brahmins and the Kshatriyas. This godhead might have been created at a time when the Kshatriyas (a hybrid caste that might perhaps have emerged in cross-breeding between white-skinned Aryans and dark-skinned Dravidian Dalitbahujans) were in revolt against the Brahmins. Jainism and Buddhism were perhaps the last of such revolts. Vishnu is said to be the upholder and preserver of all the principles that Brahma evolved. He is assigned the task of preserving and expanding Brahmin dharma. He wields the *vishnuchakram*, an extremely dangerous weapon, designed to injure all those who rebel against the Brahmins. He is supposed to be merciless in suppressing revolts. Interestingly, he is shown sleeping on a snake which suggests his wickedness more than it does his humanism. For an average Dalitbahujan the snake symbolizes evil, not virtue. He is monogamous as he is married to Lakshmi. The relationship between Lakshmi and Vishnu is no different from that between Brahma and Saraswathi. Lakshmi is supposed to aid Vishnu in his anti-Dalitbahujan designs. Her role is very clear: she must keep pressing the feet of Vishnu as he lies cogitating about the prosperity of Brahmins and the destruction of the Dalitbahujans. She is supposed to procure wealth and victory for the Brahmins, the Kshatriyas and the Vaisyas. But she must also keep a watch on Dalitbahujans. If she comes to know that a Dalitbahujan man or woman has acquired wealth or is revolting against the caste system, she is required to bring that to the notice of Vishnu who will go and exterminate such persons.

Brahminism is so diabolical that even Brahmin and Kshatriya women are assigned significant roles that keep the Dalitbahujans suppressed. Saraswathi must see to it that the Dalitbahujans do not become literate and ensure that they can never understand the brahminical methods of manipulation. Lakshmi is assigned the role of alienating Dalitbahujans from private property: land, gold and other metals. In other words, the Brahmin woman is supposed to see that the Dalitbahujans are denied the right to education and the Kshatriya woman is assigned the duty of denying the right to property to Dalitbahujans. These kinds of roles for 'upper' caste women have played an important part in assimilating them into Brahminism – but as unequal partners. In fact, as Phule repeatedly said, Brahmins were so cunning that they have assigned to Lakshmi the role of being the source of wealth and property while all Brahmin women are denied the right to property. As in the case of Saraswathi, Lakshmi, the source of wealth, is herself a poor dependent.

Assigning these roles to women has had a double-edged function. Within the caste, gender roles are strictly defined but even the oppressed gender is assimilated into the opposition against the other caste/class. Brahmin and Kshatriya men play the role of producing knowledge that lies outside the domain of production, and through which the enemies of brahminical consciousness are controlled. As a result, Dalitbahujan consciousness itself is made to consent to its oppression. If the consent system is broken, the Kshatriya God – Vishnu – is always vigilant to suppress the offenders by using violence. By creating such images of the Gods and Goddesses – Indra, Brahma, Saraswathi, Vishnu, Lakshmi – the possibility of breaking the brahminical system was arrested from several aspects: knowledge, wealth and war being predominant.

It is not very clear why Vishnu and not Brahma was chosen to be reincarnated in different forms at different times to suppress Dalitbahujan assertion. Perhaps it was because the Kshatriyas already wielded political power, but it was important to make the Kshatriya kings acquiesce in their subordination to the Brahmins. If such a message emerges from the Kshatriya Gods and Goddesses themselves, building up consent from the Kshatriyas becomes easier. To a large extent that purpose was also served because through the message of Vishnu and Lakshmi the Brahmins ensured their philosophical and ideological hegemony even over the Kshatriyas, and through the message of Lakshmi even while being out of responsible positions of running the state or conducting wars, the Brahmins could acquire wealth for the mere asking. More important, the Dalitbahujans were suppressed year after year, century after century and yuga after yuga.

The influence of the figures of brahminized women like Saraswathi and Lakshmi is enormous on 'upper' caste women in India. The image of Lakshmi gets reinforced day in and day out since she is said to be the source of wealth. During the 1990 Mandal debate many well-known women writers began to feel insecure and opposed the anti-caste movements without even realizing that these were in essence anti-caste movements. Internalization of personalities like Lakshmi and Sita by 'upper' caste women has several implications for Dalitbahujan movements and also for women's movements. In a casteized patriarchal system Dalitbahujan movements and women's movements should extend helping hands to each other. Such coordination becomes possible only when 'upper' caste women overcome the influence of Brahminism, which restricts their worldview. It is unfortunate that no women writer, not even feminists, have deconstructed the socio-political influences of these Goddesses on women – particularly on brahminical women.

Shiva and Parvathi

The third among the *trimurthies*, the one who is least powerful, and who is easily fooled, is Shiva or Maheswara. In terms of colour and costume he neither resembles Brahma and the Brahmins nor does he resemble Vishnu and the Kshatriyas. He is dark-skinned and dressed like a tribal. Though this God is associated with Brahma and Vishnu, he is assigned a third position and he does not have as defined a role as Brahma and Vishnu. Though he is also powerful and wields the *trishula* as his weapon, basically he plays the subordinate role to Brahma and Vishnu. His behaviour is a little different from that of the Brahmin and the Kshatriya Gods. He loves dancing and gets himself into all sorts of difficulties from which he needs to be rescued by Brahma or Vishnu. The story of Bhasmasura is a good example of Shiva's dependence on Vishnu.

His wife, Parvathi, or Gauri as she is also called, also does not have as specific a role as Saraswathi or Lakshmi. She joins her husband in many of his activities. They dance and roam around. But Parvathi, unlike Saraswathi and Lakshmi, questions many of the activities of her husband. She also plays certain roles which do not, strictly speaking, fall within the domain of ritual Hinduism. Perhaps this couple comes from a tribal origin. On the whole, however, Parvathi supports Saraswathi and Lakshmi in their anti-Dalitbahujan activities. The question is, then, for what purpose was the image of Shankara and Parvathi constructed? To my mind there is a definite purpose in these images. The images of Brahma, Vishnu, Saraswathi and Lakshmi were enough to control the minds of those Dalitbahujans, Vaisyas and Kshatriyas who have already come into the grip of brahminical civil society. These four figures were adequate for ensuring Dalitbahujan consent or, when necessary, suppression. This was because, by and large, the theory of karma had already been universalized among them, although, as I said in earlier chapters, these Gods were not at all known to the Dalitbahujans. To the extent that they were known, the concept of karma has created an ideological preserve of consent, and worked to ensure that the Dalitbahujans did nothing to challenge their hegemony.

What had become problematic and unmanageable, as far as the tribal population was concerned was that slowly but surely they were being pulled into brahminical civil society. However, they did not identify with Brahma and Vishnu, who looked different from them. These Gods were not adequate for creating a consent base among the tribals. So the Brahmins constructed these two images as God and Goddess who were tribals but had accepted the hegemony of Brahminism in all spheres.

Certainly the creation of the images of Shiva and Parvathi was instrumental in creating a consent base among the tribals because Shiva propagates Brahminism and forces people to accept the authority of the Brahmins by violence. These two images were successfully used to subdue the tribals. This is a part of the brahminical theory and practice of 'co-optation.'

The assimilation of Shiva, however, also created its own problems for Brahminism. Over a period of time, the tribals – particularly of South India – were being coerced into the Hindu brahminical system. But the people who came from this tribal background also created friction in Hinduism by asserting autonomy for themselves as the cult of Shiva was relatively more liberal than that of Vishnu. While Vaisnavism became an increasingly fundamentalist Brahminism, Shaivism became a liberal school of Hinduism. With the emergence of Basava's Veerashaiva movement, Shaivism posed a challenge even to Hindu Brahminism. But during the nationalist period the Hindutva school systematically resolved these contradictions among themselves by projecting the notion of a monolithic Hindutva. And as of today, the Shaivite Hindutva is as anti-Dalitbahujan as the Vaisnavite Hindu Brahminism. Of course, the militant Hindutva that was resurrected during the 80s and the 90s closed these ranks totally and presents itself as a monolithic political force (though the rift between Shiv Sena Hindutva and BJP Hindutva are expressions of the Shaivite and Vaisnavite cults, there is a unity in their use of the Rama image for votes). In future, however, in the face of a modern challenge to Hindutva from educated Dalitbahujans, the unification of Vaisnavite Hindutva and Shaivite Hindutva forces is certain. They will be united both in rebuilding the consent of the Dalitbahujans, and in using force against them. By the time Brahminism created the polytheist trimurthies, it also perfected the art of co-opting images in God forms and excluding the masses from the structure of these images. In this way the ultimate objective of subordination and exploitation of the vast masses was achieved to a large extent.

The Avatara Gods

Though the trimurthies and their wives had achieved the main objective of the Brahmins, Dalitbahujan revolts continued to take place. As a result, Brahmins went on creating more and more God and Goddess images through the technique of *avataras*. From among the later avatara Gods and Goddesses, Vamana, Krishna, Rama and Sita are important. Though Phule and Ambedkar did build up a 'Sudra' critique of some of these avataras, it is important to extend this analysis in the light of post-colonial Hindutva. Of the ten so-called avataras of Vishnu, the Buddha is an obvious co-optation. Even an average, urban-educated Indian knows this and therefore, I do not need to analyse the question of the Buddha.

Rama and Sita

The Brahmins did not mince words when they created the last and the most powerful epic images of the powerful monogamous male and female. Both Rama and Sita were said to have been born in Kshatriya families. Rama is a blue-skinned Kshatriya avatara of Vishnu, and Sita is a pale-complexioned avatara of Lakshmi. Why did the Brahmins create these images by writing the *Ramayana* and what did they expect to achieve through this epic narrative?

In North India, after the Dalitbahujan revolts were suppressed, both through consent and through war, the Dalitbahujans of that area were completely subdued. Varnadharma theory and practice became part of mass consciousness. Even the Jain and Buddhist schools that were antagonistic to Brahmin ideology were completely suppressed. Through the establishment of the Kautilyan state (economic and political) Manu's laws were implemented systematically. Brahmins ruled the roost in the system and even Kshatriya assertion no longer continued with the creation of the image of Krishna and after the writing of the Gita. The consent system was so total that no one could raise a finger against the Brahmins. All sections of the population in North India had been subjugated to such an extent that they had lost confidence in themselves and had given up all hope of change.

The Brahmins thought that this was the right time to expand their hegemony to South India, where the Dalitbahujans were ruling. The kingdoms of Tataki, Shambuka, Vali and Ravana were all Dalitbahujan kingdoms. Some Brahmins claim that Ravana was also a Brahmin. This is nonsense. Ravana was a powerful Dravida Dalitbahujan ruler. He was also a militant Shaivaite. Ravana tried to separate Shaivism from Brahminism and to create an autonomous space for Dalitbahujan Shaivism, which is what Basava finally managed to some extent. He established a powerful kingdom with its capital in Sri Lanka so that he could withstand brahminical aggression. The North Indian Brahmins decided that at a time when their dominance was total in the North, the South Indian Dalitbahujan kingdoms must be defeated and the hold of Brahminism extended. Therefore, they planned an aggression on the Dalitbahujan South. The rishis played a very crucial role in deciding on what steps Rama should take. Vishwamitra and Vasista were the driving forces in the *Ramayana* narrative. They are known as Rama's *kula gurus*, people whose words must be respected under any circumstance.

Apart from extending the hold of Brahminism to the South, the *Ramayana* narrative is also a means of subordinating women by establishing role models for them. It asserts that a wife must be subordinate to her husband, irrespective of the caste/class nature of the man; that no woman ought to be a ruler since such exercise of political power by women within the subcontinent (even among Dalitbahujans) might influence the brahminical Aryans, who had by then established a strong patriarchal system. Northern Brahminism decided to place gender roles hierarchically into brahminical patriarchy even in South India. The later Brahmins were not at all pleased about the 'unbrahminical' relationships that were made respectable by Draupadi and Radha. Draupadi became a public figure though she had five husbands and Radha was said to have had relations with Krishna, though she was not

married to him. It is surprising that Hindus give the name Radha to their female children but not of Draupadi. That is because Draupadi had five husbands. Hindus have no disrespect for a man like Krishna who had eight wives but have no respect for Draupadi who had five husbands. Hinduism respects polygamy but not polyandry. In the period of the *Ramayana*, Hinduism was settling down in patriarchal monogamy. So they decided to institutionalize patriarchal monogamy even among the Dravida Dalitbahujans, because the Dravida region still retained elements of a strong matriarchal tradition. The autonomy of men and women was systemic among South Indian masses. This is clear from the Goddess-centered rituals that are universally in vogue in South India even today.

The *Ramayana* is an ancient account of the aggression aimed at brahminizing the Dalitbahujan society of South India, turning it into a brahminizing patriarchy. With this objective the Brahmin rishies came along with Rama, Sita and Lakshmana, attacked the tribal oligarchies and destabilized several independent Dalitbahujan states. Tataki, the famous Dalitbahujan woman, was killed and her state was brought under Brahminism. Then the famous Shambuka was killed, and his kingdom usurped. The major opposition to Rama's aggression came from the ruler of Kishkinda, a tribal king called Vali. The Brahmins befriended Vali's brother Sugreeva and his nephew Anjaneya and, aided by their treachery, killed the powerful Vali. When a beautiful Dalitbahujan woman, Shurpanaka, wanted to marry Rama, the latter said she should ask Lakshmana. But Lakshmana in response cut off her nose and her earlobes. This incident enraged her brother Ravana. He kidnapped Sita to teach Rama a lesson. Of course Rama uses this incident to mobilize the same tribal Dalitbahujans to attack Sri Lanka. Somehow he reaches Sri Lanka and kills Ravana. With the killing of Ravana the Dalitbahujans of South India were conquered by the brahminical Aryans. In fact, what was worse, was after the defeat of Ravana many Brahmin rishies migrated from the North to the whole of South India, which had basically been a casteless society. It was turned into a caste-based society and the Brahmins established their ideological hegemony over the whole of South India.

Thus, in South India, Brahminism was imposed from above. There was considerable resistance to it in civil society which did not accept or practise the brahminical caste system for a long time. Though South Indian Brahmins have tried to institutionalize the caste system, using both coercion and consent, revolts against the system remained part of the history of South India. Anti-Brahmin movements like the Basava movement (in the thirteenth century) the Vemana movement and the Veerabrahma movement (both in the seventeenth century), the Jyotirao Phule movement, the Narayanaguru movement, the DMK movement, Ambedkar's movement and Periyar's movement finally resulted in the establishment of the Dravida Munnetra state in Tamil Nadu (within the Indian Union). All this is a part of South Indian non-Brahmin consciousness that gradually extended to the North in post-colonial India. The establishment of the Bahujan Samaj party in the North in 1984 is an extension of the anti-Brahmin politico-cultural tradition of the South to the North.

As I have argued earlier, in addition to the anti-Brahmin micromovements there were also several cultural traditions in civil society which were antithetical to the brahminical tradition, cultural ethos and economic system. As a result, the brahminical tradition remained only a surface system in the South. In fact, if in North India, brahminical Hinduism kept Muslim culture confined to the converts and to the state institutions, not allowing it into civil society, in South India the Dalitbahujan masses did the same to Brahminism. At one level the Brahmin priest kept himself in touch with the Dalitbahujan masses on certain occasions like marriages and deaths and extracted money, food materials, cows and land in the form of dakshina. But at another level, Dalitbahujans retained their cultural ethos, their economic notions of life, and their political and scientific tempers which were distinct.

In order to understand the alternative cultural, economic and political specificities of South Indian Dalitbahujans, we must examine some of the images of the Goddesses and the Gods that the Dalitbahujans have evolved for themselves. Our entire life-styles and philosophical motivations are closely related to these Goddess/God images even today. The Dalitbahujan cultural ethos of the future needs to be shaped by carefully studying these plural cultural traditions.

Dalitbahujan Goddesses and Gods

There are several images of Goddesses/Gods, which have caste specificities, or regional specificities but there is a basic characteristic that they hold in common in terms of their contexts and the consciousness they give rise to. The consciousness built around Dalitbahujan Goddess/God images is rooted in production processes. Though the Dalitbahujan imagination has played a role in institutionalizing these images it is also important that these images find their centre in human existence and in the relations between productive forces and nature.

In this sense, the philosophical paradigm in which Goddess/God images are developed among the Dalitbahujan masses is different. Deities do not function as means to subdue a section of society; they are not designed to exploit a section within the community; they function to create a common cultural ethic, one that re-energizes the masses so that they can engage in productive activity. To appreciate the contrast between Dalitbahujan culture and Hindu brahminical culture we should examine the Goddess/God images that are popular among the Dalitbahujan village people. It is important to note that the number of Goddesses are more than that of Gods in the Dalitbahujan narratives.

Pochamma

Pochamma is the most popular of Dalitbahujan Goddesses in Andhra Pradesh (I am sure a Dalitbahujan Goddess with similar characteristics exists all over India). Near every village, there is a small Pochamma temple. The notion of temple itself is very different in the case of this Goddess. The temple is a place where the deity exists but not in order that regular pujas be conducted for her. Pochamma is not made the object of a daily puja by the priest. Once every year the masses (and this includes all castes except Brahmins and Baniyas) go to the temple with *bonalu* (pots in which sweet rice is cooked), wash the small stone that represents the deity, and clean the temple and its surroundings. The people can approach the Goddess without the mediation of a priest. They talk to the Goddess as they talk among themselves: 'Mother,' they say, 'we have seeded the fields, now you must ensure that the crop grows well, one of our children is sick it is your bounden duty to cure her...' If one listens to these prayers, it becomes clear that these are a very human affair. There is nothing extraordinary about them. The people put small quantities of the *bonam* food (which is known as *padi*) on a leaf in front of the deity. Finally the chicken or sheep they have brought there will be slaughtered. The Dalitbahujans beat the *dappulu* (percussion instrument), while the young people dance and make merry.

What is their notion of Pochamma? She is the person who protects people from all kinds of diseases: she is a person who cures the diseases. Unlike Sita, her gender role is not specified. Nobody knows about Pochamma's husband. Nobody considers her inferior or useless because she does not have a husband. The contrast between Saraswathi and Lakshmi, on the one hand, and Pochamma on the other, is striking. Pochamma is independent. She does not pretend to serve any man. Her relationship to human beings is gender-neutral, caste-neutral and class-neutral. She is supposed to take care of everyone in the village. She herself relates to nature, production and procreation. The closeness of the relationship that exists between Pochamma and the people is evident in the belief that she understands all languages and all dialects. The people can speak with her in their own tongues; a Brahmin can go and talk to her in Sanskrit; an English person can go and talk to her in English.

Before going to Pochamma everyone bathes, and puts on clean clothes. Those who can afford it, wear new clothes. While approaching Pochamma, one does not have to wear a *pattuvastram* (silk cloth), neither does one have to fast the whole day as one would be required to do when approaching the Hindu Gods and Goddesses. People can eat whatever is available in their houses, drink toddy or arrack. This does not mean Pochamma hates vegetarians (like the Hindu Gods hate non-vegetarians now, and hated vegetarians in ancient India). One can go to Pochamma with some vegetarian food and still approach her. As she is a Goddess of the people, she regards the habits of the people with sympathy. As there is no notion of a priesthood among Dalitbahujans, everybody prays to Pochamma in his/her own way. Can a Muslim or a Christian approach her? Yes. There are no restrictions of religion in a Pochamma temple. People can, and do, go to her whatever their religious moorings. Pochamma does not specify what should be offered to her. The offering depends on the economic conditions of the family. The rich take a sari and blouse piece with the bonalu and then take them back to their respective houses. Those who cannot afford such offerings can go to the temple without anything.

Pochamma's temple is not centralized like Rama, Krishna, Venkateswara temples. She is available in every village and people do not have to travel long distances to visit her. All these things have implications for people's social and economic lives, their time and their psychological satisfaction. In other words, the spirituality that emerges around Pochamma does not divide people; it does not create conditions of conflict; it does not make one person a friend and another an enemy.

Pochamma is not a Goddess who believes in communal conflicts. Religious distinctions have no meaning for her. If a pig passes by a Pochamma temple, while there are people around, nobody takes objection; no animal, including a pig, is inauspicious in Dalitbahujan culture. There is not a single example of communal riots being initiated from Pochamma temples. Such riots have been initiated from Rama temples, Krishna temples, Narasimha temples, just as riots have been initiated from mosques.

Is Pochamma rooted in materialist culture or is she rooted in *mantric* (magical, auspicious chants) culture? There are a number of mantrics in the villages. They too believe in the power of the other world like the Brahmins do. But the village mantrics do not relate to Pochamma. They are independent persons who claim that they can change the conditions of peoples' lives by calling spirits but certainly no mantric claims that he or she controls Pochamma. Nobody is given a mediating role between Pochamma and the people. The village mantrics jump, dance and untie their long hair and begin to spell out the names of powerful trees and leaves, and names of people who discovered them. All this is known as *Shivamtuluta*, and these mantrics are known as *Shivasathulus*. Sometimes they devote themselves to specific Goddesses. There are Shivasathulus who are devoted to Pochamma. They do not mislead people for the sake of money. They work throughout the day and in the evenings they go into a trance of *shivam* (godliness). They never tell people that they can cure diseases. There are women, too, widows mostly, who believe in the power of the other world. After the day's work is over, they too get into a trance of shivam, and become *Shivasathis*. Then they dance and sing and chant the names of trees and plants and people. In fact, Shivasathi-hood is a social outlet for the widows. Is Pochamma literate or illiterate? Nobody knows the answer to such a question but the fact remains that she is not spoken of in relation to education at all. As the village masses – particularly women – are illiterate, they never relate to her or think of her in connection with education or employment. The demands of the masses basically relate to production, procreation and sickness. In that sense she is more a materialist Goddess, concerned with human life and needs.

Kattamaisamma

A Goddess whose popularity is second only to Pochamma, is Kattamaisamma. Kattamaisamma is a Goddess of water, whose deity (a small stone) is kept on the bund of the village tank. She too does not require a big temple. People believe that Kattamaisamma is responsible for ensuring that the tank is filled. She regulates the water resources. The Dalitbahujans believe that right from the seeding stage to the cutting stage, Kattamaisamma protects the crop. The paddy fields below the tanks flourish because of her blessings. Today, that kind of belief is being slowly eroded. They now think that the quality of the crop depends on fertilizers, and pesticides and hence even an average illiterate peasant uses fertilizers. In that sense, the Dalitbahujan mind is a scientific mind and can easily absorb emerging technology and science. But in spite of this, Kattamaisamma continues to play an important role in their consciousness. A whole range of rituals take place around Kattamaisamma.

Once in five years a major festival focussing on Kattamaisamma is celebrated. In some villages, several sheep, goats and chickens are killed and a big feast is organized. Rice is cooked and soaked in animal blood and sprinkled in the fields as *bali* (sacrifice). The belief here is that Kattamaisamma must see to it that the fields yield good crops and that the crops become socially useful. As we say in our language, it must have *barkati* (prosperous utility).

What is the social origin of Kattamaisamma? A primary investigation will indicate that she was a Dalitbahujan woman who discovered the technology of tank construction. She must have wandered around and studied patterns of land and water very carefully. Perhaps she is the one who found out where to locate a tank, what kind of a bund to construct, and how much water to store. Naturally the discovery of such a system would have boosted agricultural production.

Polimeramma

Yet another important Goddess that the Dalitbahujans have created and popularized among themselves is Polimeramma (the border Goddess). Polimeramma is supposed to guard the village from all the evils that come from outside, to stop them at the boundary of the village. The duty that people assign to her is the protection of the whole village, irrespective of caste or class. Once in five or ten years, a buffalo is killed at the Polimeramma temple and the blood is mixed with a huge quantity of cooked rice, while the meat is eaten by those who eat it – mainly Maalaas, Maadigaas and Muslims. The Muslims are not at all excluded from the ritual. The blooded rice is thrown to all the roof tops as bali. All the agrarian families demand such a bali, but the Brahmins and the Baniyas keep themselves apart. Even the Muslim families demand their own share of the bali, as they are part of the agrarian structure in the village.

Muslim men and women do planting, weeding, cutting of crops along with Dalitbahujan men and women. They share the food that the Dalitbahujans take to the fields. They share their individual agrarian skills. The *Peerila* (Moharram) festival is as much a Dalitbahujan festival as that of Muslims. Dalitbahujans lead the *Peeri* procession. They too hold the *peeri* (a large wooden frame with copper plates on top of it and decorated with colourful cloths called *dattees*) on their shoulders. On festive occasions the *biriyani* (a special food wherein mutton and rice are mixed and cooked) that Muslims cook is sent to Dalitbahujan homes. Thus, the taste of biriyani in Dalitbahujan homes is a contribution of Muslims. In a situation of such close relationship between Dalitbahujans and Muslims all the agrarian festivals of Dalitbahujans are also Muslim festivals. The most popular notion of barkati in Telangana villages is taken from the Urdu word *barkat*. In such a situation of close relationship between the Dalitbahujans and the Muslims, the Muslim demand for bali is an integrated process.

After the bali is sprinkled on the houses, the village is closed for one week from other villages. The idea is that the diseases and evils from other villages must not enter this village. Similarly, for one week, the people belonging to this village cannot go to other villages because such a journey would take away the prosperity of the village. During that period, there are debates about prosperity, about good and evil, all centred around production, procreation and diseases.

Part II

The Study of South Asian Society and the Emergence of Modern Forms of Social Classification

Introduction

The arrival of Europeans in search of wealth in South Asia at the end of the 15th century was to have profound effects on the social structure and economy of the region. While Mughal rule was strong throughout the subcontinent between the 16th and 18th centuries, it did not cover the whole region, and until the 18th century various European groups made alliances and traded with local kings and rulers. British territorial ascendancy after the battle of Plassey in 1757 was followed by an intensification of taxation. In 1793, the British enacted the "Permanent Settlement." Under the Mughal rule (and the earlier period of the Delhi Sultanate), there was no real concept of private ownership of land. In practice, rights to land were shared among peasants, who enjoyed hereditary occupancy or usufruct rights. The landed feudal lords who often served as village revenue officials had only limited power to alienate land from others. Lord Cornwallis's 1793 proclamation "settled permanently" the amount of revenue to be paid by these landlords to the state, giving them immunity against revenue increase by the state in addition to security of ownership. The permanent settlement thus declared landholders like the *zamindars*, *taluqdars* and *jagirdars*, as well as their subordinate intermediaries who were responsible for collecting taxes and revenues, to be land proprietors, dispossessing peasants of land rights in the process. The alienation of land from those who worked it, and the establishment of "zamindari" forms of land tenure have had long-term consequences,[1] resulting in ongoing, and increasingly militant struggles for land rights.

Along with land surveys, the first systematic descriptions of South Asians were undertaken by Orientalists who worked for the East India Company and missionaries. As Bernard Cohn points out (and Darini Rajasingham-Senanayake shows for Sri Lanka in her essay in Part IV), the first census efforts were undertaken with the objective of enumerating

Perspectives on Modern South Asia: A Reader in Culture, History, and Representation, First Edition.
Edited by Kamala Visweswaran.
© 2011 Blackwell Publishing Ltd. Published 2011 by Blackwell Publishing Ltd.

the peoples under British colonial rule so that they might be better administered. Coupled with the policy of "divide and rule," it also had the effect of consolidating caste forms of identity as different groups sought new forms of status to earn favor with the Raj. Throughout the period of East India Company rule (1757–1857) and Crown rule (1858–1947) the British consolidated territorial control over India by allying themselves with some groups to displace or conquer others. The evidence suggests that pre-modern social structures, like pre-modern social or religious identities, were more fluid than many ethnic or national identities today.

Cohn discusses one strand of "Orientalist" interpretation of India in his essay in this Part, but as Arun Guneratne explains, the popularizing of the Indo-Aryan language family as the cradle of Western civilization in the 19th century by Max Mueller accelerated the development of Aryan racial theory. Mueller was a primary translator of the Rg Veda, the oldest Sanskrit text that established a hierarchical fourfold division of Aryan society into the Brahmins (priests, scholars), Kshatriyas (kings, warriors), Vaisyas (merchants), and Sudras (peasants, craftsmen). The first three varnas were considered "twice-born" and the last, "once-born." Dalits, or former Untouchables, were outside the varnic system of caste classification, and were thus literally, "outcastes." M.N. Srinivas describes how Vedic ideals and varnic forms of classification worked themselves into Brahminical culture and became a source of Sanskritization, even as Guneratne describes how Aryan and Dravidian racial categories play out in Sri Lankan nationalism and ethnic conflict.

Srinivas, one of the founders of Indian sociology, points out that while colonial rule helped solidify caste identities; it also put into place a form of caste mobility known as "Sanskritization." In contrast to class mobility which occurs at the level of the individual, his theory accounts for how caste groups could change their position in a seemingly rigid caste hierarchy by seeking to emulate the practices of higher castes, like the Brahmins. However, he points out that Sanskritization may not result in higher status for former Untouchables (dalits); indeed as we saw in the last section, intellectuals like Kancha Iliah dispute the desirability of Brahminical culture or religion for dalits. Srinivas has shown that while the varnic system of caste designation seems to work well in North India, in South India the "dominant" (politically or economically powerful) caste in any locality is not likely to be drawn from the upper three varnas (Brahmin, Kshatriya, Vaisya) but from the Sudra category. Due to the emergence of the non-Brahmin Dravidian movement (described by Hamza Alavi in this Part), the major divisions in South India are between Brahmins and non-Brahmins. And while varnic systems of classification work in Nepal, as Rajendra Pradhan explains, major divisions in Nepali society are between upper-caste Brahmin and Kshatriya (Parbhatiya) groups, and ethnic/indigenous janajati groups; or between hill (pahari) people and plains (madhesi) peoples.

While Srinivas's framework has been critiqued, a large body of literature focused on caste mobility and caste identification developed around it through the decades of the 1950s–1990s. Caste exploitation has not disappeared (as Gopal Guru and Anuradha Chakravarty explain in their essay in Part V), but social scientists also focus on class and ethnicity as salient analytic categories. Hamza Alavi is best known for his idea that a "salariat" comprises a particular class of people who run the state bureaucracy in India, Pakistan, and Bangladesh. This class has its origins in Macauley's 1835 Minute on Education, designed to create a group of English-educated Indians who would be translators and intermediaries between the colonial government and the masses it ruled. Alavi charts the rise of Muslim nationalism and the Pakistan movement in the Muslim salariat's demand for inclusion in the colonial state apparatus. In India, the post-Independence turn to "linguistic states" (where Gujarati became the state language of Gujarat, Kannada the state language of Karnataka, etc.) effectively blunted the salariat's unity as a class. Both Alavi and Pradhan show the shifting contours of caste, regional or ethnic identity in Indian, Pakistani, and Nepali contexts.

Note

1 See Siddharth Dube, *Words like Freedom: The Memoirs of an Impoverished Indian Family, 1947–1997*, p. 27. NY: Harper Collins, 1998.

5

Notes on the History of the Study of Indian Society and Culture

Bernard Cohn

The Study of Indian Society and the Caste System

There have been recorded observations on Indian society since the third century BC. It is useful in considering more recent developments in the study of social change in India to sketch briefly the nature and content of the observations and assumptions which observers have made of the Indian social system.

Classical and Arab–Persian accounts
For the period 327 BC to 1498, there are scattered accounts of Indian society written by foreigners. These travellers included Greeks, Romans, Byzantine Greeks, Jews, and Chinese, and, increasingly from AD 1000 onward, Arabs, Turks, Afghans and Persians. Most classical accounts of Indian society follow Megasthenes, who had the advantage of direct observation of parts of India. But as Lach comments:

> Although he was an acute observer, Megasthenes was handicapped by his ignorance of the native languages. Like many Europeans since his time, he was unable to penetrate deeply into the thought, literature and history of the country simply by looking and listening, or by using interpreters.[1]

Megasthenes described Indian society as being divided into seven classes: (1) philosophers who offer sacrifices and perform other sacred rites; (2) husbandmen who form the bulk of the population; (3) shepherds and hunters; (4) those who work at trades and vend wares and are employed in bodily labour; (5) fighting men; (6) inspectors; and (7) counsellors and assessors of the king.[2] Megasthenes also noted that each of these seven 'classes' were endogamous and that one could not change his occupation or profession.[3] From the context of his account it would appear, as with many subsequent observers, that Megasthenes' data came mainly from observation of urban political centres. It is also interesting to note that, at least in the materials of Megasthenes which have survived, he makes no reference to the *varna* theory.

Perspectives on Modern South Asia: A Reader in Culture, History, and Representation, First Edition.
Edited by Kamala Visweswaran.
© 2011 Blackwell Publishing Ltd. Published 2011 by Blackwell Publishing Ltd.

Although there was regular and extensive contact between Rome and India through direct trade contact, Roman accounts, although fuller on geographic information, add little in the form of sociological information to our knowledge of the stratification system in early India.

The earliest Arabic accounts follow the classical view of Indian society in reporting the division of Indian society into seven classes.[4] Al-Biruni (c. 973–1030) appears to have been familiar with Sanskrit sources and does mention the four-varna theory of the caste system.[5] In the seventeenth century many translations were made from the Sanskrit literature into Persian by Indo-Muslim scholars.[6] Abu'l Fazl 'Allami, the author of the $\bar{A}$'in-i-Akbarī, a late sixteenth-century gazetteer and description of Akbar's court, revenue, and administrative system, presents the view that the four varnas were produced from the body of Brahma at the creation of the world. He recognizes that there are internal divisions within the four varnas, but follows Brahmanic theory in attributing these divisions to the mixture of the original varnas through intermarriage.[7]

Functionally, as can be seen in the lists of military and revenue obligations given in the A'in-i-Akbari, the Mughals clearly recognized that the operational level of the Hindu social system was not at the level of the varnas but at the level of kin-based social categories such as we are familiar with in twentieth-century literature on the Indian caste system. The split view of Indian society, which we will see is so typical of nineteenth-century European views of India, of a theoretical varna-based society which sees the four major ideological based categories of Brahman, Kshatriya, Vaishya, and Shudra as being the system, existed functionally along with the necessity on the part of the Mughals to operate with localized kin-based caste groups.

The view of the caste system of the early European travellers

The earliest direct observers of the Indian caste system in modern times were Portuguese adventurers, administrators, merchants, and priests, who began primarily on the Malabar coast to have direct experience with Indian society. Malabar at one and the same time was a highly cosmopolitan society, with enclaves of Arabs (Moplahs), Syrian Christians, Jews, and other foreign peoples, and an area in which the hierarchic principles of the caste system had been worked out in one of its most extreme forms. The Europeans were also fascinated in confronting matrilineal and polyandrous groups.

Early Portuguese observers like Duarte Barbosa[8] naively but accurately reported major cultural features of the caste system which continue to be recognized as central today: the high position of the Brahmans[9] the significance of pollution in relation to untouchability,[10] the bars to commensality among endogamous groups,[11] the relationship of occupation to caste,[12] the application of sanctions within castes to maintain caste customs,[13] and the relationship between caste and political organization.[14]

Striking in Barbosa's description is his matter-of-fact and objective approach in trying to describe what he saw and what he was told; he presents his description of the caste system organized as a hierarchy with Brahmans on top and Untouchables at the bottom. There is no reference to the Hindu theory of the varnas and no moralizing about the benefits or evils of the system. In many respects European accounts for the next 250 years do not progress much beyond Barbosa's reporting. Unlike many of the Europeans who followed him to India, for shorter or longer periods, Barbosa knew an Indian vernacular well and was recognized by his contemporaries for his linguistic abilities.[15]

Although there were others over the next 250 years who became fascinated with Indian society, most accounts by Europeans which circulated in Europe tended to focus on the Mughal courts and on political and commercial matters rather than on Indian society itself. Jean Baptiste Tavernier, a French merchant and traveller who made six voyages to the Middle East, India, and South-East Asia between about 1631 and 1667, wrote accounts of his travels that are typical of the works of this period.[16] He describes in detail the various routes and points of interest historically and commercially in his travels in India, much like a forerunner of Murray's guide to India.[17] He provides a history of the reign of Aurangzeb mainly based on oral evidence, and extensive discussions of commercial activities. Finally, Tavernier reports on various Hindu beliefs, rituals, and customs. This reporting is based on conversations with Brahmans and on eyewitness reports. The caste system receives very brief notice. Tavernier bases his views on what he 'ascertained from the most accomplished of their priests',[18] that is, that although there are believed to be seventy-two castes, 'these may be reduced to four principal [castes], from which all others derive their origin'.[19] Tavernier and other European travellers appear to have had little difficulty in finding Brahmans to discuss Hinduism with them.

Abraham Roger, the first chaplain at the Dutch factory at Pulicat in Madras, studied Hinduism from a Dutch-speaking Brahman, Padmanubha, in the 1630s. Roger's account of Hinduism was published in 1670, twenty years after his death, and contains Padmanubha's Dutch translation of Bhartrihari's *Satakas*.[20]

Developments in the Later Eighteenth and Early Nineteenth Centuries

With the establishment of British suzerainty in the later eighteenth century, the rapid acquisition of knowledge of the classical languages of India by a few British officials, the need for administrative purposes of a knowledge of the structure of Indian society, and the intensification of missionary activities, systematic knowledge of Indian society began to develop very rapidly from 1760 onward. Three major traditions of approach to Indian society can be seen by the end of the eighteenth century: the orientalist, the administrative and the missionary. Each had a characteristic view, tied to the kinds of roles which foreign observers played in India and the assumptions which underlay their views of India.

The orientalist
Although there was some knowledge of the learned traditions of India, both Hindu and

Muslim, before the middle of the eighteenth century, it was not until the post-Plassey generation that a cumulative knowledge of Persian and Sanskrit and the vernacular languages began to develop which enabled the British to begin to comprehend the depth and range of texts and their contents through which the religion, philosophy, and history of India began to become known to Europeans. Alexander Dow, an officer in the East India Company's army, was one of the first to publish a translation of one of the standard Persian histories of India, *Tarikh-i-Firish-tahi*, which was published as *The History of Hindustan* in 1768–1771. As was typical for the period, Dow prefaced his translations with a number of essays, one on the nature of Mughal government, one on the effects of British rule in Bengal, and 'A Dissertation Concerning the Customs, Manners, Language, Religion and Philosophy of the Hindoos.' To Dow, customs and manners appear to have largely meant Brahmanic prescriptions derived from his study in Persian and 'through the vulgar tongue of the Hindoos' of 'some of the principal shasters'. This he did with the assistance of a pundit from Banaras. Although Dow had tried to learn Sanskrit, apparently his official duties prevented him from mastering the language, but he was fully aware of the difficulties of understanding Hinduism through Persian translations. Matters which we would call sociological are treated in seven pages out of the fifty of his essay and cover the four varnas, which he sees as four great tribes, each of which is made up of a variety of castes; the tribes do not intermarry, eat, drink, or in any manner associate with each other. Dow presents the Brahmanical theory of the origin of the system as derived from parts of the body of Brahma. The caste system is treated in two pages. Other customs Dow thinks worth noting are astrological concerns at the birth of a child, early marriage, suttee, disposal of the dead, the privileged legal position of the Brahmans, the role of *sannyasis* as conveyers of Hinduism and types of penances which both sannyasis and the public sometimes perform.

The orientalists seem to have been convinced that the texts were indeed accurate guides to the culture and society of the Hindus. N. B. Halhed, who provided the first compilation and translation from the Dharmashastras under the title *A Code of Gentoo Laws, or, Ordinations of the Pundits, From a Persian Translation, Made from the Original, Written in the Shanscrit Language*, published in London in 1776, commented that from these translations 'may be formed a precise idea of the customs and manners of these people'.[21]

A view of Indian society which was derived from the study of texts and cooperation with pundits and *sastris* (scholars of Hindu scriptures) had several consequences. In the first instance it led to a consistent view that the Brahmans were the dominant group in the society. This was the function of the view which came from the texts themselves – a view which sees the Brahman as the centre of the social order, which prescribes differential punishments for crimes based on one's varna status, which prohibits other varnas than Brahmans from learning certain texts, and which generally exalts the sacredness of the Brahman. The acceptance of this view is all the more odd in that it flew in the face of the evidence of the political structure of late eighteenth- and early nineteenth-century India, in which there were few Brahman dynasties, and political military power rested in the hands of other groups in the society.

The acceptance of a textual view of the society by the orientalists also led to a picture of Indian society as being static, timeless, and spaceless. Statements about customs which derived from third century AD texts and observations from the late eighteenth century were equally good evidence for determining the nature of society and culture in India. In this view of Indian society there was no regional variation and no questioning of the relationship between prescriptive normative statements derived from the texts and the actual behaviour of individuals or groups. Indian society was seen as a set of rules which every Hindu followed.

The missionary

The missionary view of India developed slightly later than the orientalist view. The first

full expression of this view was contained in Charles Grant's *Observations on the State of Society among the Asiatic Subjects of Great Britain, Particularly with Respect to Morals, and on the Means of Improving It*. Grant, who was one of the early evangelicals, and who served as a commercial official in Bengal from 1774 to 1790, wrote the tract in 1792 for Henry Dundas, President of the Parliamentary Board of Control, the body responsible for the supervision of the East India Company's government.[22] Grant's view of Indian society and Indian character is summed up in the following quotation:

> Upon the whole, then, we cannot avoid recognizing in the people of Hindostan, a race of men lamentably degenerate and base, retaining but a feeble sense of moral obligation, yet obstinate in their disregard of what they know to be right, governed by malevolent and licentious passions, strongly exemplifying the effects produced on society by great and general corruption of manners, and sunk in misery by their vices . . .[23]

Grant felt that the caste system, the legal system, government, and above all the despotic role of the Brahmans who control the society are the cause of the degraded state of the Hindus. Since society and culture are based, directed, and maintained by the religious system, the only hope for the improvement of Hindus and Hindu society lies in the elimination of Hinduism. This can be accomplished by government support of a highly effective campaign by Christian missionaries to convert the Indian population to Christianity.

The early nineteenth century saw a considerable literature by missionaries and by the evangelicals on Indian society. Claudius Buchanan, Sir John Shore, William Carey, and William Ward all produced extensive works in much the same tenor as Grant's *Observations*. In these later works, especially in William Ward's *Account of the Writings, Religion and Manners of the Hindoos*, originally published at Serampore in 1811 in four volumes, but subsequently republished with some changes in content and title in 1815 and in 1820, the nature and type of 'documentation' of the condemnation of Hindu society changed. There is much more of an attempt to condemn Hindu society and to hold up the religion to ridicule with translations from the Sanskrit texts. In addition, increasing attention was paid on the basis of eyewitness and hearsay accounts of what the missionaries took to be everyday examples of the depravity of the Hindu, suttee, purdah, sale of children into salvery, veneration of the cow, worship of idols, and the caste system. The caste system was described by William Ward:

> Like all other attempts to cramp the human intellect, and forcibly to restrain men within bounds which nature scorns to keep, this system, however specious in theory, has operated like the Chinese national shoe, it has rendered the whole nation cripples. Under the fatal influence of this abominable system, the bramhuns have sunk into ignorance, without abating an atom of their claims to superiority; the kshutriyus became almost extinct before their country fell into the hands of Musulmans; the voishyus are no where to be found in Bengal; almost all have fallen into the class of shoodrus, and shoodrus have sunk to the level of their own cattle.[24]

The venom heaped on the caste system appears not to have been accidental, as the missionaries considered it necessary to destroy what they thought was the social basis of Hinduism. As long as those who converted to Christianity were merely another caste, as far as the rest of the Hindu population was concerned, and as long as an individual who converted cut himself off from the rest of society, there was little hope of diffusion of Christianity through normal channels of communication. As groups and individuals converted, the missionaries found themselves having to take on total economic and social responsibility for them as well as providing them with a different religion.[25]

The major thrust of the missionaries in their writing was to condemn Hindus and Hindu society along the lines indicated above; however, as a by-product of their proselytizing endeavours, they often made major contributions to the empirical study of Indian society. This partially came out of their need for translations of the Bible and religious tracts into the Indian vernaculars. Perhaps the first sociolinguistic study we have of an Indian language is William Carey's *Dialogues Intended to Facilitate the Acquiring of the Bengali Language*, published at the Press at Serampore in 1801. This work, which reads like a forerunner of modern language teaching materials for learning a language through the oral–aural method, is a series of dialogues between various types of Indians – zamindars and their tenants, zamindars and their officials, washermen and fishermen, cultivators, and various types of women. The different social and occupational groups are recorded as speaking presumably as they would in normal conversation.

William Adams, who came to Bengal as a Baptist minister in the early nineteenth century, was commissioned to do reports on indigenous education. These were highly laudatory of the nature of traditional vernaculr education and reported in detail on the continued vigour of indigenous education in the 1830s.[26] In the middle of the nineteenth century Robert Caldwell spent fifty years of his life in South India. His study, *Comparative Grammar of the Dravidian or South Indian Family of Languages*, was one of the first systematic accounts of the Dravidian languages and was to have considerable indirect effect on the politics of South India. Stephen Hislop, a missionary in Central India, provided some of the earliest and most useful descriptions of the tribal peoples of Central India. In the twentieth century, Charles Freer Andrews and Edward Thompson were important interpreters of changing Indian society in relation to the rise of nationalism and were consistent defenders of India and Indians in the face of official British policy.

The orientalists and the missionaries were polar opposites in their assessment of Indian culture and society but were in accord as to what the central principles and institutions of the society were. They agreed that it was a society in which religious ideas and practices underlay all social structure; they agreed in the primacy of the Brahman as the maintainer of the sacred tradition, through his control of the knowledge of the sacred texts. Both groups essentially accepted the Brahmanical theory of the four varnas and saw the origin of castes in the intermixture through marriage of the members of the four varnas. Neither group related what they must have known was the structure of the society on the ground to their knowledge of the society derived from textual study and discussions with learned Brahmans. There was little attempt on the part of either to fit the facts of political organization, land tenure, the actual functioning of the legal system or the commercial structure into their picture of the society derived from the texts. Both the orientalists and the missionaries agreed that Hinduism as practised within the realm of their observation in the late eighteenth and early nineteenth centuries was filled with 'superstition' and 'abuses' and that by and large the Hindus were debased and licentious. Their major differences lay in that the orientalists admired in theory the civilization and religion embodied in the texts and saw the difficulties of Indian society as being a fall from a golden age. The missionaries saw the society and culture as always having been corrupt, pernicious, and filled with absurdities.

The differences in view of the missionary and orientalist were related to their respective social backgrounds and their occupational roles in India. The orientalists tended to be better educated and from the upper classes of Great Britain; some, as Sir William Jones, were trained as scholars before their arrival in India and they wanted to treat Sanskrit and Persian learning with the same methods and respect as one would treat European learning. Their general political and social stance was conservative in that they accepted the status quo. They saw stability and order in the theory of caste. William Robertson, one of the Scottish moral philosophers, who, although not a Sanskrit or Persian scholar, was a disseminator of early studies of Indian tradition, argued:

> The object of the first Indian legislators was to employ the most effectual means of providing for the subsistence, the security, and happiness of all the members of the community over

which they presided. With this view, they set apart certain races of men for each of the various professions and arts necessary in a well ordered society, and appointed the exercise of them to be transmitted from father to son in succession....To this early division of the people into caste, we must likewise ascribe a striking peculiarity in the state of India; the permanence of its institutions, and the immutability in the manners of its inhabitants. What now is in India, always was there, and is likely still to continue: neither the ferocious violence and illiberal fanaticism of its Mahomedan conquerors, nor the power of its European masters, have effected any considerable alteration. The same distinctions of condition take place, the same arrangements in civil and domestic society remain, the same maxims of religion are held in veneration, the same sciences and arts are cultivated.[27]

Many of the orientalists in India were concerned with judicial affairs of the East India Company, as were Halhed, Jones, and Colebrooke. In their role as judges they were confronted with Indians who by the nature of court action appeared to be litigious, purveyors of false testimony, dishonest, and cheats. On the other hand they were studying Sanskrit legal treatises with pundits and were impressed with the learning and sophistication of Hindu law. They were trying to apply Hindu law to the cases they were hearing on the grounds that Indians would be best governed under their own law rather than under imported British law. The gap between the way Indians behaved in the courts and what the 'orientalist' judges believed was the law and the theory of the society was seen as a fall from an older and better state of society caused by the intervention of foreign rules, Muslim and European.

The missionaries with much the same perceptions and information interpreted the situation differently because of their differences in background. They largely came, particularly the Baptist missionaries, from lower orders in British society; they were committed to reform of their own society as well as of Indian society, and they were concerned with changing India rather than with maintaining the status quo.

The Growth of an Empirical Knowledge of the Structure and Functioning of Indian Society

The period 1757 to 1785 was a time in which the officials of the East India Company in Bengal had to develop an administrative system capable of maintaining law and order and producing in a regular fashion income to support the administrative, military, and commercial activities of the company and to provide a profit for its owners. Through this period the company officials had to learn from scratch a great deal about India, Indians, and how they had been governed. The assessment and regular collection of land revenue, it became clear by Warren Hasting's time, required considerable detailed knowledge of the structure of Indian society. As the East India Company in Madras, in Maharashtra, and in upper India came into contact with and had to establish relations with a wide range of states, a knowledge of Indian political history and a working knowledge of the internal political structure of Indian states became a necessity.

Persistently, inquiries into the nature of land tenure in Bengal were made, and collections of documents and records of previous rulers were assembled to determine what rights and duties various persons connected with the production of agricultural products had. Although it is clear that many of the efforts to learn the nature of Bengal rural society were confused and incomplete, none the less there were an increasing number of officials like James Grant and John Shore, who from documents and firsthand experience had considerable knowledge of the actual functioning of Bengali society. The misunderstandings leading to permanent settlement were as much a function of philosophical and social conceptions about the general nature of society and polity and the goals of British policy as they were a misunderstanding of the complicated facts of Bengali social structure.[28]

In addition to the duties which some British officials had to perform in collecting and studying information about Indian rural society, some British, official and non-official, out of interest and curiosity began to study and write on Indian society from first-hand observation in relatively objective fashion. William Tennant, a military chaplain, wrote a two-volume work, *Indian Recreations: Consisting Chiefly of Strictures on the Domestic and Rural Economy of the Mahommedans and Hindoos*, originally published in Edinburgh in 1804, which contains a collection of careful observations of agricultural practices in upper India (see vol. 2). Tennant's goal was to instruct himself about the 'condition of a numerous people, living in a state of society and manners to me almost entirely new'.[29] His information was based on personal observation, 'conversations and writings of several intelligent natives of India, both Mussulmans and Hindoos', and 'oral conversation with the most intelligent of the Honourable Company's civil and military servants'.[30] In short, he applied the techniques which were typical of the earliest generation of anthropologists down to the beginning of the twentieth century: observation and interviews with key native informants and knowledgeable Europeans. Tennant describes a particular village, thirty-six miles from Banaras, of about a thousand acres and a population of a thousand. He briefly mentions the crops and the methods of cultivation and also gives a brief description of the occupations of the principal villagers. In addition to the zamindar, the patwari, and the Byah (grain weigher), he describes the carpenters, blacksmith, washermen, barbers, potters, Chamars, Ahirs, *bárhi* (leaf plate maker), *bhat* (genealogist), shepherds, and the Brahman of the village. Tennant notes that the most numerous occupation (by implication irrespective of caste) is that of plowmen, of whom there were about 100 in the village, who received five seers of grain a day and one rupee for each of two annual plowing seasons.[31]

Another example of careful description of rural society in relation to agriculture was provided by H. T. Colebrooke (1806), one of the early Sanskrit scholars. It is interesting that Colebrooke wrote *Remarks on the Husbandry and Internal Commerce of Bengal* before he was far along in the learning of Sanskrit. His work combines statistical material and summaries of official reports with his own observations and provides a good general description of the cultivation of most of the commercial crops, cotton, indigo, sugar cane, and opium. Colebrooke believed that by and large Bengal was relatively prosperous and was capable of becoming even more so as agriculture developed and manufacturing increased. He was sure that the caste system and the religious systems were in no sense any bar to further development. After quoting an unnamed author who argued that there was a hereditary prohibition on undertaking other than one's father's occupation, and briefly summarizing the four-varna theory of caste, Colebrooke commented:

> In practice, little attention is paid to the limitations to which we have alluded; daily observation shows even Brahmens exercising the menial profession of a Sudra. We are aware that every caste forms itself into clubs or lodges, consisting of the several individuals of that caste residing within a small distance; and that these clubs, or lodges, govern themselves by particular rules and customs, or by laws. But, though some restrictions and limitations, not founded on religious prejudice, are found among their by-laws, it may be received as a general maxim, that the occupation, appointed for each tribe, is entitled merely to a preference. Every profession, with few exceptions, is open to every description of persons; and the discouragement, arising from religious prejudices, is not greater than what exists in Great Britain from the effects of Municipal and corporation laws. In Bengal, the numbers of people, actually willing to apply to any particular occupation, are sufficient for the unlimited extension of any manufacture.[32]

With the rapid expansion of the East India Company's territories in the last decade of the eighteenth century, leading up to the final defeat of the Marathas in 1818, the British became increasingly aware of the bewildering variety of peoples, histories, political forms, systems of land tenure, and religious practices which were to be found in the subcontinent. The mid and late eighteenth century western myth of 'an undifferentiated Orient characterized by the rectilinear simplicity of its

social structure, the immutability of its laws and customs, the primitive innocence of its people'[33] could not be sustained in the face of the experience that the Wellesley generation had in India. Through their direct experience, such as Munro's in the land settlements in Salem District in Madras, Malcolm's in his diplomatic duties in Mysore and with the Marathas, Tod's in his diplomatic duties in Rajasthan, Elphinstone's in his diplomatic and administrative duties in Maharashtra, as well as dozens of other officials, the British now began to have fairly deep if somewhat unsystematic knowledge of Indian society. Coincident with the relatively haphazard collection and reporting of sociological information, usually embedded in revenue reports or in historical works, the company directly supported surveys, part of whose goal was acquisition of better and more systematic information about the peoples of India. One of the earliest and most famous of these endeavours to collect information was that of Dr Francis Buchanan.

Buchanan – who later in his life took his mother's name, Hamilton, on the inheritance of her family's estate in Scotland – was born in Scotland in 1762. He had an excellent education in Glasgow and Edinburgh and became a physician; he apparently made several trips to India as an assistant surgeon on an East Indianman, and then in 1794 joined the East India Company's service as an assistant surgeon.[34] He initially served in what is today East Pakistan and began early to collect and report on botanical and zoological specimens. His work caught the attention of William Roxburgh, the great student of Indian botany. It was Roxburgh who recommended Buchanan to Lord Clive, Governor of Madras, and Lord Wellesley, the Governor General, when late in 1799 they wanted a survey made of Mysore and the Company's territories acquired after the Fourth Mysore War. Buchanan's instructions from Wellesley were to collect information on agriculture, nature of tenures, natural products of the country, manufacturing, commerce, mines and quarries, and the climate. In addition, Wellesley said: 'The condition of the inhabitants in general, in regard to their food, clothing and habitations, will engage your particular attention.... The different sects and tribes of which the body of people is composed, will merit your observance; you will likewise note whatever may appear to you worthy of remark in their laws, customs, etc...'.[35] Buchanan's report was published as a diary, in which he notes under a particular date what he observed or was told about the wide range of topics he was sent to obtain information about. He was obviously a keen observer, and his descriptions of technology, historic sites and plants are excellent. He also obtained considerable data on what we would today call ethnographic accounts of the various castes, their subdivision, and occupations. Most of his information was obtained through interviewing members of various castes, and he is frequently careful in telling us of his sources and his guess as to their reliability.

Buchanan's great work, however, was his survey carried out on the orders of the court of director's of the Company of 7 January, 1807. They wanted a statistical survey of the country, under the authority of the presidency of Bengal. If it had been completed it would cover what is today East and West Pakistan, parts of Orissa and Assam, most of present-day Bihar and Uttar Pradesh exclusive of Oudh, and the Bundelkhand districts. Buchanan was engaged in this work for seven years and completed folio volumes of manuscript. The results of this work have never been completely published and were known in the nineteenth century largely from Robert Montgomery Martin's editing of the materials, which are contained in *The History, Antiquities, Topography, and Statistics of Eastern India* ..., published in three volumes in London in 1838. Martin's volumes cover the northern part of Bengal, the Districts of Dina-jpur and Rangpur, the southern part of Assam, and the portions of Bihar south of the Ganges, and Gorakhpur district in Uttar Pradesh. In the twentieth century the Bihar and Orissa Research Society and Bihar government undertook to edit and publish the full version of Buchanan's reports which related to Bihar. In all, five volumes on four districts were published and, in addition, three volumes of Buchanan's field

journal which give his itinerary and incidental notes were also published.

The Bihar materials differ greatly in quantity and quality from the Mysore survey of Buchanan. There are extensive statistics on various aspects of the society, estimates of the number of houses classified by general types of persons who occupied them (that is, gentry, traders, artificer, and plowman), health statistics, statistics on types of farm labourers, size of families, types of houses, attempts at statistically estimating standards of living and the numbers engaged in various trades and crafts in the cities and districts. In addition to the statistical material, there are extremely well-organized and detailed descriptions of education and land tenure, as well as normative descriptions of a wide range of customs. Buchanan organized his material under five main headings, Topography and Antiquities, The People, Natural Products, Agriculture, and Commerce, Arts, and Manufacturers. Under the heading 'The People' he discussed demography, his statistics usually being based on interviews with native officials and various registers, which he frequently spot-checked. He paid a great deal of attention to the standard of living of the people and constantly tried to measure income and consumption; he also gave materials on the form and content of education in the districts he covered. He described the various sects of the Hindus and Muslims found and their ritual and theological differences. His discussion of castes was weighted to description of their occupations. Much of what he wrote about the ethnography of Bihar was presented in comparison to Bengal, which apparently was more familiar to him and his readers.

The development of the 'official' view of caste

Buchanan's work in Bengal and Bihar was the forerunner of a continuing effort undertaken by the British in India to collect, collate, and publish for official as well as scholarly use detailed information about all aspects – physical, cultural, and sociological – of every district in India, which reached its high peak with the Imperial Gazetteer of India, published in the early twentieth century. The line of work stretches from Buchanan, through efforts in the 1840s to publish district manuals and histories, through the efforts of the 1870s such as the *Statistical Account of Bengal*, edited by Hunter, to the Provincial and Imperial Gazetteers of the early twentieth century. With the publication for the first time of the census of India on a systematic and all-India basis in 1872, a whole new body of material on Indian society became available. And in North India, with the successive waves of revenue settlements which produced a great deal of material on the relation of people to the land and the organization of Indian rural society, an implicit view of the nature of Indian society and particularly the caste system began to emerge.

The 'official' view of caste was very much related to how the British collected information about the caste system. In the first instance a caste was a 'thing', an entity which was concrete and measurable; above all it had definable characteristics – endogamy, commensality rules, fixed occupation, common ritual practices. These were things which supposedly one could find out by sending assistants into the field with a questionnaire and which could be quantified for reports and surveys; or one could learn about the castes of a particular district by sitting on one's horse or in the shade of the village banyan tree as the adjunct of one's official duty. What was recorded could be collated so that the Lohars, or the Ahirs, or the Mahishyas, or the Okkaligas could be pigeonholed, and one could then go on to the next group to be described. This way of thinking about a particular caste was useful to the administrator, because it gave the illusion of knowing the people; he did not have to differentiate too much among individual Indians – a man was a Brahman, and Brahmans had certain characteristics. He was 'conservative'. His intelligence was 'superior to that of any other Race'. 'His chief fault has been extreme exclusiveness'.[36] 'Not only could one know a 'people' by knowing their caste and what its customs and rules were; what one 'knew' could be reduced to hard facts. 'The 1901 Census [of Bengal] found there were over 205 castes and tribes over 25,000 in population

in Bihar and Orissa. In Bengal there were 450 groups from one to 22,000,000. Half of them did not have over 1,000 members'.[37] India was seen as collection of castes; the particular picture was different in any given time and place, but India was a sum of its parts and the parts were castes.

The 'official' census-based view of caste therefore saw the system as one of separate castes and their customs. In order to understand caste one had to develop classifications to order the data. The most famous classification is H. H. Risley's,[38] in which he reduced the 2,000-odd castes which the census had found in India to seven types: tribal, functional and sectarian; castes formed by crossing; national castes, castes formed by migration; and castes formed by changing customs. After the castes had been counted and classified and their customs and characteristics recorded, the gnawing question remaining was – why did this 'caste' exist; what were its origins? Here origins were taken not as a direct historical question. Unlike the early orientalists the 'official' ethnographers of caste, although they recognized the Brahmanical theory as embodied in the texts, did not think the texts were documents in which could be traced the history of caste. By origin they rather meant a very broad functional question. Nesfield regarded caste as having its origin in the division of labour, and the occupation was the central determining factor in the system. H. H. Risley argued for a racial origin of caste. Ibbetson saw the major impetus to the formation of caste in 'tribal origins'. Crooke and others came out for more eclectic theories of origin. This eclecticism reaches its final form with the last of the British official ethnographers and census commissioners, J. H. Hutton. He compiled a list of fourteen 'more obvious factors which have been indicated as probably contributing to the emergence and development of the caste system'.[39]

The administrative-official view of caste not only was an outgrowth of the way in which information was collected but also reflected anthropological interests and theories of the period 1870–1910. The reflection of contemporary anthropological theory can be seen both in the general theoretical books written about the caste system and in the data assembled and classified for the series of provincial 'tribes and castes' books, for example W. Crooke's *The Tribes and Castes of the North-Western Provinces and Oudh*, published in four volumes in Calcutta in 1896. In the accounts given of the castes, which are alphabetically arranged, a good deal of space is devoted to 'marriage rules' and subdivisions of the caste, usually termed exogamous sections, which are listed by name with customs of particular sections, for example whether they worship a particular deity or have a distinctive marriage ceremony. There are descriptions of life-cycle rites for most castes. If any mythological origin stories are known about the caste or the exogamous sections, these are recorded as well. There is usually a brief description of the occupation traditionally followed by the caste. Statistics on the geographic distribution of the caste and its major sections taken from the 1891 census are presented in tabular form.

The data and their organization implicitly reflect the work of Morgan, McLennan, Lubbock, Tylor, Starcke, and Frazer. These men were concerned with the use of 'customs' – for example, marriage by capture, polyandry, or the levirate – to infer something about the origin of culture or, as they termed it, 'civilization'. Similarly, religious practices were utilized as disparate bits of information to develop stages of the development of religion. The 'customs' were reported and studied out of their contexts as hard facts which could be compared and classified as to the stage of development. The compilers of the handbooks and gazetteers, the recorders of the proverbs, myths, and practices reported in *Panjab Notes and Queries* or in *North Indian Notes and Queries* were contributing not only to an antiquarian interest in Indian society but to the eventual solution of general anthropological problems.

In 1901 an official effort was made to establish an ethnographic survey of India which would develop as part of the census of 1901. The expense and effort connected with the ethnographic survey were justified on the following grounds: 'It has come to be

recognized – that India is a vast store house of social and physical data which only need be recorded in order to contribute to the solution of the problems which are being approached in Europe with the aid of material much of which is inferior in quality to the facts readily accessible in India'.[40] The need to collect this ethnographic information was considered pressing because the 'primitive beliefs and usages in India' would be completely destroyed or transformed, another late Victorian justification for ethnography. Finally, the survey was justified on the grounds that 'for purposes of legislation, of judicial procedure, of famine relief, of sanitation and dealings with epidemic disease, and almost every form of executive action, an ethnographic survey of India and a record of the customs of the people is as necessary an incident of good administration as a cadastral survey of the land and a record of rights of its tenants'.[41] One cannot help but wonder what use knowledge of marriage customs or a cephalic index would be to an administrator.

The final question connected with the 'official' view of caste was what effect it had on Indian society. The history of British rule in India is to some extent to be seen in the unanticipated consequence of its actions. In some castes in the nineteenth century the effective unit, as in many rural areas today, was the endogamous unit, not the exogamous unit, which the administrators thought of as the effective unit in the system. Through changes brought about by literacy, aspirations for upward mobility, and new geographic and occupational mobility, the endogamous unit began to take on a wider importance. In the urban environment or in the modernized segment of the society, Indians increasingly identified themselves with endogamous groups and with the caste name 'Brahman', 'Kayasthas', 'Nadar', etc. In this process of change the census, the constant need for government applications to identify oneself by caste, the application of varying law to different castes, all seemed to have played a part.

In the census of 1901 H. H. Risley, who was census superintendent, classified castes on the basis of 'social precedence as recognized by native public opinion'.[42] Risley argued that although this turned out to be very troublesome in terms of the amount of argument and petitions submitted by Indians claiming different status than had been granted by the provincial census commissioners, it indicated that this indeed was a successful classification. Risley also noted that most of the petitions were in English, indicating that the educated classes were still very much within the caste system.[43] The question remains, however, of what was cause and what was effect. Did the notion of social precedence on a provincial basis, the enshrining of the categorical level of the caste system as against any real social grouping known in the earlier part of the nineteenth century, in effect create that level? The answer, of course, is not a simple one. The census operations were only one of many changes affecting Indian society at the time. The changes which were being simultaneously recognized included the caste sabha movements, expansion of marriage networks, establishment of caste hostels at colleges, as well as the petitioning of census commissioners for changes in rank accorded a caste in the census tables.

The village 'view' of Indian society

In the early nineteenth century another 'official view of Indian society developed alongside of and to a surprising extent not articulated with the official view of caste. This view was that India was a land of 'village republics', of self-sufficient corporately organized villages. Professor Dumont has recently traced the development of the concept of the 'village community'.[44] Dumont sees three connected but successive meanings in the term 'village community'. In the first phase the village community is seen by British writers as primarily a political society, in the second phase as a body of co-owners of the soil, while in the third phase it becomes to Indians the emblem of traditional economy and polity, 'a watch word of Indian patriotism'.[45] Two documents contain the basic ideas and descriptions of the Indian village community, the Fifth Report of 1812 and Charles Metcalfe's minutes on the village of Delhi of 1830.[46]

Although there is some variation in detail, through time the village community had certain unchanging components.[47] The village consists of a body of co-sharers of the land and of its produce. It is not too clear if this included everyone in the village or just the dominant landholding group. This group made all decisions relevant to the village, social and economic. In the South this group is represented by a headman. Decisions for and by the village are made in council (the panchayat). The economy of the village is self-sufficient, both in producing what it needs and thus needing little from the outside and in having all the crafts and services necessary for the functioning of the village economy. The village is relatively unconnected to other villages or other higher levels in the political system except that taxes are extracted by the government from the village. The village has existed in this form in unchanging fashion 'from the days of Menu',[48] or, in the famous terms of Metcalfe: 'They [the village communities] seem to last when nothing else lasts. Dynasty after dynasty tumbles down; revolution succeeds to revolution; Hindu, Pathan, Mughal, Mahratta, Sikh, English, are masters in turn; but the village communities remain the same'.[49]

In the middle of the nineteenth century Marx and Maine accepted the basic assumptions and the idea of the village community, and it was incorporated into general social and economic theory of the later nineteenth century. R. C. Dutt's important work, *Economic History of India*, originally published in 1902, seems to have been one of the principal sources used by twentieth-century scholars, publicists, and politicians for the continuation of the myth of the Indian village community, which became central to the Indian nationalists' view of their past. In this view India was both economically well off in the pre-modern period and reasonably democratically governed at the village level, and it was the evils of British imperial rule which turned India from this idyllic state into the stagnated rural economy dominated by moneylenders and rapacious landlords.

B. H. Baden-Powell's massive compilation, *The Land Systems of British India*, published in three volumes by Oxford University Press

in 1892, may be seen as the culmination of
the empirical study of the social structure of
rural India which grew out of the more than
100 years of British experience with attempting
to assess and collect land revenue. In this
work Baden-Powell gives a region-by-region
summary of the leading legislation affecting
land tenures in relation to the immediate history
of the regions at the time of their acquisition
by the British. He then tries to trace the general
effectiveness of the land tenure legislation in
terms of the collection of the revenue, discusses
the protection of rights of various groups
who were on the land during the nineteenth
century, and makes passing reference to effects
of British legislation on the distribution of
land. Baden-Powell's work is based on a close
study of the land revenue regulations, annual
and special government reports, the settlement
reports, and the district gazetteers and manuals.
He rightly argues that the empirical basis for
a study of rural India had greatly expanded
in the twenty years since 1870, when Maine
had published his *Village Communities East
and West*.[50]

Baden-Powell's *The Land Systems of British
India* was not just a compilation of data but
contained a series of arguments about the nature
of Indian village communities in relation to
the state. Baden-Powell recognized in general
that there were two claims on the produce
of the soil, the state's and the land-holder's.
He postulated that the government derived
its revenue 'by taking a share of the actual
grain heap on the threshing floor from each
holding'.[51] In order to collect this share a wide
range of offices and intermediaries between
the grain heap and the state developed through
time. These were headmen and accountants
recognized or appointed by the government,
local and district officials, and other revenue
officials of the state. Often these officials were
remunerated by the land grants, which were
turned into permanent hereditary holdings,
and at later stages revenue farmers converted
their contracts to pay the land revenue into
'ownership' of the land. In addition, rights over
the land were established by conquest. Under
this level of the system, that established by the

government and conquest, existed the village,
which was the result of a 'natural instinct'.[52]

Baden-Powell strongly disagreed with Maine,
who saw only one type of Indian village, by
arguing that there are two types of villages
which were distinct in their origin. One type
was variously called 'ryotwari' or non-landlord,
or 'severalty.'[53] In this type of village the
cultivators did not have any right as a joint
or corporate body to the whole estate. 'The
land [estate] is divided amongst themselves
and each man owns his own holding, which
he has bought, inherited or cleared from the
jungle. The holders are not jointly responsible
to the state for revenue or other obligations'.[54]
This kind of holding, according to Baden-
Powell, was closely connected with ideas
and government. It was found in Madras, the
central provinces, and Bombay. It originated,
according to Baden-Powell, in Aryan times
when a chief or raja was political leader and
had no claim as a landlord but did have the
right to grant to individuals the right to settle
on waste land.[55] The other type of village is
termed by Baden-Powell a 'landlord' or 'joint'
village. In these villages there is 'a strong
joint body, probably descended from a single
head, or single family, which has pretensions
to be of higher caste and superior title to the
"tenants" who live on the estate . . .'[56] Those
who live and work in the village do so only
by permission from the joint landholding body.
This type was found in Uttar Pradesh and the
Punjab. It took its origins from the break-up
of raja's estates, grants made to courtiers by
rajas, the conversion of land grants to revenue
officials into a patrimony, the development of
revenue farmers into landowners and 'from
the original establishment of special clans and
families of associated bands of village farmers
and colonists in comparatively later times'.[57]

Baden-Powell combined what he thought of
as direct history with evolutionary stages in the
development of property, from a tribal stage
in which land was held by a tribe, to family
property, to individual property. The logic of
the stages does not mesh with Baden-Powell's
broad-scale history, as private property is found
amongst the ryotwari villages, which derive

from an earlier period in India history than do the joint or landlord villages, in which property is held by families or lineages.

Even though Baden-Powell thought of himself as attacking Maine, his arguments are of the same type as Maine's and lead in the same direction. The Victorian students of the Indian village were interested in the village as a type from which they could infer evolutionary stages and which could be used to compare similar developments or stages in other parts of the world. For the administrator the types and classifications of villages had the same kind of advantage that the official view of caste had: they reduced the need for specific knowledge. One could act in terms of categories. Latently, the categorical or conceptual thinking about villages directed attention away from internal politics in villages and from questions of the nature of actual social relations, of the distribution of wealth, of what was happening to agricultural production; in short the Victorians were not concerned with what the actual conditions of life in the villages were but with general theoretical questions derived from social theory of the day.

The Ethnographic Tradition in the Early Twentieth Century

The census operations of the twentieth century continued to have an ethnographic and physical anthropological component. The emphasis on race and physical anthropology of the 1901 census was repeated in 1931 when B. S. Guha directed an extensive study of physical types in India as part of the census. British officials connected with the census operations continued to produce books on the caste system as a result of their work on the census, notably L. S. S. O'Malley, E. A. H. Blunt, and J. H. Hutton. However, the major development in the first forty years of the twentieth century anthropologically did not concern the bulk of the Indian population, as did nineteenth-century proto-anthropological studies, but concentrated on the tribal populations of India.

Some ethnographic study was done in the north-east of India under government auspices, by Hutton, Mills, and Hodson, who produced as

government ethnographers extensive accounts of major Naga tribes. In the period before World War I, with some government encouragement, Seligman did a study of Vedda of Ceylon, Rivers did his famous study of the Todas, and Radcliffe-Brown his study of the Andaman Islanders. Grigson, an official assigned as a resident in Central India, studied the Gonds, and Fürer-Haimendorf, supported by the Hyderabad government, studied tribal peoples in Hyderabad. The most active ethnographer of the period was a civilian, Sarat Chandra Roy, who carried out a series of important studies in Chota Nagpur on the tribals of that region. It was through Roy's energy and skill that *Man in India* was founded and thrived. Verrier Elwin, whose career encompassed work as a missionary and a Gandhian worker, also carried out important work amongst the tribals of Central India. A. A. Aiyappan was the main exception to the generalization that professional anthropologists studied tribal peoples. Aiyappan, a student of Malinowski, carried out two important functionalist-oriented studies of castes in South India, the Nayadis and the Izhavas. In addition to their ethnographic importance, both studies paid close attention to social change in relation to the status and structure of the castes studied.

Conclusions

By the 1940s the study of Indian society cumulatively had the following components: (1) a broad-scale humanistically oriented tradition which emphasized the relationship between textual studies and a static model of contemporary Indian society; (2) an administrative tradition centered on the census for the study of caste which sought to see Indian society as a collection of discrete entities whose traditions and customs could be classified and studied; (3) a tradition of economic study which sought to describe the working of village economies, with some attention to the social structure of villages; (4) an anthropological tradition centred on the study of tribal peoples; and (5) an historical administrative strain which centred on the general theory of village organization in a broad comparative framework, but without an intensive ethnographic base.

One can go back to the eighteenth century and trace in a rough chronological fashion a changing view of Indian society as it relates to the two major institutions which contemporary students of Indian society concern themselves with – caste and village. Caste, which is a European word, has for the last 200 years been used to circumscribe analytically four distinct components of the social system of India, two structural and two cultural. The orientalist view of the caste system emphasized the broadest ideological category of the system of the varnas, which functionally provides the participants in the system with a very general explanation and a very rough set of categories to account for the hierarchy of castes. The varna categories in the last 100 years, with heightened opportunity for social mobility, may be taking on new meanings for the actors in the system. In addition to the varna categories, the system contains *jat* categories, which are also cultural. A jat is a named group usually spread over a wide territory roughly occupying *vis-à-vis* other such categories the same position in the caste hierarchy of a region. Members of a jat roughly have the same traditional occupation and may have some rituals and myths in common. The jat has no structural reality in terms of corporate activities nor does it directly affect the behaviour of those who are classified in the category. In the last fifty years or so, however, for political and educational purposes there have been efforts to mobilize people around the cultural category of their jats. It was the jat which the administrative view of caste saw as one of the major parts of the system, and much of the data collected and published by the administrators related to the jat category or level of the system. A jat is still what is meant when someone uses the word 'caste'.

Jats are composed of groups of people who are by kinship and marriage tied into endogamous sections, often named, with deities, rituals, myths, and stories in common and usually localized. In a very few instances they have formal headmen and temples, and may

have accepted rules of behaviour which can be enforced by the headmen. In North Indian terminology these units are called *jatis*, and in English they are usually referred to as subcastes. The administrators were aware of this level of the system and tried, generally unsuccessfully, to collect data about them. When after World War II social and cultural anthropologists began to do intensive field work in villages, they concentrated in their study of caste system on the lowest level of the system, the exogamous section, which in eastern Uttar Pradesh are called *biradaris* (brotherhoods). A biradari is a social group made up of males who believe they are descended from a common male ancestor: they are brothers. They occupy a known territory, a village or a group of villages usually of very limited range. Frequently there are headmen, common property, and effective means for controlling the behaviour of members of the brotherhood. This grouping is exogamous. When one talks of caste ranking, intercaste relations in a village, vote banks in a caste, in fact almost any face-to-face actions in the rural social system in terms of caste, it is the brotherhood that is being talked about.

One way of looking at the history of the study of caste is as a history of the discovery of the levels of the system. This discovery is very much tied to the methods of study and presuppositions of those doing the study. In the Dharmashastras and Vedas studied by the orientalists one finds varnas. If one sends out assistants and surveys with questionnaires, as did the administrators, one finds jats, and jatis; if one does long-term, intensive fieldwork in one place, one finds brotherhoods.

By the end of World War II, with extensive changes in the methods, theories, and subject matter of social anthropology, the independence of India, and wider availability in India, Great Britain, and the United States of funds for extensive fieldwork, the stage was set for a new view of Indian society to emerge. Consciously or unconsciously much of the research in the period 1945 to 1955 by social and cultural anthropologists was based on the assumptions developed over the previous 200 years as reflected by the anthropological thinking which developed during the 1930s and 1940s.

The first publication in 1955 of two collections reporting the results of the 'first round' of modern fieldwork in India, *India's Villages* and *Village India*, reveals the shock of recognition that great correction was needed both in the anthropologist's assumptions about India derived from the traditions of study of India and in the transfer of interests in particular subject matter, methods, and theories from social and cultural anthropology as it existed in the late forties. The two collections also indicate the beginning of the new directions which anthropologists concerned with the study of India would travel in.

Notes

1 Donald Lach, *Asia in the Making of Europe* (Chicago, University of Chicago Press, 1965), I, p. 10.

2 J. W. M'Crindle, *Ancient India: as described in classical literature* (West-minster, A. Constable & Co, 1901), pp. 47–53.

3 Ibid., p. 53.

4 Henry M. Elliot and John Dowson, *A History of India as told by its own historians* (London, Trubner, 1867), I, pp. 16–17, 77.

5 Al-Biruni, *Alberuni's India* (Lahore, Govt. of West Pakistan, 1962), pp. 132–40.

6 E. Rehatsek, 'Early Muslim Accounts of the Hindu Religion', *Journal of the Asiatic Society of Bombay* (1880), 14, pp. 418–38; Sabah Al-Din 'Abid Al-Rahman, 'Study of Hindu Learning and Religion in Indo-Persian Literature', *Indo Iranica* (1961), 14, pp. 1–13.

7 Abu'l Fazl 'Allami, *A'in-i-Akbari* (Calcutta, 1786), III, pp. 82–4.

8 Duarte Barbosa, *A Description of the Coast of East Africa and Malabar in the Beginning of the Sixteenth Century* (London, Hakluyt Society, 1866), vol. 35; *The Book of Duarte Barbosa: An Account of the Countries Bordering on the Indian Ocean and their Inhabitants* (London, Hakluyt Society, Series 2, 1918 and 1921), vols. 54 and 59.

9 Barbosa (1866), p. 121.

10 Ibid., p. 129.

11 Ibid., p. 136.

12 Ibid., pp. 135, 137.

13 Ibid., p. 133.

14 Ibid., pp. 103–6.

15 Barbosa (1918), p. XXXVI.

16 Jean Baptiste Tavernier, *Travels in India by Jean B. Tavernier*, ed. Valentine Ball (London, Macmillan, 1889), 2 vols.

17 Ibid., vol. I, pp. 1–318.

18 Ibid., vol. II, p. 182.

19 Ibid.

20 Henry Yule and A. C. Purnell, *Hobson-Jobson* (London, John Murray, 1903), p. xliii.

21 N. B. Halhed, *A Code of Gentoo Laws, or, ordinations of the pundits from a Persian translation, made from the original, written in the Shanscrit Language* (London, 1777), p. xi.

22 For a Full and valuable discussion of Grant, his ideas, and career, sec Ainslie Thomas Embree, *Charles Grant and British Rule in India* (London, 1962). *The Observations* were published in the *Parliamentary Papers*, 1812–13, x, paper 282, pp. 1–112, and in *Parliamentary Papers*, 1831–32, VIII, paper 734, General Appendix no. 1, pp. 3–92.

23 House of Commons, Great Britain, *Report on East India Company Affairs* (1833), no. 14, General Appendix I, p. 41.

24 William Ward, *A View of the History, Literature and Mythology of the Hindoos* (London, Kingsbury, Parbury and Allen, 1822), vol. 2, pp. 64, 65.

25 Kenneth Ingham, *Reformers in India, 1793–1833* (Cambridge, Cambridge Univ. Press, 1956).

26 J. Long (ed.), *Adam's Three Reports on Vernacular Education in Bengal and Behar* (Calcutta, Home Secretariat Press, 1868).

27 William Robertson, *An Historical Disquisition Concerning the Knowledge Which the Ancients had of India* (1791; rpt. London, Jones & Co., 1828), appendix, pp. 52–3.

28 For an excellent discussion of the relationship of eighteenth-century European social and economic theory to British revenue policy in Bengal, see Ranajit Guha, *A Rule of Property for Bengal: An Essay on the Idea of Permanent Settlement*, Paris, 1963. For a full discussion of the

development of the policies and the growth of empirical knowledge of Bengali land system, see Walter K. Firminger, Introduction to *The Fifth Report . . . on the Affairs of the East India Company . . . 1812*, vol. I. Calcutta, 1917.

29 William Tennant, *Indian Recreations: Consisting Chiefly of Strictures on the Domestic and Rural Economy of the Mohommedans and Hindoos* (London, Longman, Hurst, Rees and Orme, 1804), 2 vols, I, p. 3.

30 Ibid., I, pp. viii, ix.

31 Ibid., II, p. 196.

32 Henry Thomas Colebrooke, *Remarks on the Husbandry and Internal Commerce of Bengal* (London, Blacks and Parry, 1806), p. 174.

33 Ranajit Guha, *A Rule of Property for Bengal: An Essay on the Idea of Permanent Settlement* (Paris, Mouton, 1963), p. 26.

34 David Prain, *A Sketch of the Life of Francis Hamilton called Buchanan: Annals of the Royal Botanic Garden* (Calcutta, Bengal Secretariat Press, 1905), vol. 10, part 2.

35 Francis Buchanan, *A Journey from Madras through the Countries of Mysore, Canara and Malabar* (London, Cadell and Davies, 1807), 3 vols, I, p. xii.

36 A. H. Bingley and A. Nicholls, *Brahmans: Caste Handbook for the Indian Army* (Simla, office of the QMG, 1897), pp. 37–42.

37 L. S. S. O'Malley, *Bengal, Bihar, Orissa and Sikkim, Census of India 1911* (Calcutta, Bengal Secretariat Book Depot, 1913) vol. 5, p. 440.

38 H. H. Risley, *The People of India* (2nd edn; London, W. Thacker, 1915).

39 J. H. Hutton, *Caste in India: Its Nature, Function and Origins* (Cambridge, Cambridge Univ. Press, 1946), pp. 89–90.

40 Government of India, 'Extract Nos 3219–3232', *Man (1901)*, I, p. 138.

41 Ibid., pp. 138–9.

42 Risley, p. 111.

43 Ibid., pp. 112–14.

44 Louis Dumont, 'The "village community" from Munro to Maine', *Contributions to Indian Sociology* (1966) vol. 9, pp. 67–89.

45 Ibid., p. 67.

46 Ibid., pp. 38–70.

47 Ibid; M. N. Srinivas and A. M. Shah, 'The Myth of the Self-Sufficiency of the Indian Village', *Economic Weekly* (1960), vol. 12, pp. 1375–8; Daniel Thorner, 'Marx on India and the Asiatic Mode of Production', *Contributions to Indian Sociology* (1966), vol. 9, pp. 33–66.

48 Mark Wilks, quoted in Dumont, p. 71.

49 Percival Spear, *Twilight of the Mughals* (Cambridge, Cambridge University Press, 1951), p. 117.

50 B. H. Baden-Powell, *The Origin and Growth of Village Communities in India* (London, S. Sornenschein, 1908), chapter III.

51 Baden Powell, *Land Systems* (1892), I, p. 97.

52 Ibid., p. 106.

53 Ibid., p. 128.

54 Ibid., p. 107.

55 Ibid., p. 128.

56 Ibid., p. 107.

57 Ibid., p. 130.

6

A Note on Sanskritization and Westernization

M. N. Srinivas

The concept of "Sanskritization" was found useful by me in the analysis of the social and religious life of the Coorgs of South India. A few other anthropologists who are making studies of tribal and village communities in various parts of India seem to find the concept helpful in the analysis of their material, and this fact induces me to attempt a re-examination of it here.

The first use of the term Sanskritization in this sense occurs in my book, *Religion and Society among the Coorgs of South India* (Oxford, 1952, p. 32):

> "The caste system is far from a rigid system in which the position of each component caste is fixed for all time. Movement has always been possible, and especially so in the middle regions of the hierarchy. A low caste was able, in a generation or two, to rise to a higher position in the hierarchy by adopting vegetarianism and teetotalism, and by Sanskritizing its ritual and pantheon. In short, it took over, as far as possible, the customs, rites, and beliefs of the Brahmins, and the adoption of the Brahminic way of life by a low caste seems to have been frequent, though theoretically forbidden. This process has been called 'Sanskritization' in this book, in preference to 'Brahminization,' as certain Vedic rites are confined to the Brahmins and the two other 'twice-born' castes."

Sanskritization is no doubt an awkward term, but it was preferred to Brahminization for several reasons: Brahminization is subsumed in the wider process of Sanskritization though at some points Brahminization and Sanskritization are at variance with each other. For instance, the Brahmins of the Vedic period drank *soma*, an alcoholic drink,[1] ate beef, and offered blood sacrifices. Both were given up in post-Vedic times. It has been suggested that this was the result of Jain and Buddhist influence. Today, Brahmins are, by and large, vegetarians; only the Saraswat, Kashmiri, and Bengali Brahmins eat non-vegetarian food. All these Brahmins are, however, traditionally teetotallers. In brief, the customs and habits of the Brahmins changed after they had settled in India. Had the term

Perspectives on Modern South Asia: A Reader in Culture, History, and Representation, First Edition.
Edited by Kamala Visweswaran.
© 2011 Blackwell Publishing Ltd. Published 2011 by Blackwell Publishing Ltd.

Brahminization been used, it would have been necessary to specify which particular Brahmin group was meant, and at which period of its recorded history.

Again, the agents of Sanskritization were (and are) not always Brahmins. In fact, the non-twice-born castes were prohibited from following the customs and rites of the Brahmins, and it is not unreasonable to suppose that Brahmins were responsible for this prohibition as they were a privileged group entrusted with the authority to declare the laws. But the existence of such a prohibition did not prevent the Sanskritization of the customs and rites of the lower castes. The Lingayats of South India have been a powerful force for the Sanskritization of the customs and rites of several low castes of Karnatak. The Lingayat movement was founded by a Brahmin named Basava in the twelfth century, and another Brahmin, Ekantada Ramayya, played an important part in it. But it was a popular movement in the true sense of the term, attracting followers from all castes, especially the low castes, and it was anti-Brahminical in tone and spirit.[2] The Lingayats of Mysore claim equality with Brahmins, and the more orthodox Lingayats do not eat food cooked or handled by Brahmins.

The usefulness of Sanskritization as a tool in the analysis of Indian society is greatly limited by the complexity of the concept as well as its looseness. An attempt will be made here to analyze further the conceptual whole which is Sanskritization.

II

The structural basis of Hindu society is caste, and it is not possible to understand Sanskritization without reference to the structural framework in which it occurs. Speaking generally, the castes occupying the top positions in the hierarchy are more Sanskritized than castes in the lower and middle regions of the hierarchy and this has been responsible for the Sanskritization of the lower castes as well as the outlying tribes. The lower castes always seem to have tried to take over the customs and way of life of the higher castes. The

theoretical existence of a ban on their adoption of Brahminical customs and rites was not very effective, and this is clear when we consider the fact that many non-Brahminical castes practise many Brahminical customs and rites. A more effective barrier to the lower castes' taking over of the customs and rites of the higher castes was the hostile attitude of the locally dominant caste, or of the king of the region. In their case there was physical force which could be used to keep the lower groups in check.

Though, over a long period of time, Brahminical rites and customs spread among the lower castes, in the short run the locally dominant caste was imitated by the rest. And the locally dominant caste was frequently not Brahmin. It could be said that in the case of the numerous castes occupying the lowest levels, Brahminical customs reached them in a chain reaction. That is, each group took from the one higher to it, and in turn gave to the group below. Sometimes, however, as in the case of the Smiths of South India, a caste tried to jump over all its structural neighbours, and claimed equality with the Brahmins. The hostility which the Smiths have attracted is perhaps due to their collective social megalomania.

Occasionally we find castes which enjoyed political and economic power but were not rated high in ritual ranking. That is, there was a hiatus between their ritual and politico-economic positions. In such cases Sanskritization occurred sooner or later, because without it the claim to a higher position was not fully effective. The three main axes of power in the caste system are the ritual, the economic, and the political ones, and the possession of power in any one sphere usually leads to the acquisition of power in the other two. This does not mean, however, that inconsistencies do not occur – occasionally, a wealthy caste has a low ritual position, and contrariwise, a caste having a high ritual position is poor.

III

The idea of hierarchy is omnipresent in the caste system; not only do the various castes form a hierarchy, but the occupations practised by them, the various items of their diet, and the customs they observe all form separate hierarchies. Thus, practising an occupation such as butchery, tanning, herding swine or handling toddy, puts a caste in a low position. Eating pork or beef is more defiling than eating fish or mutton. Castes which offer blood-sacrifices to deities are lower than castes making only offerings of fruit and flower. The entire way of life of the top castes seeps down the hierarchy. And as mentioned earlier, the language, cooking, clothing, jewellery, and way of life of the Brahmins spreads eventually to the entire society.

Two "legal fictions" seem to have helped the spread of Sanskritization among the low castes. Firstly, the ban against the non-twice-born castes' performance of Vedic ritual was circumvented by restricting the ban only to the chanting of *mantras* from the Vedas. That is, the ritual acts were separated from the accompanying *mantras* and this separation facilitated the spread of Brahminic ritual among all Hindu castes, frequently including Untouchables. Thus several Vedic rites, including the rite of the gift of the virgin (*kanyadan*), are performed at the marriage of many non-Brahminical castes in Mysore State. And secondly, a Brahmin priest officiates at these weddings. He does not chant Vedic *mantras*, however, but instead, the *mangalashtaka stotras* which are post-Vedic verses in Sanskrit. The substitution of these verses for Vedic *mantras* is the second "legal fiction."

IV

The non-Brahminical castes adopt not only Brahminical ritual, but also certain Brahminical institutions and values. I shall illustrate what I mean by reference to marriage, women, and kinship. I should add here that throughout this essay I have drawn on my experience of conditions in Mysore State, except than I have stated otherwise.

Until recently, Brahmins used to marry their girls before puberty, and parents who had not succeeded in finding husbands for daughters past the age of puberty were regarded as guilty of a great sin. Brahmin marriage is in theory

indissoluble, and a Brahmin widow, even if she be a child widow, is required to shave her head, shed all jewellery and ostentation in clothes. She was (and still is, to some extent) regarded as inauspicious. Sex life is denied her. Among Hindus generally, there is a preference for virginity in brides, chastity in wives, and continence in widows, and this is specially marked among the highest castes.

The institutions of the "low" castes are more liberal in the spheres of marriage and sex than those of the Brahmins. Post-puberty marriages do occur among them, widows do not have to shave their heads, and divorce and widow marriage are both permitted and practised. In general, their sex code is not as harsh towards women as that of the top castes, especially Brahmins. But as a caste rises in the hierarchy and its ways become more Sanskritized, it adopts the sex and marriage code of the Brahmins. Sanskritization results in harshness towards women.

Sanskritization has significant effects on conjugal relations. Among Brahmins for instance, a wife is enjoined to treat her husband as a deity. It is very unusual for a wife to take her meal before the husband has his, and in orthodox families, the wife still eats on the dining leaf on which her husband has eaten. Normally, such a leaf may not be touched as it would render impure the hand touching it. Usually the woman who removes the dining leaf purifies the spot where the leaf had rested with a solution of cow-dung, after which she washes her hands. There is no pollution, however, in eating on the leaf on which the husband has eaten.

Orthodox Brahmin women perform a number of *vratas* or religious vows, the aim of some of which is to secure a long life for the husband. A woman's hope is to predecease her husband and thus avoid becoming a widow. Women who predecease their husbands are considered lucky as well as good, while widowhood is attributed to sins committed in a previous incarnation. A wife who shows utter devotion to her husband is held up as an ideal, as a *pativrata*, i.e., one who regards the devoted service of her husband as her greatest duty. There are myths describing the devotion and loyalty of some sainted women to their husbands. These women are reverenced on certain occasions.

While polygyny is permitted, monogamy is held up as an ideal. Rama, the hero of the epic *Ramayana*, is dedicated to the ideal of having only one wife (*ekapatnivrata*). The conjugal state is regarded as a holy state, and the husband and wife must perform several rites together. A bachelor has a lower religious status than a married man, and is not allowed to perform certain important rites such as offering *pinda* or balls of cooked rice to the manes. Marriage is a religious duty. When bathing in the Ganges or other sacred river, the husband and wife have the ends of their garments tied together. A wife is entitled to half the religious merit earned by her husband by fasting, prayer, and penance.

In the sphere of kinship, Sanskritization stresses the importance of the *vamsha*, which is the patrilineal lineage of the Brahmins. The dead ancestors are apotheosized, and offerings of food and drink have to be made to them periodically by their male descendants. Absence of these offerings will confine the manes to a hell called *put*. The Sanskrit word for son is *putra*, which by folk etymology is considered to mean one who frees the manes from the hell called *put*.[3] In short, Sanskritization results in increasing the importance of having sons by making them a religious necessity. At the same time it has the effect of lowering the value of daughters because, as said earlier, parents are required to get them married before they come of age to a suitable man from the same subcaste. It is often difficult to find such a man, and in recent years, the difficulty has increased enormously owing to the institution of dowry.

Among the non-Brahmins of Mysore, however, though a son is preferred, a daughter is not unwelcome. Actually, girls are in demand among them. And there is no religious duty to get a girl married before puberty. The code under which a woman has to live is not as harsh among them as among the Brahmins. The non-Brahmins are also patrilineal, and the patrilineal lineage is well developed among them. The dead ancestors are occasionally offered food and drink. But it could be said that in the lineage of the non-Brahmins the religious element is less prominent than among the Brahmins.

V

Sanskritizatian means not only the adoption of new customs and habits, but also exposure to new ideas and values which have found frequent expression in the vast body of Sanskrit literature, sacred as well as secular. *Karma, dharma, papa, maya, samsara* and *moksha* are examples of some of the most common Sanskritic theological ideas, and when a people become Sanskritized these words occur frequently in their talk. These ideas reach the common people through Sanskritic myths and stories. The institution of *harikatha* helps in spreading Sanskrit stories and ideas among the illiterate. In a *harikatha* the priest reads and explains a religious story to his audience. Each story takes a few weeks to complete, the audience meeting for a few hours, every evening in a temple. *Harikathas* may be held at any time, but festivals such as Dasara, Ramanavami, Shivaratri, and Ganesh Chaturthi are considered especially suitable for listening to *harikathas*. The faithful believe that such listening leads to the acquisition of spiritual merit. It is one of the traditionally approved ways of spending one's time.

The spread of Sanskrit theological ideas increased under British rule. The development of communications carried Sanskritization to areas previously inaccessible, and the spread of literacy carried it to groups very low in the caste hierarchy. Western technology – railways, the internal combustion engine, press, radio, and plane – has aided the spread of Sanskritization. For instance, the popularity of *harikatha* has increased in the last few years in Mysore City, the narrator usually using a microphone to reach a much larger audience than before. Indian films are popularizing stories and incidents borrowed from the epics and *puranas*. Films have been made about the lives of saints such as Nandanar, Potana, Tukaram, Chaitanya, Mira, Thyagaraja and Tulasidas. Cheap and popular editions of the epics, *puranas*, and other religious and semi-religious books in the various vernaculars are available nowadays.

No analysis of modern Indian social life would be complete without a consideration of Westernization and the interaction between it and Sanskritization. In the nineteenth century, the British found in India institutions such as slavery, human sacrifice, suttee, thuggery, and in certain parts of the country, female infanticide. They used all the power at their disposal to fight these institutions which they considered barbarous. There were also many other institutions which they did not approve of, but which, for various reasons, they did not try to abolish directly.

The fact that the country was overrun by aliens who looked down upon many features of the life of the natives, some of which they regarded as plainly barbarous, threw the Indian leaders on the defensive. Reformist movements such as the Brahmo Samaj were aimed at ridding Hinduism of its numerous "evils."[4] The present was so bleak that the past became golden. The Arya Samaj, another reformist movement within Hinduism, emphasized a wish to return to Vedic Hinduism, which was unlike contemporary Hinduism. The discovery of Sanskrit by Western scholars, and the systematic piecing together of India's past by Western or Western-inspired scholarship, gave Indians a much-needed confidence in their relations with the West. Tributes to the greatness of ancient Indian culture by Western scholars such as Max Muller were gratefully received by Indian leaders (see, for instance, appendices to Mahatma Gandhi's *Hind Swaraj*).[5] It was not uncommon for educated Indians to make extravagant claims for their own culture, and to run down the West as materialistic and unspiritual.

The caste and class from which Indian leaders came were also relevant in this connection. The upper castes had a literary tradition and were opposed to blood-sacrifices, but in certain other customs and habits they were further removed from the British than the lower castes. The latter ate meat, some of them ate even pork and beef, and drank alcoholic liquor; women enjoyed greater freedom among them; and divorce and widow marriage were not prohibited. The Indian leaders were thus caught in a dilemma. They found that certain customs and habits which until then they had looked down upon obtained also among their masters. The British who ate beef and pork and drank liquor, possessed political and economic power, a new technology, scientific knowledge, and a great literature. The Westernized upper castes began acquiring customs and habits which were not dissimilar from those they had looked down upon. Another result was that the evils of upper caste Hindu society came to be regarded as evils of the entire society.

In Mysore State, for instance, the Brahmins led the other castes in Westernization. This was only natural as the Brahmins possessed a literary tradition, and, in addition, many of them stood at the top of the rural economic hierarchy as landowners. (Formerly, it was customary to give land to Brahmins as an act of charity. Distinguished Brahmin administrators were also given gifts of land.) They were the first to sense the arrival of new opportunities following the establishment of British rule, and left their natal villages for cities such as Bangalore and Mysore in order to obtain the benefit of English education, an indispensable passport to employment under the new dispensation.

The net result of the Westernization of the Brahmins was that they interposed themselves between the British and the rest of the native population. The result was a new and secular caste system super-imposed on the traditional system, in which the British, the New Kshatriyas, stood at the top, while the Brahmins occupied the second position, and the others stood at the base of the pyramid. The Brahmins looked up to the British, and the rest of the people looked up to both the Brahmins and the British. The fact that some of the values and customs of the British were opposed to some Brahminical values made the situation confusing. However, such a contradiction has always been implicit, though not in such a pronounced manner, in the caste system. Kshatriya and Brahminical values have always been opposed to some extent, and in spite of the theoretical superiority of the Brahmin to all the other castes, the Kshatriya, by virtue of the political (and through it the economic) power at his disposal, has throughout exercised a dominant position. The super-imposition of the British on the caste system only sharpened the contrast.

The position of the Brahmin in the new hierarchy was crucial. He became the filter through which Westernization reached the rest of Hindu society in Mysore. This probably helped Westernization as the other castes were used to imitating the ways of the Brahmins. But while the Westernization of the Brahmins enabled the entire Hindu society to Westernize, the Brahmins themselves found some aspects of Westernization, such as the British diet, dress, and freedom from pollution, difficult to accept. (Perhaps another caste should not have found them so difficult. The Coorgs, for instance, took quite easily to British diet and dress, and certain activities like dancing, hunting and sports.)

The Brahmin dietary has been enlarged to include certain vegetables which were formerly forbidden, such as onion, potato, carrot, radish, and beetroot. Many eat raw eggs for health reasons and consume medicines which they know to be made from various organs of animals. But meat-eating is even now rare, while the consumption of Western alcoholic liquor is not as rare. Cigarettes are common among the educated.

The Brahmins have also taken to new occupations. Even in the thirties, the Brahmins showed a reluctance to take up trade or any occupation involving manual work. But they were driven by the prevalent economic depression to take up new jobs, and World War II completed this process. Many Brahmins enlisted themselves in the army and this effected a great change in their habits and outlook. Before World War II, young men who wanted to go to Bombay, Calcutta, or Delhi in search of jobs had to be prepared for the opposition of their elders. But the postwar years found young men not only in all parts of India, but outside too. There was a sudden expansion in the geographical and social space of the Brahmins. Formerly, Brahmins objected to becoming doctors as the profession involved handling men from all castes, including Untouchables, and corpses.

This is now a thing of the past. A few educated Brahmins now own farms where they raise poultry. One of them even wants to have a piggery.

Over seventy years ago, the institution of brideprice seems to have prevailed among some sections of Mysore Brahmins. But with Westernization, and the demand it created for educated boys who had good jobs, dowry became popular. The better educated a boy, the larger the dowry his parents demanded for him. The age at which girls married shot up. Over twenty-five years ago it was customary for Brahmins to marry their girls before puberty. Nowadays, urban and middle class Brahmins are rarely able to get their girls married before they are eighteen, and there are many girls above twenty who are unmarried. Child widows are rare, and shaving the heads of widows is practically a thing of the past.

There has been a general secularization of Hindu life in the last one hundred and fifty years, and this has especially affected the Brahmins whose life was permeated with ritual. The life of no other caste among Hindus was equally ritualized. One of the many interesting contradictions of modern Hindu social life is that while the Brahmins are becoming more and more Westernized, the other castes are becoming more and more Sanskritized. In the lower reaches of the hierarchy, castes are taking up customs which the Brahmins are busy discarding. As far as these castes are concerned, it looks as though Sanskritization is an essential preliminary to Westernization.

To describe the social changes occurring in modern India in terms of Sanskritization and Westernization is to describe it primarily in cultural and not structural terms. An analysis in terms of structure is much more difficult than an analysis in terms of culture. The increase in the social space of the Brahmins, and its implications for them and for the caste system as a whole, need to be studied in detail. The consequences of the existence of the dual, and occasionally conflicting, pressures of Sanskritization and Westernization provide an interesting field for systematic sociological analysis.

A note to the above[6]

The British conquest of India set free a number of forces; political, economic, social, and technological. These forces affected this country's social and cultural life profoundly and at every point. The withdrawal of the British from India not only did not mean the cessation of these forces but, meant, on the contrary, their intensification.

I have elsewhere tried to argue that the traditional and pre-British caste system permitted a certain amount of group mobility. Only the extremities of the system were relatively fixed while there was movement in between. This was made possible by a certain vagueness regarding mutual rank which obtained in the middle regions of the caste hierarchy. Vagueness as to mutual rank is of the essence of the caste system in operation as distinct from the system in popular conception. And mobility increased a great deal after the advent of the British. Groups which in the pre-British days had no chance of aspiring to anything more than a bare subsistence came by opportunities for making money, and having made money, they wanted to stake a claim for higher status. Some of them did achieve higher status. The social circulation which was sluggish in pre-British times speeded up considerably in the British period. But the change was only a quantitative one.

Economic betterment thus seems to lead to the Sanskritization of the customs and way of life of a group. Sometimes a group may start by acquiring political power and this may lead to economic betterment and Sanskritization. This does not mean, however, that economic betterment must necessarily lead to Sanskritization. What is important is the collective desire to rise high in the esteem of friends, neighbours and rivals, and this should be followed by the adoption of methods by which the status of a group is raised. It is a fact that such a desire is usually preceded by the acquisition of wealth; I am unable, however, to assert that economic betterment is a necessary precondition to Sanskritization. For instance, the Untouchables of Rampura village in Mysore State are getting increasingly Sanskritized and this seems to be due to their present leadership and to the fact that the younger men are more in contact with the outside world than their parents. Also, if the report which one hears from some local men are to be believed, Rampura Untouchables are being egged on by Untouchable leaders from outside to change their way of life. Whether the economic position of Untouchables has improved during the last seventy years or so is not easy to determine, though it is likely that they also have benefited from the greater all-round prosperity which resulted when the area under irrigation increased nearly eighty years ago. In brief, while we have no evidence to assert that all cases of Sanskritization are preceded by the acquisition of wealth, the available evidence is not definite enough to state that Sanskritization can occur without any reference whatever to the economic betterment of a group. Economic betterment, the acquisition of political power, education, leadership, and a desire to move up in the hierarchy, are all relevant factors in Sanskritization, and each case of Sanskritization may show all or some of these factors mixed up in different measures.

It is necessary, however, to stress that Sanskritization does not automatically result in the achievement of a higher status for the group. The group concerned must clearly put forward a claim to belong to a particular *varna*, Vaishya, Kshatriya, or Brahmin. They must alter their customs, diet, and way of life suitably, and if there are any inconsistencies in their claim, they must try to "explain" them by inventing an appropriate myth. In addition, the group must be content to wait an indefinite period, and during this period it must maintain a continuous pressure regarding its claims. A generation or two must pass usually before a claim begins to be accepted; this is due to the fact that the people who first hear the claim know that the caste in question is trying to pass for something other than what it really is, and the claim has a better chance with their children and grandchildren. In certain cases, a caste or tribal group may make a claim for a long time without it being accepted. I have in view only acceptance by other castes and I am not considering individual sceptics who will always be there.

It is even possible that a caste may overreach itself in making claims, with the result that instead of moving up it may incur the disapproval of the others. It is also not unlikely that a claim which may succeed in a particular area or period of time will not succeed in another. A developed historical sense would be inimical to such claims but it is as yet not forthcoming among our people.

Group mobility is a characteristic of the caste system, whereas in a class system it is the individual and his family which moves up or down. One of the implications of group mobility is that either the group is large enough to constitute an endogamous unit by itself, or it recruits girls in marriage from the original group while it does not give girls in return. This implies that the original group is impressed by the fact that the splinter group is superior to it for otherwise it would not consent to such a one-sided and inferior role. A larger number of people are needed in North India than in the South to constitute an endogamous group, for marriage with near kin is prohibited in the North, and there is in addition an insistence on village exogamy. In the South, on the other hand, cross-cousin and uncle-niece marriages are preferred, and the village is not an exogamous unit. But I am straying from my main theme: what I wish to stress here is that Sanskritization is a source of fission in the caste system, and does occasionally bring about hypergamous relations between the splinter group and the original caste from which it has fissioned off. It both precedes as well as sets the seal on social mobility. It thereby brings the caste system of any region closer to the existing politico-economic situation. But for it the caste system would have been subjected to great strain. It has provided a traditional medium of expression for change within that system, and the medium has held good in spite of the vast increase in the quantum of change which has occurred in British and post-British India. It has canalized the change in such a way that all-India values are asserted and the homogeneity of the entire Hindu society increases.

The continued Sanskritization of castes will probably mean the eventual introduction of major cultural and structural changes in Hindu society as a whole. But Sanskritization does not always result in higher status for the Sanskritized caste, and this is clearly exemplified by the Untouchables. However thoroughgoing the Sanskritization of an Untouchable group may be, it is unable to cross the barrier of untouchability. It is indeed an anachronism that while groups which were originally outside Hinduism such as tribal groups or alien ethnic groups have succeeded in entering the Hindu fold, and occasionally at a high level, an Untouchable caste is always forced to remain Untouchable. Their only chance of moving up is to go so far away from their natal village that nothing is known about them in the new area. But spatial mobility was very difficult in pre-British India: it meant losing such security as they had and probably going into an enemy chiefdom and facing all the dangers there. Movement was near impossible when we remember that Untouchables were generally attached as agrestic serfs to caste Hindu landlords.[7]

I have been asked by more than one student of Indian anthropology whether I regard Sanskritization as only a one-way process, and whether the local culture is always a recipient. The answer is clear: it is a two-way process though the local cultures seem to have received more than they have given. In this connection it should be remembered that throughout Indian history local elements have entered into the main body of Sanskritic belief, myth and custom, and in their travel throughout the length and breadth of India, elements of Sanskritic culture have undergone different changes in different culture-areas. Festivals such as the Dasara, Deepavali and Holi have no doubt certain common features all over the country, but they have also important regional peculiarities. In the case of some festivals only the name is common all over India and everything else is different – the same name connotes different things to people in different regions. Similarly each region has its own body of folklore about the heroes of the *Ramayana* and *Mahabharata*, and not infrequently, epic incidents and characters are related to outstanding features of local geography.

Apropos of the heterogeneity of the concept of Sanskritization, it may be remarked that it subsumes several mutually antagonistic values, perhaps even as Westernization does. The concept of *varna*, for instance, subsumes values which are ideally complementary but, as a matter of actual and historical fact, have been competitive is not conflicting. In this connection it is necessary to add that the grading of the four *varnas* which is found in the famous *Purushasukta* verse and subsequent writings, probably does not reflect the social order as it existed everywhere and at all times. Historians of caste have recorded a conflict between Brahmins and Kshatriyas during Vedic times, and Professor Ghurye has postulated that the Jain and Buddhist movements were in part a revolt of the Kshatriyas and Vaishyas against the supremacy of the Brahmins.[8]

Today we find different castes dominating in different parts of India, and frequently, in one and the same region, more than one caste dominates.

What I wish to emphasize is that in the study of Sanskritization it is important to know the kind of caste which dominates in a particular region. If they are Brahmins, or a caste like the Lingayats, then Sanskritization will probably be quicker and Brahminical values will spread, whereas if the dominating caste is a local Kshatriya or Vaishya caste, Sanskritization will be slower, and the values will not be Brahminical. The non-Brahminical castes are generally less Sanskritized than the Brahmins, and where they dominate, non-Sanskritic customs may get circulated among the people. It is not inconceivable that occasionally they may even mean the de-Sanskritization of the imitating castes.

Notes

1 See "Soma" in the *Encyclopaedia of Religion and Ethics*, vol. XI, pp. 685–6.

2 See E. Thurston, *Castes and Tribes of Southern India*, Madras, 1909, vol. V, pp. 237ff; see also *Encyclopaedia Brittanica*, 14th ed., vol. XIV, p. 162.

3 See M. Monier-Williams, *A Sanskrit-English Dictionary*, 2nd ed. Oxford, 1899, p. 632: "*put or pud* (a word invented to explain *putra* or *put-tra*, see Mn. ix, 138, and cf. Nir. ii, II) hell or a partic. hell (to which the childless are condemned)"; and "*putra*, m. (etym. doubtful . . . traditionally said to be a comp. *put-tra* "preserving from the hell called Put," Mn. ix, 138) a son, child . . . "

4 See "Brahmo Samaj" in the *Encyclopaedia of Religion and Ethics*, vol. II, pp. 819–4.

5 Ahmedabad, 1946. See the Appendices which certain "testimonies by eminent men" to the greatness of Indian culture. Among the eminent men are Max Muller, J. Seymour Keay, M. P., Victor Cousin, Col. Thomas Munro and the Abee Dubois.

6 It is nearly a year since the preceding essay was written, and in the meantime I have given some more thought to the subject. The result is the present Note in which I have made a few additional observations of the twin processes of Sanskritization and Westernization. In this connection I must thank Dr. F. G. Bailey of the School of Oriental and African Studies, London, for taking the trouble to criticize my paper in detail in his letters to me. I must also thank Dr. McKim Marriott of the University of Chicago, and the delegates to the Conference of Anthropologists and Sociologists held at Madras on October 5–7, 1955, for criticisms which followed the reading of the paper.

7 Dr. Adrian Mayer, however, states that the Balais (Untouchables) in the Malwa village which he is studying are trying to move into the Shudra *varna*. It would be interesting to see if they succeed in their efforts. See Dr Mayer's essay, "Some Hierarchical Aspects of Caste," *South Western Journal of Anthropology*, vol. XII, No. 2, pp. 117–44.

8 See *Caste and Class in India*, Bombay, 1952, p. 65.

7

What's in a Name?
Aryans and Dravidians in the Making
of Sri Lankan Identities

Arjun Guneratne

Although most Sri Lankans would probably agree that Sinhalese and Tamils share cultural practices and beliefs, the widespread assumption, both in the island and abroad, is that they are two separate peoples with different roots in the Indian subcontinent. The twin concepts of 'Aryan' and 'Dravidian,' introduced into the island by British intellectuals in the nineteenth century, have facilitated these understandings and have been an important factor in shaping the idea that Sinhalese and Tamils are essentially different. But in nationalism, as in evolutionary biology, some of the bitterest struggles for survival and resources take place between closely related species, and the Sinhalese and Tamils are very close in their cultural relationship. It is their cultural relationship that concerns me here; a relationship explored in this book through the notion of hybridity.

The most obvious meaning of hybridity resonates with biological understandings: a hybrid species is distinct from its parents but partakes of the 'genetic essence' of both. The first definition of the term that Webster's dictionary provides is 'the offspring of two ... animals of different races, varieties, species, etc.' (1983: 888). To my mind, however, this is an unsatisfactory way of thinking about hybridity in the cultural context because it presupposes the existence, even at some distant period, of a 'pure' culture, which has subsequently hybridized by incorporating elements of other cultures. The belief in the purity of the cultural species is a necessary precondition for the development of nationalist sentiments, and is the assumption that underlies the work of a nationalist like Munidasa Cumaratunga (see Dharmadasa 1992: 261ff). It has, however, no historical validity.

While the concept of a biological species requires a high degree of impermeability between the boundaries that separate one from closely related species, the boundaries that separate one culture from another are porous in the extreme. There are no pure cultures; a culture, as a way of being in the world, as a conceptual framework through which the world is apprehended, has developed not only through

Perspectives on Modern South Asia: A Reader in Culture, History, and Representation, First Edition.
Edited by Kamala Visweswaran.
© 2011 Blackwell Publishing Ltd. Published 2011 by Blackwell Publishing Ltd.

the evolution of its own logic but also through its interactions with other ways of being in the world. The notion of a Tamil culture or a Sinhala culture as 'pure wholes' is fundamentally misleading because both conceptions are an arbitrary imposition on the flow of social thought and action. Cultures are fragmentary things and the unity we impute to them is essentially arbitrary. To make that thought clearer, consider the Dry Zone peasants drawn from two separate 'cultures' who are now engaged in a deadly struggle in northern Sri Lanka. Although they fight under the respective banners of two separate nationalisms, they have far more in common with each other (in their way of being in the world) than either does with their respective social elites who, although sharing the same ethnic labels, share little of the rituals, practices and beliefs that shape their view of life.

Webster's dictionary gives us another gloss on hybridity that resonates rather better with the notion of culture I am using here: a hybrid is anything of mixed origin (1983: 888). The emphasis falls equally on both terms: 'mixed' and 'origin.' That is, the notion of hybrid denies the possibility of 'purity' altogether. All cultures are hybrid and have always been so. They are admixtures of mixtures, and so on ad infinitum. Geertz recounts the story of the Indian who claims the world rests, ultimately, on the back of a turtle. And what does that turtle rest on, asks his English interlocutor, who wants, in a straightforward Anglo-Saxon way, to get to the bottom of things. Yet another turtle, is the reply. And that turtle? After that, sahib, the Indian says (the times are presumably colonial), it's turtles all the way down. Hybrid cultures are like those turtles in their provenance. If there exists such an oddity as a 'pure' culture, it was so far back in time, at the early dawn of *Homo sapiens*, that speculation about it is an exercise in pointlessness. Cultures have been hybrid ever since that primordial moment. This hybridity is the point of departure for this reflection on the uses to which systems of ethnic classification in Sri Lanka have been (and can be) put.

My contention is this: Sri Lanka's population derives primarily from the southern part of the Indian subcontinent. Over the centuries, as the outcome of various historical processes extending into contemporary times, two (and perhaps three) major forms of social identity have emerged: Sinhala, Tamil and perhaps Muslim. I call them major because all three are apical: none can be folded into another. The cultural elements which were brought into the island from different parts of the subcontinent were worked and reworked in different ways over the ages to produce this outcome. The semantic content of labels like Sinhala and Tamil would have varied over the centuries, assuming that is that these labels have always been meaningful. There were certainly other forms of identity that would have been meaningful to people: caste, region, and religion, for example. Which of these identities became salient at any given historical moment would have been a function of the prevailing social and political circumstances. It is in this sense that the Sinhalese and Tamils are hybrid: not that they borrow from one another's cultures, but that they are both of the same stock. That primordial stock, along with the various additions to it that time has brought, has been fashioned through the praxis of men and women as they responded to the circumstances of their lives into the many social categories and identities that inhabit the island today: Sinhalese, Tamils, Muslims, Goigamas, Karavas, Rodi, Burghers, and so on.

A system of classification deriving in part from the researches of European historians of language has helped to impose an order on this complexity and, in classificatory terms, bifurcate a complex population into contrasting groups. I suggest that what one system of classification has put asunder, another might well reunite – at least conceptually. I shall explore this idea by comparing the system of classification derived from historical linguistics (Aryan–Dravidian) with one deriving from the analysis of kinship (Dravidian). Language separates the people of Sri Lanka, but a common form of kinship structure unites them, and suggests their common origin.

In both popular culture as well as in some academic and journalistic writings, Sri Lanka is said to have been peopled initially by Aryans (supposedly the ancestors of the Sinhalese) who arrived from North India, and that subsequent to this initial settlement, other people, Dravidians, arrived in the island from South India. The Sinhalese are 'Aryan' because they speak an Indo-Aryan language but this is purely an arbitrary distinction. One could argue – as I shall do here – that they may be thought of with equal justification as a Dravidian people because they have in common with all of South India a common form of kinship, which contrasts them in a very marked way with the culture of the North. What is more, this contrast has been recognized in India since very ancient times. What Sri Lankans have in common are the concepts and structures of a particular form of kinship organization that ties them, on the one hand, to the society of South India, and contrasts them, on the other, to the social system prevailing in the subcontinent's North. One way of classifying the people of the island is as arbitrary as the other, but the second view has the distinct virtue of highlighting an attribute that *all* Sri Lankans share, thereby problematizing the essentialist claims of ethnic and 'racial' purity.

In other words, the Sinhalese may be thought of as a Dravidian people in social structure (which suggests a link to South India) but Indo-Aryan in language (which suggests a link with the North). Kinship is inherently more conservative than language in that it is less likely to change. That Sinhalese and Tamils share a common structure of kinship that is distinctly different from that prevailing in North India suggests the South Indian origin of the Sinhalese – for which evidence exists, of course, in many other areas. The language that one speaks, on the other hand, does not necessarily say very much about one's antecedents. In India, the Indo-Aryan languages are more or less congruent with North Indian kinship; the same is true for Dravidian languages and Dravidian kinship. This is not true of Sri Lanka, however, where, the majority of the population speaks an Indo-Aryan language but conceptualizes the universe of their kin in categories shared by all South Indians.

The Aryan-Dravidian Myth

The concept of the Aryan and its counterpart, the Dravidian concept, has served to divide rather than to unite Sri Lankans. They are both nineteenth century concepts whose creation we owe to the philologists and orientalists who were busy trying to unravel the relationships among what they called the Indo-Aryan languages. The early British orientalists who served the East India Company recognized the close similarities between Sanskrit, Latin and Greek, and posited that all three and their numerous offspring were descended from a proto-Indo-Aryan language, originally spoken somewhere in Central Asia. The term 'Aryan' itself was derived from references in the *Rig Veda* to a people calling itself '*arya*,' which means noble. By the middle of the nineteenth century, however, a concept originally developed as a linguistic classification had become racialized. Due to the work of German comparative philologists such as Max Müller, and to the ethnological theories of colonial administrators like Sir Herbert Risley, the common relationship among the Indo-Aryan (or Indo-European) languages became transformed into assumptions about the common racial origin of the speakers of these languages. It was argued that all people speaking Indo-European languages were related to each other by biological descent. The hypothesis was that these 'Aryans' originated in one place in Asia and then spread south into India and west into Europe and Persia (Leopold 1970).

Counterposed to the theory of the common origin of North Indian languages, and their relationship to the languages of Europe and Persia, was a theory developed in particular by Robert Caldwell. It held that the languages of South India belonged to a different family of languages, quite unrelated to the Indo-Aryan (or Indo-European) family, but closely related to one another, and preceding the Indo-Aryan in antiquity. They were collectively referred to as the Dravidian languages. The term 'Dravidian' itself comes from the Sanskrit for 'Tamil.' Not surprisingly, the category Dravidian also became racialized during the nineteenth century; the speakers of these languages were held to be of common racial origin, while the speakers of Indo-European languages in North India were believed to be of separate racial stock. European scholars of India theorized that the Dravidians had been the original inhabitants of the subcontinent until they were displaced by Aryan invaders moving into India from the northwest. These racial ideas were also utilized in an attempt to explain caste: the higher castes were the descendants of the original 'Aryans' while the low castes and the untouchables were descended from the indigenous 'Dravidian' inhabitants. These European ideas were picked up by Indian intellectuals and used for different purposes: some hailed the unity between Indian and Englishmen that this theory of common racial provenance suggested, while others used it to build up Indian self-esteem, decrying the western branch of the race as having lapsed into barbarism under the pressure of cold northern climes (Leopold 1970: 275).

These ideas were also picked up in Sri Lanka, and were used to mark out a boundary between the two main cultural components of the island's population. The Aryan myth helped to reinforce a particular view of the island's history that had begun to take shape during the latter half of the nineteenth century. Anagarika Dharmapala, for example, one of the most forceful advocates of the Aryan theory of racial origin in its Sri Lankan guise, rendered this history in the following terms:

> This bright, beautiful island was made into a Paradise by the Aryan Sinhalese before its destruction was brought about by the barbaric vandals (Dharmapala 1965: 482).

'Race' is a concept with no biological validity. It is a cultural construct reflecting cultural concerns. The population of Sri Lanka is divided not in terms of race (which continues to be a popular term to summarize these concerns), but in terms of culture and language. Nevertheless, culture is fluid and the ability to speak one or another language is not determined by one's genetic inheritance. Sri Lanka's history has been shaped, not by an initial 'Aryan' colonization followed by successive 'Dravidian' invasions, but by a continuous movement of population

from India, particularly from its southern cone – what is now Kerala, Tamil Nadu, and Andhra – that has settled among, and been assimilated to, the social groups on the island which had arrived earlier. It is very likely that, at some early point in this process, Indo-Aryan speakers achieved political overlordship over the population at large, and their language, as the language of the elite, became privileged and eventually spread to the rest of the people. Constant movement and migration of people is a commonplace of history; the population and culture of virtually every contemporary state has been formed in this way.

What the evidence shows is that Sri Lanka was populated by successive movements of people from India, and through the centuries, this diverse population has been crystallizing into the groups we identify today as Sinhala, Tamil, or Muslim. The caste system functioned in Sri Lanka, as it did elsewhere in South Asia, to allow the incorporation of new groups into the population as new castes, or to be absorbed into existing castes of equivalent standing to that of the newcomers. The *pantarams*, non-Brahmin priests of the Vellala caste of South India, who immigrated to the island in the thirteenth and fifteenth centuries, can be taken as an example of this phenomenon (Dewaraja 1972: 47–68). According to Lorna Dewaraja, they were given villages as maintenances, and absorbed into the Sinhala aristocracy. The aristocratic Sinhala title 'Bandara' is derived from the Tamil *pantaram*. At the highest levels of society, it was common for royalty to marry princesses from South India. This cultural fact is recorded in the founding myth of the Sinhalese, the Vijaya story in the *Mahavamsa*.

The opposition between the concepts Sinhala/Tamil is a modern one, arising out of a modern situation beginning in the economic and social transformation of the colonial period, and unlikely to have been meaningful to our ancestors. To assume that the Sinhala–Tamil dichotomy had the same highly politicized meaning in the past that it has today is to beg a whole host of questions. For example, why, in the context of such an ideology, would the Kandyan nobles have invited a South Indian

Tamil-speaking Nayakkar to assume the throne of Kandy? Or to reach further back into history, why does the chronicler of the *Culavamsa*, the second part of the *Mahavamsa*, speak approvingly of Nissanka Malla? Nissanka Malla was born into the royal family of Kalinga, in what is now known as Andhra Pradesh, and founded the Kalinga dynasty that presided over much of the final stages of the Polonnaruva kingdom, until Magha, also of Kalinga, and the epitome of the Sinhala conception of the 'barbaric Tamil,' put an end to it.

The point of all of this is that a careful reading of the old chronicles paints a picture of Sri Lankan history that is far too complex to be reduced to the simple binary opposition favored by nationalists and some scholars. Here is how a group of expatriate Sinhalese in Australia represent this dominant historical paradigm:

> In their long history the Sinhalese have never been chauvinistic and have treated all ethnic groups, including the Tamil people living in Sri Lanka with justice and fairness. In the case of the Tamils they had adopted this stance despite the fact that Tamils originally came to Sri Lanka in the wake of the South Indian invaders many of whom were little better than vandals and plunderers. The traditional Sinhala position had not been to divide the country into racial areas but to allow persons to live in peace and fairness under a unified Kingdom (ACSLU 1995).

Explicitly, in the nationalistic view exemplified by this statement Tamils are outsiders who are linked to invaders, no better than vandals and plunderers. There is also reference to a 'traditional Sinhala position' – the assumption being that the political concerns of people today were more or less the concerns of people in the past. For the writer, 'the Sinhalese' are a people who think in perfect harmony. The island of Sri Lanka is depicted as a Sinhala homeland; the Sinhalese, being a just and fair people, suffer the minorities to live among them. The mirror image of this rhetoric, and one that has developed partly in reaction to it, is the Tamil claim to a traditional homeland in the North

and East. But Hellmann-Rajanayagam notes:

> Tamil historical consciousness, and the resulting Tamil nationalism, is not simply 'reactive,' a product of Tamil responses to Sinhala chauvinism and the Sinhala emphasis on their own history. Tamil nationalism in Jaffna cannot be seen as separate from Tamil nationalism in south India by which it has been influenced and on which it has, to some extent, fed. But what Sinhala nationalism . . . brought about was a heightened sense of being Jaffna Tamil instead of just Tamil, thus leading to a withdrawal from the wider context of subcontinental Tamil culture and history (Hellmann-Rajanayagam 1990: 118).

Both claims to exclusive homelands are equally illegitimate, both from a liberal/progressive perspective as well as from a historical/anthropological one. However, attempts to disprove the Tamil claims miss the point. The point is that Tamil nationalism must posit the idea of a traditional homeland in order to be successful, because nationalism is inextricably linked to territory; and it is no less a construct than the idea that the island is a Sinhala homeland, which then relegates Sri Lankans of other ethnic backgrounds to a sort of second-tier citizenship. The idea that Sri Lanka is the homeland solely of the Sinhalese continues to be publicly articulated and remains a potent symbol organizing Sinhala nationalism. Inasmuch as the conceit of nationalism is that it is a form of (imagined) kinship, it seems appropriate to pursue this reflection on symbols by focusing on the kinship structure that Tamils and Sinhalese both share – the Dravidian kinship system. It can also be called the system of cross-cousin marriage.

Dravidian Kinship and Sinhala Society

It has long been recognized in India, in the Dharma Sastras, for example, that North and South India were fundamentally different from each other; each region had its own *dharma*. Although to modern eyes a central aspect of this difference is based on a linguistic contrast that has been elaborated into a racial theory in recent times (the Aryan–Dravidian opposition), this linguistic contrast was not apparent to the ancient Indian philosophers, who held that all the languages of India (including Tamil) were descended from Sanskrit (Trautmann 1981: 16). Instead, one of the central differences between the North and the South, noted since Vedic times in the Dharma Sastras, was their contrasting systems of kinship. Trautmann, on whose seminal work on Dravidian kinship I have depended for the material in this section, quotes an old Sanskrit text of Baudhayana's (500–200 BC) to this effect:

> Fivefold are the peculiar customs of the South and of the North. We will explain those of the South. They are ... (4) marriage of the mother's brother's daughter and (5) marriage of the father's sister's daughter ... For each country the [custom of] the country should be authoritative (quoted in Trautmann 1981: 303).

Different cultures have different ways of organizing the universe of one's kindred, that is, all of the people who are related to each other through ties of blood and marriage. Anthropologists have described six broad systems of classifications through which they do so, of which the system of cross-cousin marriages is one. The majority of socio-cultural forms existing in Sri Lanka and South India share this system of kinship classification.

In South Asia, there exist two well-documented kinship systems, both of which are labelled with terms borrowed from historical linguistics: the Indo-Aryan system and the Dravidian system of kinship. As Trautmann has pointed out, the Dravidian kinship system tends to correspond more or less to the Dravidian linguistic region of South Asia, with one significant exception: Sri Lanka, where the majority of the population speaks an Indo-Aryan language, but share the Dravidian kinship system with the minority, Dravidian language speakers.

A system of classification bundles up the universe of kin in different ways and gives each bundle a label; in the jargon of anthropology, these are kintypes and kin terms. In English kinship, for example, the children of all of one's parents' siblings are bundled together (a bundle of kintypes) and labelled with a common kin term, 'cousin'. Among the Sinhalese and the Tamils, however, the children of one's parents' siblings of the opposite sex are distinguished from those of one's parents' same sex siblings. The children of my father's brother or my mother's sister are placed in the same category as my own siblings, and addressed by the same kin terms (*ayya, nangi*) while the children of my mother's brother and father's sister are addressed differently (*massina, nāna*).

The fundamental rule of kinship and marriage in the North is that an individual may not marry someone who is related to him (or her) through blood; one must marry a 'stranger.' In the Indo-Aryan system, a lineage that has taken a wife from a second lineage may not give in return one of its own women as a wife to a member of that lineage. In contrast, in South India, and among both Tamils and Sinhalese in Sri Lanka, the cultural ideal favors what anthropologists term cross-cousin marriage. Baudhayana describes it from the perspective of a man, as marriage with either one's mother's brother's daughter or father's sister's daughter; over the course of time, two lineages exchange their daughters with each other. This is called cross-cousin marriage because in the parental generation the parents are siblings of opposite sexes. This distinction is encoded in the language.

However, the children of one's parents' same sex siblings (father's brother and mother's sister) stand to one in the same relationship as one's own siblings; the culture conceives of them as like one's own brother and sister, and this conception is given expression to in the kinship terms. Thus, my father's brother's son (my parallel cousin) is my *ayya* (or *malli*). The Sinhala kinship term *mama*, on the other hand, the primary referent of which is the mother's brother, is also applied to the father's sister's husband and (a significant point in analyzing Dravidian kinship) to the wife's father. The uncle is, potentially, one's father-in-law. The presumption encoded in the language is that marriage is between cross-cousins. The term *mama* also occurs in Hindi as the term for mother's brother, but the father's sister's husband is called *phupha* and the father of one's wife is called *sasur*. The Dravidian system does not distinguish between these three categories; the Indo-Aryan system does. The kinship system that structures the social relationships of Hindi speakers prohibits marriage between people related to each other by blood. From a male perspective, one's mother's brother's daughter and one's father's sister's daughter are not appropriate marriage partners even though they belong to lineages different from one's own. This is the very opposite of Sinhala kinship beliefs. Lexically, the Sinhalese terminology shows the profound influence of Tamil; the Indo-Aryan influence can be seen only in a handful of terms such as *puta, duva* and *bäna*.

The point in analyzing the lexical items used in kinship is not that they need to be the same to demonstrate a relationship between one local kinship system and another but that they have the same semantic referents. In the example above, the field of possible referents encompassed by the term for mother's brother is very different in Sinhala than it is in Hindi, although both are Indo-Aryan languages. If we compare the Dry Zone Sinhala kinship terminology with that of another exemplar of the Dravidian system, we see a close correspondence. Trautmann points out that the Sinhalese system is almost identical in both lexical items and semantic referents with the kinship terminology of the Nanjilnattu Vellalars, a Tamil-speaking caste from Kanyakumari, the southernmost district of Tamil Nadu (Trautmann 1981: 32–42; 153–155).

Trautmann concludes from his analysis of the Sinhala kinship system that Sri Lanka lies well within the hinterland of the Dravidian kinship region and is largely free of the complexity introduced by outside forces. Sri Lanka, in other words, is not on the periphery of the Dravidian kinship region nor is it in a zone of transition or contact between the Dravidian and Indo-Aryan regions. The evidence on which he bases this conclusion is a close analysis of the kinship terminology itself and the practice of cross-cousin marriage that exists among the Sinhalese. Every Sinhalese marriage is not of course between

cross-cousins, but there exists a cultural preference for this kind of marriage which is encoded in the language. Obeyesekere, in discussing traditional Sinhala marriage practices, observes that when cross-cousin marriage in Sinhala villages "was ignored in favor of marriage with an outsider ... then by local custom the permission of the eligible cross cousin was required" (Gombrich and Obeyesekere 1988: 262–63). Trautmann concludes, "The evidence taken as a whole requires that we regard the Sinhalese as a Dravidian community in respect to kinship in the present and as far back as the historical record reaches" (1981: 153).

Language and Other Symbols

If their kinship structures suggest how much Sri Lankans have in common, the languages they speak have become the symbols around which their separate modern identities have crystallized. Language is much more open to change than are kinship structures, particularly when bilingualism and the existence of a host of regional dialects is common. We sometimes forget that the standardization of language is a fairly recent phenomenon, made possible by print, modern systems of education, and other media. The traditional approach to Sri Lankan history has tended to reify language, to make of it a symbol for cultural identity, and to then project that symbol back into the past. In this way, the conflicts of the present, which are very much a modern phenomenon, come to be understood as a working out of an age-old antagonism between two distinct and definitively opposed cultural forces. This understanding of group identity primarily in ethno-linguistic terms is new; caste was at least as important as ethno-linguistic identity until recently in our political life. The first Sri Lankan ethnic group to demand federalism (in the 1920s) were the Kandyan Sinhalese, who thought of themselves then as a society distinct from that of the Sinhalese of the low country. It has taken the threat of Tamil separatism to forge a greater unity between the two principal groupings of the Sinhalese.

That language has come to define group identity is largely a modern phenomenon. In most pre-modern societies, language served an instrumental purpose, with multilinguality being not at all uncommon. The process of objectifying language has proceeded in tandem with the state-building projects of modern polities: the necessity to standardize the different dialects and forms of speech in a given region, the necessity to have a desacralized language of instruction, and not least, as Cohn has pointed out, the necessity (especially in a multilingual context) to make a choice and label it when the census taker inquires after your mother tongue (Cohn 1987). The answer the census taker receives (for this and other questions) will have a political import. It is thus that Tamil-speaking Karava become Sinhalized in modern times. On the other hand, Tamil-speaking Muslims resist being drawn into the category Tamil; their Islamic identity and their political self-interest as a community override that possibility.

What much of contemporary scholarship has shown is the historically constructed nature of the identities of Sinhalese and Tamils in modern times (see Hellman-Rajanayagam 1990, for a discussion on the development of Tamil historical consciousness). From this perspective, the claim to chronological anteriority, in which much of the nationalist rhetoric is framed, loses its point; if the content of the group identities of people in the past were different from what they are today, and if the boundaries and definitions of those identities were fluid and accommodating as the historical evidence shows, then attempts to correlate identity with territory become obviously problematic. There

are of course from the perspective of a modern multi-ethnic state much better arguments for rejecting the notion of a traditional homeland, whether of Tamils, of Sinhalese, or of Muslims.

Although contemporary ethnic identities are constructed around the symbol of language, which is then projected back into history, the distant ancestors of contemporary Sri Lankans share neither culture nor language with their descendants. The Sinhala hero-king Dutugemunu would share no common identity with Sinhalese today. We have no evidence that he (or any other king of the Anuradhapura and Polonnaruva periods) thought of himself as a Sinhalese ruling over an ethnically Sinhalese polity (although, to follow Gunawardana's logic, he may have thought of himself as a member of the Sinhala dynasty). The term Sinhala is never used at all in the *Mahavamsa*'s discussion of the Dutugemunu episode. Besides, he would not be able to communicate with any of his linguistic descendants. He would have far more in common culturally and be able to communicate with greater ease with his enemy Elara than he would with those who invoke his name as a cultural ancestor.

But why privilege language as the symbol of identity? If language serves to divide Sri Lankans, their kinship structures which communicate something very basic about the way they conceptualize their social existence, could serve just as well to unite them. As for the past, to which we are so fond of having recourse to justify our positions in the present – it is not only another country, it is another culture.

References

ACSLU (Australian Centre for Sri Lankan Unity). 1995. *The Federal Solution to the Sri Lankan Conflict: A Sequel to the Critique of the Devolution Proposals of the Sri Lankan Government*. Toowong, Queensland: Australian Centre for Sri Lankan Unity (electronic version).

Cohn, Bernard S. 1987. "The Census, Social Structure and Objectification in South Asia." In *An Anthropologist among the Historians and Other Essays*. Delhi: Oxford University Press.

Dewaraja, Lorna. 1972. *The Kandyan Kingdom, 1707–1760*. Colombo: Lake House Investments Ltd.

Dharmadasa, K.N.O. 1992. *Language, Religion and Ethnic Assertiveness: The Growth of Sinhalese Nationalism in Sri Lanka*. Ann Arbor: University of Michigan Press.

Dharmapala, Anagarika. 1965. *Return to Righteousness*. Ananda Guruge (ed.), Colombo: Ministry of Education and Cultural Affairs.

Geertz, Clifford. 1973. *The Interpretation of Cultures*. New York: Basic Books.

Gombrich, Richard and Gananath Obeyesekere. 1988. *Buddhism Transformed: Religious Change in Sri Lanka*. Princeton, NJ: Princeton University Press.

Gunawardana, R.A.L. H. 1990. "The People of the Lion: the Sinhala Identity and Ideology in History and Historiography." In Jonathan Spencer (ed.) *Sri Lanka: History and the Roots of Conflict*. London & New York: Routledge.

Hellmann-Rajanayagam, Dagmar. 1990. "The Politics of the Tamil Past." In Jonathan Spencer (ed.) *Sri Lanka: History and the Roots of Conflict*. London & New York: Routledge.

Leopold, Joan. 1970. "The Aryan Theory of Race in India: Nationalist and Internationalist Visions." *The Indian Economic and Social History Review* 7 (2): pp. 271–97.

Trautmann, Thomas R. 1981. *Dravidian Kinship*. New York: Cambridge University Press.

Webster's New Universal Unabridged Dictionary. 1983. New York: Simon and Schuster.

8

Politics of Ethnicity in India and Pakistan

Hamza Alavi

I

Ethnic issues have featured prominently in the politics of South Asian countries, as in most countries in the contemporary world. But forms and modalities of politics of ethnicity have differed from case to case. That poses large questions about the nature of ethnicity which we cannot pursue here. Our object here is rather more modest, namely to look at the social contexts and roots of ethnic politics in India and Pakistan.

Given the common history and shared cultural legacy of Pakistan and India it is remarkable to see how different are the forms that politics of ethnicity have taken in the two countries, given the fact that they are both multi-ethnic, multinational societies. The most striking difference is that ethnic movements in Pakistan take the form, primarily, of subnational movements, directed against the central power, demanding regional autonomy. The autocratic power of the central government is identified by disadvantaged regional groups as Punjabi domination. In India, no single ethnic group can be similarly identified as the dominant holder of state power at the centre. Politics of ethnicity in India have, by and large, been displaced on to local arenas, taking the form of "communalism". They revolve around demands of underprivileged or "backward" ethnic groups for positive action in their favour, for quotas in jobs and educational opportunities whereas privileged groups oppose quotas and favour their allocation on the-basis of "merit". Local competition between ethnic groups often results in communal conflict and rioting. It must be said that localized communal conflict and the issue of quotas are not absent in Pakistan. But the political scene there is overshadowed by subnationalism of regional groups. Further, in India, the so-called "untouchables", or *dalits*, as they would prefer to call themselves, are a special category of underprivileged groups. Their oppressed status is qualitatively different from that of other disadvantaged groups and is analogous to that of the black people of South Africa under apartheid. Their condition invites

Perspectives on Modern South Asia: A Reader in Culture, History, and Representation, First Edition.
Edited by Kamala Visweswaran.
© 2011 Blackwell Publishing Ltd. Published 2011 by Blackwell Publishing Ltd.

separate consideration. Finally, we have in India one or two special cases, such as that of the militant Sikh movement for an independent Khalistan, that do not fall under the broad argument that will be presented here. The Sikh case falls into a category of its own and we shall consider it briefly.

Scholarly perceptions of ethnicity have, in recent years, tended to discount notions that treated it as a manifestation of primordial sentiments, a culturally predetermined social fact that exists *sui generis*. But, nevertheless, such a notion dies hard. While it is acknowledged that entry of an ethnic group into the political arena is contingent on a variety of contextual factors that precipitate subjective perceptions of the ethnic identity, it is held nevertheless that the boundaries of groups are pre-given and exist as culturally delineated objective facts. To take an example, we find that Ballard speaks of ethnicity as a *social category*, already existing by virtue of distribution of culturally defined attributes, that is transformed into a *social group* when it is mobilized for collective action in pursuit of material interests of those who are subsumed by the category. Emphasizing that ethnicity is a political phenomenon, he draws on Marx's distinction between a class-in-itself and a class-for-itself and suggests that "We must recognize at the outset the vital distinction between a social category, that is a set of people who share common attributes of one kind or another, and a social group, where people are organized into some form of collectivity" (Ballard, 1976). Brass makes an identical distinction (Brass, 1985, 49). I believe that this is a misleading analogy.

The category of class is delineated by a set of social relations of production in a structured social matrix dividing, say, industrial workers, peasants and capitalist entrepreneurs, respectively, into objectively determinate categories, independently of subjective perceptions. In the case of ethnicity, however, there are an indefinite number of competing criteria; not just those (say) of language, religion or region but in each case further divisible and divided, according to exigencies of ethnic politics and perceptions, into subcategories or even

realigned, when one criterion (say religion) is dropped and another (say region) is taken up as the more relevant criterion for classification. There are no given ethnic categories defined by language or dialect, religion or sect, region or locality, or whatever else, that delineate groups of people independently of the line of division that is actually acknowledged and affirmed in the course of ethnic political competition.

The Pakistan experience suggests that boundaries of ethnic categories are not "objectively" pre-given for, with changes in contexts and perceptions of self-interest, radical realignments have occurred. One "objective" ethnic criterion (say religion) is abandoned in favour of another (say language or region) thus bringing together a quite different set of people into the category and community, alienating some and embracing others. The *ethnic community* therefore is not simply a politically mobilized condition of a pre-existing set of people, described as an *ethnic category*. The delineation of the "category" is itself contingent on the emergence of the "community".

For example, in the context of Muslim Nationalism in India, the criterion "Muslim" aligned a section of the people of Bengal with Muslims of other parts of India. But they were also bearers of a different identity, namely "Bengali". That potentially separated them from other Muslims and aligned them instead with Hindus of Bengal, as joint bearers of Bengali nationalism. Choice between those two competing criteria of ethnic identity was not simply a question of objective differentiation on the basis of given ethnic criteria. We might recall that in May 1947 leaders of the Bengal Muslim League together with leading Bengal Congress leaders made a bid for a United Independent Bengal, independent of both Pakistan and India. The move, accepted by Jinnah, was unsuccessful because of the opposition of the central leadership of the Indian National Congress (Mansergh and Moon, 1981, document no. 229). The alternatives, therefore, did not turn simply on subjective perception of an already given ethnic identity. The choice was decided by the influence of powerful material interests, organized in the Indian National Congress that was able to impose its will and which kept the people of West Bengal within the framework of Indian national identity and separated them from Muslims of East Bengal. We cannot speculate about how Bengali ethnic identity might have turned out had that joint initiative of Bengali Hindus and Muslims fructified. But we would do violence to history if we were to take the Muslim identity of the people of East Bengal as pre-given, independently of the manner in which the balance of political forces actually worked out in those fateful months. With shifts in interests or circumstances, ethnic realignments take place and identities change.

An examination of the politics of ethnicity in South Asia suggests that there is one class or social group whose material interests have stood at the core of ethnic competition and conflict, although other class forces too play a role in it. That class was a product of the colonial transformation of Indian social structure in the nineteenth century and it consists of those who have received an education that equips them for employment in the state apparatus, at various levels, as scribes and functionaries. For the want of a better term I call them the "salariat", for the term "middle class" is too wide, the term "intelligentsia" unwarranted and the term "petty bourgeoisie" has connotations, especially in Marxist political discourse, that would not refer to this class. For our purposes we shall include within the term "salariat" not only those who are actually in white-collar employment, notably in the state apparatus, but also those who aspire to such jobs and seek to acquire the requisite credentials, if not the actual education itself, that entitle them to the jobs.

The "salariat" is an "auxiliary class", whose class role can be fully understood only with reference to "fundamental classes", the economically dominant classes, namely the indigenous and foreign bourgeoisies and the landowning classes on the one hand and the subordinate classes, the working class and the peasantry on the other. Nevertheless, it looms large in societies in which the production base and the bulk of the population is mainly rural and agricultural, for in them the educated urban population looks primarily to the government

for employment and advancement. The salariat is not internally undifferentiated, for its upper echelons, the senior bureaucrats and military officers occupy positions of great power and prestige in the state apparatus, qualitatively different from the status of its lower-level functionaries. Nevertheless, they share a common struggle for access to a share of limited opportunities for state employment. In that struggle the salariat has a tendency to fracture (or align) along ethnic lines. Such cleavages occur because of the historical organization of division of labour and occupational specialization in India by communities, as well as uneven regional development.

Two factors affect the distribution of the salariat regionally and intercommunally. Regional disparities have much to do with early proximity to nodal points of colonial rule in India such as Calcutta, Madras and Bombay and later Delhi. Differential focus of missionary activities in the field of education has also contributed to regional and communal disparity. Hence some communities rather than others have traditionally provided cadres for service in the state apparatus, a communal specialization that has been breaking down in recent years. Communities that had traditionally provided cadres for state service had an edge over the late-comers. Under Muslim feudal rulers many Hindu communities had flourished in state employment and found themselves well-placed to exploit opportunities offered by the colonial state, such as Kayasthas and Kashmiri Brahmins of Northern India. In Sindh likewise, for example, Amils, a Hindu community, had traditionally provided cadres for state service under Muslim rulers and ethnic Sindhi Muslims were overwhelmingly rural. Members of communities that had not traditionally been employed in state service tended to be disadvantaged when they began to qualify for salariat jobs and started to look for state employment.

With the salariat, which plays a central role in ethnic politics, there are other classes which also have an interest in ethnic politics. Amongst these a class of considerable importance is the urban petty bourgeoisie, namely small traders and businessmen. Given the traditional communal division of labour, some communities tend to be already well entrenched in the respective fields when members of other ethnic communities begin to enter it. Faced with the power of those who are already well established they feel disgruntled when on entering these fields they find themselves unable to compete effectively with the old established communities. They are therefore drawn into politics of ethnicity, or communal politics.

These classes do not stand alone in the arena of ethnic or communal politics. Where prospective members of the salariat are sons of landowners or prospering peasants or, indeed, even of upper or skilled sections of the industrial working class, who work hard to give their sons an education for a better life as office workers, there is an organic link that ties members of these other classes to the salariat, and lines them up in ethnic politics. These bonds of kinship are "organic" bonds. But even beyond these, given the importance of access to officials and functionaries of government in our bureaucratized societies, politics of ethnicity attract not only kinsmen of the prospective salariats but also persons outside the kin group who have connections with them, such as fellow-villagers, inasmuch as installation of a member of an ethnic community in public office offers to the others a point of access to the bureaucratic machine. The salariat is therefore able to mobilize wide sections of the community behind itself.

In the case of subnational or regional movements, other factors enter into the equation, such as political ambitions of local-level power-holders who seek to profit from regional autonomy. Amongst these would be included powerful landlords and tribal leaders in various regions of Pakistan. They have much to gain from ethnic politics of the salariat because of the lure of political power in regional governments. They also gain when, in the rhetorical claims of ethnic solidarity, class struggle is demoted and delegitimized. Subordinate classes, the bulk of the working class and the impoverished peasantry, on the other hand, have the least to gain from politics of ethnicity. Conversely, members of a privileged ethnic group who

are in control of state power to the exclusion of others, as Punjabis in Pakistan, denounce ethnicity as parochial and narrow and appeal to larger categories, such as the nation or the "brotherhood of Islam", in the name of which they seek to deligitimize ethnic demands.

Finally, we must consider the effects of the nature of the political system on the dynamics of politics of ethnicity. India and Pakistan provide contrasting cases of this. In India the plurality of salariat groups and the absence of dominance by any one of them has necessitated a political system through which those who hold positions of power in the state are obliged to operate a process of negotiation with a wide variety of local groups in the aggregation and exercise of state power. Such processes of negotiation operate either internally within the ruling Congress Party or between the Congress and other regionally powerful parties, so that there is some sense among regional groups of a degree of participation in the process of government. In Pakistan, by contrast, the dominance of a single salariat group, Punjabis, in the military and the bureaucracy has given rise to an authoritarian political system (even during periods when there was a semblance of representative "democracy" in the country). The absence of political negotiation, under authoritarian rule, compounds the sense of alienation of subordinate ethnic groups, the outsiders. Along with that difference we need to put into balance also the relatively greater weight of class organizations in the Indian political system which puts ethnic competition into perspective. In Pakistan this is absent.

II

The people who were first inducted into the colonial salariat were from communities that had traditionally provided state functionaries in pre-colonial India and who first came in contact with colonial rule as it spread regionally from its three nodal points, namely Calcutta, Madras, Bombay and later Delhi, to other parts of India. Members of communities that had not traditionally provided cadres for government service or who came from regions that were more distant from the nodal points of colonial rule and colonial education, began to enter this field much later and in smaller numbers. That applies also to differential capacities of various trading communities to take advantage of opportunities presented by the commercialization of Indian agriculture and growth of colonial trade during the nineteenth century and onwards. Both community-wise and interregionally, the distribution of membership of the salariat and the commercial petty bourgeosie has therefore been uneven. This unevenness is at the root of subsequent ethnic competition in South Asia, for access to education and jobs in the state apparatus and participation in commerce.

The salariat was at the heart of early Indian nationalism whose main slogan was not yet independence but "Indianization" of government service and "self-government"; within the Empire. Under conditions of colonial rule the salariats (we include in this concept not only those who are actually employed in government service but also those who acquire the necessary credentials and aspire to such jobs) from different parts of India were united in that common goal. Yet even at this early stage ethnic competition within the salariat was beginning to make its appearance.

In northern India, notably United Provinces (UP), Muslims who had held a lion's share of government jobs began to lose their predominance as more and more members of other communities were recruited. Their share in the highest ranks of government service declined from 64 per cent in 1857 to about 35 per cent by 1913, a remarkable decline of privilege, for Muslims were only about 13 to 15 per cent of the total population of the UP in that period. That provided the major thrust of Muslim Nationalism in India. In the Punjab the Muslim salariat was also quite sizeable for about 32 per cent of those who were educated in English in the Punjab were Muslims who numbered over 52 per cent of the total population of the province and felt that they were underrepresented. It is not surprising that it was in these two regions that the main base of "Muslim nationalism" in India was to be found. However, the salariat by itself was too narrow a base either for Muslim nationalism or the larger Indian nationalism, to achieve their respective goals. The latter extended itself, by virtue of being adopted by the Indian national bourgeoisie, anxious to shake off the yoke of the colonial regime that obstructed its development, and by incorporating the subordinate classes who were mobilized in a mass movement. In the case of Muslim nationalism, on the other hand, a mass mobilization of subordinate classes was absent and the requisite political weight was secured by virtue of a deal that was made by leaders of the Muslim League with Muslim landlords, especially of the Punjab and Sindh, as well as those of East Bengal. This had far-reaching consequences for the successor state in Pakistan (cf. Alavi, 1983).

Muslim nationalism was by no means the only movement of its kind. In South India the non-Brahmin salariat, disadvantaged *vis-à-vis* dominant Brahmins, generated the Dravidian movement. As in the case of Muslims, the early efforts of the Dravidian movement were directed at advancing education of non-Brahmins, to break Brahmin monopoly. E. V. Ramaswamy Naicker, the *Periyar*, (Great Sage) gave a call for the formation of a separate state of "Dravidisthan", a state of non-Brahmin people of the south – Tamils, Telugu, Malayalam and Kannada – that would be independent of the Brahmin-dominated northern India and free also of domination of local Brahmins denounced as agents of the north. Naicker's dream and also his failure to mobilize the different Dravidian people behind his call for an independent Dravidisthan, illustrate very well the character and the limits of politics of the salariat.

The Telugu, Malayali and Kannada non-Brahmin salariats, it seems, had no wish to exchange Brahmin domination for Tamil domination, for Tamils were relatively more advanced than the others. These others therefore preferred to remain within the ambit of wider Indian nationalism. In Tamil Nadu itself, the Tamil Language movement and the associated anti-Hindi Language movement, the anti-northerners movements, etc., continued with varying degrees of fervour, all variations on the original Dravidian anti-Brahmin movement responding to changing circumstances. There were other regionalist movements in militarily sensitive Nagaland and there was a movement for an independent Nagaland. There was, understandably, a great deal of anxiety in India during the 1950s about such regionalist and secessionist movements. By the early 1960s a National Integration Council went to work at the centre, setting up two Committees, one on "National Integration and Communalism" and other on "National Integration and Separatism". But the Nagaland movement lost steam when its demands were partially conceded by virtue of elevation of Nagaland as a state within the Indian Union. The Dravidisthan movement led by the DMK likewise settled down to wheeling and dealing with the central government when they won control of the state from the Congress Party. Indeed, much earlier, at the time of India's military conflict with China, the DMK even declared that it would not raise the separatist issue during the National Emergency at the time. Separatism was never a very serious issue for India, although for a time regionalist rhetoric existed.

More typical of ethnic movements that were to grow after independence was one that was launched in Bihar in the 1930s to reserve employment opportunities in the state for "sons of the soil" in opposition to the more advanced Bengali salariat that dominated the field of state employment there (Nirmal Bose, 1967, 47–50). There were to be similar movements of "sons of the soil" elsewhere in India, against immigrants, seeking to reserve opportunities within the respective states for locals (Weiner, 1978, passim).

The "Scheduled Castes Movement", or the dalit movement, was concerned initially mainly with demands of educated members of those castes. Problems concerning the bulk of the "untouchables", landless labourers, were pushed into the background. Later dalit movements were to become more broadly involved. Unlike Muslims or Dravidians, they did not have a regional focus so that their politics could not take the same form but emerged instead as pressure group politics for abolition of discrimination in all walks of life, against dalits, the "untouchables".

Given the relatively earlier and greater development of Bengali and Tamil (Brahmin) salariat classes, located at the principal centres of early colonial rule in India, they came to be preponderant in government employment. It became a part of the conventional wisdom of colonial rulers that these rather than other regional groups had a natural talent for administrative service. Bengalis were sent not only to the adjoining provinces but also to the UP and even Punjab. Urdu as well as Persian (the pre-colonial language of administration) were taught at the Fort William College in Calcutta so that Bengalis were able to learn not only English but also the languages that prepared them for work all over northern India. Likewise Tamils (Brahmins) were posted in various parts of southern India. However, other regional and linguistic groups soon began to establish themselves in state service. Educational, cultural and literary associations and movements sprang up everywhere to facilitate that process.

Early ethnic movements in India, apart from the Muslim, Dravidian, Bihari and dalit movements mentioned above, mobilized behind demands for realignment of state boundaries along linguistic lines. Even the Sikh movement had presented itself as a movement for creation of a Punjabi (language) state. Following a Report of the States Reorganization Commission (appointed in 1953), the demand for linguistic states was accepted in principle and, by and large, implemented by the 1960s. The movement of linguistic states was associated with demands against immigrant groups in each region, on behalf of "sons of the soil". They did not take the form of regional movements against the centre, as in Pakistan, for they did not perceive the centre itself to be dominated by any one ethnic group. When the principle of linguistic realignment of state boundaries was conceded there were inter-state disputes over the boundaries and such matters as division of river waters – for example that between Andhra, Mysore and Maharashtra or between Punjab and Rajasthan.

The Centre even took upon itself the role of a mediator and adjudicator in such inter-state disputes, for these movements were not for regional autonomy, much less for secession. The main ethnic conflicts in India have instead been between local communities and groups of states, against each other. Given the plurality of centres of colonial administration and colonial education, numerous well-developed regional salariat groups had emerged in India balancing each other in the Indian State, ruling out a sense of ethnic domination from the centre by any single one of them. Even the Dravidisthan rhetoric could not be more precise than a vague conception of domination by Brahmins and northerners in general. This is probably the main explanation for the difference in the form that politics of ethnicity have taken in India and Pakistan.

While movements on behalf of "sons of the soil" continue in several states of India (such as Assam) where immigrants have been a significant factor in the equation, by and large ethnic conflict in India is now mainly between local communities of each region, between those that are more advanced and others that are less privileged. These conflicts are fought out (often literally so) essentially in local political arenas. The objective is twofold – first, to achieve (larger) formally allocated quotas of jobs and places in institutions of higher education for particular communities and, second, to secure places in individual cases through patronage controlled by politicians who hold high office. Ministries of Education and of Health (which control admissions to medical colleges) are among the most prized political appointments because of the opportunities for patronage that go with them. Ethnic rhetoric is therefore important in electoral politics.

A Directive Principle of the Indian Con-stitution requires the Indian State to promote educational and economic interests of the weaker sections of the people, in particular "Scheduled Castes", i.e. *dalits* or untouchables, and "other socially and educationally Backward Classes" (the word "classes" as used here is meant to be a euphemism for "castes"). The state enforces "preferential policies", establishing quotas in education and jobs in favour of underprivileged communities. Unlike the concept of "Scheduled Castes" that of

"Backward Classes" is vague and is interpreted differently in different regions and contexts. Broadly it refers to communities other than Brahmins, or Brahmins together with some more advanced non-Brahmins. The Backward Classes Commission, set up in 1953, identified no fewer than 2,399 backward groups – about 32 per cent of India's population – but there are regional variations (Galanter, 1978, p. 1816). In practice the designation of Backward Classes and their quotas has been left to the states and local authorities to decide. This is another reason why politics of ethnicity in India are displaced onto the local level and not directed against the Centre, for the issues have to be resolved locally.

There are two reasons at least why ethnic conflict, or "communalism" has escalated in India over recent years. First is the fact that the Indian educational system is producing vast numbers of educated unemployed, persons who possess formal credentials for whom there are no realistic prospects of the jobs to which they aspire. Competition for scarce jobs (and for scarce places in institutions of higher education that provide access to jobs) is intense. Second, members of less privileged communities, the Backward Classes, look up to state employment as a major avenue for upward mobility and go to great lengths to give their children an education to qualify for it. This has fostered extreme right-wing politics that border on fascism. The Shiv Sena (God's Army) with a major base in Bombay is an example. It recruits its support from Maharashtrians, including better-off, skilled sections of the working class, who aspire for their sons to be educated and qualify for office jobs. South Indians are singled out by them as targets for vicious fascist attacks. All over India ethnic violence and communal riots have become a part of the everyday scene. Communal violence attracts and is reinforced by political opportunism, which seeks to exploit emotive slogans, and also by racketeers of all kinds who profit from it, for appeals to ethnicity can provide a cover for thuggery.

In recent years ethnic politics have moved to rural areas, with the growing prosperity of the better-off farmers who possess viable landholdings, labelled by the Rudolphs as "bullock capitalists" (Rudolph and Rudolph, 1987). These members of the "Backward Classes", having prospered economically in the 1960s, have emerged as a significant political force in the Indian countryside, having upset the traditional balance of political forces. They are vocal in their demands for quotas for admissions to institutions of higher education for their children and for jobs in government.

The case of *dalits* or "untouchables" is qualitatively different from that of the aspiring salariats who have provided the main thrust of ethnic politics in India. It is true that the movement – the Scheduled Caste Federation – begun by Dr Ambedkar was mainly oriented towards the rising white-collar middle-class elements emerging from a *dalit* background. But nevertheless, the better-off *dalit* shares with his or her brothers and sisters in lower classes discrimination and oppression from higher castes. Indeed the upwardly mobile *dalit* is often the principal target of ethnic violence, whereas *dalits* at the bottom of the social heap may be ignored (Pradip Bose, 1981). It is not easy for upwardly mobile *dalits* to conceal their identity from potential employers, landlords or neighbours. Given the barriers of ritual pollution erected against them they find it difficult not only to get a suitable job that they merit but also to rent an apartment or to eat in public eating-houses and restaurants, although institutions of the city afford some anonymity and protection. *Dalits* are targets of constant indignities. This draws members of different *dalit* classes closer together than is the case with the others. Their problem is that of survival in a hostile environment, a total problem that encompasses all aspects of their life and not merely that of securing admission to an educational institution or a job, a once-for-all problem for the others. In recent decades therefore militant *dalit* movements have arisen to secure remedies that must go beyond quotas in university admissions and allocation of jobs, which draw in all sections of the *dalit* population.

On the face of it the Sikh movement for a Punjabi *suba* (state), and more recently for an independent Khalistan, may appear to fall outside the general pattern of ethnic politics in India. The militant Sikh movement, for an independent Khalistan has some special features that set it apart. Unlike regionalist movements in Pakistan, where dissident movements for regional autonomy and national self-determination are generated in underprivileged provinces, the Indian Punjab (and Sikhs) could well be described as being amongst the most privileged in India. From among Indan states, Punjab has the highest income per capita. Numbering only about 2 per cent of India's population, Sikhs have a massive presence in the Indian army and the police and not much less in civilian government jobs. Being the bread-basket of India, agriculture is the foundation of Punjab's prosperity. About 80 per cent of its cultivated area is irrigated. Its most productive agricultural economy is highly modernized and mechanized. Although Punjab does not have much by way of large-scale industries, it has flourishing small- and medium-sized industries. During the First Indian War of Independence (the so-called "Indian Mutiny") in 1857 Sikhs gave "loyal" support to the British and fought on behalf of the colonial regime. That "loyalty" was rewarded by grants of land and jobs in the colonial army and bureaucracy. It should be added parenthetically that Sikhs did later play a distinguished role in the national freedom movement and produced as many heroes and martyrs in the national cause as any other community of Indians. But the fact remains that under the colonial regime they, along with most Punjabis, were much favoured and their privileged position is undiminished.

Sikh Jats (powerful landowners) dominate Sikh politics through the communalist Akali Dal party which, in turn, is supported by the Shiromani Gurdwara Prabhandak Committee (SPGC) which controls the Sikh religious establishment. The SPGC has, since 1925, administered the several hundred Sikh shrines and places of worship with access to vast resources derived from control of religious property and offerings of devotees, estimated in 1985 to amount to over $12 million (Kapur, 1986, xv). It derives great power from patronage through the disbursement of these funds and appointments to jobs in the shrines and religious organizations.

As in the case of other salariat groups in India, educated Sikhs turned towards religious reform, notably through Singh Sabhas (Sikh Associations) whose object, *inter alia*, was to promote the Punjabi language and Sikh education (Barrier, 1970, xxiv–xxv). By 1902 the various Singh Sabhas came together in "an organisation known as the Chief Khalsa Diwan [which] was formed to serve as a centre for communication among educated Sikhs … From the outset [it] was dominated by prominent members of the Sikh gentry and large landowners" (Kapur, 1986, 18). The movement that resulted in the formation of the SPGC and its takeover of Sikh Gurdwaras, was a part of that Sikh reform movement. However, given the favoured position of Sikhs under the colonial regime and their disproportionate representation in the army and other branches of state employment, the Sikh movement did not need to make demands for quotas in education and employment, as in the case of other minority communities.

Their main demand was to secure a state within India, in which Sikhs would be in a majority. It is noteworthy that even this Sikh communal party couched that demand as one for a Punjabi (language) state. Punjabi was essentially a Sikh language in India, for Hindus of the region are Hindi-speaking and language was easily a surrogate for the religious community. After much pressure and agitation by the Akali Dal a new state of Punjab was finally constituted in 1966, after trifurcation of the old Punjab. But even here Sikhs numbered only 54 per cent of the population, Hindus numbering 44 per cent.

III

The pattern of politics of ethnicity in Pakistan has been radically different from that in India in two respects. First, ethnic movements in Pakistan have primarily taken the form of subnationalism although a secondary theme of localized ethnic conflict has not been absent.

Second, there has been a succession of ethnic definitions and redefinitions as circumstances have changed. To begin with, the peoples of Pakistan were defined as Muslims by virtue of the claims of Muslim nationalism. However, the social roots of Muslim nationalism were quite shallow. Indeed it is quite remarkable that the Pakistan movement was weakest in Muslim majority provinces of India. In the Punjab political power lay in the hands not of the weak Punjabi urban Muslim salariat but rather in the hands of powerful landowners who were organized behind the secular right-wing landlord party, the Unionist Party, which brought together Punjabi Muslim, Hindu and Sikh landowners into their class organization, and who despised (even when they patronized) the urban salariat groups.

In Sindh the pattern was virtually identical except for the fact that an ethnic Sindhi Muslim salariat was virtually non-existent, for Muslims in Sindh were either landowners or peasants. Sindhi urban society was overwhelmingly Hindu, consisting of Amils who traditionally provided cadres for the state apparatus of Muslim rulers of Sindh, and Bhaibands who were a community of traders. They were driven out of Sindh by deliberately organized urban riots in January 1948. Muslims in Sindh who were included in salariat occupations before the Partition were mostly migrants either from northern or western India. The position was similar in Sarhad (the land of the Pathans) and Baluchistan. In Bangladesh the party in power for a long time before independence was the secular Krishak Proja Party led by Fazlul Haq. It was only when Independence was in sight that an accommodation was made with the Muslim League which took office in the province. The region where the Muslim League was the strongest was in the UP and Bihar where the Muslim salariat was highly privileged in holding high-level government jobs more than in proportion to the Muslim population of the region, but was nevertheless insecure because the ratio of its privilege was rapidly declining as more and more Hindus were coming into salariat positions. "Muslim nationalism" was a movement that was aimed essentially to secure their positions (for an analysis of the Pakistan movement see Alavi, 1987).

By virtue of the claims of the Pakistan movement, the salariat groups, as above, adopted the ethnic identity of "Muslim" and proclaimed the "Two Nation" theory, that asserted that Indians were divided into two nations, Muslims and Hindus. The moment that Pakistan was established, Muslim nationalism in India had fulfilled itself and had outlived its purpose. Now there was a fresh equation of privilege and deprivation to be reckoned within the new state. Virtually overnight there were ethnic redefinitions. Punjabis, who were the most numerous, could boast of a greater percentage of people with higher education and were most firmly entrenched in both the army (being 85 per cent of the armed forces) and the bureaucracy. They were the new bearers of privilege, the true "Muslims" for whom Pakistan was created. The weaker salariats of Bengal, Sindh, Sarhad and Baluchistan did not share this and accordingly they redefined their identities, as Bengalis, Sindhis, Pathans and Baluch who now demanded fairer shares for themselves. Bengali, Sindhi, Pathan and Baluch nationalist movements exploded into view the day after Pakistan came into being, the state in Pakistan now being seen as an instrument of Punjabi domination.

Articulation of Bengali and Pathan identities, respectively, was relatively unproblematic. In Sindh and Baluchistan this was not quite so straightforward. In Baluchistan, if one were to interpret cultural and linguistic criteria very rigidly it would be possible to identify a number of different groups, namely Baluch proper, Brahuis (or Brohi), Lassis, Makranis and, in the north-east districts, Pushtuns who are Pathans rather than Baluch. The literature of Baluch nationalism repudiates attempts to differentiate amongst them and has produced historical accounts of convergent origins of the different sections of the Baluch people. The dominant Punjabi ideology, on the other hand, emphasizes the differences.

The situation in Sindh is much more complicated for Sindh is a multi-ethnic province. Hence contradictions of politics of ethnicity are concentrated there. That arises initially and

principally from the pattern of settlement of refugees from India, known as Muhajirs. Forty years ago the Punjabi ruling oligarchy ensured that refugees from East Punjab (and only those) were settled in West Punjab so that Punjab in Pakistan remained ethnically homogeneous. All other refugees, mainly Urdu-speaking refugees from northern and central India, were settled in Sindh. They were kept out of the Punjab although Punjab is a much larger province and had a greater capacity to absorb the refugees. On the other hand, communal riots were deliberately instigated in Sindh to drive out Sindhi Hindus who were the overwhelming majority of the urban population. The population of Sindh was thus radically and irrevocably restructured.

Some of the Urdu-speaking refugees from India who were funnelled into Sindh settled on the land. But the bulk of them took the place of the urban Sindhi Hindus who were driven out of Pakistan, either as traders or professionals. Muhajirs also provided the bulk of the industrial working class in Sindh immediately after the Partition. The ethnic Sindhi Muslim urban population, was minute. Whereas before Partition Sindh's cities were predominently *non-Muslim* (the Muslims that were there originated mostly from outside Sindh) now they are predominantly *non-Sindhi*. Initially overwhelmingly Muhajir in composition, the pattern of Sindh's urban population changed later as Pathan and Punjabi workers began to pour into the industrial cities of Sindh.

As a result only 52 per cent of the population of Sindh consists of those whose first language is Sindhi (census 1981). Urdu-speakers, the Muhajirs, are more than 22 per cent of the total population. But they predominate in the urban areas of Sindh where Urdu-speakers were reckoned to number over 50 per cent of the population. The disproportionate number of ethnic non-Sindhi population is less pronounced in smaller towns, which after all are mere extensions of the rural society. But non-ethnic Sindhis are in overwhelming majority in the three major industrial conurbations of Sindh, namely Karachi, Hyderabad and Sukkur.

In Karachi, the capital of Sindh and a metropolis of over 8 million people, 54.3 per cent of the population (in 1981) were Muhajirs, i.e. those whose first language is Urdu. 13.6 per cent were Punjabi speakers and 8.7 per cent Pushto-speaking Pathans. Those whose first language was Sindhi, were a mere 6.3 per cent. These census figures probably underestimate the numbers of Pathans and Punjabis in Karachi, many of whom live in slums or *katchi abadis* as they are called; experts believe that they have been underenumerated. An estimated 40 per cent of the population of the city live in the slums. Sindhis in Karachi, on the other hand, belong to the lower middle class and above, many of them being absentee landlords. Reliable figures are hard to come by but it is widely believed by informed persons that Pathans number far more than 8.7 per cent of the city's population as suggested by the Census data. Likewise in Hyderabad and Sukkur Sindhis are a small minority.

A different complication about the situation in Sindh arises from the influx of privileged groups from outside. These are mostly Punjabis. Large tracts of valuable land in Sindh, brought under irrigation since independence, have been allotted to Punjabis, members of the armed forces or senior bureaucrats or their relatives. They tend to be mostly absentee landlords and have brought with them Punjabi tenants or labourers whom they can better control (and rely upon) than local Sindhis. In urban areas, too, valuable land is allotted to persons in these categories. In the last decade or so a new trend has established itself. Because of the elaborate network of state control over business, members of the traditional business communities, mainly Gujerati-speaking, finding it increasingly difficult to cope with obstacles put in their way by the government, are moving out and their place is being taken by a new class of army related Punjabi capitalists. Their kinship connections are a vital element in negotiating bureaucratic hurdles which, in the past, were managed by simple bribery. Punjabis increasingly dominate most positions of wealth and power in society. The police force in Sindh is almost wholly Punjabi. Both Sindhis and Muhajirs have increasingly found themselves pushed into the background and resent it.

At the time of the Partition, Muhajirs were well-established in the bureaucracy, though not in the armed services which are about 85 per cent Punjabi, the rest being Pathans. The well-established Muhajir presence in the bureaucracy was a source of patronage and protection for them. They identified therefore with the Pakistan state and with Islamic ideology, and were hostile towards regional ethnic movements. They backed the fundamentalist Jamaat-e-Islami or the traditionalist Jamiat-e-Uleme-e-Pakistan (JUP). The bureaucracy, with its substantial Muhajir component, was presided over in Pakistan by the CSP (the Civil Service of Pakistan), successor to the colonial "Indian Civil Service", the so-called "Steel Frame" of the colonial regime. It was the senior partner in the military–bureaucratic oligarchy that has ruled Pakistan since its inception (cf. Alavi, 1987). It was powerful enough to keep the military at bay even during the Martial Law regimes of General Yahya Khan. The situation changed radically after Bhutto's reform of the bureaucracy which effectively broke its back. Ironically that removed the main barrier that had stood in the way of hegemony of the army which is now supreme. With it has come unchallenged Punjabi hegemony in the country. It has taken a little time for the effects of this shift in the ethnic balance of the state apparatus to manifest itself in the politics of ethnicity in the country, which crystallized in 1986.

Hitherto Muhajirs had agitated against the quota system for jobs and admission into institutions of higher education. As late as December 1986 a Jamaat-e-Islami-oriented Muhajir Urdu weekly carried an article entitled "Quota System: Denial of Justice and the Sword of Oppression" (*"Quota System: Adal ki nafi aur zulm ki Talwar"*, *Takbeer*, 24 December 1986). The quota system dates back to the 1950s when it was introduced, in deference to Bengali demands. Unlike India where they are based on local communal criteria, quotas in Pakistan are regional, 10 per cent of the places being awarded "on merit", 50 per cent being for the Punjab, 19 per cent for Sind, of which 11.4 per cent for rural Sind and 7.6 per cent for urban Sind, 11.5 per cent for Sarhad, 3.5 per cent for

Baluchistan and the rest for Azad Kashmir and Federally Administered Territories. In Sind it was calculated that the urban quota would be oriented towards Muhajirs and the rural quota towards ethnic Sindhis. The problem with the quota system, however, is that given Punjabi control of the administrative machinery in all provinces, it is not too difficult for a Punjabi to obtain a false "Certificate of Domicile" in say Quetta in Baluchistan or Hyderabad in Sindh, and poach quotas from other regions, depriving the locals.

With the collapse of bureaucratic power and consolidation of Punjabi-dominated army power, Muhajirs began to feel that they were losing out heavily under the existing system, and that they had little to gain from agitating for abolition of the quota system. In March 1984 a new movement called the Muhajir Qaumi Mahaz (MQM) (the Muhajir National Front) was set up, its initial impetus deriving from a students' organization. They demanded that Muhajirs should be recognized as the fifth nationality of Pakistan and that they should be allotted a 20 per cent quota at the Centre and between 50 per cent and 60 per cent in Sindh. They want quotas in Sindh to be reserved exclusively for Sindhis and Muhajirs, whom alone they consider to be the rightful communities of Sindh, so that the places should not be made available to any others.

The rise of the MQM on the national scene was quite sudden and dramatic, precipitated by certain events in September 1986. Only a few months earlier it would have been thought unbelievable that Muhajhirs would rally behind the slogan saying that "*Ham nain Pakistan aur Islam ka Theka nahin liya hai*" (i.e. "We have not signed contracts to uphold Pakistan and Islam"). Having for decades declared their identity as Pakistanis and Muslim, and opposed all ethnic movements in the name of Pakistan and Islam, they have now repudiated both of these criteria in favour of the notion of Muhajir nationality. There was an overnight ethnic redefinition. They abandoned the Islamic fundamentalist Jamaat-e-Islami and the traditionalist Jamait-e-Ulema-e-Pakistan and rallied massively behind the new MQM. Instead of moving towards an end to

communalism, however, the rise of the MQM signifies a further consolidation of communalism in Pakistan.

Developments in Sind are still in a state of flux. In 1983 a powerful exclusively Sindhi (and therefore rural-based) militant movement arose in opposition to the military regime on a scale that fully stretched its repressive capacities. Nevertheless the movement was unsuccessful. Some Sindhi leaders and intellectuals recognize that this was so because of their inability to establish a united front with Muhajirs, the majority of the urban population, without whose participation a purely rural-based, non-revolutionary, movement can achieve little. They are sufficiently realistic in their grasp of the situation in Sindh to accept that Muhajirs are now part of the Sindhi people and must stand shoulder-to-shoulder with Sindhi speakers in Sindh. That recognition and a desire to establish solidarity with Muhajirs has led an influential section of the Sindhi leadership to redefine the Sindhi identity.

Sindhi identity has always been a little problematic in that multi-ethnic province, for many people from other regions have settled there, amongst them, notably the Baluch who speak Baluchi at home even though they consider themselves to be Sindhis and are acknowledged as such by other Sindhis. Indeed, some Baluch hold positions of leadership in the Sindhi movement. Now, in the aftermath of the failure of the 1983 movement, many Sindhi leaders, both on the right of the political spectrum and the left, extend the concept of Sindhi identity to other groups in the province whereas others would resist that.

The former argue that being Sindhi is not a matter of place of origin or language. If that were otherwise how could the Baluchis in Sindh have been accepted amongst them as Sindhis for so long and so many of them acknowledged as Sindhi leaders? The Baluch were Sindhis because they had roots in Sindh. They would extend that principle to Muhajirs. The Muhajirs, they say, were uprooted from India and deposited in Sindh "by fate and the forces of history". They have struck fresh roots in Sindhi soil. These Sindhi leaders repudiate paternalistic designation of Muhajirs as "New Sindhis", a term that has been widely used in the past but which, implicitly, denies Muhajirs full status as Sindhis. They are "Sindhis", they say, without qualification. Descent is no criterion of ethnicity they say, nor language nor religion. It is a question of roots.

In the eyes of these Sindhi leaders and intellectuals, Punjabis in Sindh, nevertheless, do not qualify for inclusion within the expanded notion of Sindhi identity. The Punjabis, mostly bureaucrats and members of the armed forces who have been allotted land in Sindh by the Government, have come into Sindh, they argue, on the strength of state power, as conquerors and usurpers. They do not have roots in Sindh for their roots lie in the Punjab. They should be expelled from Sindh and the lands that they have been given should be restored to Sindhi hands.

It is most significant that such ethnic redefinitions are taking place, impelled by the need for fresh political alignments, towards a united front with Muhajirs and away from a more narrow definition of Sindhi identity that isolates the predominantly rural Sindhi-speakers in Sindh. It takes into account the realities of political forces in Sindh and a recognition that without a united front of the peoples of Sindh, Sindhi-speakers on their own will get nowhere.

As for the future there is no simple answer to the problem of ethnic competition in Pakistan and India, though one would suggest that its narrow class bases and interests need to be recognized in order that it is handled as it deserves to be. An opposition to ethnic movements, without regard to the just demands of the underprivileged groups would play into the hands of the privileged who want a free hand for themselves in the name of merit and efficiency. On the other hand an unqualified line-up behind ethnic demands, under the slogan "the national contradiction takes precedence over class contradictions", means that the forces of the common people are not mobilized in the struggles against injustices but rather that the initiative is handed over to powerful landlords or political adventurers and opportunists or the way is left open for the issue to be exploited by gangsters. That means that politics in the country fail to generate forces that can take society forward towards an egalitarian and just society.

References

Alavi, H. 1983. "Class and State in Pakistan" in H. Gardezi and J. Rashid eds. *Pakistan: The Roots of Dictatorship*. London: Zed Books.
_____. 1987. "Pakistan and Islam: Ethnicity and Ideology", in Fred Halliday and Hamza Alavi eds. *State and Ideology in the Middle East*. London: Macmillan.

Ballard, R. 1976. "Ethnicity: Theory and Experience", *New Community V*, 3.

Barrier, N. G. 1970. *The Sikhs and their Literature*. Delhi: Manohar Book Service.

Bose, N. K. 1967. *Problems of National Integration*. Simla: Institute of Advanced Study.

Bose, Pradip K. 1981. "Social Mobility and Caste Violence", *Economic and Political Weekly*, 18 April 1981.

Brass, Paul. 1985. *Ethnic Groups and the State*. London: Croom Helm.

Galanter, Marc. 1978. "Who Are the Backward Classes?", *Economic and Political Weekly*, 28 October.

Kapur, Rajiv. 1986. *Sikh Separatism: The Politics of Faith*. London: Allen & Unwin.

Mansergh, N. and Moon, P., eds. 1981. *Constitutional Relations Between Britain and India: The Transfer of Power 1942–47*, vol. X. London: HMSO.

Rudolph, L. I. and Rudolph, S. H. 1987. *In Pursuit of Lakshmi: The Political Economy of the Indian State*. Chicago: The University of Chicago Press.

Weiner, M. 1978. *Sons of the Soil: Migration and Ethnic Conflict in India*. Princeton: Princeton University Press.

9

Ethnicity, Caste and a Pluralist Society

Rajendra Pradhan

It is difficult to find elsewhere in the world a country as small in area as Nepal with such a variety in population. Nepal is a cultural mosaic inhabited as it is by an amazingly diverse array of ethnic, caste, linguistic and religious communities. The 1991 Census of Nepal recorded 60 caste and ethnic groups (mostly Indo-Aryan and 'Mongols') and 70 languages and dialects (mostly Indo-Aryan and Tibeto-Burman). In terms of religions, the census lists Hinduism, Buddhism, Islam and local faiths, but the Hinduism–Buddhism interface itself provides so many variations that it is often difficult to put a name on the belief system.

This cultural fertility is a consequence of several waves of migration over two thousand years, with some consolidation, as a result of the political unification of the territories occupied by migrant communities. The ethnic groups, speaking Tibeto-Burman languages such as the Gurung, Tamang and Limbu, migrated at different times from regions across the Himalaya far to the north and east, with the Sherpa and some of the Tibetan-speaking groups having arrived more recently from the same general direction. The Nepali-speaking Bahun (Brahmin), Chhetri (Kshatriya) and Thakuri as well as the service caste dalits, collectively known as Parbatiya ('hill people'), migrated in from the west and south. The ethnic group known as the Newar is a composite of several communities who migrated into Kathmandu Valley over two millennia. In the tarai plains, some 'indigenous' communities such as the formerly forest-dwelling Tharu, Sattar and Santhal have probably been around for over two millennia as well, whereas others such as the farming Maithili-speakers of the eastern tarai arrived later.

Over the centuries, these different communities, each with its own language, religion and culture, settled in different parts of Nepal's plains, hills and high valleys. They established separate but fluid political units, mainly small chiefdoms and principalities, although there were also larger political units such as the kingdom of the Mallas in the west and of the Lichchhavis based in Kathmandu Valley.

Perspectives on Modern South Asia: A Reader in Culture, History, and Representation, First Edition.
Edited by Kamala Visweswaran.
© 2011 Blackwell Publishing Ltd. Published 2011 by Blackwell Publishing Ltd.

In the second half of the eighteenth and the first decade of the nineteenth century, Prithvi Narayan Shah, ruler of the small hill principality of Gorkha at the centre of present-day Nepal, and his immediate descendants conquered and politically amalgamated these different political units into the Gorkhali empire, now known as Nepal. Some migration into the eastern tarai continued even after the political unification of the country.

The Tibeto-Burman-speakers settled in regions where, owing to the difficult terrain and the unfordable rivers, they developed as discrete communities in distinct pockets. For example, the Limbus and Rais have their own regions in the eastern part of Nepal; the Tamangs reside in the area around Kathmandu Valley; the Gurungs reside in the hills of central Nepal around Pokhara Valley; and the Magars in regions south and west of the Gurung habitat. The peopling of this landscape by the Indo-Aryans was different, for they spread through the length and breadth of the country, aided by the Gorkhali conquest. It can thus be generally said that while the Tibeto-Burmans give Nepal its extraordinary demographic diversity, the Indo-Aryans have provided the connections that have bound the country together as one.

The 1991 census data is considered flawed by some because of the biased manner in which the different categories of the population were recorded, but it does provide us with a general picture of how this national cultural diversity is currently structured. In a country as geographically and demographically complex as Nepal, there are various ways to look at the population: by religion, language, region (hill or plain), caste/ethnicity; and because there are inter-cutting identities as well, it makes the study even more complex. The census classifies 86.5 per cent of the population as Hindu, 7.8 per cent as Buddhist, 3.5 per cent as Muslim and 2.7 per cent as 'others' (Kiranti, Christians, Jains and Sikhs). In terms of mother tongues spoken, 77 per cent use Indo-Aryan languages (14 in all), 20 per cent speak Tibeto-Burman languages (17 in number) and three per cent speak other languages, including Munda and

Dravidian. Speakers of Nepali as their mother tongue constitute just over 50 per cent of the population (See Table 1).

In terms of caste and ethnic break-up, the country is essentially a conglomeration of minorities, with the two largest groups comprising but 16 per cent (Chhetri) and nearly 13 per cent (Bahun) of the population. None of the other groups constitute more than 10 per cent of the population. In term of groupings, the 1991 census recorded 40.3 per cent of the population as hill-based Parbatiyas (Chhetri – 16.1 per cent, Bahun – 12.9 per cent, and the three 'untouchable' and other service castes, dalits – 11.3 per cent). The janajati ethnic groups, of both hill and plains taken together, constitute 35.5 per cent of the population, whereas the hill ethnic groups alone make up 26.5 per cent of all Nepalis. The major hill ethnic groups are the Magar, Newar, Tamang, Rai, Gurung and Limbu. The Tharu (6.5 per cent) constitute the largest ethnic group in the plains.

Another way to classify the population of the country is between the Pahadi and Madhesi. The former is the term applied to the hill communities of Nepal, comprising both the caste-structured Parbatiya as well as the ethnic janajati. They constitute 66.8 per cent of the population. Due to migration in the last half century, a large proportion of this Pahadi population now lives in the Tarai plains. As a counterpoint to the Pahadi are the Madhesi, people of tarai origin, among whom are found caste, linguistic, religious as well as ethnic groups. Together, the Madhesi make up the rest (32.1 per cent) of the population.

Like the Pahadis, the Madhesi are not linguistically or religiously homogeneous. The 12 ethnic groups from the Tarai, including the Tharu, Kumal, Majhi and Rajbanshi, constitute 9 per cent of the total national population. Madhesi Hindus, with 20 castes, make up 15.9 per cent of the national population and speak a variety of languages and dialects. Maithili (11.8 per cent) is spoken in the east, Bhojpuri (7.5 per cent) in the central tarai, and Awadhi (2 per cent) to the west of the Narayani river. Tarai Muslims also have a significant presence, making up 3.5 per cent of the national population.

Despite its overwhelming cultural diversity, Nepal is predominantly a Hindu kingdom with a Hindu polity, though not necessarily a Hindu society. Over the centuries, nature-worshipping, animist or Buddhist communities have been gradually 'Hinduised', mainly due to the conquest of non-Hindu communities by Hindu kings and the migration of Parbatiyas to different parts of Nepal. Whereas the ethnic groups of the hills have been historically confined to the different regions of Nepal, the Parbatiya spread out across the country, providing the motive force for Hinduisation. This process intensified after the political unification of Nepal and more so during the Rana era (1846–1951); there was no let-up during the Panchayat regime (1961–1990) either, and to some extent is continuing even today. The 1991 census recorded 86.5 per cent of the population as Hindu, although that figure is disputed by many who are convinced about an inherent bias in census-taking.

What is called the Hinduisation of Nepal was actually 'Parbatiyasition', that is, the spread and imposition of the culture of the Parbatiya, most significantly their language, Nepali (originally known as Khas or Khas Kura), and religion, Hinduism. Even though Kathmandu Valley itself had long been a centre for Hindu devotion and pilgrimage, it was the Gorkhali kings who spread the faith in its diverse forms across the mid-hills of Nepal. The process of Parbatiyasition was, and to a degree continues to be, facilitated by the state, because a majority of the ruling elite since the time of King Prithvi Narayan have been 'high-caste' Parbatiyas, who were actively supported by the Newar elite of Kathmandu, the majority of whom were also Hindu. The subordinated communities responded with accommodation and assimilation, but also with out-migration or resistance, sometimes violent.

Regardless of the reality on the ground, Nepal is usually represented as a Hindu kingdom where different castes as well as ethnic, linguistic and religious groups have co-existed peacefully. The state and the ruling elite take pride in what they see as 'unity in cultural diversity' and never tire of repeating King Prithvi Narayan's famous statement: 'This country is a flower garden of four *varnas* and thirty-six *jats*.' There is some truth to this claim because Nepal, unlike so many countries, has remained relatively free of ethnic, religious, linguistic and caste violence. However, the subordinate groups are beginning to question this picture of tolerance and pluralism. Particularly since the restoration of multi-party democracy in 1990, the open political atmosphere has allowed the emergence of an energetic movement of ethnic assertion, whose leadership might regard Nepal as a pluralistic society, but one that is characterised by hierarchy, dominance and oppression.

As is only natural for a country with such a multiplicity and interlinked collection of identities, there are different views when it comes to identifying the dominant, oppressive community. According to the janajati (mainly hill-ethnic) leadership, claiming to represent the 'original inhabitants' of Nepal, this dominant and exploitative group is made up of Bahuns, the Chhetri warrior castes and the Thakuri ruler class. According to the leaders of the Madhesi people of the tarai, it is the Pahadi hill people in general, whether Parbatiyas or janajati, who have been dominant and discriminatory. In their mind, the Pahadis have arrogated to their hill and mountain terrain the definition of Nepal's self-identity, and have pushed the plains people to the status of second-class citizens. On the other hand, 'low' caste dalits argue that it is the 'upper' castes and ethnic groups, whether from the hills or the plains, who dominate and discriminate. Thus, leaders of the dominated groups variously point to the Parbatiya, Pahadi, Madhesi, janajati and 'upper' caste groups as the sources of economic, political and cultural discrimination. In other words, they raise issues pertaining to the political economy as well as the politics of cultural diversity and inter-caste relations in Nepal.

Different models of a culturally pluralist society have been articulated by the state and by different communities over the past two centuries. Throughout this period, the ruling elite in Kathmandu Valley have tried to impose their vision of a plural society within the framework of their understanding of Hindu society and polity, a fact that is reflected in the laws and codes promulgated by different rulers. Following the work of anthropologist Joanna Pfaff-Czarnecka, it is useful to discuss three periods: a) the establishment of the Gorkhali empire up to the end of the Rana regime (1769–1950); b) the Panchayat period (1961–1990); and c) the decade following the restoration of democracy in 1990. How did the different population groups negotiate these periods, and in which circumstances did they seek assimilation and accommodation or resistance and separation? This will help in understanding the debate that has been taking place nationally since 1990 concerning ethnicity, caste, state and society. It is important to study the models of plural society proposed by the state and the dominant communities on the one hand and by the leadership of the ethnic movement on the other, and refer to a possible model for an ideal pluralist Nepali society.

Hierarchy, Diversity and the Hindu Polity 1768–1950

The political unification by conquest and other means of the 60-odd political units populated by different ethnic communities, posed a challenge to the ruling Parbatiya Hindus. Rather than imposing a uniform culture throughout the newly expanded kingdom, their primary concern was exercising political control and extracting revenue from the newly conquered territories. At the same time, the elites did need an overarching framework to integrate the diverse communities of the newly expanded kingdom, and also to establish it as a pure and true Hindu land, an 'asal Hindustan' as Prithvi Narayan Shah called it. The model that was already available to them and most suited to their plans was the caste system, which provided the legal and social structure into which Nepal's diversity could be organised and subsumed in a single hierarchical – Hindu – order.

This explains Prithvi Narayan's celebrated definition of his new kingdom as a garden of four *varnas* and thirty-six *jats*. The 'unifier' king, tenth direct ancestor of Nepal's King Gyanendra, used this formula to include all of his subjects, Hindu and non-Hindu, caste-based as well as ethnic. *Varna* refers to people of all castes, and *jat* in its more general meaning refers to communities, including castes as well as ethnic and religious communities. There are those who question whether Prithvi Narayan accepted cultural diversity, but there is no doubt that he understood the reality of the plural character of his rapidly expanded realm. Some scholars have argued for the Indian case that at least some interpretations of the Hindu theory of kingship and polity did not preclude cultural pluralism, and it could be argued that the model society Prithvi Narayan of Gorkha espoused was that of cultural pluralism within the broad framework of a hierarchical caste system. Cultural differences were accepted, but with different communities and castes ranked in a hierarchical order depending on the degree of similarity and difference with the cultural norms and practices of the 'upper-caste' Nepali-speaking Hindus. Nevertheless, it can be said that the 'unifier king' was more accepting of cultural diversity and provided greater autonomy to the different cultural groups than did his successors.

By the middle of the nineteenth century, the new ruling elites had consolidated their power and were firmly ensconced in the palaces of the Malla kings in Kathmandu. The kingdom became progressively more integrated and centralised, both politically and administratively. Meanwhile, with the blessings of the state, the land-hungry Parbatiya populace began migrating in ever-larger numbers to territories populated by ethnic communities. While the rulers were mainly concerned with extracting revenue for themselves and in consolidating their hold over the kingdom, as time went by they became increasingly interested in imposing a more homogeneous cultural matrix on the kingdom as well.

This process of Hinduisation, spearheaded by the migrating Parbatiya, progressed rapidly after Jang Bahadur Kunwar seized power in 1846 and established the hereditary Rana *shogunate*, which effectively ruled the country until 1951 while maintaining Prithvi Narayan's Shah successors in the royal palace as titular monarchs. The era of conquest was over, and consolidation required a more 'unified' kingdom, and in trying to establish Nepal as a true Hindu land, the Ranas were less tolerant of cultural plurality. Eight years after Jang Bahadur seized power, he promulgated the first Muluki Ain (a national 'civil code'), a set of laws that was to be valid throughout the kingdom. The code dealt with many subjects such as land tenure, inheritance and even sexual relations, but by far the most important portion dealt with inter-community relations. The Muluki Ain articulated a more worked-out vision of a plural society within a caste system than Prithvi Narayan's model. It conceptually integrated all the different linguistic and ethnic groups as well as existing castes into one overarching hierarchy. All groups in mid-nineteenth century Nepal, therefore, came under the following five categories:

1   Wearers of the holy thread (*tagadhari*): Bahun, Rajput, Chhetri, various Newar castes, etc.
2   Non-enslavable alcohol-drinkers (*namasinya matwali*): Magar, Gurung and some Newar castes, etc.
3   Enslavable alcohol-drinkers (*masinya matwali*): Limbu, Kirat (Rai), Tharu and the general category of Bhote, including Sherpas, the group now known as Tamang and other groups with close Tibetan cultural affiliation, etc.
4   Impure but touchable castes: Newar service castes – butchers, washermen, tanners – Europeans and Muslims.
5   Impure and untouchable castes: Parbatiya (blacksmiths, tanners, tailors) and Newar (fishermen and scavengers) service castes.

There were obvious challenges in trying to force-fit the diverse communities into these categories, particularly because some of the groups were not 'castes' by any definition of the term. The first, fourth and fifth categories incorporated the Hindu caste groups proper, with the exception of European and Muslims. The second and third categories (*matwalis*), with the exception of Newars, on the other hand, were janajati ethnic groups outside the pale of the caste hierarchy till then. Some were made 'enslavable' and others not, seemingly in accordance with the communal power play during those days of national consolidation. And because the Newars of Kathmandu Valley were structured internally along the lines of religion (Hindus and Buddhists) and also had a complex caste system of their own, they had to be dispersed among four of the five 'caste' categories.

Though all groups within these broad five categories were not 'castes', the Muluki Ain prescribed caste status for them based on Hindu notions of purity and pollution in many domains of social life, such as inter-caste commensality of boiled rice, acceptance of water, and sexual relations. The code also proscribed certain practices, such as consumption of beef, which was not taboo among many ethnic communities. On the other hand, the Muluki Ain did allow for some degree of autonomy in some areas, especially concerning marriage and inheritance. Further, the Muluki Ain was to some extent neutral as far as Muslims, Buddhists or other religionists were concerned, neither encouraging nor prohibiting their practice of faith.

The five categories thus represented permutations of the two basic caste and non-caste communities, with structuring and ranking according to the norms of 'high-caste' Parbatiya Hindus. Although the Muluki Ain recognised and accepted some degree of cultural diversity, it translated cultural differences into hierarchical 'caste' categories. For example, the ethnic communities that consumed alcohol were categorised as *matwali* and ranked lower than most of the Parbatiyas. Punishment for infringing laws, especially concerning inter-caste relations, were more severe for them than for the wearers of the holy thread. Since the Muluki Ain had structured the social universe into a broad caste-based classification, there was a lot of pressure on non-Hindus to conform to Hindu norms, at least in their public behaviour and inter-caste relations.

The spread of Parbatiya Hindu culture was, of course, not only a result of state domination and subjugation of the minorities; ethnic communities themselves responded in various ways to the new dispensation. For example, Magars and Thakalis – particularly the elite among them – sought to integrate themselves into the dominant culture by using Bahun priests, celebrating some Hindu festivals, and opting for the Nepali language. The Gurung of the central Nepali hills, meanwhile, divided their lineage-based community into two major categories, the higher status grouping which they termed 'four castes' (*char jat*) and the lower status grouping known as 'sixteen castes' (*sohra jat*), in emulation of the Hindu caste system. There was thus an attempt to reduce the differences with the dominant Parbatiya community, and at the same time amplify the differences within other ethnic groups. The widespread recruitment of Gurung, Magar, Rai and Limbu soldiers into the British and Indian armies also helped spread Parbatiya culture among the ethnic groups. Nepali became the *lingua franca* in these armies and rather than employ different priests according to ethnicity, Bahun priests were used to perform rituals for the soldiers.

In large measure, the ethnic communities either assimilated into the dominant culture or turned insular to protect what they had remaining. However, some resisted the process of Parbatiya-isation, actively or passively. This seems to be one of the reasons why the Limbus of Nepal's far east migrated in large numbers to adjacent Sikkim and Darjeeling. Towards the end of the Rana regime, the Limbus staged a revolt against Parbatiya incursions into their homeland which threatened their unique form of communal land-holding (known as *kipat*). The Tamangs, who, due to their proximity to Kathmandu Valley, were among the most subjugated of the large hill ethnic groups of Nepal, are known to have on occasion resisted the imposition of Parbatiya culture. Meanwhile, communities living in remote areas where the state had not managed to establish its dominance, such as the Sherpas of the eastern high valleys, simply ignored the central dictates.

Equality, Homogeneity and the Parbatiya Culture 1961–1990

The Rana regime was overthrown in 1951 but this did not result in major changes as far as the relationship between the ethnic groups, non-Hindus and 'low' castes were concerned. Nepal continued to be ruled by 'high-caste' Parbatiyas, and the laws from the Rana period were essentially retained. Though an interim constitution was put in place, the Muluki Ain of the Ranas remained in force. The ruling elites obviously wanted to enhance political and cultural unity within the framework established earlier – a fact reflected in their policies regarding language and religion.

The government attempted to promote Nepali as the national language and the sole medium of instruction in schools. The first National Educational Planning Commission went so far as to argue in the early 1950s that, 'If the younger generation is taught to use Nepali as the basic language then other languages will gradually disappear, and greater national strength and unity will result.' Similarly, the Hindu ruling elite tried to show the numerical dominance of Hindus in Nepal by classifying even some non-Hindu ethnic groups as Hindus. This is reflected in the instructions given to the enumerators of the 1952–54 census: 'Assign as Hindus the worshippers of the five deities (Ganesh, Shiva, Vishnu, Sun, Devi) such as Bahun, Chhetri, Magar, Gharti, Gurung, Sarki, Damai, etc.' It is because of such insensitive policies and directives that language and religion have emerged as the two major contentious issues as far as the hill ethnic groups are concerned. In the tarai, language is the major focus of Madhesi activists who are fighting Pahadi domination.

After nearly a decade of confusing political arrangements following the overthrow of the Rana regime in 1951, Nepal experimented briefly with multi-party democracy in 1959–1960. In December 1960, King Mahendra overthrew the elected government of B.P. Koirala and later instituted the Panchayat political system, with himself as absolute monarch. The Panchayat period (1960–1990) witnessed a concerted effort to implement the ideals of nation-state, that is, to forcibly evolve a nation with a common culture and language. To achieve this end, there was a move towards greater centralisation of politics and administration, with an emphasis on transportation and communication as a means of modernisation and development. The spread of Nepali-based education and growing employment opportunities in the rapidly-expanding government bureaucracy and development projects were other ways in which the nation-building project continued. The Panchayat elite viewed cultural diversity as an impediment to nation-building, modernisation and development, and hence great emphasis was placed on homogeneity in the population.

At the beginning of the Panchayat era, due to the dynamics of domestic politics and the perceived need to join the rest of the world, the state sought to replace the hierarchical social order based on the caste system by recognising cultural diversity and equality of all citizens before the law. Caste and ethnicity were no longer significant legal categories although they continued to remain socially valid. The caste system, though not explicitly abolished, was absent from the new Muluki Ain introduced in 1963 by King Mahendra.

Ethnic communities as legal categories disappeared from the legal discourse, but they did resurface to some extent in the national census as linguistic and religious categories. Demographic classification in the census remained discriminatory, since it recorded a large number of people who practised other faiths as Hindus. Linguistic classification of the population provided only a rough, and perhaps misleading, data on the ethnic communities because many of them had given up their mother tongues or were bilingual, leading to their classification as Nepali-speakers. The law as well as the census thus attempted to 'erase' caste and ethnic identities of the population to bring about a more egalitarian society as well as to wipe away cultural differentiation that existed in a diverse land.

The Madhesi population posed a sensitive problem for the state and the ruling elites, especially because of Nepal's economic and political dependence on India and the open border between the two countries. The ideals of nation-state pushed the Kathmandu government to implement policies that would ensure a common language and culture. However, many Madhesi communities had highly developed languages and cultures which could not be so easily suppressed, especially given the ease of trans-border movement of people and ideas and the commonalities between the populations on both sides. Close cultural, economic and kinship ties across the border helped the Madhesi population in general to resist assimilation into the dominant national Nepali (Parbatiya) culture.

The Panchayat state's policy was to encourage massive migration of the Pahadi people to the tarai. The eradication of malaria, the construction of roads and other infrastructure and the clearing of forests and opening up of new lands made the tarai plains a magnet for people from the hills. In order to forestall the people south of the border from moving into the newly cleared territory, the government encouraged Pahadis to move to the plains.

Equality, Pluralism, and Cultural Dominance 1990–2001

The attempts by cultural or ethnic organisations to preserve their space in a culturally homogenising Nepal had begun in the Rana era, sometimes working out of India. This process continued, albeit in a low key, during the Panchayat period as well, and the number of such organisations grew over the years, and particularly after the 1980s. The authorities allowed them to function but only as long as they did not become overtly political. It was only after the restoration of democracy in 1990 that ethnic, religious and linguistic communities as well as 'low-caste' groups, emboldened by the rights bestowed by the Constitution, organised themselves to protect their cultures, languages and religions.

Long subdued and unable to make their demands under the authoritarian regime led by the king, the citizens at large aspired for a new social order. The long-suffering ethnic, linguistic and religious communities hoped for an egalitarian, pluralistic society in which they would be treated as equals by the dominant Parbatiyas, where cultural differences would be accepted and valued, and where their cultures and languages would receive state recognition and support.

The Constitution of 1990, drafted by representatives of political parties and some independents, responded to some of these aspirations. It declared Nepal to be a 'multi-ethnic, multilingual . . . Hindu and constitutional monarchical kingdom'. The Constitution granted equal rights to all citizens before the law and prohibited any form of discrimination based on religion, race, caste or ethnicity. It bestowed on the various communities the right to profess and practise their traditional religion (although it prohibited conversion), to protect and preserve their culture and language, and to educate their children in their own mother tongues up to the primary level. It also recognised the languages spoken by the different communities in the country as national languages (*rastriya bhasa*). The Constitution thus gave official recognition to cultural diversity based, to some degree, on the notion of equality. It was in response to the Constitution's egalitarian provisions that the 1991 census for the first time classified and recorded the population according to linguistic, religious as well as ethnic affiliations.

However, for all its liberalism, the Constitution also managed to circumscribe cultural pluralism with two important qualifications: first, its definition of Nepal as a 'Hindu kingdom' and second, its declaration of Nepali as the language of the nation (*rastra bhasa*) and official language. The primacy given to Hinduism and the Nepali language, mainly due to pressure from Parbatiya Hindus from across the political spectrum, indicated that the dominance of the Parbatiya ruling elite had continued into the modern democratic era. (All of Nepal's major political parties, as well as the Maoists who claim to support ethnic assertions, are dominated by 'high-caste' Parbatiyas, particularly Bahuns.) Thus, behind the official model of cultural pluralism and equality, a hierarchy of cultures or the dominance of one culture over others

(through language and religion) can be discerned. The state does make efforts to promote the cultures and languages of the non-Parbatiya, but these tend to be more symbolic than real.

Non-hierarchical Pluralism: the Politics of Cultural Difference

The cultural, ethnic and linguistic discontent that had been simmering for decades surfaced after what has been called the 'Kathmandu Spring' of 1990. Numerous new ethnic, linguistic, religious and caste-based organisations were established while the existing ones became more active. These organisations were involved in two kinds of activities. The first was to inculcate a sense of cultural self-pride. The emphasis here was on promoting the use of their mother tongues, particularly among the young, and to recover their own histories through research or by reviving or reinventing traditions and customs. The second was to force changes in state policies and laws in two areas: one concerning the protection and development of their cultures and languages, and the other relating to affirmative action or positive discrimination that would ensure a more equitable share of economic and political resources in areas such as education and government jobs – both of which are dominated by 'high-caste' Parbatiyas, especially Bahuns, and also by 'high-caste' Hindu Newars.

Language became the most visible and emotive issue around which the activists mobilised within and among communities. While most communities were willing to accept Nepali as the *lingua franca* in the country, they demanded active state support for the development of their own individual languages, insisting on their use as the medium of instruction in schools in their traditional homelands, especially up to the primary level. They also sought recognition of their languages as the official language in their strongholds, in addition to or even in place of Nepali. And, finally, they objected to the requirement of proficiency in the Nepali language for entry into government service, arguing that it automatically favoured the Parbatiya, and particularly the Bahun among them.

The other major issue around which ethnic and religious communities have cooperated is in demanding that the Constitution declare Nepal to be a secular state rather than a Hindu kingdom. The demand for a secular state by non-Hindus perhaps has more to do with the history of Hindu dominance and enforcement of Hindu norms among non-Hindus than with the currently defined nature of the state, for it is open to question whether Nepal is in fact a 'Hindu state' today as it undoubtedly was before 1950. It is certainly true that Nepal is predominantly Hindu in terms of the dominant culture and religion, the percentage of population who profess this religion, and some of the laws carried over from the earlier periods, for example, laws relating to inheritance and the prohibition on cow slaughter. However, the Constitution itself and most of the other laws are not based on Hindu law. Nepali society may not be secular, but in many ways, the state is. But what is important is the perception of non-Hindus. A declaration of Nepal as a secular state would signal to all that the state does not discriminate on the grounds of religion and considers all faiths to be equal. It may also force the state to remove all the vestiges of (Hindu) religious law which remain on paper today.

Ethnic and linguistic activists have also demanded that the state provide them with better access to economic and political resources, such as jobs in the civil service. There is currently a great disparity between the 'upper-caste' Parbatiyas and Newars on the one hand and the rest on the other, regarding employment in the civil service, in the education sector, in leadership of political parties, in the development and NGO sector, and so on. For a large section of the ethnic, linguistic and religious communities, economic and political issues are perhaps more important than cultural and linguistic issues. Ethnic leaders have accordingly been demanding reservations in government jobs for non-Parbatiyas. For the Newars, who are relatively better off than other ethnic communities, culture and language tend to be more important than economic and political issues.

Some activists have also advocated a federation of mini-nations within Nepal, or in extreme cases, even separate states based on

'nationalities' in the traditional homelands of the major ethnic and linguistic communities. While the majority of the ethnic and linguistic organisations may not have such aspirations, the very existence of such voices indicates the extent to which ethnic assertion has progressed under the free atmosphere of the democratic era. Unfortunately, as the ethnic activists have discovered, freedom to air one's views does not mean much when the 'establishment' does not respond to even the most minimal demands. Fears are sometimes expressed that these sharply-worded demands for autonomy may lead to sectarian or ethnic violence or even a balkanisation of Nepal. While such a possibility cannot be ruled out, it appears that a majority of the leadership of the non-dominant communities would not support such action. What they aspire for is a genuine plural society, where all cultures and languages are treated as equals, and where opportunities are not concentrated among the Parbatiyas.

Cultural diversity is accepted and celebrated by most Nepalis. At the same time, ethnic activists like to stress their difference from the dominant Hindu communities. During a conference in 1994, the federation of 21 ethnic groups known as the Nepal Federation of Nationalities (NEFEN), along with some other groups, renamed themselves 'indigenous peoples' in reaction to the United Nations' call for a Decade of Indigenous People. They defined their 'indigenousness' in opposition to Hindus, i.e., as those communities which possess their own traditional language, culture and non-Hindu religion, and whose society was traditionally egalitarian rather than hierarchical or caste-based. Other characteristics of this indigenousness included displacement from original homelands, deprivation of traditional rights to natural resources, and neglect and humiliation of their culture and language by the state.

This celebration of cultural diversity and distinct cultural identities by the (hill) ethnic communities, unfortunately, falls somewhat short of celebrating a genuine egalitarian society and for that matter a genuine pluralistic society. For example, ethnic activists have not shown much solidarity with the dalit castes, which are economically and politically more deprived than most of the ethnic groups. Neither has the ethnic leadership, which is primarily hill-based, shown much empathy for the non-ethnic communities of the tarai. This could either be because the tarai communities are considered Hindus, or, more likely, because they are considered lacking in 'Nepaliness', a characteristic often defined in terms of Pahadi (hill) identity. In this way, the hill ethnics are themselves harking back to the hill-origins of the Nepali nation state and its definition as such by the ruling elites.

The Madhesi have equal, if not more, cause for grievance with the state and the ruling groups. As with the hill ethnic groups, their languages and cultures are devalued and they have limited access to the economic and political resources at the centre. However, unlike the hill ethnic communities, their very loyalty to the country and even their nationality is suspect among the hill-centric establishment as well as among the Pahadi population in general. Madhesis are seen by many hill people – even among the leadership of the discriminated ethnic groups – as 'foreigners' of 'Indian origin'. As a result, the Madhesi people face many social hurdles, the most significant of which exhibits itself in the difficulty Madhesis have in acquiring citizenship papers. This is not only because, culturally and linguistically, the Madhesi are similar to Indian citizens across the border, but also because many of them are recent migrants.

The Madhesi population, with the exception of the Tharu and 'upper-caste' Maithili-speakers, has not been as active as the hill ethnic groups in demanding equal treatment. The Sadbhavana Party has been championing the cause of the Madhesis, but it has yet to succeed in providing an overarching unifying umbrella for them, partly because the people of the tarai too are divided by language, religion and caste.

Models of Plural Societies

There is no country in the world that today does not have two or more communities living within the same political unit. Since cultural pluralism has now become a worldwide reality, how to deal with difference is a challenge everywhere. How should culturally dominant groups perceive and treat groups and communities that are different from them? And how should the subordinate groups perceive and treat other communities, including the dominant community? Failure to tackle this challenge – and instead trying to force the issue through assimilation or radical separation – has, historically and in contemporary times, led to racial, communal and ethnic violence, and, in extreme cases, to ethnic cleansing and balkanisation. Nepalis, therefore, need to learn from other contemporary plural societies as well as their own history to face this challenge.

One global tendency has been for nation states to move towards homogeneity of cultures and the erasure of differences, either by assimilation into the dominant culture (the 'melting-pot' of the United States), or 'disappearing' the minority community through 'ethnic cleansing' (Nazi Germany, or the Hutu-Tutsi conflict of Rwanda), or partition based on differences, whether of religion (India-Pakistan) or ethnicity (the Balkans). The alternative is allowing heterogeneity of cultures within nation states, and there is wide acceptance of the reality of nation states made up of pluralistic societies.

There are, or were, several types of plural societies, each with different ways of perceiving and treating cultural difference. The most common is the hierarchical pluralistic society, as exemplified by colonial societies and the old Nepali model, where one racial, ethnic, religious, or linguistic community stands dominant. Rarer are the non-hierarchical pluralistic societies, for example the Dutch and the Swiss models, where the different communities are considered equals. In both types of pluralistic societies, we find societies characterised either by separation of communities based on difference or by interaction and cooperation between different communities. An extreme example of the former type is the apartheid era South Africa. This separation of communities based on race was common to all white colonial societies.

In Nepal, there have been three models of society, as reflected in the laws enacted by different political regimes over the past two hundred-odd years. These three models may be seen as part of a kind of dialectical movement. In the first model, during the Gorkhali and Rana regimes, cultural pluralism was recognised but differences were translated into hierarchy with reference to the caste system and Parbatiya values. The antithesis to this model was the Panchayat model of the nation state, which did not recognise cultural difference and instead envisioned a society where all citizens were equal and assimilated into a single homogeneous, national culture. Ethnicity was not the basis for legal identity. The synthesis of the two models, one plural and hierarchical and the other homogeneous and non-hierarchical, is the plural and non-hierarchical model envisioned by the Constitution of 1990. Ethnicity has again become one of the bases for legal identity. However, in this model too, as we have seen, the culture, religion and language of the Parbatiya remain dominant. In other words, the 1990 Constitution too does not offer a model of a truly egalitarian, non-hierarchical plural society.

The model of pluralism offered by many leaders of the non-dominant ethnic, linguistic and religious communities is that of a non-hierarchical, plural society which values differences and encourages and facilitates the diverse communities to maintain their separate identities. However, even their model suffers because the proponents are not really concerned about the plight of 'low' castes on the one hand, or the Madhesi communities on the other. The Pahadis, including the ethnic groups, have a deep-set and historically-conditioned disdain for the dalit, and are suspicious about the nationalist credentials of the Madhesi.

Furthermore, in their model of pluralism, the different communities would not only maintain their distinct identities, they would also have little interaction or cooperation between each other on an everyday basis. The radicals among the ethnic activists would even reject pluralism altogether and establish separate nation-states or nations for different communities. Their models, thus, do not envisage a dynamic society where the different communities, while maintaining their separate identities, interact and influence each other. In this sense, it seems as though the ethnic leadership wants to replace the fuzzy and even fluid boundaries between the different communities – which is a reality in many cases – with more impermeable boundaries in which groups and identities are rigidly defined and immutable. They are thus attempting to stop or reverse the historical process that shaped the formation of different communities and their identities in relation to other communities, forgetting that identity is always relational. The Newar, Tamang, Rai, Tharu and even the Parbatiya, for example, are all categories (ethnonyms) that are used for populations who were not necessarily homogeneous within themselves in the past, and are not so even in the present.

Fortunately, most members of these subordinated communities aspire for a non-hierarchical plural society in which cultural differences are valued and members of different communities interact and cooperate as equals, and in which they can negotiate their dual identities both as members of their distinct communities and as Nepalis with a common expanded culture, which includes cultural elements and symbols from the diverse communities. In other words, they wish for a society that is constituted of culturally diverse, distinct and equal communities, which also interact with each other and are united as members of a single nation-state.

Further Readings

Bista, Dor B. *People of Nepal*. Kathmandu: Ratna Pustak Bhandar, 1987.

Bista, Dor B. *Fatalism and Development: Nepal's Struggle for Modernization*. Calcutta: Orient Longman, 1991.

Burghart, R. *The Conditions of Listening: Essays on Religion, History and Politics in South Asia*. Delhi: Oxford University Press, 1996.

Caplan, Lionel. *Land and Social Change in East Nepal: A Study of Hindu-Tribal Relations*. (2nd ed.). Kathmandu: Himal Books, 2000.

Hoefer, Andras. *The Caste Hierarchy and the State in Nepal: A Study of the Muluki Ain of 1854*. Innsbruck: Universitatsverslag Wagner, 1979.

Gellner, David, Joanna Pfaff-Czarnecka and John Whelpton (eds). *Nationalism and Ethnicity in a*

Hindu Kingdom. The Politics of Culture in Contemporary Nepal. Amsterdam: Hardwood Academic Publishers, 1997.

Pradhan, Kumar. *The Gorkha Conquests: The Process and Consequences of the Unification of Nepal with Special Reference to Eastern Nepal*. Calcutta: Oxford University Press, 1991.

Salter, Jan and Harka Gurung. *Faces of Nepal*. Kathmandu: Himal Books, 1996.

Sharma, Prayag Raj. 'Caste, Social Mobility and Sanskritisation: A Study of Nepal's Old Legal Code'. *Kailash*, vol. 5 no. 4: 1977.

Himal. vol. 5 no. 3: 1992; vol. 6 no. 2 and 5: 1993; and vol. 7 no. 1: 1994. Kathmandu.

Part III

Partition, Nationalism, and the Formation of South Asian National States

Introduction

The first stirrings of Indian nationalism are conventionally dated to the 1857 "Sepoy Mutiny" (called by some, "India's first war of Independence") or to 1885 with the founding of the Indian National Congress. It is clear, however, that there were sporadic forms of resistance to colonial rule before this time, and also that a period of social reform pre-dating the second half of the 19th century was important for sowing the seeds of nationalist consciousness.

After Muslim land-owners in North India were stripped of their properties as punishment for their prominent role in the 1857 rebellion, the British continued their policy of divide and rule by appealing to cooperative groups to leverage them against those groups which had revolted. Though these disparate groups tried to unite under the banner of the Indian National Congress, splits developed. The Muslim League was formed in 1906 with some encouragement from the British, who wanted the support of wealthy zamindars for the Partition of Bengal. Beginning in 1905, the Congress-led Swadeshi movement defeated the attempt to partition Bengal with boycotts and demonstrations; as a result the British moved the capital from Calcutta to Delhi in 1911. Gandhi penned "Hind Swaraj" ("Indian Self Rule") in 1909 to argue the ethical basis for resistance to British colonialism. Between 1919 and 1924 he also sought to bring Muslims back into Congress-led nationalism by supporting the Khilafat movement (to restore the Turkish Caliphate abolished after World War 1). This period also marks the emergence of mass-based peasant protests in Awadh against exploitative zamindars where Gandhi attempted to fold discontented peasants back into Congress by counseling them to set aside their differences with the zamindars. However, E.V. Ramaswamy Naicker ("Periyar"), founder of the non-Brahmin movement, formed the Justice Party in 1921 because he felt the Congress was too Brahmin-dominated. B.R. Ambedkar formed the Independent Labour Party (later the Republican Party of India) in

Perspectives on Modern South Asia: A Reader in Culture, History, and Representation, First Edition.
Edited by Kamala Visweswaran.
© 2011 Blackwell Publishing Ltd. Published 2011 by Blackwell Publishing Ltd.

1936 for Dalits after the Poona Pact[1] compromise convinced him that Congress would not push for Dalit interests. We can see then, that Congress-led nationalism was fissiparous and was unsuccessful in incorporating major sections of Indian society.

The creation of a Hindu-majority India and Muslim-majority Pakistan was the outcome of two processes. First, Muslim leaders felt the Congress would not share power with Muslims in areas of the subcontinent where they had a majority. Second, the growing impact of Hindu nationalist (or Hindu supremacist) influences within Congress through the Arya Samaj and other social reform movements of the late 19th century tended to increase, if not create, Hindu–Muslim tension. There is a common misconception that it was the Muslim League that first articulated the notion that Muslims comprised a separate people, and thus nation. In fact, notions that "Hindus" were a separate people or nation first emerged in the late 19th century, and Lala Lajput Rai may have been the first to articulate a form of "two-nation" theory in 1899.[2] Mohammed Iqbal, in his presidential address to the Muslim League in 1930, advocated a separate state for Muslims. However, the Muslim League did not put forward the demand for a Muslim State until 1940 at its meeting in Lahore, and it did not call for the Partition of British-ruled India. It is instructive to note that the 1940 "Lahore Resolution" also never mentions the word Pakistan (an acronym of the letters of the names of the north and western Muslim-majority provinces – Punjab, Afghan Border States, Kashmir, Sindh, Baluchistan – coined in 1933 by Cambridge student Chaudhury Rahmat Ali).

Partition resulted in the division of British-ruled India into the separate nation-states of India and Pakistan. Mohammed Ali Jinnah, one of the founders of Pakistan, may not have had in mind a separate sovereign state for Muslims, but rather autonomous Muslim-majority states in a federated system. In this scheme, respect for the rights of Hindu minorities in autonomous Muslim majority provinces would be counter-balanced by respecting the rights of Muslim minorities in Hindu minority provinces).[3] Jawaharlal Nehru and Sardar Patel were unwilling to share power and cast the deciding votes for Partition. Yet, as Hamza Alavi points out in his article (in Part II), the legislators in the Punjab, the largest Muslim majority area, actually voted against Partition. (They did so in Bengal as well.)[4] The newly created state of Pakistan was comprised of the Muslim majority areas in western India, and an eastern wing carved out of Bengal (See Map 4). Yet these two halves of Pakistan were ethnically and culturally distinct. Bengali Muslims spoke Bangla, not Urdu, and as the most populous region of Pakistan were denied full recognition, including language rights. This led to the emergence of a secular Bengali nationalist movement; after a war in 1971 in which India backed East Pakistan's struggle for Independence, the nation-state of Bangladesh was formed.

Kashmir, a Muslim majority state, should have gone to Pakistan at the time of Partition. But the Hindu Maharaja of Jammu and Kashmir signed a (contested) letter of accession to India, and in 1948 Pakistan fought India and gained part of the territory which it named "Azad Kashmir," while another part was absorbed as the "Northern Territories." India and Pakistan have been to war three times over Kashmir. More than 600,000 troops are now stationed in Indian-occupied Kashmir. Today, a growing number of Kashmiris want "azadi" or independence from both India and Pakistan; still others fault India for reneging on the terms of three separate 1948 UN resolutions authorizing an independently administered plebiscite for Kashmiris to vote on their country of citizenship.

India's constitution declares it to be a secular state, and it has attempted to enshrine "unity in diversity" as the ethic of secular nationalism by guaranteeing minority rights.

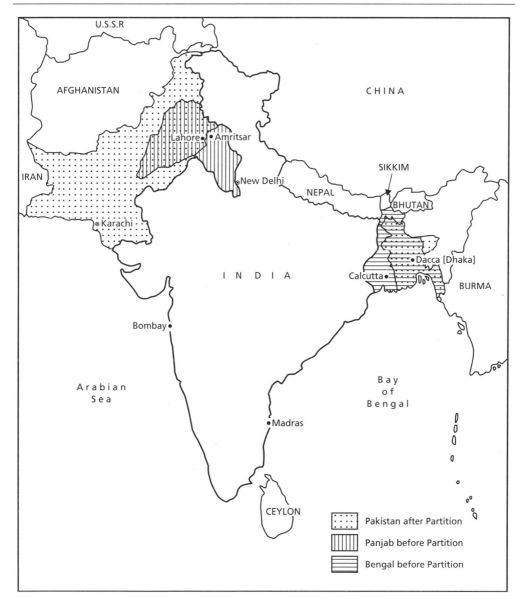

Map 4 Partition of India, 1947.
(Redrawn with permission)

In 1947, Jinnah, too, had not only envisioned Pakistan as a homeland for Muslims, but as a secular state. He said, "... you are free to go to your temples, you are free to go to any other place of worship in this State of Pakistan ... You may belong to any caste or creed – that has nothing to do with the business of the state ... we are starting with this fundamental principle that we are all citizens and equal citizens of one state." The first (1956) constitution of Pakistan declared it an "Islamic Republic," but also guaranteed minority rights, religious freedom and contained non-discrimination provisions until it was abrogated by military rule in 1958. Islam did not become the state religion until it was introduced into Pakistan's 1973 constitution. Islamic law in Pakistan was not instituted until Zia ul-Haq came to power in a military coup in 1977. Bangladesh followed the same pattern as Pakistan. The Awami League, the party headed by Sheikh Mujibir, which led the Bangladeshi nationalist struggle, originally proclaimed Bangladesh to be a secular state, and its constitution guaranteed minority rights. After Zia-ur Rehman came to power in a military coup in 1975, Islamization was introduced. India and Sri Lanka remain nominally secular, but as we will see in Part IV, forms of Hindu and Buddhist nationalism threaten the secular fabric of both countries.

Partition is remembered as one of the most traumatic events in modern South Asian history. As Ritu Menon and Kamla Bhasin note, however, it is only recently that people's experiences of this trauma (also reflected in novels, short stories, and films) have challenged official views of Partition. The violence of Partition described by Menon and Bhasin and by Nighat Said Khan also affected women in specific ways with consequences for continued communal conflict today. The legacy of Partition for Bangladesh is also distinct: unlike in India and Pakistan, women survivors of sexual violence of the 1971 war were called "birongonas," heroic women, and recognized by the state.[5]

Although Afghanistan did not experience Partition, and it remained a monarchy until 1973, like Pakistan and Bangladesh, it also experienced tension between secular-socialist forces and Islamist movements. Some parallels can be drawn to the ways in which women come to symbolize community and nation in India and Pakistan, so that violence against women, or violation of their modesty, is thus seen to be an attack on the community or nation. Similarly, the "woman question" described by Val Moghadam and Naila Kabeer came to mark the articulation of Afghan and Bangladeshi nationalism in South Asia in particular ways. Finally, both Afghanistan and the Maldives (which ended its monarchy in 1968) also mark the "founding myths of state" (to use Rizwan Ahmed's term) by attaching monarchial power to Islam in different ways, and with complex legacies for current politics. A mixed (but positive) record of progressive monarchy described by Moghadam for Afghanistan is one reason why some Afghans today would like to see it restored.

Notes

1 During the Roundtable Conferences of 1930–2, Ambedkar pushed for Dalits to be awarded separate elec-torates, as Muslims, Sikhs, and Christians had been. Gandhi protested separating Dalits from caste Hindus, and began a fast unto death. Concerned that Gandhi might die and that Untouchables would face reprisals, Ambedkar withdrew the demand for a separate electorate in exchange for a greater number of reserved seats in elections. This compromise is called the "Poona Pact."

2 See Chetan Bhatt, *Hindu Nationalism: Origins, Ideologies, and National Myths*, p. 41. Oxford: Berg, 2001.

3 See Sugata Bose and Ayesha Jalal, *Modern South Asia*, 145–6. London: Routledge, 2004.

4 See Sugata Bose and Ayesha Jalal, *Modern South Asia*, 151–3. London: Routledge, 2004.

5 This veneration of rape victims had problematic consequences for women, however. See Bina D'Costa, *Nationbuilding, Gender and War Crimes in South Asia*, London: Routledge, 2010.

10

Abducted Women, the State and Questions of Honour

Three Perspectives on the Recovery Operation in Post-Partition India

Ritu Menon and Kamla Bhasin

Official and even historical accounts of Partition see it as the unfortunate outcome of sectarian and separatist politics, and as a tragic accompaniment to the exhilaration and promise of a freedom fought for with courage and valour. They have looked at the causes and consequences of the division of the country, analysed the details of the many 'mistakes' and 'miscalculations' made, examined the genesis of the call for a Muslim Homeland, and so on. But when we start looking for social histories or for accounts that try to piece together the fractured reality of the time and of the event itself from a non-official perspective – a perspective from the margins, as it were – we encounter a curious void. Perhaps it has been too painful, too difficult to separate personal experience from corroborated fact, too hazardous, at least for those who tried to record it, to claim 'objectivity'. Indeed, so far only some 'fiction'

seems to have tried to assimilate the enormity of the experience.

For those of us who may or may not have lived through Partition but who did witness the massacre of Sikhs in 1984 and heard the survivors, especially the widows, recall the violence and brutality of 1948, the question of how such events are recorded, and by whom, returns to haunt us and acquires greater urgency with each subsequent episode. Recent considerations of how such accounts are to be written, of the place of personal testimony and of bearing witness, of the desirability of reconstructing biographies or trusting memory or the collective re-telling of tragedy, have highlighted the importance of each of these aspects in presenting an alternative construction of what took place.[1] They have raised the question of the authenticity of such recording – individual bias, political stance, ideology, class and gender, all

Perspectives on Modern South Asia: A Reader in Culture, History, and Representation, First Edition.
Edited by Kamala Visweswaran.
© 2011 Blackwell Publishing Ltd. Published 2011 by Blackwell Publishing Ltd.

become factors that are critical to any analysis or representation. When one is trying to unravel the complexity of an event that took place forty-five years ago but still reverberates in the general consciousness, the enterprise becomes even more treacherous. But without such an attempt, the myriad individual and collective histories that simultaneously run parallel to official accounts of historic moments, and are their sequel, almost inevitably get submerged; with them may also be submerged the countering of accepted – and acceptable – versions, to be buried eventually in the rubble of what Gyan Pandey has called the 'aberrations' of history.[2]

What is presented here is in the nature of an exploration, an attempt to communicate an experience of Partition through those whose voices have hitherto been absent in any re-telling of it: women who were destituted in one way or another by the event, as forced mass migrations led to an extreme disruption of life at all levels and exposed them to a kind of upheaval that could only proclaim the dark side of freedom. In their recall, the predominant memory is of confusion, dislocation and a severing of roots as they were forced to reckon with the twin aspect of freedom – disintegration and bewildering loss: of place and property, no doubt, but more significantly, of community, of a network of more or less stable relationships, and of a coherent identity. Overriding all these was a violence that was horrifying in its intensity, and one which knew no boundaries; for many women, it was not only 'miscreants', 'outsiders' or 'marauding mobs' that they needed to fear – husbands, fathers, brothers and even sons, could turn killers.[3] That terrible stunning violence and then the silencing pall that descended like a shroud around it have always just hovered at the edges of history; the story of 1947, while one of the attainments of independence, is also a gendered narrative of displacement and dispossession, of large-scale and widespread communal violence, and of the realignment of family, community and national identities as a people were forced to accommodate the dramatically altered reality that now prevailed.

The location of women at the intersection of all these forces, rather than at their periphery,

casts an entirely new light on the apparent fixity of defining features of identity like community, religion, nationality. We propose to do this through an examination of the Central Recovery Operation of the Government of India, carried out between 1948–56, which sought to recover those women who had been abducted and forcibly converted during the upheaval, and restore them to their respective families and countries, where they 'rightfully belonged'.

The material is presented in three voices: the voice of the government, bureaucrats and Members of Parliament; the voices of women themselves; and lastly, those of the social workers to whom the work of rehabilitation and resettlement of recovered women was entrusted. Through these three perspectives we hope to demonstrate how ambiguous and conflictual the relationship was between the governments of India and Pakistan; between government officers, social workers and the women to be recovered; between the State and its citizens; between Hindus, Muslims and Sikhs; and finally between the women and their families and society. We argue that it was a particular construction of the identity of the abducted woman that determined the entire recovery operation, one that raises serious questions regarding the Indian State's definition of itself as secular and democratic. We further argue that the State, in its articulation of gender identity and public policy, underlined the primacy of community identity and, implicitly and explicitly, departed from its neutrality in assigning values to the 'legitimate' family and community 'honour', and that it did so through a regulation of women's sexuality. Indeed, through legislation and executive and police action; it effectively reconstituted the multiple patriarchies at work in women's lives within the family and community, and as embedded in institutions and social mores. Finally, it is our contention that it is only when this shift of perspective takes place that the discourse of the State can be interrogated and its assumed secularity challenged.

Our archive is constituted of extensive and intensive interviews with women who survived the trauma of dislocation, of whom many are to be found in homes, rehabilitation centres and shelters even today, in Punjab and Haryana; in-depth interviews with women social workers who were entrusted with the work of rescue, recovery and rehabilitation; interviews with those government officials who were in charge of the various agencies that were set up to coordinate relief and rehabilitation; private papers, diaries and autobiographical accounts of those who were engaged in this activity; government documents, and reports of fact-finding committees, private and public; and the Constituent Assembly of India Legislative Debates, 1949.[4]

I

The Hindustan–Pakistan Plan was announced on 3 June 1947 whereby a new political entity, Pakistan, was created, of which West Pakistan was to comprise the Muslim-majority provinces of Sind the NWFP and 16 districts of Punjab; the remaining 13 districts of undivided Punjab were to be part of India. Although the exact boundary line between the two countries had still to be determined by the Boundary Commission, the exchange of populations had started taking place even before 15 August. Within a week of independence about 11 lakh Hindus and Sikhs had crossed over from West to East Punjab, and in the week following, another 25 lakhs had collected in the refugee camps in West Punjab.[5] By 6 November, 1947 nearly 29,000 refugees had been flown in both directions; about 673 refugee trains were run between 27 August and 6 November, transporting 23 lakh refugees inside India and across the border – of these 1,362,000 were non-Muslim, and 939,000 were Muslim. Huge foot convoys, each 30–40,000 strong were organised by the Military Evacuation Organisation and Liaison Agency to move the bulk of the rural population, especially those who still had their cattle and bullock-carts with them. The estimate is that in 42 days (18 September to 29 October) 24 non-Muslim foot columns, 849,000 strong, had crossed into India.[6] By the time the migrations were finally over, about eight million people had crossed the newly created boundaries of Punjab and Bengal, carrying with

them memories of a kind of violence that the three communities had visited upon each other, unmatched in scale, brutality and intensity.

No-one, they say, foresaw either the rivers of people that would flow from one part of Punjab to the other or the blood that would be shed as they were ambushed and killed in the tens of thousands. The official estimate of lives lost during Partition is placed at half a million, but the number of those destituted would have been much higher. The movement of refugees, though undertaken with military escort as far as possible, was both hazardous and traumatic; convoys were ambushed, families separated, children orphaned, and women abducted, left as hostages or killed by their own families in large numbers. Elsewhere, we have discussed the specific kinds of violence that women experienced at this time both within the family and at the hands of the 'other'; our focus here is on abducted women, and their recovery by both India and Pakistan over almost a decade after Partition.

The material, symbolic and political significance of the abduction of women was not lost either on the women themselves and their families, on their communities, or on leaders and governments. As a retaliatory measure, it was simultaneously an assertion of identity and a humiliation of the rival community through the appropriation of its women. When accompanied by forcible conversion and marriage it could be counted upon to outrage both family and community honour and religious sentiment. The fear of abduction, or of falling into the hands of the enemy compelled hundreds of women to take their own lives, equal numbers to be killed by their own families, and literally thousands of others to carry packets of poison on their persons in the eventuality that they might be captured. And many committed suicide after they were released by their captors for having been thus 'used' and polluted.

Leaders expressed their concern and anger at the 'moral depravity' that characterised this 'shameful chapter' in the history of both countries; the fact that 'our innocent sisters' had been dishonoured was an issue that could not be looked upon with equanimity. 'If there is any sore point or distressful fact to which we cannot be reconciled under any circumstances, it is the question of abduction and non-restoration of Hindu women. We all know our history,' said one MP in Parliament, 'of what happened in the time of Shri Ram when Sita was abducted. Here, where thousands of girls are concerned, we cannot forget this. We can forget all the properties, we can forget every other thing but this cannot be forgotten.' And again, 'As descendants of Ram we have to bring back every Sita that is alive.'[7] A letter dated 4 April, 1947 from Nehru to Evan Jenkins, Governor of Punjab, says: 'There is one point, however, to which I should like to draw your attention, and this is the question of rescuing women who have been abducted or forcibly converted. You will realise that nothing adds to popular passions more than stories of abduction of women and so long as these ... women are not rescued, trouble will simmer and might blaze out.'[8] Malik Feroze Khan Noon, on a visit to Bihar, made a public announcement that if women were returned within a week it would be assumed that those returning them had been protecting them and had not committed any offence.[9]

At the level of policy, the first initiative was taken at the 23–25 November, 1946 session of the Indian National Congress at Meerut, at which a resolution was adopted, which stated:

The Congress views with pain, horror and anxiety the tragedies of Calcutta, East Bengal, Bihar and some parts of Meerut district.... These new developments in communal strife are different from any previous disturbances and have involved murders on a mass scale, as also mass conversions ... abduction and violation of women, and forcible marriage.

Women who have been abducted and forcibly married must be restored to their houses; mass conversions have no significance or validity and people must be given every opportunity to return to the life of their choice.[10]

Communal tension and the ensuing violence escalated at such a rapid pace, however, especially after March 1947, that on 3 September, 1947 leaders and representatives of the governments of India and Pakistan met and resolved that steps be taken to recover and restore abducted persons. Thus, on 17 November, 1947 the All India Congress Committee passed a resolution which stated:

During these disorders, large numbers of women have been abducted on either side and there have been forcible conversions on a large scale. No civilised people can recognise such conversions and there is nothing more heinous than the abduction of women. Every effort must be made to restore women to their original homes with the co-operation of the governments concerned.[11]

On 6 December 1947, an Inter-Dominion Conference was held in Lahore at which the two countries agreed upon steps to be taken for the implementation of recovery and restoration, with the appointment of Mridula Sarabhai as chief social worker. The primary responsibility of recovery was that of the local police, assisted by a staff of one AIG, (Assistant Inspector General) two DSPs (Deputy Sub-Inspector of Police), 15 inspectors, 10 sub-inspectors, and 6 ASIs (Assistant Sub-Inspector).[12] Between December 1947 and July 1948 the number of women recovered in both countries was 9,362 in India and 5,510 in Pakistan. Recoveries dropped rather drastically after this date – one reason put forward being the withdrawal of the MEO (Military Evacuation Organisation) from both territories – and it was felt that a more binding arrangement was necessary for satisfactory progress. Accordingly, an agreement was reached between India and Pakistan on 11 November, 1948, that set out the terms for recovery in each dominion. Ordinances were issued in both countries, in January 1949 for India, and May 1949 for Pakistan; in the case of India it was to remain in force till January 1950, in Pakistan till it was abrogated.

The official estimate of the number of abducted women was placed at 50,000 Muslim women in India and 33,000 non-Muslim women in Pakistan. Although Gopalaswami Ayyangar (Minister of Transport, in charge of Recovery) called these figures 'rather wild', Mridula Sarabhai believed that the number of abducted women in Pakistan was ten times the 1948 official figure of 12,500.[13] Till December 1949 the number of recoveries in both countries was 12,000 for India, and 6,000 for Pakistan, and the age-wise break-up was as follows:[14]

	In Pakistan	In India
	[in percentages]	
> 12 yrs	45	35
12 > 35 yrs	44	59
35 > 50 yrs	6	4
50 and above	5	2

At the Constituent Assembly (Legislative) session held in December 1949, considerable dissatisfaction was expressed at the low rate and slow pace of recovery in Pakistan, especially from Sind, Baluchistan, Azad Kashmir, and the 'closed' districts of Gujrat, Jhelum, Rawalpindi and Campbellpur. Additionally, there was extreme disquiet at the mention of 2,000 non-Muslim women being held by government servants in Pakistan and at a Cease Fire being agreed to in Kashmir without negotiating the return of Hindu women abducted there. Some members even went so far as to call for 'open war to recover our sisters and daughters lying helpless in Pakistan', or at the very least for retaliatory measures, suggesting that only an exchange of women be considered – what they give is what they will get.

To facilitate recovery and because the ordinance in India expired on 31 December, 1949, Gopalaswami Ayyangar moved a Bill in Parliament on December 15, called The Abducted Persons (Recovery and Restoration) Bill, for the consideration of the house. It extended to the United Provinces of East Punjab and Delhi, the Patiala and East Punjab States Union [PEPSU] and the United State of Rajasthan, and consisted of 10 operative clauses, which the Minister termed 'short, simple, straightforward . . . and innocent'; relevant clauses are reproduced below.

2. *Interpretation*

    (1) In this Act, unless there is anything repugnant in the subject or context,

    (a) 'abducted person' means a male child under the age of sixteen years or a female of whatever age who is, or immediately before the 1st day of March, 1947, was, a Muslim and who, on or after that day and before the 1st day of January, 1949, had become separated from his or her family and is found to be living with or under the control of any other individual or family, and in the latter case includes a child born to any such female after the said date;

. . .

4. *Powers of police officers to recover abducted persons*

    (1) If any police officer, not below the rank of an Assistant Sub-Inspector or any other police officer specially authorised by the Provincial Government in this behalf, has reason to believe that an abducted person resides or is to be found in any place, he may, after recording the reasons for his belief, without warrant, enter and search the place and take into custody any person found therein who, in his opinion, is an abducted person, and deliver or cause such person to be delivered to the custody of the officer in charge of the nearest camp with the least possible delay.

    (2) In exercising any powers conferred by sub-section (1) any such police officer may take such steps and may require the assistance of such female persons as may, in his opinion, be necessary for the effective exercise of such power.

. . .

6. *Determination of question whether any person detained is an abducted person*

    (1) If any question arises whether a person detained in a camp is or is not an abducted person or whether such person should be restored to his or her relatives or handed over to any other person or conveyed out of India or allowed to leave the camp, it shall be referred to, and decided by, a tribunal constituted for the purpose by the Central Government.

    (2) The decision of the tribunal constituted under sub-section (1) shall be final: Provided that the Central Government may, either of its own motion or on the

application of any party interested in the matter, review or revise any such decision.

7. *Handing over of abducted persons to persons authorised.*

   (1) Any officer in charge of a camp may deliver any abducted person detained in the camp to the custody of such officer or authority as the Provincial Government may, by general or special order, specify in this behalf.

   (2) Any officer or authority to whom the custody of any abducted person has been delivered under the provisions of sub-section (1) shall be entitled to receive and hold the person in custody and either restore such person to his or her relatives or convey such person out of India.

8. *Detention in camp not to be questioned by Court*

   Notwithstanding anything contained in any other law for the time being in force, the detention of any abducted person in a camp in accordance with the provisions of this Act shall be lawful and shall not be called in question in any Court.

9. *Protection of action taken under Act*

   No suit, prosecution or other legal proceeding whatsoever shall lie against the Central Government, the Provincial Government or any officer or authority for, or in respect of, any act which is in good faith done or intended to be done in pursuance of this Act.

As is evident the Bill, although it may indeed have been short, was not as simple, straightforward or innocent as the Minister would have the house believe. More than 70 amendments were moved by 20 members in an extended debate on the Bill that took a full three days to pass. Every clause, sub-clause and section was discussed threadbare, and serious objections were raised on everything from the preamble to the operative clauses. The main objections related to the definition of abduction, and the time-frame to which the Bill referred (1 March, 1947 and 1 January, 1949); the

virtually unlimited powers given to the police with complete immunity from enquiry or action and no accountability at all; the denial of any rights or legal recourse to the recovered women; the question of children; the constitution of the tribunal; camp conditions and confinement; forcible return of unwilling women; unlimited duration for the Bill to remain in force; and the unequal and disadvantageous terms of the agreement for India vis-a-vis Pakistan.

The amendments moved by members sought to mitigate man of the gross irregularities they pointed out, and to qualify or modify certain other procedural aspects that were set out. But despite their strenuous efforts the Hon'ble Minister declined to incorporate a single amendment or modification proposed (bar one, limiting the duration of the Bill to December 1951) and it was passed, unchanged, on 19 December, and notified in the Official Gazette on 28 December, 1949.

But more on this later; we will turn now to the women themselves.

II

Even were it desirable, it would be difficult to present an accurate profile of the abducted woman during that turbulent time. From the official figures quoted earlier, it is clear that of those recovered, the majority were below the age of 35, and primarily from the rural areas. From what we have been able to gather through interviews and some documents, however, the circumstances of their 'abduction' varied widely. Some were left behind as hostages for the safe passage of their families; others were separated from their group or families while escaping, or strayed and were picked up; still others were initially given protection and then incorporated into the host family; yet again as in the case of Bahawalpur State, all the women of Chak 88 were kept back, and in Muzaffarabad district of Azad Kashmir, it is said that not a single Sikh male was left alive, and most of their women and young girls were taken away to the provinces. Some changed hands several times or were sold to the highest or lowest bidder as the case might be; some became second or third wives; and very, very many were converted and married and lived with considerable dignity and respect. A Sikh schoolteacher we met had spent six months with a Muslim neighbour in Muzaffarabad after the October 1947 raid, before she crossed over safely to Srinagar; her younger sister who had been abducted could never be located, despite sustained efforts by the family and the International Red Cross. In the mid-Eighties she returned to Muzaffarabad where she stayed for six months, visiting every Hindu and Sikh woman who had remained behind, talking to them of their lives and circumstances. Of the 25–30 women she met, she informed us that only one could be said to be unhappy and in unfortunate circumstances. All the others, though nostalgic and distressed at not being able to meet their natal family freely, seemed to her to be settled and held in regard both by the community and their new families. And there were a few among them whose circumstances had in fact improved. 'After all,' she remarked 'where is the guarantee of happiness in a woman's life anyway?'

It is by no means our intention to suggest that the predicament these women found themselves in was not traumatic or fraught with anxiety and uncertainty; merely that it would be false to presume that their lot was uniformly grim, their 'abductors' without exception 'bestial' or unreliable and craven, and to assert, as Mridula Sarabhai did, that recovery was 'an effort to remove from the lives of thousands of innocent women the misery that is their lot today and to restore them to their legitimate environment where they can spend the rest of their lives with *izzat* [honour]'.[15] Nor is it our case that the recovery effort should never have been made; going by the few accounts that exist and on the basis of the interviews we have conducted with women themselves and those to whose care they were entrusted, the majority of women recovered were rehabilitated in greater or smaller measure or restored to their families. Our purpose here is to look beyond these at the many discordant notes that were struck in the process of recovery; at the conflicting claims that were made and voices that were raised; at the silence that was almost unfailingly imposed

on the women after the event, and at what all these tell us about the particular vulnerability of women in times of communal violence when each one of their identities – gender, community and nationality – is set up against the other and contested.

Let us listen then to what the women themselves have to say of their experience. The first is an account by a social worker who was the Superintendent at Gandhi Vanita Ashram, Jalandhar, for several years, and worked with recovered women. The second is a reported case; and the third has been reconstructed from family accounts, letters and taped messages sent by the woman to her brother.

1. 'Some time in 1950 I was required to escort 21 Muslim women who had been recovered, to Pakistan. They did not want to return, but the Tribunal had decided that they had to go. They were young, beautiful girls, and had been taken by sardars. They were determined to stay back because they were very happy. We had to use real force to compel them to go back. I was very unhappy with this duty – they had already suffered so much, and now we were forcing them to return when they just didn't want to go. I was told, "*Ey tan aiveyeen raula pa raiyan ne, enada ta phaisla ho chuka hai, enanu ta bhejna hi hai*." (These girls are simply creating a commotion for nothing, their case has been decided and they have to be sent back.)

'The girls were desperate. The news got around and I received two anonymous letters saying, "If you take our women away to Pakistan we will kidnap you too." Those women cursed me all the way to Amritsar, loudly and continuously. When we reached Wagah, it was evening and we found that there were about 15 other jeeps that had also accompanied us – all belonging to their relatives! They were hoping that should any one of the girls manage to escape, they would pick her up and take her back. As far as I could see, they were all Sikhs. I told the Pakistan SI who was with me that to transfer them at this point into Pakistani jeeps was a risky business – the girls will raise a real hue and cry and we won't be able to restrain them. We had no lady police – in those days there were hardly any – and I won't allow the policemen to manhandle any woman, whether she's a Hindu or a Muslim. And if they resist, we will have no choice but to use force. Now our jeeps couldn't go across without permission. Finally, we managed to get cleared, and as soon as we reached Pakistan, these same women who had made such a commotion, became absolutely quiet. This the Pakistan SP had already told me, would happen.

'Naturally, as soon as we reached Pakistan, the women realised their complete helplessness – what else can you call it? It was complete helplessness, they had been transferred from one set of butchers (*kasais*) to another... what could they do?

'When the jeeps came to a halt, the SP dismounted, went round to the back of the jeeps, opened the door and rained abuses on those poor women. He shouted at them and said, "Now tell me, which one of you wants to go back to India? Tell me and I'll let you off right now to find your way back. Let's see how far you get." They shouted back at me – after all, I was the one who had brought them – they kept saying, "Why are you destroying our lives?" Earlier, when I had brought them from Jalandhar jail saying, this is a government agreement, our girls are also being returned, they had shouted at me: "Who are you to meddle in our lives? We don't know you, what business is it of yours?"

'In Lahore, the camp for recovered Muslim women was in the Women's Penitentiary. When we reached there, the women got down and each one of them made a burqa of her chunni and emerged in parda. They knew that if they protested now, they would regret it.'

2. S. is 58, a sturdy Punjabi woman from Mirpur (in Azad Kashmir). Abducted by Muslims when she was about 15 or 16 years old she lived in Pakistan till 1956 when she was recovered by the military at her brother's insistence, and brought to Jalandhar. She was happily married in Pakistan to a man in the police service, had three children – two girls and a boy – whom she brought with her.

S. was returned to India very much against her wishes. We were told that after she came back, she refused to see her brother, did not leave the ashram and socialised very little with the women there. She almost never spoke of her life in Pakistan, except to say that she had been well-treated and was content, and that her children were well looked after. In the ashram she educated herself, took a degree in Hindi Visharad, started to teach in a local school, and in May 1990 retired as its headmistress. She now lives in a house that she has built herself, with her widowed daughter and her son and daughter-in-law.

S. was eloquent about her present life, spoke with pride about having been able to stand on her own feet, and of being helped greatly by the ashram and the women there, but absolutely refused to speak of her past. '*Dafa karo*', she kept saying, '*hun ki yaad karna hai. Dafa karo. Main sab bhula ditta hai. Hun main izzat nal rah rahin aan, main kyon puranian gallan yaad karniyan ne. Mere baccheyan nu vi nahin pata. Hun sudhar nahin ho sakda, kuj nahin ho sakda.*' (Leave it. What use is it recalling the past? Forget about it. I've banished it all from my mind. I lead a respectable [honourable] life now, why look back to the past – even my children don't know anything about it. Nothing can be done now. It can't be resolved.) For years she believed in no religion and no god, till very recently, when she joined a Radha Soami sect.

3. K. was 16, and had gone to visit her grandparents in village Hattiyan Dupatta (Muzaffarbad Distt. of Azad Kashmir), when she was picked up by the Kabailis (tribals). She passed from one man to another, tried to commit suicide by throwing herself off the roof of her captor's house, but was caught and taken away by a *zaildar*. She was rescued by her parents' erstwhile neighbour, a *patwari* (village headman who keeps all land records), who kept her in his house for some time before he persuaded her, for her own safety, to marry his son who was in fact younger than her.

Her father went to Lahore, stayed there for three months and tried to trace her through the Red Cross, but failed. When they finally managed to make contact with her, he went again to Pakistan and tried hard to persuade her to return. She did indeed journey to Lahore to meet him, but refused to go back because she was carrying her husband's first child. Her father returned, heart-broken and minus his daughter, and died shortly thereafter.

K. had two sons and four daughters, commanded great respect in her family and community and according to the accounts of those who visited her, lived well and with great dignity. She had complete freedom, we were told, didn't believe in Islam, was not obliged to read the Koran or say her namaaz. The common description of her was that she was like a dervesh whose words had almost oracular importance. She never moved out without a pistol (is supposed to have shot dead three intruders who entered her house when she was alone), always kept a lathi by her side, was quite militant – and wrote reams of mystic poetry.

K's brother, whom we met, said she was filled with longing for her family after she met her father, and wrote and wrote and wrote, letters that spoke heartrendingly of the wall of separation that had come between them, of the misfortune that divided them forever.

Who has aimed these arrows of separation?
Neither you, nor me.
He has released these arrows of separation
That forever divide you and me.

When her brother wrote once that for them she was forever lost, she responded with, "How can you talk of purity and honour? How can you denounce me for what was no fault of mine?" When he visited her 40 years later, she sat guard by his bedside, all night, every night, for the two months that he stayed with her. But she did not visit them in India even once, nor did she ever return to their ancestral village in Muzzafarabad.

These three narratives (as well as the disputed cases heard by the Tribunal, and the several stories we were told of women who had managed to escape from the transit camps on both sides), offer clear clues regarding the particular circumstances of abducted women's lives and the individual adjustments they made in order to achieve a degree of equilibrium that would enable them to take up the threads of living again. At the same time they are an

indication of the strong resistance by, and often refusal of, many women to conform to the demands of either their own families or their governments, to fall in line with their notions of what was legitimate and acceptable. Some women who resisted returning to their countries resorted to hunger strikes, others refused to change out of the clothes they had been wearing either when they were recovered or when they had been abducted. Their protest could be powerful and searing. One young recovered girl confronted Mridula Sarabhai thus: 'You say abduction is immoral and so you are trying to save us. Well, now it is too late. One marries only once – willingly or by force. We are now married – what are you going to do with us? Ask us to get married again? Is that not immoral? What happened to our relatives when we were abducted? Where were they?... You may do your worst if you insist, but remember, you can kill us, but we will not go.'[17]

The challenge posed by those 21 Muslim women to the social worker – 'Who are you to meddle in our lives?' – was a challenge directed at the State itself, a State that had already lost any legitimate claims it might have made to intervene in their lives by its complete failure to prevent the brutality and displacement that accompanied Partition. 'There was so much distrust and loathing for us in their hearts,' we were told by a social worker who was Rameshwari Nehru's right hand person for eighteen years. 'They would say – "if you were unable to save us then, what right have you to compel us now?" ' To assurances that they were India's and Pandit Nehru's daughters and that the government was duty-bound to look after them, they retorted angrily, 'Is this the freedom that Jawaharlal gained? Better that he had died as soon as he was born... our men have been killed, our homes destroyed.'

For those who were recovered against their wishes, the choice was not only painful but bitter. Abducted as Hindus, converted and married as Muslims, recovered as Hindus but required to relinquish their children because they were born of Muslim fathers, and disowned as 'impure' and ineligible for membership within their erstwhile family and community, their identities were in a continual state of construction and reconstruction, making them, as one woman said to us, 'permanent refugees'. We were told that often, those women who had been abandoned by their families and subsequently recovered from Pakistan, simply refused to return to their homes, preferring the anonymity and relative autonomy of the ashram to a now alien family.

III

In all, approximately 30,000 women, Muslim and non-Muslim, were recovered by both countries over an eight year period. Although most of the recoveries were carried out between 1947–52, women were being returned to the two countries as late as 1956, and the Act was renewed in India every year till 1957, when it was allowed to lapse. Recoveries were more or less abandoned in the two or three years prior to this, largely because Mridula Sarabhai came in for some adverse criticism, and resigned. The total number of Muslim women recovered was significantly higher – 20,728 as against 9,032 non-Muslims.

On 16 January, 1948, Nehru made a public appeal through the newspapers, in which he said:

I am told that there is an unwillingness on the part of their relatives to accept those girls and women (who have been abducted) back in their homes. This is a most objectionable and wrong attitude to take and any social custom that supports this attitude must be condemned. These girls and women require our tender and loving care and their relatives should be proud to take them back and give them every help.[18]

Mahatma Gandhi who, after the Noakhali riots of October 1946, had resolved to go and 'wipe away the tears of the outraged womanhood of Noakhali' expressed similar sentiments. He said,

I hear women have this objection that the Hindus are not willing to accept back the recovered women because they say that they have become impure. I feel that this is a matter of great shame. These women are as pure as the girls who are sitting by my side. And if any one of those recovered women should come to me, then I will give them as much respect and honour as I accord to these young maidens.[19]

Quite early in the recovery process, social workers came up not only against resistance on the part of families or of the women to be claimed, but also against those whose status could not easily be determined. These were the disputed cases, and generally consisted of those who said they were in either country out of choice, had voluntarily stayed back, or had been married to either a Hindu or a Muslim as the case may be, before 15 August, 1947. There is no doubt that many were compelled or coerced into saying so for a variety of reasons, but it is also clear from the cases that came up before the joint tribunals that there were enough who protested against forcible recovery in the only way open to them – refusal to comply.

In a letter dated 3 March 1948 to K. C. Neogy, Jawaharlal Nehru wrote:

I have just had a telephone message from Sushila Nayyar from Patiala. She told me that a great majority of the (Muslim) women recovered refused to leave their new homes, and were so frightened of being taken away forcibly that they threatened to commit suicide. Indeed, last night 46 of them ran away from the camp through some back door. This is a difficult problem. I told Sushila that she can assure these women that no one is going to send them forcibly to Pakistan, but we thought it desirable for them to come to Delhi so that the Pakistan High Commission and others could then find out what their desires were. This would finally settle the question. In any event I assured her that we would not compel any girl to be sent to Pakistan against her wishes.[20]

The question could not so easily be laid to rest, however, for the issue became a matter of prestige for both countries: how many Hindu and Muslim women were returned and in what condition, and how the authenticity of conflicting claims was to be established gradually took precedence over the humanitarian aspects of recovery. The issue, in addition to being focused on the identity of the women as, of course, being either Muslim or Hindu, also extended to their being citizens of their 'respective countries', needing to be reclaimed. Kamlabehn Patel, who worked in the Lahore camp for four years in close association with Mridula Sarabhai, said to us: 'The identification was done according to the countries they belonged to, this one is Indian, this one a Pakistani. Partition was internally connected with Islam, the individual, and the demand for a separate homeland. And since this label was attached, how could the women be free from it?' Speaking of the disputed cases, she continued, 'The government of India said any person abducted after the 31st of August, either women or children, must go to their respective countries, whether they desire to or not.'[21]

The major part of the recovery operation extended upto 1952, although as mentioned earlier, women were being claimed and returned as late as 1956 through official channels. The public appeals made by Gandhi and Nehru indicate that the number of families unwilling to accept women who had been 'defiled' by the Muslims was by no means insignificant. According to one social worker, the problem became so pressing that the Ministry of Relief and Rehabilitation was constrained to print and distribute a pamphlet that sought to educate the public on the subject it said that just as a flowing stream purifies itself and is washed clean of all pollutants, so a menstruating woman is purified after her periods. Similarly, the All India Women's Conference Report of its 21st session in Gwalior mentions that the Delhi Branch organised public meetings in different localities during Recovery Week in February 1948. It says, 'Some of the office-bearers and a few members did propaganda work in connection with abducted women by going about in a van through streets of New Delhi and speaking to the public on loudspeakers.' No details of this propaganda are given but one can guess its contents without being too far off the mark.

The anticipation of just such a rejection by the very family and community that was to provide them succour was one reason why many women resisted being recovered. Kamlabehn says, 'The women who came to our camp put us this question: "Where will we go if our relations don't keep us?" And we used to reassure them that, you are India's daughter, Pandit Nehru's daughter, and as such the government is duty-bound to look after you. We shall keep you in a camp.'[22]

Pregnant women were obviously more vulnerable than others. Kamlabehn told us that lists of all the pregnant women would be made and sent to Jalandhar; there, the women would be kept for three months or so, be given a complete 'medical check-up' (a euphemism, we soon learnt, for abortions, illegal at the time) and only then be presented to their relatives, 'Because,' she said, 'if they came to know that the woman is pregnant, they would say, let her stay in the camp and have her child.'

Meanwhile the government passed an ordinance to say that those women whose babies were born in Pakistan after Partition would have to leave them behind, but those whose children were born in India, could keep them. According to Kamlabehn: 'For the government this was a complex problem. In Indian society, a child born to a Hindu mother by a Muslim father was hardly acceptable, and if the relatives of the women did not accept such children, the problem of rehabilitation of a large number of women and children would arise.' A special conference was held in Lahore to discuss the implications of this, where the majority of social workers felt that it would be wise to leave all such children with their fathers instead of allowing their mothers to bring them over to India where, eventually, they were likely to end up in orphanages. A senior civil servant, a joint secretary in the Ministry of Relief and Rehabilitation, said the only practical solution was to treat such children as 'war babies' and not be guided by emotional considerations while arriving at a decision in this regard. It was only a sharp difference of opinion between Rameshwari Nehru and Mridula Sarabhai on the issue, and the insistence of those social workers who opposed such a callous solution to the problem, that saved the day for the women. A compromise was arrived at whereby the women would take their children with them to Jalandhar and, after 15 days, decide whether they wanted to keep them or not. 'It was our experience,' says Kammobehn, 'that most of the unmarried young mothers were not keen to part with their infants ... and older women were not keen to take their children, for they had other children earlier.'

When the question of separating women from their children arose and was sought to be decided 'practically' and 'unemotionally,' Kammobehn told us,

> I said to Mridulabehn that I would not attend this meeting because my opinions are the opposite of yours. I will say frankly what I feel about this matter at the meeting, otherwise I will not come ... Mridulabehn was worried about the future of these girls: how to settle them, who will marry them? Rameshwari Nehru was of the opinion that if they were Muslims themselves, why should they leave their children in India? So I said in the meeting: the soldiers responsible for their birth go back to their respective countries and the infants have to be brought up by their mothers. Nobody separates them from their mothers. The stalwarts and the seasoned social workers like Rameshwari Nehru should therefore visit Lahore and impart necessary training for separating the child – on our part we have neither the strength nor the capability for that work. If all of you do not approve of my suggestion, I would like to dissociate myself from this work.

Before long, strong differences between Rameshwari Nehru (who opposed forcible recovery) and Mridula Sarabhai (who wished to press on) began to surface; Mridula Sarabhai believed that no woman could be happy with her abductor, Rameshwari Nehru, not so. Within a few months of recovery work having been undertaken systematically, she advised the government to stop it altogether because she was convinced that 'we have not achieved our purpose ... Figures alone are not the only criterion against which such work should be judged.' Viewed from the 'human and the women's angle', as she proposed to do, removing them (the women) from the home in which they were now settled would 'result in untold misery and suffering'. From what she

could gather, the number of such women was 'appreciably great'; moreover there was no way of ascertaining what happened to them once they were recovered and returned. 'By sending them away we have brought about grief and the dislocation of their accepted family life without in the least promoting human happiness,' she said. And finally, the woman's will was not taken into consideration at all; she was 'once again, reduced to the goods and chattel status without having the right to decide her own future or mould her own life'. Her pleas found few supporters and little sympathy within officialdom, however, and in July 1949 she resigned as Honorary Advisor to the Ministry of Relief and Rehabilitation.[23]

It would be incorrect to claim that the social workers all spoke in one voice, or that they did not also subscribe to prevailing notions of 'difference' between Muslims and non-Muslims in the matter of 'honour' and acceptability, and of social – and government – responsibility in the task of restoring these women to a life of 'dignity'. Indications are that they carried out the search and 'rescue' missions with some perseverance, especially in the first flush of recovery; in time, however (and this factor assumes significance in the light of what is discussed later) and with first-hand experience of the implications of their actions, they began to express their disagreement with decisions that they believed worked against the women and rendered their situation even more precarious. Indeed, when it seemed to them that the women's plight was particularly poignant, more than one social worker admitted to having 'helped' them 'escape' the police and bureaucratic net. In December 1949, Mridula Sarabhai was constrained to point out that 'the approach of the people *and even the social workers* is not correct. Public opinion must assert that the honour and dignity of women will be respected and that in our country abduction will not be tolerated', as it was 'in itself, immoral, apart from its being criminal....'[24]

These differences direct us to examine the role played by social workers in the recovery operation, and the triangular relationship that developed between the government, the women to be recovered and the intermediaries. That this relationship was ambivalent and became increasingly troubled is, we would suggest, precisely because the government's construction of the abducted woman's identity was being called into question. It was a construction that defined her, first and foremost, as the member of a community and then invested her with the full responsibility of upholding community honour. Second, it denied her any autonomy whatever by further defining her as the victim of an act of transgression which violated that most critical site of partiarchal control – her sexuality. For an elaboration of this, however, we need to return to the Bill, the circumstances under which it was formulated and the debates around it.

The Recovery Operation of the Government of India, albeit humanitarian and welfarist in its objectives, was neverthless articulated and implemented within the parameters of two overriding factors; first, the relationship of the Indian State with Pakistan and second, its assumption of the role of *parens patriae* vis-a-vis the women who had been abducted. As the former, it was obliged, as a 'responsible and civilised' government of a 'civilised' country to rightfully claim its subject-citizens; as the latter it was morally bound to relocate and restore these same subjects to their family, community and country. This dual role and responsibility simultaneously cast Pakistan itself as the abductor-country and India as the parent-protector, safeguarding not only her women but, by extension, the inviolate family, the sanctity of the community, and ultimately, the integrity of the whole nation; Additionally, and recurrently, the moral, political and ideological importance of India's secularism was upheld as an ideal that had to be vigorously championed and defended; it was this, more than anything else, that enabled the Indian State to *define itself in opposition to the Pakistani one*.

IV

Why, it may be asked, did the Indian government bend over backwards in its efforts to reclaim women, sometimes several years after their abduction had taken place, and through

such extraordinary measures as were proposed in the Bill? Why should the matter of *national* honour have been so closely bound up with the bodies of women and with the children born of 'wrong' unions? The experience of Pakistan suggests that recovery there was neither so charged with significance nor as zealous in its effort to restore moral order. Indeed, informal discussions with those involved in this work there indicate that pressure from India, rather than their own social or political compulsions, were responsible for the majority of recoveries made. There is also the possibility that the community stepped in and took over much of the daily work of rehabilitation, evidenced by findings that the level of destitution of women was appreciably lower in Pakistan. We were told that both the Muslim League and the All Pakistan Women's Association were active in arranging the marriages of all unattached women, so that 'no woman left the camp single'. Preliminary interviews conducted there also hint at relatively less preoccupation with the question of moral sanction and 'acceptability', although this must remain only a speculation at this stage.[25]

Nevertheless, some tentative hypotheses may be put forward. For India, a country that was still reeling from Partition and painfully reconciling itself to its divided self, reclaiming what was by right its 'own' became imperative in order to establish its credentials as a responsible and civilised state, one that fulfilled its duties towards its citizens both in the matter of securing what was their due, and in confirming itself as their protector.[26] To some extent, this was mirrored in the refugees' own dependency in turning to the *sarkar* as their *mai-baap* (parent) at this time of acute crisis.

But the notion of 'recovery' itself as it came to be articulated cannot really be seen as having sprung full-blown in the post-Partition period, as a consequence of the violence that accompanied the exchange of populations.

If we pause to look at what had been happening in Punjab from the mid-nineteenth century onwards with the inception and consolidation of the Arya Samaj and the formation of a Punjabi Hindu consciousness, we might begin to discover some elements of its anxiety regarding Muslim and Christian inroads into Hindu-ness and the erosion of Hindu dharma values and life-styles through a steady conversion of Hindus to these two faiths. With the creation of Pakistan, this anxiety found a new focus, for not only had it been unable to stem conversions to Islam, it had actually lost one part of itself to the creation of a Muslim homeland. Recovery then became a symbolically significant activity (its eerie resonance in the current frenzy to recover sacred Hindu sites from the 'usurping' Muslims, is chilling), just as earlier the *shuddhi* programme of the Arya Samaj, even if it resulted in bringing only one convert back into the Hindu fold, served to remind the Hindu community that losing its members to Islam or Christianity was not irreversible. Recovering women who had been abducted and forcibly converted, restoring them both to their own and the larger Hindu family, and ensuring that a generation of newly born Hindu children was not lost to Islam through their repatriation to Pakistan with their mothers, can be seen as part of this concern. Because, in fact, such a recovery or return might not be voluntary, necessary legal measures had to be taken to accomplish the mission. In one sense, it would seem that the only answer to forcible conversion was – forcible recovery.

This unhappiness and, indeed, outrage at forcible conversion is palpable through all the debates on abducted women, and the extension of the definition of the term to *any male child below the age of 16*, further indicates the depth of the disquiet. Although the State, especially one that called itself secular, could not be seen to be subscribing to this anxiety, it could certainly act in the national interest and in the interest of its male citizens and their communities, by upholding their honour; in this case, through restoring their 'sisters' and its own subjects to where they belonged – with their respective Hindu or Muslim families and in their own Hindu or Muslim countries.

By becoming the father-patriarch, the State found itself reinforcing official kinship relations by discrediting, and in fact declaring illegal, those practical arrangements that had in the meantime come into being, and were *functional and accepted*.[27] It was not only because abduction was a criminal offence that it was sought to be redressed – its offence was also that, through conversion and marriage, it transgressed prescribed norms in every respect. (After all, as one Member of Parliament pointed out, the government was nowhere near as anxious to take action against the abduction of Muslim women by Muslims or Hindu women by Hindus, because here no offence against community or religion had been committed, no one's honour compromised.) This was why such alliances could neither be socially acknowledged nor granted legal sanction, and why the children born of them would forever be 'illegitimate'.

This reinforcement of the legitimate family required the dismembering of the illegal one by physically removing the woman/wife/mother from its offending embrace and relocating her where she could be adequately protected. It also entailed representing the woman as ill-treated and humiliated, without volition or choice and – most importantly – without any rights that might allow her to intervene in this reconstruction of her identity and her life. Only thus could social and moral order be restored and community and national honour, vindicated.

It is rather unlikely that we will ever know what exactly abduction meant to all those women who experienced it because it is rather unlikely that they will ever talk of it themselves, directly; society still enjoins upon them the silence of the dead around an event that, to it, was shameful and humiliating in its consequences. Yet society and State, father, husband and brother, virtually to a man, placed upon women the special burden of their own attempt to renegotiate their post-Partition identity, 'honourably'.

Notes

1   The various reports on communal violence, over the last ten years or so, by the PUDR. Independent Initiative on Kashmir, the PUCL and citizens and human rights groups; Uma Chakravarti and Nandita Haksar, *The Delhi Riots: Three Days in the Life of a Nation* (Delhi: Lancer International, 1987); Amrit Srinivasan, "The Survivor in the Study of Violence" in Veena Das (ed.) *Mirrors of Violence: Communities, Riots and Survivors* (Delhi: Oxford University Press, 1990); Veena Das, "Our Work to Cry, Your Work to Listen" in Das (ed.), *Mirrors of Violence, op.cit.*; Gyanendra Pandey, "In Defence of the Fragment: Writing About Hindu-Muslim Riots in India Today", *Economic and Political Weekly*, Vol. XXVI, 1991, among others.

2   Gyanendra Pandey, "In Defence of the Fragment", op.cit.

3   A detailed account of the nature and circumstances of this violence is to be found in our "Surviving Violence: Some Reflections on Women's Experience of Partition", a paper presented at the IVth National Conference of the Indian Association of Women's Studies, Jadavpur (Calcutta), February 1990.

4   Our discussion has also benefitted from the findings of the Pakistan study, carried out in West Punjab and Sind. Although detailed information has still to be analysed, a preliminary examination of it suggests some critical differences and also, unexpected resonances.

5   M.S. Randhawa, *Out of the Ashes: An Account of the Rehabilitation of Refugees from West Pakistan in Rural Areas of East Punjab* (Bombay, 1954).

6   Satya Ral, *Partition of the Punjab* (Bombay: Asia Publishing House, 1965).

7   Constituent Assembly of India (Legislative) Debates, December 1949.

8   Confidential papers of Evan Jenkins, IOL/R13/1/176

9   Ibid., March 1947.

10 Constituent Assembly Debates, op.cit.

11 Ibid.

12 Satya Ral, *Partition of the Punjab* (Bombay: Asia Publishing Housing, 1965).

13 Aparna Basu, *Rebel With a Cause: Mridula Serabhai, A Biography* (Delhi: Oxford University Press, 1995).

14 Constituent Assembly Debates, op.cit.

15 Aparna Basu, op.cit.

16 The Gandhi Vanita Ashram in Jalandhar was set up for the rehabilitation of destitute women, after Partition. Subsequent to the signing of the Inter-Dominion Agreement on the recovery of abducted persons, it was designated the receiving institution for women recovered from Pakistan; its counterpart in Lahore was Sir Ganga Ram Hospital.

17 Aparna Basu, op.cit.

18 Appeal published in *The Hindustan Times*, 17 January, 1948. *Selected Works of Jawaharlal Nehru*, second series, Vol. 5 (Delhi: Jawaharlal Nehru Fund, 1987) p. 119.

19 Quoted in G.D. Khoala, *Stern Recokning: A Survey of the Events Leading Upto and Following the Partition of India*. (Delhi: Oxford University Press, 1949, rpt. 1989).

20 *Selected Works of Jawaharlal Nehru*, op.cit., p. 114.

21 Kamlabehn Patel in a personal interview.

22 Kamlabehn Patel, personal interview and her book, *Mool Suta Ukhadslar*, (Bombay-Ahmedabad: R.R. Sheth & Co., 1985).

23 Private papers of Rameshwari Nehru, Nehru Memorial Museum and Library, Delhi.

24 Report of the Relief and Rehabilitation Section, presented at the Indian Conference of Social Work (Delhi Branch), December 1949.

25 We owe this information to Nighat Said Khan, researching the Pakistan experience.

26 Organisations like the RSS and Akhil Bharatiya Hindu Mahasabha, for instance, were clamouring for the return of Hindu women, and the Hindu Mahasabha even included the issue of the recovery of women in its election manifesto of 1951.

27 We are grateful to Veena Das for having drawn our attention to this; for an elaboration of this point, see Das, "Of National Honour and Practical Kinship", in her book, *Critical Events*: (Delhi: Oxford University Press, 1995).

11

Identity, Violence and Women: A Reflection on the Partition of India 1947

Nighat Said Khan

"It was when the Hindus said, go to your country, that we saw Pakistan as another country" and "if Pakistan had not been created, at least we could have lived in peace" highlight several of the key concepts that underlie Partition and the creation of Pakistan: the construction of identity; the notion of country; real and symbolic peace posited against external and internal violence. Yet, despite the fact that Pakistan has still not come to terms with itself, and not yet recovered from the trauma of partition, Pakistanis have continued to treat this history as an event that is recorded and discussed from the distance of the third person narrative. This eerie silence is imposed and encouraged, not only by the state, but by those who have recorded this history, and indeed those who lived it. This opens up areas of ideological control and internalization of ideology on the one hand, and the issue of authenticity in the recording of history on the other; as also the role of class, gender, ideology, and individual experience in the construction of knowledge. So far the political and intellectual voice has dominated

the debate on Pakistan, and also to some extent, the fictional voice; as opposed to the the experiential voice, which may offer greater insights into issues of identity, nationhood and country, violence, and women, which continue to plague us.

This paper seeks to explore some of these underlying concepts as they are articulated by those with personal experiences, in an attempt to shift the discussion of Partition from focussing only on the "Pakistan movement" and from the leadership of the Muslim League. Specifically, the focus here is to give voice to women who have experiential knowledge of these events, as migrants and as women, in order to move towards an understanding of the construction of identity, nationhood, and violence, and women as signifiers of these constructions. The shattering violence that engulfed independence and the creation of Pakistan; dislocation; the loss of the self while supposedly trying to attain it; the reconstruction of home, and family, and the self, played itself out on women with much greater force; and

Perspectives on Modern South Asia: A Reader in Culture, History, and Representation, First Edition.
Edited by Kamala Visweswaran.
© 2011 Blackwell Publishing Ltd. Published 2011 by Blackwell Publishing Ltd.

these continue to play a role in the construction of identity in women as women.

My arguments in this paper concern themselves with a brief analysis of over 100 interviews conducted with women migrants from India, in terms of how they view the creation of Pakistan and the impact that it had on them; with the stunning violence that surrounded this creation, a violence that in its scale and its articulation does not fit into norms that may be acceptable in such historical events; and with the issue of subjectivity, especially the role that it plays in the recording and the analysis of events.

Womens' Perceptions of Partition

Of the 100 interviews done in rural and urban Sind and Punjab, 90 were of middle and lower income women, while 10 were upper, mainly professional, women. Significantly only the 10 women with professional backgrounds said that they had made a conscious choice to come to Pakistan. The rest did not come to realize a dream, but fled instead, from a disaster. Most of these had lived among Hindus and Sikhs and almost all remembered no conflicts or problems until Partition was announced. The comment, "if Pakistan had not been created we could have lived in peace" signifies an underlying perception that the violence only started after the decision to divide India and the actual establishment of borders. It was that decision that made the Hindu say "go to your country" and it was that violent push to leave that brought these people here, and not, as is often understood, that they identified with the creation of Pakistan.

Some were even unaware of Pakistan until some years after its creation. Almost all had never heard of the Muslim League, or the movement for Pakistan and only four from urban Sind and one from rural Punjab had worked for it. Only 14 said that they had understood the implication of Partition, or felt that there was a need for it, and even fewer understood the concept of a separate country with borders that could not be crossed. In Sind, where nearly all had family still settled in India, came with the intention to go back once "things had settled down". This is different from the Punjab where families and

whole villages migrated and in many cases got land from the state. Yet even in the Punjab the people fled to the new country and did not actually choose to come. Almost all were stunned by the violence, especially from those with whom they had lived "in harmony" and over half either lost members of their families or were the victims of violence themselves, and only seven feel that they could live with Hindus and Sikhs again. Significantly, these seven are all widows, and all have members of their natal family in India, a thought that I will explore later.

Many describe the instant that the decision was made to leave: that there was no time to put anything together or to make arrangements, or even to say goodbye. Women, were by and large, not consulted in making this decision, but this was invariably because, as they say, there was no time to consult with anyone. In only one instance, however, was the initiative taken by a woman. All the women talked about the violence, and specifically the violence against women, and almost half spoke of sexually motivated violence, and the violence of women being abandoned, or lost, or abducted. As survivors of this cataclysmic historical event, there was no sense of pride in having survived and there is a perceptible yearning for a past that will not leave them. This yearning is translated into how they perceive their lives now. Only sixteen describe their lives as "better" now, economically and socially. Whereas it is difficult to judge whether they might have been economically better off had partition not taken place, the migrants from India have not been assimilated socially into the Pakistani fabric even at the micro level. They are still seen as refugees or *panahgir* (those seeking safety), and identify themselves as such. This is true also in the Punjab despite the fact that in the Punjab the migrants share a Punjabi identity, culture, and language.

The above has been culled from the recorded interviews with each of the women included in our study. We did not have a questionnaire as such, but did use a format to rationalise some of the information. The responses themselves, however, indicate much more than is listed above, and allow one to explore dimensions that the format in itself does not highlight.

On Identity, Violence, and Women

The Muslim and Pakistani identity of these women is in direct relationship to the "other" as it were, and not an identity in and of itself. Responses such as the "Hindu made us see ourselves as Muslims"; "it was the Hindus and the Sikhs that made us Muslims"; "it was when the Hindu said go to your country that we saw Pakistan as a country"; "the Hindus drove us out"; "when *they* turned on *us*" indicate that one's perception of oneself is in direct relation to how others perceive one, and further that it is in relation to the other that identity is constructed and reinforced. Few of these women would relate to Partition other than in terms of what was done to them, and how destructive it was. The sense of loss of a country; a home; family, especially the natal family, permeates the present. Yet life and personal histories are truncated into two distinct categories: pre-Partition and post-Partition, leading to a division of the self. The horror of the Partition lingers and consumes, and continues to determine how one relates not only to the outside world but to oneself. There is a continuing inability to deal with dislocation, especially with these women whose children are old enough to make their own lives and in some cases have gone away, and some of whom may have lost their husbands.

The notion "country" is described variously as *mulk, quam*, and *watan*, all aspects of nationhood and identity, but all of which are also used to to describe sub-nationalities. In fact these women use the same terms to describe what they left behind, as in "we left our watan and came here". The *watan* is *in* India but is *not* India. What then does the term country mean, outside of its geographic and political boundaries? Implicit in the definition of country is a sense of home; of an emotional relationship with the outside; with the space that one inhabits and one's connection with it. Few of the women have this relationship with the new country, especially not in terms of emotional space, and home for them is what they left behind. Identity with the country is, therefore, also truncated with political loyalties

being given to the space that they now inhabit, and emotional loyalties given to one's home in another.

The dislocation for women was even more traumatic than it was for men. Almost all of the ones that we spoke to were married at the time of Partition, and came here with their husbands and in many cases, the husbands' family, but almost all of them got dislocated from their own natal families. This further broke their links with their own homes and families and with that the support, physical and emotional, that women do get from their natal home even after they enter their marital homes. Women were thus dislocated at two levels (and in the case of Biharis in Karachi who came after 1971, at two levels twice) from the home and from the family. They also lost the security of friendships and other relationships that define social structure and social space, since in this new home, the permissible freedoms for women were further limited. The concept of *Mehram* and *Na mehram* which determine who a woman can or cannot meet, or which man she might be seen in the company of, drove many of these women in to the *chardevari* (four walls) of their houses. Women were therefore further cut off from relating to the outside world, and further caught within themselves and their marital families. The yearning for the earlier home is invariably a yearning not only for the space that it signifies, but also a yearning for the natal home; for friendships; and for a freedom to relate that they had had previously. Those wanting now to go back are all widows. Since the husband is no longer there to connect them to the marital home, and since in many cases the children are no longer there to give them a sense of belonging, or of being needed, identity with the physical space loses what meaning it had previously. Their history, pre-Partition, locates them and they reconstruct their present aloneness in images of the past.

The overwhelming memory and perception of Partition is the relentless violence of it. Although we the researchers, were familiar with it, we were unprepared for the scale and dimensions of it. The pain and horror was not just of what happened but whom it was done by; people that they had lived with and related to and loved. "Suddenly they turned on us", or "we knew them", punctuated many of these discussions. The fact that Muslims also did the same was understood as revenge and therefore, at some level, permissible. Women described the violence unselfconsciously but often in the third person. Many said that they had seen the violence but gave details only on instances that they said they had heard about. The experiential has either been silenced, or there is a tacit commitment not to bear personal witness when someone they knew was involved as perpetrator or victim.

Violence is invariably perceived as having been done by the other and often by others to others. Not a single woman admitted to violence having been done by her or her kin. This points not only to the concept of violence itself, but to what was considered permissible in this instance. The parameters of what is permissible are historically determined. For instance slavery, war booty, rape, the use of the sword as opposed to the gun, are no longer considered morally acceptable even in conditions of war, by the community of nations. Apart from the philosophic doubt about violence itself in any circumstances, the violence during Partition went beyond all of this and exposed to personal and national scrutiny the beast within. It showed that in a situation of perceived threat, real or imagined, people are capable of things that they would not normally do, and that each one of us, can, in certain circumstances, be violent. While it is comforting to think, and indeed may be necessary to believe, that violence is inhuman and therefore not normal, the violence during the Partition indicates that madness or insanity lies in each, and that insecurity, pain, anger and revenge will often be articulated in violence. The intensity of the violence of partition may be directly linked to the intensity of pain, bitterness, sense of betrayal, loss and revenge that people felt in relation to the other, that is, the intensity of emotion produced the intensity in the violence.

The other aspect of this violence that needs further exploration, is that the movement for Pakistan, and the Partition, do not fall into the categories that normally define such movements.

At one level it was an independence struggle and a war of liberation; it was also a civil war; a war between two nation states; and in some instances, a class war. Most of these situations would justify violence, albiet in a different form. But it is interesting that this war, or liberation struggle, produced no military or revolutionary heroes. The violence was never heroic, and it had to be legitimated and mediated through concepts such as "self defense", "revenge", "honour" etc., for if anything, this was an internecine war and was always perceived as such. The silence around it therefore, is perhaps understandable, since admitting to killing and raping one's own kin defied the parameters of permissible violence. I would further suggest that both the states would inculcate and encourage this silence, not because they could not face the dimensions of it, but because it was perceived as internecine. That recognition, at least on the part of Pakistan, would open for scrutiny the two-nation theory, for if the Muslims considered themselves to be one with the Hindus and the Sikhs, to the extent that they could not admit how many of the other they killed, or how much they destroyed, let alone glorify it, then the identity of Pakistan was at risk.

The violence directed against women took on additional forms, most of them located in sexuality. I will discuss six aspects of this here. The first is the molestation and rape done by the men of one community to women of the other as a way of "dishonouring" the other as real and symbolic subjugation. Inherent in this are notions of women as property, or belonging to, of those without identity. However, I would suggest that while this is one explantion for rape in conflict situations, we should also be looking to male psychology and to the relationship between violence and rape. In Manto's *Thanda Ghost* (an Urdu short story) the rape is propelled by the woman's beauty, which the rapist cannot resist. He must posses her, first by abducting her and then by raping her several times. In this he is not simply dishonouring another community, he is making a statement about himself and how he perceives the individual woman. The second level of violence was the countless stories of women being disfigured by their limbs or other parts of their bodies being hacked. While men also were the victims of such violence, what was peculiar to women is that it often took on sexual connotations. Invariably women's breasts were cut off, their vaginas split, or they were hacked into two. We came across very few instances where penises were hacked. This, I argue, is also connected to the honour of the community for a woman who is not sexually alive and active, or cannot produce and nuture children, is an affront to that community, since community must reproduce itself. Women in this case as well are seen without identity other than the identity of their male kin. Women were also repeatedly stripped, and often made to dance naked in the streets, a form of violence that seems particular to this region, since notions of purity, chastity, and morality demand that women must be clothed and that they, especially Muslim women, do not dance. Again these are linked to "dishonouring" the men in the woman's community.

A third and fourth type of violence specific to women, was the killing of women by male kin, usually fathers and brothers, and by suicide, in order to "save the honour" of the women. There are countless accounts of women being stabbed, or thrown into a well, or poisoned when men perceived "their" women to be at risk. The threat of rape, molestation and abduction was considered more fatal than death itself, since to live a life without honour was a fate worse than death. Similarly, women were encouraged and helped to commit suicide in the event that this dishonour might be possible. Many women did internalise this concept of honour and did commit suicide in these circumstances. It appears though that it was not the honour of the women per se, that had to be safeguarded, but the honour of their male kinsmen. We did not come across a single instance where "the women were (not) told by the men to kill themselves" or when they made arrangements for suicide unaided by the men.

A fifth type of violence was instances of women being bartered for the safety and lives of others in the family. Usually it was a daughter who was "sacrificed", or other young kinswomen. The decision was made by male kin, and in one instance, by a mother to protect her son. Decisions such as these are connected with the concept that daughters are only in their natal homes on a temporary basis and that they must eventually leave for their "real" home, that is the marital home. The sacrifice of a daughter is not, therefore, the same as the sacrifice of a son, and most such decisions hid behind a marriage, for often it was rationalised that these women had been married off.

The sixth form of violence was that of women abducted by the other community. Usually these women were either abducted in a raid or plunder, or were caught when they got left behind in the home or by the caravan, and sometimes snatched from the family. Many of these were kept as wives by their abductors. These abductions reached such a scale that the states on both sides of the border negotiated an agreement to recover abducted women. From the figures available, almost half of them were recovered. This recovery, however, is a complex issue and requires a different discussion since the conditions in which these women found themselves were not uniformly bad. In some cases their captor/husbands treated them well and they integrated themselves in their marital homes, and they resisted their lives being disrupted again by the state "recovering" them.

All six aspects of specific violence against women make women extensions of male identity and regard them as male property; and in each woman signifies male honour. The silence that surrounded these women after Partition and in the process of reconstruction of the country and of the self, speaks again of male honour that itself needed to be reconstructed. Since men are meant to protect their women and since in this case they were unable to give this protection, meant that they had to conceal what they could not face. The silence of these women was necessary in reconstituting patriarchal society.

12

The Quest for National Identity: Women, Islam and the State in Bangladesh

Naila Kabeer

Introduction

The contradictions and uncertainties which have dogged the state's Islamisation policy in Bangladesh stem partly from a central ambivalence in prevailing notions of national identity, an ambivalence which relates to the significance attached by different political constituencies to the place of 'Islamic' versus 'Bengali' values in determining national identity. A historical perspective is necessary to comprehend the nature of this ambivalence because it is rooted, in the first place, in the manner in which Islam was introduced and absorbed into Bengali society and, in the second, in the processes by which Bengali Muslims were incorporated into the wider Islamic community.

The next section discusses the concept of the national entity and illustrates its complexities in the case of the Bengali Muslim collectivity. It is followed by an examination of the effects of state policy in the Pakistan era in heightening the contradictions between official definitions of nationhood and the cultural identity of the Bengali Muslims. Finally, the continuing quest for national identity in post-liberation Bangladesh is analysed. Particular attention is paid to the interactions and conflicts which surfaced at different phases of the nation's history between official constructions of nationhood and the state's position on the 'woman question'.

The Nation as Ideological Construct

Anderson's conceptualisation of the nation as an 'imagined community' is helpful in pointing to the *ideological* construction of national communities and therefore to their historical contingency.[1] National identities come into existence as a consciousness of specific forms of difference. The boundaries of demarcation are frequently transitory and fluid, drawing on a diverse array of forms: 'a myth of common ancestry, a sense of common territoriality, a

Perspectives on Modern South Asia: A Reader in Culture, History, and Representation, First Edition.
Edited by Kamala Visweswaran.
© 2011 Blackwell Publishing Ltd. Published 2011 by Blackwell Publishing Ltd.

common language and body of cultural symbols and/or common phenotypical appearance, in physique or in garments...'[2]

The case of Bangladesh will serve to illustrate the fluid and contingent nature of the national community. The demarcating principles of the Bengali Muslim collectivity have been reshaped several times during this century in response to diverse ideological and political forces.[3] When Pakistan came into existence as a homeland for the Muslims of the Indian subcontinent, Islam was inevitably invoked as the unifying principle of national identity, capable of transcending all differences between its geographically and culturally divided population. It continued to figure prominently as the *raison d'être* of the subsequently truncated Pakistani state. Unable to ignore or unify its dissatisfied minority nationalities, Pakistan's rulers still relied on Islam to keep the nation intact: in the words of the late President, Zia-ul Haq, 'Take Islam out of Pakistan and make it a secular state; it would collapse'.[4]

Since liberation from Pakistan, the search for a national identity in Bangladesh has been driven by a different set of forces. Bangladesh is relatively homogeneous in cultural, linguistic and ethnic terms. It has a sizeable (10 per cent), but politically weak, minority of Hindus as well as a small tribal population. The problem of national identity for the Muslim majority today focuses less on forging the basis for internal unity and more on establishing its difference from the Hindu Bengalis of India, thereby justifing its claims to an independent state and, more recently, to a closer alignment with the oil-rich nations of the Middle East. The quest for the defining principles of 'Bengali Muslim' nationhood is complicated, however, by the fact that while Islamic religion and Bengali culture are the very essence of the community's separate identity, its historical experience has prevented the two from being successfully moulded into a coherent unity. In fact, the country's persisting preoccupation with its own identity may reflect its uncertainty that such a cohesion can ever be achieved. It may also contribute to the current lack of political stabilty in Bangladesh.[5]

The Rise of the Muslim Community in Bengal

Bangladesh consists of the eastern, deltaic districts of the province of Bengal and roughly approximates the areas of Muslim majority in the eastern section of the Indian subcontinent. In 1947 it became the eastern wing of Pakistan, the new homeland for the Muslims of India, which was carved out from the eastern (East Bengal) and northwestern extremities of the subcontinent. Islam was the basis for the creation of this geographically, culturally and ethnically divided state, separated by a thousand miles of hostile Indian territory. The bloody war for Bengali liberation in 1971 proved that religious ties were too fragile, uneven and tenuous in themselves to hold the two wings together.

The Islam of Bengal was not the Islam of Pakistan; it bore the imprint of very different historical and social forces. There are some suggestions that the original settlers of Bengal were migrants from south-east Asia who introduced their own agrarian practices and animist belief-systems into the region.[6] Hinduism, Buddhism and then Islam have each in turn been imposed on the pre-existing 'little tradition' and were permeated and transformed by it.[7]

The resilience of the early folk beliefs has been related to the 'extraordinary geography' and 'frontier' character of Bengal.[8] Situated at the far eastern periphery of India, at the delta of its two largest rivers, and cut off from the rest of the subcontinent periodically by massive floods, Bengal was isolated for several centuries from the dominant cultures of the region. The Aryan conquerors did not establish Brahmanical Hinduism in Bengal until the fifth century. The Brahmin elite, which based itself in the more accessible western part of Bengal, incorporated the local Bengali tribes into the Brahminical hierarchy as a ritually inferior caste. The indigenous Bengalis responded by enthusiastically embracing every major anti-Brahminical movement that flourished in the region – Buddhism, Vaishnavism and finally Islam.[9]

Islam came to Bengal in the wake of the Muslim conquest in the thirteenth century. Its egalitarian principles made for massive conversions among the despised low-caste population of Bengal, but it did not live up to their expectations. A caste-like division emerged within the Muslim community between the *ashraf* those of noble or foreign extraction, and the *ajlaf*, indigenous converts of lowly origins. Bengali Muslims found themselves integrated into the Islamic *umma* (community) without transcending their former subordinate status. They sought solace in the preachings of the Sufis, holy men and mystics of Persian origin, whose respect for Islamic principles of equality brought them into closer contact with the artisans and cultivators of rural Bengal, making them more effective leaders than the distant urban-based *ulema* (Islamic clergy). The Sufi traditions co-existed easily with other devotional cults in Bengal, and came to represent non-conformity and rebellion in opposition to the established centres of *ulema* orthdoxy.[10]

Thus two forms of Islam flourished in Bengal. There was the Islam of the villages, a fusion of Hindu and Muslim traditions among cultivators and artisans who had lived and worked together for centuries and who shared the cultural legacy of the early pioneers of the delta. Within this syncretic system, it was impossible to disentangle the origins of various beliefs and customs about the land and the seasons, about pollution, seasonality and birth, about kinship and fate, about ghosts, demons and holy men which were shared by Muslim and Hindu peasant alike and were essentially Bengali beliefs.[11]

In marked contrast was the faith practised by the urban-based, foreign-born Islamic elite who strongly resisted assimilation into indigenous Bengali culture. They maintained their distance from the local population, as much from low-born Muslim converts as from Hindus, by stressing their foreign extraction, by adhering closely to orthodox Islamic practices and by speaking only Persian, Arabic and, later, Urdu.

It was this Islamic elite who became the leading Bengali representatives of the Muslim League and the most vociferous supporters of the demand for a separate Muslim homeland. Although they claimed to speak for all Bengali Muslims, they were from the outset made up of people, like Syed Amir Ali, Nawab Abdul Latif and Nawab Salimullah, who spoke in languages that were not understood by the majority of their 'imagined' constituency, who looked to West Asia for their cultural references and who regarded local culture and customs as irremediably Hinduised.[12]

This, then, was the situation at the time of partition. Two parallel belief-systems, both claiming to be Islam, co-existed uneasily within the Bengal delta: the orthodox Islam of the elite and the more syncretic and personal version of the Bengali peasant. Erected on this 'quicksand of a persisting identity problem between the self-image of Bengali Muslims and Muslim Bengalis'[13] was the solid weight of the state of Pakistan, brought into existence on the basis of Muslim separateness. The experience served to intensify, rather than resolve, the problematic nature of the Bengali Muslim identity.

National Integration and Cultural Difference in the Pakistan Era

From its inception, state power in Pakistan was monopolised by a Punjabi-based, military-bureaucratic oligarchy whose policies towards the east wing reduced it to the status of a colony and sowed the seeds of the country's subsequent disintegration. While these policies took the form of both economic and political discrimination,[14] it was probably the state's activities on the cultural front that finally brought home to Bengalis the full extent of their alienation from the Islamic Republic and accelerated their passage to independent nationhood.

The assault mounted by the Pakistani state on Bengali culture met little resistance from Bengal's Islamic elites, who shared the attitudes of the ruling oligarchy. However, West Pakistani antipathy to Bengali culture was further intensified by racial arrogance towards the smaller and darker Bengalis and nourished by the suspicion that, though nominally Muslim, their 'relatively recent' conversion from low-caste Hindu status made them unreliable co-religionists.[15] The cultural and linguistic affinity between the Hindus and Muslims of Bengal was also profoundly threatening to a state which had only Islam to hold together its fragmented and divided people.

Reluctant to rely on religious allegiance alone, successive regimes in Pakistan embarked on a strategy of forcible cultural assimilation towards the Bengalis.

The process began soon after partition and was targeted on the Bengali language, the primary vehicle for the specific identity and separate culture of the Bengali people. Urdu, with its echoes of the sacred language, had come to symbolise the movement for a Muslim homeland and in 1948 was declared its state language. The Bengali resistance to this move was spearheaded by the student movement, which did not share the Pakistani antagonism to Hindu culture, but chose rather to emphasise the common *bhadrolok* ('respectable classes') values and aspirations which informed the middle-class way of life for Bengalis on both sides of the political divide with India. The Language Movement resulted in the death of six student protestors and the overwhelming defeat of the Muslim League in the 1954 provincial elections. The victors were the United Front, led by the Bengali nationalist Muslim Awami League founded in 1949. The new party subsequently dropped the 'Muslim' epithet and henceforth became the voice of the disenfranchised middle classes of East Bengal. Bengali was finally given equal status with Urdu as state language in the Constitution of 1956.

However, the language issue symbolised a struggle about power, rather than speech, and the essential problems remained unresolved. Cultural issues came to the forefront again under Ayub's regime. A Bureau for National Reconstruction was set up to purge the Bengali Language of Sanskrit/Hindu elements and purify it with Arabic, Persian and Urdu. The songs of Tagore were banned from the state-controlled radio and television. Restrictions were imposed on the dissemination of Bengali literature, and grants offered to artists and literati who were prepared to work for 'national integration'. A policy of assimilation-through-miscegenation made its first appearance in the system of financial incentives for inter-wing marriages.[16]

Alienated by the regime's attempts to appropriate the mantle of Islamic purity for its own cultural traditions, the Bengali middle class was forced to confront more clearly the dilemmas of identity: were they Muslims first or Bengalis first? Resistance to Pakistani cultural hegemony helped to crystallise what was exclusive to the Bengali Muslim community: its common history and distinct way of life, reaffirmed continuously through shared cultural references, rituals and modes of communication. Although initially the province of the middle classes, Bengali nationalism had become a mass movement by 1971.

Bengali Women and the Pakistani State

Despite the significance attached to Islam as the basis of nationhood, the political leadership in Pakistan regarded itself as Muslim modernist, prepared to make pragmatic use of Islam for political ends but prepared also to reform its more anachronistic features. It was through Ayub Khan's initiative that the Family Law Ordinance, which modified the right of men to marry and divorce at will, was passed in 1961. On this occasion Bengali women united with women from West Pakistan in defending the bill against its detractors among the *ulema*. They united again in the 1960 presidential elections, to challenge the decision of the Combined Opposition to Ayub Khan to adopt the demand for a 'true' Islamic state and the abrogation of the Family Law Ordinance as a concession to the fundamentalist *Jamaat-e-Islami* presence in the coalition.

As a result of the modernist posture adopted by ruling groups, there were few direct attempts by the state to reshape the behaviour of Bengali women in accordance with orthodox notions of Islam. The official policy of purging Bengali culture of its 'Hindu' elements was fuelled by the fear that cultural differences could destroy the foundations of the national collectivity, rather than by a drive towards Islamisation *per se*. If Bengali women experienced official disapproval, they did so as part of the generalised attack on their culture rather thas as its specific targets.

Nevertheless, the dress and deportment of Bengali women took on increasing symbolic value as expressions of their cultural difference. On one level, it led to the politicisation of normally uncontroversial aspects of everyday middle-class life. The right to sing the songs of Tagore and to wear *bindis*[17] became acts of political dissent because they conflicted with the values of official Islam, as did the practice of the Bengali middle classes of training their daughters in the arts – singing, dancing and drama – and allowing them to perform in public.[18]

Bengali women celebrated their cultural identity within the conventional political sphere as well. Over the years, 21 February, formally observed as the Day of the Language Martyrs, had come to be enacted as an annual reaffirmation of Bengali identity. Women wearing white saris (the colour of mourning among both Hindus and Muslims in Bengal) joined in processions to lay wreaths at the monument to the martyrs. As the nationalist movement gathered force in the months preceding the declaration of Bangladesh's independence, massive demonstrations were held in Dhaka in which large contingents of women, dressed in traditional festive yellow and red saris, wearing *bindis* on their foreheads and singing Bengali nationalist songs, including the banned songs of Tagore, spearheaded what was effectively a cultural resistance to the Pakistani regime.[19]

The affronted sensibilities of the Muslim fraternity were avenged in the bloodbath that was unleashed on Bangladesh. In the nine months of occupation that followed, Bangladeshi civilians were picked up for interrogation by Pakistani soldiers with the question that haunted them with increasing intensity: are you a Muslim or a Bengali? Perhaps the most tragic victims of Pakistani hatred and suspicion were the estimated 30,000 Bengali women who were raped by Pakistani soldiers, purportedly in their mission to 'improve the genes of the Bengali people'[20] and thus populate Bangladesh with 'pure' Muslims. The policy of assimilation-through-miscegenation revealed the terrible deluded logic of racial supremacy.

The Politics of the Post-Liberation State

Bangladesh emerged from the nightmare of 1971 as an independent state. It has been ruled ever since by an unstable alliance between an underdeveloped national bourgeoisie and the military and civil bureaucracy. Shifts in the balance of power within the ruling alliance have generated persistent contradictory pressures on national development strategies and have led to periodic conflicts and reversals in state policy. The post-liberation years in Bangladesh have been marked by coups, counter-coups, growing impoverishment and an increasing dependence on external assistance. During this time, the state has completed a full ideological circle which has taken it from a position of official secularism to one of giving constitutional recognition to Islam, only a step short of the Islamic Republic status of pre-liberation days.

The Awami League, under the leadership of Sheikh Mujib, led the nationalist movement against Pakistan and formed the first government after Independence. It won a massive mandate from the people, first in 1970 and then in 1973, and Mujib himself enjoyed tremendous personal popularity. Its political support was derived mainly from the salariat classes – the managers, bureaucrats and professionals – who had been deprived of opportunities for advancement under the Pakistani regime. It was also backed by the rich peasantry who, with sufficient state patronage, could be relied on to contain unrest among the rural poor and to muster votes at election time.

The Awami League government sought to implement a moderately socialist programme, nationalising banks and key industries and imposing controls over foreign exchange, imports and foreign investment. In the area of foreign policy, it opted for a non-aligned status for Bangladesh, negotiating aid and assistance from diverse sources, including India and the socialist countries.

However, its socialist rhetoric and nationalisation policies were not popular with the United States. One of the factors behind the devastating famine of 1974 was the US decision to withhold food shipments (over the question of Bangladesh's trade relations with Cuba) at a time when the country was suffering from floods of catastrophic proportions.[21] The government was forced to accept financial help from the newly formed Aid-to-Bangladesh

Consortium, chaired by the World Bank, subject to conditions which sought to reverse government policy through greater stress on economic liberalisation and the private sector.

Within the country, the government's popular base was progressively eroded. Corruption and mismanagement of the economy by the Awami League and their cronies, the shortfall of essential goods, rapid growth in inflation rates, the government's glaring failure to utilise the foreign aid flowing into the country for productive purposes and, perhaps most importantly, the hostility of the traditionally anti-Indian army to a pro-Indian ruling party all combined to bring a loss of credibility and support by influential sections of society.[22] Mujib was assasinated in August 1975 by a small group of junior army officers, who justified their action on the grounds of the corruption and incompetence of the Awami League government and its alleged subservience to India.

After a brief succession of coups, Zia-ur Rahman took power as the man most acceptable to the different factions within the military establishment and set the country firmly on its present pro-Islamic and pro-US course. Zia's political survival depended on distancing himself ideologically from the Awami League as far as possible in order to generate his own civilian base. He projected himself as a modernist, espousing a progressive version of Islam and committed to the enhancement and prosperity of private capital. The rapid de-nationalisation of the economy under Zia created a newly-rich class of entrepreneurs and traders whose interests were tied to those of the government in power and who became its allies.

However, electoral victory represented the acid test in his bid for domestic and international legitimacy; it was the most effective demonstration that the Awami League was not the sole party with a popular base. A broader-based political support was also necessary to insure him against the likelihood of a future coup by some aspiring military rival. Zia used the breathing space afforded by martial law to found his own party – the Bangladesh National Party (BNP) – using the various forms of patronage available to a government in power.

In the end, Zia's quest for civilian legitimacy proved to be his downfall. The military resented sharing power and resources with his newly established allies in the BNP and increasingly distanced themselves from him. He was assassinated in 1981 and succeeded by General Ershad. Ershad has imitated many of Zia's tactics – to the extent of founding his own political party and seeking electoral legitimation – but has not repeated his mistakes. The presence of the military is now more extensive and more overt: in industry, in commerce, in the diplomatic service and within central and local government. Ershad, in other words, is not going to risk being alienated from his military power base.

In the midst of the political turbulence and shifting strategies of the post-independence years, two consistent features have been in evidence. First, there has been increasing impoverishment and social differentiation. The rural development strategies pursued by successive governments emphasised yield-enhancing rather than redistributive effects, and recent studies indicate that the growth of landlessness is accelerating and that the standard of living has deteriorated for most rural families since the 1960s.[23]

The other consistent feature is an increasing dependence on aid. Aid disbursed as a percentage of GDP rose from 10 per cent in 1972/73 to 14 per cent in 1981/82.[24] However, there have been significant changes in the sources of aid. Aid from India and the socialist bloc decreased after the assasination of Mujib, whereas aid from the developed capitalist countries became much more important as did aid from the OPEC countries, particularly Saudi Arabia.

The magnitude of aid donated to Bangladesh has given the international donor community a far-reaching influence over the country's affairs. Both at the national level through IMF/World Bank conditionality, and at the local level, through the implementation of development programmes and projects, the effects of aid are evident in almost every sphere of people's lives. By 1982, most of the earlier nationalist policies had been modified or reversed, and the developmental emphasis had shifted to the private sector and export-orientated economic growth.

The preoccupation with national identity has not been abandoned in the post-liberation era; there are continuing tensions between the claims of *Din-ul-Islam* and *Bangla Samaj*, the sacred and the cultural community. However, different forces shape the ideological construction of national boundaries in the post-liberation era; it is now spearheaded by the state's search for political legitimation rather than by the politics of anti-colonialism. In this continuing process, women have entered the public arena in new, explicit ways that are often directly linked to the political projects of the post-liberation regimes.

The Awami League, State Secularism and Women's Rights

The increasing significance assigned to women in official discourse and state policy did not become apparent until after the assassination of Mujib. The liberation struggle had been fought on the grounds of Bengali 'culture-as-nationalism'. Women participated in the movement for Bangladesh, but raised no challenge to their position within the cultural community. Most middle-class women appeared willing to rely on the good intentions of the nationalist government to represent their interests and remedy social injustices.

Unchallenged in its paternalistic vision of gender relations, the good intentions of the post-liberation government towards 'the womenfolk' were circumscribed within narrow limits. The 1972 Constitution of Bangladesh recognised for the first time the equality of the sexes in all spheres, but went on to reserve for members of one sex some classes of employment or office on the grounds that 'it is considered by its nature to be unsuited to members of the opposite sex' (Clause 3, Article 29). Fifteen parliamentary seats were reserved for women, to be filled through nomination by the ruling party rather than through the electoral process. While the importance of education for women was recognised, it was seen strictly in terms of their domestic role: according to the First Five Year Plan, 'The level of schooling of women determines the efficiency of household management. Educated women pay better

attention to nutrition, health and child-care than the uneducated . . . '

Mujib's regime was mainly preoccupied with coping with the ravages of war, famine and deteriorating law and order. It had little scope to deal specifically with the situation of women, except in connection with the rehabilitation of women who had been raped, widowed or otherwise affected by the war. Despite a variety of measures towards this end, it is likely that Mujib will be best remembered for declaring women who had been raped *birangona* (war heroines). The term was an attempt to disguise the sexual violence of the crime so as to make social ostracism of its victims less severe. However, it merely highlighted the social hypocrisy and unease surrounding the issue of female virtue in Bangladesh and many of the women were rejected by their families. A 5 per cent quota of government employment reserved for rape victims was, needless to say, never filled, since it merely served to identify them.[25]

In the broader policy arena, there were few initiatives for women under Mujib's regime. Women continued to be perceived in development planning efforts primarily in relation to fertility control and their critical role in realising population objectives; the only reference to women's income-generating activities in the country's First Five Year Plan is in connection with such objectives.

Nevertheless, at the ideological level the longstanding commitment to secularism by the Awami League must be regarded as more compatible with the ideas of women's emancipation than the theocratic rhetoric of the Pakistani state. Secularism in this context was taken to imply not the absence of religion, but equal status for all religions in the eyes of the state. The spheres of marriage, divorce, inheritance and guardianship for each religious community remained under the jurisdiction of its own personal status laws. What was new was the constitutional ban on communalism, on religious discrimination in any form, on state bias in favour of any religion and on political parties based solely on religion. Secularism was made a basic principle of the new constitution and Bangladesh was declared a People's Republic rather than an Islamic one. The choice of a national anthem, composed by Tagore, and of a national flag devoid of Islamic symbolism, were other signifiers of the secular leanings of the Awami League government.[26]

The Awami League's espousal of secularism as state ideology was, of course, derived from its analysis of the divisive role played by religion in the nation's history rather than from any particular commitment to gender equality. But it can be argued that there is a fundamental contradiction between official secularism and the extreme forms of gender discrimination which may be countenanced within a state-sanctioned religious framework. The Awami League's secularism effectively favoured the 'customary, communal, pliable' version of Islam which made up the folk traditions of Bengali Muslims over the 'divine, centralist and establishment-based' version favoured by theocratically-run states as well as by fundamentalists within the country.[27] Secularism removed the power of enforcing religious codes of conduct from the Muslim clerical establishment and permitted less rigid and immutable models for women's behaviour to emerge, models which were more open to change through contest and struggle.

Women and Developmentalism in the Bangladesh State

By the time Mujib was assassinated, changing currents in the international donor community were converging to form new strands of donor policy. The influence of the international women's movement was making itself felt in the politics of foreign aid. It challenged the assumptions and priorities that had so far dominated development aid and demanded that women's interests be specifically taken into account rather than left to a dubious trickle-down process or be interpreted entirely in terms of their reproductive roles. The effects of these new trends were visible in the policies of aid donors to Bangladesh who began to earmark separate budgets for women's programmes and for research on women's issues. These developments had their positive effects in the

Bangladesh context by introducing a new and potentially progressive vocabulary – the vocabulary of women's emancipation – into official discourse on women, by giving women's productive contributions a greater visibility and by increasing the number of development projects directed at women.

The coup that brought Zia-ur Rahman to power coincided with the United Nations International Women's Year (1975) and the declaration of the United Nations Decade for Women. Zia took up the cause of Women in Development (WID) with great public zeal. The second Five Year Plan (1980–85) was the first in two decades of development planning in the country to give explicit consideration to strategies for integrating women into the development process. A full-fledged Ministry of Women's Affairs was set up, the number of parliamentary seats reserved for women was doubled to 30 and 10 per cent of public sector jobs were to be reserved for women. Resources were channelled to rural women through the Women's Rehabilitation Foundation, mandated to assist poor women, and through various rural public works, women's co-operatives and as an expanded range of population-linked programmes.

These efforts to improve the condition of women did not spring from entirely disinterested motives. On the contrary, Zia was able to make considerable political capital out of his championship of Women and Development policies. Having come to power by military means, he was faced with the problem of generating a political base for himself. The strategy of using state patronage to persuade rural interest groups to support regimes in power was not pioneered by Zia. But the opportunities for patronage inherent in the distribution of foreign development resources, together with the additional funding now available for women's projects, offered new and different channels of patronage to offer to the rural power brokers.

Zia's display of concern for women's welfare had other practical payoffs. It helped mobilise an important constituency for himself and his newly founded party in their bid for electoral legitimation.[28] As the enormous potential contained in state championship of WID became apparent, he moved rapidly to nail its colours to his party's mast. The *Bangladesh Jatiya Mahila Sangshtha* (National Women's Organisation), for instance, was initially set up in 1976 to co-ordinate organisations and programmes dealing with women and children and to run its own programmes in training and service delivery for women. Its membership was nominated through the district bureaucracies, ensuring a fairly broad spectrum of the rural middle-classes rather than a narrow faction within the political spectrum.

By 1979, however, all its most important members had joined Zia's newly founded political party, including its Chairwoman who also became Minister for Women's Affairs. During the parliamentary elections of 1979, the *Sangshtha* used its powers of patronage to mobilise truckloads of women for political rallies in support of Zia. Recruitment onto *Sangshtha* committees was subsequently changed to nomination by the new women members of parliament who were themselves appointed by Zia's ruling party; the politically-neutral character of the BJMS was thus abandoned and it became a vehicle for Zia's political ambitions.

So closely identified with the BNP did the *Sangshtha* become that when Ershad came to power, he opted to channel official resources through the redesigned Ministry of Social Welfare and Women's Affairs and to transform the *Sangshtha* into a subordinate, government-sponsored agency. In other respects, Ershad has continued Zia's policy of public commitment to WID policy. In addition to the conventional range of development activities for women, he has also pushed through certain legal initiatives. Family courts have been set up since 1985 with exclusive jurisdiction to deal with cases relating to parental and conjugal rights, thereby expediting their resolution. A number of ordinances have also been enacted which make crimes against women (abduction, trafficking, rape, acid-throwing and dowry-murder) subject to capital punishment.

To sum up, there is no doubt that both Zia and Ershad attached considerable significance to the place of WID in state policy. It is evident in their frequent and public declarations on the subject, generally couched in the WID language of 'ensuring women's participation' and 'integrating women into development'. It is also evident in the variety of projects and legal measures devised to advance women's welfare and provide them with incomes.

The Drift to the Islamic State

The process of dismantling state secularism was started by Zia in 1977 through Proclamation Order No. 1. This inserted the declaration *'Bismillah-ar-Rahman-ar Rahim'* (In the name of Allah, the Beneficient, the Merciful) at the beginning of the constitution; deleted the principle of secularism and replaced it by 'absolute trust and faith in the Almighty Allah'; and added a new clause which stated 'The state shall endeavour to consolidate, preserve and strengthen fraternal relations among Muslim countries based on Islamic solidarity'. Zia also proposed the designation of 'Bangladeshi', instead of the previous one of 'Bengali', to describe citizens of Bangladesh (reported in *Bichitra*, 27 April 1981). The redefined term played down the cultural aspects of the national identity, with its unavoidable connotations of a common heritage with Hindu West Bengal, and imposed instead a territorial definition which clearly demarcated the two communities. The ban placed on religious parties by the Awami League was lifted and many ex-Muslim Leaguers now aligned themselves with Zia's Bangladesh National Party.

Attempts to close the gap between state and religion have been continued by Ershad. A *Zakat* fund was established with the President at its head.[29] All television broadcasts have to be preceded by the call to prayer and female television presenters are required to present a modest appearance. Although a signatory to the World Plan of Action of the UN Decade for Women, the Bangladesh Government refused to ratify a number of clauses (relating to inheritance, marriage, child custody and divorce) in the Convention on the Elimination of All Forms of Discrimination Against Women, on the grounds that they conflicted with the *Shari'ah*.

Ershad, even more than Zia, needs to provide himself with a mantle of legitimacy. Zia was at least able to base his nationalist credentials on his active role in the liberation struggle. Ershad, by contrast, spent the entire period of the struggle interned in West Pakistan. His new party, *Jana Dal*, has a similar programme to the BNP, but has not succeeded in wresting away support for the BNP, which remains unified under the leadership of Zia's widow, Begum Khaleda Zia. Ershad's strategy is to play the Islamic card, without having to share power with the fundamentalist parties. This has not proved to be an easy task and accounts for his irresolute path to Islamisation.

In January 1983 he declared to a meeting of Islamic scholars that 'the place of Islam as a religion will be maintained above all in the constitution of the country. Our struggle is to fight the enemies of Islam and turn Bangladesh into an Islamic state'.[30] This was followed by a proposal that the Martyrs Day celebrations on February 21 be opened with readings from the Quran. This was immediately denounced by students belonging to the secular opposition parties as a negation of the achievements of the February 21 Movement, as 'changing basic state policy and promoting the interests of a group and a person in the name of religion'.[31] Twenty-three opposition leaders also issued a statement warning that declaration of an Islamic State would lead to civil war and communal strife. Ershad beat a hasty retreat and there were no readings from the Quran. He later told reporters that he realised it was a mistake to have allowed his emotions to have carried him away on those occasions.

In November 1987 a fresh wave of political activity nearly brought the government down. Incensed by a proposal to introduce military representatives into the newly-decentralised local government structure, the three main oppositional alliances led a series of general strikes and demonstrations, demanding fresh elections under a caretaker government. Ershad agreed to hold elections, but rejected the idea of a caretaker government. The elections were held in March 1988 and while Ershad's party swept the polls, it was a meaningless victory. The main opposition parties boycotted the elections and it was estimated that less than 3 per cent of the electorate turned out (*The Daily Telegraph*, 5 March 1988) in what was dubbed 'the voterless election'.

Ershad's first act in the new Parliament was to push through the Eighth Amendment in which Article 2A declares: 'The state religion of the Republic is Islam, but other religions may be practised in peace and harmony in the Republic'. Justifying the Amendment, Ershad declared that the distinct identity of the people of Bangladesh in their culture, language, geographical entity, independent sovereignty and other spheres of nationalism could only be defined through Islam (*Daily Ittefaq*, 21 June 1988). However, the move was widely seen as a cynical political act, an attempt to contain the secular opposition and to make inroads into the fundamentalist constituency. A large number of rallies and demonstrations were held in protest against what was seen as a violation of the liberal nationalism which brought Bangladesh into existence – 'the spirit of '71'. They were supported not only by the mainstream opposition parties and trade unions, but also by a wide spectrum of women's organisations, student groups, the Supreme Court Bar Association, the Combined Professionals' Action Committee, the Federation of Bangladesh University Teachers and various prominent intellectuals and ex-freedom fighters.

It is still not at all clear what the longer-term implications of the Amendment are going to be. According to Justice Sobhan, a constitutional expert,

> At present, it might be a simple declaration, but in later phases of implementation it may call for certain very negative measures. For example, it may imply added constraints on women, including the imposition of the *purdah* system, end to demands for equal rights for women, certain amount of judicial discrimination and religious injunctions in various spheres of personal life (*Courier*, 22 April 1988).

On the other hand, it may be a merely cosmetic decision. The alternative view reported in the same issue of *Courier* was that 'the declaration would be as good or as bad as choosing *doyel* [local species of robin] as the national bird'. According to this view, 'the government is not interested in theocracy. Its motives are more political than religious. It would never go for further "Islamising" the Constitution'.

The Islamic Community: International Support and the Internal Constituency

The restoration of Islam to a central place in state ideology has been analysed so far as the strategy of military rulers in search of an ideology, but there were other considerations which assisted the process. Official Islamisation was also an attempt to create and capitalise on forces which would help to contain the secular and liberal opposition within the country.

During Mujib's ban on religious politics, the main fundamentalist party, *Jamaat-e-Islami*, had continued its activities unofficially through various social and community organisations such as the Masjid Mission and the Bangladesh Islamic Centre. Initially through clandestine and subsequently through open recruitment, it expanded its base from 425 full members and 40,000 associate members in 1968/69 to 650 and 100,000 respectively by 1980.[32] It continues to operate through a combination of well-organised proselytising and social welfare work (mobile clinics, medical services, education and charity). It has been particularly successful in recruiting a youthful cadre through the operations of its Youth and Student *Shibirs* (Encampments) and, significantly, it is for the first time successfully recruiting among women through a separate women's front.

A growth in non-political grassroots religious consciousness is also discernible. It is exemplified by the *Tabliq-Jamaat*, one of the largest but least known religious movements in the Muslim world today, whose annual assembly in Tongi (Bangladesh) draws together over a million people from all over the world. The *Tabliq-Jamaat* has no organisational structure or political aspirations, but assists the fundamentalist cause by creating an environment of revivalist Islam.

Various reasons have been advanced for this growth in Islamic consciousness. To some extent, it represents a rise in anti-Indian sentiment in reaction to Indian intransigence on the Farakka Barrage, its naval presence in the Bay of Bengal and other acts of hostility which have periodically disrupted the relationship between the two countries. Another reason offered is the import of conservative values by Bangladeshi migrants returning from the Middle East.[33] Another undoubtedly important reason can be termed the Saudi factor. The West is, after all, not the only source of funds for Bangladesh. The OPEC countries, most importantly Saudi Arabia, entered the ranks of major aid donors since the oil boom of the early 1970s. While it is not clear to what extent moves to reassert Islamic values were in deference to Saudi sensibilities, it should be noted that Saudi Arabia refused to recognise the new state of Bangladesh until the assassination of Mujib and Zia's accession to power. The change of regime expedited the flow of aid from the Middle East, with Saudi Arabia as the most important source.

The main vehicles identified by the Saudis to disseminate Islamic values have been the Islamic non-governmental organisations, the *madrassa* (religious education) system and the fundamentalist parties, all of which are believed receive a great deal of official and unofficial aid from Saudi Arabia. The outcome of Saudi munificence has been the creation of alternative networks of patronage (scholarships, vocational training, student accommodation, employment and medical aid) which materially bolster the appeal of the Islamic constituency. Particularly noteworthy has been the remarkable expansion in the numbers and influence of community-oriented 'Islamic NGOs' – *Chattagram Al Jamiya Islamia, Jamat al Sabah, Dakheli Complex, Masjid* Mission, *Rabitat-ul-Islam, Mashjid Samaj* – all of whom draw on funds from the Middle East.[34] The training of imams by the Islamic Foundation to carry out village administration, basic health care, including maternity courses, and agricultural extension work exemplifies the entry of religious forces into the field of community development.

Various research organisations have also been set up to propagate Islamic values and build up a cadre of Islamic intellectuals to service the expansion in religious centres and the educational system. They seek to challenge head-on the ideology and rhetoric of developmentalism, clearly labelled 'Western'. The publications of the Islamic Foundation, for instance, are sold at unprofitably low prices to counter 'the fact that tons and tons of books on other ideologies in the best print and finest paper ... are being distributed free in this country'.[35]

Predictably, the rising Islamic intelligentsia pays special attention to the conspicuous place accorded to women in the state's developmentalist discourse, denouncing 'the so-called progressive intellectuals' who 'in symphony with their Western masters' attempt to argue for equality between the sexes.[36] The Islamic Economics Research Bureau recently published a collection of papers presented at a seminar on Islamic Economics (to which the Saudi ambassador was invited as Special Guest). Three papers dealt specifically with women, all of them focusing on the issue of employment. One common feature of these articles is their attempt to subvert WID arguments to provide support for their own very different positions. Thus, in common with many feminists within and outside Bangladesh, one article contests the 'Western' idea that housewives do not work, but draws from this the conclusion that women do not require further employment opportunities.[37] The other aspect of these articles is their overriding fear of the sexual chaos which might result from women and men working together: 'the close proximity of opposite sexes arouses lust and love for each other which on many occasions lead to immoral and scandalous affairs'.[38] The message is simple: tampering with the 'natural' principle of separate spheres for men and women can lead to the total collapse of the moral order.

Contradictions and Tensions in State Policy

Clearly, state attempts to win the support of the Islamic constituency have different gender implications from those associated with promoting Women and Development policy. In contrast to goals of women's emancipation and economic participation, the Islamic lobby in Bangladesh seeks to confine women to a domestic role and to impose controls on their mobility. Zia's strategy, and that of Ershad after him, has been a blatant balancing act between the conflicting gender ideologies implicit in different aid packages and a refusal to acknowledge their inherent contradictions.

Women have not benefited, for instance, from the money being poured into the religious education system by the government and the *Madrassa* Board. They are generally excluded from the new *madrassas*, the Islamic Centre for Vocational Training and the Islamic University currently being set up by the government. Such discriminatory provision of education clearly contravenes the commitment to sexual equality still contained within the Constitution as well as the declared intention of the state to increase educational opportunities for women.[39] Measures curtailing women's visibility in the public domain also contradict the state's declared policy of encouraging women's employment in the public sector and women's participation in competitive sports. Thus the earlier policy of recruiting women into the metropolitan police has been gradually modified so that women are now restricted to roadside traffic booths or check points: obviously maintaining a female police force which operated on the streets 'did not quite tally with the values being cultivated by an aspiring Islamic state'.[40]

These shifts and contradictions within state policy are possible because the state regards the issue of women's rights – and of Islam itself – in essentially instrumentalist terms. It is significant that the most organised political force on the religious right – the *Jamaat-e-Islami* – has remained in the opposition, unimpressed, it would appear, by the government's Islamic posturing. Some degree of coherence in overall government policy is made possible by the fact that both the Saudis and the US have the long-term interests of private capital at heart. Consequently, while Saudi influence is apparent in some public sector policy and within the community, it has generally refrained from interfering with the workings of the private sector.

The Emergence of Women's Movements

When the totality of successive policies of the Bangladesh state is taken into account, its championship of women's rights can be seen in an extremely cynical light. In its pursuit of political legitimacy and international aid, it professes to believe in both the emancipation of women as well as in its opposite. The clash is most evident in the sphere of gender relations because the position of women is a key factor distinguishing the two ideological packages. At the same time, it is precisely the existence of these conflicting interests and pressures on the state that has permitted some genuine advances to be made in women's interests. The WID influence has helped to challenge the monopoly of archaic ideological preconceptions about women at all levels of Bangladesh society. It has also opened up new possibilities for organisation and struggle around women's interests.

Since Liberation, political activities around women's rights have emerged as a distinct area of mobilisation. The women's wings of the two main parties – the BNP and the Awami League – are primarily active around welfare issues but also support equal rights for women. However, since they operate with a limited view of women's roles, their demand generally translates into putting pressure on the state to reform family and personal status law.

Women's rights are given a broader interpretation by the women's organisations associated with various left-wing parties. The most active of these is *Mahila Parishad* linked to the Communist Party, which now has over 30,000 members. *Mahila Parishad* has been active on a wide range of issues: it has fought for the rights of women workers both in factories and in middle-class occupations like banking, kept up the pressure on the government to implement the 10 per cent quota for women in employment and (in contrast to the BNP and Awami League) opposed reserved parliamentary

seats for women as an anti-democratic ploy to strengthen the party in power. More recently, it spearheaded a campaign against the practice of dowry and against violence against women and opened up shelters for women who had been victims of violence. Some of the laws passed by the government on these issues were a consequence of *Mahila Parishad*'s campaigns.

Despite its undeniable strengths, *Mahila Parishad*'s institutional links with the Communist Party have prevented it from giving an independent significance to women's oppression. The struggle for women's rights tends to be subsumed within the 'wider' struggle for socialism and democracy; the politics of gender in personal relations and everyday life and the ideological bases of women's subordination receive scant attention from its members. This was evident, for instance, in the national campaign against male violence which reached its peak in the summer of 1985. While *Mahila Parishad* took a leading role in denouncing male violence, it joined forces with the left opposition in linking it with the breakdown of law-and-order under Ershad's regime and focusing its efforts on bringing down the government. Protests by other women's groups that women were being portrayed in *Mahila Parishad*'s campaign as passive victims and that the issue of domestic violence (reported in the press far more frequently than recognised in the law-and-order explanation) was being side-stepped, were generally dismissed by *Mahila Parishad* as divisive, irrelevant and likely to alienate male support.

The other main location of struggles for women's rights is in grassroots development organisations which flourish outside the confines of official efforts. A significant number of these non-governmental organisations allocate a central place to women's oppression in their programmes for change. Rather than reproduce the welfarism that characterises most development initiatives, NGOs such as *Proshika, Nijera Kori* and *Saptagram* have shifted their primary objective from meeting the immediate needs of poor and landless women and men to that of their longer-term empowerment.

Notes

1 Benedict Anderson, *Imagined Communities: Reflections on the Origin and Spread of Nationalism* (London: Verso Press, 1983).

2 Nira Yuval-Davis, 'National Reproduction: Sexism, Racism and the State'. Paper presented at the British Sociological Association Conference (Manchester 1982) p. 3.

3 The first partition of Bengal in this century took place in 1905 in an attempt by the British Raj to weaken the power of Indian nationalism in the region and play up Hindu-Muslim differences: as H. H. Risley, Home Secretary to India, asserted, 'Bengal united is a power. Bengal divided will pull in different ways' (cited in Premen Addi and Ibne Azad. 'Politics and Society in Bengal' Robin Blackburn (ed.), in *Explosion in a Subcontinent* (London: Penguin Books, 1975) p. 111). The Muslim League was founded in Dhaka in the following year with the objectives of advancing Muslim interests in the subcontinent and promoting loyalty to British government. However, protest against partition shook not just (Hindu) Bengal, but the rest of India and it was annulled in 1911.

4 Tariq Ali, *Can Pakistan Survive? The Death of a State* (Middlesex: Penquin Books) 1983, p. 133.

5 David Kopf, 'Pakistani Identity and the Historiography of Muslim Bengal' in Richard L. Park (ed.), *Patterns of Change in Modern Bengal* South Asia Series Occasional Paper no. 29 (Asian Studies Centre East Lansing, Michigan State University, 1979) p. 111.

6 See for instance Clarence Maloney, K. M. Ashraful Aziz and Profulla C. Sarker, *Beliefs and Fertility in Bangladesh* (Dhaka: ICDDRB, 1981); A. M. A. Muhith, *Bangladesh: Emergence of a Nation* (Dhaka: Bangladesh Books International Ltd., 1978).

7 Examples of this for Bangladesh can be found in Therese Blanchet, *Meanings and Rituals of Birth in Rural Bangladesh* (Dhaka: University Press Ltd, 1984). For West Bengal see Lina M. Fruzetti, 'Ritual Status of Muslim Women in Rural India' in Jane J. Smith (ed.), *Women in Contemporary Muslim Societies* (London: Associated University Press, 1980).

8 See Blanchet, *Meanings and Rituals . . . .* and also Ralph W. Nicholas, 'Vaishnavism and Islam in Rural Bengal' in David Kopf (ed.), *Bengal Regional Identity* (Asian Studies Centre, Michigan State University, 1969).

9 Addi and Azad 'Politics and Society . . .'.

10 Romila Thapar, *A History of India Volume 1* (London: Penguin Books, 1968).

11 See, for instance, Blanchet, 'Meanings and Rituals' and Fruzetti, 'Ritual Status of Muslim Women'. See also contributions in Rafiuddin Ahmed (ed.), *Islam in Bangladesh: Society Culture and Politics* (Dhaka: Bangladesh Itihas Samiti, 1983).

12 In relation to Amir Ali, for instance, Kopf comments, 'His *Short History of the Saracens* (1900) illustrates clearly the heterogenetic identity of the Muslim Bengali intelligentsia; so intense was Amir Ali's concern with the temporally remote happenings of physically remote Arabia, that if one did not already know his Bengali origins, one could easily imagine the author to have been born an Arab' (in 'Pakistani Identity and . . .', p. 120).

13 Kopf, 'Pakistani Identity . . .', p. 112.

14 See Keith Callard, *Pakistan: A Political Study* (London: George Allen and Unwin Ltd, 1957), for an analysis of the political devices by which the Punjabi oligarchy secured its hegemony over the rest of the country. An analysis of the economic exploitation of East Pakistan is contained in Richard Nations, 'The Economic Structure of Pakistan and Bangladesh' in Blackburn, *Explosion in a Subcontinent*.

15 Tariq Ali, *Can Pakistan Survive*.

16 Zillur Rahman Khan, 'Islam and Bengali Nationalism' in Rafiuddin Ahmed (ed.), *Bangladesh: Society Religion and Politics* (South Asia Studies Group, University of Chittagong, 1985).

17 The vermilion spot traditionally worn by Hindu women as symbol of their marital state, but now widely adopted by both Muslim and Hindu Bengalis as a cosmetic feature.

18 Rehnuma Ahmed, 'Women's Movement in Bangladesh and the Left's Understanding of the Women Question', *Journal of Social Studies*, no. 30 (1985), pp. 27–56.

19 Rehnuma Ahmed, 'Women's Movement . . .'.

20 Tariq Ali, *Can Pakistan Survive*, p. 91.

21 Rahman Sobhan, *The Crisis of External Dependence: The Political Economy of Foreign Aid to Bangladesh* (London: Zed Press, 1982).

22 Rounaq Jahan, *Bangladesh Politics: Problems and Issues* (Dhaka: Dhaka University Press, 1980).

23 Rahman Sobhan, *The Crisis of External Dependence*.

24 See, for example, Shapan Adnan, Mahmud Khan, Malik Md. Shahnoor, Hussain Zillur Rahman, Mahbub Ahmed and Mahbubul Akash, *A Review of Landlessness in Rural Bangladesh: 1877–1977* (Department of Economics, University of Chittagong, 1978); Harry W. Blair, 'Ideology, Foreign Aid and Rural Poverty in Bangladesh: Emergence of the Like-Minded Group', *Journal of Social Studies*, vol. 34 (1986), pp. 1–27; F. Tomasson Januzzi and James T. Peach (eds), *The Agrarian Structure of Bangladesh: An Impediment to Development* (Boulder, Colorado: Westview Press, 1980). See also Rahman Sobhan, *The Crisis of External Dependence*.

25 Sigma Huda, 'Women and Law: Policy and Implementation', paper presented at a seminar on Women and Law organised by Women for Women, 13–15 September 1987, Dhaka.

26 The Awami League's gestures towards secularism stand in marked contrast to Bhutto's stance in Pakistan during the same period. Despite his left-wing populism, Bhutto's version of socialism carried the prefix of 'Islamic', he retained the status of Islamic Republic for Pakistan and declared Islam the state religion. A list of the symbols incorporated by Bhutto in his 1973 Constitution, which went beyond those in the Constitutions of 1956 and 1962, are cited in Khawar Mumtaz and Farida Shaheed, *Women of Pakistan: Two Steps Forward, One Step Back* (London: Zed Press, 1987).

27 B.K. Jahangir, *Problematics of Nationalism in Bangladesh* (Dhaka: Centre for Social Studies, 1986) p. 79.

28 Meghna Guhathakurta, 'Gender Violence in Bangladesh: The Role of the State', *Journal of Social Studies* no. 30 (1985), pp. 77–90.

29 *Zakat* represents the charitable obligations of wealthy Muslims sanctioned by Islam. The President's prominent role in the distribution of this fund serves to emphasise his association with a particular form of public patronage while simultaneously establishing his Islamic credentials.

30 Peter Charles O'Donnell, *Bangladesh: Biography of a Muslim Nation* (Boulder, Colarado: Westview Press, 1987) p. 255.

31 Ibid.

32 Talukder Maniruzzaman, 'Bangladesh Politics: Secular and Islamic Trends' in Rafiuddin Ahmed (ed.), *Islam in Bangladesh*.

33 Rehnuma Ahmed, 'Women's Movement...

34 Tanvir Mokkamel, *Samrajyabader Pancham Bahini* (Dhaka: Jatiya Shahitya Prakashini, 1987).

35 K.M. Mohsin, 'Trends of Islam in Bangladesh' in Rafiuddin Ahmed (ed.), *Islam in Bangladesh*.

36 Zohurul Islam, 'Women's Employment: Problems and Prospects' in *Thoughts on Islamic Economics*, Proceedings from a seminar on Islamic Economics held by the Islamic Economics Research Bureau, Dhaka, 1980, p. 250.

37 Shah Abdul Hannan, 'Women's Employment: Its Need and Appropriate Avenues' in *Thoughts on Islamic Economics*, Proceedings from a seminar on Islamic Economics held by the Islamic Economics Research Bureau, Dhaka, 1980, p. 240.

38 Muhammad Musharraf Hossain, 'The Employment for Women' in *Thoughts on Islamic Economics*, p. 270

39 Salma Khan, *The Fifty Percent Women in Development and Policy in Bangladesh* (Dhaka: University Press Ltd, 1988).

40 Meghna Guhathakurtha, 'Gender Violence in Bangladesh'.

13

Nationalist Agendas and Women's Rights

Conflicts in Afghanistan in the Twentieth Century

Valentine M. Moghadam

The case of Afghanistan is illustrative of the dilemmas feminists face in assessing the merits of nationalist movements in terms of their gender dynamics and outcomes for women. In the 1980s, two opposing movements – one Marxist-modernizing; the other Islamist-traditionalist – fought a long bloody war over divergent nationalist agendas and conceptions of "women's place." Although the Islamist movement was explicitly antifeminist, it received more international support (even from many European feminists) than did the modernizing government, because the mujahideen were perceived as attempting to liberate their country from Soviet domination. If there was a "feminist nationalist social movement," to use Lois West's term, in Afghanistan, I argue that it describes the efforts of the Marxists – men and women in and around the government and party – to modernize Afghanistan and enhance the status of the female population.

The 1980s conflict was not the first in Afghan history to be fought over "the woman question." In the early twentieth century, efforts by reformers and nationalists to improve the status of women, to establish an education system, and to modernize the economy and society met with the fierce resistance of traditionalists and ulema (Islamic clergy).

This chapter seeks to explain why women's rights and women's emancipation have been such vexed issues in Afghanistan, and in so doing provides a historical perspective on the Woman Question. I hope to show that notwithstanding the neglect of the gender dimension in nearly all accounts of the 1980s conflict in Afghanistan, the woman question was an integral part of the conflict between the tribal-Islamist mujahideen and the ruling People's Democratic Party of Afghanistan (PDPA), which came to power in the Saur (April) Revolution of 1978. The attempts by the PDPA to improve and enhance the status of women followed a Third World pattern of linking modernization, development, and socialism with women's emancipation. Civil war in Afghanistan was to a great extent a battle between modern revolutionaries and traditional social groups.

Perspectives on Modern South Asia: A Reader in Culture, History, and Representation, First Edition.
Edited by Kamala Visweswaran.
© 2011 Blackwell Publishing Ltd. Published 2011 by Blackwell Publishing Ltd.

At the center of the battle was the question of women. The conflict in the 1980s, then, was a continuation of the conflict in the 1920s.

I will argue here that the issue of women's rights in Afghanistan has been historically constrained by (a) the patriarchal nature of gender and social relations deeply embedded in traditional communities, and (b) the existence of a weak central state, that has been unable, since at least the beginning of this century, to implement modernizing programs and goals in the face of "tribal feudalism." The two are interconnected, for the state's weakness is correlated with a strong (if fragmented) society resistant to state bureaucratic expansion, civil authority, regulation, monopoly of the means of violence, and extraction – the business of modern states. These factors were behind the defeat of the modernizing nationalists in the 1920s. In the 1980s, war, the fundamentalist backlash, and a hostile international setting forced the Afghan leadership to shift from social revolution to national reconciliation, relegating the emancipation of women to a more stable future. And in April 1992 the government of Afghanistan collapsed and the mujahideen assumed control.

Part I of this chapter describes social structure in Afghanistan. Part II describes the early efforts to reform and modernize Afghan society. Part III describes the second major effort by modernizing nationalists to develop and transform the society – the Saur Revolution of 1978. Part IV reflects on feminism, nationalism, and "gendered cultural relativism."[1]

Part I. Social Structure in Afghanistan

Historically, the population of Afghanistan has been fragmented into myriad ethnic, linguistic, religious, kin-based, and regional groupings.[2] Afghan nationalism, properly speaking, is at best incipient because the concept of a nation-state, or of a national identity, is absent for much of the population, and has been promoted primarily by modernizing elites since the nineteenth century.[3] During most of the country's recent history, the fragmented groupings composed warring factions. Battles were fought principally over land and water, sometimes women and "honor," usually sheer power – or what Massell, writing of early-twentieth-century Central Asia, described as primordial cleavages and conflicts.[4]

One of the few commonalities in this diverse country is Islam. Afghan Islam is a unique combination of practices and precepts from the *Sharia* (Islamic canon law as delineated in religious texts) and tribal customs, particularly Pushtunwali, the tribal code of the Pushtuns, who constitute about half the population. On certain issues, Pushtunwali and Islam disagree.[5] For example, the absence of inheritance rights for females is contrary to Islamic law but integral to the complex web of the tribal exchange system. Contrary to the Islamic ban on usury, there has been widespread usury, a practice that has kept rural households in perpetual indebtedness. Exorbitant expenditure in marriages (for example, on dower such as *sheerbaha* and *walwar*) has also contributed to the rural household's debt accumulation. The Islamic dower, the *mahr* (a payment due from groom to bride that is an essential part of the formal Islamic marriage contract), has been abused. In the Quran it is a nominal fee, and in many Muslim countries its purpose is to provide a kind of social insurance for the wife in the event of divorce or widowhood. In the Afghan patriarchal context, the *mahr* (or *walwar* in Pashtu) is the payment to the bride's father as compensation for the loss of his daughter's labor in the household unit.[6]

Afghan rural and poor women work extraordinarily hard, but their ability to contribute substantially to household survival or the family income takes place within a patriarchal context of women's subordination and intrahousehold inequality. In such a context, a woman's labor power is controlled and allocated by someone else, the products of her labor are managed by others, and she receives no remuneration for work performed. In areas where carpet making is a commercial enterprise, male kin are allowed to exploit women's labor without any wage payment, as Afshar has found for Iran and Berik has described for Turkey. In extended patriarchal, patrilineal households, as Kandiyoti has argued, collective (male) interests dictate strict control of a woman's labour deployment throughout her lifetime.[7]

Part II. Modernizing Nationalism: The Early Years

Reforms to improve the status of women began during the reign of Abdur Rahman Khan, who ascended the throne in 1880. He abolished a longstanding customary law that, in violation of Islamic law, bound a wife not only to her husband but to his entire family as well: a widow who wanted to remarry had to marry her dead husband's next of kin, often against her will.[8] Among Abdur Rahman's other measures was a law requiring the registration of marriages (*sabt*). He also modified a law pertaining to child marriages, permitting a girl who had been given in marriage before she had reached the age of puberty to refuse or accept her marriage ties when she attained maturity. Still another law allowed a wife to sue her husband for divorce or alimony in cases involving cruelty or nonsupport.[9]

Mahmud Tarzi (1866–1935), a royal adviser, was the first Afghan to take a positive stand on feminism, dedicating to famous women in history a series of articles that discussed the many abilities of women. Because in his view the health, welfare, and education of Afghan families were essential to Afghan progress, he attacked the extravagant expenditures incurred in connection with multiple marriages, which often financially ruined families.[10] His views were supported by the ruler, Habibullah Khan, who attempted to limit the burdensome expenses incurred in connection with marriage. To meet the costs, most Afghans had to borrow, at times paying as much as 75 percent interest. In 1922 Habibullah put a ceiling on the amount that could be spent, urging his people to abandon the customary public celebrations in favor of private parties. By establishing Habibiyeh College, Habibullah also sought to broaden the education system. Despite the founding of the Afghan Ministry of Education, government attempts to improve and standard-ize the curriculum were not totally successful.

Gregorian writes that the mullahs, especially those outside Kabul, resented the government's control of education, the teacher-training center, and the teaching of English and of modern subjects in general, and vehemently resisted all further innovation.[11]

Habibullah Khan was assassinated in 1919, and his son, King Amanullah who ruled from 1919–1929, had the enormous task of convincing the religious establishment that modern secular education and Islam were not incompatible, and that the schools he built did not threaten the sanctity or spiritual message of Islam in Afghanistan.[12] His most audacious acts were to begin a study-abroad program for Afghan students and to open the first schools for girls.

In examining Amanullah's reform program and the organized resistance to it, one discovers parallels with the experience of the PDPA government some fifty years later. According to Gregorian, Amanullah's general program to improve the position of women was promoted by his wife, Queen Soraya (who founded the first women's magazine, *Ershad-e Niswan*), the reformer Mahmud Tarzi and his wife, the small intelligentsia, and the modernist and nationalist Young Afghans, who were impressed by developments in Turkey, Iran, and Egypt. In 1921 Amanullah enacted the Family Code, which undertook to regulate marriages and engagements. Child marriages and intermarriage between close kin were outlawed as contrary to Islamic principles. In the new code Amanullah reiterated Abdur Rahman's ruling that a widow was to be free of the domination of her husband's family. He followed his father's example and placed tight restrictions on wedding expenses, including dowries, and granted wives the right to appeal to the courts if their husbands did not adhere to Quranic tenets regarding marriage. In the fall of 1924, Afghan women were given the right to choose their husbands, a measure that incensed the traditionalists.[13]

The presence in Kabul of a considerable number of unveiled women, especially Turkish women who had abandoned the veil and adopted modern dress, undoubtedly encouraged the efforts of the new Afghan feminists. However, their greatest support came from Amanullah himself, who believed that the keystone of the future structure of new Afghanistan would be the emancipation of women.[14] The Afghan press, including bulletins of the War Office, took part in the emancipation campaign. In 1928, during the final months of his rule, Amanullah made a frontal assault on the institution of purdah, which "hid half the Afghan nation." Because of his efforts and the personal example of Queen Soraya, some one hundred Afghan women had reportedly discarded the veil by October 1928.

By this time, Afghan legislation was among the most progressive in the Muslim world. No other country had yet addressed the sensitive issues of child marriage and polygyny. Afghan family law on these issues became the model for similar reforms in Soviet Central Asia in 1926.[15] It is not surprising that the family law of 1921 was a major cause of the uprising instigated by the clergy in 1924.

The first organized reaction against Amanullah reforms was directed against the controversial administrative code, the Nizam-nameh, which he promulgated in 1923. Among other things, the code attempted to liberalize the position of women and to permit the government to regulate the various family problems formerly dealt with by the local mullah. A few traditionalist mullahs inveighed against the new code, asserting that it was contrary to the precepts of Islamic law. Their cause was picked up in 1924 by the Mangal tribe of the Khost region, and in March armed warfare broke out. The religious and tribal leaders were particularly exercised over the sections of the code that deprived men of full authority over wives and daughters, and they were further incensed at the opening of public schools for girls.

The Khost rebellion continued for more than nine months. Gregorian writes that both the rebels and the government side suffered enormous losses, and that the cost of the rebellion represented the total government receipts for two years. The king was forced to postpone various modernization projects and to revoke or modify many important sections of

the Nizam-nameh; the schooling of girls, for example, was limited to the under-twelve age group. In 1928 the Loya Jirga, the traditional Afghan consultative body, rejected Amanullah's proposal to set a minimum age for marriage of eighteen for women and twenty for men. The Loya Jirga also vehemently opposed modern, Western education for Afghan girls in Afghanistan or outside it.

In the autumn of 1928, a group of female students was sent to Turkey for higher education, and the Association for the Protection of Women's Rights (Anjoman-i Hemayat-i Neswan) was established to help women fight domestic injustice and take a role in public life. The queen presided over several committees to strengthen the emancipation campaign. These unprecedented measures, which violated traditional norms, offended the religious leaders and their following, especially in rural areas. Reaction against the campaign for women's emancipation was a major factor in the outbreak of violent disturbances in November and December.

When the king banned the practice of polygyny among government officials, it caused an uproar among the religious establishment. A tribal revolt ensued, led by Bacha-i Saqqo, a Tajik rebel claiming Islamic credentials. As the political situation deteriorated, Amanullah was compelled to cancel most of his social reforms and to suspend his controversial administrative measures. The Afghan girls studying in Constantinople were to be recalled, and the schools for girls were to be closed; women were not to go unveiled or cut their hair; the mullahs were no longer to be required to obtain teaching certificates; compulsory military recruitment was to be abandoned; and the old tribal system was to be reinstated.[16]

As a last, desperate concession, the unhappy king agreed to the formation of a council of fifty notables, to be chosen from among "the most respected religious luminaries and tribal chieftains," and promised to abide by their advice as well as to conform to Islamic law as interpreted by the orthodox religious leaders. Any measure the government proposed to enact was to be ratified by this council. But in the end, all of these concessions were to no avail. The rebels attacked Kabul, and Amanullah abdicated and left Afghanistan.

Not until the 1950s were reforms attempted again. In 1950 a law was passed banning ostentatious life-cycle ceremonies. It prohibited many of the expensive aspects of birth, circumcision, marriage, and burial rituals but was difficult to enforce. The Marriage Law of 1971 once again tried to curb the indebtedness arising from the costs of marriage. The Civil Law of 1977 abolished child marriage and established sixteen as the minimum age of marriage for girls, but the law was ignored. Furthermore, it left the husband's right to unilateral divorce basically untouched.[17]

The above overview suggests the enormous difficulty faced by Afghan modernizers. The Afghan state had been too weak to implement reforms or to undertake modernization in an effective way, and was constantly confronted by religious and tribal forces seeking to prevent any change whatsoever, particularly in regard to their power. Nevertheless, as in many other Third World countries in the 1960s, a left-wing modernizing elite organized itself to address the country's problems and to steer Afghanistan away from its dependency on US aid money.

III. The Saur Revolution and Women's Rights

In 1965 a group from the small Afghan intelligentsia formed the People's Democratic Party of Afghanistan (PDPA). Evoking the Amanullah experiment, the PDPA envisaged a national democratic government to liberate Afghanistan from backwardness. Among its demands were primary education in their mother tongue for all children and the development of the country's various languages and cultures. Its social demands included guarantees of the right to work, equal treatment for women, a forty-two-hour week, paid sickness and maternity leave, and a ban on child labor. That same year, six women activists formed the Democratic Organization of Afghan Women (DOAW), whose main objectives were to eliminate illiteracy among

women, forced marriage, and the brideprice. The 1964 Constitution had granted women the right to vote, and thus in the 1970s four women from the DOAW were elected to Parliament. Both the PDPA and the DOAW were eager for profound, extensive, and permanent social change.[18]

Among the most remarkable and influential of the DOAW activists was Anahita Ratebzad. In the 1950s she studied nursing in the United States, and then returned to Kabul as director and instructor of nursing at Women's Hospital. When the faculty for women at Kabul University was established, she entered the medical college and became a member of its teaching staff upon graduation in 1963. She joined the PDPA in 1965 and was one of the four female candidates for Parliament. In 1968 conservative members of Parliament proposed enactment of a law prohibiting Afghan girls from studying abroad. Hundreds of girls demonstrated in opposition. In 1970 two mullahs protested public evidence of female liberation such as miniskirts, women teachers, and schoolgirls by shooting at the legs of women in Western dress and splashing them with acid; among those who joined the mullahs was Gulbeddin Hekmatyar (who went on to be a leading figure in the mujahideen, one of the "freedom fighters" hailed by President Reagan). This time five thousand girls demonstrated.[19]

In April 1978, the PDPA seized power in what came to be called the Saur (April) Revolution, and introduced a program to change the political and social structure of Afghan society. Three decrees were its main planks: Decree No. 6 was intended to put an end to land mortgage and indebtedness; No. 7 was designed to stop the payment of brideprice and give women more freedom of choice in marriage; and No. 8 consisted of rules and regulations for the confiscation and redistribution of land.[20] The decrees were complementary, but Decree No. 7 seems to have been the most controversial. On November 4, 1978, President Noor Mohammad Taraki declared: "Through the issuance of decrees no. 6 and 7, the hard-working peasants were freed from bonds of oppressors and money-lenders, ending the sale of girls for good as hereafter nobody would be entitled to sell any girl or woman in this country."[21] The six articles of Decree No. 7 were as follows:

Article 1. No one shall engage a girl or give her in marriage in exchange for cash or commodities.

Article 2. No one shall compel the bridegroom or his guardians to give holiday presents to the girl or her family.

Article 3. The girl or her guardian shall not take cash or commodities in the name of dower [*mahr*] in excess of ten dirham [Arabic coinage] according to Shari'at [Islamic law], which is not more than 300 afs. [about US $10] on the basis of the bank rate of silver.

Article 4. Engagements and marriage shall take place with the full consent of the parties involved: (a) No one shall force marriage; (b) No one shall prevent the free marriage of a widow or force her into marriage because of family relationships [the levirate] or patriarchal ties; (c) No one shall prevent legal marriages on the pretext of engagement, forced engagement expenses, or by using force.

Article 5. Engagement and marriages for women under 16 and men under 18 are not permissible.

Article 6. (1) Violators shall be liable to imprisonment from six months to three years; (2) Cash or commodities accepted in violation of the provisions of this decree shall be confiscated.[22]

The PDPA government also embarked upon an aggressive literacy campaign that was led by the DOAW, whose function was to educate women, bring them out of seclusion, and initiate social programs. PDPA cadre established literacy classes for men, women, and children in villages, and by August 1979 the government had established six hundred new schools.[23]

The PDPA program was clearly audacious, aimed at the rapid transformation of a patriarchal society and a power structure based on tribal and landlord authority. Revolutionary change, state-building, and women's rights subsequently went hand in hand. This led one commentator to write:

The novel character of the new regime [in Afghanistan] soon became apparent. It committed itself to land reform, to equality of the nationalities, to emancipating women, to a solution of the nomadic question. So it was that at a time and in a place suspected by few, and in a country renowned only for colonial war and narcotic plenitude, a revolutionary process of some description had begun.[24]

The emphasis on women's rights on the part of the PDPA reflected (a) its socialist/Marxist ideology; (b) its modernizing and egalitarian outlook; (c) its social base and origins (urban middle-class, professionals educated in the United States, the USSR, India, or western and eastern Europe; and (d) the influence of women members of the PDPA, such as Anahita Ratebzad. In 1976 Ratebzad had been elected to the central committee of the PDPA; after the Saur Revolution, she was elected to the Revolutionary Council of the Democratic Republic of Afghanistan (DRA) and appointed minister of social affairs. Other influential PDPA women in the Taraki government (April 1978–September 1979) included (no last name) Firouza, director of the Afghan Red Crescent Society (Red Cross); and Professor R. S. Siddiqui (who was especially outspoken in her criticism of "feudalistic patriarchal relations"). In the Amin government (September–December 1979), the following women headed schools and the women's organization, as well as sat on government subcommittees: Fawjiyah Shahsawari, Dr. Aziza, Shirin Afzal, Alamat Tolqun. These were the women who were behind the program for women's rights. Their intention was to expand literacy, especially for girls and women; encourage income-generating projects and employment for women; provide health and legal services for women; and eliminate those aspects of Muslim family law that discriminate against women – unilateral male repudiation, a father's exclusive rights to child custody, unequal inheritance, and male guardianship over women.

Patriarchal resistance to change

PDPA attempts to change marriage laws, expand literacy, and educate rural girls met with strong opposition. Fathers with unmarried daughters resented Decree No. 7 most because they could no longer expect to receive large brideprice payments, and because it represented a threat to male honor. According to Beattie, "By banning brideprice – and especially by declaring that women could marry whom they pleased – it threatened to undermine the strict control over women on which the maintenance of male honor depended."[25]

The right of women to divorce was one of the most significant measures introduced by the PDPA. Although the divorce law was never officially announced, owing to the outbreak of tribal Islamist opposition to the regime, the family courts (*mahakem-i famili*), mostly presided over by female judges, provided hearing sessions for discontented wives and sought to protect their rights to divorce and on related issues, such as alimony, child custody, and child support.

PDPA attempts to institute compulsory education – provided for in the Constitution of 1964 but ignored by the population – were opposed by traditionalists and by fathers keen to maintain control over their daughters. Believing that women should not appear at public gatherings, villagers often refused to attend classes after the first day. PDPA cadre viewed this attitude as retrograde and resorted to various forms of persuasion, including physical force, to change minds. Often PDPA cadre were either ousted from villages or murdered. In the summer of 1978 refugees began pouring into Pakistan, giving as their major reason the forceful implementation of the literacy program among women. In Kandahar, three literacy workers from the women's organization were killed as symbols of the unwanted revolution. Two men killed all the women in their families to save them from "dishonor."[26] An Islamist opposition began organizing and conducted several armed actions against the government in spring 1979.

Internal battles within the PDPA (especially between its two wings, Parcham and Khalq) exacerbated the government's difficulties. In September 1979 President Taraki was killed on orders of his deputy, Hafizullah Amin, a ruthless and ambitious man who imprisoned and executed hundreds of his own comrades in addition to further alienating the population.[27] The Pakistani regime of Zia ul-Haq was opposed to leftists next door, and supported the mujahideen armed uprising. In December 1979 the Soviet army intervened, beginning a long military engagement in the civil war on the side of the PDPA government. Amin was killed and succeeded by Babrak Karmal, who initiated what was called "the second phase" (*marhale-i dovvom*).

PDPA and DOAW attempts to extend literacy to rural girls have been widely criticized for heavy-handedness by most commentators on Afghanistan. Three points regarding this criticism are in order. First, literacy campaigns are common during or following popular revolutions and movements for national or social liberation: the Bolsheviks, Chinese, Cubans, Vietnamese, Angolans, Palestinians, Eritreans, and Nicaraguans had extensive literacy campaigns. Second, the PDPA's rationale for pursuing the rural literacy campaign with some zeal was that all previous reformers had made literacy a matter of choice; male guardians had chosen not to allow their females to be educated, hence 98 percent of Afghan women were illiterate. It was therefore decided that literacy was not a matter of (men's) choice but, rather, a matter of principle and law. Third, state coercion to raise the status of women had been employed elsewhere, notably Soviet Central Asia and Turkey in the 1920s, and other governments have issued decrees that have been resisted. The last point is not to condone the use of force but to point out that rights, reforms, and revolutions have been effected coercively or attained through struggle.

It should be noted that not everyone in the PDPA and the DOAW was in favor of the pace of the reforms. According to Soraya, many DOAW activists, including herself, thought they should be sought in a more measured fashion. As a result of her antagonism toward Hafizullah Amin, Soraya, like many in the Parcham wing, was imprisoned and even tortured. She and the others were released after the Soviet intervention, the death of Amin, and his replacement by Babrak Karmal.[28]

In 1980 the PDPA slowed down its reform program and announced its intention to eliminate illiteracy in the cities in seven years and in the provinces in ten. In an interview that year Anahita Ratebzad conceded errors, "in particular the compulsory education of women;" "the reactionary elements immediately made use of these mistakes to spread discontent among the population."[29] Despite the moderation (including concessions such as the restoration of Muslim family law),[30] the Peshawar-based opposition – supported by Pakistan, the United States, China, the Islamic Republic of Iran, and Saudi Arabia – intensified its efforts to destroy the Kabul regime. In contrast to other states, the Afghan state was unable to impose its will through an extensive administrative and military apparatus. As a result, the program for land redistribution and women's rights faltered. The efforts to raise women's status through legal innovations regarding marriage were stymied by patriarchal structures highly resistant to change, by a hostile international environment, and by an extremely destructive civil war.

There can be no doubt that the manner in which land reform and women's emancipation were implemented immediately after the Saur Revolution was seriously flawed. Some of the bold symbols of the revolution – red flags, the term *comrade*, pictures of Lenin, and the like – were also ill-advised, considering the extremely conservative and patriarchal social structure, and they contributed to the hostility. Nevertheless, the conflict in Afghanistan must be understood as contestation over two unalterably opposed political-cultural projects: development and reform on the one hand, tribal authority and patriarchal relations on the other.

The literature on Afghanistan has been exceedingly partisan, and much of it very pro-mujahideen, with a noticeable reluctance to discuss the positive aspects of the PDPA state's social program, notably its policy on women's rights. One political journalist, however, has written that "one genuine achievement of the revolution has been the emancipation of (mainly urban) women."

> "There is no doubt that thousands of women are committed to the regime, as their prominent participation in Revolutionary Defense Group militias shows. Eyewitnesses stated that militant militiawomen played a key role in defending the besieged town of Urgun in 1983. Four of the seven militia commanders appointed to the Revolutionary Council in January 1986 were women."[31]

As one enthusiastic teenage girl said to me at a PDPA rally in Kabul in early 1989: "This revolution was made for women!"

The early PDPA emphasis on the women question subsided in favor of a concerted effort at "national reconciliation," that began in January 1987. In the Constitution of November 1988, the result of a Loya Jirga, or traditional assembly, PDPA members and activists from the Women's Council tried to retain an article stipulating the equality of women with men; it was opposed by the non-PDPA members of the assembly. A compromise was reached in Article 38:

> Citizens of the Republic of Afghanistan – men and women – have equal rights and duties before the law, irrespective of national, racial, linguistic, tribal, educational and social status, religion, creed, political conviction, occupation, kinship, wealth, and residence. Designation of any illegal privilege of discrimination against rights and duties of citizens are forbidden.[32]

Notes

1 This chapter draws on my previously published work, especially chapter 7 in *Modernizing Women: Gender and Social Change in the Middle East* (Boulder: Lynne Rienner, 1993); and "Reform, Revolution and Reaction: The Trajectory of the Woman Question in Afghanistan," in *Gender and National Identity: Women and Politics in Muslim Societies* ed. V. M. Moghadam (London: Zed Books, 1994).

2   Louis Dupree, *Afghanistan* (Princeton: Princeton University Press, 1980); Olivier Roy, *Islam and Resistance in Afghanistan*, 2nd ed. (Cambridge: Cambridge University Press, 1990).

3   Vartan Gregorian, *The Emergence of Modern Afghanistan* (Stanford: Stanford University Press, 1969); Thomas Hammond, *Red Flag Over Afghanistan* (Boulder: Westview Press, 1984), p. 5; Mark Urban, *War in Afghanistan* (New York: St. Martin's Press, 1988), p. 204.

4   Gregory Massell, *The Surrogate Proletariat: Moslem Women and Revolutionary Strategies in Soviet Central Asia, 1919–1929* (Princeton: Princeton University Press, 1974), p. 9.

5   On Pushtunwali and Islam, see Roy, *Islam and Resistance in Afghanistan*, pp. 34–7; John C. Griffiths, *Afghanistan* (Boulder: Westview Press, 1981), pp. 111–12; Inger Boesen, "Conflicts of Solidarity in Pukhtun Women's Lives," in *Women in Islamic Society* ed. Bo Utas, (Copenhagen: Scandinavian Institute of Asian Studies, 1983).

6   On the brideprice and property rights, see Nancy Tapper, "Causes and Consequences of the Abolition of Brideprice in Afghanistan," in *Revolutions and Rebellions in Afghanistan* ed. M. Nazif Shahrani and Robert L. Canfield (Berkeley: Institute of International Studies, 1984); and *Bartered Brides: Politics, Gender and Marriage in Our Afghan Tribal Society* (Cambridge: Cambridge University Press, 1991). A comprehensive study is in Mohammad Hashim Kamali, *Law in Afghanistan: A Study of the Constitutions, Matrimonial Law and the Judiciary* (Leiden: E.J. Brill, 1985). See also Raja Anwar, *The Tragedy of Afghanistan* (London: Verso, 1988), esp. chap. 11, "The Contradictions of Afghan Society."

7   Haleh Afshar, "The Position of Women in an Iranian Village," in *Women, Work and Ideology in the Third World*, ed. H. Afshar (London: Tavistock, 1985), esp. pp. 75–76; Günseli Berik, *Women Carpet Weavers in Rural Turkey: Patterns of Employment, Earnings, and Status* (Geneva: ILO, 1987), esp. chap. 4; Deniz Kandiyoti, "Rural Transformation in Turkey and Its Implications for Women's Status," in UNESCO, *Women on the Move* (Paris; UNESCO, 1984), pp. 17–30.

8   Urban, *War in Afghanistan*, p. 138. See also Lajoinie, *Conditions des femmes en Afghanistan*, p. 61. This is known as the levirate.

9   Gregorian, The *Emergence of Modern Afghanistan*, p. 139.

10   Ibid., p. 172.

11   Ibid., p. 198.

12   Ibid., p. 241.

13   Ibid., p. 244.

14   Ibid., p. 244.

15   See Massell, *The Surrogate Proletariat*, p. 219.

16   Gregorian, *The Emergence of Modern Afghanistan*, p. 264.

17   Kamali, *Law in Afghanistan*, pp. 86–87.

18   Interview with Soraya, DOAW founding member and past president, Kabul, February 6, 1989, and Helsinki, October 8, 1990. Soraya identified three of the four women parliamentarians: Anahita Ratebzad, Massouma Esmaty Wardak, and Mrs. Saljugi.

19   This paragraph draws from Nancy Hatch Dupree, "Revolutionary Rhetoric and Afghan Women," in Shahrani and Canfield, *Revolutions and Rebellions in Afghanistan*.

20   Hugh Beattie, "Effects of the Saur Revolution in Nahrin," in Shahrani and Canfield, *Revolutions and Rebellions in Afghanistan*, p. 186.

21   Quoted in Tapper, "Abolition of Brideprice in Afghanistan," p. 294.

22   Beattie, "Effects of the Saur Revolution in Nahrin."

23   Suzanne Jolicoeur Katsikas, *The Arc of Socialist Revolutions: Angola to Afghanistan* (Cambridge, MA: Schenkman, 1982), p. 231.

24   Fred Halliday, "Revolution in Afghanistan," *New Left Review* 112 (November/December 1978): 3.

25   Beattie, "Effects of the Saur Revolution in Nahrin," p. 191.

26   See Dupree, *Afghanistan*.

27   See Anwar, *The Tragedy of Afghanistan*, eps. chaps. 14, 15.

28   Interview with Soraya, Kabul, February 6, 1989.

29   Quoted in Dupree, *Afghanistan*, p. 330.

30   The formal reinstatement of Muslim Family Law did not apply to party members. Interview with a PDPA official, New York, October 28, 1986.

31   Urban, *War in Afghanistan*, p. 209.

32   Interview with Farid Mazdak, PDPA official, Kabul, February 9, 1989.

14

The State and National Foundation in the Maldives

Rizwan A. Ahmad

Metonyms of Foundation

On 10 September 1994, *Aafathis*, the Maldivian morning daily, announced that it was 867 years to the day since the Maldives had been converted[1] to Islam by the Arab saint Abu al-Barakat al-Barbari. The headline article related the events of the conversion, the most detailed account of which is to be found in the travel narrative of Ibn Batuta, who visited the Maldives between 1343 and 1344 and again in 1346. Ibn Batuta, who briefly held the post of *Qazi* (chief judge) in the islands, relates:

> The cause of these islands becoming Mohammedan was, as it is generally received among them, and as some learned and respectable persons among them informed me, as follows. When they were in a state of infidelity, there appeared to them every month a spectre from among the genli. This came from the sea. Its appearance was that of a ship filled with candles. When they saw him, it was their custom to take and dress up a young woman who was a virgin, and place her in the idol-temple which stood on the sea-shore and had windows looking towards him. Here they left her for the night. When they came in the morning, they found her vitiated and dead. This they continued doing month after month, casting lots among themselves, and each, to whom the lot fell, giving up and dressing out his daughter, for the spectre. After this there came to them a western Arab, named Abu'l Barakat the Berber. This was a holy man, and one who had committed the Koran to memory. He happened to lodge in the house of an old woman in the island of Mohl.[2] One day, when he entered the house, he saw her with a company of her female inmates weeping and lamenting, and asked them what was the matter. A person who acted as interpreter between him and them said, that the lot had fallen upon this old woman, who was now adorning her daughter for the spectre: for this it was she was crying: this too was her only child. The Mogrebine, who was

Perspectives on Modern South Asia: A Reader in Culture, History, and Representation, First Edition.
Edited by Kamala Visweswaran.
© 2011 Blackwell Publishing Ltd. Published 2011 by Blackwell Publishing Ltd.

a beardless man, said to her: I will go to the spectre tonight instead of thy daughter. If he takes me, then I shall redeem her: but if I come off safe, then that will be to the praise of God. They carried him accordingly to the idol-house that night, as if he had been the daughter of the old woman, the magistrate knowing nothing whatsoever of the matter. The Mogrebine entered, and sitting down in the window, began to read the Koran. By and by the spectre came, with eyes flaming like fire; but when he had got near enough to hear the Koran, he plunged into the sea. In this manner the Mogrebine remained till morning, reading his Koran, when the old woman came with her household, and the great personages of the district, in order to fetch out the young woman and burn her, as it was their custom. But when they saw the old man reading the Koran, just as they had left him, they were greatly astonished. The old woman then told them what she had done, and why she had desired him to do this. They then carried the Mogrebine to their King, whose name was Shanwan, and told him the whole affair; and he was much astonished at the Arab. Upon this the Mogrebine presented the doctrine of Islamism [sic] to the King, and pressed him to receive it; who replied: Stay with us another month, and then, if you will do as you now have done, and escape from the spectre with safety, I will become a Mohammedan. So God opened the heart of the King for the reception of Islamism before the completion of the month, of himself, of his household, his children, and his nobles. When, however, the second month came, they went with the Mogrebine to the idol-house, according to former custom, the King himself being also present; and when the following morning had arrived, they found the Mogrebine sitting and reading his Koran; having had the same rencontre with the spectre that he had on the former occasion. They then broke the images, rased the idol-house to the ground, and all became Mohammedans. The sect into which they entered was that of the Mogrebine; namely, that of Ibn Malik. Till this very day they make much of the Mogrebines, on account of this man. I was residing for some time in these islands, without having any knowledge of this circumstance; upon a certain night, however, when I saw them exulting and praising God,

as they were proceeding towards the sea, with Korans on their heads, I asked them what they were about; when they told me of the spectre. They then said: Look towards the sea, and you will see him. I looked, and behold, he resembled a ship filled with candles and torches. This, said they, is the spectre; which, when we do as you have seen us doing, goes away and does no injury. (Ibn Batuta, 1984: 179–80)[3]

Ibn Batuta's account, popularly known in the Maldives as the *Rannamari story*, after the *jinn* of the sea he mentions, is at variance with the version of events related in the Maldivian state chronicle, the *Tarikh*, translated by H.C.P. Bell (1940).[4] This records:

When God wished to uplift the people of the Maldives from the pit of ignorance, to save them from the ways of Unbelievers, the wrong path, and idle life, and the worship of idols, and to show them the right path and the light of Islám, the most religious God fearing Chief of Saints of that age, who was acquainted with the hidden secrets of the Everlasting World, whose knowledge was as deep as the Ocean, whom we to this day acknowledge to be the *Maulána Shaikh Yúsúf Shams-ud-din of Tabríz* was inspired by God with the desire to visit the Máldives.

After that he disappeared from his native town, called Tabríz (in Persia), and appeared at the Máldives.

He (the Saint) called upon the natives, then steeped in ignorant worship of idols instead of the Almighty God, to become Muslims.

Until they had been shown great miracles, not a single man offered to embrace the Faith of Islám.

One such miracle displayed was a colossal giant, whose head well-nigh touched the sky. By reason of their great fear, the King and all the inhabitants of Mále became Muslims.

Thereupon, this Saint of Tabríz bestowed the title *'The Sultán Muhammad'* on the King, who had been proclaimed (at his accession) upon beat of *Koli* (gong) *'Sri Bavanáditta'* by the Máldivians.

Afterwards the Sultán sent to every Island of the Máldives persons who converted all the inhabitants, whether willing or unwilling, to the

Muslim Faith; so that throughout the Máldives there were none but Muslims.

The Sultán and his subjects were converted by 'Tabrízigefánu' on the 12th day of the month Rabí-ul-Ákhir, in the year 548 of the *Hijra*, being the 17th year of the rule of the *Khálif* Muqtafi-al-Amru'llahi at Baghdád, and the 13th year of Sultán Muhammad's reign over the Máldive Islands.

He (the Sultán) lived thirteen … years after becoming a Muslim.

It is related, that on the advice of 'Tabrízigefánu', rules were made for the administration of the Country, and religious laws were enforced. Religious knowledge was widely disseminated; signs of idolatry effaced; and Mosques built in all the Islands for the due observance of Friday congregational prayers (*Jum'a*)

Not long afterwards, whilst the Government was being carried on smoothly, *Tabrízigefánu*, the greatly reverenced, died at Mále, was buried in a tomb, now famed and widely venerated. (May God bestow on him Everlasting Peace, and may he, through his saintliness, bring us prosperity.)

After his death, the Sultán lived for a few years. He was the first King of Maldives to become a Muslim. As Ruler, he was just and pious, observing religious and secular laws: and honest in all his dealings. *Shariat* (Muslim laws) were drawn up in proper form.

This Sultán loved his subjects. When meting out justice, no difference was made between relatives and others. He was wise, considerate, mild-tempered, kind, and generous in almsgiving. He contributed the *Zakát* (alms), was an observer of Fasts, and regularly offered up prayers – in short, he was a Saint.

One day it is said that he (the Sultán) told the (Mále) inhabitants that he was preparing to go on (the *Hajj*) Pilgrimage, that a vessel would arrive the following Friday, and that he would sail in it.

On that Friday, a ship arrived, and anchored off Mále. At the conclusion of the *Jum'a* (Friday) prayers, (the Sultán) left the Mosque and hastened to the seashore. Thence, without attendants or provisions, he embarked with the ship's crew alone; and the vessel passed from sight like lightning flash or flight of bird. Deprived thus of their Ruler, the people were

filled with great wonder. This occurred in the *Hijra* year 561.

Altogether he (the Sultán) had occupied the throne for twenty-five … years, twelve … years as an Infidel and the remaining thirteen … years as a Muslim. (Bell, 1940: 203–4)

From the outset, it can be noted that the accounts differ in their respective attribution of the Islamic conversion of the Maldives to either a Maghrebi saint, Abu al-Barakat, or a Persian saint, Yusuf Shamsuddin. Further, while the former *shaykh* sought to quell fear to effect religious transformation, the latter sought to inspire it. Those Maldivians who express a preference and seek to accredit Yusuf Shamsuddin in the matter, argue that the use in Dhivehi (Maldivian), of Persian religious terms – *namadu* (from the Persian *namaaz*) for prayer as opposed to the Arabic *salat*, and *roda* (from the Persian *rozah*) instead of *sawm* for fasting – demonstrates the validity of their claims. Further, as Forbes notes, a wooden panel inscribed in Arabic, dated AH 738/AD 1338, which used to hang in the Hukuru Miskit (Friday Mosque) in Malé, records that: 'Abu'l Barakat Yusuf al-Tabrizi arrived in this country, and the *sultan* became a Muslim at his hands in the month of *Rabi 'al-Akhir* 548' (Forbes, 1983: 71 n. 28). The panel, which predates Ibn Batuta's arrival in the Maldives by five years, could account for his accreditation to *Barbari* as the result of a misreading of the *nuktah* (scriptural dots); something which would allow either of the names to be inferred and *Barbari* to be substituted for *Tabrizi*. Those who argue for Abu al-Barakat's origins in the Maghreb validate their claim by arguing that, as Ibn Batuta stated, the *Maliki madhhab* (school of Sunni religious practice), predominant in North Africa, was followed in the Maldives prior to the adoption of the *Shafi'i madhhab* in the 16th century.[5]

The *Rannamari story*, I argue, enacts (following White, 1975: 9) a *romantic* emplotment – a drama of national redemption and transcendence of worldly limitation. The community of the *Dhivehin* (Maldivians), subjects of the state newly established by Koimala, are portrayed as steeped in *infidelity* (*kufr*). As a result, in the face of the supernatural unknown, the community is powerless to counter its affliction by demonic disruption and violation.[6]

As an account of the conversion of the islanders, the *Rannamari story* culminates in the encounter between the Saint and King. In the reading I propose, the King as metonymic representative of a weak state, is unable to protect the people from disorder, and is clearly to be seen as submitting to Barakat, the metonymic personification of Divine Law; something demonstrated in his knowledge of Quran and miraculous negation of demonic power. Such an intervention finds a rich source in Islamic Sufi literature, where the confrontation of ascetics with Iblis – the Islamic Devil – are celebrated as the empowerment of the soul perfected through detachment from earthly trappings (Awn, 1983: 77). Thus Sufi holy men (*shaykhs*) are *mahfuz*, protected by God through their attainment of higher spiritual stations. Not only are they considered able to defend against satanic offensives, but are also capable of physically overpowering Iblis (Awn, 1983: 111).

In both accounts, the King is seen to submit to the Divine Law the Saint represents, translating state power into a body of religiously guided action. In the process, however, the King's rule is ensured, being legitimated by his very subordination. The accounts of conversion therefore provide an argument for the authority of government, depicted as implementing the Divine Code from which, as its guarantor, the state secures its legitimacy. It is the refoundation of the state based on *true religion* and Islamic Law (*Shari'a*) that the accounts demonstrate, giving precedent to governmental rule, as the perpetuation of that Law. The accounts also encode a claim to a totalized royal governance, with a further assumption of an achieved encompassment of an isomorphic popular sentiment by the state: 'All became Muslims', as a royal will *guided* the 'popular will' to true religion.[7]

In reference to Koimala and Kalaminja, it can be seen that Dhivehin *history* is shown *essentially* to commence with the conversion to Islam; 1153 being *year zero*. This inauguration of *authentic* Islamic existence is also depicted

as instantaneous and unproblematic – 'All became Muslims' – part of the need to reconcile an undeniable past state of *infidelity*, with the current profession of Islam. Indeed, the pre-Islamic period of Dhivehin origins is to a great extent limited and effaced (like the idolatry of the narratives), with a collapse of focus into the period around the 12th-century events.[8]

Both the *Tarikh* and the *Rannamari story*, then, present an account of the idealized regeneration of the state in the conditions of Islam it adopts and propagates – a charter which combines powerfully with the moment of *true* social foundation.[9]

Religion and the State

Before the ceremony at which the first written constitution was proclaimed (on 22 December 1932), Sultan Shamsuddin visited the tomb of the Arab saint, Abu al-Barakat al-Barbari, at the Meduziyyara in Malé (DIB, 1993a: 4). According to Bell, the sultan would weekly recite the *fatihah* at the entrance to the shrine, after attending *jummah* (Friday congregational prayers) at the nearby Hukuru Miskit. Bell also noted: 'Only on seven particular days in the year can even the sultan pass in over the threshold to worship; at all other times the mosque and tomb are kept rigidly shut off against ingress.'[10]

From the interpretation of the *Rannamari story* above, it will be apparent that royal visits to the saint's tomb served to re-enact the monarch's metonymic status as state subordinated to religion. In the sultanate, the legitimacy of royal governance was evoked in an avowed deference of state power to Islam; and in the circumscription of governmental rule by *Shari'a* (Islamic Law). Thus in the *Tarikh's* first part, entitled *Treatise of Advice to Sovereigns*, rulers are counselled that they must 'find a way to govern the world, whilst following religion'. A 'just ruler' must live according to *Shari'a*, 'purging himself from acting contrary thereto'; though inspiring fear in one's subjects is also recommended (Bell, 1940: 202–3).

But the sultan was not merely to be seen as constrained by religion. The king was also depicted as the guarantor of faith, and in this capacity would issue grants (*Fat-kolu*) for the upkeep of mosques, sealed with a royal curse: 'Any miscreant... minded to frustrate and nullify these actions will descend to Hell with... those who commit the sins of destroying the *Ka'aba* Shrine [in Mecca], burning the *Qurán*, and worshipping Images' (Bell, 1940: 193). Furthermore, Pyrard describes how the state's custodianship of religion also involved the instruction of the king's subjects by the *Fandiyaaru* (*Qazi*):

All he meets without exception he causeth to say their creed, some prayers in Arabic, and then asks them the interpretation of the same in the Maldive language. If they know it not he hath them whipped and scourged on the spot by his officers. (Pyrard, 1888: 199–200)

Displays of royal deference to religion serve to instantiate official assertion today that the Maldives 'continued as a unified Islamic society', in which *the people* consented to the state's 'authoritative interpretation of the Islamic Law' (Ahmed et al., 1990: 7 and 9). Moreover, the monarch's legitimation through submission to *Shari'a* also provides precedent for current constitutional arrangements.

On 15 March 1968, a national referendum returned an 81 percent majority in favour of the abolition of the sultanate. After a further referendum on 27 September, and with a vote of 97.16 percent, Ibrahim Nasir was elected president of the republic. Nasir assumed office on 11 November 1968 – the day that a new constitution (still current at the time of my field-work in 1993–4) came into force.[11]

Article 2 of the 1968 Constitution states that the 'Maldives is a composite, sovereign and fully independent *Islamic State*' (emphasis added), and Article 3 declares: 'Maldives shall be a Republic, its Religion shall be Islam'.[12] The Constitution also specifies that the president and all ministers should be 'Muslim of Sunni Sect' (Articles 24 and 51), and that members of the Citizens' Majlis and Citizens' Special Majlis, be 'Muslim' (Article 63).[13] Moreover, the president, ministers and members of the Majlis are all inducted after taking oaths which include a pledge to 'respect the religion of

Islam' (Articles 25, 52 and 64, in Hecker, 1986: 11–12, 17 and 19–20), and presidential power is also explicitly circumscribed by religion: 'All powers vested in the President of the Republic are confined within the limits laid down in the Shariath' (Article 36). By thus validating its organization, the state itself gains religious credentials and this leads to a further stipulation: 'The President of the Republic is the supreme authority to propagate the religion of Islam in Maldives' (Article 32; Hecker, 1986: 13). It must be noted here that such a conflation, when combined with presidential election, must reduce religious authority to contingency.

Nasir was replaced by Maumoon Abdul Gayoom[14] in 1978, and the day after his inauguration, the new president led Eid festival prayers in Malé, in a demonstration of his newly validated religious authority (Colton, 1978: 32). Having obtained a master's degree in Islamic Studies from Al-Azhar University in Cairo, Gayoom (his supporters claim) had been selected for the presidency by the Majlis as the person best qualified to maintain religion.[15]

The new incumbent commenced to enact Article 32 of the Constitution as an active propagation of faith – purportedly transforming his predecessor's practice of merely employing the provision as a limitation on dissent. Thus the *Far Eastern Economic Review* reported that Gayoom had taken to preaching every evening (1982: 200). In 1984, Gayoom opened the largest mosque in the Maldives – the Masjid Al-Sultan Muhammad Thakurufanu Al-Auzam (part of Malé's 'Islamic Centre') – which can accommodate 5,000 worshippers.[16] And the government has continued to build new mosques throughout the Maldives – a visible substantiation of the state's perpetuation of religion. Of course, donations to fund construction and renovation, the laying of cornerstones and the opening of new mosques by the president or one of his ministers, all afford opportunities for conspicuous piety. And *jummah* prayers also allow a minister's attendance to be noted by his prominent participation at the front of the congregation.[17]

Gayoom occasionally still leads *jummah* prayers, and preaches to the citizenry through televised, religious discussion programmes, or when he tours islands. As supreme religious authority, only the president is empowered to deliver a *khutba* (Friday sermon). All other *imams* (prayer leaders) must read out officially sanctioned texts (from which they are not permitted to deviate), issued each week by a sermon committee of presidential appointees.[18] The president also appoints a special committee to oversee the selection of government-sponsored pilgrims for the *hajj*, and if Gayoom himself is making the pilgrimage, his daily progress is reported prominently by state media.[19]

At the level of its immanent claim, the Maldivian state represents a mediation of Islamic *universality* and national *particularity*. And this entails that national enunciation always emerges from a field of national-religious-state concurrence; a field that (in official assessment) not only presupposes the integrity of religion, nation and state, and their original coalescence at the point of social (re)foundation, but their coincidence and joint implication in any act of dissent.[20]

Notes

1 The employment of the term *conversion* is to be understood as a posited rupture and discontinuity, and is not to be taken as validating the claim of assent to a stable, coherent and uncontested doctrinal core. As will be seen below, the *event* of conversion, official dated as AH 584/AD 1153, does encode a claim to the 'discovery, already at work in each beginning, a principle of coherence and the outline of a future unity' (Foucault, 1972: 22).

2 Malé, the island capital of the Maldives.

3 This is the version of events which appears in the tourist literature: Balla and Willox, 1993; Bevan, 1994; Farook, 1985; Hussain, 1991; Maniku et al., 1977. It is also recorded in James Frazer's *The Golden Bough*.

4 Bell, the first Archaeological Commissioner of Ceylon (Forbes, 1983: 44) visited the Maldives in 1879, 1920 and 1922, and it was during the last two visits that he was able to examine the *Tarikh*. As he noted, the copy he studied 'was admittedly not the actual Chronicle', ostensibly commenced by *Qazi* Haji Hasan Tajuddin who died in AH 1139/AD 1726–7, and subsequently continued by his nephew *Qazi* Haji Muhammad Muhibuddin from AH 1137/AD 1724–5 to AH 1174/AD 1760–1 and grandson *Qazi* Ibrahim Sirajuddin up to AH 1237/AD 1821–2 (Bell, 1940: 201–2). The original chronicle was said to have perished during the sacking of Malé by Malabari forces in 1752. The paper of the copy examined by Bell bore a watermark of 1820 and, after being presented to the Ceylon Government by Sultan Muhammad Shamsuddin

III (second accession 1903), has since been lost (Forbes, 1980: 72). The *Tarikh* according to Bell consisted of three parts: *A Treatise for Rulers; A Condensed History of the Prophets prior to Muhammad*; and *A History of the Maldive Sultans*. It is the third part, presented in abridged form by Bell (1940: 18–43), covering the 83 reigns of 76 monarchs, which commences with the account of conversion by Yusuf Shamsuddin and the date of the event, 12 Rabi ul-Akhir AH 548 (AD 1153) – the date officially recognized in Maldives today – is logged. However, as Forbes (1980: 73) points out, the *Tarikh*, written in Arabic, a language with which Bell was unfamiliar, may have been made accessible for compilation by the translation efforts of local Maldivians fluent in English. Of course, one can only speculate about the significance of the foundational accounts prior to Bell's arrival.

5 Bell notes: 'Ibn Batuta, as a native of Tangier, would assign the credit of the Conversion to Abu-l-Barakat, the Berber, a Maghrabin' (1940: 19n.).

6 Of course in Tabrizi's intervention, the demonic is manifested as a demonstration of his power of social transformation.

7 The *Tarikh* intimates that things were very *straightforward*: 'Afterwards the Sultan sent to every island of the Maldives persons who converted all the inhabitants, whether willing or unwilling, to the Muslim Faith; so that throughout the Maldives there were none but Muslims' (Bell, 1940: 203). In addition, the Gan, Addu *Fila fat-kolu* dated AH 1063/AD

1652–3, records: '(Thereafter), lands belonging to those persons who became Muslims willingly were separated and allotted to them; (and) lands belonging to non-converts, with all other lands, made over to the Government (*Fura Bandára*), in order to ensure provision of State Revenue for the maintenance of the Muslim Faith (*Islán Dín*)' (Bell, 1940: 192).

8   While my concern is not with the validity of theories of origin, it is perhaps worth mentioning that Bell subscribed to what De Silva (1970: 154) terms the 'Sinhalese-origin hypothesis'. This posits a Sinhalese colonization of the Maldives at the beginning of the Christian era. Bell based his belief, amongst other things, on the examination of ruins during his 1922 archaeological expedition in various atolls, which he identified as Buddhist monasteries, stupas and 'image houses'; though these lay in a dilapidated state due to 'the fanatic zeal and iconoclastic ruthlessness of the earlier Muslim converts'. Bell also cites the similarity between Elu (termed 'pure Sinhalese') and Dhivehi (Bell, 1940: 16, 107, 108). De Silva for his part posits a 'simultaneous separation hypothesis' based on his identification of 'pre-Sinhalese Indic material' in Dhivehi (1970: 138, 151). With regard to origins, it should also be noted that Forbes (1981) claims: 'By the fourth century BC trade contacts appear to have been established between the Near East and Sri Lanka' (p. 64), and that 'Arab knowledge of the Maldive Archipelago in pre-Islamic times may be taken for granted' (p. 66).

9   Maloney's (1980) work on the accounts of conversion is pitifully inadequate. After devoting a whole chapter on various accounts concerning Koimala and Sinhalese sources, his only comment after recording the Barakat account is: 'This myth is full of symbolic significance, and supersedes all earlier myths' (p. 99)!

10   From Bell's (1921) *The Maldive Islands: Report on a Visit to Male*, quoted in Forbes (1983: 60–1). The *fatihah* is the opening chapter of the Quran, recited here as a *du'a* (individual prayer). The mosque referred to is the Medu Miskit (Central Mosque) which adjoins the Meduziyyara. The state's subordination to religion was also elaborately staged at the ceremony to mark the sultan's enthronement. A pavilion was erected 'facing the shrine of the Saint Shamsu Tabraiz', and three 'chief men,

representing the north, middle and south atolls', pledged allegiance to the new monarch 'on condition that he protects the poor and rules with justice according to Mohamedan [sic] laws and Maldivian customs'. After a prayer, a 'procession, announcing to the people the accession of their new ruler, made the tour of the principal thoroughfares of the island... [T]he State palanquin, on which was borne a richly ornamented copy of the Koran ... was also borne along with the procession' (emphasis added; Keane, 1907: 54–7). Of course, the bearing of a copy of the Quran on the state palanquin would seem to imply equivalence through transposition.

11   Hecker (1986: 7); *Almanac of Current World Leaders* (1969: 12[1]: 55); DIB (1993a: 7). The date is recognized in the Maldives as Republic Day.

12   Hecker (1986: 7–8). The 1968 Constitution opens with: 'In the Name of Allah, The Beneficient [sic], The Merciful. Praise be to Allah, the Lord of the Universe. Peace and Blessings be upon Mohamed [sic], the last of the Apostles, and Messengers, and his family and all his companions' (p. 6). The 'Islamic faith of the State' is symbolized by a star and crescent on the national emblem, while a white crescent symbolizes the 'Islamic faith of the nation' on the Maldivian flag (DIB, 1992: 3).

13   Such a stipulation accords with the de facto limitation of Maldivian citizenship to nominal Sunni Muslims, though the express formulation of such a specification is missing from Article 4 of the 1968 Constitution, which states: 'Every child born of a Maldivian father and also every child born of a Maldivian mother other than by a marriage with a foreign father is a Maldivian citizen' (Hecker, 1986: 8). As Forbes notes, there is a widespread belief that the Constitution specifies adherence to the *Shafi'i madhhab* as a requisite of citizenship, though there is no article to that effect (1981: 60).

14   In June 1978, Nasir, in a surprise announcement, informed the Majlis that he would not be seeking re-election, when his current term as president expired later that year. The Majlis nominated Gayoom (the Minister of Transport) for the presidency, and in July, Gayoom was confirmed after securing a 92.9 percent vote in the national referendum. The 1968 Constitution stipulates that the Citizens' Majlis after selecting a presidential candidate by secret

ballot, 'proposes his name to the public for election'. If the candidate 'obtains a majority he is elected President of the Republic'. The term of office of the president is five years from the day he is sworn in, and the president-designate takes the following oath: 'I swear by Allah that I shall respect the religion of Islam, the Constitution of Maldives, and the rights of the citizens, and I shall not be unfaithful to any one of them' (Hecker, 1986: 10–12, 15). Gayoom first assumed office on 11 November 1978, and has since been re-elected three times: in 1983 with a 95.6 percent endorsement; in 1988 with a 96.4 percent endorsement; and in 1993 a 92.8 percent endorsement.

15 After completing his degree, Gayoom returned to Maldives in 1971, and occupied several government posts during Ibrahim Nasir's presidency, including Deputy Head of the Department of External Affairs, Permanent Representative to the United Nations, and Minister of Transport (Ahmed et al., 1990: 16). Nasir employed Gayoom's fluency in Arabic by assigning him 'special responsibilities for petrodollar negotiations with Arab countries' (*Far Eastern Economic Review*, 1978: 254).

16 The Islamic Centre cost US$7 million to construct and was funded by aid from Saudi Arabia, Brunei, Kuwait, the United Arab Emirates, Malaysia, Pakistan and Egypt (*Far Eastern Economic Review*, 1985: 198).

17 The state as guarantor of Islam, also supplicates for the well-being of the nation through the recitation of *munaja* – a prayer read aloud in the Islamic Centre in the small hours of each day.

18 Many of the approved *khutbas* were prepared by Muhammad Jameel, father of Foreign Minister Fathullah Jameel. Both Jameels also graduated from Al-Azhar.

19 I discuss elsewhere the contestation of the president's religious authority by Saudi-trained Wahhabis.

20 The state's religious prerogative allowed the deployment of a charge of religious as well as national secession, at the time of the formation of the breakaway United Suvadivan Republic (1958–64) on the three southernmost atolls.

References

Ahmed, Asim, Abdulla Saeed and Jennifer Sharples (1990) *Maldives: Twenty-five Years of Independence*. Bangkok: Media Transasia Ltd.

Almanac of Current World Leaders (1968–). Santa Barbara, CA: International Academy.

Awn, Peter (1983) *Satan's Tragedy and Redemption: Iblis in Sufi Psychology*. Leiden: E. J. Brill.

Balla, Mark and Bob Willox (1993) *Maldives and Islands of the East Indian Ocean*. Hawthorn, Victoria: Lonely Planet.

Bell, Harry Charles Purvis (1940) *The Maldive Islands: Monograph on the History, Archaeology and Epigraphy*. Colombo: Ceylon Government Press.

Bevan, Stuart (1994) *Maldives*. Hawthorn, Victoria: Gadabout Guides.

Colton, Elizabeth (1978) 'Turning Towards the Future', *Far Eastern Economic Review* (1 Dec.).

De Silva, M.W. Sugathapala (1970) 'Some Observations on the History of Maldivian', *Transactions of the Philological Society* 137–162.

DIB (Department of Information and Broadcasting) (1992) *Information 16: National Emblems*. Malé, Maldives: Department of Information and Broadcasting.

DIB (1993a) *Information 15: Constitutional History*. Malé, Maldives: Department of Information and Broadcasting.

Far Eastern Economic Review (1978–96) *Far Eastern Economic Review: Asia Year-book*.

Farook, Mohamed (1985) *The Fascinating Maldives*. Malé, Maldives: Novelty Printers and Publishers.

Forbes, Andrew D.W. (1980) 'Archives and Resources for Maldivian History', *South Asia* 3(1): 70–82.

Forbes, Andrew D.W. (1981) 'Southern Arabia and the Islamicisation of the Central Indian Ocean Archipelagoes', *Archipel* 21: 55–92.

Forbes, Andrew D.W. (1983) 'The Mosque in the Maldive Islands: A Preliminary Historical Survey', *Archipel* 26: 43–74.

Foucault, Michel (1972) *The Archaeology of Knowledge and The Discourse on Language*, trans. A.M. Sheridan Smith. New York: Pantheon Books.

Hecker, Hellmuth (1986) 'The Maldives', trans. Adnan Hussain, in Albert P. Blaustein and Gisbert H. Flanz (eds) *Constitutions of the Countries of the World*. New York: Oceana Publications.

Hussain, Ali (1991) *Mysticism in the Maldives: Eyewitness Accounts of Supernatural Encounters*. Malé, Maldives: Novelty Printers and Publishers.

Ibn Batuta (1984) *The Travels of Ibn Batuta*, trans. Samuel Lee. London: Darf Publishers.

Keane, John (1907) 'State Ceremonies in the Maldive Islands', *Empire Review* 13(73): 51–58.

Maloney, Clarence (1980) *People of the Maldive Islands*. New Delhi: Orient Longman.

Maniku, Adam, B.I. Saleem, Hassan Maniku and Mohamed Shareef (1977) *Discover Maldives*. Malé, Maldives: Fotoart.

Pyrard, François (1888) *The Voyage of François Pyrard of Laval to the East Indies, the Maldives, the Moluccas and Brazil*, trans. Albert Gray, 2 vols. London: Hakluyt Society.

White, Hayden (1975) *Metahistory: The Historical Imagination in Nineteenth-Century Europe*. Baltimore, MD: Johns Hopkins University Press.

Part IV

States and Communal Conflict in South Asia

Introduction

Political conflict in South Asia occurs frequently between communities – ethnic or religious – hence the term "communal conflict." In India, communal conflicts most often arise between Hindus, Sikhs, Christians, and Muslims and carry religious overtones and justifications, though analysts like Stanley Tambiah point to their function as instrumental or political in nature. There is also conflict between (former Untouchable) "dalits" and Sudras ("Other Backward Castes") and upper-castes. In Pakistan, and to some extent Bangladesh, communal conflict is ethnic or sectarian, between majority Sunni Muslims and minority Shias or Ahmadiyas. There are also small groups of Christians and Hindus in these countries, and in 1992 when conflict broke out over the Babri Masjid (a 16th century mosque destroyed by Hindu nationalists), Hindus and their temples were objects of attack in both countries. In Pakistan and Afghanistan, however, much of the dominant conflict today is also between ethnic groups or "tribes." In Nepal, the conflict is primarily ethnic and class-based, with high-caste Hindu groups of the Kathmandu valley being challenged by "madhesi" groups of the plains and the more isolated and impoverished ethnic groups who live in the mountains. In Bhutan, a large immigrant Nepalese population – about 30% of the total Bhutanese population – is subject to discrimination and hardship. In Sri Lanka, conflict occurs primarily between the ethnic majority Sinhalese and the Tamil minority. While Sinhalese Buddhist nationalism is a unifying force for the Buddhist majority, Tamils are split into Hindu, Christian, and Muslim communities.

Building upon themes explored in Parts II and IV, Pankaj Mishra and Darini Rajasingham-Senanayke examine how Hindu nationalism in India and Buddhist nationalism in Sri Lanka have undermined plural, multicultural societies in both countries. In India, the rise of the Bharatiya Janata party (BJP), which came to power at the national level in 1998, resulted from the mobilization of a family of organizations (the "Sangh Parivar") begun in the early 20th century (while some would argue its seeds can be found in late 19th century social reform movements). Similarly, Sinhala nationalism has its roots in the 19th century racial theory of "Aryans" and Dravidians, as Rajasingham-Senanayke argues. As we saw in the readings in Part III, these forms of religious nationalism frequently take women as their object; women may become active members of such groups as well as the passive symbols of their communities.

At 1.2 billion people, India is often called the world's largest democracy, and there are indeed, long traditions of democratic politics throughout South Asia, as we will see in Part VI. But it is also the case that electoral politics throughout South Asia result in communal violence when different communities are "vote-banked." The state management of communal voting blocs and their deployment in pre-election violence to harass or intimidate minority communities results in what Stanley Tambiah calls the "paradox of democracy." This notion stands in stark contrast to the idea that ethnic or communal conflict is highest in "weak states" like Afghanistan which lack a strong center and therefore the ability to control communal conflict. In his essay, Nazif Shahrani shows that in the case of Afghanistan, prolonged ethnic conflict underlies the history of the Taliban insurgency. The roots of this ethnic conflict are found in the territorial boundaries set for Afghanistan during the "Great Game" played by Britain and Russia in the region, in a continuing history of foreign intervention that has played upon and exacerbated those conflicts in combination with a highly centralized state.

Pankaj Mishra describes the history behind the Babri Masjid/"Ram Janmabhoomi" (birthplace of Ram) conflict and the emergence of the "Sangh Parivar" family of Hindu nationalist organizations that began with the founding of the Rashtriya Swamsevak Sangh in 1925. Hindu nationalist organizations claim that the Babri Masjid was built at the site of a former temple to Lord Ram, and could thus be destroyed with impunity. About 1,000 Muslims were killed in Hindu nationalist-led violence after the destruction of the mosque by its cadres. Significantly, no one was ever brought to trial for these killings, and the mosque has not been rebuilt. To the contrary, construction of a new temple dedicated to Lord Ram is ongoing. Significantly, the Delhi Historians Group, and a state-appointed archeological team, found no linguistic, historic, or archeological evidence to back the claim that a Ram temple had ever stood at the site.[1] A recent (and controversial) Indian court-ruling awarded shared but unequal custody of the site to Hindu and Muslim communities.

Note

1   See Sarvapalli Gopal et al., "The Political Abuse of History: Babri Masjid-Rama Janmabhumi Dispute," *Social Scientist* 18(1/2) 1990, pp. 76–81; Also *The Babri Masjid Question*, Vols. 1 and II, A.G. Noorani (ed.). Delhi: Tulika, 2003.

15

Reflections on Communal Violence in South Asia

Stanley J. Tambiah

Ethnic conflict is said to be rampant today. To all those instances familiar to us from the recent past, we may add the latest explosions in Southern Russia, in Eastern Europe, and in India's Kashmir.

A great deal has been written on the historical antecedents of ethnic conflicts, and on the political, religious, economic, and social circumstances in which many of them have broken out. These accounts include the effects of global processes that stem from metropolitan centers upon satellite countries, the assumptions and the problems of nation-making, and the politics of ethnic and other group entitlement claims in plural societies.

In contrast to this rich literature, relatively little is known about the nature of the destruction and dislocations caused by violence that is enacted during ethnic conflicts. This issue involves at least three large domains of inquiry, which I have labeled the anthropology of collective violence, the anthropology of displaced persons, and the anthropology of suffering.

Although my present research and writing touch on all three of these domains, my address will be concerned with some aspects of only one of them, namely, the anthropology of collective violence.[1] This topic is closely linked to a wide array of political, economic, and social and cultural issues that affect societies both internally and externally. My concluding remarks will pick up one of those issues, the relationship between ethnic violence and democracy, and offer some thoughts on what linkages might exist between these two.

Within the ambit of collective aggression, I will limit my remarks to the phenomenon of civilian riots, the most frequent and dramatic expression of ethnic conflicts, and exclude the violence that is associated with the actions of professional armed security forces and guerrilla movements.

There have been many attempts by scholars to specify ethnicity, ethnic identity, and consciousness, and I shall not become involved in that redundant exercise here. Recently, I have

Perspectives on Modern South Asia: A Reader in Culture, History, and Representation, First Edition.
Edited by Kamala Visweswaran.
© 2011 Blackwell Publishing Ltd. Published 2011 by Blackwell Publishing Ltd.

discussed my views on this thorny issue at some length (Tambiah 1989), but I want to remind you of the nature of this persistent, boisterous, and many-headed beast by retelling two stories:

A member of Parliament representing Orissa State once said over thirty years ago in the course of a debate: "My first ambition is the glory of Mother India. I know in my heart of hearts that I am an Indian first and an Indian last. But when you say you are a Bihari, I say I am an Oriya. When you say you are a Bengali, I say I am an Oriya. Otherwise, I am an Indian" (Harrison 1960).

About thirteen years ago, a reporter asked Abdul Wali Khan, the son of the "frontier Gandhi," Abdulla Ghaffar Khan, the founder of the National Awami Party: "Are you a Pakistani, a Muslim, or a Pathan?" Wali Khan replied that he was all three. The reporter pressed him as to his primary identity. Wali Khan replied that he had been a Pakistani for thirty years, a Muslim for 1,400 years, and a Pathan for 5,000 years.[2]

Three Ethnic Riots in South Asia

Particular instances of ethnic riots usually differ as to the groups and issues that are in contention, and the circumstances in which they occur. That is certainly true of the three recent occurrences in South Asia I will discuss today. The Sinhala–Tamil riots in Colombo in 1983, the Sikh–Hindu eruptions in Delhi in 1984, the Pathan–Bihari clashes in Orangi, Karachi, in 1985 and 1986 involve different groups, widely separated from each other, and were triggered and fueled by differing concrete circumstances.

Yet it is these three occurrences, and many others lesser in scale, that I shall group together in this discussion. Examples of the latter are the Hindu–Muslim clashes in Moradabad in the 1980s, the Bombay riots of 1984, and the flareups in various parts of India – Uttar Pradesh, Karnataka, Bihar, Madhya Pradesh, Gujarat, Maharashtra and Rajasthan – caused by the so-called Ram Janmabhoomi–Babri Masjid controversy, which has intensified the militancy of both Hindus and Muslims and also seriously affected the outcome of the most recent national and state elections. I propose

to identify certain general features that they all share and thereby open a window onto the phenomenon of collective violence itself.

Let me begin by naming several preliminary characteristics. The three riots I have identified typically, although not exclusively, involved urban populations.[3] Those who actually engaged in the physical acts of aggression, as well as those who mobilized and directed the violence, were primarily drawn from certain identifiable segments or categories of that population.

The riots were not simply disconnected occurrences but formed part of a larger incidence of violence that occurred in a wide range of social contexts and political circumstances that can be ordered on a scale of increasing violence, premeditation, and participation. This larger universe ranges from abuse in family life to petty crime and robbery, to the use of henchmen and thugs to settle business disputes, and to organized thuggery during political elections. The ethnic riots are in one sense the last in this series. And when I refer to widespread violence in society at large, I do not by any means exclude the terrorism and violence practiced by the state, principally as routine practice in relation to the public by police and security forces. It is common knowledge that the police practice physical violence on those arrested, especially if they are of lower status, and use coercion to extract information and confessions. And the tendentious participation during riots of police, army, other security forces, and paramilitary groups recruited by the state, either as onlookers slow to take preventive action or as vigorous participants favoring the cause of one side or another, is a fact of life recorded in country after country. Neutrality on the part of those entrusted with maintaining law and order is rarely witnessed in societies where ethnic conflict is rife.

Another dimension of ethnic riots in many cities and towns is that, occurring as intermittent events, they constitute another kind of series, with antecedent riots influencing the unfolding of succeeding occurrences. Thus, the 1983 riots in Sri Lanka, the most virulent so far on that island, were preceded, to mention only the most destructive ones, by the riots of 1958, 1977, and 1981. The city of Colombo was involved in all of them. In the city of Meerut in Uttar Pradesh, India, where the Muslims comprise about 45 percent of the population, tensions between them and the Hindus have led to communal rioting on eight occasions since Independence; the last occurrence was in May 1987, when both civilian Hindus and the "provincial armed constabulary" committed atrocities.[4] The same story could be repeated of many other Indian and Pakistani cities, implicating the same or different antagonists. A variation that is not infrequent in large metropolitan cities that contain a mosaic of differentiated communities is offered by two commentators on the Bihari–Pathan clashes in Orangi (Karachi). They remarked that Karachi "has seen anti-Qadiani riots in the early fifties, anti-Pathan riots in 1965, anti-Qadiani riots again in 1969–70, Sindhi–Muhajir riots in 1973, and a yearly encounter of Shia–Sunni sectarian riots before the Orangi troubles of 1985" (Ali and Shaheed 1987). Since then, clashes between Pathans and Biharis occurred in February and July of 1987, and in May and October of 1988.

Case 1: The Hindu–Sikh Riots of 1984

Let me now, by way of illustration, give you a sketch of a famous case. The Hindu–Sikh Riots that took place in Delhi in late 1984 have been amply documented[5] both officially and unofficially, and answers can be given to some precise questions.

The duration of the riots was, as usual, brief. They began in the late afternoon of October 31, and had virtually abated by November 3, a period of about three to four days. Indira Gandhi's cremation on November 3 was the cathartic climax to a national tragedy, and the prelude to the subsidence of the orgy of violence.

The triggering event, traumatic and deeply unsettling when it took place, was the assassination of Mrs. Indira Gandhi, the Prime Minister, by two of her Sikh guards. She was shot at 9:15 A.M on October 31, and was rushed to the All India Institute of Medical Sciences (AIIMS) for treatment. By 11:00 A.M. the All India Radio

reported the attack, and by 2:30 P.M the evening edition of several papers in the capital carried news of her death by assassination and divulged the Sikh identity of the assailants.

Soon after the All India Radio announced her death, the large crowds that had gathered at the AIIMS went on a rampage. They proceeded in four different directions – toward the Defense Colony, toward R. K. Puram, toward Prithviraj Road, toward Hauz Khas – indulging in arson and violence on the way. The rioting continued until late into the night of October 31, with the main incidents reported in areas of South Delhi.

The collective violence of the riots was one-sided in that non-Sikhs, mostly Hindus, attacked the Sikhs. The Union Territory of Delhi had a population in 1984 of around 6.2 million, and some 6.3 to 7.5 percent of this total was Sikh, a small minority wedged into the interstices of a largely Hindu universe.

The interesting question is, if we are to follow the language used by the Report of the Misra Commission, how crowds that had formed spontaneously after being traumatized by a national tragedy, unleashed riots which by the next morning (November 1) took the shape of organized and purposive violence that systematically committed arson, looting, and killing. (Indeed, the Parliamentary announcement, in setting up the Official Misra Commission, unproblematically referred to the phenomenon as "incidents of organized violence.") During the second day, the riots exploded in various parts of the city, and vented their most destructive fury in the settlement colonies at the periphery, such as Sultanpuri and Mangolpuri in West Delhi, Trilokpuri, Kalyanpuri, and the trans-Jamuna colonies in the east, and other places like Sagar Puri and Palam in the Delhi Cantonment. These settlements are described as the poorer sections of Delhi. They contained both Sikh and non-Sikh dwellers who made their living mainly as urban workers, artisans, small businessmen, and lower echelon workers of the Congress (I) Party; they also harbored the so-called "criminal elements." But we should not infer that they were people without property, assets, incomes, and savings, as the scale of destruction and the targets of attack demonstrated.

The destruction that was wrought in a few days was awesome. The Delhi Administration reported to the Misra Commission that a total of 180 *gurudwārās* (Sikh temples) and 11 educational institutions run by members of the Sikh community were affected by arson, looting, and burning. That places of worship, store-houses of community goods, and educational institutions and equipment were targeted indicates the purposiveness of the intent to diminish the collective assets of the Sikh community.

At the level of individual Sikh families and households, the loss of property was widespread. The *Report of the Citizens' Commission* (1984:35) states that many Sikh houses, large and small, were burned, and that trucks, taxicabs, three- and two-wheel scooters, cars, and motorcycles were burned by the hundreds. It continues, "Factories and business premises, together with machinery and stock-in-trade were looted, damaged, or destroyed."

The same report remarks (p. 23) that a remarkable unity in the pattern of the crimes committed strongly suggests that at some stage the objective became to "teach the Sikhs a lesson" (The same expression, applied to the Tamils, was heard in Colombo in the 1983 riots). The scale of killing, maiming, and burning of human beings exceeded the carnage of ethnic riots at other times and places in India. The official figures, as estimated by the Misra Commission, are that somewhere between 3,874 and 2,037 persons were killed (the lower figure coming from the Delhi Administration). In particular, the agonizing documentation by Uma Chakravarty and Nandita Haksar in their *The Delhi Riots. Three Days in the Life of a Nation* (1987) conveys the horror and pain of the brutalities inflicted. I shall here merely cite the Misra Commission's prosaic statement (1986:23) that "It is in evidence that hundreds of people [were] killed and burnt while they were half dead or while they were in an unconscious state or had already died.... There is evidence that hundreds of charred bodies were recovered."

As in other cases of South Asian riots (and this observation is not necessarily limited to South Asia), the Delhi mobs were almost exclusively composed of male attackers, mostly young men and mature adults.

Let me first deal with the victims of the Delhi riots before I advert to the identity of the attackers. The vast majority of those killed were males, husbands and sons, mostly youth and young men, many of them students or job-holders, and male adult household heads who were usually the main breadwinners. The evidence shows that some women and children were also killed in the outlying settlements, and that some women were raped by packs of men.

To kill and reduce the male population is to reduce the occupational and working strength and the fighting capacities of the enemy. To rape and degrade their women, to burn their homes and loot their property is to further invade their inner social space, violate family life, and disorient their sense of sociocultural continuity. A further consequence of such a pattern of killing is to create for women both hardship and peril in their positions as relatively young widows, incoming wives and daughters-in-law in the deceased husbands' households, and as mothers of dependent children. I cannot on this occasion develop these issues further, except to indicate that ethnic violence is frequently directed towards reducing the enemy's alleged economic well-being and margin of advantage, leveling and reducing the enemy's status while violating and appropriating its property, and reducing the means by which the enemy produces and reproduces its social and cultural distinctiveness.

Who were the participants in the Delhi Riots? It is tempting and comforting to say that the aggressors were strangers and enemies and not friends and neighbors. No such neat binary contrast quite fits the case in point. It can, however, be said that the more mob violence moved toward the active mobilization of people, equipping them with the means of destruction and inciting them to violence, the greater the likelihood of a guiding role by conspiring "outsiders," aided by informers and collaborators within.

Among the residents of the settlement colonies, while many neighbors and friends, both Hindu and Muslim, gave shelter, refuge, and protection to the beleaguered Sikhs as far as it was possible and safe to do so, there is ample evidence that colony residents in the shape of Congress (I) activists and block leaders (pradhan), and the lower echelons of the Congress (I) Party, were involved. Local Congress offices were frequently the sites for mob assemblies, for burning bodies, and for launching raids.

These link persons to the Congress (I) mobilized their local clients and thugs, provided them with liquor, and directed sellers of kerosene oil, whose sale was restricted to permit holders, to distribute the fuel for arson. They also provided information about the targets – Sikh houses, business establishments, schools, and gurudwārās. When such organized mobs went into action, local "low caste" elements, for example, the bhangis and chamars, appear to have been readily available as supporters of Congress (I).

Another set of participants in the arson and looting were the Gujjar and Jat farmers from the villages bordering settlement colonies such as Trilokpuri, Mangolpuri, and the trans-Jamuna colonies. Much of their land had been taken over as sites for resettlement colonies, and they had their own scores to settle.

Still another set of participants, willing or forced, were bus drivers, such as those who worked for the Delhi Transportation Corporation (based in South Delhi). The evidence is solid that public vehicles were used to transport rioters from place to place, especially on the second day. These mobile gangs, spreaders of rumors, shouters of slogans, instigators of violence among the public, and themselves strike forces, were a critical element in the rapid sparking and spread of violence at key junctions of the city.

A list compiled by the authors of Who are the Guilty? (1984) gives the occupations of some of the persons identified by informants as those who participated in the rioting, arson, and murder in the settlement colonies. This list gives some specificity to the faces in the crowd, most of them belonging to the ordinary gainfully employed citizens who constituted the majority of the local populace: shop-keeper;

railway worker; tailor; mason; dealer in cement; TV shop owner; video shop owner; teashop owner; furniture dealer; Congress (I) pradhan; Congress (I) worker; meat-shop owner; dairy owner; shoemaker; groceryshop owner; cloth and chappal seller; liquor seller; sweeper; rickshaw repairer; milkman; cloth and tailoring shop owner; land owner and goala; auto-rickshaw driver; kerosene seller; property dealer; carpenter; mechanic; vegetable seller; owner of godown; flour mill owner; paper seller; barber; owner of 3-star hotel; dhoby (washerman); opium dealer; local goonda (thug).

One sees that the occupational spectrum was wide, ranging from low-wage workers, providers of services, and artisans to shop owners, small businessmen, and, occasionally, even more prosperous property owners. In the listing, lower echelon Congress (I) workers; kerosene oil sellers; sweepers (low caste); shop-keepers selling a variety of goods from cloth and shoes to videos and television sets, and artisans such as masons, carpenters, barbers, mechanics, are the types that occur most frequently. All told, the riot participants, the vast majority of them Hindus, were representative of a cross-section of the inhabitants one may expect to find on the periphery of India's large cities.

My account will be incomplete if I do not allude to the behavior of the Delhi police force, especially because their behavior was not uncommon but widely replicated elsewhere. In late 1984, the Delhi police force was about 27,142 strong, of whom the vast majority were of the rank of constable (22,000) and head constable (3,000). Delhi was divided into 5 police districts, 63 police stations, and 25 police posts.

It is generally regarded that the force was numerically inadequate, but not so inadequate that it could not have taken preventive and regulatory action during the anti-Sikh riots, even under the explosive conditions stemming from Mrs. Gandhi's assassination.

All reports, including the official Misra Commission Report, reprimand the police, especially the lower ranks from constables to Station House officers, for being ineffective. There is cumulative evidence of dereliction of duty, especially during the worst phases of destruction in the settlement colonies: correct and timely information was not transmitted to the district police control rooms; police stations when contacted on the telephone or directly by prospective victims did not respond; more seriously, the police deliberately absented themselves from crowd scenes, or stood passively by, or accompanied crowds while they committed arson and killing before their eyes; even worse, sometimes they acted in collusion, distributing diesel oil from their jeeps, and disarming Sikhs but not their assailants. In a few cases, they participated in the looting and in the escape of rioters in their custody.

It is understandable that Indian commentators would reprimand the Delhi police force, some 25,000 to 30,000 strong, for unprofessional conduct. But without seeming to condone their actions, I want to make the observation that the vast majority of the constables and lower echelons cannot have been socially and ethnically different from the majority of the riot participants, with whom they must have consorted in everyday life, and whose politics they must have shared.

Case 2: The Karachi Riots of April 1985

My sketch of the Delhi riots of 1984 highlighted how a highly traumatic event acted as the immediate catalytic agent for crowd formation and crowd emotions, and how the rioting, if "spontaneous" at the beginning, soon became organized. It focused on the victims and the assailants and the scale of the damage inflicted; it also gave some (but not enough) sense of the manner in which groups of participants with their own agenda entered the flow of events.

My next example, one of Karachi's many riots, is intended to give some idea of how categories and groups of participants with their own particular agenda entered the flow of events. The riots that took place in Karachi in April 1985 can be deconstructed to reveal that certain violent incidents arising out of local and unrelated clashes escalated into a spiraling cycle of violence that was eventually and inevitably interpreted and labeled as an ethnic conflict between the Pathans and Biharis.[6]

My sense is that the Karachi case is by no means unique and is not only fairly typical of the ethnic riots that occur in that city but also of many such episodes elsewhere in South Asia. (For example, the well-documented 1915 Sinhala–Muslim riots in Sri Lanka illustrates the same dynamics.)[7]

In Pakistan the label Muhajir embraces in general the immigrants from India at the time of partition in 1947, and the subsequent immigrants from Bangladesh in 1971, who are themselves labeled as Biharis. The Pathans in question have come mostly from the northwest Frontier Province and include as well some Afghan immigrants.

That riots in Karachi frequently and typically crystallize in a familiar manner implies that there are sociocultural differences and conflicts of interest between those labeled as Pathans and as Muhajirs/Biharis, both living in a common urban space.

Orangi township, Karachi's largest squatter settlement ("katchi abadi"), contains an estimated population of about one million. "Ethnically speaking, the township has representations from every ethnic group in Pakistan, but is dominated by the Biharis and Pathans, each of whom constitutes approximately 25 percent of the population. The remaining 50 percent of the population is a mixture of Punjabis, Sindhis, Baluchis, Bengalis, Muhajirs, and the more recently arrived Afghan refugees" (Ali and Shaheed, 1987).

As in the case with many other South Asian (and Third World) metropolitan cities, the proliferation and mushrooming of large squatter slums are related to the massive migrations from rural/tribal areas to the growing cities. These cities hold the promise of industrial and commercial wage labor, attract waves of immigrants from diverse points of origin, and thus continue to grow as a mosaic of "ethnic" enclaves jostling each other. Orangi is the product of both these developments.

As background to appreciating the wayward logic of the Karachi riots in question, it is important to know that the transport business in Karachi is the ethnic monopoly of the Pathans, and that wild driving by Karachi's competitive and passenger-hungry bus drivers causes many deaths and frequently triggers street violence by an exasperated public. For example, from January 1986 to August 1987, there were 78 deaths and 17 minor riots associated with reckless driving.

The Pathan–Bihari clashes that took place in April 1985 in Metropolitan Karachi's Township of Orangi began with an identifiable fatal accident that happened in a commercial area of Karachi called Nazimabad. In this instance, the death of a schoolgirl of Sir Syed College brought out the girls of that school in a public demonstration. Their manhandling by the police, who were generally believed to be sympathetic to Pathan transporters, not only engaged the public at large but also the male students of a right-wing organization, who battled the police. Predictably, the mismanagement by the police led to the usual rampage resulting in the burning of vehicles, barricading of streets, and skirmishes with the police.

The next big incident took place at the Banaras Chowk, a nodal point in the city with bus and truck depots, and bus terminals. As a transportation center, Banaras Chowk links the large squatter settlement of Orangi to Karachi proper via Nazimabad and is dominated by Pathan transporters and workers. A clash there between them and the students, who in trying to attend the schoolgirl's funeral had to pass Banaras Chowk, precipitated the next and more virulent phase of the riots.

The incidents, now distorted through rumors and labeled as a Pathan–Bihari conflict, in turn precipitated violence between Pathan and Bihari residents of Orangi, where both communities had their local concentrations in Karachi's largest squatter settlement. The Biharis who were attacked, and attacked in retaliation, were shopkeepers and urban dwellers employed in a variety of trades and wage activities. On the Pathan side, aside from the transport workers, others involved in shopkeeping and other activities of the "informal economy" also became implicated. From 50 to 100 persons were killed, and at least 300 shops and houses were looted and set on fire.

This example illustrates well how a bus accident, in which a schoolgirl was killed, led to a protest rally staged by her schoolmates, which, in turn, was supported by a male public at large which also included militant youths who belonged to a right-wing student body.

The original issue of the death of a schoolgirl ballooned into a more general protest against the inequities of the public transport system and that, again, into an anti-Pathan backlash. But there are more twists and turns to the story. Mischievous and distorted rumors circulated, unchecked by the government and its media; and armed, angry Pathans took to the streets in their locality in Orangi, where concentrations of Bihari, their alleged enemies, also lived. Neighborhood boundaries were breached, clashes proliferated, deteriorated, and narrowed into a stark Pathan–Bihari bloodbath. Thus, incidents that took place in the part of the city called Nazimabad came to roost in the Orangi slums many miles away; and the Biharis who had nothing to do with the original events – neither the schoolgirl who died nor her schoolmates were Bihari – were drawn by processes of "distorted" communication, rumors, and prior ethnic sensitivities into violent clashes with the Pathans.

Concluding Comments

The cross-sectional composition of the South Asian, and many Third World, riot crowds of our time distinctly and integrally links them to a participatory democracy, population movements, and sprawling urbanization. The politicization of ethnicity (Tambiah 1989), a hallmark of our time tied to the politics of elections, has much to do with the winning of the benefits distributed by the modern state committed to welfare, development, and employment programs. This political equation, combined with huge demographic aggregations and the capabilities of the mass media, the radio, television, and print capitalism so effectively deployed today, make present-day ethnic riot crowds very different from the crowds of preindustrial Europe. The contrast is striking when we take into account the "universalistic" slogans of popular democracy that have been transplanted to the political arenas of newly independent states.

While ethnic violence is not a feature limited by any means to that category of states we call democratic, it is certainly clear to anyone examining either the events of our own day or those of the past, that democracies, or even efforts to create democracies, all too frequently produce outbursts of ethnic rioting. Myron Weiner (1989:9) recently raised this very issue about India: "How does one explain why India's democratic institutional structure persists, and how does one explain the paradox of a democratic system continuing to function in the midst of sharp social cleavages and large-scale violence?" India's democratic system continues to flourish, says Weiner; although "conflicts among religions, castes and tribal communities have shown no signs of abating," and although the record of democracy is not an unblemished one, as illustrated by the period of emergency from 1975 to 1977. The same question, with some modification and greater skepticism, can be asked about Sri Lanka (and other places).

Indian democracy has recently staged its ninth national elections, and it is widely celebrated for good reasons. It has developed a number of successful mechanisms for mediating disputes, adjusting interests, and settling claims. However, the paradox posed by Weiner has to be answered, and my answer is that participatory democracy, mass militancy, and crowd violence are not disconnected. They were, and are, not disconnected in Europe: In Britain, for instance, the latter part of the nineteenth century saw the parallel rise of democracy and industrial militancy through the two suffrage acts and the emergence of the new unionism. (Incidentally, the poll tax riot that recently burst in London reminds us that crowd violence to deal with political grievance is always a possibility.) And before that, the French Revolution had ushered in the crowd as an enduring political force with the storming of the Bastille as the unforgettable event of crowd politics. Thereafter, political doctrines of democracy had to speak directly of the people, for or against it, and governments had to shape techniques to control the militant crowd that

signified people's power, just as intellectuals had to accommodate it as a potent factor in their social and political theories.[8]

It seems to me that students of South Asian politics should make ample room today for ethnic politics and collective violence as an integral component of their theories of democracy at work. We have, on the one hand, the ideal normative description of democracy as a rational system of representative government where citizens as individuals – with "one man – one vote" – make rational choices according to their interests and values as to what parties to support and which candidates to elect. And this theory also holds that the governed hold their governors to account through periodic elections and by recourse to judicial process.

But democracy in South Asia is also a manner of conducting mass politics. The mobilization of the crowds and the wooing of their support – through election speeches, rallies, mass media propaganda, and dispensation of favors through election machines – is the central process of persuasion and vote-getting. This reliance on crowds opens the door to the invention and propagation of collective slogans and collective ideologies, to the appeal to collective entitlements for groups in terms of divisive "substance codes" (to borrow a term from McKim Marriott). Today, ethnicity is the most potent energizer, embodying and radiating religious, linguistic, territorial, and class identities and interests; it is also an umbrella under which personal, familial, commercial, and other local scores are sought to be settled.

In the practice of democracy in India, Pakistan, Sri Lanka, and Bangladesh, the Weiner paradox is facilitated by presenting public policies through the media as if they are outcomes of rational debate, and by parading public rituals and spectacles as the process of consultation of the masses and of seeking their legitimization and consent.

Other processes in the practice of democracy also stimulate the generation of communal violence. An increasing number of commentators, both Indian and Western, are drawing our attention to the dangers of the Indian State becoming a relatively independent and dominant actor, with its own interests that dictate specific policies in relation to ethnic and cultural groups in the polity. Engaged in its unrealistic project of creating a homogenized nation state, it frustrates the cultural and social pluralism of India.[9]

Notes

1 The other two domains are topics too diverse for anything more than brief mention here. One is the study of displaced persons, the refugees, and others who have taken flight and have faced relocation. Their liminal existence; their placement in camps; their discipline and control by authorities; their subjection to invidious comparisons with the local populace; their additional infirmities if they have transgressed national state boundaries and their placement in the limbo of "non-nationals"; their attempts to reconstruct their own identity and their theodicy of suffering in mytho-historical terms – these are some of the features of the anthropology of displacement and dislocation. This train of inquiry ultimately merges with the stituation of overseas communities established as a result of diaspora and their complex attitudes and relations with their own kind at home, and with their host populations.

The other is the study of the experiences, sufferings and coping patterns of the victims and survivors. The trials of suffering, torture, and witnessing the brutal deaths of husbands and sons, and kinsmen and friends; the traumas of women becoming widows; of women raped and humiliated; of the inability of survivors to conduct normal mortuary rites and grieving for their dead; and of the loss of home and property and business. These ordeals and the means of coping with them at all levels from the individual to the collective, as well as the social and psychic costs that deter restoration and rehabilitation, are features of the anthropology of collective suffering.

2 I owe this story to Dr Tariq Banuri.

3 Ethnic riots also occur in border regions whose local inhabitants and "tribes" feel their "homelands" are being appropriated by immigrants and "aliens," and that they themselves are being demographically swamped by the new colonists. Similar attitudes are generated in interior provinces where new peasant resettlement schemes are instituted and populated by peasants transplanted from other overcrowded and poverty-stricken areas. See, for example, Myron Weiner (1978).

4 See report by Amnesty International (International Secretariat, London) *India, Allegations of Extrajudicial Killings by The Provincial Armed Constabulary in and around Meerut*, 22–23 May, 1987. November 1987.

5 My sources are: *Report of the Citizens' Commission*, 1984. *Who are the Guilty?*, 1984. Uma Chakravarty and Nandita Haksar, 1987. *Report of Justice Ranganath Misra Commission of Inquiry*, 1986.

6 My chief source is Ali and Shaheed, 1987. In fact, another spate of violence occurred in the following year from December 12–17 (1986) whose immediate or proximate origins also had little to do with its eventual crystallization as another case of the Pathan–Muhajir ethnic conflict. See Akamal Hussain, 1987.

7 An essay on these riots written by me will be published in a projected volume on Ethnic Conflict and Collective Violence.

8 See J. S. McClelland (1989) for a discussion of this theme.

9 See Paul Brass, *Ethnic Groups and the State*, 1985, pp. 1–58. Also *Daedalus, Another India*, Fall 1989, essays by Ashis Nandy, "The Political Culture of the Indian State," pp. 1–26, and Rajni Kothari, "The Indian Enterprise Today," pp. 51–67.

References

Ali, Amineh Azam and Farida Saheed. 1987. "Karachi Riots, April 1985. A report of the Pathan-Bihari Clashes in Orangi." Paper read at the Kathmandu Conference of the International Centre of Ethnic Studies, 15 February 1987.

Amnesty International. 1987. *India, Allegations of Extrajudicial Killings by the Provincial Armed Constabulary in and around Meerut, 22–23 May, 1987*. London: International Secretariat.

Brass, Paul. 1985. *Ethnic Groups and the State*. London: Crown Helm.

Chakravarty, Uma and Nandita Haksar. 1987. *The Delhi Riots. Three Days in the Life of a Nation*. New Delhi: Lancer International.

Harrison, Selig S. 1960. *India: the Most Dangerous Decades*. Princeton: Princeton University Press.

Hussain, Akmal. 1987. "The Karachi Riots of December 1986: Crisis of State and Civil Society in Pakistan." Paper read at the Kathmandu Conference of International Centre for Ethnic Studies, February 15–17, 1987.

McClelland, J. S. *The Crowd and the Mob. From Plato to Canetti*. London: Unwin Hyman.

Report of the Citizen's Commission, Delhi 31 October–November 10, 1984. 1984 Delhi: Tata Press Ltd.

Report of the Justice Ranganath Misra Commission of Inquiry. Vols 1 and 2. 1986. New Delhi: S. N.

Tambiah, Stanley J. 1989. "Ethnic Conflict in the World Today." *American Ethnologist*. 16 (2):335–349.

Weiner, Myron. 1978. *Sons of the Soil: Migration and Ethnic Conflict in India*. Princeton: Princeton University Press.

———. 1989. *The Indian Paradox. Essays in Indian Politics*. London: Sage Publishers.

Who are the Guilty? 1984. Report of a Joint Inquiry the Causes and Impact of the Riots in Delhi from 31 October–10 November. Peoples' Union for Democratic Rights; Peoples' Union for Civil Liberties. New Delhi: Excellent Printing Services.

16

Ayodhya

The Modernity of Hinduism

Pankaj Mishra

1. History as Myth

Ayodhya is the city of Rama, the most virtuous and austere of Hindu gods. Traveling to it
in January 2002 from Benares, across a wintry
North Indian landscape of mustard-bright fields,
hectic roadside bazaars, and lonely columns of
smoke, I felt myself moving between two very
different Hindu myths, or visions of life. Shiva,
the god of perpetual destruction and creation,
rules Benares, where temple compounds secrete
Internet cafés and children fly kites next to open
funeral pyres by the river. But the city's aggressive affluence and chaos seem far away in Ayodhya, which is small and drab, its alleys full of the
dust of the surrounding flat fields. The peasants
with unwieldy bundles under their arms brought
to mind the pilgrims of medieval Indian miniature painting, and sitting by the Saryu River at
dusk, watching the devout tenderly set afloat tiny
earthen lamps in the slow-moving water, I felt
the endurance and continuity of Hindu India.

After that vision of eternal Hinduism, the
numerous mosques and Moghul buildings in
Ayodhya came as a surprise. Most of them
are in ruins, especially the older ones built
during the sixteenth and seventeenth centuries,
when Ayodhya was the administrative center
of a major province of the Moghul empire,
Awadh. All but two were destroyed as recently
as December 6, 1992, the day, epochal now
in India's history, on which a crowd led by
politicians from the Hindu nationalist BJP
demolished the mosque they claimed the
sixteenth-century Moghul emperor Babur had
built, as an act of contempt, on the site of the
god Ram's birthplace.

None of the mosques is likely to be repaired
anytime soon; the Muslim presence in the town
seems at an end for the first time in eight
centuries. This was the impression I got even
in January 2002, a month before anti-Muslim
rage exploded in the western Indian state
of Gujarat, at Digambar Akhara, the large,
straw-littered compound of the militant sadhu
sect presided over by Ramchandra Paramhans.
In 1949, Paramhans initiated the legal battle to
reclaim Babur's mosque, or the Babri Masjid,

Perspectives on Modern South Asia: A Reader in Culture, History, and Representation, First Edition.
Edited by Kamala Visweswaran.
© 2011 Blackwell Publishing Ltd. Published 2011 by Blackwell Publishing Ltd.

for the Hindu community; in December 1992 he exuberantly directed the demolition squad.

The sect, Paramhans told me, was established four centuries ago to fight the Muslim invaders who had ravaged India since the tenth century AD and erected mosques over temples in the holy cities of Ayodhya, Benares, and Mathura. The sadhus had been involved, he added, in the seventy-six wars for possession of the site of the mosque in Ayodhya, in which more than two hundred thousand Hindus had been martyred.

Two bodyguards nervously watched my face as Paramhans described this history. More armed men stood over the thin-bricked wall of the compound. The security seemed excessive in what was an exclusively Hindu environment. But as Paramhans explained, caressing the tufts of white hair on the tip of his nose, the previous year, he had been attacked by homemade bombs delivered by what he called "Muslim terrorists."

Paramhans, who died in 2004 at the age of ninety-three, headed the trust in charge of building the temple, which the leaders of the BJP had vowed to build on the site of Babur's mosque. When I spoke to Paramhans in late January 2002, he expected up to a million Hindu volunteers to reach Ayodhya by March 15, defying a Supreme Court ban on construction at the site of the mosque, and to present another fait accompli to the world in the form of a half-built temple.

Thousands of Hindu activists from across India traveled to Ayodhya through the first few weeks of February. Many of them were from the prosperous state of Gujarat, whose entrepreneurial Hindus, often found living in Europe and the United States, have formed a loyal constituency of the Hindu nationalists since the 1980s. On February 27, some of these activists were returning on the train from Ayodhya when a crowd of Muslims attacked and set fire to two of the cars just outside the town of Godhra in Gujarat. Fifty-eight Hindus, many of them women and children, were burned alive.

Murderous crowds of Hindu nationalists seeking to avenge the attack in Godhra rampaged across Gujarat for the next few weeks. Wearing the saffron scarves and khaki shorts of Hindu nationalists, they were often armed with swords, trishuls (tridents), sophisticated explosives, and gas cylinders. They had the addresses of various Muslim families and businesses, which they attacked systematically. The police did nothing to stop them and even led the charge against Muslims. A BJP minister sat in police control rooms while pleas for assistance from Muslims were routinely disregarded. Hindu-owned newspapers printed fabricated stories about Muslim atrocities and incited Hindus to avenge the killings of Hindu pilgrims.

In the end, more than two thousand people, mostly Muslims, were killed. About 230 mosques and shrines, including a five-hundred-year-old mosque, were razed to the ground, some replaced with Hindu temples. Close to one hundred thousand Muslims found themselves in relief camps. Corpses filled mass gravesites; they often arrived there mangled beyond recognition, with fetuses missing from the bellies of pregnant women that had been cut open.

The chief minister of Gujarat, a young up-and-coming leader of the Hindu nationalists called Narendra Modi, quoted Isaac Newton to explain the killings of Muslims. "Every action," he said, "has an equal and opposite reaction." The Indian prime minister at the time, Atal Bihari Vajpayee, who visited the site of the massacres a whole month after they began, expressed shame and lamented that India's image had been spoiled. "What face will I now show to the world?" he said, referring to his forthcoming trip to Singapore. Later, at a BJP meeting, he rejected demands from the opposition and the press for Modi's sacking and proposed early elections in Gujarat. In a public speech, he seemed to blame Muslims. "Wherever they are," he said, "they don't want to live in peace." He added, referring to Muslims and Christians, "We have allowed them to do their prayers and follow their religion. No one should teach us about secularism." A resolution passed by the RSS (Rashtriya Swayamsevak Sangh – National Volunteers Organization), the parent group of Hindu nationalists, from which have emerged almost all the leaders of the BJP, the VHP (Vishwa Hindu Parishad), and the Bajrang Dal, and whose mission is to create a Hindu state, described the retaliatory killings as "spontaneous," stating, "The entire Hindu society had reacted," and even making the following declaration: "Let Muslims understand," the RSS said, "that their real safety lies in the goodwill of the majority." Both Vajpayee and his senior-most colleague, L. K. Advani, are members of the RSS, which was involved in the assassination of Mahatma Gandhi in 1948.

In Ayodhya in January, Paramhans had told me, "Before we take on Pakistani terrorists," he said, "we have to take care of the offsprings Babur left behind in India; these one hundred thirty million Muslims of India have to be shown their place." This message seems to have been taken to heart in Gujarat, where the Hindu nationalists displayed a high degree of administrative efficiency in the killing of Muslims. In Gujarat's cities, middle-class Hindu men drove up in new Japanese cars, the emblems of India's globalized economy, to cart off the loot from Muslim shops and businesses.

The rich young Hindus in Benetton T-shirts and Nike sneakers appeared unlikely combatants in what Paramhans told me was a *dharma yudh*, a holy war, against the traitorous 12 percent of India's population. Both wealth and education separated them from the unemployed, listless small-town Hindus I met in Ayodhya, one of whom was a local convener of the Bajrang Dal (Hanuman's Army), the storm troopers of the Hindu nationalists, which has been implicated in several incidents of violence against Christians and Muslims across India, including the 1998 murder of an Australian missionary in the eastern state of Orissa. In response to a question about Muslims, he dramatically unsheathed his knife and invited me to feel the sharpness of the triple-edged blade, in the form of the trident of the Hindu god Shiva.

But despite their differences, the rich and unemployed Hindus shared a particular worldview. This was outlined most clearly for me, during my travels across North India in early 2002, by students at Saraswati Shishu Mandir, a primary school in Benares, one of the fifteen thousand such institutions run by the RSS. The themes of the morning assembly I attended were manliness and patriotism. In the gloomy hall, portraits of the more militant of Hindu freedom fighters mingled with such signboarded exhortations as GIVE ME BLOOD AND I'LL GIVE YOU FREEDOM, INDIA IS A HINDU NATION, and SAY WITH PRIDE THAT YOU ARE A HINDU. For over an hour, boys and girls in matching uniforms of white and blue, marching up and down in front of a stage where a plaster of paris statue of Mother India stood on a map of South Asia, chanted speeches and songs about the perfidy of Pakistan, of Muslim invaders, and of the gloriousness of India's past.

This message clearly resonates at a level of caste and class privilege, flourishing in a society where deprivation always lies close at hand. But the school and most of its pupils and the surrounding area were firmly middle-class; just beyond the gates, banners advertising computer courses hung from electric poles bristling with illegal connections. The out-of-work upper-caste advertising executive I met at my hotel in Benares seemed to be speaking of his own insecurities when he suddenly said, after some wistful talk of the latest iMac, "Man, I am scared of these mozzies. We are a secular modern nation, but we let them run these madrassas, we let them breed like rabbits, and one day they are going to outstrip the Hindu population, and will they then treat us as well as we treat them?"

The Muslims of course have a different view of how they have been treated in secular, modern India. In Madanpura, Benares's Muslim locality, a few minutes' walk from Gyanvapi, one of two Moghul mosques the Hindu nationalists have threatened to destroy, I met Najam, a scholar of Urdu and Persian literatures. He is in his early thirties and grew up with some of the worst anti-Muslim violence of postindependence India. In the slaughter in Benares in 1992, he saw Hindu policemen beat his doctor to death with rifle butts.

"I don't think the Muslims are angry anymore," he said. "There is no point. The people who demolished the mosque at Ayodhya are now senior ministers in Delhi. We know we will always be suspected of disloyalty no matter what we say or do. Our madrassas will always be seen as producing fanatics and terrorists. We know we are helpless; there is no one ready to listen to us, and so we keep silent. We expect nothing from the government and political parties. We now depend on the goodwill of the Hindus we live with, and all that we hope for is survival, with a little bit of dignity."

Hindu devotees throng the famous Viswanath Temple in Benares all day long, but few, if any, Muslims dare to negotiate their way through the scores of armed policemen and sandbagged positions to offer namaz at the adjacent Gyan-vapi Mosque. It is not easy for an outsider to enter the Indian Muslim's sense of isolation. There was certainly little in my own background that could have prepared me to understand the complicated history behind it. As Brahmins with little money, we perceived Muslims as another threat to our aspirations to security and dignity. My sisters attended an RSS-run primary school where pupils were encouraged to disfigure the sketches of Muslim rulers in their history text-books. At the English medium school I went to, we were taught to think of ourselves as secular and modern citizens of India and view religion as something one outgrows.

In the 1970s and 1980s, when I heard about Hindu–Muslim riots or the insurgencies in Pun-jab and Kashmir, it seemed to me that religion was the cause of most conflict and violence in India. The word used in the newspapers and in academic analyses was "communalism," the antithesis of the secularism advocated by the founding fathers of India, Gandhi and Nehru, and also the antithesis of Hinduism itself, which was held to be innately tolerant and secular.

Living in Benares in the late eighties, I was unaware that this ancient Hindu city was also holy for Muslims, unaware too of the seventeenth-century Sufi shrine just behind the tea shack where I often spent my mornings. It was one of many in the city, which both Hindus and Muslims visited, part of the flowering of Sufi culture in medieval North India. It was only in 2002, after talking to Najam, the young Persian scholar I met in Benares, that I discov-ered that one of the great Shia philosophers of Persia had sought refuge at the court of a Hindu ruler of Benares in the eighteenth century. And it was only after returning from my most recent trip to Ayodhya that I read that Rama's primacy

in this pilgrimage center was a recent event, that Ayodhya was for much of the medieval period the home of the much older and prestigious sects of Shaivites, or Shiva worshipers (Rama is only one of the many incarnations of Vishnu, one of the gods in the Hindu trinity, in which Shiva is the most important); many of the temples and sects currently devoted to Rama actually emerged under the patronage of the Shia Muslims who had begun to rule Awadh in the early eighteenth century.

Ramchandra Paramhans in Ayodhya had been quick to offer me a history full of temple-destroying Muslims and brave Hindu nationalists. Yet Paramhans's own militant sect had originally been formed to fight not Muslims but Shiva-worshiping Hindus, and it had been favored in this long and bloody conflict by the Muslim nawabs, who later gave generous grants of land to the victorious devotees of Rama. The nawabs, whose administration and army were staffed by Hindus, kept a careful distance from Hindu–Muslim conflicts. One of the first such conflicts in Ayodhya occurred in 1855, when some Muslims accused Hindus of illegally constructing a temple over a mosque, and militant Hindu sadhus (mendicants) massacred seventy-five Muslims. The then nawab of Awadh, Wajid Ali Shah, a distinguished poet and composer, refused to support the Muslim claim on the building, explaining:

> We are devoted to love; do not know of religion. So what if it is Kaaba or a house of idols?

Wajid Ali Shah, denounced as effeminate and inept and deposed a year later by British impe-rialists, was the last great exponent of the Indo-Persian culture that emerged in Awadh toward the end of the Moghul empire, when India was one of the greatest centers of the Islamic world, along with the Ottoman and the Safavid empires. Islam in India lost some of its Arabian and Per-sian distinctiveness, blended with older cultures, but its legacy is still preserved amid the squalor of a hundred small Indian towns, in the grace and elegance of Najam's Urdu, in the numerous songs and dances that accompany festivals and marriages, in the subtle cuisines of North India, and the fineness of the silk saris of Benares, but one could think of it, as I did, as something just there, without a history or tradition. The Indo-Islamic inheritance has formed very little part of, and is increasingly an embarrassment to, the idea of India that has been maintained by the modernizing Hindu elite over the last fifty years.

That idea first emerged in the early nineteenth century, as the British consolidated their hold over India and found new allies among upper-caste Hindus. In India, as elsewhere in their empire, the British had largely supplanted, and encountered stiff resistance from, Muslim rulers. Accordingly, the British tended to demonize Muslims as fanatics and tyrants and presented their conquest of India as at least partly a humanitarian intervention on behalf of the once-great Hindu nation that had been oppressed for centuries by Muslim despots and condemned to backwardness.

Most of these early British views of India were useful fictions at best since the Turks, Afghans, Central Asians, and Persians who together with upper-caste Hindu elites had ruled a variety of Indian states for over eight centuries were rather more than plunderers and zealots. The bewildering diversity of people that inhabited India before the arrival of the Muslims in the eleventh century hardly formed a community, much less a nation, and the word "Hinduism" barely hinted at the almost infinite number of folk and elite cultures, religious sects, and philosophical traditions found in India.

But these novel British ideas were received well by educated upper-caste Hindus who had previously worked with Muslim rulers and then begun to see opportunities in the new imperial order. British discoveries of India's classical sculpture, painting, and literature had given them a fresh invigorating sense of the pre-Islamic past of India. They found flattering and useful those British Orientalist notions of India that identified Brahmanical scriptures and principles of tolerance as the core of Hinduism. In this view, such practices as widow burning became proof of the degradation Hinduism had suffered during Muslim rule, and the cruelties of caste became an unfortunate consequence of Muslim tyranny.

A wide range of Hindu thinkers, social reformers, and politicians followed the British in dismissing the centuries of Muslim domination as a time of darkness and upholding imperial rule with all its social reforms and scientific advances as preparation for self-rule. Some denounced British imperialism as exploitative, but even they welcomed its redeeming modernity and, above all, the European idea of the nation – a cohesive community with a common history, culture, values, and sense of purpose – which for many other colonized peoples appeared a way of duplicating the success of the powerful, all-conquering West.

Muslim leaders, on the other hand, were slow to participate in the civilizing mission of imperialism; they saw little place for themselves in the idea of the nation as espoused by the Hindu elite. British imperialists followed their own strategies of divide and rule; the decision to partition Bengal in 1905 and to have separate electorates for Muslims further reinforced the sense among many upwardly mobile Indians that they belonged to distinct communities defined exclusively by religion.

It is true that Gandhi and Nehru worked hard to attract low-caste Hindus and Muslims; they wanted to give a mass base and wider legitimacy to the political demands for self-rule that intensified in the early twentieth century under the leadership of the Congress Party. But Gandhi's use of popular Hindu symbols, which made him a mahatma among Hindu masses, caused many Muslims to distrust him. Also, many Congress leaders shared the views not of Gandhi or of the poet Rabindranath Tagore, who criticized Western-style nationalism, but of such upper-caste ideologues as Veer Savarkar and Guru Golwalkar, the spiritual and ideological parents of Hindu nationalists of today.

2. The Rashtriya Swayamsevak Sangh: Indian-Style Fascism

On the evening of January 30, 1948, five months after the independence and partition of India, Mahatma Gandhi was walking to a prayer meeting in the grounds of his temporary home in New Delhi when he was shot three times in the chest and abdomen. Gandhi was then seventy-nine years old and a forlorn figure. He had been unable to prevent, and so was widely blamed by many Hindus for, the bloody creation of Pakistan as a separate homeland for Indian Muslims. The violent uprooting of millions of Hindus and Muslims across the hastily drawn borders of India and Pakistan had tainted the freedom from colonial rule that he had been so arduously working toward. When the bullets from an automatic pistol hit his frail body at point-blank range, he collapsed and died instantly. His assassin made no attempt to escape and even, as he would later claim, shouted for the police.

Millions of shocked Indians waited anxiously for further news that night, fearing unspeakable violence if Gandhi's murderer proved to be a Muslim. There was much relief, and also some puzzlement, the next morning when the assassin was revealed as Nathuram Godse, a Hindu Brahmin from western India, a region relatively untouched by the murderous passions of the partition.

Born in a lower-middle-class family, Godse began his career in 1932 as a Hindu activist with the RSS, which had been founded by a Brahmin doctor called Hegdewar in the central Indian city of Nagpur seven years previously. The RSS was, and remains, dedicated to establishing a Hindu nation by uniting Hindus from all castes and sects and by forcing Muslims, Christians, and other Indian minorities to embrace Hindu culture. Godse received both physical and ideological training from members of the RSS and absorbed their ideas about the greatness of pre-Islamic India and the havoc wrought upon Hindus by eight centuries of Muslim invasions and tyranny.

During his trial, Godse made a long and eloquent speech in English explaining his background and motives. He claimed that Gandhi's 'constant and consistent pandering to the Muslims,' whom he described variously as fanatical, violent, and antinational, had left him with no choice. He blamed Gandhi for the "vivisection of the country – our motherland" and denounced the latter's insistence upon nonviolence, saying that it was "absurd to expect [four hundred million] people to regulate

their lives on such a lofty plane." He claimed it was the terrorist methods of Hindu and Sikh freedom fighters, not Gandhi's nonviolence, that had forced the British to leave India, and hoped that with Gandhi dead, "Indian politics would surely be practical, able to retaliate," and the nation, he claimed, "would be saved from the inroads of Pakistan."

Godse requested that the judge at his trial show him no mercy, and he did not appeal against the death sentence passed on him. He went to the gallows in November 1949 shouting such slogans as "Long Live the Undivided India" and singing paeans to the "Living Motherland, the Land of the Hindus." The Indian government under Pandit Nehru banned the RSS a few days after Gandhi's murder and arrested thousands of its members. The ban was lifted a year later, after the RSS agreed to have a written constitution and confine itself to "cultural" activities, a promise it quickly broke.

Not much is known about the RSS in the West, although both the former prime minister Atal Bihari Vajpayee and his deputy, L. K. Advani belong to it and have never repudiated its militant ideology, the ideology of Hindu nationalism that seeks aggressively to "Hinduize" South Asia and has often threatened to plunge the region, which has the largest Muslim population in the world and two nuclear-armed nations, into catastrophic war.

After September 11, 2001, the Hindu nationalists presented themselves to the West as reliable allies in the fight against Muslim fundamentalists. But in India their resemblance to the European fascist movements of the 1930s has been clear for a long time. In his manifesto *We, or Our Nationhood Defined* (1938), Guru Golwalkar, director of the RSS from 1940 to 1973, during which time both Mr. Vajpayee and Mr. Advani joined the organization and rose to become senior leaders of its political wing, said that the Nazis had manifested "race pride at its highest" by purging Germany of the Jews. According to Golwalkar, India was Hindustan, a land of Hindus where Jews and Parsis could only ever be "guests," and to which Muslims and Christians came as "invaders." Golwalkar was clear about what he expected from both the guests and the invaders:

> The foreign races in Hindustan must either adopt the Hindu culture and language, must learn to respect and hold in reverence Hindu religion, must entertain no idea but those of the glorification of the Hindu race and culture, i.e. of the Hindu nation and must lose their separate existence to merge in the Hindu race, or may stay in the country, wholly subordinated to the Hindu nation, claiming nothing, deserving no privileges, far less any preferential treatment – not even citizen's rights. There is, at least should be, no other course for them to adopt.

Golwalkar and his disciples in the RSS and Congress saw India as the sacred indigenous nation of Hindus which had been divided and emasculated by Muslim invaders, and which could be revived only by uniting India's diverse population, recovering ancient Hindu traditions, and weeding out corrupting influences from Central Asia and Arabia. This meant forcing Indian Muslims to give up their allegiance to such alien lands and faiths as Mecca and Islam and embrace the so-called Hindu ethos, or Hindutva, of India, an ethos that was, ironically, imagined into being with the help of British Orientalist discoveries of India's past.

By the 1940s the feudal and professional Muslim elite of India had grown extremely wary of the Hindu nationalist strain within the Congress. After many failed attempts at political rapprochement, this elite finally arrived at the demand for a separate homeland for Indian Muslims. The demand expressed the Muslim fear of being reduced to a perpetual minority in a Hindu majority state and was, initially, a desire for a more federal polity for postcolonial India. But the leaders of the Congress chose to partition the Muslim-majority provinces in the west and east rather than share the centralized power of the colonial state that was their great inheritance from the British.

This led to the violent transfer of millions of Hindus, Sikhs, and Muslims across hastily drawn artificial borders. The massacres, rapes, and kidnappings further hardened sectarian feelings; the RSS, which was temporarily banned after Gandhi's assassination, found its most dedicated volunteers among middle-class Hindu refugees from Pakistan, such as the former home minister, Lal Krishna Advani, who was born in Muslim-dominated Karachi and joined the RSS as early as 1942. The RSS floated a new party, the Jana Sangh, later to become the BJP, which entered electoral politics in independent India in 1951 with the renewed promise of a Hindu nation; although it worked for much of the next three decades in the gigantic shadow of the Congress Party, its sudden popularity in the 1980s now seems part of the great disaster of partition, which locked the new nation-states of India and Pakistan into stances of mutual hostility.

In Pakistan, a shared faith failed to reconfigure the diverse regional and linguistic communities into a new nation. This was proved when the Bengali-speaking population of East Pakistan seceded, with Indian help, to form the new state of Bangladesh in 1971. Muslims in India continue to lack effective spokespersons, despite, or perhaps because of, the tokenist presence of Muslims at the highest levels of the government. Politically, they are significant only during elections, when they form a solid vote bank for those Hindu politicians promising to protect them against discrimination and violence. Their representation in government jobs has steadily declined.

Secularism, the separation of religion from politics was always going to be difficult to impose upon a country where religion has long shaped political and cultural identities. But it was the only useful basis on which the centralized government in Delhi could, in the name of modernity and progress, establish its authority over a poor and chaotically fractious country. However, when Sikh and Muslim minorities in the states of Punjab and Kashmir challenged the great arbitrary power of the Indian government, Nehru's heirs, his daughter, Indira, and grandson Rajiv, were quick to discard even the rhetoric of secularism and to turn Hindu majoritarianism into the official ideology of the Congress-run central Indian government.

The uprisings in Punjab, and then Kashmir, were portrayed by the Indian government and the middle-class media as fundamentalist and terrorist assaults on secular democracy. In fact, although tainted by association with Pakistan and religious fanaticism, the Sikhs and Kashmiri Muslims expressed a long-simmering discontent with an antifederalist state in Delhi, a state that had retained most of the power of the old colonial regime and often wielded it more brutally than the British ever had. The uprisings were part of a larger crisis, one that has occurred elsewhere in postcolonial nations, the failure of a corrupt and self-serving political and bureaucratic elite to ensure social and economic justice for those it had claimed to represent in its anticolonial battles.

By the 1980s, when the Hindu nationalists abruptly rose to prominence, the Congress had disillusioned lower-caste Hindus and looked incapable of preserving even the interests of its upper-caste Hindu constituency. It kept raising the bogey of national unity and external enemies. But the disturbances in the border states of Kashmir and Punjab only gave more substance to the Hindu nationalist allegation that the Congress with its "pseudosecularism" had turned India into a "soft state," where Kashmiri Muslims could blithely conspire with Pakistan against Mother India.

It was in the 1980s, with the Congress rapidly declining and the pseudosocialist economy close to bankruptcy, that the Hindu nationalists saw a chance to find new voters among upper-caste Hindus. Like the National Socialists in Germany in the early 1930s, they offered not so much clear economic policies as fantasies of national rebirth and power. In 1984 the VHP announced a national campaign to rebuild the grand temple at Ayodhya; the mosque the first Moghul emperor Babur, had erected was, they said, a symbol of national shame; removing it and rebuilding the temple were a matter of national honor.

Both history and archaeology were travestied in this account of the fall and rise of the eternal Hindu nation. There is no evidence that Babur had ever been to Ayodhya or that this restless, melancholic conqueror from Samarkand, a connoisseur of architecture, could have built an ugly mosque over an existing Rama temple. Rama himself isn't known to recorded history; the cult of Rama worship arrived in North India as late as the tenth century AD, and no persuasive evidence exists for the Rama temple that apparently once stood on the site of the mosque.

But the myths were useful in reinforcing the narrative of Muslim cruelty and contempt. At first, they found their keenest audience among wealthy expatriate Hindus in the UK and the United States, who generously bankrolled a movement that in upholding a strong self-assertive Hinduism seemed to allay their sense of inferiority induced by Western images of India as a miserably poor country. In India the anxieties that persuaded many upper-caste Hindus to support the BJP were much deeper. In 1990 the government in Delhi, then headed by defectors from the Congress Party, decided to implement a long-standing proposal to reserve government jobs for poor "Backward-caste" Hindus. Upper-caste Hindus were enraged at this attack on their privilege. The BJP saw the plan for affirmative action as potentially destructive of its old goal of persuading lower-caste groups to accept a paternalistic upper-caste leadership as part of presenting a united Hindu front against Muslims.

Later that year the leader of the BJP, L. K. Advani, decided to lead a ritual procession on a faux chariot – actually a Chevrolet – from Gujarat to Ayodhya, where he intended to start the construction of the Rama temple. Appropriately, he set out from the temple in Somnath, Gujarat, which, looted by a Turk conqueror in the eleventh century AD, was lavishly rebuilt in the early 1950s by devout Hindu leaders of the Congress Party. This wasn't just playacting, however; more than five hundred people, most of them Muslims, were killed in the rioting that accompanied Advani's progress across India. Hindu policemen were indifferent and sometimes even participated in the violence. When I was in Benares recently, a friend casually pointed out a distant relative of his walking down the street. He was a retired police officer who liked to boast of how he had shot and killed fourteen Muslims during a riot in the city of Meerut.

It is strange to look back now and recall just two decades ago the temple–mosque controversy was hardly heard of outside Ayodhya. Local Hindus first staked a claim on the mosque in the mid-nineteenth century, and British officials allowed them to worship on a platform just outside the building. In 1949, two years after independence, a Hindu civil servant working together with local abbots surreptitiously placed idols of Rama inside the mosque. The story that Lord Rama himself had installed them there quickly spread. The local Muslims protested. Prime Minister Nehru sensed that nothing less than India's secular identity was threatened. He ordered the mosque to be locked and sacked the district official, who promptly joined the Hindu nationalists.

The idols, however, were not removed, and Muslims gradually gave up offering namaz at the mosque. During the three decades that followed, the courts were clogged with cases concerning Hindu and Muslim claims on the site. In 1984 the VHP began a campaign for the unlocking of the mosque. In 1986 a local judge allowed the Hindus to worship inside the building. A year later Muslims held their largest protest demonstration since independence in Delhi.

Until 1984, however, Babur's mosque remained relatively unknown outside of a small circle of litigious, property-hungry abbots in Ayodhya. Religion was a fiercely competitive business in Ayodhya. The local abbots fought hard for their share of donations from millions of poor pilgrims, and, more recently, wealthy Indians in the United States and the UK, and they were notorious for murder and pillage; the attack on Ramchandra Paramhans that he blamed on Muslim terrorists was probably the work of rival abbots. But as the movement for the temple intensified, entrepreneurs of religiosity such as Paramhans were repackaged by Hindu nationalist politicians as sages and saints and turned into national celebrities. Rama himself suddenly evolved from the benign, almost feminine, calendar art divinity of my childhood to the vengeful Rambo of Hindu nationalist posters.

The myths multiplied in October 1990, when Advani's Chevrolet chariot procession was stopped and police in Ayodhya fired upon a crowd of Hindus attempting to assault the mosque. The largest circulation Hindi paper in North India, *Dainik Jagran*, spoke of "indiscriminate police firing" and "hundreds of dead devotees" and then reduced the death toll the next day to thirty-two. The rumors and exaggerations, part of a slick propaganda campaign, helped the BJP win the elections in four North Indian states in 1991. The mosque seemed doomed. When on December 6, 1992, a crowd of mostly upper-caste Hindus, equipped with shovels, crowbars, pickaxes, and sometimes just their bare hands, demolished Babur's mosque, the police simply watched from a distance.

Uma Bharti, one of the more vocal of Hindu nationalist politicians cheer-led the crowd, shouting, "Give one more push and break the Babri Masjid." The president of the VHP announced the dawn of a "Hindu rebellion," while a leader of the BJP said for "those who want to see the flag of Pakistan flutter over Kashmir, the process of showing them their right place has begun."

That evening the crowd rampaged through Ayodhya, killing and burning thirteen Muslims, some of whom were children, and destroying scores of mosques, shrines, and Muslim-owned shops and houses Protests and riots then erupted across India. Altogether two thousand people, mostly Muslims, were killed. Three months after the massacres Muslim gangsters in Bombay retaliated with bomb attacks that killed more than three hundred civilians.

In Delhi, the elderly Congress prime minister, Narasimha Rao napped through the demolition. The next day he dismissed the BJP governments, banned the RSS and its sister organizations, and promised to rebuild the mosque. The leaders of the BJP tried to distance themselves from the demolition, saying that it was a spontaneous act of frustration, provoked by the anti-Hindu policies of the government. However, the Central Bureau of Investigation (CBI) concluded that such senior leaders of the BJP as L. K. Advani, subsequently home minister of India, had planned the demolition well in advance. As for the anti-Muslim violence, Advani claimed in an article in *The Times of India* that it would not have taken place had Muslims identified themselves with Hindutva, the same sentiment echoed after the riots in Gujarat.

Six years after the demolition, the BJP, benefiting from India's "first past the post" electoral system, became the dominant party in the ruling National Democratic Alliance (NDA) in Delhi. Despite its being forced to share power with more secular parties, the BJP's ideological fervor seemed undiminished, if ultimately unfulfilled. Certainly, the Hindu nationalists have tried hard to whip up Hindu passions. In early 1998, during their first few months in power, they conducted nuclear tests, explicitly aiming them against Pakistan, which responded with its own tests. The VHP and Bajrang Dal distributed radioactive earth from the nuclear test site as sacred offerings; they were also responsible for an unprecedented series of mob attacks on Christians across India. About half of these occurred in Gujarat, but Advani claimed that there was "no law and order problem in Gujarat" and at a meeting of Hindu nationalists shared the dais with the new chief of the RSS, K. S. Sudarshan. The latter spoke of "an epic war between Hindus and anti-Hindus," asked Christians and Muslims to return to their "Hindu roots," and also attacked secular intellectuals as "that class of bastards which tries to implant an alien culture in their land."

John Dayal, the vice president of the All India Catholic Union, told me that the RSS has spent millions of dollars in trying to convert tribal people to Hindu national-ism. Dayal, who monitors the missionary activities of the RSS very closely, claimed that in just over eighteen months the RSS distributed 350,000 trishuls, or tridents, in three contiguous tribal districts in Central India.

Dr B. L. Bhole, a political scientist I met at Nagpur University, saw a Brahminical ploy in these attempts. He told me that the RSS had tried to turn not just Gandhi but also Dr Ambedkar, the greatest leader of the Dalits, into a Hindu nationalist icon. K. S. Sudarshan, the current supreme director of the RSS, had recently garlanded the statue of Dr Ambedkar at the park in Nagpur where the latter rejected Hinduism and converted to Buddhism in 1956.

Dr Bhole thought this outrageous. He had joined local Dalit activists and intellectuals in ritual "purifying" the statue after Sudarshan's visit.

Dr Bhole said, "The RSS can't attract young middle-class people anymore, so they hope for better luck among the poorest, socially disadvantaged people. But the basic values the RSS promotes among low caste people and tribals are drawn from the high Sanskritic culture of Hinduism, which considers the cow as holy et cetera and which seeks to maintain a social hierarchy with Brahmins at the very top. The united Hindu nation they keep talking about is one where basically low-caste Hindus and Muslims and Christians and other com-munities don't complain much while accepting the dominance of a Brahmin minority. But the problem for the RSS is that most of the low-caste Hindus and tribals don't want to learn any Brahmin mantras. They form an increasingly independent political group within India today; they no longer want any kind of Brahmin pater-nalist leadership. Even such low-caste leaders of the BJP as Uma Bharti want to focus on tangible rights for their community; they won't be fobbed off with nationalist ideology. Their assertiveness is really the greatest achievement of democratic politics in India, which has so far been dominated by upper-caste Hindus."

Dr Bhole said, "The RSS has been most suc-cessful in Gujarat, where low-caste Hindus and tribals were indoctrinated at the kind of schools you went to; they were in the mobs led by upper-caste Hindu nationalists that attacked Muslims and Christians. But the RSS still doesn't have much support among low-caste people outside Gujarat. For the RSS, this is a serious setback, and the only thing they can do to increase their mass base is keep stoking anti-Muslim and anti-Christian passions and hope they can get enough Hindus, both upper-caste and low-caste, behind them."

The consistent demonizing of Muslims and Christians by Hindu nationalists may seem gratuitous – Christians in India are a tiny and scattered minority, and the Muslims are too poor, disorganized, and fearful to pose any kind of threat to Hindus – but it is indispensable to the project of a Hindu nation. Hindu nationalists have always sought to redefine Hindu identity in opposition to a supposedly threatening "other." They hope to unite Hindu society by constantly invoking such real and imagined threats as are posed by the evangelical Christians and militant Muslims.

Visiting villages and towns across North India in the last few years, I found Muslims full of anxiety about their fate in India. They spoke to me of an insidious and regular violence, of the frequent threats and beatings they received from local Hindu politicians and policemen.

The growth of religious militancy in South Asia is likely to enthuse many Hindus. As they see it, Gujarat proved to be a successful "laboratory" of Hindu nationalism, in which carefully stoked anti-Muslim sentiments eventually brought about a pogrom, and a Muslim backlash seemed to lead to even greater Hindu "unity."

The victory of the BJP in Gujarat indicated that this plan was going well. It hinted that well-to-do Indians were likely to support the Hindu nationalists, even the extremists among them, as long as they continued to liberalize the Indian economy and help create a consumer revolution. But neither the BJP nor their supporters had reckoned with the larger, neglected majority of India's population, which expressed its skepticism about Hindu unity by voting out the BJP in the general elections in May 2004.

Opinion pollsters, political pundits, and journalists had predicted an easy victory for the ruling NDA (National Democratic Alliance), the coalition of BJP and its allies, which claimed in its advertising campaign to have created an "India Shining" in the previous six years. But it was the opposition Congress that emerged as the single largest party in the 545-seat Indian Parliament. These results surprised most middle-class Indians, for it was during the BJP's six years in power that India's urban prosperity achieved by the economic reforms initiated in 1991 became most visible. The BJP had supported the reforms, which benefited greatly those who were best placed to take advantage of new opportunities in business and trade and the economy's fast-growing service

sector (information technology, jobs offshored by Europe and America), the educated middle class, the BJP's primary constituency, which, despite growing fast in recent years, still makes up less than 20 percent of India's population.

The reforms also attracted a generation of rich Indians who live in the United States and the UK and were eager for cultural and economic links with their ancestral land, a desire that turned nonresident Indians into the BJP's most devoted followers and sponsors and helped the BJP itself evolve rapidly, despite its Hindu nationalism, into a keen advocate of economic globalization. During its six years in power, new freeways, shopping malls, brand-name boutiques, Starbucks-style coffee bars, and restaurants with exotic cuisine and London prices transformed the cities of Bangalore, Hyderabad, Delhi, Chennai, and Bombay. Newfound wealth created a heady mood among the middle class, what the leaders of the BJP called the "feel-good factor" (so important that in March 2004 the BJP was initially reluctant to send the Indian cricket team to Pakistan out of the fear that it might lose and make the cricket-obsessed nationalist middle class feel not so good anymore). Most English-language newspapers began to print entire daily supplements in order to cover film premieres, fashion shows, champagne-tasting sessions in five-star hotels, and the lifestyles of beauty pageant winners, models, Bollywood actors, and other celebrities. The general air of celebration overwhelmed many formerly left-wing intellectuals, academics, and journalists. Convinced that the BJP would be in power for many years, they aligned themselves openly with the party and lobbied for political and diplomatic posts. Some of the most influential TV news channels, newspapers, and magazines, including *India Today*, once India's best news-magazine, were content to become an echo chamber for the BJP's views.

Not surprisingly, the BJP, and its supporters and advisers in the media, couldn't see beyond the "India Shining" of the Hindu middle class and turn their attention to the 70 percent of Indians living in the countryside. They barely noticed the Indians who live in slums or in equally degrading conditions in the big cities, the fact that while high-tech hospitals in the big cities cater to rich Indians and foreigners, or medical tourists, public health facilities in small towns and villages decline rapidly; that communicable diseases such as malaria, dengue, and encephalitis have revived; that half of all Indian children are undernourished and more than half a million of them die each year from diarrhea; that an estimated five million Indians are infected with HIV/AIDS.

A powerful ideology often shaped the reforms the BJP espoused: that the free market can usurp the role of the state. This meant that government often withdrew from precisely those areas where its presence was indispensable. Though India had more than sufficient food grains in stock, the government's failure to distribute it effectively led in recent years to an unprecedented rise in the number of drought-affected villagers starving to death in many of the most populous states.

As for the mosque, which appears now in memory as a melancholy symbol of a besieged secularism, there seems little hope it will ever be rebuilt. It has fallen victim not just to the ideologues but to less perceptible changes in India's general mood in the last decade. The talk of poverty and social justice; the official culture of frugality; the appeal, however rhetorical, to traditions of tolerance and dialogue – all these seem to belong to the past, to the early decades

of idealism. A decade of proglobalization policies has created a new aggressive middle class, whose concerns dominate public life in India. This class is growing; the current numbers are between 150 and 200 million. There are also millions of rich Indians living outside India. In America, they constitute the richest minority. It is these affluent, upper-caste Indians in India and abroad who largely bankrolled the rise to power of Hindu nationalists. In the global context, middle-class Hindus are no less ambitious than those who in the Roman Empire embraced Christianity and made it an effective mechanism with which to secure worldly power. Hinduism in the hands of these Indians has never looked more like the Christianity and Islam of popes and mullahs and less like the multiplicity of unselfconsciously tolerant faiths it still is for most Indians.

It was this modernized Hinduism that Gujarat in 2002 provided a glimpse of, as Benetton-clad young Hindus carted off the loot of digital cameras and DVD players in their new Japanese cars. It is this Hinduism that Ayodhya presents both a miniature image and a sinister portent of, with its syncretic past now irrevocably falsified, its mosques destroyed, its minorities suppressed, an Ayodhya where well-placed local abbots helped by elected politicians wait for new lucrative connections to the global economy and prove, along with much else, the profound modernity of religious nationalism.

17

Identity on the Borderline: Modernity, New Ethnicities, and the Unmaking of Multiculturalism in Sri Lanka

Darini Rajasingham-Senanayake

Borders Old and New and the Problem of Hybridity

Stories at the border and peripheries of the modern nation-state often problematize nationalist narratives of history and identity invented at hegemonic centres, in this case Colombo and Jaffna, to justify and legitimize violence. As the battle for territory, between the government's armed forces and the LTTE fighting for a separate state, has progressed, Lanka's internal regional and administrative borders have shifted, hardened and softened as a de facto partition has been established and slowly eroded across the Vanni region. The border constitutes a broad swath of land between territory controlled by the government in the south, and the LTTE in the north. Sometimes it has harbored the clandestine headquarters of the LTTE leadership. The border for many years prevented the movement of persons from north to south and vice versa. The border-partition

was also constituted of displaced persons, refugee camps and military camps, which alternatively plot a new perimeter across the island. Estimates were that 78% of the internally displaced due to the armed conflict that escalated in 1983 are ethnically Tamils, 13% are Muslims, and 8% are Sinhalas.[1]

Forced population displacement due to violence between the armed groups has resulted in the destruction of multicultural and hybrid communities and traditions of co-existence along the border. Yet in *purana* (old) villages and settlements Sinhalas, Tamils, Muslims, Christians, Buddhists, Hindus, continue to co-exist, speak each other's languages, worship one another's gods, albeit with increasing difficulty and a great deal of ambivalence. Many on the border have been repeatedly displaced during cycles of war and détente between the government and LTTE (Deng 1994). Those who have returned to their villages do so because they are tired of living on handouts in

Perspectives on Modern South Asia: A Reader in Culture, History, and Representation, First Edition.
Edited by Kamala Visweswaran.
© 2011 Blackwell Publishing Ltd. Published 2011 by Blackwell Publishing Ltd.

refugee camps. In 1994 when the Kumaratunge government came to power with talk of peace negotiations, the displaced local minorities returned to fields gone wild and homes ravaged by elephants, but with hopes of peace and promises of resettlement allowances from the newly elected People's Alliance government. But in the course of the conflict, cycles of forced displacement and ethnic cleansing, a once hybrid and multicultural border area has been destroyed. A new military border – the Forward Defence Line (FDL) has replaced a border of cultural mixing. Simultaneously, civilian administration and law and order had broken down, and alternative and competing authority structures emerged in the form of paramilitary security regimes and a political economy driven by violence in the region (Rajasingham-Senanayake 2001).[2]

Geographically, the new border or FDL stretches in a gentle arch from east to west dividing the island horizontally – further south on the coasts and further north inland. In some places it extends over miles – traversing lush vegetation or the dusty plains and scrub jungle of the dry zone. Since 1983 the villages in the area have come to be known as "border villages" in the popular media, and among the relief and development NGO community. Along this border, war and peace resonate in curious ways. The boundary has its own (hidden) economy of fear, co-operation and co-existence: the Sri Lanka army, LTTE cadres, other paramilitary groups, border villagers, and other bit players in the conflict sometimes maintain an uneasy truce (Rajasingham-Senanayake 1999). Enemies sometimes co-operate for the good of others – particularly refugees and civilians – and for personal profit. At other times it is in these zones that the war is most bitterly fought. It is in this swath of land that the bloodiest memories of massacres that perpetuate the logic of blood for blood are rooted. Places shift names at the border too, as did Manal Aru which became Welioya – from Tamil to Sinhala – with land colonization and conflict.

Culturally, the Vanni border region comprises one of the most diverse areas outside the island's capital city of Colombo. Ethnically, it comprises internally displaced Tamils, Sinhalas, Moors, Malays, Burghers, and some intermarried. Religiously, it comprises Buddhists, Muslims, Christians, Hindus, those who worship all or some or none of these pantheons or associated gods. The new border zones are overseen and administered also by international (aid) agencies – from the United Nations High Commission for Refugees, to OXFAM and other non-governmental relief/development organizations – with the support of the Sri Lanka government and the LTTE. The Sri Lanka government, however, would not officially admit the existence of this extensive border zone which has come to constitute a de facto partition because it would consist of recognition of the LTTE's partial victory in its search for separation.

Yet in another sense this is an old border zone; an area that was described by John Still, colonial administrator, member of the Archaeological Commission of Ceylon (under H.C.P. Bell), officer of the Land Settlement Department (1908) and Colonial Labour Officer (1911), thus:

In the north of Sri Lanka as in England there is a border where two races meet . . . The northern frontier where the Tamils and Sinhalese join hands, ran through a region known as the Wanni, a word whose close kin to the Sinhala adjective "wal" meaning wild or woodland, and perhaps to the western "wald," "weald," wold and probably wild. And the Wanni is very wild. Along its southern fringe the people are Sinhalese, for the most part though a few Veddhas still linger there whose own language is lost, and who speak Tamil and Sinhalese so impartially that they change from one tongue to another in the middle of a conversation without effort or any preference either way. North of these and throughout the rest of the Wanni, the people are Tamils of various castes who unite but in calling each other Wanniyar (1930: 123).

In his chapter titled "Border Lands," Still noted:

Its [Wanni] jungles are rich in ruins of shrines once holy, both Buddhist and Hindu, but curiously enough its most holy place where active worship still persists belongs to neither of these creeds, though it is approached by the followers of both. The old temples are forgotten and Islam has never had a foothold there. The wood-god cult is wholly unorganized, and remains a matter of private and personal converse with god. But in the very middle of the forest, hidden further from cities than any other church in Ceylon, there is an old Roman Catholic mission, so catholic indeed that men and women of all creeds flock there on pilgrimage, and I have even known a strict Mahomedan to go there from Anuradha-pura, carrying with him his sick baby son in full faith that he would be healed there. As on the summit of Adam's Peak, where all religions meet without rancour, so at Madhu in the Wanni do men and women of many creeds find some common denominator which reduces their diver-gent faiths to hopes possessed by all: and in the wilderness of this old border land of many wars they find a place of truce (1930: 150).

Still's often moving ethnography, *Jungle Tide*, was written in a period before the scientific discrediting of racial theory and the debunking of the Aryan myth of superior races, when race theory held sway in the mind of colonial administrators afflicted by the "white man's burden." Still believed that Sinhalas and Tamils were of two distinct races, but then he also thought that the Scots and the English were of two different races. It is easy to discern the problem of (race/ethnic/caste) classification of native identity writ large in his descrip-tions of the "wild" inhabitants of the border areas – wild, arguably, because of the appar-ently ambiguous nature of their identity. For, looking beneath the surface, relating past and present ethnography, were the Sinhala speakers really Sinhala, were the Tamil speakers really Tamil, what of the bilinguals? When did these groups cease to be Veddas? Was it not, in short, a hybrid people with multiple and overlapping linguistic, ethnic, caste identities that inhabited the Vanni? The problem of classifying peoples with ambiguous "ethnic" identities is glossed in this description, which nevertheless dwells extensively on the meaning and origin of the term "wanni." Linguistic difference appears to have signified racial difference to the British ethnographer.

Clearly, from Still's description, ethno-linguistic hybridity, co-existence and mingling was a way of life among Sinhala and Tamil-speaking groups. The church at Madhu, evocatively described by John Still as a mul-ticultural centre of faith and healing, remains, even after years of war, a multicultural safe area for refugees of all communities displaced by the conflict. Both parties to the combat, the LTTE and the military, have respected its boundaries. This fact is perhaps testimony to the power of local sacred spaces and a common history of co-existence and worship. The LTTE and the military had respected that local sacred space, even where they have not hesitated to mow down whole border villages of the "wrong" ethnicity.

The ethnographic record of the border zone is rich with evidence of complex patterns of cultural co-existence and conflict, hybridity and multiculturalism among diverse castes and com-munities in the Vanni. A pattern of bilingualism and interpellated caste and ethno-religious iden-tity is evident in a reading of the *Manual of the Vanni Districts* (comprising large parts of cur-rent Vavuniya and Mullaithivu) by J.P. Lewis, of the Ceylon Civil Service. The *Manual* was pub-lished in 1895, but drew from almost a hundred years of "diaries extent in the two Kachcheries" up to 1892, including those of George Turnour and H. Pole. Reading the *Manual* one has a sense of the non-discrete and interpellated nature of caste/ethnic identity, as well as the problem that classifying and enumerating the native pop-ulation in these circumstances presented to the colonial administrator.

In the chapter "Races, Castes, Occupations and Religions," Lewis remarks upon the prob-lem of the confusion of caste/ethnicity/linguistic markers and boundaries with regard to the "Veda" caste people living in the Vavuniya district:

These people are Tamil in dress and language, though some of them speak Sinhalese, and some of the women have married Tamils of other castes. I suppose that they are not of the same origins as the Sinhalese Veddahs (so-called).

A caste peculiar to the Vanni is one that takes its name therefrom, viz. the Vanniya caste. There is a Sinhalese caste of the same name found only in the North-Central Province and the Vavuniya District. The Tamil Vanniyas are descendants of Vanni chiefs . . . According to the Census of 1891 there was one "Veddah" in Vavuniya who gave the North Central Province as his birthplace. He was no doubt not a Veddah, but a man of the Vanniya caste, who sometimes call themselves and are called Veddhas. I do not believe that they know what the term means (*Manual*: 87).

Note here the linguistic seepage and (con)fusion of the categories "Veda," "Veddha," "Vanniya," caste/ethnic identity. The author sorts out the confusion of identity labels and markers in a number of speculations, and with the final claim that the particular native does not know "the meaning of the term." Lewis might well have been correct since a singular "ethnic" identity that was central to the colonial classifier was probably a non-concept for that particular native peasant. More significant here is the colonial classifier's condescending **attribution** of an identity upon the native, in the guise of a claim of the native's ignorance. Elsewhere in the *Manual* we are informed that:

> There were 12 Sinhalese Buddhists in Mullait-tivu, no doubt the Galle traders there. Vavu-niya also possessed 4 "Tamil Buddhists" but I have not been more fortunate in regard to these *curiosities* than I have with respect to the three "Sinhalese Hindus" (*Manual*: 90).

Hybrid identities that blurred the presumed mutually exclusive categories Tamil-Hindu and Sinhala-Buddhist, and individuals who believed in both Hindu and Buddhist deities (as do most Buddhists and Hindus in contemporary Sri Lanka), were regarded as anomalies. The colonial classifier's confusion about how to classify socio-cultural and religious groups was eventually projected back onto the "native," who was constructed as either ignorant or a "curiosity." Hybridity was clearly frowned upon. Note the condescending use of the term "curiosities" to speak of the hybrid native – the Tamil-Buddhist and the Sinhala-Hindu – who

did not fit the neat scientific classification that was being constructed, wherein Sinhalas and Tamils, Hindus and Buddhists, are constructed as mutually exclusive. Recall that A is either B or not-B (law of excluded middle term) and A cannot be B and not-B at the same time (law of noncontradiction), according to the scientific method of classification. In short, hybridity was a problem for the colonial authorities because it disrupted the precarious and prejudiced race-based colonial classificatory system that European imperialism devised to map, classify, represent and govern the natives.

This is not, however, to posit the absence of cultural, social and political borders and con-flicts between groups in the border areas, but merely to point out that identity was a dense and overlapping set of categories – not necessarily articulated in neat ethnic, linguistic, religious or caste terms. The multicultural identity of many of the residents was also evident in the cultural geography in some parts of the Vanni where a single place could have both Tamil and Sinhala names, as had Mandukkodai, or Madu Kanda (*Manual*).

Complex patterns and practices of spatial, structural and cultural hybridity and boundary demarcation among cultural groups clearly existed and still do in the *purana* (old) villages of the currently war-torn Vanni districts. But patterns of co-existence between Sinhala and Tamil linguistic groups have been considerably eroded since 1983. State-sponsored post-colonial settlements, in a national context of heightened tensions between Sinhala and Tamil politicians, have generated new local tensions. Post-colonial land colonization processes have re-resulted in the erasure of diversity, as hap-pened when Manal Aru (Tamil) was renamed Weli Oya (Sinhala).

Nevertheless, during my ethnographic field-work in 1996 to 1998 in Vavuniya district in the midst of the conflict, the history of co-existence was constantly referred to by the older gen-eration of *purana* villages. One remarkable, spritely, ninety-year-old Sinhala villager, Siriwardene, who lived near Sidambarapuram Refugee Camp, about 10 kilometres from Vavuniya town, said to me in July 1997:

We do not have problems with our Tamil neighbours in the next village. This is a war that has come to this region from somewhere else, the attackers are outsiders. But it has affected our relationship with them. In the old days we used to visit them and play cards and they would come, but now there is an army camp to protect our village, and it is difficult to have to cross the checkpoint and explain why one is going there. We don't go anymore and they don't come after the attacks.

An elderly Tamil woman once said to me with nostalgia, speaking of a time before the armed conflict came to the region: "We visited each other's villages, exchanged cattle during the plowing season, attended the same temple festivals and ceremonies, held the same festivals, and attended one another's marriages and funerals."

In Vavuniya, clearly, there was a pattern of co-existence that had elements of ethnic and caste *spatial* segregation, which was counterbalanced and interpellated by social mingling and linguistic hybridity. Sometimes, young people fell in love and intermarried across caste and/or ethnic lines and often were ostracized. Some low caste families and communities had converted to Christianity or switched ethnic identity as a means of caste mobility. At the local-level caste was the most important social category, as evident in the cultural geography of caste-based village demarcation.

In the Vanni borderlands then there were and are numerous axes of difference and identity conflicts on sectarian, caste, religious and cultural lines. Colonial administrators used the categories "Race, Caste, Occupation, and Religions" (title of Chapter 4 of the *Manual*) to understand social differences in the Vanni district. Later, caste classifications were to lose their salience in the official census. But caste was and remains a salient, significant and highly elaborated social border and reality in everyday contexts and interactions. The interpellated and overlapping practice of identity in the border area constituted a problem for the scientific classification and enumeration of individuals and communities when the question of instituting colonial and subsequently representative

government for the natives arose. To understand how this problem was sorted out, with caste disappearing from the census and race based notions of ethnicity achieving dominant focus, we turn now to the problem of classification in the colonial census.

From Caste to Race: Inventing Ethnicity via the Colonial Census

The first modern census was carried out in the island in 1871, at the same time that a census was taken in Great Britain and Northern Ireland. Prior to that, censuses in Ceylon had consisted of population estimates based on accounts of village headmen of the Kandyan highlands, which were then added to the count of the maritime provinces which had been enumerated under the Dutch Governor Van der Graaf in 1789 (Panditaratne and Selvanayagam 1973). The 1814 and 1824 censuses provided information on castes and religions in Ceylon. In the early years "caste" was the primary category used to differentiate between different communities, as was also the case in India (Cohn 1987). Yet until the census of 1911, the census was a fairly haphazard exercise, and during the period between 1827 and 1871 no censuses were held.

By the 1871 census the term "race" appeared for the first time along with the category of nationality, with 78 "nationalities" and 24 "races" being recorded in Ceylon. There was a certain amount of incoherence in these categories. "Sinhalese" and "Tamil" were races as well as nationalities while the Kandyans were another nationality. The history of the colonial census in the island reveals a systematic simplification of the complexity and diversity of the island's people and cultures by British colonial administrators over time. As Wickramasinghe (1995) notes, the term *caste* was initially used vaguely in Ceylon. It encompassed recognized caste groups such as the Vellalas, but also regional groups such as Europeans, Portuguese and Malays; it also recognized occupational groups such as washers and potters, as well as larger amorphous groups such as "Moors" and "Malabars." It appears that until 1824 Sinhalese and Tamils were perceived not as clear-cut ethnic groups but first and foremost as members of a number of caste groups of various sizes. At the same time, categorical confusion and indeterminacy in the pre-1871 censuses also reflect the absence of a modern scientific, race-based system of classification. When juxtaposed with the later scientific censuses, they tell a story of how the colonial racial imagination was developed and articulated with local categories. For, by the 1881 census, there was a clear consolidation of race-based communal differences. There were only seven "races" left, namely, Europeans, Sinhalese, Tamils, Moormen, Malays, Veddas, and Others. From then on "races" rather than castes became the main category of classification, and identity was more or less fixed territorially as well. As I have argued elsewhere (Rajasingham-Senanayake 1992), race conceptions of ethnic difference functioned as a deep and invisible time-line for positing internal or genotypal sameness in the face of phenotypal changes, mixedness or miscegenation or hybridity.

Notably, the structure of the colonial census reveals an absence of significant Sinhala–Tamil geo-political polarization during the early part of British colonial rule. Rather, it indicates that regional differences between groups speaking the same language – as for instance, between the low-country Sinhalas and up-country Kandyans – were more salient than those between the coastal Tamil and Sinhala groups. The dominant group in the South was the Sinhalas; in the central hills, the Kandyans; and in the north the Tamils. Indeed it is arguable that the Kandyans considered themselves to be a distinct ethnic group from the low-country Sinhalas even as late as 1925, when the Kandyan National Assembly (KNA) asked for regional autonomy for the Kandyan provinces within a federal state. It is hence also that Tamil politicians had not considered themselves a minority, since low-country Sinhalas and up-country Kandyans were considered to be and seemed to consider themselves as two separate and distinct groups. The salient geo-political borders, albeit colonially engineered, were then not always ethno-national, or between

north and south, as has been posited by modern nationalist historians who quote the *Pali-Vamsas*, as evidence of perennial conflict between Sinhalas and Tamils. Rather, the border between coastal regions and the hill country was the main geo-political, rather than ethno-racial divide in the island for many centuries, ironically at precisely the time that ethno-racial categories discourses on identity were being consolidated.

The stabilization of ethno-racial categories towards the latter part of the nineteenth and early twentieth centuries in the colonial census, echoes processes of identity consolidation in Britain and in many parts of the colonial world as race theory achieved scientific credence. But while the shifting structure of the colonial census says little about local categories for marking difference, it points to instability and ambiguities of ethnic identity categories that so often appear natural and primordial. It also points to the productive ambiguities and conflations of meaning that the translation of exogenous categories like "race" created in the colonies.

In Ceylon the consolidation of ethno-racial identity entailed the slow eclipse of caste in official classification. There was no equivalent term among any of the local languages for the European concept of "race." The closest Sinhala term for race, "jathi/jathiya" connotes various types of linguistic, religious and cultural differences, and most often connotes caste difference. The term "jathiya" was and still is used to connote "race," "ethnic" and "nation," not to mention caste. The translation of "race" to "jathi" enabled and enables a semantic slippage which permitted mapping religious, linguistic and cultural differences along a single overarching frame of race. In other words, the term "jathi" collapses non-equivalent types of difference. Religious, linguistic, cultural, phenotypal markers coalesce in the contemporary concept of ethnicity via racial categories. The connotational slippages encapsulated in the term "jathi" mask the fact that race serves as an anchor for otherwise disparate classificatory frames – that is, linguistic, religious, caste classification – in an overarching hierarchical and unipolar system of, and for, understanding differences.

A process of native identity translation, classification, and transformation begun in colonial times instituted race-based identity categories that configured identity politics in post-colonial Sri Lanka, where Sinhala-Buddhists and Tamils have emerged as bi-polar ethnic groups. For in the post-colonial period, communal – or what are now termed ethno-racial or national – identities were mapped on to conceptions of race, thereby reconstituting a complexly layered set of identity configurations, practices and discourses. What is clear is that interpellated linguistic and religious categories have been consolidated along an ethno racial fault line in post-colonial Sri Lanka. Thus, despite the fact that Hindus and Buddhists share many common religious practices, they are viewed as belonging to different, mutually exclusive religions. Race has served as a root metaphor which congeals linguistic, religious and cultural markers in the formation of modern Sinhala-Buddhist and Tamil (ethnic) identities. The non-equivalency of the two identity formations, one which emphasizes religion and language (Sinhala-Buddhist), and the other linguistic differences (Tamil), is indicative of this process of constructing difference. The shifting categories of the colonial census then demonstrate the point that identity formations are politically determined and hence historically fluid. At different moments they congeal and collapse different types of salient identity markers, be they linguistic, religious, ethnic, gendered, caste or class based – a process that was evident until recently in identity negotiations across ethnicity and caste in the border areas of the Vanni.

Along with the colonial census a dominant tradition of colonial and post-colonial sociology, anthropology and history also contributed to the invention and consolidation of modern ethno-racial identity politics in Lanka. But the construction of ethnicity as *the* predominant identity formation and lived experience, both in public and in scholarly discourse in Sri Lanka, is relatively recent. It has occurred with the slow

eclipse of caste as a substantive and lived identity formation in the public political discourse and in the anthropological and historical scholarship on identity and conflict in the island.

A short survey of the pre-1983 ethnographic writing on the island reveals the preoccupation with caste, kinship, and land tenure as dominant identity and conflict formations. The primacy of caste identity as the dominant socio-political and lived reality is also evident in the anthropological and historical scholarship. Thus the early colonial and post-colonial anthropological, ethnographic and travel narratives focused on caste structures, kinship and marriage practices (Leach; Yalman), and tribal communities such as the Veddas (Scligmann). Subsequent attention was focused on the land tenure practices (Obeyesekere; Tambiah). It was only after the 1983 pogrom orchestrated by segments of the state that the post-colonial sociological tradition and imagination of the island focussed on ethnicity. Since then the strength of communal or ethnic identities came to be read in inverse relation to the weakness of caste identities in the island. Consider, for instance, Eric Meyer's description of identity politics:

> It is appropriate to place the case of identity politics in the island in the broader Indian context. In the colonial imagination Lanka's distinctive features are the weakness of the caste system, the strength of communal identities... (1985).

But as a number of analysts have argued (Silva 1999; Jayawardena 2000; Uyangoda 1998), caste remains a sociologically and politically important identity formation, which has been repressed and become the hidden structure or doxa of social and political identity and conflict in the post-colonial period.[3] Caste continues as both a political reality and the repressed signifier that has enabled the invention and consolidation of a bi-polar Sinhala–Tamil "ethnic" divide in the post-colonial period. But in the post-colonial imagination, where race-based ethnic identity categories have been consolidated, the caste system and the ethnic system have been constructed as separate classificatory systems and domains, which might overlap but do not meld into each other. An ethnic or caste group rarely switches ethnicity via migration or conversion.

The point here is to mark the discursive transformation that the institution of "scientific" race-based identity classifications effected in the encounter with "native" identity formations and social systems. A number of scholars, foremost among them Michel Foucault, have shown how the modern regime, its technologies and regimes of governmentality, reconstituted bodies and subjectivities via a range of institutional logics. Post-colonial subaltern studies scholarship has extended this analysis to the colonial world (Said 1978; Cohn 1987). Here, I have argued that the application of the rules of the Scientific Method of classification in the colonial census was a fundamental aspect of the process of colonial governmentality that was to transform a more fluid system of identity negotiation. Elsewhere I have traced how colonial and post-colonial modes of and for instituting representative government, which are central to the process of modern nation-state building in the island, resulted in the bi-polar configuration of Sinhala and Tamil linguistic communities as mutually antagonistic (Rajasingham-Senanayake 1999). Modern Sinhala and Tamil nationalist histories have then drawn from colonial racial science and orientalist histories of Aryan and Dravidian "races" in Asia to invent the charter myths of conflict between the Sinhalas and Tamils in recent times.[4] In turn the conflict has generated more ethnocentric histories that read far back in time recognizably modern identity formations.

The Border as Metaphor of National Conflict: Unmaking of Multiculturalism

History repeats itself, but not as the nationalists tell it. The reordering of identities and of internal political boundaries in the island of Sri Lanka, Ceylon, Serendip (many of the borders shifted with the name and perspective), is not new. Political feuding among the island's various principalities or, what anthropologist Tambiah terms "galactic polities," as well as four

and a half centuries of Portuguese, Dutch and British colonialism in the coastal plains of Sri Lanka, meant the periodic shift and reconstitution of internal geo-political units, identities and boundaries, even as local communities adapted to the dominant political authority. The Vanni region was no exception to this. The current conflict in the Vanni may thus be seen as continuous with a long history of the settlement and mixing of people through various migrations, trade and colonizations – an old phenomena. What is new and different is the extremities of violent unmixing of peoples. Sri Lanka's de facto ethnic partition then replaces an ancient border zone of ethnic and cultural mixing.

But if the new border rents the territorial and geographic unity and sovereignty of the island of Sri Lanka, it was a fiction of unity constructed by (post)colonial administrators, ethnic nationalists, and scholars (none of them being exclusive) since early this century. What also is noteworthy is the character of the boundary now emergent after the British colonial unification of the lowlands and highlands in 1815. For unlike pre-independence and pre-British boundaries that were geo-political, the current boundary is ethno-national in character. The British, after all, rewrote the map of Ceylon by uniting the predominantly Sinhala Kandyan highlands, whose last king was of Tamil descent and whose court language was Tamil, with the far more ethnically mixed lowlands in 1815.

Contrary then to what LTTE homeland propaganda and Sinhala nationalists claim, north–south conflict was not the major fault line of identity in the island, nor was conflict always ethnic in character, until this century. More often than not, conflict occurred between low-country peoples and the up-country or the hill kingdom of Kandy – a pattern of boundary demarcation evident in most parts of South and South-East Asia where modern state-building projects have penetrated remote mountain areas and communities.

It is then to modern (read post-colonial) nation-building and related development projects that we must turn to explain how a multicultural border area has been transformed into an ethnic partition, in an armed conflict that is destroying patterns of hybridity, multiculturalism and co-existence in the island. The current Vanni partition is the invention of three migratory movements: state-sponsored settlement under the Mahaveli development project; settlement of Southern Tamils from the plantations fleeing riots; and competitive ethnic settlements carried out by Buddhist societies, the church, and NGOs like those arising out of the Gandhian movement.

The emergence of a de facto partition in a border zone of cultural mixing is a metaphor of the hardening and fixing of ethnic identity in post-colonial Sri Lanka. Since conflict between the secessionist LTTE and the Sri Lanka government escalated after the pogrom riots of 1983, the social demography of the north and east, where the fighting has been concentrated, and, to a lesser extent the south of the island, has been transformed by forced migrations and the delinking of inter-communal ties. Yet this process began much earlier. A slow but ever increasing exodus of Tamils occurred from the Sinhala-dominated south due to periodic anti-Tamil riots condoned and arranged by segments of the Sinhala-dominated post-colonial state, while the LTTE has practised ethnic cleansing in the northern areas they claim as their homeland since 1990.

The unmixing of peoples in the south has been a gradual and incomplete process, with Tamils moving northward or overseas since the first anti-Tamil riots in 1958, ten years after Sri Lanka became independent. Clearly ethnic unmixing in the north, east and Vanni regions has been more recent, dramatic and systematic, beginning in 1983 and culminating with the LTTE's policy of ethnic cleansing when Sinhalese and Muslims who constituted minorities in the Tamil-dominated north were asked to leave their homes in 1990.

At the time, the LTTE warned the departing Sinhalese and Muslim: "Do not even dream of coming back." The result is that today the Jaffna peninsula which is ravaged by war between the LTTE and Sri Lanka military, is denuded of

non-Tamils, and contains a depleted Tamil population traumatized by war and repeated displacements. The only non-Tamils in the north are Sri Lanka military personnel, who effectively constitute an occupying force, while many Tamils in the south live under close surveillance by the military and fear of arbitrary search and arrest. The Tamils' search for routes of migration overseas continues.

Violence, state-sponsored and anti-state, has erased a history of co-existence and hybridity. Seventeen years of war has also resulted in the militarization of civil society, restrictions on people's mobility from north to south or vice versa, and the development of an ethnic enclave mentality, whereby local minorities are viewed by local majorities as security threats. The violence has undone much of the cultural mixing that occurred over centuries of migration to and within this island situated at the intersection of major sea routes East and West – Chinese, Semitic and Christian. For historically, the south of Sri Lanka has been dominated by Sinhala-speaking peoples including Tamils, Muslims, Christians, various Euro-Asian communities, as well as tiny Malay and Chinese communities, while the north of the country has been dominated by Tamil-speaking peoples including Sinhalas, Muslims and others who partly assimilated with the regionally dominant linguistic communities. Despite past and present localized conflicts between various groups, ethnic co-existence and cultural hybridity was, and still is, a way of life along the coastal areas and in urban centres of the island, but is gradually being eroded. In the context of proliferating scholarly and nationalist myths that Sinhalese and Tamils have been in perennial conflict, and given the violence, suffering and displacement that has occurred in different ways among all communities in this island, remembering that until relatively recently native and foreign ethnographers almost routinely remarked on the more or less peaceful co-existence of its diverse and hybrid cultures is less than sobering.

Notes

1   The population of displaced people has fluctuated
from 1.2 million to half a million at various points
in the conflict. At the end of December 1995
the Ministry of Rehabilitation and Reconstruction estimated that there were 1,017,181 internally displaced people in Sri Lanka while 140,000
were displaced overseas, some of the latter having
sought asylum status. Figures of displaced persons are, however, controversial. The University
Teachers for Human Rights, Jaffna (1993) estimates that half a million Tamils have become
refugees overseas. The decennial census of Sri
Lanka scheduled for 1991 was not taken due to
the conflict.

2   It is this border/partition that operation Jaya
Sikurui (victory assured), begun and abandoned
almost two years later by the Sri Lanka army
to clear the main supply route to the northern
capital of Jaffna in 1997, set out but failed to
erase.

3   As Uyangoda notes, caste politics plays itself
out in the "inner court yards" of national politics
dominated by ethnic categories and conflicts
(*Pravada*, 2000).

4   This too has been contested by R.A.L.H.
Gunawardana.

References

Cohn, B. 1987. *An Anthropologist Among the Historians and Other Essays*. Delhi: Oxford University
Press.

Deng, Francis. 1994. Report of the Representative of
the Secretary General, Mr. Francis Deng, submitted
pursuant to Commission on Human Rights Resolution 1993/95. Profiles in Displacement: Sri Lanka.
E/CN. 4/1994/44 add. 1

Jayawardena, Kumari. 2000. *Nobodies to Somebodies:
The Rise of the Colonial Bourgeoisie in Sri Lanka*.
Colombo: Social Scientists' Association.

Leach, Edmund. 1960. *Aspects of Caste in South
India, Ceylon, and North-West Pakistan*. Cambridge: Cambridge University Press.

Lewis, Esq. J.P. 1895 and 1993. *The Manual of the
Vanni Districts*, Ceylon. Navrang. Colombo: Lake
House Bookshop.

Obeyesekere, Gananath. 1975. "Sinhala Buddhist
Identity in Ceylon." In George De Vos and Lola
Romanucci-Ross (eds.) *Ethnic Identity: Cultural
Continuities and Change*. Palo Alto, California:
Mayfield Publishing.

Panditaratne, B.L and S. Selvanayagam. 1973.
"The Demography of Ceylon, – An Introductory
Survey." In K. M de Silva (ed.) *History of Ceylon*
Vol. 3., University of Ceylon.

Rajasingham-Senanayake, Darini. 1992. "Afterlife of
Empire. Colonialism and the Roots of Race." Paper
presented at Annual Meeting of AAA, San Francisco, 1992.

_____1999a. *Ethnic Futures*. Pfaff-Czarnecka et al.
New Delhi: Sage.

_____1999b. "Dangers of Devolution: Hidden
Economies of Armed Conflict." In Robert Roberg

(ed.) *Creating Peace in Sri Lanka*. Washington DC:
Brookings Institute Press.

_____2001. "Transformation of Legitimate Violence
and Civil Military Relations." In Mutiah Alagapa
(ed.) *Coercion and Governance*, Stanford Stanford
University Press.

Said, Edward. 1978. *Orientalism*. London: Penguin
Books.

Seligmann, Charles Gabriel. 1909. "Among the Veddas of Ceylon". In *Travel and Exploration* 1(2), pp.
110–120. London.

Silva, Tudor. 1999. *Caste, Ethnicity and Problems of
National Identity*. In *Sociological Bulletin*, Vol. 48
(1&2) March-Sept. 1999.

Still, John. 1930. *The Jungle Tide*. Edinburgh and
London: William Blackwood.

United States Committee for Refugees. 1991. *Sri
Lanka: Island of Refugees* (October).

University Teachers for Human Rights, Jaffna. 1994.
Someone Else's War. Colombo: MIRJE

Uyangoda, Jayadeva. 1998. *Caste in Sinhalese Society, Culture and Politics*. Colombo: Social Scientists' Association.

_____2000. "The Inner Courtyard." *Pravada*, Vol. 6,
Nos. 9&10, pp. 14–19.

Wickramasinghe, Nira. 1995. *Ethnic Politics in Colonial Sri Lanka 1927– 1947*. New Delhi: Vikas Publications.

Yalman, Nur. 1971. *Under the Bo Tree. Studies
in Caste, Kinship and Marriage in the Interior
of Ceylon*. Berkeley: University of California
Press.

18

War, Factionalism, and the State in Afghanistan

Nazif M. Shahrani

After September 11, 2001

Following the tragic attacks in New York City, Washington, D.C., and Pennsylvania on September 11, 2001, people in the United States, shocked and in disbelief, wondered who had committed such acts and why. When U.S. government authorities cautiously revealed the identities of the alleged perpetrators to be members of the al-Qaeda terrorist network, believed to be led by the Saudi Arabian national Osama bin Laden, with headquarters in Taliban-held Afghanistan, everyone wanted to know the facts about the Taliban: Where did they come from? What internal and external forces created and supported them? What brand of Islam were they brandishing? What was the relationship between the al-Qaeda terrorists and the Taliban regime in Afghanistan?

Those of us concerned with the long-term study of the more than two-decades-long conflict in Afghanistan were not at all surprised by the links between the alleged perpetrators of these horrors on U.S. soil and those who had been waging terrorist wars for the previous five years against a large segment of the Muslim peoples of Afghanistan. Indeed, we were appalled by the lack of international concern prior to September 11 for the plight of the victims of Taliban and al-Qaeda terrorist wars in many parts of Afghanistan (see Maley 1998; Rashid 2000; and Shahrani 1998, 2000a, 2000b). Contrary to the assumptions of the advocates of the "clashes of civilizations" thesis that would blame all of Afghan "culture" for what had happened, we knew that the inhabitants of the western, central, and northern parts of Muslim Afghanistan who did not belong to the ethnic-linguistic and sectarian community of the Taliban, as well as all Afghan women and girls, had themselves been the targets of a systematic and sustained terror campaign in the name of Islam by the extremist Taliban movement and their international terrorist allies since 1995.

Although the answers to even the most basic questions about the Taliban were largely unknown before September 11, it was not long before even more complicated ones were raised:

Perspectives on Modern South Asia: A Reader in Culture, History, and Representation, First Edition.
Edited by Kamala Visweswaran.
© 2011 Blackwell Publishing Ltd. Published 2011 by Blackwell Publishing Ltd.

Why and how did Afghanistan become the safe heaven for al Qaeda and other terrorist groups? What explained the meteoric rise of the Taliban as an extremist Muslim militia movement in post-Soviet Afghanistan? Why and how did the *mujahideen* fighters in Afghanistan fail so miserably to form a workable national governance structure after successfully fighting the former Soviet occupation forces and their puppet communist regimes? How had the long-established, ideologically organized mujahideen parties lost their political significance, giving way to intense intercommunal proxy wars fought by coalitions of tribal, regional, and ethnolinguistic-sectarian forces, financed and managed by foreign powers? What in the history of Afghanistan and its political culture provided the space for the rise of such an extremely harsh and violent militant movement at the dawn of the 21st century? Was this an expected manifestation of recognizable historical patterns in the country? or was it an aberration and a product of novel circumstances of post-jihad Afghanistan?

From Holy War to Holy Terror

One way to begin to answer some of these questions is to focus on the transition in Afghanistan from military successes following the Soviet withdrawal to political disasters, or as Olivier Roy has put it, "From Holy War to Civil War" (1995). The explanations offered have focused on the role of outside forces especially following the Soviet withdrawal from Afghanistan in 1989; the effects of meddling by outside powers (both governmental and nongovernmental) in a fragile multinational state; and the presence of deeply contradictory moral codes within the Afghan political culture.

International security experts, Zalmay Khalilzad and Daniel Byman,[1] provide an example of the first type of explanation. They assert that,

As the United States departed [after the withdrawal of Soviet Red Army from Afghanistan], a vicious civil war spread throughout the country. Once the Soviet-backed regime fell,

war, anarchy and fragmentation followed. The conflict became increasingly one of ethnic and sectarian groups, particularly Pashtuns, Tajiks, Uzbeks, and the Shiah Hazaras.... The war also became a proxy war between Iran and Pakistan, with each power backing different factions. [Khalilzad and Byman 2000:67; also see Khalilzad et al. 1999][2]

The role of outside powers and foreign forces in the factional wars of the post-jihad period (1992 to the present) is undeniable and fully documented (Maley 1998; Rashid 2000).

Afghan leaders also look to external factors for an explanation for Afghanistan's current crisis (with, I hasten to say, considerable justification). They blame foreign conspiracies against Afghanistan for the country's internal political chaos. This explanation suggests that foreign powers (governments both near and far and, more recently, multinational corporations such as Unocal of California, Delta Oil of Saudi Arabia, and Bridas of Argentina) have tried to undermine the gains of a militarily successful jihad and Islamic revolution, and have interfered directly in the country's internal affairs in order to further their own policy goals in the region by financing and managing proxy wars.

Other international relations and regional security experts (e.g., Goodson 2001; Rubin 1995) explain the chaos in Afghanistan by invoking the notion of a "weak/failed state syndrome." According to Goodson, for example, Afghanistan

Is an extremely weak state, almost the archetypal one, made all the weaker by...years of war. [It]...Is the axle on which several regions swivel [especially the relatively weak post-Soviet Central Asian Muslim states]. [It]...also borders on or is influenced by several [competing] regional powers [some of them with nuclear capabilities such as Russia, China, India, and Pakistan, as well as Iran, Saudi Arabia, and Turkey]. Finally, Afghanistan has been the on-again, off-again recipient of superpower and international attention and manipulation, which has contributed to its weakening. [2001:12]

For Goodson, states that have failed to build strong centralized government with capabilities "to *penetrate* society, *regulate* social relationships, *extract* resources, and *appropriate* or use resources" are weak states that pose serious threats to the international order in the new millennium (Migdal 1988:4, in Goodson 2001:11). Certain unchanging "political, social, economic, demographic, and even geographic" (Goodson 2001:11) factors in such societies are implicated in hampering attempts to build strong and stable centralized state institutions. In Afghanistan, one such factor is said to be the existence of many quarrelsome ethnic, tribal, and religious-sectarian communities that occupy rough mountainous terrain, jealously guarding their communal autonomy. These fragmentary constituencies of a weak state are allegedly prone to resorting to violence for resolving interpersonal and intercommunal problems.[3] They are also thought to be susceptible to manipulations by meddling outside powers, which may account for the ultimate failure of the weak Afghan state.

A final, and more novel, explanation for the predicament of the peoples of Afghanistan is offered by David Edwards (1996). He suggests a cultural thesis in which Afghanistan's political chaos is seen to derive "less from divisions between ethnic and religious-sectarian groups or from the ambitions of particular individuals than they do from the moral incoherence of Afghanistan itself" (1996:3). According to Edwards, this moral incoherence is the product of the conjunction of three contradictory and incompatible moral systems or codes that undergird Afghan political culture: the ultraindividualistic codes of honor *(nang)*, the universalist moral system of Islam, and the codes of monarchical state rule.

None of these explanations is entirely satisfactory in itself. To understand the current situation in Afghanistan, we must at once recognize that its political and military chaos is not an isolated or unique phenomenon, and at the same time acknowledge the particular social and political dynamics of Afghanistan's history that have set the parameters for current events. This involves recognizing that internal communal conflicts in Afghanistan are part of a much wider

affliction common to many postcolonial (and now post-Soviet) states and multinational societies, especially smaller and poorer ones, which have found themselves in a geostrategic location within the post-Soviet, unipolar New World Order. Thus, Afghanistan's current, complicated situation can only be understood by focusing on its failed attempts at nation-state building *within* the broader geopolitical circumstance of foreign manipulation and proxy wars that have given rise to particular forms of ethnic factionalism.

Nation-State Building and Social Fragmentation

The failure of Afghan governments to achieve their goal of building a strong, sovereign, centralized, and unified nation-state is generally justified and explained by government officials and researchers alike by pointing to intrinsic factors such as the conflictual and fragmentary character of Afghan society. The country's difficult topography, ethnolinguistic and religious-sectarian cleavages, and tribal loyalties are all cited as contributing factors. From this perspective, the problems of state building are safely severed from the larger economic and political context of which they are a part, and Afghan citizens themselves are blamed for their troubles.

The geophysical characteristics of Afghanistan and the sociocultural and social structural heterogeneity of Afghan society have played some part in affecting the processes of state building in the country. However, the transformations of existing sociocultural pluralism into articulated forms of social structural fragmentation along ethnic, religious-sectarian, regional, and tribal parameters, I argue here, can be understood as calculated responses to the imposition of an utterly inappropriate model of a "modern" nation-state governance structure with its discriminatory policies and practices in Afghanistan. As we will see, it was the incessantly centralizing state policies and practices of internal colonialism, generally aided and abetted by old colonialist powers, which produced a cumulatively negative impact on state-building efforts in Afghanistan.

Social Identity and Governance

Ethnicity and kinship, which are expressed linguistically through the same terms, *qawm* (people, tribe, community), *wulus* (nation, tribe, relatives), and *tyfah* (clan, tribe, group), represent the same or similar ideological frameworks in Afghanistan. Together with Islam, they provide the most fundamental bases for individuals and collective identities and loyalties, and they are the most persistent and pervasive potential bases for the organization of social formations, for the mobilization of social action, and for the regulation of social interaction among individuals and between social groups. As generalized social organizational principles, Islam, ethnicity, and kinship have been equally available to individuals and collectivities in Afghan society at large, as well as to those who have controlled the central government powers. They have been applied and manipulated not only to further common or similar collective national goals, but also to pursue separate, often divergent, and sometimes conflicting and contradictory aims by individuals, groups, and state institutions (for further details see Shahrani 1986, 1998).

Ethnic, kinship, and religious ideologies, like other social organizational principles, are filled with internal ambiguities, contradictions, limitations, and conflicts. Therefore, the use of these principles by individuals, organized pluralities, and governments for instrumental purposes has often resulted in unforeseen consequences. However, social organizational principles, whether based on ethnicity, kinship, religion, or any other sources of social identity, are not in themselves causal in the actual organization of social relations. Rather, individuals, organized social pluralities, and governments apply such principles according to the specific political, economic, and historical contexts in which they find themselves. It is within the context of the operations of real economic and political forces, both internal and external to the particular society, that the value of particular ethnic, kinship or religious identities, loyalties, and ideologies, and their efficacy in organizing social relations, mobilizing for a cause, as well as their relation to the state, can be studied. It

is also within the changing historical contexts of the political economy of both the state and society that the nature of relations between the ongoing formation and reformation of ethnic, tribal, and religious-sectarian groupings in the country, and the formation and transformation of the government power structures at the center, can be examined and understood (also see Shahrani 1986, 1998, 2000a, 2000b).

The relationship of social identity to changing power relations and attempts at state-building in Afghanistan must therefore be examined in relationship to its structure of governance and its political ecology – that is, the relationships of Afghanistan's political economy and political culture to its broader national and regional history. First, it is necessary to identify the major sociocultural principles that provide cultural ideas and norms for conceptualizing and ordering identities and informing politics of difference between social groupings that articulate the relations of domination, as well as resistance, between social groups and communities, as I have done elsewhere (see Shahrani 1998, 2000a, 2000b). Second, it is essential to assess the history of the modern state in Afghanistan and its relationship to its heterogeneous communities of citizens during the last one hundred years as I do below, focusing on the period of Mohammadzai/Durrani dynastic rule preceding Soviet intervention, the decade of the jihad struggle against communism and Soviet occupation (see also Roy 1990; Shahrani and Canfield 1984), and the ongoing postcommunist and post-jihad struggle for control of state power.

Heterogeneous Communities and the State

At first glance, the problems in Afghanistan might seem to have begun with the communist coup in 1978, which ignited the war that has continued for 24 years. That was not, however, the beginning of the problem, which actually extends back to the creation of the first modern state under the name 'Afghanistan' more than a century ago. The foundation of the modern state of Afghanistan was laid when Britain invaded

Afghanistan from the Indian subcontinent in 1879 for the second time in 40 years. The British could not adequately control the country because of a prolonged, bloody civil war underway over royal succession. Britain had lost many fighters during its wars of conquest and was faced with stiff resistance by many warring groups headed by competing princelings of the Muhammadzai/Durrani ruling clan of the Pashtun tribes, groups that had been fighting each other for the Kabul throne for some time. The British picked Abdur Rahman, one of the princelings, and pronounced him "King of the Afghans. They provided him with weapons and money to be used to create a buffer state between czarist Russia and British India.

The borders of Afghanistan – drawn by Britain and czarist Russia during the onset of this "Great Game" in Central Asia in the closing decades of 19th century – were gerrymandered to split members of ethnic groups between or among different neighboring states. Along the northern frontiers, for example, the peoples of Turkistan, the Turkic and Tajik-speaking Muslim Central Asians such as the Uzbek, Turkmen, Kazak, Kirghiz and Tajiks, were divided. A large area of southern Turkistan between the Hindu Kush mountains and Amu Darya (Oxus River) was included within the borders of the new buffer state of Afghanistan, which existed until 1967 when the government in Kabul eliminated the province of Turkistan by means of an administrative "reform," replacing it with a number of newly named smaller provinces: Balkh, Jawzjan, Samangan, and Faryab. This politically motivated administrative fiat by the Pashtun-dominated Afghan government in the 1960s paralleled Joseph Stalin's policy of National Delimitation. In 1924 Turkistan was replaced with five language-based Central Asian Soviet Socialist Republics: Uzbekistan, Turkmenistan, Kazakstan, Kyrgyzstan, and Tajikistan. Further east in western China, Sharqi Turkistan – a large territory occupied by the Turkic-speaking Muslim Uyghur, Kazak, and Kirghiz peoples – became officially known in China as Xinjiang province. Thus, as a result of the creation and re-creation of national frontiers that began with the drawing of boundaries

of Afghanistan in the 1880s, the larger identity and territorial reality of Turkistan was wiped clean from the face of the world map.

On the western frontier, the Farsiwan, a Persian-speaking people who speak the same dialect as people in eastern Iran, were located on both sides of the Iran–Afghanistan borders. The area to the south and southeast populated by the Baluch population was divided among three countries: Afghanistan, Iran, and British India (now Pakistan). The Pashtun/Pathans (the Afghans) were divided by the Durand Line on the eastern borders, leaving most of the Pashtun/Pathans on the British-India side, which, after the partition, became part of Pakistan. The Durand Line, Afghanistan's eastern frontiers with Pakistan, was drawn by the British to effectively divide the Pashtun between two separate states. The predominantly Mongol-looking, Persian-speaking, Shi'i Hazara became the only large community that was contained wholly within the boundaries of Afghanistan because of their location in the central highlands around Bamyan.

The demarcation of these borders as part of the Great Game by Britain during the reign of Emir Abdur Rahman (1880–1901), laid the foundation for the troubled status of Afghanistan as a modern nation-state. Backed by Britain, Emir Abdur Rahman terrorized the people within these freshly marked borders. He and his Muhammadzai/Durrani Pashtun clan hailed from Kandahar, the recent spiritual headquarters of the Taliban, as well as the home of Hamid Karzai, the leader of the current U.S.-installed Interim Administration in Afghanistan. The Pashtun in this southwestern area of Afghanistan belong to different tribes than those living further east along the borders with Pakistan. After decimating the leadership of the eastern Ghilzai Pashtun tribes whom he did not trust, Emir Abdur Rahman moved against the Hazaras in the center of the country. The Hazaras resisted Abdur Rahman's conquest (as they also recently opposed the Taliban invasions) of their territory and, as a result, were subjected to extremely harsh punishments: entire villages were massacred, people were skinned alive, and women and children were enslaved. A particularly gruesome form of torture perpetrated against the Hazara people was to form a rim of dough around the shaven heads of men so that boiling oil could be poured on them to fry their brains. Stories of such atrocities remain a permanent part of public memories in this area of the country and are still in circulation (see Mousavi 1997).

Emir Abdur Rahman employed violence and torture in his rampages of conquest and subjugation of all of the peoples within his designated domain. In the east, where the inhabitants were not Muslims (Kafiristan), he forcibly converted them and renamed the area Nooristan (Land of Light). The same brutalities were used in subjugating Uzbek, Turkmen, Tajik, and other ethnic communities in the northern region. Throughout the entire country during the 21 years of his reign, people were brutally terrorized into submission. Emir Abdur Rahman created a relatively strong centralized state through the use of such tactics, by advocating a conservative and xenophobic interpretation of Islamic ideology, and by the liberal use of foreign money and weapons. Indeed, Emir Abdur Rahman – nicknamed by his British colonial masters, the "Iron Emir" for his cruel two-decade-long rule – laid the foundation for an ill-suited centralized state structure that lasted for most of the 20th century.

The Iron Emir was intensely suspicious of his citizens, especially of those Pashtun who did not belong to his own clan or tribe and the non-Pashtun groups in the center and northern regions of the country. In order to insure his sovereignty over the non-Pashtun peoples in the north and central regions of the country, Emir Abdur Rahman mobilized large groups of Durrani Pashtun nomads from the south to occupy large areas of pastureland in central Afghanistan belonging to Hazaras (see Ferdinand 1962; Kakar 1979; Mousavi 2000). He also resettled tens of thousands of Pashtun tribesmen from the south in the strategic parts of Afghan Turkistan along the borders with Central Asian Khanates under czarist Russian control (Tapper 1973). By doing so, he laid the ground for the enforcement of century-long policies that were nothing but a crude form of internal colonialism run by the ruling clique in Afghanistan.

This system of governance lasted until the 1960s when a very small window of opportunity for democratic experimentation opened up as a result of constitutional changes (1964–73). It was during this brief period that some freedom of the press and rudimentary forms of political activity were allowed. Under pressures from the former U.S.S.R., the government did not object to the formation of Afghanistan's Communist Party (Khalq, in 1965), although it strongly opposed the Islamist youth movements. By 1973, King Zahir Shah (r. 1933–73) was overthrown by his own paternal cousin and brother-in-law, prince Muhammad Daoud, with help from the leftist military officers belonging to the Parcham faction of the Communist Party. Five years later, in 1978, the communists killed Muhammad Daoud and massacred his entire family. They also installed a communist regime and, in 1979, faced with overwhelming popular resistance, they "invited" the Soviets to invade the country, beginning Afghanistan's 24-year-long war.

Long-simmering communal tensions rose to the surface after the collapse of the autocratic monarchic state and were further aggravated because of the prolonged proxy wars, leading to the creation of the Taliban and their regime's brutal policies of ethnic cleansing directed against the Hazara, Uzbek, Farsiwan, and Tajik populations in western, central, and northern Afghanistan. The intercommunal wars that had spiraled out of control since the mujahideen military victory in April 1992 are in fact the virulent manifestations of the century-long policies of internal colonialism carried out by Pashtun-dominated governments, supported in large measures by decades of Cold War politics in the region.

During the anti-Soviet and anti-Communist struggles of 1978–92, communities everywhere across Afghanistan organized themselves militarily to defend their own territories. They also created civilian structures at the local level to provide basic health and educational services with the help of international NGOs, as well as for the administration of justice. By 1989, with financial and military help from the United States and some Muslim countries,

Afghans serving as the foot soldiers of this proxy war managed to defeat the Red Army, forcing the Soviets to withdraw their troops from Afghanistan in April 1989. But the communist regime they left behind in Kabul lingered until 1992. In the meantime, Pakistan and Iran encouraged their respective client Afghan political parties to fight not only the communist regime and the Soviets but also amongst themselves. The ethnic dimension of Afghan conflict was purposefully heightened and manipulated by Afghanistan's neighbors: Pakistan, the former Soviet Union, and Iran.

The United States reportedly had invested some three billion dollars in the anti-Soviet war and then, after the Soviet defeat and troop withdrawal in 1989, simply abandoned Afghanistan. When America walked away, it left behind a country that was shattered economically, politically, and in every other conceivable sense, and left to the mercy of its quarrelsome neighbors. In 1992, when the communist regime in Kabul finally fell, Pakistan quickly cobbled together a so-called broad-based government of the mujahideen in which the only party they did not favor, the one headed by a non-Pashtun, Burhanuddin Rabbani, managed to take control of Kabul. Feeling slighted by the "usurpation" of power by the non-Pashtun groups from the rightful Pashtun rulers, Pakistan urged Hekmatyar, the leader of Hizb-i Islami (Islamic party), to take control of the capital from the Tajiks militarily, resulting in the bombardment of Kabul for two years and in unimaginable crimes between 1992 and 1994. The resistance against Hekmatyar's onslaught in Kabul was fierce given the Shia Hazaras' powerful presence in some major areas of the city. The Uzbek forces of Abdur Rashid Dustom that had played a critical role in the collapse of the communist regime and mujahideen takeover of Kabul by the Tajik forces of Ahmad Shah Massoud, all fought together initially to resist Hekmatyar. Alliances of forces shifted repeatedly and the interethnic factional fighting in and around Kabul grew worse. Lacking any alternative vision of governance, the leading contenders in these struggles envisioned, if successful, the same system of government dating back to

Abdur Rahman: a centralized state in which the ruling faction could impose itself on the rest of the unwilling communities in the country with help from their close kinsmen and friends and support by a foreign sponsor.

Two years of warfare by Gulbuddin Hekmatyar against Kabul could not secure the prize that his Pakistani sponsors wished for him to win. And, at that point, the country had, more or less, been divided into five or six different semi-Independent regions. In the western region, the Persian-speaking Farsiwan communities had created an alliance under Ismail Khan with the city of Herat as its center. Ismail Khan had disarmed its own population, enforced a legal system, and began to reopen schools. General Abdul Rashid Dostam, who is vilified as a Northern Alliance warlord by his Pakistani detractors in the media, in fact, had managed to unify several provinces in northwestern region, where he had also brought peace and order. In the area under his control, centered around the city of Mazar-i Sharif and predominantly inhabited by Uzbeks, the conditions for the local population improved: They had local autonomy and thriving commercial ties with the newly independent Central Asian republics. Schools and universities functioned and radio, television, and print media enjoyed considerable freedom and support. The northeastern parts of the country, together with mountain valleys just north of Kabul such as Kohistan, Kohdaman, Panjsher, and Tagaw wa Nijraw, were ruled by the Shura-i Nazzar (Northern Council) under the command of the late Ahmad Shah Massoud. These areas were more or less peaceful. In the center, the Hazara Shias controlled their own territory and sectarian community with virtual autonomy. In the east, the Pashtuns had created a coalition of several provinces under Shura-i Mashreqi (Eastern Council), peacefully running their own affairs.

By late 1994, factional fighting was mostly limited to the national capitol, Kabul, and to Kandahar, a predominantly Pashtun tribal area where chaos reigned. Not surprisingly, in 1994 it was in Kandahar that Mullah Mohammed Omar emerged along with a group of ex-mujahideen fighters who challenged some of the most notorious of the local warlords. Initially, he succeeded in attracting considerable popular support in and around the city of Kandahar for bringing a semblance of order to that unruly city.

By 1995, a plan by a consortium of oil companies, including Unocal and Delta Oil of Saudi Arabia, was underway to build a natural gas pipeline through Afghanistan from Turkmenistan to the Pakistani seaports of Gwadar. Immediately, Pakistan saw the potential usefulness of the newly rising Pashtun force in Kandahar and adopted Mullah Omar's small movement, naming it "Taliban," the movement of seminary students. Pakistan offered them money, weapons, and logistical support and wanted them to secure a corridor for Pakistan so that Unocal and its partners could build the Turkmenistan–Pakistan oil/gas pipeline across western parts of Afghanistan. Early in 1995, the Taliban secured the allegiance of local Pashtun commanders, mostly through bribes, all across the southern and southeastern Pashtun belt approaching Kabul. Then in the autumn of 1995 they attacked the forces of Ismael Khan in western Afghanistan. Because the population of Herat had been disarmed by its own leaders, the area quickly fell to the Taliban and Ismael Khan took refuge in Iran. But the capture of Herat by Pakistani forces for the Taliban did not end the war. Emboldened by their easy victory, the Taliban and their Pakistani patrons proceeded to take the rest of the country by force, pursuing a policy of total war. During this period of Taliban conquest, large-scale massacres of civilians occurred as the peoples of northern and central Afghanistan defended their territories against the Taliban and their Pakistani allies. The defenders argued that when the war against the Soviet Union was fought, no Pashtun had come from any other part of Afghanistan to help liberate the territories inhabited by the Uzbeks, Tajiks, and Hazaras. These territories were defended by their local inhabitants who had liberated themselves from Soviet occupation forces and Afghan communists, even though non-Pashtun Afghans had joined their Pashtun compatriots in southern Afghanistan to liberate Pashtun areas. Non-Pashtun peoples of Afghanistan put up stiff resistance to the Pashtun army led by the Taliban, who were supported by the government of Pakistan, which planned to conquer their territories and resubjugate them to a form of internal colonialism.

In 1995, Osama bin Laden, who had initially come to Afghanistan in 1981 to fight in the jihad against the Soviet invaders, returned to Afghanistan. Enraged by the Gulf War, bin Laden became a vocal opponent of the U.S.-led coalition war within Saudi Arabia, organizing antiwar demonstrations resulting in his exile from Saudi Arabia to Sudan. In 1995, ISI, the Pakistani Intelligence Service, brokered a deal to move bin Laden and his entourage from Sudan to Pakistan and into Afghanistan, an act that laid the foundation for a Taliban–bin Laden alliance. Bin Laden financed the Taliban's war against their non-Pashtun enemies, with his al Qaeda militants fighting alongside Taliban forces, and supported the training of other disgruntled Muslim militant groups from virtually anywhere around the world.

Notes

1   Zal (Zalmay) Khalilzad, an Afghan American, formerly working with the RAND Corporation, is currently a member of President George W. Bush's National Security Team and the Special Envoy of the President of Afghanistan. His role as the principal architect of U.S. policies toward Afghanistan since September 11, 2001, cannot be underestimated.

2   Hence, these authors advocated for the return of the United States in the region and resumption of its presumed responsibilities to help bring peace. Not surprisingly, after the events of September 11, 2001, and the start of the war on terrorism campaign, the United States has returned to Afghanistan in full force.

3 One of the frequently cited facts introduced to prove the violent nature of Afghan society is that during the 20th century, seven out of 12 political leaders of the country met violent deaths (Habibullah I, Habibullah II, Nadir Shah, Daoud, Taraki, Amin, and Najibullah), while Amanullah, Zahir Shah, Rabbani, and Mllah Omar, four of the survivors, were violently deposed, and Karmal was sent into exile. This fact, however, tells more about the nature of the political succession in the country and the violent nature of the Afghan *state* than it does about the peoples of Afghanistan.

References

Edwards, David B. 1996 *Heroes of the Age: Moral Fault Lines on the Afghan Frontier*. Berkeley: University of California Press.

Ferdinand, Klaus 1962 *Nomad Expansion and Commerce In Central Afghanistan*. Folk 4:123–159.

Goodson, Larry P. 2001 *Afghanistan's Endless War: State Failure, Regional Politics and the Rise of Taliban*. Seattle: University of Washington Press.

Kakar, Hasan 1979 *Government and Society in Afghanistan: The Reign of Amrir 'Abd al-Rahman Khan*. Austin: University of Texas Press.

Khalilzad, Zalmay, and Daniel Byman 2000 *Afghanistan: the Consolidation of a Rogue State*. Washington Quarterly 23(winter):1.

Khalilzad, Zalmay, Daniel Byman, Elle D. Krakowski, and Don Ritter 1999 *U.S. Policy in Afghanistan: Challenges and Solutions*. Washington, DC: Afghanistan Foundation.

Maley, William 1998 *Fundamentalism Reborn: Afghanistan and the Taliban*. London: C. Hurst and Company.

Mousavi, Sayed Askar 1997 *The Hazaras of Afghanistan: An Historical, Cultural, Economic and Political Study*. New York: St. Martin's Press.

Rashid, Ahmed 2000 *Taliban: Militant Islam, Oil and Fundamentalism in Central Asia*. New Haven, CT: Yale University Press.

Roy, Olivier 1990 *Islam and Resistance in Afghanistan*. 2nd ed.. Cambridge: Cambridge University Press.

———— 1995 Afghanistan: From Holy War to Civil War. Princeton: Darwin Press.

Rubin, Barnett R. 1995 *The Fragmentation of Afghanistan: State Formation and Collapse in the International System*. New Haven, CT: Yale University Press.

Shahrani, Nazif M. 1986 *State Building and Social Fragmentation in Afghanistan: A Historical Perspective*. In *The State, Religion, and Ethnic Politics: Afghanistan, Iran, and Pakistan*. Ali Banuazizi and Myron Weiner, eds. Pp. 23–74. Syracuse, NY: Syracuse University Press.

————. 1998 The *Future of the State and the Structure of the Community Governance*. In Afghanistan In Fundamentalism Reborn? Afghanistan and Taliban. William Maley, ed. Pp. 212–242. London: C. Hurst and Company.

————. 2000a *The Taliban Enigma: Person-Centred Politics and Extremism in Afghanistan*. ISIM Newsletter 6:20–21.

————. 2000b *Resisting the Taliban and Talibanism in Afghanistan: Legacies of a Century of Internal Colonialism and Cold War Politics in a Buffer State. Perceptions*. Journal of International Affairs 4: 121–140.

Shahrani, Nazif M., and Robert Canfield 1984 *Revolutions and Rebellions in Afghanistan: Anthropological Perspectives*. Berkeley: Institute of International Studies, University of California, Berkeley, Research Series, 57.

Tapper, Nancy 1973 The Advent of the Pushtun Maldars in Northwestern Afghanistan. *Bulletin of the School of Oriental and African Studies* 36(1):55–79.

Part V

Development and Liberalization

Introduction

The eight countries of South Asia form the South Asian Association for Regional Cooperation (SAARC). With a high-functioning stock market, India has the strongest economy in the region, and is thus the dominant force in SAARC. Indeed as one of the newly minted BRIC nations (Brazil, Russia, India, China), it is also seen as poised for greater global economic prominence. Between 2008 and 2009, the number of Indian billionaires doubled from twenty-six to fifty-seven. Despite India's recent economic success, and its hegemony in the region, it shares with all the countries of South Asia high rates of rural poverty and landlessness.

In 1990, about half of Asia's poor lived in South Asia, and 40 percent lived in East Asia. By 2007, three-quarters of Asia's poor lived in South Asia and only 21 percent lived in East Asia. India comprises three quarters of South Asia's population, where 72 percent of the population is rural and 75 percent of the poorest live in rural areas. These figures, however, still mask the fact (as Guru and Chakravarty point out in their essay), that three-quarters of India's poor are Dalits, though they make up only 16 percent of the population. In India the rural poverty rate is 37 percent and in urban areas, 31 percent. In Bangladesh the rural poverty rate is 55 percent and in urban areas it is 46 percent. In Pakistan the rural poverty rate is 13 percent and the urban rate is 10 percent, while in Sri Lanka; the rates are 7 percent and 5 percent respectively. Most of South Asia's poor live in rural areas and have little land or no land. In India, where struggles for land rights during the twentieth century led to some land reform, absolute landlessness is at 22 percent (though here again, three-quarters of all Dalits are landless), while in Bangladesh it is 58 percent and in Pakistan it is 77 percent.[1] In Bangladesh, landlessness has been increasing: in 1988 it was 46 percent, but by 1995 it was nearly 50 percent.[2] As we will see in the next

Perspectives on Modern South Asia: A Reader in Culture, History, and Representation, First Edition.
Edited by Kamala Visweswaran.
© 2011 Blackwell Publishing Ltd. Published 2011 by Blackwell Publishing Ltd.

section, increasing landlessness and displacement is one of the motors of Naxalite and Maoist political struggle.

The number of people who live below the poverty line of $1 per day is 33 percent in India and 55 percent in Bangladesh. In India, over 90 percent of rural women workers are unskilled and 90 percent of them work in the informal/unorganized sectors. The wage rates for women in agriculture are 30–50 percent less than for men and female casual laborers have the highest incidences of poverty for any occupational category, male or female. While South Asia now accounts for about three-quarters of Asia's poor, South Asia had more poor people in 2004 than it did in 1990. While some of this increase may be due to population growth, the claim that liberalization has decreased the numbers of South Asia's poor is questionable.

Under colonialism, the economies of South Asia were subjected to similar crises and challenges, producing what David Ludden calls a "development regime" which includes the institutions of economics, education, technology, media, and policy. For Ludden, development regimes are also historic formations, and the main shift he describes in his essay is from a single imperial development regime to multiple national development regimes, which are nonetheless unified by globalization and "economic liberalization."

Economic liberalization is now a feature of all the economies of South Asia. In Sri Lanka it started in the late 1970s with relaxation of laws to enable foreign investment, and the establishment of free trade zones, or FTZs, discussed in Sandya Hewamanne's article. While FTZs are an established part of Sri Lanka's economy, the attempt to establish them three years ago in West Bengal, India met with violence and protest. Since so much of South Asia's economy hinges upon India's growth, most of the recent debate on liberalization has focused on India. For smaller countries like Bhutan, as Tashi Choden explains, India plays a more direct and immediate role than western investment has played in India.

"Economic liberalization" or structural adjustment of the economy to bring it in line with the demands of international lending agencies took off in India in 1991 (though some economists date it to the 1970s). In this section, Amartya Sen characterizes the economic reforms as involving a "greater reliance on the market mechanism," translating into "public policies including deregulation and the reduction of governmental controls, greater autonomy of private investment, less use of the public sector, more opening of the economy to international trade, less restrictions on the convertibility of the rupee" (1998: 1). Proponents of liberalization claim that it has allowed for high levels of economic growth. Skeptics claim that these levels of growth are exaggerated, or do not take into account that there is no trickle-down effect to the poorest at the bottom. They argue that even when an economy experiences growth, a substantial number of the poor may slide into poverty, and growth may not even touch the large numbers of people who have been poor for generations. Sen questions the value of high growth rates when illiteracy remains high and basic health care is nonexistent. He calls for a "human capabilities" approach to development that moves "well beyond liberalization."

Sen and Dréze note that India's high rate of GDP has to be evaluated on a state by state or regional basis, and must take into account that most of the increase of growth has been in the tertiary or service sector, where the much vaunted high-tech industry is located.[3] Indeed, in the first decade of economic reform, there was no economic growth in the primary, or agricultural sector, where most Indians labor. Dréze takes us through several comparisons: intrastate (within India) and interstate (between India and China) to underscore the value of investing in education and health – a feature that allowed both Kerala and pre-reform China to maximize development. Sen is also known for identifying the "problem of the missing women" – the fact that the female to male ratio (FMR) is much lower in many areas of North India than in Sub-Saharan Africa (where female literacy is also higher). While economists have sought to redress gender imbalances in society by bringing women into development, this has also resulted in women becoming the targets of development so that they are seen as either passive subjects, or transgressive ones as Seira Tamang, Lamia Karim, and Sandya Hewamanne point out in their essays. On the one hand a kind of "woman question" emerges (as discussed in Part IV); on the other hand, non-governmental organizations may actually increase class divisions or promote microcredit which might intensify forms of patriarchal social control over women.

Part of the debate on liberalization in India has focused on the role of the state in development. It has been argued that by decentralizing state functions, or privatizing them – by letting businesses or non-governmental organizations (NGOs) take on the function of state agencies – that competition will allow for greater efficiency and a higher quality of services. While some have argued that the problem was not with the state model itself, but rather that the state was not strong enough to deal with multiclass politics and social fragmentation, others have also cautioned against decentralization. When the state fails to deliver essential services, as in the case of disaster relief, NGOs step in. In contrast to the devastating 2005 earthquake in Kashmir, or the severe massive flooding throughout Pakistan in 2010, the 1999 Orissa cyclone and the 2001 Gujarat earthquake generated massive donations from abroad. At the same time, it allowed Hindu nationalist groups to set up relief agencies as a means of spreading their ideological message. Today, the RSS, the parent organization of the Hindutva movement runs thousands of NGOs focused on "seva" or service. In many contexts in South Asia, NGOs have been in an oppositional relationship to the state. While some welcome NGOs as implicit to the practice of democracy; others, like Karim are more skeptical, finding that the much-lauded micro-credit revolution in Bangladesh hides coercive social structures which negatively impact women.

Notes

1   Akhter U. Ahmed, Ruth V. Hill, Doris M. Wiesmann, and Lisa C. Smith "Asia's Poorest and Hungry: Trends and Characteristics" Draft paper for Policy Session on Agricultural and Rural Development for Reducing Poverty and Hunger in Asia: In Pursuit of Inclusive and Sustainable Growth, International Food Policy Research Institute (IFPRI) and Asian Development Bank (ADB) ADB Headquarters, Manila, Philippines, August 9–10, 2007. http://www.ifpri.org/2020ChinaConference/pdf/manilac_ahmed.pdf: accessed on 9/12/07.

2   Ganesh Thapa, Rural Poverty Reduction Strategy for South Asia, ASARC Working Paper 2004-06, Presented at an International Conference on Ten Years of Australian South Asia Research Centre organized at the Australian National University, Canberra from 27–28, April 2004.

3   Jean Dréze and Amartya Sen, *India: Development and Participation*, pp. 316–17. Delhi: Oxford, 2001.

19

Development Regimes in South Asia
History and the Governance Conundrum

David Ludden

I Development Regimes

Development can be understood as an activity, a condition, an event, or a process. In natural science, it unfolds according to principles that humans do not control, but in social science, development is entirely the product of human decisions. Economic development is the subject of this essay: it can be understood as a very complex set of institutional activities that employ public and private assets to enhance the wealth and well-being of an entire population. Its institutions span the gamut, including families, communities, firms, media, governments, political parties, NGOs, and agencies and associations of many kinds. Development is a reflexive process, wherein policies, institutions, outcomes and analysis interact. It is distinct from its many objects of theory and measurement, such as economic growth. The process of development cannot be reduced to any specific set of policy goals, empirical trends, or normative statements, for it includes the definition of goals, setting of priorities, choice of policies, critical reflection,

debate, relationships among people who decide what trends are important, and political efforts to change the direction of policy.

What appears to be objectively true about development at any moment in time is the product of debate, selection and erasure. Mainstream and dissenting opinions acquire empirical veracity as their contending forces generate and deploy appropriate data. The result is a vast literature on all varieties of development, using various yardsticks. In economic development, for instance, the aggregate increase in national wealth is a common measure of progress but national autonomy, food security, equity, poverty reduction, and social stability are typically important policy priorities. A state's stability, revenue, military might, and cultural legitimacy may actually preoccupy development policy practice more than economic indicators. Contending forces conditioning development jostle for influence in policy practice and use various measures of success to bolster their positions in development debates.

Perspectives on Modern South Asia: A Reader in Culture, History, and Representation, First Edition.
Edited by Kamala Visweswaran.
© 2011 Blackwell Publishing Ltd. Published 2011 by Blackwell Publishing Ltd.

Economics and economies

The objective, scientific nature of economic development seems secure at first sight, but that appearance is deceptive. There is, most fundamentally, a definitive difference between 'the economy' and any particular 'economy'. The 'economy' studied by economics consists of various elements and mechanisms described in economic theory, but 'an economy' includes natural endowments, social power, and political history, all officially confined by state boundaries that have no place in economic theory. The 'world economy' in which 'globalisation' occurs is a kaleidoscopic configuration of national economies, most of whose operations elude the conceptual field of economic theory.

The application of economics to development in any economy requires that economic ideas and empirical statements be understood by participants in the development process as compelling representations of reality in their own context. Thus, economic development embraces much more than economics: it includes all the institutional and material conditions that constitute economies. Most critically, economic development includes historical processes in which some particular set of economic ideas and empirical statements become convincing to leading participants in the development process.

Power and authority

A development regime is an institutional configuration of effective power over human behaviour, and that also has legitimate authority to make decisions that affect the wealth and well-being of whole populations. It includes an official state apparatus but also much more. And, as we will see, one single state can participate in various regimes. A development regime includes institutions of education, research, media, technology, science and intellectual influence that constitute a development policy mainstream. The power and authority of a regime resides not only in government but also in physical instruments of power over nature and in cultural instruments of authority over people's minds and morality. It is a techno-regime with a discursive regimen.

Composed of self-conscious, reflective, articulate people who work in specific contexts to direct the development process, a development regime is a documented historic formation. Its organised influence generates ideas and empirical knowledge that are most compelling for leading participants in the process of development in particular places and times. The history of development thus centres on regimes that chart trajectories of development from the past to the present and into the future [Ludden 1992].

II An Imperial Regime

In south Asia, pre-modern regimes developed regional economies for many centuries, but the first development regime emerged under the British empire after 1840. Built upon conquered regions, south Asia's first development regime subordinated conquered regional economies to imperial designs of globalisation.

In 1929, one erudite British agricultural officer, William Moreland, concluded from his research that the 'idea of agricultural development was already present in the 14th century.' His conclusion can now be extended much further back in time, because now we know that ancient and medieval rulers in south Asia invested heavily to increase productivity, most visibly by building irrigation, roads and cities. By the 18th century, state investments had helped to develop agriculture, commerce, and manufacturing most remarkably around capital cities in Bengal, Gujarat, Indo-Gangetic plains, and peninsular river basins [Raychaudhuri and Irfan Habib 1970; Habib 1982].

Pre-modern regimes endeavoured to increase state revenue in political and social environments unfavourable to modern goals of development, because military and political struggles often destroyed investments in farming, manufacturing, and banking [Moreland 1929]. Though pre-modern states did accomplish economic development in their day, they were certainly not organised around the process of development in the modern sense of that term, because their efforts focused specifically on ruling elites.

The modern idea of economic development to increase the wealth of whole populations spread around the world in the 19th century. Its referent population was then, and still remains, the nation. One key early text was Adam Smith's Wealth of Nations, published in 1776, which attacked the British Crown for its support for elitist monopolies like the East India Company and which advocated commerce that would benefit the whole nation.

The British nation came into being during the imperial expansion of Crown authority overseas. British conquest in south Asia was underway in Adam Smith's day and continued into the late 19th century. At the same time, Britain became the world's foremost industrial nation. British India became an official collection of regions in the world-economy of British imperialism. The British Empire organised a development regime that embraced Britain, British India, and also Ceylon and other colonial territories, all of which became territorially demarcated and distinctively national segments of an imperial economic design, whose legacy is still with us today.

The business of empire

By 1793, debates had begun in Britain about managing Britain's 'Asiatic possessions' in the national interest, something Adam Smith never considered.[1] Two basic principles emerged. First, the empire must pay for itself. The East India Company fell foul of this principle, forcing the British parliament to assume direct control over Indian finance. Secondly, British business had to benefit. The Company ceased to serve this purpose adequately and imperial policy shifted onto laissez faire lines. In 1813, the British parliament ended the Company's monopoly to allow private merchants freer access to British territories overseas. In 1833, Britain opened India further by making English the official language of state law, administration and education [Barber 1975].

The administrative articulation of Empire with British business interests moved ahead noticeably in 1833, when the abolition of slavery triggered petitions from Caribbean sugar planters, who being deprived of slave labour, spurred the Indian government to send shiploads of indentured workers from Calcutta to English sugar plantations in the West Indies. By 1833, tariffs against Indian cloth were protecting Lancashire industrialists, who sent cloth virtually free of tariff to British India, driving countless weavers into destitution. English merchants sold Bengal opium in China to buy porcelain teacups and tea for English housewives and factory workers to sweeten with sugar from Caribbean plantations. Meanwhile, English businessmen came more often to work in India and displaced Indians from commercial partnerships with British firms, as India's overseas trade moved more and more into British hands.

By the 1840s, the British parliament was directly engaged with the national business interest in empire. For instance, a commission considered ways and means to increase cotton supplies to Lancashire, so as to reduce England's dependence on the American South. Bombay Presidency attracted special attention, along with Egypt.[2] Resulting efforts to boost cotton exports from India and Egypt accomplished their goal, and when the US Civil War broke out in 1860, Egypt and the Bombay Presidency could fill the void in cotton supplies created by the Union blockade of Confederate ports.

Investing in infrastructure

A new round of imperial globalisation, attached to industrial capitalism, had thus begun by the mid-19th century. With it emerged a modern development regime, whose initial construction began piecemeal during the decades between 1823 and 1854, when the real value of taxes in British India rose rapidly, as prices in India dropped steadily. During this long price depression, it became more cost effective to invest Indian taxes in India, where tax money could buy more in real terms than if remitted to England. At the same time, British businesses sought ways to invest state money overseas to improve the supply of raw materials and consumer goods. In the 1840s, as parliament considered how to invest state money to improve cotton supplies, government in British India began building infrastructure to cheapen imports and exports, to expand military operations, to increase revenue, and to extend the field of British private capital investment.

So began the promotion of state infrastructure investments in economic development. It focused first on plantations, railways, cities, roads, ports, shipping and irrigation. In the 1840s, an irrigation engineer, Arthur Cotton, led the way by arguing that Indian crop production could increase manifold with state irrigation that would pay for itself with higher taxes on more valuable land.[3] In 1853, governor general Dalhousie announced a plan to build an Indian railway with state contracts that guaranteed English companies a minimum 5 per cent return, and to secure that return, government kept control of railway construction and management. In 1871, the government of India obtained authority to raise loans for productive purposes, and large irrigation projects began, following earlier success raising revenues from small projects.

Globalisation and development

A development regime had emerged in south Asia by 1880, and it fed the unprecedented burst of globalisation that spanned the following five decades. By 1880, four basic modern development ideas were well established. First was the idea that the state would lead the development process in the public interest. Secondly, major state investments in infrastructure would boost private investment, expand and integrate markets, accelerate economic growth, enrich the state and benefit the public at large. Direct benefits to the people of British India would derive for instance from state irrigation projects that employed native contractors and benefit landowners who used new irrigation to produce commodity crops for expanding markets. Third, economic progress would benefit 'the poor', who for example were to be protected from famine by large irrigation works. And last but not least, advances in science and technology would be instruments of human progress in all nations, led by imperial regimes.

Underlying and energising this imperial development regime, vast market integration spawned regions of specialised commercial production around the Indian Ocean. Ceylon was a plantation economy. Coffee plantations expanded from 50,000 to 80,000 acres between 1847 and 1857, and peasants devoted another 48,000 acres to coffee for export. Coffee acreage expanded another 35,000 acres in the 1860s. In the 1880s, leaf disease killed coffee cultivation, which was rapidly replaced by tea, rubber, coconut and cinchona. British-owned plantations in Ceylon and Assam (including Sylhet) replaced China as the major suppliers of English tea. British investors eventually drove out most peasant plantation crop producers and controlled export markets.

Labour supplies posed the major constraint for plantations, and the solution was found in (eventually permanent) labour migration. Tea planters depended on labour migration from southern Tamil districts into Ceylon and from northern India into Assam. British plantations in Malay colonies likewise depended on migratory Tamil workers. By 1880, the modern age of vast labour migration to major sites of capital investment had begun.

The mobility of commodities, labour and capital that defines 'globalisation' increased more between 1870 and 1914 than ever before. Since then, it has only expanded. Our recent globalisation is another great burst whose magnitude has yet to surpass the first. By 1900, distant lands around the Indian Ocean – from the west Asia and eastern Africa to south and south-east Asia – had become extensively attached. Many of those attachments broke after 1945, and most have yet to be restored, while the west Asia connection has alone expanded.

By 1900, British Burma and East Africa developed within circuits of mobility anchored in British India. In Burma, Tamil Chettiyar bankers financed agricultural expansion in the Irrawaddy River delta, which generated huge exports of rice for world markets, including India, where urbanisation increased demand for imported rice. In East and South Africa, merchants from Gujarat and workers from Bombay, Calcutta and Madras provided labour and capital for railway construction, forming urban nuclei for modern economies. Between 1896 and 1928, 85 per cent of the emigrants leaving Indian ports went to work on plantations in Ceylon, Malaya, the Caribbean, Fiji and Mauritius.

Spatial specialisation

Regional economic specialisation, based on consciously targeted capital investment and state-organised labour mobility, became a hallmark of the national economies that emerged in south Asia during this round of globalisation. Though regional specialisation is most visible in plantation and mining regions, it embraced the entire subcontinent.

Imperial development before 1920 gave economic regions in south Asia a distinct export-orientation, which faded in the first decades after 1947, but returned with a vengeance during the second great burst of globalisation after 1980. In 1914, almost all goods arriving at south Asia ports were destined for export: these were mostly cotton, wheat, rice, coal, coke, jute, gunny bags, hides and skins, tea, ores and wool. Most cotton came to Bombay from Maharashtra. All tea came to Calcutta and Colombo from Assam, Darjeeling and Ceylon. Most export rice came to Rangoon. Wheat came primarily from fields under state irrigation in Punjab and western United Provinces (Uttar Pradesh). Oilseeds came to Bombay from Hyderabad territory (Andhra Pradesh), the Central Provinces (Madhya Pradesh) and Bombay Presidency (Maharashtra). Coal, coke and ores came from mines around Jharkhand into Calcutta and Bombay. Eastern Bengal (Bangladesh) produced almost all the world's jute.

Specialised industrial regions also emerged in British India. Imported machinery was rapidly domesticated in new Indian factory towns. The first Indian cotton mill had appeared in 1853 in Bombay. The Factory Act (1881) imposed working rules on Indian factories to reduce comparative advantages they enjoyed by virtue of low local labour costs and cheap raw materials. The impetus behind the Factory Act sounds familiar today, as western countries endeavour to raise compliance with international standards among industrial competitors in Asia.

But the Factory Act did not suppress industrialisation in British India. In 1887, J N Tata's Empress Mill arose at Nagpur, in the heart of cotton country, and the Tatas became India's industrial dynasty. Tata Iron and Steel Works at Jamshedpur consumed increasing supplies of ore and coal, which by the 1920s rivalled exports from Calcutta. In 1914, India was the world's fourth largest industrial cotton textile producer: cotton mills numbered 271 and employed 2,60,000 people, 42 per cent in Bombay city, 26 per cent elsewhere in Bombay Presidency (mostly Nagpur), and 32 per cent elsewhere in British India, at major railway junctures. Coal, iron, steel, jute and other industries were developed at the same time, producing specialised regional concentrations of heavy industrial production around Bombay, Ahmedabad, Nagpur, Kanpur, Calcutta, Jamshedpur and Madras [GoI 1921]. In 1913, manufactured goods comprised 20 per cent of Indian exports, valued at 10 per cent of national income, figures never surpassed.

In 1914, war stimulated policies to enhance India's industrialisation to make India less dependent on imports. The Great Depression, 1929–1933, again boosted incentives for industrial growth by reducing prices for farm output compared to manufactures. As a result, industrial output in British India grew steadily from 1913 to 1938 and was 58 per cent higher in 1936 than in 1914, compared to slower, more uneven rates of growth in the UK and Germany [Morris 1983].

A national economy

By 1920, British India was a national economy within the Empire, with its own distinctive institutions and material conditions. Though dominated by agriculture, it included a large public sector and major industries. Native investors and nationalist politicians were by this time vocal advocates for increasing state development efforts: they were aspiring and increasingly influential leaders of the development regime.

By 1920, British India was also a land of opportunity for global investors. The US Consul at Bombay, Henry Baker, had called India 'one of the few large countries of the world where there is an "open door" for the trade of all countries'.[4] England was still British India's dominant trading partner, but losing ground. In

1914, the UK sent 63 per cent of British India's imports and received 25 per cent of its exports; and by 1926, these figures stood at 51 per cent and 21 per cent, respectively. By 1926, total trade with the UK averaged 32 per cent for the five major ports (Calcutta, Bombay, Madras, Karachi and Rangoon). Bombay and Rangoon did 43 per cent of their overseas business with Asia and the west Asia. Calcutta did a quarter of its business with America.[5]

South Asia's early 20th century globalisation also appears in migration data. In 1911, the British in British India numbered only 62 per cent of all resident Europeans. Four times more immigrants came into British India from other parts of Asia than from Europe; seven of 10 came overland from Nepal (54 per cent) and Afghanistan (16 per cent). In 1911, Nepalis entering British India (280,248) exceeded the resident British population by 50 per cent; and overall, Asian immigrants were three times as many. In addition, by 1921, emigration far exceeded immigration. Between 1896 and 1928, 83 per cent of 1,206,000 emigrants left British India from Madras (which accounted for only 10 per cent of total overseas trade), and they mostly went to work in Ceylon (54 per cent) and Malaya (39 per cent). Bombay emigrants went mostly to East and South Africa; Calcutta emigrants, to Fiji and the West Indies [Schwartzberg 1978].

In 1920, Britain still controlled the highest echelons of south Asia's political economy, but by then, the overall process of capital accumulation inside south Asia had escaped British control. Before the first world war, London's political position in south Asia seemed secure. After the war, London's power declined visibly, both in relation to other imperial nations and in relation to nationalist forces in south Asia, which mobilised then on an unprecedented scale to wrest control of their national development from the British.

III National Regimes

In the 1920s, a national development regime emerged inside British India. In 1920, the Indian government obtained financial autonomy from Britain. Nationalist forces focused their critique of government sharply on economic issues. The Indian National Congress had first met in Bombay, in 1885, and then met every year in late December in a different city of British India. Following the great Deccan famines, Dadabhai Naoroji had published in 1879 The Poverty of India to document the negative economic impact of imperial policies on India. It was, in effect, a nationalist revision of Adam Smith, with even greater impact, because of its political location. Naoroji presided at Congress meetings in 1886, 1893 and 1906, where delegates from all the provinces discussed government policy and argued for lower taxes and increased state development expenditure. In 1905, the Congress launched a Swadeshi movement to induce Indian consumers to buy Indian-made cloth rather than British imports. Economic nationalism had been established [Chandra 1966].

Perils of globalisation

The end of this first globalisation phase in the history of development regimes in south Asia came in the 1930s, when the Great Depression dramatised beyond doubt the perils imposed on a nation when its economy is open wide to the world economy under imperial managers. Depression sparked peasant and worker's movements demanding economic security, and it spurred nationalist efforts to make government accountable to the nation.

By this time, the government in British India had gained experience as economic manager and investor in infrastructure. The government owned and managed most mineral and forest resources. Government agricultural departments, colleges, and experiment stations supported scientists and engineers who worked on state-funded development projects. Yet, the vast state sector of the imperial economy was managed within a laissez faire, free-market policy framework that favoured big investors and delivered benefits disproportionately to foreigners.

During the 1930s, nationalists concluded from hard empirical data interpreted within mainstream nationalist economic thought that a laissez faire free-market development regime discriminated against politically subordinate regions: it enriched imperial nations with taxes, remittances and countless indirect benefits; and it provided imperial investors profits, and their consumers, cheap raw materials and consumer goods, while draining wealth from colonies and depriving subordinate nations of the just rewards of enterprise. Having reached this conclusion, national leaders devised new ambitions for development.

In 1931, Jawaharlal Nehru pushed economic thought in a new direction by saying, 'the great poverty and misery of the Indian People are due, not only to foreign exploitation in India but also to the economic structure of society, which the alien rulers support so that their exploitation may continue'. He went on to proclaim, 'In order therefore to remove this poverty and misery and to ameliorate the condition of the masses, it is essential to make revolutionary changes in the present economic and social structure of society and to remove the gross inequalities' [Zaidi 1985].

Planning regimes
The 1930s and 1940s brought peoples of south Asia as bitter an experience of state failure as any population has ever endured, including mass suffering, death and dislocation during the Great Depression, Bengal Famine and Partition. Disastrous experience of failed imperial governance induced nationalists to lay the groundwork for nationally planned economic development, which stressed autonomy, security and national integration under strong central state leadership. In 1951, prime minister Nehru chaired India's Planning Commission, and in the 1950s, all south Asian countries wrote national plans stressing self-sufficiency and addressing problems of national economic growth, poverty and inequality.

The 25 years between 1950 and 1975 were the heyday of nationally planned development in south Asia. Uniquely in Bangladesh, however, independence arrived only in 1971, and during most of the heyday of the planning era, the regime centred in West Pakistan had rejected legitimate demands for regional development in East Pakistan. Though Pakistan started national development in what became Bangladesh, it also delivered intensely discriminatory, uneven development, which spawned mass discontent, upheaval, and eventually brutal war. In 1971, Bangladesh emerged determined to pursue progressive, planned national development for all citizens.

Notably for Bangladesh, but to some degree for all post-colonial regimes, national planning faced serious constraints: financial, infrastructural, administrative, political and intellectual. All these were quite severe in Bangladesh. The imperial regime had stranded this region on the outer margins of public and private priorities. Administrative and judicial systems, transport and educational infrastructure, and financial resources were notoriously weak, compared to other parts of British India. To address these weaknesses, Lord Curzon had established the province of East Bengal and Assam, in 1905, but this innovation died in 1911, under nationalist pressure. Regional development in eastern Bengal remained subordinate and marginal under both imperial and early national regimes. Raw materials, zamindar rents, interest payments, tax revenues and plantation and industrial profits moved systematically out of eastern Bengal to enrich people in Calcutta, Delhi, London and Islamabad; while the inflow of public and private investment was minimal. Imperial development had designed all dependent regions to serve dominant metropolitan regions, but even so, comparatively large public and private investments had flowed into favoured regions of British India, particularly the western Ganga basin and Punjab [Ludden 2005].

During the heyday of planning, systematic inequalities in wealth and power among social groups and regions remained starkly visible in development thinking. The Bangladesh freedom struggle dramatised inequalities, which in other ways also became prominent in India, Sri Lanka and (West) Pakistan. Planning regimes tackled inequalities with administrative and legal action, supported by the burgeoning academic field of 'development studies', endowed in these decades with policy-oriented research centres focused on nations emerging from imperial regimes. In post-colonial countries, the political character of development – and the necessity of changing power relations in order to redesign development regimes, to serve national citizens – pervaded mainstream development thought.

In that historic context, development theory and practice converged on planning, whose central goal was to reorient development around national priorities. Imperial regimes had turned resources of subordinate regions into objects for laissez faire allocation by markets in the world economy. National planning separated national and global market priorities, enclosing national economies and instituting state redistributive systems to make national markets serve national citizens [Myrdal 1968].

Most national regimes around the world became more self-contained in the 1950s and 1960s. Traumas following the earlier burst of globalisation made most national regimes more inward looking and self-protective. Foreign direct investment (FDI) declined globally from roughly 10 per cent of world output in 1913 to less than 5 per cent in the 1960s, when the rate of increase in world merchandise exports remained well below the 1.7 per cent that pertained from 1870 to 1914.

In south Asia, as elsewhere, national plans focused on national markets. Planners devised priorities for allocating public and private resources, acquired internally and externally. External funding came in grants and loans directly from countries that sought to wield influence in former imperial dependencies, and indirectly also from the richest countries, for the same reason, through Bretton Woods institutions, the World Bank and International Monetary Fund (IMF). Among the rich capitalist countries, the US became most aggressively expansive.

Following the basic working principles of their imperial predecessor, national planning regimes in south Asia strove to enhance and supplement private investment. They were not anti-market, but rather, pro-national market. Planning instituted a combined public–private apparatus for monitoring and managing national economies. Planning agencies organised

initiatives like cooperative societies and community development programmes. Governments set up public food procurement and distribution systems. They expanded national health and education. They added to large inherited portfolios of state-owned assets heavy industries, public utilities, banks and insurance [Bagchi 1989; Bardhan 1984; Chaudhuri 1979; Frankel 1978; Kothari 1971].

IV Regime Change

During the heyday of national planning, economic progress became a central feature of national life. Public intellectuals and organisations representing farmers, workers, businesses and many other economic interests became intensely involved in development debates. Public interest groups of many kinds mobilised politically. As in earlier nationalist times, economic self-interest preoccupied urban middle classes, which became more populous, diverse and politically active.

To address development demands pressed by all these groups, national politicians deployed deficit spending, which increased their need for external funding. International and bilateral funding agencies, as well as national donors and lenders, thereby obtained more leverage on post-colonial national economies. Funding needs and national pride pushed politicians in south Asia to emphasise economic growth, and increasing national wealth per capita eventually became an end in itself, which turned policy priorities toward the interests of investors, as competitive politics pushed governments to undertake larger projects demanding more external finance.

Pragmatic strategies
While in theory, expanding popular political participation would favour the inclusion of all citizen interests in the development process, in fact and in practice, financial pressures to meet citizen demands made governments more dependent on people with money to invest in development. Launched in the 1960s, the green revolution represents a strategic amalgamation

of these contending forces, for on the one hand, being based on the intensive use of pesticides, fertiliser, tractors, tube wells and high-yielding hybrid seeds, it favoured investors in agriculture and industry, and on the other hand, because it raised wheat and rice yields tremendously, it secured basic food requirements for national populations and spread benefits widely, though unevenly. Green revolution provided a strategic blueprint for national development by encouraging regimes to: (i) increase national wealth and security by; (ii) spreading new productive technologies; (iii) with the help of lavish state subsidies that; (iv) favour richer investors; (v) so as to generate more private investment; and (vi) bring producers throughout national economies into more wealth productive systems of combined state-and-market asset allocation.

South Asian planning regimes substantially reorganised market economies inside their borders. This activity was in tune with development thinking, which supported land reform and redistributive policies to favour disadvantaged groups. Development theory also supported industrial import substitution and public sector production of basic goods and services, essential for public welfare and for business alike, including transportation, energy, banking and insurance.

Yet in theory and practice, national economies remained predominantly market-oriented, and mostly under private control. Private enterprise still dominated agriculture and industry. Even in India, where national planning had the largest impact, 80 per cent of industrial production remained in the private sector, where public output lowered input prices and state import protection expanded national markets for private enterprise. The result was slow but steady economic growth and visible progress in shifting development benefits toward groups that would not have benefited as much from free-market allocation in post-colonial economic conditions, especially farmers, industrial workers, and big business [Tomlinson 1997; Johnson 1983].

Unplanned problems

Regulatory systems established under planning regimes also pushed national markets in

unforeseen directions, which became counter-productive. Most notably, bureaucratic controls on imports, exports, and business generally spawned corruption as well as black and grey markets. Foreign exchange shortages put private and public sector companies into financial competition, driving profit seekers underground. One estimate put the value of India's black market at nearly half the GDP in the late 1970s.

In addition, political pragmatism mixed development administration with political patronage. This sparked opposition from groups left out of the patronage circuit, deprived of development benefits. In the 1970s, this opposition became volatile in Pakistan, Bangladesh, India and Sri Lanka. Charges of corrupt, inefficient, domineering and discriminatory state development practices became effective weapons in competitive politics. By the 1970s, leading and aspiring participants in national regimes clashed openly over control of development. Bureaucrats, politicians, the military, domestic investors, and international financiers were tearing at the fabric of national planning regimes.

Transitional decades

In retrospect, we can see a transformation in national regimes beginning in the late 1960s that yielded new development regimes by 1990. The transition began slowly, soon after Nehru's death in 1964, when famines struck India in 1967. Bangladesh independence gained political force at the same time, and then in 1974, famine hit Bangladesh. In both famine periods, foreign aid became critical, and in response, national regimes put new energy into the green revolution. Planners concentrated on investing state funds in sites of intensive cultivation, where well endowed landowners controlled local labour, finance, and political institutions. Critics called this strategy 'betting on the rich'. Defenders called it the only road to national food security.

This strategic blueprint led states to adopt development plans that called for increasingly expensive investments, which demanded more external finance, more in the form of debt. At the same time, the World Bank dramatically increased its lending under Robert McNamara, who led the charge to increase development loans and aid from rich countries and private banks.

These new loans came with new conditions, collectively called Structural Adjustment Programmes, which began in the 1970s, and gained force and reach in the 1980s and 1990s. Under these programmes, the World Bank and IMF demanded that borrowing governments drastically reduce their regulatory and provisioning role in their economies, to assume the role of supporter and facilitator for private investors, who would, according to emerging mainstream economic thought under the so-called Washington consensus, engage rationally in market activity to allocate resources most efficiently for the increase of national wealth. Freeing markets from state control became the mantra of the international development mainstream [SAPRIN 2004; Leys 1996].

Planning regimes unravelled under structural adjustment. Sri Lanka, Bangladesh and Nepal led the way in south Asia, starting slowly in the 1970s and accelerating in the 1980s. With declining relative prices for primary product exports, the burden of external debt grew heavier, while raising funds for large development projects, (epitomised by the Mahaveli scheme in Sri Lanka, then the largest irrigation project in the world) became more pressing. At the same time, rising oil prices brought Europe and North America recession, inflation, and petro-dollars in need of circulation, while they brought south Asia higher costs for industrial growth, middle class consumption, and the green revolution.

The smaller countries first began borrowing on a much larger scale and succumbed quickly and decisively to structural adjustment. In 1981, India began to rely on foreign debt, and by 1991, internal and external pressures forced economic liberalisation. In the 1980s, neo-liberal free-market orthodoxy conquered the economic mainstream, where harsh critics of state planning, provisioning, and regulation become most influential. Development strategies emphasised private sector leadership in market-driven economic growth, emphasised imports and exports, and shifted the balance of power in national state-and-market asset allocation towards national and international business interests [Hossain et al 1999].

V The Governance Conundrum

Development regimes in south Asia operate today inside the same national states that managed them in 1975. But today's regimes are fundamentally different, and their transformation has accompanied – if not caused – major shifts in national politics.

In India, private capital and state governments have both gained increasing independence from New Delhi. The Congress Party lost its old hegemony, national government came to be composed of shifting coalitions of regionally-based parties, and state chief ministers now compete fiercely to attract FDI to their individual states, all of which has effectively made each Indian state a distinct development regime. In Nepal, electoral democracy was established in 1991, opening development to wide public debate, as foreign investments grew, and as did a Maoist insurgency carving the nation into regions of war and allowing the king to stage a royal coup in February 2005, purportedly to secure Kathmandu against revolution. Sri Lanka has endured civil war since 1981, and the nation that existed in 1970 has effectively disappeared. In Bangladesh, struggles over development brought military coups and a popular movement that established democracy in 1991, amidst a deep dependency on international finance and trade. In Pakistan, a government wracked by struggles for regional autonomy has experienced disruptions from two decades of war in Afghanistan, leading to more stringent authoritarian dependence on the US.

History in the present
Contemporary development regimes are currently in flux. Dismantling government controls to expand the private sector has accompanied domestic and foreign demands for more public scrutiny and popular participation to make state regimes more accountable and transparent to citizens and investors at home and abroad.

A vast reinterpretation and reorientation of national government is occurring. States are officially intact, and nations remain the basis of development, but national states no longer govern development.

No wonder governance is now such a prominent concern in development discourse. No coherent set of institutions has the power and authority to establish norms and enforce rules that govern development.

How is development governed today? The question is more than contentious: it is a conundrum, which we can analyse historically and spatially. As we have seen, imperialism established modern development regimes, which redesigned regional economies to serve the world of markets managed by imperial nations. The British Empire designed territories of development in south Asia, which nationalists captured and redesigned by disciplining markets inside independent states. Thus, the spatial framework of development shifted from empire to nation, in the middle decades of the 20th century.

In the last 20 years, another shift has occurred. States have lost much of their disciplining power over markets, and thus their leadership role in development. As that has occurred, national territory has lost its definitive role as the spatial framework that determines who is authorised to govern development and what people development must serve. Territorial boundaries had previously defined participants, populations, and priorities in the development process. Now links between development and territory are ambiguous. Leaders of development have diversified, they are now scattered all over the world, and their border crossing is ubiquitous.

National states still define official territories of development, but national powers to govern development vary tremendously. In general, these powers decline as national wealth does, until they reach virtually zero in the world's poorest countries.

Growing inequality of wealth and power among nations is an increasingly visible feature of the development process, but also increasingly, invisible in the mainstream development discourse, which treats all countries as equally

sovereign territories in the world of globalisation. Disproportionate rich country influence is pervasive globally, in government circles, business, finance, technology, international agencies, consumerism, education, media, fashion, language, and other realms. A new imperial formation is emerging and globalisation today has much in common with globalisation a century ago. Then there was British Empire, now there is US Empire. Even India, the most powerful economy and state in south Asia, has now succumbed under its current leadership to pragmatically strategic subordination to the US.

Yet imperial authority is a thing of the past. In a world of nations, empire can no longer provide legitimate governance. But most states cannot provide effective governance for development. So who then will govern development?

Balanced precariously between the real power of contemporary imperialism and the real authority of national states, in the shifting sands of globalisation, leadership in development today has no clear guidelines of organisation. Leaders have disparate loyalties and priorities. Their institutions pursue disparate goals. Their relationships with one another are messy, filled with competition, conflict, resistance, and negotiation among old, new, emerging, and aspiring leaders. Television images of protesters at World Bank and WTO meetings, or of the carnivalesque World Social Forum raised against staid G-8 meetings, represent only the most visible surface of the disorderly contestation underway in development regimes today.

Can finance govern?
The overarching influence of finance capital in development suggests it may now be dominant. Financial interests take many forms but have in common their ability to suborn and discipline the needy. The first order of business in development work today is gathering finance, and the power and authority of financial institutions have grown exponentially in the last 20 years. The striking absence of diversity in poor country economic policies and the uniformity of policy trends and economic problems in these countries following structural adjustment

result from the vast power and authority of Bretton Woods institutions.

Most international funding agencies have followed the World Bank leadership when using money to increase their influence over development. In the age of structural adjustment, they have by-passed national governments and supported the rise of non-governmental organisations (NGOs), which now play independent leadership roles. 22,000 NGOs operate in Bangladesh, and the largest, BRAC, rivals ministries. Launched on a small scale in 1976, the Grameen Bank now counts its clients in the millions and values its loans in billions of dollars. In India, NGOs employ more people than the central government. Using individual access to financing, and working independently of government, NGOs have effectively scattered governance in the development process among countless fragmented geographies and institutions, many with strong intellectual and other links with international agencies, and though grounded in specific countries, also dispersed around the world.

Funding worth hundreds of billions of dollars circulates in networks of development finance, which is wide open for NGO entrepreneurship. Yet garnering these funds no more makes an NGO a mere tool of funding agencies than receiving NGO goods and services makes pawns of village beneficiaries; and no more, indeed, than taking a bank loan makes a business a banker's mute instrument. NGOs have minds and agendas of their own and funding agencies need NGOs, as well as governments, to utilise funds effectively and keep finance circulating. The growth of NGOs reflects the rise of a relatively autonomous leadership sector in development, while state dependence on donors and lenders indicates that governments remain indispensable.

Immeasurably more money moves through business networks, seeking profits. Numerous multinational corporations control more finance than all development agencies combined. Indeed, it might be said that what goes under the name of 'development funding' only makes sense economically when synchronised with business interests. Making places and people attractive for investors now seems the dominant concern for most development agencies. From this perspective, we can see the World Bank as a conduit for the power and authority of major business interests and of its major rich country financiers.

Yet financiers and businesses need sustainable sites for profitable investment, which they cannot create themselves. However dependent governments and NGOs may be on funding agencies that serve profit-seekers, businesses rely on governments, and now also on NGOs, to secure investment environments in national territories to which all the world's population are variously attached [Ludden 2003]. Structural adjustment did not intend to demolish national governments, but rather to make them better serve financial leaders in an emerging global development regime, which articulates the power of many rich countries in authoritative international institutions, including the World Bank, IMF, UN, OECD and WTO.

A global regime

In global development discourse, each national state governs its economy, and each 'developing economy' is developing itself, in a global context, but in south Asia and elsewhere, national development regimes can also be understood realistically as officially but not operationally independent territories in a global development regime. Imperial histories underpin the global regime, which includes difference and competition as well as collaboration among its leaders. Yet the integration and coherence of the global regime have increased dramatically in the last 20 years, under the authority of the World Bank and increasing impact of globalisation.

As a result, each country in south Asia now inhabits more than one development regime. National regimes still operate, but each has various local and regional sub-units with distinctive rules of operation, and each must also abide by international rules. In this light, we can consider, for instance, the Tuesday Group – composed of diplomats from donor countries who meet each week in Dhaka to make their will known to government – as a part of the Bangladesh regime. US embassy and World Bank offices act like global headquarters in Dhaka. Numerous

NGOs and government agencies, such as DFID in Dhaka, serve as articulating institutions that knit together local, national and global regimes with cross-border activities to connect rich and poor capital cities with 'target' sites and populations throughout Bangladesh.

Thus, populations served by development regimes are now difficult to delineate geographically. Each country's national citizenry is ostensibly its target population, but national regimes must please donors, lenders, investors, and financiers, whose compelling interests lie elsewhere as well.

Like the leaders of imperial development in British India, contemporary leaders all claim to be serving 'the poor'. Viceroy Lord Curzon once famously quipped that he had done more for India's poor than all the raving nationalists who attacked him. With this in mind, it is worth considering that programmes which proclaim their goal to be poverty reduction also have other functions. Moreover, their geographical reach is important today, as national states steadily lose the capacity to undertake poverty reduction effectively on their own, inside their own borders.

All the major globally active development institutions have now adopted Millennium Development Goals (MDGs). This unprecedented common framework for policy thought and action adds coherence to the global regime, whose leaders seem to agree that national states only serve their own poor peoples adequately by meeting uniform targets set by international agencies. 'Targeting the poor', 'listening to the poor', and 'learning from the poor', also preoccupy NGOs, donors, funding groups, and action groups of many kinds, with various territorial attachments. 'The poor' now represent a global population living in countries saddled with MDG performance targets under global surveillance. Poor people are thus no longer conceived primarily as national citizens. They are targets, beneficiaries, and participants in a development process wherein leading financiers, intellectuals, activists, policy-makers, and disciplinarians travel the globe, measuring, monitoring, cajoling, and rewarding state performance according to global standards rendered acceptable in most countries through the operations of international agencies like the World Bank and United Nations.

Notes

1   *Historical View of Plans for the Government of British India and Regulation of Trade to the East Indies and Outlines of a Plan of Foreign Government, of Commericial Economy, and of Domestic Administration for the Asiatic Interests of Great Britain,* J Sewell and J Debrett, London, 1973.

2   British Parliamentary Papers, *Reports from Committees, 1847-1848,* Volume 9, 'Report from the Select Committee on the Cultivation of Cotton in India'.

3   Arthur Thomas Cotton, *Lectures on irrigation works in India; Delivered at the School of Military Engineering, Chatham, Autumn Session, 1874,* Collected and Published by Uddaraju Raman, Vijayawada, 1968.

4   US Department of Commerce, *Special Consular Reports, No. 72, British India, with Notes on Ceylon, Afghanistan, and Tibet,* Washington, Government Printing Office, 1915, p.9.

5   *Annual Statement of the Sea-Borne Trade of British India with the British Empire and Foreign Countries for the Fiscal Year Ending Match 31, 1926,* Calcutta, Government of India, 1926, Table 10.

References

Bagchi, Amiya Kumar (1989): 'Development Planning' in Murray Milgate and Peter Newman (eds), *The New Palgrave: A Dictionary of Economics,* John Eatwell, London.

Barber, William (1975): *British Economic Thought and India 1600–1858: A Study in the History of Development Economics,* Oxford University Press, Oxford.

Bardhan, Pranab (1984): *The Political Economy of Development in India,* Oxford University Press, Bombay and Delhi.

Chandra, Bipan (1966): *The Rise and Growth of Economic Nationalism in India: Economic Policies of Indian National Leadership,* People's Publishing House, New Delhi.

Chaudhuri, Pramit (1979): *India's Economy: Poverty and Development*, St Martin's Press, New York.

Frankel, Francine R (1978): *India's Political Economy, 1947–1977: The Gradual Revolution*, Princeton University Press, Princeton.

Government of India (1921): *Inland Trade (Rail and River-borne) of India, 1919–1920*, Department of Statistics, Government of India, Calcutta.

Habib, Irfan (1982): *An Atlas of Mughal Empire: Political and Economic Maps With Notes, Bibliography and Index*, Oxford University Press, Delhi.

Hossain, Moazzem, Iyanutul Islam and Reza Kibria (1999): *South Asian Economic Development: Transformations, Opportunities and Challenges*, Routledge, London.

Johnson, B LC (1983): *Development in South Asia*, Penguin, Harmondsworth, England.

Kothari, Rajni (1971): *The Political Economy of Development*, Orient Longman, Bombay.

Leys, Colin (1996): *The Rise and Fall of Development Theory*, EAEP and Indiana University Press, Nairobi and Bloomington.

Ludden, David (1992): 'India's Development Regime' in Nicholas Dirks (ed), *Colonialism and Culture*, University of Michigan Press, Ann Arbor, pp 247–287.

_____ (2003): 'Maps in the Mind and the Mobility of Asia' in *Journal of Asian Studies*, 62, November 3, pp 1057–1078.

_____ (ed) (2005): *Agricultural Production and South Asian History*, David Ludden, preface to the second edition, Oxford University Press, Delhi, pp 7–24

Moreland, William (1929): *The Agrarian System of Moslem India*, Cambridge, reprint 1968, Oxford University Press, Delhi, pp 205–206.

Morris, Morris D (1983): 'The Growth of Large-Scale Industry to 1947' in Dharma Kumar (ed), *The Cambridge Economic History of India*, vol. II, c1757–c1970, Cambridge University Press, Cambridge.

Myrdal, Gunnar (1968): *Asian Drama: An Inquiry into the Poverty of Nations*, Random House, New York.

Raychaudhuri, Tapan and Irfan Habib (ed) (1982): *The Cambridge Economic History of India*, Vol 1 circa c. 1200-c.1750, Cambridge University Press, Chicago, p 115.

Schwartzberg, Joseph E (1978) (ed): *A Historical Atlas of South Asia* University of Chicago Press, Chicago, p 115.

Structural Adjustment Participatory Review International Network (SAPRIN) (2004): *Structural Adjustment: The Policy Roots of Economic Crisis, Poverty and Inequality*, Zed Books, London.

Tomlinson, B R (1997): *The New Cambridge History of India: The Economy of Modern India, 1860–1970*, Foundation Books, New Delhi.

Zaidi, A Moin (ed) (1985): *A Tryst With Destiny: A Study of Economic Policy Resolutions of the Indian National Congress Passed during the Last 100 Years*, New Delhi, p 54.

20

Radical Needs and Moderate Reforms

Amartya Sen

1. Ends, Means and Practical Reason

Economic policies in India have undergone much change over the last few years, and more changes are in the process of being implemented. The central approach underlying these reforms, initiated in 1991, involves a greater reliance on the market mechanism, and this translates into a class of public policies including deregulation and reduction of governmental controls, greater autonomy of private investment, less use of the public sector, more opening of the economy to international trade, less restrictions on the convertibility of the rupee, and so on. While many critics had wanted faster reforms (and a quicker change – basically in the same direction), there can be little doubt about the gathering force and the growing reach of the reforms, or about the break that has been initiated in the established conventions of Indian planning and policy-making. Nothing quite like this has happened earlier in the Indian economy, since independence – or for that matter, before it.

Outside India the reforms have been fairly universally welcomed, but they have been, since their inception, the subject of severe debate within India. The controversies have been extensive, and the arguments on each side quite forceful and firm.

There are two elementary points of departure. First, there must be an attempt to link the strategies of development to something more fundamental, in particular, the *ends* of economic and social development. Why do we seek development? What can it achieve, if fruitful? How are the successes and failures of policies – including the 'reforms' of traditional policies – to be judged? It is only with an explicit recognition of the basic ends that debates on means and strategies can be adequately founded.

The second basic departure takes us beyond the scrutiny of ends, to the investigation of means. What are the means that have to be employed to achieve these ends felicitously? While the debates on the current reforms concentrate on a particular class of means related to the use or non-use of markets (such

Perspectives on Modern South Asia: A Reader in Culture, History, and Representation, First Edition.
Edited by Kamala Visweswaran.
© 2011 Blackwell Publishing Ltd. Published 2011 by Blackwell Publishing Ltd.

as incentives for private investment, reliance on international trade, and so on), there are many other means, especially dealing with the 'social' side of economic operations and successes, which typically tend not to figure in these debates. To the foundational lacuna of neglecting the scrutiny of the basic ends is, thus, added the more immediate gap of ignoring the examination of some powerful means that help us to achieve those ends. In fact, we argue that achievement of even the limited objectives of the current reforms will depend crucially on conscious and organized pursuit of the social means on which economic performance and results are frequently conditional.

2. Regional Diversities and Contrasts

Given the extremely heterogeneous character of the Indian economy and society, India's achievements and failures cannot be understood in composite terms, and it is essential to examine the experiences in sufficiently disaggregative form – and in adequate detail. In the set of studies in this book, the regional perspective has been extensively explored, concentrating on three states in particular: Kerala, West Bengal, and Uttar Pradesh. Kerala's achievements in the social fields have been quite remarkable, including an achieved life expectancy of well over 72 years (69 for males and 74 for females by 1991) that compares well with China's (69 years) and South Korea's (71 years) achievements, despite the much greater economic advancement of these other countries. At the other end, Uttar Pradesh remains one of the most backward states in India, and had this state of 140 million people been an independent country, it would have been not only one of the largest, but also one of the most socially deprived countries in this world – giving its citizens less than some of the worst-performing economies in sub-Saharan Africa. We have to ask why – and to what extent – Kerala has succeeded, and why Uttar Pradesh has failed so badly in precisely those fields. West Bengal's experience is more mixed, including some remarkable achievements and some conspicuous failures. Again, we have to identify

the successes and deficiencies there, and link them with the nature of policies pursued and the overall political economy of West Bengal.

The internal diversities in India offer a great opportunity to learn from each other. This is part of the objective of this set of studies. This must not, however, be taken to suggest that the lessons for India must come mostly from 'inside'. On the contrary, there is a great deal to be learnt from successes and failures of other countries as well. Even Kerala, successful as it is in many social fields, must learn more about how to generate and stimulate straightforward economic growth – an area in which it has been conspicuously unsuccessful.

Some 'lessons from abroad' have often been aired in the current economic debates, particularly in motivating the on-going reforms and deregulation. It is, however, important, in learning from other countries, to take an adequately comprehensive and discriminating view of their experiences. I shall argue, later on in this chapter, that some parts of the essential lessons – related in particular to the generation of social opportunities – have been particularly neglected in the typical readings of these experiences.[1] This collection of studies is aimed at scrutinizing the lessons from other countries as well as from within India itself.

One of the broad conclusions to emerge is the need for much more radical change in the Indian economy and society, in order to achieve the basic goals that were unambiguously outlined at the time of India's independence, but which still remain largely unaccomplished. The problem with the economic reforms currently under way is not that they are not needed, nor that they are overexacting, but that they are basically inadequate and unbalanced.[2] The departures are too moderate – and too tolerant of parts of the established tradition of economic planning in India. More – rather than less – radicalism is needed at this time.

3. Intrinsic Value and Instrumental Role of Human Capabilities

In his famous speech on India's 'tryst with destiny', on the eve of independence in August

1947, Jawaharlal Nehru reminded the country that the task ahead included 'the ending of poverty and ignorance and disease and inequality of opportunity'. Some achievements have indeed been made in these general areas, including the elimination of substantial famines, fairly successful functioning of our multiparty democratic system, and the emergence of a very large and quite successful scientific community – achievements that compare favourably with what has happened in many other parts of the world. However, it is not hard to see that much of the task that Nehru had identified remains largely unaccomplished, and that we have fallen quite far behind the best performers. We have to ask what obstacles we face, how they can be eliminated, and whether we are already on course in remedying the underlying deficiencies.

Nehru's list of the tasks that India faces is well worth remembering in taking stock of where we are, and more particularly where we are *not*. As Nehru pointed out, the elimination of ignorance, of illiteracy, of remediable poverty, of preventable disease, and of needless inequalities in opportunities must be seen as objectives that are valued for their own sake. They expand our freedom to lead the lives we have reason to value, and these elementary capabilities are of importance on their own.[3] While they can and do contribute to economic growth and to other usual measures of economic performance, their value does not lie only in these instrumental contributions. Economic growth is, of course, important, but it is valuable precisely because it helps to eradicate deprivation and to improve the capabilities and the quality of life of ordinary people.

We must not make the mistake – common in some circles – of taking the growth rate of GNP to be the ultimate test of success, and of treating the removal of illiteracy, ill-health, and social deprivation as – at best – possible means to that hallowed end. The first and the most important aspect of Nehru's listing of what we have to do is to make clear that the elimination of illiteracy, ill-health, and other avoidable deprivations are valuable for their own sake – they

are 'the tasks' that we face. The more conventional criteria of economic success (such as a high growth rate, a sound balance of payments, and so forth) are to be valued only as means to deeper ends. It would, therefore, be a mistake to see the development of education, health care, and other basic achievements *only* or *primarily* as expansions of 'human resources' – the accumulation of 'human capital' – as if people were just the *means* of production and not its ultimate *end*. The bettering of human life does not have to be justified by showing that a person with a better life is also a better producer.

This issue of intrinsic importance is an appropriate starting point, because we must assert first things first, but our analysis cannot, of course, stop at basic issues only. Something that is of intrinsic importance can, *in addition*, also be instrumentally momentous, without compromising its intrinsic value. Basic education, good health, and other human attainments are not only directly valuable as constituent elements of our basic capabilities, these capabilities can *also* help in generating economic success of a more standard kind, which in turn can contribute to enhancing the quality of human life even more. Many of the ingredients of a good quality of life – including education, health, and elementary freedoms – clearly do have instrumental roles in making us more productive and helping us to generate more outputs and incomes. As I shall presently discuss, the lessons of economic and social progress across the world over the last few decades have forcefully drawn attention to the instrumental importance of education, health, and other features of the quality of human life in generating fast and shared economic growth (on top of the direct intrinsic importance they have). It will, of course, be a mistake to see the enhancement of human capabilities as being invariably effective in raising economic performance, since the political economy of *actual use* can be very different from the *potential* possibilities generated. But without generating those possibilities the question of their use would not even arise, and this is a lesson that many other countries have learned with very good effect.

In looking back at what Jawaharlal Nehru saw as our 'tryst with destiny', we must both assert (1) the inalienable eminence of basic capabilities and the quality of life in judging the success of economic and social policies, and (2) the contingent but significant practical importance of many of these capabilities (especially those related to education, health, and elementary freedoms) in promoting economic growth, and through it further advancing the quality of life that people can enjoy. While the improvement of human life is its own reward, it also offers – as it happens – other rewards which in turn can create the possibilities of further augmentation of the quality of life and our effective freedom to lead the lives we have reason to seek.

The subject of development economics, since its inception in its modern form in the nineteen-forties, has been full of sombre theses of a multitude of 'vicious circles', and there is a general air of pessimism that has characterized this discipline. In that context, the importance of this 'virtuous circle' in achieving economic and social progress can scarcely be overemphasized.

4. On Learning from Others and from India

India can learn a lot from the experiences of other countries which have done, in different ways, better than we have. More on that presently, but we must also note the fact that India has much to learn from India itself. We live in a most diverse country, and in many spheres our records are extremely disparate. The average levels of literacy, life expectancy, infant mortality, etc., in India are enormously adverse compared with China, and yet in all these respects Kerala does significantly better than China. For example, in adult female literacy rate, India's 39 per cent is well behind China's 68 per cent, but Kerala's 86 per cent rate is much higher than China's. Indeed, as will be presently shown, in terms of rural female literacy, Kerala has a higher achievement than *every* individual province in China. Similarly, compared with China, Kerala has higher life expectancies at birth (69 for males and 74 for females, compared with China's 68 and 71 years, respectively), a lower fertility rate (1.8 *vis-à-vis* China's 2.0), and a much lower rate of infant mortality (17 and 16 per thousand live births, respectively, for boys and girls in 1991, compared with China's 28 and 33 years, respectively).[4]

There are a great many things that we can learn from within the country, by using the diversity of our experiences, particularly in the use of public action. In some respects, Kerala – despite its low income level – has achieved more than even some of the most admired high-growth economies, such as South Korea. All this has to be recognized and its lessons used in policy-making elsewhere in India. But at the same time, we must also note that Kerala has much to learn from the experiences of other countries on how to stimulate economic growth. Kerala's performance in that sphere has been quite dismal, even compared with many other Indian states. The political economy of incentives is of crucial importance in translating the potential for economic expansion, implicit in human development, into the reality of actual achievement in the economic sphere. Kerala has to learn as well as teach.

While the encouragement of economic incentives and opportunities has varied between different parts of the country, there has been a generally counterproductive regulational environment in India that has restrained economic growth all over the country over many decades. We can profit a good deal from trying to understand what other countries have been able to do in generating economic growth and in utilizing that growth for improving qualities of human life. In the recent reforms, this issue of learning from the experiences of more successful economic performers has loomed large. I shall presently have more to say on the lessons to draw from the experiences of other countries, and in that context, I shall have to argue that some crucial features of the experiences of the more successful countries may have been seriously missed. But before that, the importance of removing counterproductive controls and regulations must be discussed.

5. Counterproductive Regulations and Necessary Reforms

Comparison of India with the experiences of other countries is often made to motivate changes in economic policy, for example, to defend a programme of economic reforms – involving liberalization of trade, deregulation of governmental restrictions, encouragement of private initiative, and so on. In this context, attention is paid to the remarkable achievements of South Korea, Hong Kong, Singapore, Thailand, and other countries – including China in recent years – which have made splendid use of market-based economic opportunities. Such comparisons are indeed illuminating, and there is much to learn from these countries.

The counterproductive nature of some of the governmental restrictions, controls, and regulations has been clear for a long time. They have not only interfered with the efficiency of economic operations (especially for modern industries), but also have often failed lamentably to promote any kind of real equity in distributional matters. The privileges were often exploited for the sectional benefit of those with economic, political, or bureaucratic power, or those with the opportunity to influence people with such power. A radical change was certainly needed for these basic reasons, in addition to the short-run crises that actually prompted the change that did occur.

The scope of and rewards from greater integration with the world market have been and are large, and India too can reap much more fully the benefits of economies of scale and efficient division of labour that many other countries have already successfully used.[5] While greater reliance on trade is sometimes seen as something that compromises a country's economic independence, that view is hard to sustain. Given the diversity of trading partners and the interest of the different partners to have access to the large economic market in India, the fear that India would be an economic prisoner in the international world of open exchange is quite unfounded. This does not deny the importance of getting the terms and conditions right, including having fair

regulations from GATT (or its successor) and other international institutions. But in general there is little reason for fearfully abstaining from the benefits offered by the greater use of the facilities of international trade and exchange.

I am not commenting here on the appropriateness or sufficiency of the exact pattern of current economic reforms that is being introduced in India. Rather, I am pointing to the necessity and general desirability of economic reforms that remove counterproductive regulations and restrictions and allow greater use of the opportunities of international exchange. There is a strong case for such a change, and that case is not overwhelmed, in general, by any real reasons for fearing exploitative trading relations. The wisdom of going in this direction does not, however, deny the importance of many other policy changes that are also needed, on a priority basis, to pursue economic prosperity through greater integration with the world market.

6. India and China: Comparisons and Contrasts

In judging how India has been doing, it is useful to contrast its experiences with those of China. Whenever India is compared with much smaller countries, such as Hong Kong or Singapore, which have very successfully integrated with world markets, there is understandable scepticism about the relevance of these comparisons; these are effectively city states and can do many things that a country of the size of India cannot. In contrast, China, which is of a similar size – in fact larger – than India, provides an interesting and instructive comparative picture. This is not just because of size (though that is relevant too), but also because China too started off from being in a state of much poverty and deprivation. Also, the Chinese civilization, like the Indian, has a long tradition of trade and commerce (along with traditional, non-market, social conventions), and furthermore, both India and China have the additional similarity of having large expatriate communities which could play important

Table 1   Adult Literacy Rates, 1991

	Males	*Females*
India	64	39
China	87	68
Kerala	94	86
UP	56	25

Source. Census data (see Drèze and Sen, 1995, Statistical Appendix).

instrumental roles in achieving more integration with the world of international commerce and trade. The comparison with China is, thus, quite significant in understanding where India is and in scrutinizing what it can and should do.

Table 1 presents comparative figures on adult literacy rates in India and China. India is well behind China in this field – particularly so in the realm of female literacy. In addition to the figures for the Indian average, Table 1 also gives data for two states within India that respectively do much better (Kerala) and much worse (Uttar Pradesh) than the Indian average. Uttar Pradesh's male and female literacy rates of 56 and 25 per cent, respectively, lie very much behind China's 87 and 68 per cent, but on the other side, Kerala's 94 and 86 per cent lie well ahead of China's achievements.

China too is, of course, a heterogeneous country of many provinces. Several features of this comparison are obvious. First, the Chinese provinces generally do very much better than the Indian states. Second, nevertheless the best performer among all the Indian states and Chinese provinces put together is Kerala, and the worst performer is Tibet, so that the extremes go in the opposite direction to the relative pictures of means and modes. Third, while

Kerala is comfortably on top, following Kerala come a whole bunch of Chinese provinces before the next Indian state comes into the league. Similarly, while Tibet is indubitably at the bottom, above it come a big group of Indian states before we get to the next low performing Chinese province. Finally, there is some evidence that with the exception of Tibet, the Chinese provinces are more closely bunched together than are the Indian states. It is that bunched modal achievement of China that is so far above the run of Indian states.

Table 2 turns to matters of life and death, and presents the comparative picture of life expectancies at birth, infant mortality rates, total fertility rates, and female–male ratios in the population. Again, China is well ahead of India on the average, and tremendously ahead of Uttar Pradesh, but still significantly behind Kerala in each of these respects.

The distinction of Kerala is particularly striking in the field of gender equality. The female–male ratio in the population tends to be well above unity, because of the survival advantages that females have over males in terms of age-specific mortality rates whenever they receive comparable attention and care. In Europe and North America, the female–male ratio tends to be around 1.05 on the average, though it would have been somewhat lower had there not been extra male mortality in past wars the demographic effects of which still linger. In contrast, in many countries in Asia and north Africa, the female–male ratio is well below unity, and this is the case in India too.[6] But China's female–male ratio of 0.94, while higher than India's 0.93, is not really very high, whereas Kerala's ratio is close to 1.04, and is

Table 2   Life and Death, 1991

	Life Expectancy		*Infant Mortality Rate*	*Female–male Ratio*	*Total Fertility Rate*
	Males	*Females*			
India	59	59	80	0.93	3.6
China	68	71	31	0.94	2.0
Kerala	69	74	17	1.04	1.8
UP	57	55	98	0.88	5.1

Source. Drèze and Sen (1995), Statistical Appendix.

much higher than unity even after note is taken of greater emigration of men out of the state. This is a comparable ratio to that obtaining in Europe and North America and shows how much more equal Kerala is in terms of some elementary matters of gender parity, compared with China as well as the rest of India.

But leaving out the particular issue of gender equality, China's overall performance is enormously better than India's. While Kerala does better than China in terms of life expectancy, fertility rates, and infant mortality, the gap between the two, in each of these fields, is typically a good deal less than that between the average pictures of India and China.

7. India's Educational Backwardness and Lessons of Kerala

In view of the remarkable expansion of higher education in India (we send about six times as many people to the universities and other higher educational establishments as China does, relative to its population), it is extraordinary how little we have progressed in basic education. When I gave my Lal Bahadur Shastri Memorial Lectures in 1970 (entitled 'The Crisis in Indian Education'), the contrast between our attention to higher education and neglect of elementary teaching had seemed intolerably large.[7] But that gap has, if anything, *grown* rather than shrunk over the last 25 years. I had tried to argue that there were deep-seated class biases in the pressures that have determined Indian educational priorities, and that the inequalities in education are, in fact, a reflection of inequalities of economic and social powers of different groups in India.[8] The educational inequalities both *reflect* and help to *sustain* social disparities, and for a real break, much more determined political action would be needed than has been provided so far by either those in office, or by the parties that have led the opposition. The weakness, in this field, of even parties of the 'left' is particularly striking, given the fact that elementary education has been one of the few really solid achievements of the countries led by communist parties – in

places as diverse as Soviet Union, China, Cuba, and Vietnam.

The traditionally elitist tendencies of the ruling cultural and religious traditions in India may have added to the political problem here. Both Hinduism and Islam have, in different ways, had considerable inclination towards religious elitism, with reliance respectively on Brahmin priests and on powerful Mullahs, and while there have been many protest movements against each (the medieval poet Kabir fought against both simultaneously), the elitist hold is quite strong in both these religions. This contrasts with the more egalitarian and populist traditions of, say, Buddhism. Indeed, Buddhist countries have typically had much higher levels of basic literacy than societies dominated by Hinduism or Islam. Thailand, Sri Lanka, and Myanmar (Burma) are good examples.

There is even some evidence that when Western imperialists conquered countries in Asia and Africa, they tended to expand – rather than counteract – the biases that had already existed in the local cultures. For example, the British in India took little interest in elementary education, but were quite keen on creating institutions of higher learning in the good, old Brahminical mode, whereas the same British in Buddhist Burma gave much encouragement to the expansion of elementary teaching, even though they tended to do rather little for higher education.[9]

There is, however, some encouraging information in the remarkable heterogeneity that characterizes India in the field of elementary education. Advances of basic education have often come from forces that have railed against traditional politics (including protests against the historical hold of caste practices), or against traditional cultures (sometimes in the form of missionary activities). While the latter may explain the higher achievements in elementary education in, say, Goa or Mizoram, Kerala has had the benefit of both types of breaks (education-oriented lower-class movements as well as missionary activities), in addition to the good fortune of having royal families in Travancore and Cochin that happened to be atypically in favour of elementary education.

In drawing policy lessons from Kerala's experience of public action, note must be taken of two particularly instructive features. First, a real difference has been made by political activism in the direction of educational expansion for the lower-caste – and lower-class – groups. In the general picture of political apathy towards elementary eduction that is characteristic of much of India, Kerala is a big exception, and the results vindicate the attention that has been paid to this.[10] There is, thus, much evidence here of the importance of political leadership and initiative and of popular involvement in making a real difference in the realization of basic capabilities of the people at large.[11] The lessons to draw are of relevance not only for policy-makers and political leaders in office, but also for opposition parties and the politically-conscious public at large.

Second, the historical heterogeneity *within* Kerala itself is also quite instructive. When the state of Kerala was created in independent India, it was made up, on linguistic grounds, of the erstwhile native states of Travancore and Cochin, and the region of Malabar from the old province of Madras in British India (what is now mostly Tamil Nadu). The Malabar region, transferred from the Raj, was very much behind Travancore and Cochin in social development (including literacy and life expectancy – and mortality rates generally). But by the eighties, Malabar had so much 'caught up' with the rest of Kerala that it could no longer be seen in divergent terms.[12] The initiatives that the state governments of Kerala took, under different 'managements' (led by the Communist Party as well as by the Congress), succeeded in transforming Malabar into being basically at par with the rest of Kerala. Since Kerala has had a rather special history, it is important to note that a region need not be imprisoned in the fixity of history, and much depends on what is done here and now. In this too Kerala itself offers a lesson for the rest of India on what can be done by determined public action, even without having the favourable historical circumstances of Travancore and Cochin.

Table 3   Literacy and Schooling: India (1987–88)

	India	Kerala	UP
I. Rural literacy rate (Children 10–14)			
Males	73	98	68
Females	52	98	39
II. Percentages of rural children attending school			
Age 5–9: Males	52	87	45
Females	40	83	28
Age 10–14: Males	66	93	64
Females	42	91	31
III. Percentage of children 12–14 ever enrolled			
Rural: Males	74	100	73
Females	49	98	32
Urban: Males	89	100	81
Females	81	99	61

Source. Drèze and Sen (1995), Table 6.1, based on Census and National Sample Survey data.

The heterogeneity within India is illustrated and explored in Table 3 which gives information on the literacy rates of rural children in India as a whole and in the two states of Kerala and Uttar Pradesh. It turns out that while nearly all the children in the age group of 10 to 14 years are literate in Kerala, one-third of the UP male children and more than three-fifths of the UP female children of that age group are clearly illiterate. The picture is similarly dismal for school attendance for India as a whole and even more so for Uttar Pradesh.

Finally, it is totally remarkable that in rural India in the age group 12 to 14 years, more than a *quarter* of the boys have *never* been enrolled in any school and more than *half* the girls have *never* been enrolled either. As expected, in Kerala nearly all the boys and girls of this age group have had some schooling, and on the other side, in Uttar Pradesh the percentage of rural children of this age group who have been totally out of school is even higher than in India as a whole. In fact more than two-thirds of the UP girls between 12 and 14 have never had the benefit of any schooling at all. This is an appalling picture of neglect of basic education, and shows how very backward the bulk of India is – in terms of an important element of 'the task' that Nehru identified in 1947 – and furthermore, how abysmal the failure is in India's largest state. With more than 140 million people, had Uttar Pradesh been a country on its own, it would have been one of the largest countries in the world and would have been – or close to being – the lowest in terms of school education in the entire world.

Indeed, in the field of elementary education, India is not only behind China or Sri Lanka or South Korea, but also worse off than the average of 'low income countries other than India and China' (as defined by the World Bank), the comparative data for which are given in Table 4. Even in comparison with sub-Saharan Africa – perhaps the most problematic region in the world now with its record of recurrent famines – India does not shine. While it just about matches the literacy rates of Nigeria, it falls well behind the achievements of many of the African states, including Botswana, Zimbabwe, Kenya, and Ghana (Table 4). If India's relative performance is 'middling' in many fields of economic and social development, its record is far below that – close to the very bottom – in the fields of literacy and elementary education.

Table 4   Adult Literacy Rates, 1990: Developing Countries

	Total	Female
India[a]	52	39
China	78	68
Average of low-income countries excluding China and India	55	44
Zimbabwe	67	60
Botswana	74	65
Kenya	69	58
Nigeria	51	39
Ghana	60	51

Note. [a] Age 7+, 1991.
Source. Drèze and Sen (1995), Statistical Appendix, Table A.1, for India and China; *World Development Report 1994*, Table 1, for other countries.

8. The Economic Handicap of Educational Backwardness

While education and the development of human ability and skill must not be valued *only* as instruments to other ends, their instrumental importance must *also* be acknowledged (as was discussed earlier). In the analysis of 'growth-mediated' social progress, public education can be both *favourable* to economic growth (through expanding the opportunities of economic expansion) and *favoured* by economic growth (through generating more resources for such support).[13]

The economic roles of school education, learning by doing, technical progress, and even economies of large scale can all be seen as contributing – in different ways – to the centrality of direct human agency in generating economic expansion. Recent work on economic growth has brought out sharply the role of labour, education, and experience, and the so-called 'human capital'. This has helped to fill the large gap identified as a 'residual' in the basic neo-classical model of economic growth, and recent growth theory has done much to bring out the function of direct human agency in economic growth, over and above the contribution made through the accumulation of physical capital. Our attempt to learn from the experiences of 'the East Asian miracle' and other cases of growth-mediated progress cannot ignore the wealth of insights that the recent theoretical and empirical analyses have provided.[14]

The crucial role of education and skill makes it all the more essential to pay attention to public policy to expand basic education and to promote skill formation. The role of widespread basic education has been quite crucial in countries that have successfully grown fast making excellent use of world markets: for example, the so-called four 'tigers' in East Asia (namely South Korea, Hong Kong, Singapore, and Taiwan), and more recently, China and also Thailand. The modern industries in which these countries have particularly excelled demand many basic skills for which elementary education is essential and secondary education most helpful. While some studies have emphasized the productive contribution of learning by doing and on-the-job training, rather than the direct impact of formal education, the ability to achieve such training and learning is certainly helped greatly by basic education in schools prior to taking up jobs.[15]

In the context of learning from the experiences of the fast-growing economies of East Asia, it is important to recognize that all these countries – South Korea, Hong Kong, Singapore, Taiwan, Thailand, and post-reform China – had enormously higher levels of elementary education at the time they went for fast economic growth and greater integration with the world economy. The point is not that these countries have a much higher base of elementary education *now* than India currently has, but that they *already had* radically higher levels of elementary education in the nineteen-seventies, when they went rapidly ahead, compared with what India has *now*.

Table 5 presents some comparative figures on this. India's current level of adult literacy at 52 per cent is not only enormously lower than the current figures for China, Thailand, South Korea, or Hong Kong, but compares very unfavourably with the adult literacy rates of around 70 per cent at the time these countries respectively launched their rapid economic expansion (from 1980 in China and around 1960 or thereafter in Hong Kong, South Korea, and Thailand).

There has been an astonishing failure of adequate public action in expanding elementary and secondary education in India. While 'too much' government has been identified, with some plausibility, as a problem of past policies

Table 5   Adult Literacy Rates, 1960–90

	1960	1980	1992
India	28	36	52[a]
South Korea	71	93	97
Hong Kong	70	90	≈100
China	n.a.	69	80
Thailand	68	86	94

Note. [a] Age 7+, 1991.
Source. Drèze and Sen (1995), p. 38.

in India, in fact in the field of basic education (and also those of elementary health care, land reforms, and social security), 'too little' government action – rather than 'too much' – has been the basic problem.[16] This is not to deny that India can quite possibly achieve high rates of growth of GNP or GDP even with present levels of massive illiteracy. It is more a question of the strength and the nature of the economic expansion that can occur in India today, and the extent to which the growth in question can be participatory.[17]

The social opportunities offered by market-based economic growth, particularly of integration with modern world markets, are severely limited when a very large part of the community cannot read or write or count, cannot follow printed or hand-written instructions, cannot cope easily with contemporary technology, and so on. The objective of integration with the world market – important as it is – is deeply hampered by India's unusually low level of basic educational development. The inequality in Indian educational policies and achievement thus translates into inequalities in making use of new economic opportunities. The *distributive* failure supplements the effect of educational backwardness in restricting the *overall* scale of expansion of employment-generating modern production.

The persistence of endemic illiteracy and educational backwardness in India has many adverse effects. It limits, in general, the freedom and well-being of the Indian masses, and has a direct role in the relative deprivation of women in particular. It sustains high levels of mortality and fertility rates. It contributes to the comparative lack of pressure for social change, and to the moderateness of political demand and pressure for effective public attention in such fields as health care.[18] But in addition the lack of elementary education also makes the goals of economic expansion very much harder to realize. We have to face here two quite distinct but interrelated problems that limit the attainment and use of economic growth. First, elementary education is extremely important for successful integration with the world market. The nature and range of the commodities sold by, say, South Korea since the seventies or China from the eighties bring out clearly how crucial basic education is for catering to the world market, with production to specification and reliable quality control. Second, the wider the coverage of the population that takes part in the integration with the world market, the more 'participatory' the process of growth would tend to be, raising the income-earning power of large parts of the nation. Even if India were to grow very fast with its highly technical industries (making use of special skills that India has cultivated and drawing on the trained middle-class labour force), such as modern computer software or engineering products, the bulk of the Indians may still receive little reward from it.

9. The Role of Pre-reform China in Its Post-reform Success

In learning from China, we have to pay particular attention to what has been achieved in China in the post-reform period. But if the analysis presented here is correct, we must resist the common tendency now to 'rubbish' what China had already done before the reforms. The spread of basic education across the country is particularly relevant in explaining the nature of Chinese economic expansion in the post-reform period. The role of mass education in facilitating rapid and participatory growth has been quite crucial in the integration of the Chinese economy with the world market. The big step in the direction of mass education was decisively taken in China in the pre-reform period. The literacy rates in China by 1982 were already as high as 96 per cent for males in the 15–19 age group, and 85 per cent even for females in that age group. This social asset made participatory economic expansion possible in a way it would not have been in India *then* – and is extremely difficult in India even *now*.

A similar thing can be said about widespread health care and systems of nutritional attention, which China developed in the pre-reform period, but from which post-reform China has benefited a great deal. The importance of basic health and nutrition in economic development has received much attention in the recent literature.[19] In assessing the economic success of post-reform China, the groundwork done in the pre-reform period would have to be adequately acknowledged.

Another area in which the Chinese post-reform expansions have benefited from pre-reform achievements is that of land reforms, which has also been identified as having been of great importance in the east Asian economic development in general.[20] In China, things went, of course, much further than land reforms, and the extremism of communal agriculture certainly was a considerable handicap for agricultural expansion in the pre-reform period. But that process of collectivization of land had also, *inter alia*, abolished landlordism in China. When the Chinese government opted for the 'responsibility system', it had a land tenure pattern that could be readily transformed into individual farming without intermediaries, not weighed down by the counteracting weight of tenurial handicaps (as in many parts of India).[21]

It is interesting that the institutional developments that have favoured participatory economic growth throughout east Asia (in particular, the spread of basic education and health care, and the abolition of landlordism) had come to different countries in the region in quite different ways. In some cases, even foreign occupation had helped, for example, in the land reforms in Taiwan and South Korea. In the case of China, the pre-reform governments had carried out, for programmes of their own, radical changes that proved to be immensely useful in the economic expansion based on marketization in the post-reform period.

These connections are extremely important to note in having an adequately informed interpretation of the Chinese successes of recent years, and in drawing lessons for it for other countries. If India has to emulate China in market success, it is not adequate just to liberalize economic controls in the way the Chinese have recently done, without also creating the social opportunities that post-reform China enjoyed through education, health care, and land reform – to a great extent inherited from pre-reform achievements of that experimental country. The force of China's market economy rests on the solid foundations of social changes that had occurred earlier, and India cannot simply jump on to that bandwagon without paying attention to the enabling social changes – in education, health care, and land reforms – that made the market function in the way it has in China.

10. Economic Development through Social Opportunity

The central issue in economic development is to expand the social opportunities open to the people. In so far as these opportunities are compromised – directly or indirectly – by counterproductive regulations and controls, by restrictions on economic initiatives, by the stifling of competition and its efficiency-generating advantages, and so on, the removal of these hindrances must be seen to be extremely important. The expansion of markets has a crucial role to play in this transformation.

But the creation and use of social opportunities on a wide basis requires much more than the 'freeing' of markets. They call emphatically for an active public policy that could enable people to use the opportunities that the possibility of more trade – domestic and international – offers. Perhaps above all, it calls for a rapid expansion of basic education – overcoming the massive illiteracy and educational backwardness that characterize much of India.[22] This requires the provision of literacy and elementary education as fundamental opportunities for all (rather than leaving the majority of women and a large proportion of men illiterate), and the spread of secondary education on a very much wider basis (rather than that opportunity being confined fairly narrowly to particular classes). India's record in both these respects is quite dismal, despite the fact that literacy and school education have been part of the rhetoric of Indian planning since independence.

There are also other expansions of social opportunity that call for urgent attention. These include the need for more widespread and better health care, greater access to provisions of social security, more effective and sweeping land reforms, and in general, enabling the more constrained sections of the population to lead a less restrictive life, including being more free to make use of the facilities that the spread of markets could provide.

11. The Need for a Bigger Departure

Policy debates in India have to be taken away from the overwhelming concentration on issues of liberalization and marketization. The nostalgia of the old debates 'Are you *pro* or *anti* market?', or 'Are you *in favour* or *against* state activities?' seem to have an odd 'hold' on all sides, so that we concentrate only on some issues and ignore many – often more important – ones. While the case for economic reforms may take good note of the diagnosis that India has too much government in some fields, it ignores the fact that India also has too little government activities in many other fields, including basic education and health care, which makes people's lives miserable and which also limits the possibility of economic expansion. We may need 'more markets', but we also have to go 'more *beyond* the markets'. What needs curing is not just 'too little market' or 'too much market', but 'too little market' in some areas and 'too little *beyond* the market' in others.[23]

To emulate the use of markets in China or South Korea, without taking note of their vast and highly productive experience in public education and health care, and without understanding the role of these governmental activities in encouraging economic expansion cannot be adequate. It is, at best, 'piece-meal copying' of others – not really 'learning' from others. We have to go well beyond liberalization to get somewhere.

The radicalism that is needed cannot be met by just removing restraints through deregulation and reform, and it must also embrace the positive duties of a responsible government to create social opportunities that are valuable in themselves and which can also help the process of economic development. While learning from the successes abroad, we have to take note of the totality of the experiences in making them so successful, and in applying these lessons from elsewhere, we have to bear in mind the need for a fuller view of the government's role. The contrasts between the experiences of different states in India and their enormous variations in achieving social progress are of interest not only for their direct role in raising well-being and in reducing human deprivation, but also for the indirect part they can play in enhancing the nature and quality of economic growth.

Notes

1 This diagnosis has been developed in greater detail in the companion volume (Drèze and Sen, 1995).

2 For a more comprehensive development of this line of analysis and its extensive implications, see Drèze and Sen (1995).

3 The capability perspective in assessing individual advantage and social progress has been presented and analysed in Sen (1980, 1985a, 1985b), Drèze and Sen (1989), and Nussbaum and Sen (1993). For extensions, applications, and critiques, see also Rawls (1982, 1993), Roemer (1982, 1994), Atkinson (1983, 1989), Nussbaum (1988), Arneson (1989, 1990), Pogge (1989), Crocker (1991), Cohen (1989, 1990, 1994), Hossain (1990), Schokkaert and van Ootegem (1990), van Parijs (1990), Sugden (1993), Herrero (1994), among other contributions.

4 The sources of these data include Coale (1993), Office of the Registrar General of India (1993), World Bank (1994), UNDP (1994), and Drèze and Saran (1995); see also the Statistical Appendix in the companion volume (Drèze and Sen, 1995). The life expectancy estimates for India for 1991 are 'provisional' and draw on unpublished works at the Registrar General's Office, for which we are most grateful.

5 The actual scope of international division of labour depends to a great extent on the importance of economies of scale, which the recent literature on growth and trade has illuminatingly explored; see particularly Krugman (1986, 1987), Romer (1986, 1987a, 1987b), Helpman and Krugman (1990), and Grossman and Helpman (1991).

6 On this subject, see my paper, 'Missing Women', in the *British Medical Journal* (Sen, 1992), and the literature cited there. For a general review of the literature (including critiques of the estimates of Drèze and Sen, 1989, and of Ansley Coale, 1991) and some new estimates of his own, see Klasen (1994).

7 'The Crisis in Indian Education', Lal Bahadur Shastri Memorial Lecture, given in New Delhi on 10–11 March 1970, for The Institute of Public Enterprise, Hyderabad. Reprinted in Malik (1971) and partially in Chaudhuri (1972).

8 The argument, presented in my Lal Bahadur Shastri Lecture (Sen, 1970), that 'the rot in Indian education is ultimately related to the structure of Indian society' (reprinted in Malik, 1971, p. 273) unfortunately continues to hold, and there has been in the last quarter of a century quite inadequate public effort to overcome the legacy of those social inequalities.

9 The relevance of these issues was briefly discussed in my paper 'How Is India Doing?', *The New York Review of Books*, 1982; see also Drèze and Sen (1995), chapter 6. On a personal note, as a young child in Mandalay, I remember being struck by the throng of Indian professors in Burma (my father was one of them for a while) coming from a country with extremely little literacy to one where most people appeared, even then, to be able to read and write. The divergence between India's extensive development of higher education and its extraordinary neglect of basic education comes out most sharply in contrast with the opposite tendency in countries like Burma.

10 See particularly V.K. Ramachandran's chapter on Kerala in this volume. Ramachandran goes through the long history of Kerala's educational expansion, and the emergence and development of other forms of public intervention, and outlines the role of public participation and local leadership in bringing about the changes the results of which make Kerala stand out so sharply in India.

11 West Bengal, the state other than Kerala in which left-wing parties have been in office for substantial lengths of time, have tended in the past to share the conservative scepticism

(common in India) of elementary education, and its record in school education, while better than that of many states, has been relatively indifferent. However, there has been in very recent years a shift of governmental policy in the direction of emphasizing elementary education, and there are some early signs of rapid progress beginning to be made in this field. See the chapter on West Bengal, by Sunil Sengupta and Haris Gazdar, in this volume.

12 On this, see T. N. Krishnan (1994).

13 On this, see Drèze and Sen (1989), chapter 10.

14 On different aspects of the relations involved, see Krugman (1986), Romer (1986), Barro (1991), Stokey (1991), Young (1991), Mankiw, Romer, and Weil (1992), Lucas (1993), among other contributions.

15 Despite having quite a different focus of emphasis in the past, the World Bank has also acknowledged these connections in its recent study of 'the East Asian miracle', which draws on a vast range of empirical works: 'We have shown that the broad base of human capital was critically important to rapid growth in the HPAEs [high-performing Asian economies]. Because the HPAEs attained universal primary education early, literacy was high and cognitive skill levels were substantially above those in other developing economies. Firms therefore had an easier time upgrading the skills of their workers and mastering new technology' (World Bank, 1993, p. 349).

16 These issues are discussed extensively in the companion volume (Drèze and Sen 1995).

17 On the characteristics of participatory growth and their relevance in enhancing living conditions, see Drèze and Sen (1989), chapter 10.

18 On the relation between education and other aspects of social choice, see Tapas Majumdar (1983, 1993).

19 See, for example, Dasgupta and Ray ((1986, 1987)).

20 See, for example, Amsden (1989), Wade (1990), and World Bank (1993).

21 Within India, West Bengal has done much more than any other state in carrying out land reforms. On this see the chapter on rural poverty in West Bengal (by Sunil Sengupta and Haris Gazdar). But the traditional inequities in land holdings are very strong in many parts of India.

22 There is also considerable evidence that the rate of return to basic education tends to be higher in countries that are more 'open', with less restriction on trade. On this and related issues, see Birdsall and Sabot (1993a, 1993b).

23 The argument in this direction has been more extensively presented in the companion volume (Drèze and Sen, 1995).

References

Amsden, Alice (1989), *Asia's Next Giant: Late Industrialization in South Korea* (Oxford: Oxford University Press).

Arneson, R. (1989), 'Equality and Equality of Opportunity for Welfare', *Philosophical Studies*, 56.

_____ (1990), 'Primary Goods Reconsidered', *Nous*, 24.

Atkinson, A.B. (1983), *Social Justice and Public Policy* (Brighton: Wheat-sheaf, and Cambridge, MA: MIT Press).

_____ (1989), *Poverty and Social Security* (New York: Harvester Wheat-sheaf).

Barro, Robert (1991), 'Economic Growth in a Cross Section of Countries', *Quarterly Journal of Economics*, 106.

Birdsall, Nancy and Richard H. Sabot (1993a), 'Virtuous Circles: Human Capital Growth and Equity in East Asia' (mimeo, Washington, DC: World Bank).

Birdsall, Nancy and Richard H. Sabot, eds. (1993b), *Opportunity Foregone: Education, Growth and Inequality in Brazil* (Washington, DC: World Bank).

Chaudhuri, Pramit, ed. (1972), *Aspects of Indian Economic Development* (London: Allen & Unwin).

Coale, Ansley J. (1991), 'Excess Female Mortality and the Balance of the Sexes: An Estimate of the Number of "Missing Females"', *Population and Development Review*, 17.

_____ (1993), 'Mortality Schedules in China Derived from Data in the 1982 and 1990 Censuses', Office of Population Research, Princeton University, Working Paper 93– 7.

Cohen, G.A. (1989), 'On the Currency of Egalitarian Justice', *Ethics*, 99.

_____ (1990), 'Equality of What? On Welfare, Goods and Capabilities', *Recherches Economiques de Louvain*, 56.

_____ (1994), 'Amartya Sen's Unequal World', *New Left Review*.

Crocker, David (1991), 'Toward Development Ethics', *World Development*, 19.

Dasgupta, Partha and Debraj Ray (1986), 'Inequality as a Determinant of Malnutrition and Unemployment: Theory', *Economic Journal*, 96.

Dasgupta, Partha and Debraj Ray (1987), 'Inequality as a Determinant of Malnutrition and Unemployment: Policy', *Economic Journal*, 97.

Drèze, Jean and Mrinalini Saran (1995), 'Primary Education and Economic Development in China and India: Overview and Two Case Studies', in Kaushik Basu, Prasanta Pattanaik and Kotaro Suzumura, eds., *Choice, Welfare and Development* (Oxford: Oxford University Press).

Drèze, Jean and Amartya Sen (1989), *Hunger and Public Action* (Oxford: Clarendon Press).

_____ (1995), *India: Economic Development and Social Opportunity* (Oxford and Delhi: Oxford University Press).

Grossman, Gene M. and Elahanan Helpman (1991), *Innovation and Growth in the Global Economy* (Cambridge, MA: MIT Press).

Helpman, Elahanan and Paul R. Krugman (1990), *Market Structure and Foreign Trade* (Cambridge, MA: MIT Press).

Herrero, Carmen (1994), 'Capabilities and Utilities', mimeo, Universidad de Alicante, Spain.

Hossain, I. (1990), *Poverty as Capability Failure* (Helsinki: Swedish School of Economics).

Klasen, Stephan (1994), '"Missing Women" Revisited', mimeo, Harvard University, forthcoming in *World Development*.

Krishnan, T.N. (1994), 'Social Intermediation and Human Development: Kerala State, India', mimeo, Centre for Development Studies, Thiruvananthapuram.

Krugman, Paul R. (1986), *Strategic Trade Policy and the New International Economics* (Cambridge, MA: MIT Press).

_____ (1987), 'The Narrow Moving Band, the Dutch Disease, and the Consequences of Mrs Thatcher: Notes on Trade in the Presence of Scale Economies', *Journal of Development Economics*, 27.

Lucas, Robert (1993), 'Making a Miracle', *Econometrica*, 63.

Majumdar, Tapas (1983), *Investment in Education and Social Choice* (Cambridge: Cambridge University Press.

_____ (1993), 'The Relation between Educational Attainment and Ability to Obtain Social Security in the States of India', research paper, World Institute for Development Economics Research, Helsinki.

Malik, S.C., ed. (1971), *Management and Organization of Indian Universities* (Simla: Indian Institute of Advanced Study).

Mankiw, Gregory, David Romer, and David Weil (1992), 'A Contribution to the Empirics of Economic Growth', *Quarterly Journal of Economics*, 107.

Nussbaum, Martha (1988), 'Nature, Function and Capability: Aristotle on Political Distribution', *Oxford Studies in Ancient Philosophy*.

Nussbaum, Martha and Amartya Sen, eds. (1993), *The Quality of Life* (Oxford: Clarendon Press).

Office of the Registrar General of India (1993), *Sample Registration System: Fertility and Mortality Indicators 1991* (New Delhi: Ministry of Home Affairs).

Pogge, T.W. (1989), *Realizing Rawls* (Ithaca, NY: Cornell University Press).

Rawls, John (1982), 'Social Unity and Primary Goods', in Amartya Sen and Bernard Williams, eds., *Utility and Beyond* (Cambridge: Cambridge University Press).

_____ (1993), *Political Liberalism* (New York: Columbia University Press).

Roemer, John (1982), *A General Theory of Exploitation and Class* (Cambridge, MA: Harvard University Press).

_____ (1994), 'Primary Goods, Fundamental Preferences and Functionings', mimeo, University of California, Davis.

Romer, Paul M. (1986), 'Increasing Returns and Long-Run Growth', *Journal of Political Economy*, 94.

_____ (1987a), 'Growth Based on Increasing Returns due to Specialization', *American Economic Review*, 77.

_____ (1987b), 'Two Strategies for Economic Development: Using Ideas and Producing Ideas', in World Bank, *Proceedings of the World Bank Annual Conference on Development Economics 1992* (Washington, DC: World Bank).

Schokkaert, E. and L. van Ootegem (1990), 'Sen's Concept of the Living Standard Applied to the Belgian Unemployed', *Recherches Economiques de Louvain*, 56.

Sen, Amartya (1970), 'The Crisis in Indian Education', Lal Bahadur Shastri Memorial Lecture, The Institute of Public Enterprise, Hyderabad; reprinted in Malik (1971) and partially in Chaudhuri (1972).

Sen, Amartya (1980), 'Equality of What?', in S. McMurrin, ed., *Tanner Lectures on Human Values*, vol. 1 (Cambridge: Cambridge University Press); reprinted in Sen, *Choice, Welfare and Measurement* (Oxford: Blackwell; Cambridge, MA: MIT Press, 1982).

_____ (1982), 'How Is India Doing?', *The New York Review of Books*.

_____ (1985a), *Commodities and Capabilities* (Amsterdam: North-Holland).

_____ (1985b), 'Well-being, Agency and Freedom: The Dewey Lectures 1984', *Journal of Philosophy*, 82.

_____ (1992), 'Missing Women', in *British Medical Journal*, 304 (March).

Stokey, Nancy (1991), 'Human Capital, Product Quality and Growth', *Quarterly Journal of Economics*, 106.

Sugden, R. (1993), 'Welfare, Resources, and Capabilities: A review of *Inequality Reexamined* by Amartya Sen', *Journal of Economic Literature*, 31.

UNDP (1994), *Human Development Report 1994* (New York: UNDP).

van Parijs, Phillip (1990), 'Equal Endowments as Undominated Diversity', *Recherches Economiques de Louvain*, 56.

Wade, Robert (1990), *Governing the Market: Economic Theory and the Role of the Government in East Asian Industrialization* (Princeton: Princeton University Press).

World Bank (1993), *The East Asian Miracle* (Oxford: Oxford University Press).

_____ (1994), *World Development Report 1994* (Oxford: Oxford University Press).

Young, Alwyn (1991), 'Learning by Doing and the Dynamic Effects of International Trade', *Quarterly Journal of Economics*, 106.

21

Who Are the Country's Poor? Social Movement Politics and Dalit Poverty

Gopal Guru and Anuradha Chakravarty

Appointed in 1953, the first Backward Classes Commission observed that a low position in the caste hierarchy was the key determinant of social and economic backwardness. No less in contemporary times, caste continues to be deeply imbricated in the perseverance of poverty. The proportion of Scheduled Castes classified as marginal landholders (owning about a third of a hectare) has risen from 68.9 percent in 1980–1981 to 72.2 percent in 1990–1991, and the proportion of scheduled caste landless agricultural laborers is growing.[1] In 1993–1994, the proportion of rural Scheduled Castes and Scheduled Tribes falling below the poverty line was 49.0 and 49.5 percent respectively, as compared to 32.8 percent of rural, non-scheduled households generally.[2] According to a report from Human Rights Watch, "An estimated forty million people in India, among them fifteen million children, are bonded laborers, working in slave-like conditions in order to pay off a debt. A majority of them are Dalits."[3]

This strong colinearity of low caste status and poverty has long been recognized. But debates have raged over the reasons for and the fitting response to this social and economic reality. For Gandhi, the problem was not caste (*varna*) but untouchability. For Nehru, the problem was first and foremost poverty: Supplant poverty with equitable growth and the excrescences of caste would fade. For B. R. Ambedkar, the Untouchable leader and statesman, as long as caste as a social system persisted, so would grievous deprivation.

In this chapter, even as we are most persuaded by Ambedkar's understanding, we address the political complexity of dismantling caste concurrent with the intent to redress poverty. In India's democratic polity, we argue, organizing against caste has required organizing on the basis of caste. In the process of addressing this "democratic paradox," we trace how the common thread running through the varied approaches of India's political formations has been the shortchanging of strategies that address

Perspectives on Modern South Asia: A Reader in Culture, History, and Representation, First Edition.
Edited by Kamala Visweswaran.
© 2011 Blackwell Publishing Ltd. Published 2011 by Blackwell Publishing Ltd.

the wrenching problems of material poverty. We organize the discussion that follows, first by exploring the caste basis of Indian poverty; we then turn to the development of state policies and to the ways these policies shaped the approaches of social movements as they sought to combat poverty. We subsequently consider three particular responses: the radical challenge and failed adaptation of the Dalit Panthers, the capture of state power by the BSP with its attendant compromises and contradictions, and finally, the soft resistance to the State's neoliberal agenda by dalit NGOs.

Dalitization of Indian Poverty

Following from the dominant logic of class analysis of Indian poverty, both mainstream neo-classical economists and radical Marxist analyses have generally neglected the study of the economic consequences of the caste system. In the few instances that neoclassical approaches have been applied to examine the independent effects of caste on the economic structure, the animating questions have pertained to the origins and persistence of caste as an economically inefficient institution or of the impact of caste on unemployment patterns. The literature is largely silent on the issue of income distribution.[4] In its turn, the Marxist literature's tendency to treat the social structure of caste as the residue of feudal or semifeudal modes of production constrains our ability to understand the economic impact of caste under conditions of capitalism and the globalized market. Also, the Marxist understanding of social relations as superstructure determined by the economic base limits an appreciation of the independent impact of social structure on the control of the means of production, specific patterns of appropriation of surplus value, etc.[5]

Obviously, these approaches for understanding the nature of poverty in India miss an important point, i.e., the mutually reinforcing effects of caste and class hierarchies condemning those at the bottom to a doubly-reinforced structural trap. Various independent surveys at the national level and across different states have concurred that the dalits are backward on

more criteria than any other caste grouping[6] Suffering from cumulative disabilities, the dalits are backward on all counts such as mental and physical health, dwelling status, sources of livelihood, land ownership, debt levels, etc.[7] Contemporary indices reveal some characteristic features of the economic status of dalits. They have a high dependence on wage labor – particularly unskilled manual labor. They comprise a negligible proportion of the self-employed. Unemployment levels are twice that of the other caste groups, and the daily wage earning is the lowest among all castes. All of these factors collude to result in low consumption expenditures limited to the barest subsistence, little to no savings, and very high poverty levels.[8] Although about 16 percent of the total population of India,[9] the dalits comprise fully three-quarters of the ranks of the poorest of the poor. An indication of the very long-term historical impact of this structural trap is manifested in the slow and barely perceptible process of inter-generational mobility out of this position at the bottom of the economic and social hierarchies.

The two available exits from this severely disempowering location are the State and the market. Unfortunately, the market has proven ruthless and the State unreliable. The State in its commitment to social justice and fundamental rights of citizens has over the years enacted a series of legislations designed to abolish the practice of untouchability, to carry out land reform, to declare as illegal the institution of bonded labor, etc.[10] Through a policy of reservations in government employment, on elected assemblies and in public educational institutions, the State has also sought to create opportunities for dalits to exercise political power, to attain economic security and the capacity for upward mobility. Unfortunately, the State stands implicated for its failure to enforce the above laws, for its active collusion with the propertied classes and upper castes preventing the full implementation of land reform and for the failure of its "development" agenda to impart either the necessary education for gainful employment or to create sufficient jobs for educated dalit youth.

The case of land reform is a telling example of the extent to which the State has abdicated its commitment to justice, leaving the dalits to face the ruthless logic of market forces. Eighty-one percent of India's dalit population lives in villages. More than three-quarters of this population are landless agricultural laborers, sharecroppers and rural non-farm workers. The program of land redistribution did not rely much on confiscation and redistribution. Instead, some redistributed land was sliced away from the local commons; other portions were made available to dalit families as upper-caste landowners sold off tiny slivers of land in a gesture toward meeting the new laws.[11] This inconclusive and half-hearted program resulted in ownership by dalit families of generally uncultivable land ranging from a tiny percentage of an acre to a couple of acres at the maximum. Less than 1 percent of dalit farmers have access to irrigation facilities. Upper caste farmers usurp available water resources as well as using rights to transport and other infrastructure connecting the village to the market.[12] This produces and sustains economic relations of severe dependence of dalits on the landed classes. These upper and middle caste families have retained ownership of hundreds of acres of land – some of it in blatant violation of land ceiling laws, some of it exempted by the State from the land ceiling laws, and most of it as disguised holdings. The income of dalit families from agricultural labor or cultivation of their miniscule land holdings is barely enough to ensure two full meals a day. It means the utter inability to generate savings or to make small productive capital investments, to provide for adequate clothing or much-needed medicine.[13] In fact, 48 percent of the dalit population in rural India lives below the poverty line.[14]

This desperate poverty also means that despite high enrollments in government schools (87 percent according to government figures), families cannot afford to lose a pair of working hands during the long gestation period that goes with the completion of school education. This factor, along with faint employment prospects in the future, leads to a high dropout rate among dalit students (66.7 percent) as families begin to use

schools largely as crèches, keeping young children there only until the point that they become more useful in helping to provide subsistence for the family.[15] As market prices of food grains and other essential commodities soar, the iron grip of poverty tightens, setting in motion the migration of dalit peoples to urban and semi-urban areas. Here, the dalits constitute a new urban proletariat, working in stone quarries and brick kilns from dawn to dusk in deplorable conditions for wages below the market rate.[16] Tribals join the ranks of the dalits in these occupations – having been dislocated from their forested lands by crushing poverty – to be bought and sold between middlemen and then delivered to proprietors for what is for all practical purposes a new system of bonded labor.[17] The informal sector with its low incomes, irregular work, and lack of organizational structures for workers is another arena that absorbs the dalit masses. Ragpicking, construction work, scavenging for coal or scraps of metal in the drains, rickshaw pulling, etc. are a few of the primary activities in this sector – requiring only unskilled labor. Their huts and shanties in the slums are not safe from the government's eviction and demolition squads trying to "clean up" the city.[18] In order to earn a livelihood from ragpicking and scavenging, they root about in mounds of garbage with stray dogs and pigs for company – thereby conflating the ritual pollution line with the poverty line. A competitive enterprise, this work also requires that scavenging zones be guarded against violation at all times of the day or night. As they work round the clock, the doubly reinforced social and economic structural trap remains firmly shut.

What then are the options for survival open to dalits? It is an established fact that government jobs (e.g., bureaucracies, public enterprises, railways, army) are the main source of employment in the formal sector. The economic security along with the social prestige associated with it has enabled the emergence of a class of dalits that is vastly better off, socially conscious and more politically aware than its brethren in the urban slums or villages. The State program of investing in the education of dalits through provision of free schools, hostel facilities, scholarships, and training centers has met with relative success, as evinced by a slow but definite growth in literacy levels. In the year 1961, the literacy level among dalits was 10.27 percent. This rose to 21.38 percent in 1981 and stands at 37.4 percent in recent years.[19] Now a certain number of dalits can also compete with upper-caste candidates for middle-level positions.[20] However, given the shrinkage of the welfare state (not offset by the growing availability of jobs in the private sector which does not observe affirmative action policies), dalits face the risk of further marginalization. Without some fundamental social and economic change, dalits will continue to be at a far remove from top-level educational qualifications and access to white-collar jobs.[21] Where self-employment opportunities are concerned, these are more difficult to come by for the dalits than for other social groups. The hotel and hospitality industry, for example, is closed (except for the most menial of tasks like sweeping) because of the ritual pollution aspect. Without access to credit facilities or lobbies in the corridors of power, capital-intensive industries such as that of oil and petrol are also off limits to dalit peoples.[22]

As life becomes a series of movements from margin to margin, dalits cannot but question the fruits of economic development. Symptomatic of the growing alienation from the State are the metaphors they use to think about their lives and livelihood. The revolutionary poet Narayan Survey has suggested that for the dalits, the *roti (bhakri)* is not only round as the moon but also just as distant.[23] "Poison bread"[24] is another symbol of the diminution of human dignity each time dalits eat leftover food from the homes of the upper castes as a matter of routine survival, or are forced to consume wild leaves or the flesh of dead animals during bad times such as droughts.

The Evolution of Policy and Movement Response

Efforts to oppose the scourge of untouchability and the idea of caste ascription have a long history. Indeed, as Myron Weiner has argued, "More than one hundred years of social reform movements, public pronouncements by political leaders, constitutional declarations, and legislation" have undermined the "orthodoxy" – the belief in – if not the "orthopraxy" – the practice of – caste hierarchy.[25]

The paradox of *"naming"* and thereby *inscribing* caste in order to *disinter* its strictures from its deeply embedded place in Hindu society also reaches back into pre-democratic colonial times, even as post-Independent democratic practices reinforce these processes. The 1953 Backward Classes Commission report referred to at the opening of this chapter was not the first official acknowledgement of the role of caste as an independent factor in determining the class structure. The Untouchables and the lower castes[26] had been categorized under the rubric *"backward classes"* in the 1870s by the colonial administration in Madras. By 1925, particularly in the Bombay and Madras presidencies, seats were reserved in local assemblies and educational institutions for the *backward classes* – an overarching category constructed to include the *"depressed classes"* (Untouchables and Tribals) and low castes other than the *depressed classes*. The colonial state then created through the Government of India Act 1935 a new nomenclature *"scheduled castes"* for the Untouchables who became entitled to the benefits of an affirmative action policy in the spheres of education and representation in the state apparatus.

The efforts to dismantle the detriments of untouchability through the targeted practice of preferential identification continued with the Constitution of independent India. Article 17 abolishes untouchability, while Article 46 simultaneously requires the state to promote with special care the educational and economic interests of the weaker sections, particularly the so-named Scheduled Castes and Tribes. Similarly, Article 335 provides for preferential treatment of Scheduled Castes and Tribes in appointments to government services and posts; and Articles 330 and 332 provide for seat reservations in parliament and the state legislative assemblies, while still other constitutional provisions do the same for the local councils (*panchayats*). Interestingly, the post-colonial state has continued to institutionalize this particular identity for Untouchables and beginning in the early 1990s further codified the term *"other backward classes"* (OBCs) by authorizing job preferences designating eligibility by the social and economic status of the lower castes.

In the Constitutional Assembly debates, however, a strong preference emerged to overlook the structuring effects of caste on the grossly iniquitous economic system. Nehru's socialist leanings implied that economic change and modernization would become the preferred instruments to do away with caste, other abhorrent social legacies, and of course, poverty. The imperative of national unity also contributed to this tendency to underplay the consequences of the divisive caste structure. Another powerful force operating in this context was "colonial shame," or the need to deny British characterizations of India as backward and caste-ridden.[27] Thus a whole nexus of causes conspired to neglect the fundamentally social basis of poverty in India. Defeating Ambedkar's argument in Parliament that the backward classes were "but a collection of certain castes,"[28] Nehru's Congress government successfully engineered the dominant consensus that held that the most appropriate strategy to combat poverty and implement social justice was one centered around economic class identification rather than that of caste. In fact, by 1961, this government had decided that although the scheduled castes and scheduled tribes would continue to enjoy the benefits sanctioned by the Constitution, it would not be useful to compile a caste-based list of OBCs, nor would it be desirable to have a reservation policy for OBCs at the Center.[29]

From this time until the mid-1970s, the political opportunity structure continued to be fairly stable and generally inopportune for explicit caste-based political mobilization as well as other identity movements more generally. This is not to deny that the broad structure of constraints and opportunities was undergoing a slow and perceptible change. A split in the hegemonic Congress party followed Nehru's

death in 1964. The economy also landed in serious trouble leading to falling support for the party. With these changes, some political space began to open up for mobilization by competing parties and identity-based social movements. As the mid-1970s approached, "dalit" identity emerged as a powerful frame used by the scheduled castes to galvanize a political movement around their pressing concerns. It resonated with Ambedkar's famous argument (*contra* Gandhi) that the scheduled castes had political interests separate from the rest of the Hindu masses and should therefore mobilize on that distinct social basis.[30]

However, even as the Constitution and its pursuant legislation permitted, indeed, seemed to require claims-making based on caste, the degree to which class and poverty matters were to be incorporated in movement agendas was a more indeterminate question. In the 1970s, the mobilization frames that were constructed proved to be predominantly class-based. For example, the Dalit Panthers emerged as a radical movement of urban slum-dwelling scheduled caste youth in Maharashtra. A substantial section of the Dalit Panthers embraced a discourse animated by the ideas of revolutionary Marxism, and although the movement did not involve armed struggle, it was a call to the dalit peoples to demand an improvement in their rapidly deteriorating conditions of life. In socialist magazines and through brief flirtations with Marxist groups, the Panthers expressed their total rejection of the ideology of the caste system and determined to break the reinforcing effects of the economic and social hierarchies, of which the dalits were at the very bottom. In other parts of the country, the increasingly assertive dalits threw in their lot with the Naxalites, a radical Marxist-Leninist group which organized armed struggles of the rural poor against the exploitation of the upper-caste landed classes and colluding state governments.[31]

Indeed, economic class continued to be the mainframe of Indian politics as Indira Gandhi and the Congress party surged into power in the 1972 general elections on the wave of the hugely successful manifesto "*Garibi Hatao!*"[32] which resounded deeply with the impoverished masses. Class-based populist strategies of mobilization around the program of nationalizing industries and imposing land reforms during the imposition of Emergency between 1975–77 are also indicative of the incentives for class mobilization inherent in the political opportunity structure. Emergent dalit movements adapted to this opportunity structure that opened up space for contentious political mobilization and simultaneously ensured its articulation through a class-based lens.

It was not until the late 1980s, when the Mandal Commission recommendations were resuscitated by V. P. Singh's government, however, that caste became an overtly political issue at the national level with significant electoral incentives for political parties mobilizing on that basis. Caste questions began to occupy center stage in national debates about modernity and citizenship in India. In the following years, the politics of identity continued to become increasingly important as the Babri Masjid was demolished and in its wake bloody communal riots (re)established religion as another live political issue. A notable feature of this new political opportunity structure is that it has generated not only identity-based social movements but has also prompted the direct quest for political power through electoral competition. In the state of Uttar Pradesh, for example, two main contenders for political power are the *Bahujan Samaj Party* (BSP: a dalit-based political party) and the *Bharatiya Janata Party* (BJP: a Hindu-right political party). On the one hand, the BSP seeks to defend its dalit constituency from co-optation by the BJP's upper-caste-dominated, all-encompassing Hindu fold; on the other hand, the BSP seeks to thwart the BJP's Hindu revivalist politics by projecting a secular front comprising the dalits, scheduled tribes, some lower castes and other members of religious minority groups, particularly Muslims. In the intertwining of the politics of caste and religion, dalit politics has been recast and redefined along these dimensions, but somewhere along this road, the focus on class and poverty as the important political issues of the day has been lost.

Identity Formation as Strategy to Deal with Poverty

Still another strategy emerged in the middle of the next decade of the 1990s. Without explicitly referring to a class-based strategy for the mobilization of the impoverished, and rejecting the default position that the struggles of the dalits must be waged by dalits alone, this movement speaks in the majoritarian language of liberal democratic politics. It identifies a *bahujan samaj* (majority community) that does not deny the divisions and differences between its constitutive parts, yet hopes to contain the contradictions in the name of the numerical majority of the oppressed. It is aided significantly by the incentive of a direct route to capture of state power that its majority strength implies. This purposive political framing by the political party BSP draws inspiration from the ideas of Jotirao Phule in mid-nineteenth century Maharashtra, and Swami Achhutanand in early twentieth century Punjab and the United Provinces. These reformers had articulated the expression "*bahujan samaj*" to indicate that should the Untouchables and *shudras* (low castes) unite politically, they could comprise the majority of the population and be in a position to govern themselves.[33] The BSP is not only following through on the promise of the *bahujan*, but also responding to the logic of the changed political opportunity structure that is enabling of identity-based political mobilizations around caste and religion. Thus, it has sought a broad strategy of inclusiveness without denying the diversity and specificity of identities within its political constituency comprised of dalits, scheduled tribes, some OBC castes and religious minorities such as Muslims. The BSP's projection of itself as a dalit-based secular party is an attempt to challenge and subvert the logic of the upper-caste dominated Hindu revivalist BJP. Important questions remain, however. Is the *bahujan* identity merely one of political convenience, or is the practice of a *bahujan* politics shaping and constituting a cross-caste community of solidarity that the "dalit" frame has not been able to create? And what of poverty? Unfortunately, in doing away with the weaknesses of the "dalit" frame, the BSP has compromised the dalit movement's main virtue, i.e., its central focus on the urgent question of impoverishment. Given the threatening nature of globalization in terms of the shrinkage of state employment opportunities, reduction of social spending, and the rise in food prices, this neglect could be an egregious betrayal of the pauperized *bahujan*.

Finally, there have been efforts to unite the scheduled castes, low castes and tribal peoples under the broad banner of race. The *Dravida* movement began in the late nineteenth century as an appropriation of colonial discourse on the Brahmin-dominated Aryan invasion into the Indian subcontinent. This was a strategy to reject the Sanskritizing influence of the twice-born castes and to build in its place an egalitarian, ethnicized identity as the original inhabitants of the land. The *Self-Respect movement* was later founded by Periyar who had left the Congress arguing for a new society based on equality (*samadharma*) and a rejection of the caste system. The dravidian identity in particular, and the politics of race in general, have continued to inspire the formation of political parties and other social movements led by non-Brahmins in the southern states. The Dalit Panthers were deeply interested in the struggles of African-Americans in the United States and named themselves after the Black Panther movement that emerged in 1966. Elsewhere, dalits see themselves as the black Untouchables of India.[34] Indeed, the politics of race remains significant as a category for the mobilization of dalits and other oppressed peoples though it has never become a primary site of dalit struggle.

The Dalit Panthers – Failed Adaptation of an Emerging Radicalism

In 1972, hundreds of dalit youth raised their pens in a powerful protest against their dehumanizing poverty and the "Hindu feudal order."[35] Most of the Panther youths were children of poor peasants, landless laborers, or urban workers. As first-generation educated,

yet continuing to experience hunger, unemployment, and social discrimination on account of their "untouchability," they mobilized in revolt against these oppressive economic and social conditions. Their voices rose from the slums and factories, tea-houses and public libraries, exposing the inadequacies of Independence, developmentalism, and social justice. They demanded land redistribution through the just implementation of the land ceiling acts, control of food grain prices, daily minimum wages for laborers, benefits for unemployed dalits, confiscation of foreign capital, control of the means of production, the removal of casteist and communal prejudices in employment and educational institutions, and an equal treatment for all in the name of human dignity. The Panthers' Manifesto concluded "true independence is one that is snatched forcibly out of the hands of the enemy. One that is like bits thrown to a helpless beggar is no independence."[36]

There was discernibly a vital disconnect between their revolutionary aspirations and the strategies they adopted for radical struggle. Instead of a revolutionary armed struggle, as one would perhaps expect from a reading of the Manifesto, theirs was a movement focused on developing a revolutionary consciousness by countering the ideological hegemony of the upper castes which, based on the ancient scriptures and religious–moral philosophy, legitimated the oppression of dalits. The young poets and writers of the Dalit Panthers publicized their trenchant critiques in socialist magazines and at dalit literary conferences. In their contestation of the ideological, moral and cultural superstructure of the political–economic system, the Dalit Panthers adhered to a Gramscian brand of Marxism rather than a Marxist–Leninist approach to system change. They missed, however, a key insight of Gramscian Marxism: although challenging discourses are necessary instruments of system change, this is inherently a long-term process and does not constitute a direct or immediate route to the achievement of desired outcomes. What becomes indispensable to bringing about actual change is the degree of political organization, the strength of political alliances, and the relations of force within a particular historical bloc of contention.[37] In these vital respects, the Dalit Panthers found themselves unprepared. They could not adjust to the political flux produced in the wake of the de-institutionalization of the Congress party; nor could they engage other important political actors who had become active as political space opened up both at the national and regional levels. They seemed hesitant to take any initiative beyond cultural activism.[38] Ultimately, organizational weaknesses and fundamental differences between its leadership on the direction that Panther activism should take split the organization from within. The inability also to develop a coherent agenda of class-caste struggle, the failure to build political alliances around such an agenda and to position itself in the rapidly changing scenario hastened the decline of the Dalit Panther movement.

The confusions of the Dalit Panthers during the pre-Emergency days extended well into the Emergency period and speak volumes about the paralysis that engulfed the organization. Instead of building relationships with political forces on the left or developing a viable economic program as an alternative to that of the Congress whose economic vision had over twenty-five years of independence yielded little to the dalits, the Panthers found themselves in support of Indira Gandhi's call to banish poverty, nationalize industries, etc. There was also a strong reluctance on the part of the faction led by Raja Dhale to participate in the rural struggles led by the radical Naxalites in Bihar and Andhra Pradesh who were at that time facing the inevitable problems in bringing the lower castes and dalits together in an armed struggle on the lines of a class war.[39] The conspicuous lack of effort by the Panthers themselves to organize the rural dalits has been a valid criticism of their political strategy. Certainly no dalit movement can be effective without mobilizing the vast masses of rural India.[40]

In the tradition of Ambedkar, the Dalit Panthers also harbored a deep suspicion of the mostly Brahminical leadership of the socialist parties. Jayprakash Narayan's socialist movement building on a rural–urban coalition failed to attract the Dalit Panthers. In organizational terms too, the Dalit Panthers floundered. Though membership grew to around 25,000 by the mid-70s, there were no cadre-training programs, no full-time workers for the organization, and no established method of generating resources for their work. Branches of the Dalit Panthers emerged spontaneously with an uncertain relationship to the main leadership or central commitments of the movement. The Dalit Panthers began to resemble a large, indisciplined crowd rather than a focused political organization. Finally, as the differences between Namdeo Dhasal and Raja Dhale became more irreconcilable, the Panthers underwent the first split in 1974, followed in quick succession by three more splits in 1975, 1976, and 1977.[41]

During this period, its activism was broadly centered on organizing meetings, processions and propaganda to protest atrocities against dalits. Over the next two decades, the Dalit Panthers were immersed in the struggle to defend the state assembly decision to rename the Marathwada University with the name of Dr Ambedkar. This decision by the state assembly had sparked pogroms against dalits as villages were attacked, thousands of poor people fled their homes, and women were raped. Over time, some organizational splinters of the Panthers were absorbed into the Congress and main-stream politics.[42] There remained, however, several organizations by the name of Panther,[43] drawing inspiration from the effervescence of the 1970s, and determined to continue the struggle of dalit assertion in the villages and slums of India. This strong "expressive link"[44] can be counted as one of the Panthers' main successes.

The other major success of the Panthers has been the vital legacy of dalit cultural assertion. Baburao Bagul, the prominent dalit poet, declared "dalit sahitya is not a literature of vengeance. ... dalit sahitya first promotes man's greatness and man's freedom and for that reason it is an historic necessity."[45] Beginning in the 70s in a major way, dalits have emerged as creators of culture in their own right. There is today a great profusion of novels, short stories and poems, debates on cultural memory and social change,[46] and considerable effort underway in various parts of the country to recover, record and preserve dalit folk traditions.[47] Literary contributions by dalits have also included innovations of style and content. Using a starkly minimalist approach in the use of language, the poets and writers of the Dalit Panthers exploded their subaltern world into a complacent middle class, upper-caste consciousness. Namdeo Dhasal's collection of poems *Golpitha*, based on life in Bombay's red-light district, aroused considerable indignation among middle-class intelligentsia. The deliberate use of crude and direct language to represent the violence and stark poverty of their lives has often disturbed middle-class sensibilities. It is worth quoting from Vijay Tendulkar's[48] introduction to Dhasal's *Golpitha* poems:[49]

> In the calculations of the white collar workers, "no man's land" begins at the border of their world, and it is here that the world of Namdeo Dhasal's poetry of Bombay's Golpitha begins. This is the world of days of nights; of empty or half-full stomachs; of the pain of death; of tomorrow's worries; of men's bodies in which shame and sensitivity have been burned out; of overflowing gutters; of a sick young body, knees curled to belly against the cold of death, next to the gutter; of the jobless; of beggars; of pickpockets; of Bairaga swamis; of Dada bosses and pimps; of Muslim tombs and Christian crosses; of film star Rajesh Khanna and the gods on the peeling wall above the creaking bed.

Because refined cultural tastes and literary sophistication is generally defined by an upper class position, high culture is often used as an instrument to mark class boundaries and exclude lower classes from access to social and cultural commodities.[50] Thus, the confident and bold use of language, metaphor and images unpalatable to the upper castes and upper classes testifies to the spirit of resistance among dalit writers. And in the creation of an original and authentic dalit literary work there is enacted the more radical practice of cultural assertion and social empowerment.

Bahujan Samaj Party – Redefinition and the Politics of Compromise

The BSP is the vehicle through which a certain class of dalits has aimed, through electoral victory, to capture State power and control public policy. It represents the efforts of a generation of dalits who have benefited from the State's development programs and affirmative action policies in education, employment and politics. Despite the general failure of the postcolonial State in eradicating poverty or improving the quality of life for the vast majority of dalits, it is surely a portent of future possibilities that this small success (i.e., the emergence of a class of upwardly mobile and politically conscious dalits) has in its turn become an investment into a future of empowerment for the dalit masses. With an authoritative say in the allocation of resources and the direction of public policy, it may be possible to bring about the kind of fundamental changes that previous governments have generally been constrained to do. This trajectory of change, though bound to be gradual, could also be considerably deep, because inherent in the use of State power by dalits are multiple possibilities for crafting a future such as were unavailable before.

The launch pads for the BSP were two earlier organizations built by Kanshi Ram. The *All-India Backward and Minority Employees Federation (BAMCEF)*, founded in 1973, was a forum to establish networks and spread an Ambedkarite social consciousness among educated dalit government employees in the west and north Indian states. This was followed in 1982 by the *Dalit Shoshit Samaj Sangharsh Samiti (DS-4)*, which functioned as a "quasi-political party"[51] and mobilization organ of the dalit masses particularly in rural areas. It organized rallies and peoples' parliaments,[52] launched fund-raising drives,[53] contested elections, and published its own newspaper, *The Bahujan Times*. This publication could not sustain itself and died out, followed by the weekly *Bahujan Sangathak*[54] which continues to be regularly published today in various languages under the auspices of the BSP. Formed in 1984, the BSP carefully propagates the political relevance of a *bahujan* (majority) community that includes, besides the dalits, various other poor and oppressed sections of the population such as the scheduled tribes, some OBC castes particularly the MBCs, and Muslims. It is to enact and symbolize this community that BSP leaders refer to their work in terms of a movement, not that of a political party. For all practical purposes, however, the BSP is a dalit-based political party committed to the pursuit of power.

The *bahujan* identity has achieved some success in forging a unity between these different social groups on the strength of which the BSP has, in the 90s, emerged as an important national-level party, also winning a place in governing coalitions in Uttar Pradesh several times. Significantly, each time that the BSP has participated in a coalition government, there have been indications as to how tense and tenuous the *bahujan* identity can be. For instance, despite being coalition partners with the BSP in the 1993 UP government, Mulayam Singh Yadav's OBC-based *Samajwadi Party* (SP) worked to undermine the cohesiveness of the *bahujan* community by trying to wean away Muslim and MBC votes toward itself. Deeper problems surfaced as well, such as the resistance of the SP toward the appointment of dalits (instead of dominant OBCs, such as the *Yadavs*) in the bureaucracy; the growing resentment of the OBCs toward dalits in the rural economy leading to violent clashes between them, etc.[55] It came as no surprise when this coalition government was torn apart from within and collapsed. Two years later, in 1995, the BSP entered into a political alliance with the BJP to form the state government in UP. As an upper-caste dominated Hindu revivalist party, the BJP happens to be the antithesis of everything the BSP purportedly stands for. It was inevitable that this partnership should be a "fragile and contradictory"[56] one; if the contradictions of the 1993 alliance were not readily apparent at the start, this time around the tensions stood out in bold relief. The BSP had to be alert to the BJP's potential to subvert the *bahujan* community by absorbing dalits and lower castes into its Hindu fold on the basis of

an anti-Muslim agenda; it also had to defend its program for the empowerment of dalits from the stiff resistance put up by the BJP. This government collapsed by the end of that year, only to be resuscitated after the assembly polls of 1997. The endless recriminations continued between these two parties, particularly when the BJP attempted to reverse programs put in place by Chief Minister Mayawati, such as the recruitment of dalits to key positions in the bureaucracy, implementation of reservation quotas for MBCs, increased expenditures on health and family planning schemes for the dalits, etc. This government, too, did not manage to last its tenure.

There is one important difference between situations like those outlined above and that of the present government in UP. The 2002 post-election alliance (once again) between the BSP and the BJP is marked by a balance of power preponderantly in favor of the BSP and Chief Minister Mayawati. The BJP, having lost considerable political ground at the national level in the aftermath of the Gujarat riots and the assembly polls in several states, has high stakes in the survival of this particular government. For the time being at least, the BSP has been able to proceed with programs aimed at its *bahujan* constituency without strenuous opposition from its partner-in-government. However, a new strategy used by the BSP to counter the influence of the BJP has made vulnerable the authenticity of this very constituency. This is the practice of issuing party tickets to upper-caste candidates. Though it is not clear if this will be enough to wean away upper-caste Hindu votes from the BJP, it does open to question the integrity of the *bahujan* community. Will this dilute the BSP's commitment to the dalits and other backward groups? What about its commitment to secular politics? Will the carefully constructed unity of the *bahujan* and the agenda lying at its heart be compromised in the heat of electoral competition and identity politics? It is very likely that capitulation by the BSP on issues perceived by the dalits to be of great importance could cost the party their support. Clearer answers than this will emerge only with the passage of time.

There is one particular critique, however, that can be made with reasonable accuracy. This pertains to the BSP's abdication of the poverty question. Urgent issues at the heart of dalit welfare, such as land redistribution and minimum wages, have been generally ignored, and the single-minded quest for political power has not been accompanied by a comprehensive economic or social vision for the dalits and other constituent members of the *bahujan* community. When in power, the party has, on the one hand, focused on building a cultural consciousness by renaming roads and building statues to honor dalit leaders. This is important in itself, but given the neglect of fundamental structural questions, substantial improvements in the life conditions of dalit masses appear to be far from likely. On the other hand, the BSP has been busily engaged in a "transfer of power,"[57] as reservation quotas are filled and dalits appointed in large numbers to high administrative posts. Though this is a long-term system change underway, the direct benefits of this empowerment are more likely to go to the upwardly mobile, educated dalit class than to the vast numbers of impoverished and illiterate masses. Failure to attend to the critical question of poverty indicates the exercise of power without purpose – an egregious error for a dalit-based political party that has come so far.

NGOs and Soft Resistance to the State's Neoliberal Agenda

A reformist strand of NGO activism believes in the potential of capitalism to achieve greater social good, but acknowledges that unrestrained global capitalism generates inequities, subverts democracy, and creates conditions for instability and violence. In keeping with this philosophy, they press States for guarantees of basic incomes, protectionist measures for vulnerable social groups, and greater opportunities for such groups to participate in and benefit from globalization. In contrast, radical NGO activism sees globalization as inherently damaging to social democracy, economic justice, and cultural pluralism. Though deglobalization seems to be the

only appropriate solution to these problems, radical opposition campaigns at the global level such as the NGO-dominated battle of Seattle have yet to gain a momentum critical enough to bring about a substantive reversal of the globalization project.[58]

A survey of NGO activism on the Indian stage similarly reveals the absence of radical politics, particularly on the question of dalit poverty. Among dalit-led NGOs, there seem to be two main focii of activism. On the one hand, there are organizations engaged in information dissemination, skill generation, and capacity building among dalits. These projects, like the ones conducted by the *Women's Voice* in Bangalore, enable impoverished dalit families to create avenues for self-employment and learn other technical skills. On the other hand, there are dalit-led NGOs such as *Drushti* in the Bidar district of Karnataka,[59] that are mobilizing the dalits for political agitation on questions such as minimum wages essential to their survival. This kind of activism has yielded some successes in parts of Andhra Pradesh, specifically in the coastal Andhra and Telengana regions.

Focused specifically on human rights issues such as the daily occurrence of atrocities against dalits (and therefore related only indirectly to the poverty question) are NGOs like the *Peoples Union for Civil Liberties* (PUCL) under a primarily non-dalit leadership.[60] Other NGOs such as the *Mazdoor Kisan Sang-harsh Samiti* (MKSS)[61] seek to weld together a broad class-based coalition of workers, peasants and other toiling masses. But it has not demanded fundamental changes in the social and economic structures that produce poverty; nor is the MKSS agitation (focused on issues such as corruption, the need for transparency and the right to information) explicitly linked to the question of impoverishment. It is also unfortunate that there has been a general failure on the part of NGOs concerned about dalit peoples to galvanize an all-India social movement. The reasons for this are many; for example, the inability of activists to generate consensus on the question of according primacy to reservation policy and denunciation of caste atrocities *or* to issues relating to poverty.[62]

There is, however, one strategy that is being increasingly adopted by NGOs building transnational alliances with non-governmental organizations in other countries. Identified as a "boomerang"[63] pattern of activism, domestic NGOs working on the concerns of dalits are able to bring pressure to bear on the State by activating their transnational networks. Thus, member NGOs in other countries begin to pressure their respective states or, if necessary, an inter-governmental forum, so that these actors are in turn persuaded to urge, pressure, and compel the original State to implement the required policy changes. In this manner, domestic NGOs are able, by activating external sources of influence, to bring about the desired change when a solely domestic advocacy campaign would not have been sufficient. The growing preference for this kind of activism is evidenced by the proliferation of transnational linkages such as the *International Dalit Solidarity Network*, the

World Council of Churches' *Dalit Solidarity Program*, and the growing participation of dalit activists in UN activities such as the *Seminar of experts on Racism, Refugees and Multiethnic states* (Geneva, 1999), the *First session of the Preparatory Committee for the World Conference against Racism* (Geneva, 2000), and the organization of international conferences such as the *Global Conference against Racism and Caste-based Discrimination* attended by social activists from South Africa, Japan, Germany, Denmark, Netherlands, United States, United Kingdom, Sri Lanka, Pakistan, Nepal, Bangladesh and of course India (New Delhi, March 2001). The agenda of dalit activists at this particular conference was the inclusion of the question of dalit rights onto the agenda at the *World Conference against Racism* to be held at Durban. It is worth noting that they were able to succeed in this endeavor.[64]

Notes

1 National Commission to Review the Working of the Constitution; A Consultation Paper on the Pace of Socio-Economic Change under the Constitution, Chair: Justice Dr K. Ramaswamy, May 11, 2001, chapter 9, 5 (http://lawmin. nic.in/ncrwc/finalreport/v2b1-4.htm).

2 Ira N. Gang, Kunal Sen, and Myeong-Su Yun, "Caste, Ethnicity, and Poverty in Rural India," Department of Economics, Rutgers University, School of Development Studies, University of East Anglia and the Department of Economics, Tulane, February 2004 (http://oll.temple.edu/ economics/Seminars/GangSenYun-IndiaPoverty-Caste.pdf).

3 Human Rights Watch, "Broken People; Caste Violence against India's Untouchables," New York, March 1999. Summarizing this nexus between caste and poverty in India's "heartland" of Uttar Pradesh, Valerie Kozel and Barbara Parker write that the vast majority of respondents, rich and poor alike, saw social identity (low caste) as a strong predictor of "who is and is not poor, who is illiterate, who is employed in low-paid, low status agricultural

labour, and who lives in poorly constructed housing with limited access to basic services." Kozel and Parker, "A Profile and Diagnostic of Poverty in Uttar Pradesh," *Economic and Political Weekly*, January 25, 2003. None of this is to suggest that there has not been change. In a recent survey of Rajasthan in which he discusses the emergence of a new strata of "political entrepreneurs," Anirudh Krishna writes: "Caste continues to be a primary source of social identity in these villages, people live in caste-specific neighborhoods, and the clothes that they wear reveal their caste identity. Yet insofar as political organization is concerned, caste no longer has primary importance." Krishna, "What Is Happening to Caste? A View from Some North Indian Villages," *Journal of Asian Studies* 62, no. 4 (November 2003): 1171–93.

4 See S. K. Thorat and R. S. Deshpande, "Caste System and Economic Inequality: Economic Theory and Evidence," in *Dalit Identity and Politics*, ed. Ghanshyam Shah (New Delhi: Sage Publications India Pvt. Ltd., 2001), for an

excellent overview of the economic literature dealing with the economic consequences of caste. For an application of the neo-classical approach to the caste system, see George Akerlof, "The Theory of Social Customs of which Unemployment May Be One Consequence," *Quarterly Journal of Economics* 94, no. 4 (June 1980); George Akerlof, "The Economics of Caste and of Rat Race and Other Woeful Tales," *Quarterly Journal of Economics* 90, no. 4 (November 1976); and Deepak Lal, ed., *"Hindu Equilibrium," Cultural Stability and Economic Stagnation*, vol. 1 (Oxford: Clarendon Press, 1988).

5   See, for example, E. M. S. Namboodiripad, "Caste, Classes and Parties in Modern Political Development," *Social Scientist*, November 1977, and B.T. Ranadive, "Caste, Class and Property Relations," *Economic and Political Weekly*, February 1997.

6   To mention only a few sources, see Census of India 1991; National Sample Surveys over the years – particularly the rural labor inquiry reports, the landholding surveys and the employment/unemployment surveys; Second Backward Classes Commission (Venkatswamy report) 1986: 2 volumes, Government of Karnataka.

7   This is the finding of forty IAS officers in several villages across the country in 1995. See Sanjay Sinha, "Profile of the Poorest among Poor," *The Administrator* XLII (January–March 1997): 173–83.

8   See Thorat and Deshpande, 57–71.

9   Scheduled castes in India (data sheet): Planning Commission (Backward classes and Tribes Division) Government of India, November 2000.

10   Minimum Wages Act 1948; Zamindari Abolition Act 1952; Untouchability Offences Act, 1955 and the Protection of Civil Rights Act, 1976; Bonded Labor System (Abolition) Act 1976; SC and ST (Prevention of Atrocities) Act, 1989. These are the more prominent among the myriad legislations designed to empower the dalits and other impoverished sections of the population which are mostly the low castes comprising the OBCs. There are also the justiciable fundamental rights guaranteed in the Constitution and the nonjusticiable Directive Principles that are supposed to guide State policy in its program of social justice.

11   See Oliver Mendelsohn and Marika Vicziany, *The Untouchables: Subordination, Poverty and the State in Modern India* (Cambridge: Cambridge University Press, 1998), 30–36.

12   P. Sainath, *Everybody Loves a Good Drought* (New Delhi: Penguin Publications, 1996), 123; Tangraj, *Dalit in India* (Mumbai: Vikas Adhyayan Kendra), 23.

13   For an account of the land reform project in Uttar Pradesh and the survival strategies of several generations of an impoverished and powerless dalit family, see Siddharth Dube, *In the Land of Poverty: Memoirs of an Indian Family 1947–97* (New York: Zed Books Ltd., 1998), chapter 12.

14   Scheduled castes in India (data sheet): Planning Commission (Backward Classes and Tribes Division) Government of India, November 2000.

15   See Gopal Guru, "Education as Baby-sitting," *The Hindu*, 27 May 2000.

16   See Mendelsohn and Vicziany, *The Untouchables*, chapter 6, for an account of the mobilization of workers in the stone quarries of Faridabad. About eight of every ten laborers in these quarries is a dalit – the others are Tribal peoples. This struggle faltered in the face of the failure of the Central Government to enforce the laws that already existed; the blatant contempt by Haryana's state government of Supreme Court directives in favor of the laborers; and the corrupt nexus between the ruling party in Haryana and the contractors.

17   Mahasweta Devi, "Contract Labor or Bonded labor?" *Economic and Political Weekly*, June 6, 1981. For an insight into the extreme exploitation of people at the intersection of low caste, low class, and gender, see also a collection of narratives on the exploitation of impoverished dalit and tribal women. Mahasweta Devi, *Outcaste: Four Stories*, trans. Sarmistha Datta Gupta (Calcutta: Seagull Books Pvt. Ltd., 2002).

18   See, for example, the editorial "Bombay: Whose Grandfather's Property?" in *Dalit Voice* (April 1–15, 1983), a fortnightly newspaper published in Bangalore, Karnataka. Reprinted in Barbara Joshi ed., *Untouchable! Voices of the Dalit Liberation Movement* (London: Zed Books, 1986), 69–71. In 1999, one such eviction effort in Bombay made headlines as a dalit woman whose little hut was demolished hit Commissioner Khairnar in anger and desperation.

19   Vijendra Kumar, *Rise of Dalit Power in India* (Jaipur: ABD Publishers, 2001), 7. Also see Tangraj, *Dalit in India*, 23.

20 Mendelsohn and Vicziany, *The Untouchables*, 266–68.

21 Jan Breman (*Wage Hunters and Gatherers: Search for Work in the Urban and Rural Economy of South Gujarat* [Delhi: Oxford University Press, 1994], 8) has pointed out that "it seems reasonable to assume that workers in the formal sector are mostly recruited from the higher social strata whose education level is much higher; conversely, low social position and informal sector activities are likely to go together."

22 Advocacy for non–farm-related, self-employment opportunities for dalits is gaining momentum in India, but there is need to pay greater attention to the problems peculiar to the dalit situation. See, for example, Martin Ravallion, "What is needed for a more pro-poor growth process in India," *Economic and Political Weekly*, March 25, 2000. It should be mentioned here that dalits are taking the initiative in establishing their own sources of credit and finance, e.g., Siddharth Bank (Pune), Ambedkar Bank (Jalgaon), and the Dalit Chambers of Commerce (Ahmedabad). Because they are very recent phenomena, there are no concrete evaluations available of these institutions.

23 See Narayan Survey, *Sanad* (Mumbai: Granthali, 1987), 34. Dalit writers such as Surajmal Chaun also echo this sentiment. See his autobiography, *Gehu Ki Roti* (Hindi).

24 See Arjun Dangle, *Poison Bread* (New Delhi: Orient Longman, 1983).

25 Myron Weiner, "The Struggle for Equality: Caste in Indian Politics," in *The Success of India's Democracy*, ed. Atul Kohli (Cambridge: Cambridge University Press, 2001).

26 "Low castes" refers to the vast number of castes subsumed under the nomenclature, *Shudras* (those other than the twice-born Hindu castes), but even so, the low castes are positioned as a group a rung above the Untouchables in the caste hierarchy.

27 On this point, see Nicholas B. Dirks, *Castes of Mind: Colonialism and the Making of Modern India* (Princeton, N.J.: Princeton University Press, 2001), 281.

28 Parliamentary Debates, vol. XII–13 (part II), col. 9006.

29 See Christophe Jaffrelot, *India's Silent Revolution: The Rise of the Lower Castes in North India* (New York: Columbia University Press,

2003), 228. Various states, however, went ahead with reservation for OBCs. In this regard, the southern states were much more progressive than other parts of the country.

30 With this in mind, Ambedkar had argued in favor of separate electorates for the scheduled castes. He was opposed to Gandhi, who advocated that the scheduled castes be called "harijans" (literally "God's people") to be incorporated into a reformed Hindu fold. This position denied that the scheduled castes represented a distinct political constituency. Ultimately, the Poona Pact (1932) was signed with Ambedkar conceding the demand for separate electorates, achieving in its place the right of reserved seats on elected assemblies.

31 Mendelsohn and Vicziany, *The Untouchables*, 204.

32 Literally meaning "Remove Poverty!"

33 See Jaffrelot, *India's Silent Revolution*, chapters 5 and 6.

34 See V. T. Rajshekhar, *Dalit: The Black Untouchables of India*, 3rd ed. (Atlanta: Clarity Press, 1995).

35 The Dalit Panthers' Manifesto (Bombay 1973) declared that Hindu feudal rule has been much more ruthless in suppressing the dalits than either the Muslim rulers or British imperialists. It further argued that all the arteries of production, the bureaucracy, judiciary, army, and police forces are in the hands of Hindu feudal land-lords, capitalists, and religious leaders, enabling them to serve their vested interests.

36 See the Panthers' Manifesto in Joshi, ed., *Untouchable!*, 141–7.

37 For Antonio Gramsci's selected writings on hegemony, relations of force, and the idea of the historic bloc, see David Forgacs, ed., *An Antonio Gramsci Reader: Selected Writings; 1916–1935* (New York: Schocken Books Inc., 1988), 189–221.

38 On the important issue of preparedness for radical struggle, Omvedt writes that "Much of the Panther elan had been built up in dialog and clash with the brahmanic elite, its figureheads, and its symbols; now they seemed unable to move beyond this. They found themselves the center of radical attention in a way for which they were unprepared." Omvedt, *Reinventing Revolution*, 53.

39 See Sumanta Banerjee, *In the Wake of Naxalbari: A History of the Naxalite Movement in India* (Calcutta: Subarnarekha Publications, 1980).

40 See Lata Murugkar, *Dalit Panther Movement in Maharashtra: A Sociological Appraisal* (Bombay: Popular Prakashan, 1991), 100.

41 For a detailed account of the organizational dilemmas that plagued the Dalit Panthers, see Murugkar, *Dalit Panther Movement in Maharashtra*, chapter 4.

42 Guru, "Language of Dalit–Bahujan Political Discourse."

43 For instance, an organization by the name of Dalit Panther was born in Uttar Pradesh in the 1980. They were a militant group using fiery rhetoric and violent demonstrations to press their claims. By 1986, however, the UP Panthers had waned and its leadership arrested on charges of threat to national security. See Vivek Kumar and Uday Sinha, *Dalit Assertion and the Bahujan Samaj Party: A Perspective from Below* (Lucknow: Bahujan Sahitya Sansthan, 2001), 53.

44 Omvedt, *Reinventing Revolution*, 57.

45 Quoted in Zelliot, *From Untouchable to Dalit*, 278.

46 See, for example, D. R. Nagaraj, *The Flaming Feet: A Study of the Dalit Movement in India* (Bangalore: South Forum Press and ICRA, 1993) for an insight into the social and political debates embedded in the emerging dalit literary oeuvre in Karnataka.

47 For an account of the profusion of works of dalit folk traditions, see Eleanor Zelliot, *From Untouchable to Dalit*, 317–33.

48 A major playwright and dramatist in Marathi theatre.

49 Quoted in Zelliot, *From Untouchable to Dalit*, 277.

50 For a defining work on the social critique of the judgment of taste, see Pierre Bourdieu, *Distinction: A Social Critique of the Judgement of Taste*, trans. Richard Nice (London: Routledge, 1986).

51 Sudha Pai, *Dalit Assertion and the Unfinished Democratic Revolution*, 91.

52 Kanshi Ram argued that the peoples' Parliament would provide dalits with "the opportunity for debate and discussion on their burning problems which are side-tracked in the national Parliament.... Such a debate by peoples' Parliament without any power will be a constant reminder for the oppressed and exploited masses to make the national Parliament a truly representative one as early as possible." Cited in Kumar and Sinha, *Dalit Assertion and the Bahujan Samaj Party*, 62.

53 For a fascinating account of Kanshi Ram's fundraising strategies, pursued independently of big business support by going directly to the impoverished masses for a single rupee per head in donation, see Kumar and Sinha, *Dalit Assertion and the Bahujan Samaj Party*, 65–69.

54 *The Bahujan Times* had a precursor in *The Oppressed Indian*, a monthly magazine published in English by the BAMCEF. This too faded away eventually.

55 See Pai, *Dalit Assertion and the Unfinished Democratic Revolution*, chapter 4.

56 Pai, *Dalit Assertion and the Unfinished Democratic Revolution*, 178.

57 Jaffrelot, *India's Silent Revolution*, v.

58 For a comprehensive discussion of the multiple dimensions of globalization, see Jan Aart Scholte, *Globalization: A Critical Introduction* (New York: Palgrave, 2000). For the distinctions between reformist and radical responses to globalization, see pp. 33–39.

59 *Drushti* is led by Rev. Karkaer Namdeo. There are also several dalit-based NGOs in Andhra Pradesh such as those under the leadership of Chinnaih in Hyderabad.

60 Other prominent human rights NGOs are, for example, the *Society of Depressed People for Social Justice* and the *All India Human Rights Group*.

61 Active in the state of Rajasthan in western India. See Aruna Roy, "Democracy, Ethics and the Right to Information," Dept. of Education, Delhi University, December 19, 2000.

62 See V. Suresh, "Dalit Movement in India," in *Region, Religion, Caste, Gender and Culture in Contemporary India*, vol. 3, ed. T. V. Satyamurthy (New Delhi: Oxford University Press, 1996), 379.

63 See Keck and Sikkink, *Activists without Borders*, 13.

64 At Durban, however, the *National Campaign on Dalit Human Rights* was not able to make much headway with their demand for an international recognition of dalit rights. For an analysis of the unpreparedness of dalit activists to deal with hard–nosed intergovernmental diplomacy at Durban, see *Human Rights Features*, "Caste Away – or How the Dalit Cause Was Lost in Durban," www.hrdc.net/sahrdc/hrfeatures/HRF44.htm (accessed July 25, 2003).

22

Politics of the Poor? NGOs and Grass-roots Political Mobilization in Bangladesh

Lamia Karim

Bangladeshi NGOs in the Global Economy

The 1992 Earth Summit in Rio strengthened the role of the NGOs by globally inaugurating them as the allies of marginalized groups worldwide and institutionalized them into a greater partnership with the United Nations, the World Bank, and world governing bodies through a series of programs and summits.[1] Commenting on this capacity of the NGOs to do good work, UN General Secretary Kofi Annan in his speech at the Global Issues Forum in Berlin said that the *raison d'être* of many NGOs is to put pressure on governments and to "hold their feet to the fire." In speaking of the important role of NGOs in the twenty-first century, Annan went on to add:

> We have entered an era of even greater diplomacy where there are few limits to what civil society can achieve.... I think it is clear that there is a new diplomacy, where NGOs, people from across nations, international organizations, the Red Cross, and governments can come together to pursue an objective. When we do – and we are determined, as has been the case in the landmines issues and the International Criminal Court – there is nothing we can take on that we cannot succeed in, and this partnership of NGOs, the private sector, international organizations and governments, in my judgment, is a powerful partnership of the future.[2]

NGOs did not come to occupy this role by accident. Their long-term grassroots work in communities has converged with the interests of the United Nations and the Western countries to form a global government that transcends the nation-state and has the authority to implement global rules and regulations (WTO and CEDAW regulations, for example) within the nation-state. As Annan's comments show, this new global alliance has the indigenous NGO as a partner that works inside states to protect the interests of marginalized groups. The local NGO

Perspectives on Modern South Asia: A Reader in Culture, History, and Representation, First Edition.
Edited by Kamala Visweswaran.
© 2011 Blackwell Publishing Ltd. Published 2011 by Blackwell Publishing Ltd.

lobby in the developing country can, through its transnational linkages, bring internal tyranny, oppression, and injustices in front of a global body (the Hague, for example). However, such transnational advocacy also weakens the powers of the nation-state, making it more vulnerable to global forces and mandates. According to some critics from the left, such NGOs are the "community face of neoliberalism" (Hardt and Negri 2000:313). They are complicit with global capital in that while international capital puts pressure from the outside, NGOs work from within to undermine the powers of the state.

Where do Bangladeshi NGOs fit into the global structure of the NGO movement? A 1996 World Bank Report called Bangladeshi NGOs "one of the most effective agents of change in the 21st century" (World Bank Report 1996:5). NGOs in Bangladesh service over twenty-four million people in seventy-eight percent of the 65,000 villages in the country (World Bank Report 1996:5). They cover a wide spectrum of ideologies from modernist to free-market to feminist to Islamist and they offer a wide array of services from reproductive healthcare to microcredit to non-formal primary education to voter education. Bangladeshi NGOs have made impressive strides in microcredit, non-formal primary education, child immunizations, diarrhea preventative saline formulas, sanitation, reproductive healthcare, potable water provisioning, and voter education, for example. However, Bangladeshi NGOs are best known for their work in microcredit made popular by the Grameen Bank, the poster child of the World Bank and the United Nations.

With over 2.3 million borrowers of whom ninety-four percent are women, and a much celebrated ninety-eight percent rate of loan recovery, the Grameen Bank has provided the world financial community with the following seductive information:

a. The poor have debt and the poor pay their debt.
b. The poor are willing to pay a high price for their debt.
c. The Bank should go to the poor.

It should be mentioned here that this "ninety-eight percent rate of return" does not tell the reader how the money is *recovered* from its poor borrowers. In my research I found that the money is often recovered through intimidation, force, and violence against poor female members. I discuss this point in a subsequent section.

The Grameen model has provided data for the replication of microcredit on a global scale. At the 1995 Beijing Conference on Women, the Bank was upheld as a model for the economic empowerment of women to be replicated globally. Following the Summit, the World Bank opened the Consultative Group for the Assistance to the Poorest (CGAP) to assist in the replication of the Grameen model and to provide more credit to the poor in developing countries. In 1997, the Microcredit World Summit was held in Washington, DC where the Grameen model was again the centerpiece of discussion. The key resolution at the Summit was to provide microcredit to 100 million of the world's poor, and especially to poor women, by the year 2005.

By promoting a minimalist approach to credit – the borrower knows best – Grameen Bank has introduced ideas of self-help, individualism, and small entrepreneurship into the development community. Add to that the image of a poor Bangladeshi woman who, with only the Bank as her ally, transforms her life and becomes a small trader selling chickens and eggs. The Grameen approach promotes the neoliberal philosophy of a rolled back state by stressing that the individual knows best and is responsible for herself. It is no coincidence then that the Grameen Bank begins to get considerable attention from the world community in the late 1980s when privatization and neoliberal ideas of the state also gain ground globally.

NGOs in Contemporary Bangladesh

Through their programs and links to Western donor nations, NGOs continue to play a very prominent role in national politics. It is important to add here that I do not analyze the current national politics in Bangladesh which is played out between the two major political parties, the Awami League (AL) and the Bangladesh Nationalist Party (BNP).[3] With over 1,200 directly foreign funded NGOs[4] and with 13,000 registered NGOs, Bangladesh has emerged on the development map as the "NGO capital of the world." The trend to funnel donor money through the NGOs is very evident in Bangladesh. Most of the financing to NGOs comes as grants-in-aid (World Bank Report 1996:43). Figures from the NGO Affairs Bureau (NGOAB) reveal that between 1990 and August 1998 the cumulative amount of foreign funds disbursed through the Bureau stood at Tk. 1,364,421,079 for 5096 NGO projects. When the Bureau was first established in 1990, its annual disbursement stood at Tk. 217,169,685 for 8 projects. (Tk.=Taka, the unit of currency in Bangladesh.) In 1994–95, twenty percent of foreign funds earmarked for public investment was disbursed through NGOs (World Bank Report 1996:6). In 1997, the EU channeled twenty-five percent of its aid to Bangladesh (480 million ECUs) through the NGO sector.

It is evident from the above that NGOs in Bangladesh are highly dependent on donor funds for the sustainability of their projects. It is important to note, however, that foreign aid is channeled through the large NGOs. A 1992 study revealed that only 30 large NGOs in Bangladesh get eighty percent of the total foreign funds given to NGOs and of that sixty percent was controlled by the eight largest NGOs (BRAC, Proshika, CARITAS, CCDB, ASA, Gano Shahajya Sangstha,[5] Nijera Kori, Ganoshasthya Kendro) (World Bank 1996:45). Such visibility, resources, and support from Western donor agencies give the leading NGOs tremendous power to effect changes in the lives of most people they work with. This funding structure has created a pyramid structure within the NGO community, leaving the large bulk of the smaller NGOs dependent on the largesse and growth of the ten or so large NGOs.[6] From a donor perspective channeling money through a few dedicated NGOs maintains a streamlined and rigid structure of accountability. This ability to control such large quantities of money has allowed people associated with the ten largest NGOs to become a new class of social elites.

In a country with a very high unemployment rate, the leading NGOs offer the promise of jobs to the youth and the educated middle class. It is estimated that these NGOs employ 200,000 young men and women as fieldworkers. The NGOs have also introduced some novel ideas into rural communities. NGOs recruit college-educated men and women to work at the field level. In contrast to the government bureaucrat who seldom goes for field visits, the educated NGO worker comes in daily contact with the villagers, visiting them in their homes. According to Hashemi, "this going to the poor breaks down some of the threatening distance between the urban educated and the poor, that is so much a part of rural social stratification" (Hashemi 1997b:4). In reality, it introduces a new power elite into the existing dynamic of rural social relations. This power elite symbolizes the onrush of modern ideas and capital into the rural economy. BRAC and Proshika have also introduced some radical ideas about women in rural culture. Women fieldworkers of these NGOs ride bicycles and motorbikes to work in a traditional Muslim society where the public conduct of women is still strictly regulated. Compared to the NGO bureaucrats working in Dhaka, the NGO fieldworkers[7] have an unenviable position. They work six days a week with only one day off. Their day usually begins at 7:00 a.m. when they have to report for work. The work day normally stretches well into the night, often until 9:00 or 10:00 p.m. Most of the fieldworkers I interviewed said that the only reason they worked for the NGO was because of the "specter of unemployment."

Another group of key people inducted into the NGO structure are local research consultants, the producers of "scientific" knowledge. University professors and researchers who work as consultants on NGO projects enjoy considerable privileges in a materially impoverished country. In fact, working as a consultant on an NGO project is a source of much needed additional income for middle-class people. Salaries of university professors cover the costs of minimal living standards in Dhaka. NGO income provides one with access to better housing, healthcare, private schooling for children, automobiles, that is, to all the accoutrements of status in a poor country. The "professor as NGO consultant" situation has become so serious that the authorities of Dhaka University issued an official warning to professors who spend their time as "consultants" on various NGO projects instead of discharging their duties to the university.[8] For example, one of the leading NGO research institutions gave a local university professor one-year project funding for US$15,000. The annual salary of the university professor was US$3,000. These lavish contracts function as a way of creating, and at the same time cementing, new dependencies between the NGO and a cohort of local consultants.[9] It must be mentioned here that these figures pale next to what Western consultants earn who often have neither local language skills nor cultural familiarity, but who nonetheless pass off as "experts" by virtue of being citizens of the grant-giving donor nation. It is *really* the donors who seek such poverty research monographs and create a new need for knowledge about the poor (BRAC Research 1998; Doriddo Gobeshona Sharangsho 1998). All the leading NGOs – BRAC, Proshika, and Grameen Bank – have their own research institutions. They pay local NGOs handsomely to do so. The donors, in turn, need such data about the efficacy of different aid programs to justify to their governments the ongoing need for grants to Bangladesh. Within the development industry, the sustenance of the donor community depends on the continuance of these grants to the developing countries.

A new group of people becoming inducted into the NGO structure are high-ranking government bureaucrats. In the 1990s the World Bank, Asian Development Bank, and several Western donor agencies began to foster government–NGO relations in all sectors of the economy locally. One such partnership is the GO–NGO Consultative Council (GNCC). GNCC is a group that facilitates "better under-standing" and "complementarity" between the government and the NGO sector (Dutta 1999). Through GNCC, large NGOs (BRAC, Proshika, and others) have set up liaisons with the govern-ment by rotating government officials on two- to three-year deputations at the NGO headquarters. This liaison resolves conflicts arising between the NGO and the state. These officers enjoy all the perks of high-ranking NGO bureaucrats, including handsome salaries, company cars, and travel to donor countries to attend meetings and seminars.[10] In fact such close collaboration makes one wonder if Kofi Annan's comment "the raison d'être of the NGOs to hold the government's feet to the fire" has in this context changed into a golden handshake between the government and the NGO establishment.

The result of such NGO patronage is that it can tie up the future and livelihoods of a key group of people – academics, college-educated youth, and, more recently, government officials, who would have been their most likely critics – into its own maintenance and reproduction. This induction of the educated middle class into the NGO circuit is an unexpected conjuncture between the growth process of an institution in need of English-educated talent and a country with a small group of English-educated people.[11] Moreover, the structure of social dynamics in Bangladesh, which is kin-based and face-to-face, makes it difficult for criticisms of NGOs to emerge in the urban research spaces. In such societies manners are a way of conducting business, embarrassment is generally avoided, and people *do not* openly criticize those on whom they have to depend on for future favors.

While the NGO establishment has been able to induct certain groups of people into its structure, there is nonetheless a growing and robust critique of the activities of NGOs among people who are left-identified, students, and those professionals (doctors, engineers, business people, teachers) who are not part of the NGO network. Among the complaints of these critics are: that the NGO bureaucrats are not elected representatives of the people: that their operations are not transparent; that they do not pay taxes to the government although many of them have profitable commercial enterprises;[12] that they are beholden to their financial sponsors who happen to be Western industrialized nations, and thus, even if well intentioned, their programs are straitjacketed by the demands of their sponsors.[13]

History of NGOs

In 1972, war-torn Bangladesh faced the heavy task of relief and rehabilitation. Prior to independence in 1971, most of the NGOs were Christian or foreign-based voluntary organizations. In the post-independence phase, indigenous NGOs such as BRAC, Proshika, Ganoshastho Kendro (GK), Gono Shahajya Sangstha (GSS, now defunct), Nijera Kori, Grameen Bank, and the Association for Social Advancement (ASA) began to grow. In the aftermath of the war of 1971, the government faced the formidable task of resettling at least ten million people with the physical infrastructure of the country in shambles. The departing Pakistani army had blown up bridges, highways, and rail tracks, thus disconnecting various parts of the country. The developmental NGO occupied this infrastructural vacuum and began its work in charitable reconstructive efforts. Its ethos came from a missionary sense of "doing good" for the poor – landless and marginal farmers, women, and children – combined with a sense of patriotism. The real growth and expansion of NGOs occurred during the 1980s under the military dictatorship of General Ershad. In the 1970s and early 1980s there had been a rise in secret societies and left politics in Bangladesh. By supporting the growth of the NGO establishment, General Ershad effectively bifurcated the left by introducing a resource rich organization to work with the poor. The left and the NGO sector both fought over the same clientele, the rural poor. In fact, one of the top NGO leaders in Bangladesh, Dr Zafarullah of Ganoshastho Kendro is reputed to have said, "Now we NGOs can do the job. We do not need the left." Many former cadres of the communist parties joined NGOs as a way of helping the poor. A former communist party activist who had done grassroots political organizing in villages said in an interview, "During this time we had constant fights with the NGOs. We would go to the villages and find out that the NGO workers had urged villagers not to come to our meetings. NGOs did anti-left propaganda. They would tell villagers, why go to them? What can they give you? Thus instead of fighting the military state, we fought the NGOs who we saw as depoliticizing our work."[14]

By establishing a good working relationship with the NGO sector, General Ershad attempted to legitimize his rule as a benevolent dictator. He courted the NGO sector as a countervailing force to the major nationalist political parties. BNP and Awami League, that opposed his party (Jatiya Party) and military rule on the one hand, and the left parties on the other. By doing so, he also satisfied the demands of the donors by allowing the NGOs to carry on relief and rehabilitation efforts quite unhampered. During Ershad's rule the routinization of NGO operations began. In 1990 he opened the NGO Affairs Bureau (NGOAB) to oversee the flow of foreign funds to NGOs.

However, by 1990 the NGO lobby shifted allegiance away from Ershad and formed an alliance with the national political parties (Awami League and Bangladesh Nationalist Party) that were trying to oust him from power. This shift in alliance coincided with the new policy agenda of donors that now favored trade liberalization and democratic governance (Feldman 1997:59; Lewis 1997:36). The emphasis on "good governance" opened up a vacuum in the political space that the NGOs could occupy as the "allies of the poor." This shift in donor emphasis as well as changes in national politics offered them an additional site of action – the local political structure. In contrast to the 1980s when they fought the rural power structure on their own, in the 1990s NGOs could depend on support from donors interested in good governance issues (USAID, CIDA) and from the national parties that see NGOs as huge vote banks. The transition to democracy also resulted in the open politicization of NGOs and bifurcation of NGOs along national party lines. In spite of registration laws that do not allow them to participate in politics, the NGOs have become increasingly political, even if it is true that there is no unified vision of what the role of NGOs should be in national-level politics. Proshika advocates a proactive political role for NGOs, terming it as a duty of NGOs to help the poor in their struggle against rural oppression and disenfranchisement. In 1997

Proshika/Nijera Kori formed an institutional alliance which sponsored 44,138 women candidates for 12,894 Union Council seats and 12,822 of these candidates won (*Adhuna* 1997:19) The Union Council is the lowest tier of government at the village level. Each Union Council has nine members; three of those member seats are reserved for women candidates. This huge win was rendered in the press as a triumph of the feminization of rural power structure.

On the ground, however, such triumphs have very different resonances. In my study area. I interviewed four Proshika-sponsored women who had successfully run for public office. Fearing a loss of power, their husbands had asked their wives to run for local political office under Proshika sponsorship. I also met several men who had joined Proshika in 1996 to use its resources to run in the upcoming Union Council elections. All of these women and men were middle-class people who had joined the ranks of the NGO to improve their lives both materially and politically. These people representing the rural power structure were creative in appropriating the goals of Proshika for their own political purposes. It remains to be seen how these compositional changes affect rural power structures in the future.

Politics, Credit, and Emergent Identities

The four leading NGOs – Proshika, BRAC, ASA, and Grameen Bank – all work with microcredit. As mentioned earlier, debt is a powerful dynamic in culture because it creates relations of dependence. Debt also links the present and future together. Present behavior determines future payoffs. Restructuring local social relations through debt relations has had adverse effects on the ability of the poor to fight NGO-imposed conditions that often go against local norms. Stakes in dependent social relations that are market-driven can and do erode other forms of political expression.

Speaking of this trend. Professor Badruddin Umar, the party leader of *Bangladesh Kheth-Majoor Union* (Bangladesh Agricultural Workers Union), said.

NGOs provide employment: they do not generate employment. It is not that kind of process.... It exploits the situation of unemployed youths in our country and creates conditions that do not allow for other forms of recruitment, political recruitment for example, from occurring. To rural people, they (NGOs) preach a kind of economism instead of a political progressive consciousness. Their goal is the extension of credit instead of industrial development. In this way, political outlook is hijacked. Rural people say to us, political party organizers, "NGOs give us money, what will you give us?" When I go to the villages. I tell people I cannot give you money or loans. I can tell you of ways in which you can improve your conditions. That's not much anymore. People are now disinterested in hearing such talk.[15]

While I was in the field, local villagers would often ask me whether I represented an NGO and had come to give them *reen* (loans). In my eighteen months of research, not a single person once asked me if I were going to open an NGO school or provide them with healthcare, sanitation, or organize them into groups for training. Such anecdotal evidence goes to show to what extent loans have become associated with NGO work in the lives of local people, and how credit has come to govern their world of imaginative possibilities.

There are both practical and ideological implications of this widespread work in credit/debt-based programs. The program model of group formation ties individual behavior with group responsibility. Failure to pay a loan on the part of any member results in the NGO putting pressure on the group, either by withholding future loans or by forcing the remaining members to pay up for the defaulting member. In turn, the group members put pressure on the defaulting member and force her to come up with the money even if it means selling her possessions and in extreme cases selling off her house to pay for the loans (Karim 1998; Rahman 1999). It is a vicious cycle of pressure emanating from a closed circuit of dependent relations and offering no way out to the defaulting member. In my research I found that ninety percent of the loaned money went to the men. Women usually default when their husbands, who are the end users of loans, cannot pay their installments due to sickness, theft, business failure, or a natural calamity. The women are the bearers of credit although not its users. The NGO uses a woman's social vulnerability – her powerlessness to fight them or to run away from the village (the way a man can) – to recover money. In every meeting I found four or five members who were unable to pay their loan installments. As a result, the prevailing situation among group members is one of strife and not one of solidarity.

Many NGO field-workers who force the women to find means of recovering money are deeply uncomfortable about their role in masterminding these conflicts, but they see no way out of the situation. Below is a comment from a manager of a leading NGO in the area in which I conducted my research.

> I joined the NGO to help the poor. But are we helping the poor? No, I don't think so. We are committing *julum* (oppression) on the poor. I don't see any improvement among the poor. When they cannot pay their loans on time, we force them to pay up even if they have to sell possessions, sometimes even taking the rice from the mouths of their children. Once in a while I help them from my own pocket. It is against NGO regulations. But what can I do? If I could get another job, I would give this up in an instant. I am here because of unemployment.[16]

Microcredit, by providing inputs to the individual, creates the out-of-the-home worker. The lending process isolates women as individual entrepreneurs and introduces competition, self-interest, and individualism into their networks of social relations. Those women engaged in income-generating projects (e.g., chick rearing) do not think of themselves as laborers but as owners of petty capital. For example, when I interviewed these women about the costs of production, they did not include their labor time as part of the cost of production. Credit relations has the capacity to mystify the real relations of capital ownership. But, as already stated, failure to keep up the loan payments results in the confiscation of goods by the NGO, leaving these women worse off.

Another effect of microcredit is the reproduction of usury in culture. In my research area I found that fifty percent of women borrowers of microcredit who lived close to the market, usually lend out the money to small traders at a rate of 120%, which is the going rate for the village moneylender. In one of my study villages, 100 households out of 230 NGO beneficiary households were engaged in moneylending. The small traders need cash capital, and they can invest it in a productive base. In the rural economy, there are few opportunities to invest and poor women do not have the skills or access to markets or other institutional structures that would enable them to invest in a productive base. Money lending becomes a smart option for women, because they can lend without leaving their homes. Among women this activity is not considered as "*shudh*" (moneylending) but as "*taka khatai*" (we invest money). Money is seen as an investable commodity and not just as a means of commodity exchange. Before the onrush of microcredit, *taka dhaar* (to loan money without interest) was a common practice in the villages. The lender knew the borrower and would extend loans based on social knowledge. These were usually small sums of money. Now social relations are mediated through relations of power negotiated through debt. Such extensive moneylending through formal NGOs and informal borrower lending structures has resulted in making NGOs less willing to advocate social justice issues that conflict with community norms because they do not want to hurt their money lending business. The NGO beneficiaries are also less willing to engage in political activities that may disturb the status quo because they are in debt to others. But as the following example shows, women are quite powerless to fight the NGO when it seeks them out as targets of social mobilization programs.

Proshika, however, has taken a different approach from the other credit organizations in this respect. Since 1997 it has taken an active role in promoting a politics of the poor. In this emergent NGO-led politics, the struggle against poverty and social justice becomes a struggle against militant Islamic groups. Proshika, which has a close relationship with the party in power, Awami League, conducts this politics under a nationalistic discourse called *shadhinatar juddher chetona*, a politics geared towards establishing the promises of the independence struggle of 1971. The following section reveals the limitations inherent in such a rhetoric.

The Deployment of Poor Women as Political Subjects

On December 7, 1998, between 8,000 and 10,000[17] poor women and men who were members of Trinomul Sangathan (the grassroots organization of ADAB which is now controlled by Proshika) marched into Brahmanbaria town around 12:45 p.m. to attend a rally ostensibly to commemorate the spirit of the war of independence of Bangladesh. The sponsors of the rally (Proshika/ADAB) had originally planned a *mela* (fair) that would feature patriotic songs, a puppet show, rural handicrafts, and vegetables. The clergy of the local madrassah, the Jamia Islamia Yunusia Madrassah, had repeatedly warned Proshika that a rally of "*nogno* women" (*nogno* means bare, here bare means baring it all without shame or modesty) would not be allowed in Brahmanbaria and threatened carnage and mayhem if they dared to do so. According to the madrassah clergy, women's rallies are un-Islamic and the commingling of non-kin men and women is strictly forbidden in Islam. The clergy also objected to a puppet show, which they considered to be a form of idolatry.

As the conflict between Proshika and the local clergy over the right of women to participate in a public rally intensified, the local administration sided with the clergy and declared a ban on any rallies in town. For reasons unknown, the Proshika leadership under Qazi Faruque offered a direct challenge to the clergy. Faruque, along with top women NGO bureaucrats, led the slogan-chanting procession of 8,000 women and men into town. They went past the madrassah and congregated at a local college ground. Soon youths and clergy belonging to the Yunusia Madrassah attacked the rally with stones, sharp sticks, and knives.

They tore down the stage, chased away the bureaucrats, beat and publicly humiliated the women attendees. They tore off their clothes and verbally abused them. For a day and a half total lawlessness reigned in the city. Hordes of men carrying knives, Chinese axes, and sharp sticks roamed the streets burning and looting NGO and commercial property. They burned BRAC, Proshika, and Grameen Bank offices, and torched BRAC and Proshika schools. Homes of at least 200 NGO members were looted and burned.

When many of the assaulted women returned to their villages, their husbands/families refused to take them back because they had been touched by other men. When they could return home, they were subjected to taunts and physical abuse. These women were triply violated: once by the clergy, then by their community, and finally by Proshika, which had failed to offer them any protection.

The motivations of the clergy are not the focus of this paper. It should be noted though that as the guardians of Islamic laws and morality in Brahmanbaria, they could not let a rally of women right in front of their madrassah go unchallenged. For purposes of this paper, I want to consider the motivations of Proshika. *Why did Proshika hold the rally when they could not guarantee the safety of the poor women assembled?* For Proshika the conflict was reduced to a management issue, a technical issue of how to forecast and manage such conflicts in the future.[18] In the aftermath of the conflict, Proshika, through ADAB, held conferences and seminars on the rise of Islamic fundamentalism and called this event a "social disaster." ADAB officials informed me that other social ills – black-marketing, killings, cheating on national exams – do not fall under this category. This category "social disaster" targets Islamic militants who stand in opposition to the NGO's way of doing things. In the public forum, Proshika leadership interpreted the Brahmanbaria incident as an attempt by militant Islam to threaten secular forces in the country and to establish a Taliban-style government in Bangladesh. While the first point is true, there is little evidence to support the second point.[19] Most Bangladeshis say these Taliban conspiracy tales are manufactured for Western donor consumption and they dismiss them as "nonsense." This storytelling of Islamic militancy is a powerful rhetorical device to find sympathetic allies within the donor community at a time the West has discovered Osama Bin Laden and the Talibans as the forces of evil. Not surprisingly, the Canadian Aid Organization (CIDA is the primary sponsor of Proshika) lauded Proshika as a stalwart fighter against "Islamic fundamentalism."

In this strident NGO rhetoric of democratic rights of the poor, it was forgotten that the poor women in question were not fully informed and willing agents of such actions. Through their entrapment in debt relations to Proshika, they were forced to attend this rally. I interviewed about twenty women who had attended the rally. These women did not know of the controversy surrounding the fair, nor were they told that the fair had been changed to a rally, and had they known of the falwa they would not have attended. The women said they went to the rally because they were obligated to by Proshika and feared the "loss of future loans," and they wanted to see the "puppet show." They also said that they "went to see Faruque Bhai and other important people from Dhaka." The husbands of these women and several male community leaders noted that "Proshika has no business taking our women to marches." Many of these husbands asked their wives to go to the rally because they feared the loss of loans.

What did the fair mean to these women? It meant a day off from the daily grind of their lives. Going to a fair becomes a special day when they can put on nice clothes, watch puppet shows, and have some time off from their in-laws, husbands, and children. In the clientist culture of Bangladesh, rich and important folks coming to visit them is an acknowledgment of their importance as people and this must not be understated. As several women said to me. "Rich people are coming to see us, and we will not go. How can that be?" For many of these women the rally was also a *darshan* – a pilgrimage to pay respects to a holy man, Qazi Faruque, who as the new patron occupied this role in their worldview.

In the late 1990s, the Proshika/ADAB alliance conducted this politics of the poor under the rubric of "*shadhinotar juddher chetona*" (spirit of the struggle of freedom) and called for an end to "Islamic fundamentalism" in the country. Coincidentally, this new mosaic in NGO politics occurs at a time when the U.S. and the Western nations have discovered the Taliban government as the new threat to democracy in the world. Conflicts between NGOs and the clergy are usually the result of local power struggles and are not part of international conspiracy theories. By conflating issues of social and economic justice with Islam and a nationalist discourse that emanated from the freedom struggle of 1971, such politics gets constrained by the limits of these conceptual frames. Bangladeshi nationalism emerged from the concerns of middle-class Bangladeshis and their struggle against Pakistani cultural, political, and economic domination. This nationalism did not address the needs of rural people nor did it have a well-developed plan of economic transformation. The "spirit of the liberation struggle" in its most utopian ideal was the establishment of a *Sonar Bangla* – a golden Bengal that existed in some mythical past when Bengal was a land of abundance. By invoking this discourse, Proshika plays into the nationalist politics of Awami League that claims to be the makers of this history of Bengalis' struggle for freedom. It also uses this rhetoric of the freedom struggle to carry out a frontal attack on the militant Islamic[20] groups in the country. These Islamic groups in varying degrees oppose the work of NGOs, especially in relation to women's participation in the public sphere. Fighting Islamic militancy on the one hand, and making the ideational framework of the liberation struggle meaningful to the lives of the majority of Bangladeshis on the other, are noteworthy efforts. However, Proshika engages in this nationalism-inflected politics of the poor through its power over the lives of its borrowers and erodes their ability to determine their own stakes in such issues. In doing so, it shifts the costs of social adjustments to the poor, and ends up by using the poor women as shock troops against forces that stand in its way.

The trajectory that the NGO movement has followed in Bangladesh is peculiar to its specific history. NGOs elsewhere will have different stories of empowerment and struggles to narrate. I analyzed here how debt relations introduced through the lending policies of microcredit NGOs have resulted in new instruments of control over targeted groups, such as poor women. Through extensive lending practices, these NGOs have brought poor women into new webs of social and financial

obligations. Once inside these networks, it is difficult for poor people to resist because NGOs offer them money and other needed services. Women, who are supposed to be the beneficiaries of NGO programs, are often victimized by NGO policies on multiple levels, from loan repayments to becoming deployed as political subjects to achieve the goals of an NGO leader. In the context of Bangladesh, it is both timely and necessary for such stock-taking of NGO operations to occur because of their ability to invent themselves as the saviors of the poor.

Notes

1 See the websites of the UN and World Bank for a list of NGO related programs.
2 See http://www.undp.org.fj/docs/news/un-ngos .htm. Annan, Kofi. "Secretary General calls partnership of NGOs, private sector, international organizations and governments powerful partnership for future."
3 AL is associated with the independence of Bangladesh. Its founder, Sheikh Mujibur Rahman, was the first Prime Minister of the country. He was later assassinated in a military putsch. AL is considered to be a more pro-Bengali nationalist party. The widow of the assassinated military leader, General Ziaur Rahman, leads BNP. Ideologically, BNP is aligned with Islamic nationalism. High levels of corruption, inefficiency, nepotism, ballot-stealing, and banditry characterize politics in Bangladesh and make a mockery of the basic democratic rights of its citizens. Locally, it is called the politics of *goonda-giri*, that is, the politics of musclemen and rent-seekers.
4 NGOAffairs Bureau figures as of August 1998.
5 GSS is now defunct and exists in name only. Allegations of sexual harassment were brought against its leader, Mahmudul Hasan, who was a leader in the NGO-led civil society initiative in Bangladesh. A donor representative told me that German donors did not like his political work and helped to bring him down.
6 NGOs in Bangladesh vary in size from 23,000 full-time employees (BRAC) to a one-person NGO (*Kormojibi Nari*). Starting an NGO is an attractive option for people because (a) it has

tax-exempt status; and (b) it is a way of making money.
7 Here I collectively refer to the fieldworkers of BRAC, Grameen Bank, ASA, and Proshika.
8 *Bhorer Kajog*. "Dhaka University takes initiative to halt consultancy business and part-time job of teachers." April 12, 1999.
9 While I was conducting my fieldwork, I had occasion to both witness how such grants are arbitrated and heard of many such perks being distributed by NGOs to their friends.
10 In Bangladesh where travel to foreign countries is prohibitively expensive, the opportunity to travel abroad is a much desired perk.
11 After independence in 1971, in keeping with the demands of Bengali nationalists, Bengali was made the national language of the country and the medium of language instruction was changed to Bengali.
12 In this respect BRAC is a good example. It runs Aarong, a handicraft store, which is a commercial venture. BRAC and Proshika both have commercial presses. These two NGOs have plans to open private universities soon. Increasingly, these large NGOs are taking up multiple commercial ventures for which they do not pay taxes.
13 A good example of this debate was carried in *Dhaka Courier* in its August–October issues (1989).
14 Interview with Tanvir Mokammel, former communist activist and filmmaker.
15 Interview with Professor Badruddin Umar.
16 Conversation with a manager of a leading NGO.

17 This number is from the Special Human Rights Report written by Advocate Aksir Ahmed of Brahmanbaria. *Samaj Chetona* (a socialist weekly) gives the figure to be around 4,000–5,000. The correct figure probably falls somewhere in-between.

18 Jim Ferguson (1994) offers a detailed critique of the reduction of poverty to a technical and management issue in *The Anti-Politics Machine*.

19 This point is based on my conversation with a cross-section of people in Brahmanbaria and Dhaka.

20 While there are many militant Islamic groups in Bangladesh, the *Islamic Oikyo Jote*, an alliance of several parties, is their most formidable opponent.

References

Adhuna 1997 "Grassroots Democracy." Year 7, no. 1 (Oct.-Dec.).

BRAC 1998 "Abstracts of Reports and Papers completed in 1998." In *BRAC Research*. Dhaka: BRAC Publishers.

Dutta, Aroma 1999 "A Brief History of NGO Development in Bangladesh." http://www2.worldbank.org/hm/participate/0076.html. p.2.

Feldman, Shelley 1997 "NGOs and Civil Society: (Un)stated Contradictions." In *The Role of NGOs: Charity and Empowerment*. Jude Fernando and Alan Heston. eds. *Annals of the American Academy of Political and Social Science*. Vol 554. November.

Ferguson, James 1994 *The Anti-Politics Machine: "Development," Depoliticization and Bureaucratic Power in Lesotho*. Minneapolis: University of Minnesota Press.

Grameen Poverty Research 1998 *Doriddo Gobeshona Sharangsho (Poverty Research Summaries)*. Dhaka: Grameen Trust Publications.

Hashemi, Syed M. 1997b "NGOs-State Relations in Bangladesh." Paper presented at the conference on NGOs in Aid: A Reappraisal of 20 Years of NGO Assistance, Bergen, Norway.

Hardt, Michael and Antonio Negri 1997 "Mixed Constitutions." In *Empire*. pp. 304–332. Cambridge: Harvard University Press.

Karim, Lamia 1998 "Women as Money Make the World Go Round." Paper presented at the Annual Anthropological Meetings in Philadelphia, December 2–6.

Lewis, David 1997 "NGOs, Donors and State in Bangladesh." In The Role of NGOs: Charity and Empowerment. Jude Fernando and Alan Heston, eds. *Annals of the American Academy of Political and Social Science*. vol. 554. November.

Proshika Activity Report 1997 *Freedom from Poverty: Another Step Forward*. July 1997-June 1998. IDRC Proshika: Dhaka 1998.

Rahman, Aminur 1997 "Microcredit Initiatives for Equitable and Sustainable Development? Who Pays?" *World Development* 27 (1): 67–82.

United Nations 1999 Human Development Report. New York: Oxford University Press.

World Bank Report 1996 *Pursuing Common Goals*. Dhaka: World Bank Publications.

23

The Politics of 'Developing Nepali Women'

Seira Tamang

Since 1990 and the advent of democracy, there has been an exponential growth in the forms and types of activities undertaken for the women of Nepal by state and non-state players. Consequently, the past 12 years of democracy appear to have been quite fruitful for women. For example, inadequate as they may be, laws and legal decisions have been made to ensure women's right to property, abortion and to their bodies (via a recent court decision on marital rape). Overall, advocacy on women's issues has been widely undertaken by the state, non-governmental organisations and the media. But, while there has been undeniable progress in some areas, these markers of change and their contexts need to be studied carefully in order to more fully gauge their successes, limitations and contradictions. More specifically, it is necessary to situate the initiatives undertaken in the name of women within the historical context of nationalist imperatives sponsored by the Panchayati state, and its legacies that remain with us to this day. Such a perspective reveals that the particular project

of *bikas* – development – has compounded the structured inequalities relating to class and ethnicity, and it has erased the heterogeneity of women's lived experiences in Nepal. The project of development has furthermore also enabled the co-option of women's activism.

Anthropological works on Nepal, while to some extent complicit in the construction of state-sponsored identity and other categories, have been helpful in pointing out the heterogeneity of the country's population and the very different manner in which the different groups structure relations between men and women. It becomes clear from these studies that a huge variety of 'gendered norms' exist. To take the most well-known examples, orthodox Hindu groups emphasise the sexual purity of women; Thakali and Sherpa communities take pride in the business acumen and marketing abilities of their females; and Tibetan-origin groups inhabiting the northern rimland of Nepal practise polyandrous marriage. It is clear that not all women in Nepal have been sequestered in the realm of the domestic, nor has wage-labour,

Perspectives on Modern South Asia: A Reader in Culture, History, and Representation, First Edition.
Edited by Kamala Visweswaran.
© 2011 Blackwell Publishing Ltd. Published 2011 by Blackwell Publishing Ltd.

business and other realms of 'the public' been uniformly imagined only as masculine; neither has the sexuality of women been consistently and narrowly regimented.

It is also clear that the cultural and social norms of these many groups are not ahistorical and unchanging. Amidst the complex interplay of socio-economic and political forces, the necessity for adaptation has led to changes in the way in which men and women play their social roles within their different communities.

Furthermore, in her book *On the Edge of the Auspicious: Gender and Caste in Nepal*, Mary Cameron reveals the manner in which changing economic forces have had both positive and negative ramifications for the 'low-caste' women of Bhalara in Bajhang District of Nepal's far-west. In the context of increasing poverty, dalit women have been gradually moving away from artisan-related production to paid agricultural and non-agricultural work. Becoming free labourers in the agricultural economy has meant that the security of the earlier inter-caste patron–client relationships has disappeared. On the other hand, a few of these women have gained economic power in their homes and communities, and in some cases, have even begun using the remittances of husbands working in India to make loans to 'high-caste' families in exchange for the use of land.

These examples serve to highlight the need to take account of ethnicity, caste, class and religion when discussing the lives of women in Nepal. While neither the existence of patriarchy nor discrimination against the women of Nepal is being denied, it is clear that different societal norms (informed by class, caste, ethnicity and religion) result in different definitions of 'masculine' and 'feminine'. Women from different communities experience different realities according to the dissimilar patriarchal arrangements within those communities. The roles played by men and women are certainly not uniform, and 'to be a woman' in Nepal will vary between, as well as within, variously defined societies. It may well be more productive to talk not of 'patriarchy' but multiple patriarchies. As the term 'gender' makes clear, rather than biological categories, men and women are

social and political categories that are produced historically.

The Gendered Politics of *Bikas*

The importance of understanding the nature of the historical construction of social and political categories is especially important given Nepal's specific history. During the Panchayat years (1961–1990), the Nepali state sought to impose and legitimate a hegemonic Hindu national culture by homogenising the ethnically and religiously heterogeneous population. Key to the legitimisation of Panchayat rule was the doctrine of 'development' – *bikas* – as '*the national project.*' The fortuitous conjuncture of the post-World War II global project of international development and the Panchayat elite's own need to legitimise itself led to massive injections of foreign assistance into Nepal. This enabled the expansion of infrastructure and state institutions, which in turn facilitated the dissemination of Panchayat ideology. This intertwining of the global and national agendas of development had important ramifications for the women of Nepal.

For, at the very time that the Panchayat government was seeking to impose its definition of 'the Nepali', the international project of development had set itself the task of developing 'the Nepali woman'. This linkage to development is essential to understanding the history of gender in the country. The creation of 'the Nepali woman' was as much the work of development agencies in search of 'the Nepali woman' to develop as it was the result of the active dissemination of state-sponsored ideology. The patriarchically oppressed, uniformly disadvantaged and Hindu, 'Nepali woman' as a category did not pre-exist the development project. She had to be constructed by ignoring the heterogeneous forms of community, social relations, and gendered realities of the various peoples inhabiting Nepal. This erasure of differences ensured an easy target population for development. It also simultaneously legitimised the creation of a single national culture based on Hindu norms extolled by the Panchayat regime. The fiction of 'the Nepali *mahila*' was thus an effect rather than a discovery of the institutions, practices and discourses of international development and *bikas*.[1]

An analysis of Panchayat-era training course syllabi, manuals and reports as well as journal articles produced by the Panchayat Training Materials Production Centre is revealing, for it tells us that Panchayati conceptions of the 'modern Nepali woman' involved an active feminisation and thus the narrowing of roles deemed acceptable and indeed necessary for the kingdom's women. The emphasis, in the name of *bikas*, was on the domestic roles of cooking, cleaning and working exclusively within the household; the more flexible gender roles prevalent within various ethnic groups were dichotomised to conform to Hindu notions of a strict division between the masculine realm of the public and the feminine realm of the private.

Both the Nepali state and international donors spearheaded the effort continuing to this day – to 'empower' the 'traditionally patri-archically bound, agency-less, Hindu Nepali women' (my iteration of a common phrase). The ongoing emphasis on the need to 'main-stream gender into development' misses the fact that *bikas* has actually always been 'gendered', being premised on women and men playing definite and defined roles. Post-1990 Nepal may have seen a change in individual state elites, but 'high-caste' Bahun and Chhetri hegemony continues to perpetuate the projected image of the 'Hindu Nepali' citizen. Although janajati activism by ethnic campaigners has weakened this construct somewhat, its ramifications in terms of the definition of gender roles remain unchallenged. It is in this context that one has to scrutinise the role of the leaders in women's issues in Nepal.

Nepali *Netris* and the Politics of Development

We know from example how women have been the vicarious recipients the world over of caste, ethnic and other privileges accorded to their husbands or fathers. In Nepal, both caste- and family-specific privileges have been central

in propelling women to leadership positions. A cursory glance at the names of speakers attending national and international conferences on women, writers of papers and articles, and leaders of various development training sessions during the Panchayat era, confirms the overwhelming presence of Bahun, Chhetri and, to some extent, Newar women in influential positions. Post-Panchayat Nepal has seen little change in the class, caste and ethnic composi-tion of the women in positions of leadership. This too can be seen from a simple perusal of the names of authors of papers, conference participants, members of various committee, and NGO leadership. Given their relatively privileged access to education and social and political networks, it has been 'upper-caste' Hindu women who are most advantageously positioned to take hold of employment as well as leadership opportunities.

The fact that employment opportunities in the post-1990 era have been mostly in the develop-ment arena, and more especially in 'women and development', has had further ramifications. Whether as 'expert consultant', office worker or field officer – categories created by the develop-ment apparatus – it has been these 'upper-caste' Hindu women who have performed the key role of 'native informants' for the non-Nepali speaking donor experts and aid bureaucrats. Unquestioned in their authority – being Nepali and being female – to produce information about 'Nepali women', the speeches, reports and other writings of these elite women reflect little, if any, acknowledgment of the relative positions of power and privilege from which they speak. These elite women's experience of being a woman in Nepal is circumscribed by a very specific ethnic, caste, class and religious milieu. Thus their ability to 'understand' the experience, wants and needs of other women living in Nepal under very different societal constraints is necessarily limited. Questions concerning middle-class, urban African and Asian scholars producing scholarship on or about their rural or working-class sisters which assumes their own middle-class/ethnic cultures as the norms have been raised elsewhere, such as by Chandra Talpade Mohanty. However, in

Nepal, these concerns have rarely been voiced and the *netris* (female leaders) continue to voice the wants and needs of 'Nepali women' unproblematically.

The continual use of the term 'Nepali women are...' and 'Nepali women need...' by these representatives helps create and propagate the omnipresent fictive 'Nepali *mahila*': uniformly poor, illiterate and choked by Hindu patriarchal domination, not to mention tradition and superstition. These being the conditions from which the netris themselves have presumably escaped, such portrayals further legitimise the elite women's representative and 'expert' role – to continue to speak 'for' the other women. As subjects of 'development', then, the women of Nepal are homogenised as those 'who do not know' and who are in need of having 'their consciousness raised'.

Whereas 'sisterhood is global' is the slogan of choice among Kathmandu-based women/gender and development offices, in the field the dynamics are somewhat different, and the arrival of the expert from the capital is far from being a 'sisterhood bonding' experience. Janajati women,[2] for example, relate stories of 'upper-caste' women from Kathmandu arriving in their villages armed with a list of the former's supposed 'needs', already pre-determined in 'the office'. The Gurung, Tamang or other janajati women are thought to be too uneducated to understand 'these things'. In 'participatory' gatherings, 'unapproved' remarks or concerns by janajati women are often met with stern glances or cutting remarks from the Bahun or Chhetri development worker as this writer discovered in the course of her research. Issues of internalised stereotypes aside, remarks by the janajati women such as – 'we are slow to understand and those Bahun women, who are so quick and *chalak*, boss us around' – reveal that these women are all too conscious of the power dynamics which define relations between development representatives and the rural ethnic women. This is more than what can be said for most consumers of women-and-development reports and speeches in the country.

Furthermore, such power dynamics are not restricted to the 'field'. As more janajati women enter the development workforce, encounters with Bahun and Chhetri women – invariably in higher positions of power within the offices – reveal the same hierarchical and repressive structures. Janajati women's own perceptions of critical issues pertaining to women of Nepal tend to be considered irrelevant or 'too political' to be presented to the higher echelons of power. This sieving process means that female gatekeepers deprive the donor agencies of a more heterogeneous, and indeed more problematic, picture of 'Nepali women'.

These hurdles in the field and at the Centre have deep implications for the manner in which policies for women are carried out. For example, in the much-debated struggle for women's property rights, little consideration was given to the implications of the property rights bill from the perspective of various ethnic and other communities. Consequently, the bill has neither been assessed in terms of its impact on the already existing informal access to property rights, nor in terms of its role in allowing the state to regulate social relations at the cost of the traditional authority exercised by the community. Thus, while theoretically a positive step for women's rights, the passage of the bill may well have unintended consequences that are more detrimental in the long run for many women in Nepal who do not fall within the narrowly defined category of 'the Nepali woman' implicitly understood as being 'Hindu' and 'upper caste'.

Controlling the Political

Concerns about giving more power to the state is important in reconceptualising the role played by the Nepali state. The state cannot be viewed simplistically, either as an obstacle to or as a channel for reforms. It must be seen as actively shaping not just gendered identities, but also the manner in which resistance to the state can be mounted. The following section reveals the manner in which state-initiated reforms on political actions during the Panchayat era served to actively demarcate what constitutes 'legitimate' and 'illegitimate' activities by women – demarcations that continue to inform current activist initiatives.

The Panchayat state systematically regulated non-governmental organisations in order to neutralise the potential for mass mobilisation. Not only political parties, but all organisations were controlled to ensure that they were free of anti-Panchayat political elements. The Nepal Women's Organisation (NWO) was one of the Panchayat's legally recognised six 'class organisations', and its main programme areas consisted of literacy, legal aid, skill development and family planning services. Cleansed of politically subversive elements, the NWO and the other organisations were actively used to legitimise the gendered Panchayat order.

In this context, the introduction of women-in-development (WID) by donor agencies in the 1970s served the ideological function of legitimising 'women-in-development' as defined by the Panchayat state. International backing with its concomitant prestige-laden values, enabled Panchayat elites to delegitimate 'political' concerns as 'anti-national'. In conjunction with the 'welfare' approach dominant in the global arena of development, the political dimensions of rights were subsumed under the rhetoric of *bikas* and emphasis was given to notions of service and 'the national good'.

Given this backdrop, it is not surprising that most issues continue to be framed in terms of 'development', 'uplift' and 'empowerment' in the development discourse for women in Nepal. The language of rights, with its political contours, has only recently crept into the activist rhetoric, with the coming to the fore of property rights and abortion issues. The idiom of 'rights' in the political arena defines women as autonomous, purposeful actors capable of making choices in the full knowledge of their legal and political personhood. However, dominant accounts of the under-valuation of women's work; the necessity of girl's education; domestic violence and the trafficking of women, to name a few examples, are framed in a language in which – very much according to the language of *bikas* – women are portrayed as agency-less subjects in need of assistance in order to fulfill their potential. Indeed, *bikas* is premised on the specific defining of women as not being full individuals, and not having the

capacity for free choice and self-development. Thus, rather than participants in their own advance, women become mere target populations. This outlook is only perpetuated by the elite female native informants and development consultants, for whom paternalistic empathy rather than solidarity defines their relations with their 'un-developed' sisters.

Reconsidering the manner in which gender and development have hitherto been understood in Nepal also necessitates a closer look at the term 'gender'.

The Mainstreaming of 'Gender' Reconceptualised

Much has already been written about the manner in which borrowed concepts and trendy development jargon enter Nepal, only to later dissipate meekly with the arrival of a later entrant. As far as the new development terminology is concerned, questions have also been raised not only about the relevance of using certain conceptual imports in the Nepali context but also whether the words and concepts being invoked have been properly understood by those using them. Some may argue that it is in the very nature of policies, projects and programmes that they require a certain simplification or pruning of complex theories in order to render their meanings more concise and 'implementable'. While that may be true to some extent, in the Nepali context the simplifications have resulted in a weakening of the political power of concepts as they are made to fit the discourse of *bikas* in a sanitised form.

It is significant, for instance, that while notions of 'women' and 'gender' have proliferated in the *bikas* discourse – as indicated in the abundant presence of phrases such as 'gender and development', 'women and governance', 'governance and gender equity', and 'gender and education', they have also been rendered interchangeable or synonymous. Analyses which use 'gender' as a concept appear no different from those using 'women'. Apart from an obligatory reference emphasising the difference between sex (a biological notion) and gender (a social construct), and, sometimes, a preamble concerning the historical march from WID (Women in Development) to WAD (Women and Development) to GAD (Gender and Development), the innumerable papers presented and reports written reveal no descriptive or analytical variation from the 'Status of Women in Nepal' volumes completed two decades ago. The latter, USAID-funded, volumes were doubtless ground-breaking insofar as such comprehensive research had not earlier been carried out on the general background and status of women in Nepal. However, written in the late 1970s and early 1980s, they were also firmly grounded in the WID tradition with its focus on women, their economic potential/contribution and the need for education and civil rights to overcome the 'irrationality' of prejudice and superstition which was said to hold back the innate rationality of women.

Since INGOs, NGOs and the various institutions 'doing' development require the requisite stamp of 'gender sensitivity', it is no surprise that 'gender' trainings, lectures and conceptual-clarity workshops have found a fertile market in Kathmandu. As with prepackaged vacation tours tailored to individual needs, these 'gender trainings' can run as easily for months and weeks as days or even half-day sessions. No minimum amount of 'training' appears to be stipulated in order to gain 'gender-trained' certification. Despite the plethora of such training activities, however, 'gender' continues to be a much misunderstood concept, with the so-called gender 'faculties' themselves often displaying confusion over the terminology. Consequently, even as the rhetoric of 'gender sensitisation' achieves near-universal appeal in Nepal, the concept itself has clearly lost its political potency.

Furthermore, the seemingly well-meaning emphases on gender 'equity', 'gender sensitivity' and a commitment to the 'gender' perspective in looking at various socio-economic issues actually translates into an insidious assertion of gender difference: namely, that women and men have different roles in society that need to be recognised and respected, counted, and so on. In other words, 'gender' as mediated by the discourse of *bikas*, is being used to forward claims for women qua *women*. There is no sense

here of a challenge to the conservative notion that women and men are somehow naturally suited to different tasks and activities. In other words, the constant reference to 'gender' is a convenient device to *essentialise* women, thus implicitly acknowledging an unchanging feminine essence that transcends the particularity of women's lives. This takes away from women's struggles to push back the boundaries of what has been defined as being 'naturally' feminine in order to reveal its socially constructed basis.

'Gender', as predominantly used in Nepal, does not question the origins of the roles of men and women, the power that lies behind the maintenance of those roles, and the socially constructed nature of the reality that presents the functions performed by men and women as 'natural', 'biologically derived' and 'timeless'. The lack of attention given to the historically constructed nature of categories such as 'woman' and the dominant focus of women's struggle against an unchanging, all-oppressive Hindu patriarchy reifies dominant social relations, making them appear immutable. What is ignored is that the specific form of 'traditional Hindu patriarchy' that exists in Nepal today is actually quite 'modern', traceable via legal and developmental activities to the attempts by the male, Hindu, Panchayat elites to construct unifying national narratives with which to legitimate their rule over a heterogeneous populace. The invention of 'tradition' has always been a key aspect of nationalist politics, whether as part of an anti-colonial struggle as in India or constitutive of a nationalist struggle to develop as in Nepal.

Furthermore, because of its 'constructedness', gender is never found in a 'pure' form. It is always interwoven with other social relationships and inequalities such as class and caste and ethnic identity and so on. In the face of caste prejudice and economic poverty, for example, dalit women face a very different form of oppression than affluent Hindu, 'high-caste' women. Indeed, dalit women may see patriarchy as being secondary in importance to the caste structures that oppress them and their menfolk. Equally, insofar as Hindu 'high-caste' women receive both the caste and class privileges of their father and husbands, they can be seen as being as culpable for the oppression of dalit women – a topic that has not even been touched in unreflexive accounts of 'the Nepali woman's' 'oppression' by 'women leaders'.

Clearly, the category of 'gender' and its implications has not been fully worked through in all its political dimensions by Nepalis thinkers and those in the development business. Posed in non-threatening and conservative modes of analysis, the potency of the idea that the roles of both Nepal's men and women have been historically malleable has been lost in much the same way that the edge of feminist politics in political transformation and mobilisation has been blunted. It is consequently important to take stock of the extent to which women's issues have been simplified, purged of the political, and de-historicised, and yet subsumed under the fashionable rubric of 'gender' over the last 12 years of democracy. In view of a general lack of independent research conducted outside the realm of the development theatre, and a co-option of many of the country's intellectuals into the *bikas* agenda, such analyses are even more crucial.

Women Who Know What They Want

Placing current initiatives within a historical context reveals a rather problematic picture of the post-1990 democratic period and its implications for women in Nepal. However, it is clear that alternatives to non-*bikas* feminist thought have existed in the past and continue to exist, as exemplified by the women's magazine, *Asmita*, and its promotion of the politics of transformation. It is also clear that women who have entered the newly-emerging public spheres, are beginning to find their voices and claiming constitutionally and internationally defined rights. These legal rights, while not sufficient in themselves, do hold the promise of a further democratisation of Nepali society and politics. Once a social right such as the right to property is granted to and defended by one group, for example, related rights can be more easily claimed by previously excluded peoples.

Despite limitations, international players do have a positive role to play in this endeavour. An international event such as, say, the United Nations Fourth World Conference on Women in Beijing in 1995, provides networking forums that strengthen the validity, force and impact of feminist claims within national boundaries.

It is nevertheless important that a rethinking of 'feminist' politics begin to take place within Nepal itself. Such re-conceptualisation needs to not only reclaim the political idioms of rights, but to acknowledge the multiple forms of patriarchies and oppression faced by women. As such, there is no one valid form of feminism; there are several. The recognition of difference in the priorities of different women's groups and movements should not be seen as necessarily endangering 'the feminist' movement, or as an insidious attempt to create divisions among women. On the contrary, this recognition of difference is crucial for the possibility of dialogue between women in their united struggles against patriarchies and discrimination, and in the re-working of gendered identities which might ultimately lead towards a more just and democratic Nepal.

All over the world, feminists have begun to think through a 'politics of solidarity in difference'. Such an orientation is premised on a 'grammar of political conduct' or a 'framework agreement' in which the process and not the outcome is valued, thus allowing different voices to be heard. Dialogue is emphasised, and identities and interests recognised to be fluid. Each participant brings into the conversation her own membership and identity, but is also able to shift her own orientation in order to understand women whose background and identity are different from her own. Such a method of building solidarities without erasing difference, it seems, is critical for the progress of women from Nepal's diverse communities.

Furthermore, most conservative challenges to women's rights are based on arguments of 'culture' and the concomitant 'threat' of the imposition of 'western feminist' thought on the nation. 'Tradition' and/or 'culture' is generally used to justify such gender inequalities as purdah, or women's inheritance rights. However, by understanding the very constructed nature of 'culture' and 'tradition' and thus the flexibility and variation of 'custom', this deployment of culture as a justification of gender inequalities can be challenged. For example, the idea that easy divorce for women is not acceptable in 'Nepali culture' and is an import from the West, can be challenged with references to divorce practices in the Limbu community. While taking care not to obscure the patriarchal structures within Limbu society, the consequent emphasis on the inherent flexibility of gender roles within 'Nepali culture', or more properly, 'cultures of Nepal', can open up spaces from which women from all communities are able to implement different remedial policies and strategies demanded by the different and diverse contexts in which they are situated.

'Culture', thus seen as 'open', 'flexible' and changing, also permits an understanding of the active role played by the state in defining 'culture'. Current feminist interventions in Nepal have consisted of viewing the state as merely obstructing women's attempts to secure their rights. The state has not been viewed as actively constructing gendered roles for women as an intrinsic part of the imposition of hegemonic notions of 'a Hindu Nepali culture'. An understanding of the role of power in dominant articulations of culture – at the level of the state and community – enables women to challenge notions of 'tradition' that would deny their own voices and the voices of others in shaping norms and values.

And lastly, connected to the above, much can be learnt by gender analysis that goes beyond the collection of sex-aggregated data which reveals the differential impact of development activities on women and the effect that gender roles and responsibilities have on development efforts. While quantitative gender analysis is necessary, it appears to be forgotten that it needs to be complemented by qualitative gender analyses. The latter, which is more time-consuming and thus in conflict with the ever-present time constraints of development deadlines, entails the tracing of historical, economic, social and cultural forces in order to clarify how and why these differential impact roles and responsibilities have come about. In such analyses and orientations lies the key to women seeking to expand their rights and democratic space in post-1990 Nepal.

Notes

1 In view of the fact that women's groups in Nepal were in existence since 1917, it can be argued that 'the Nepali woman' as a category was not so much created by 'development' and *bikas*, as given official legitimacy and wider dissemination. However, this essay argues that the notion of 'Nepali woman' prevalent today – the 'backward, illiterate, helpless Nepali *mahila*' – is qualitatively different from 'the Nepali woman' conceptualised in the social and *political* reform movement during the Rana period. It is the construction of 'Nepali *mahila*' in need of aid in order to develop that is the key.

2 While not the focus of my work, the experiences of lower caste women within these networks of gendered power relations would very likely reflect similar silencing hierarchies.

Further Readings

Acharya, Meena. 'Feminist Movement in Nepal.' Paper for Regional Seminar-Cum Workshop on Women and Media, August 9–15, 1993.

Adhikari, Shyam Prasad. 'Role of Women in Rural Development.' *Panchayat Darpan*, Year 15, Issue 1, 1984.

Cameron, Mary. *On the Edge of the Auspicious: Gender and Caste in Nepal*. Chicago: University of Illinois Press, 1998.

Devi, Leela. 'Home Science: A Strategy for Women Education.' *Education Quarterly* 23, 3&4, 1978.

Ekh Barseh Mahila Karyakartha Talimko Pathyakrum 2040–2041. Jawalakhel, Nepal: Mahila Prasikchan Kendra

Enslin, Elizabeth. 'Imagined Sisters: the Ambiguities of Women's Politics and Collective Actions.' In *Selves in Time and Place: Identities, Experience and History in Nepal*, Debra Skinner, Al Pach and Dorothy Holland (eds). Boulder: Rowman and Littlefield, 1998

Onta, Pratyoush. 'Ambivalence Denied: The Making of Rastriya Ithihas in Panchayat Era Textbooks.' In *Contributions to Nepalese Studies*, vol. 23 no. 1, 1996

Sen, Gita and Caren Grown. *Development, Crises, and Alternative Visions: Third World Women's Perspectives*. New York: Monthly Press, 1987

Tamang, Seira. 'Assembly-Line Sisters.' *Himal South Asian*, vol. 12 no. 9, 1999

———. 'Gender, State and Citizenship in Nepal.' PhD dissertation, American University, 2000

Upadhaya, Shizu. 'The Status of Women in Nepal – 15 Years On', *Studies in Nepali History and Society*, vol. 1 no. 2, 1996

24

"City of Whores"

Nationalism, Development, and Global Garment Workers in Sri Lanka

Sandya Hewamanne

Intersection of the Modern and Dangerous

The Colombo–Negombo highway runs past the entrance to the Japan–Sri Lanka Friendship Road, which leads to both the country's only international airport and the Katunayake Free Trade Zone (FTZ). This highway is considered one of the country's best and most dangerous arteries. The intercity buses speed along this road, almost always exceeding the legal speed limit. One of the most difficult tasks at the Katunayake FTZ is to cross this road. Vehicles do not stop or slow down, forcing hapless pedestrians to find the right gap between two vehicles to cross.

One day in August 1998, several FTZ worker friends and I had to wait a while at the pedestrian crossing before crossing the road. When we were well into the middle of the road we spotted a van coming at breakneck speed toward us, almost as if willing us to stop crossing and let it pass. While my friends started to back off, I

decided to show the driver that we had the right of way, and I pointed to the yellow crossing and stood my ground. The van skidded to a halt and the driver started yelling at us, using the filthiest words I have ever heard. I remember repeated references to "no-good whores."

My long-term field research in the area surrounding the Katunayake FTZ in 1999–2000 showed me that street vendors, shopkeepers, bus conductors, and even policemen often referred to FTZ working women as whores. It was not uncommon for FTZ workers walking in groups near the main bus terminal, the shopping plaza, or the night bazaar to find men asking for sexual favors in the most graphic terms. This understanding that FTZ workers, as a group, were women with loose morals was related to their position as young unmarried women who lived away from their families in an urban area and the unique way they negotiated city life. This also had much to do with the particular spatial and discursive production of the city as it intertwined with the

Perspectives on Modern South Asia: A Reader in Culture, History, and Representation, First Edition.
Edited by Kamala Visweswaran.
© 2011 Blackwell Publishing Ltd. Published 2011 by Blackwell Publishing Ltd.

discourses on nation, modernity, and female morality.

While Katunayake had not witnessed the same intensity of modernist industrialization as have some other cities in the world, it was nevertheless a space that had been intensely affected by structural adjustment programs. The rapid urbanization and industrialization of Katunayake, resulting from the transnational production at the FTZ and the related globalized sociocultural flows, affected the lived experiences of the people in this new urban space in varied ways. While neighbors reinvented themselves as the moral guardians of the FTZ's migrant women workers, many agents and institutions, including the media and NGOs, involved themselves in spatial and conceptual production of the new city and its gendered citizen subjects.

My article explores the fragmented production of the gendered and classed subjects within the particular modern-urban project of the Katunayake FTZ. The essay first focuses on the discursive production of Katunayake as a city and then analyzes NGO activities that sought to create social and political spaces to enable women's participation even while seeking to create particular subjectivities that limited that very participation. The essay thereafter explores how FTZ women workers responded to this modern urban project by negotiating an identity that in many ways refused the particular subjectivity enforced upon them by middle-class and capitalist narratives. I focus on the way workers engaged in oppositional cultural practices and created and participated in gendered public spaces, which were constantly contested by male and middle-class elements. Analyzing the new spaces and cultural practices in order to delineate the gender and class critique contained within these new practices, I assert that their performances in public spaces conveyed a specific identity as migrant FTZ garment workers and registered their differences from men, other women, and their counterparts in other working-class spheres. Through registering difference, they participated in politics of citizenship. While the discourses surrounding FTZ employment identify it as

bringing modernity to rural women, workers refused these modernizing narratives by negotiating an identity that transgressed the image of an "ideal modern female subject." Based on long-term ethnographic research carried out in the Katunayake FTZ, the essay also argues that while FTZ workers' participation in stigmatized cultural practices and spaces was explicitly transgressive and critical at some levels, they also demonstrated acquiescence to different hegemonic influences, especially capitalist hegemony. In that sense their oppositional practices marked the way transnational flows of ideas and resources shaped responses to marginalization in a way that discouraged transformational political activities.

Katunayake FTZ and the "Respectable Women"

When Sri Lanka established its first FTZ in Katunayake in 1978, thousands of rural young women migrated to the area seeking work. This was not surprising as the government, in order to attract investors, had touted the availability of "well disciplined and obedient women workers, who can produce more in a short time."[1] Today more than 100,000 women work at the FTZ factories, while about 70,000 more work in smaller factories in the vicinity. They live in insecure, poorly built, and overcrowded rooms and have poor access to running water, electricity, and health and sanitary services. While negotiating the burgeoning city, the women have to struggle to access public goods and services and to keep the disciplining forces of the state and other various agents away. The other subaltern groups within cities, such as slum dwellers, have the "vote," which they use as a bargaining chip to access their rights to public goods. The structure of the FTZ employment is such that workers are assumed to be in the city for a short time. This allows the city to relegate the FTZ workers to the status of "semipermanent strangers." However, there is no lack of agents and institutions seeking to produce subjectivities for the female migrant workers.

When people referred to the FTZ area as "city of whores" or as the "love zone," it produced particular gendered and classed subjects of a local urban project. It also set the FTZ workers apart from the city's "respectable women." Local residents of the FTZ area liken the "free-living women" (*ayale yana*) among them to a great (cultural) disaster (*maha vinasayak*). The reasons for such anxiety derive from an ideal image of the Sinhala Buddhist woman that was constructed in the late nineteenth and early twentieth centuries. Primarily constructed as a response to colonial discourses on women and culture, this ideal projected women as passive and subordinate beings who should be protected within the confines of their homes. As a result, women leaving their parental homes to live alone in urban, modernized spaces aroused intense anxieties about cultural degradation and female morality.

Protestant Buddhist traditions and discipline constructed "decent and correct" manners and morals, as well as a proper attitude toward sexuality for middle-class women. Early Christian missionaries and educationists saw Sinhala Buddhist women as unrestrained and sought to make them more civilized, obedient, and serene in manner.[2] Male members belonging to the early-twentieth-century nationalist movement also saw instilling virtues of Victorian femininity, domesticity, discipline, and restraint as essential to transforming Sinhala Buddhist women into a symbol of national greatness. These discourses played a significant role in recasting women as religious, moral, educated, and accomplished. Many sections of society enthusiastically embraced these codes of gendered behavior, which were comingled with anti-imperialist rhetoric.

The importance given to virginity also contributed to the anxieties over women living alone in the city and having unsupervised leisure time, because it provided the opportunity to transgress norms relating to premarital sex. Furthermore, a discursively constructed notion regarding the moral superiority of the village also burdened rural women.[3] Notions of superior morals and undisturbed traditions were superimposed on women, initiating expectations that village women were naive, innocent (in the sense of being sexually ignorant), and timid and that they were also the unadulterated bearers of Sinhala Buddhist culture. Therefore, when they migrated to the city and started enjoying their time away from patriarchal control, fears about their morality became a major preoccupation for urban, middle-class nationalists.

Although the socioeconomic circumstances of lower-class women were not conducive to following hegemonic norms of respectability, in rhetorical and written expressions all Sinhala Buddhist women were measured by this unitary notion of respectability. FTZ garment factory workers, who were rural women now living in the city away from their villages and freely moving around, came under harsh criticism, and their conduct became the space where deep anxieties and ambivalences over notions of development, modernity, and sexuality were played out.

Discursive Production of the City

When former president Ranasinghe Premadasa initiated the Two Hundred Garment Factory Program (200 GFP) in 1992, it was heralded as a solution to many problems faced by rural youth. The 200 GFP aimed to establish a garment factory in each of the two hundred Assistant Government Agent Divisions (AGA) in the country and was to generate nearly 100,000 jobs. More than 80 percent of the jobs generated by the 200 GFP, in keeping with the perception of women as "nimble-fingered and docile," were filled by women. Every factory was inaugurated with pomp and pageantry by the president himself. It was through his inaugural speeches that Premadasa managed to reconcile the ideal woman image, modernity, and the city/village dichotomy. In one speech, Premadasa referred to the depraved and debased activities into which the FTZ workers had been forced in the city and pledged that with the opening of village factories such consequences would be avoided.[4] Owing mainly to these speeches and various forms of media reinterpretations, people started to see the 200 GFP as designed to prevent rural women from migrating to distant cities for employment. Village factories soon came to be known as places that saved "innocent" young rural women from coming under immoral influences in the city. The meanings generated by the propaganda surrounding the 200 GFP intensified the already stigmatized image of FTZ workers, and as a result even village factory workers projected their "purer" morality in comparison to the Katunayake FTZ worker. According to Caitrin Lynch, village factory officials preferred rural workers to the workers in urban FTZs because the latter workers abused their freedom, were spoiled, and acted more stubborn because they were away from their parents. Furthermore, these village factory officials contended that cities were full of bad people who led village girls astray, and they also cited reports of illicit sexual activities of village women in Colombo as evidence.[5]

Literary work also recreated the notion that the FTZ is a space where innocent rural women got corrupted and faced tragedies. Two recent films, *Kinihiriya Mal* and *Sulang Kirilli*, focused in different ways on FTZ village workers who got entangled in sexual relationships and other city attractions that resulted in tragic consequences. Several teledramas focused on rural women's troubles in city FTZs and depicted "what happens to women who take the fast road." These media have had a profound influence on people in Katunayake, who frequently used such stories to explain their views of FTZ work and female morality. The influence of such discourses was evident in workers' own writings, which have appeared in two monthly magazines called *Dabindu* and *Niveka*, published by the NGOs of the same names.

The following poem is an example of how the author understood migration in terms of how modern and dangerous city life contaminated the pure and innocent village upbringing:

Little sister
You came to the city from the village,
Why did you change?
You cut your hair short
Started wearing trousers and short dresses –
You were the most innocent girl in the village

What happened to you after coming to the city?
We can't correct the city
But we can keep in mind to
Protect the village [customs].[6]

Social Construction of Subaltern Citizenry

Katunayake was thus discursively created as a city full of urban evil no less scary than Colombo. In that space, rural women encountered new global cultural flows and acquired new knowledges – or in the popular perception, they got "corrupted." When a young rural woman first arrived in the FTZ and assumed duties at an assembly line, she also inherited a subjectivity that positioned her in a particular way vis-à-vis other industrial workers, men, and middle-class women. The contradictory image of the workers as sexually promiscuous and as innocent victims of evil men was created through media and artistic representations. The spatial production of the city surrounding their lives also depended on the particular understanding of these women as morally degenerate and needing help and protection. Even though politicians found it easy to ignore the appalling work and living conditions of this "nonvoting female community," they spent lavishly to create a little park called *Pem Uyana* (garden of love) close to Katunayake's main bus terminal. The politicians celebrated this as a place where FTZ workers could spend time with their boyfriends without going to rooming houses. There were two assumptions underlining this idea: (1) women were often taken by men to rooming houses, where they then engaged in premarital sexual activities, and (2) women were unwilling participants and would cease going to rooming houses if public/private space was provided to communicate with their men friends. It is also important to note that the park was constructed as a place for FTZ workers and not for the Katunayake city, thereby making a distinction between "normal female citizens" and the "peculiar newcomers." When I visited this garden in 2000, it was a lonely place with unkempt flower bushes and hedges. According to the workers and NGO officials, nobody used the place and young couples especially avoided it. Both *Dabindu* and *Niveka* magazines published workers' opinions in which they lamented the image created about them by the very existence of the garden and critiqued the way politicians overlooked much more immediate needs such as a rest area for women workers' visiting family members.

In fact, the authorities had done surprisingly little spatial ordering with regard to the actual accommodation of the migrant worker population. According to Sally Engle Merry, management of space has been deployed by many authorities lately as part of transnationally circulating notions of urban governance.[7] Rather than restricting the female migrants in certain areas, the Sri Lankan authorities let them find their own accommodations among the neighboring families. The reason for this apparently stemmed from the understanding that migrant village women were purer, with a strict sense of shame and fear, and thus they needed the family environment. Local families, who needed the extra income, provided accommodation to women by building lines of substandard rooms in their backyards. Reports of behavioral and sexual transgressions soon started to surface, and the nonmigrant population began to be alarmed about possible contamination. This led to young women from the area projecting an image that differentiated them from the collective fashion tastes and behavior of FTZ workers.[8]

Spatial ordering has long been a strategy of registering social distance.[9] Most local families started displaying middle-class accoutrements, thanks to the economic activities generated by the presence of FTZ workers. Several families that earned enough money moved out of the area while still renting their houses in Katunayake to FTZ workers. Some others started displaying demarcations such as a barbed-wire fence that separated the boardinghouse area from the owner's house while still letting him supervise the residents' behavior from his porch.[10] Others who could not afford to move out or clearly separate themselves from the workers sought to display difference through their strict control of women's movements. City dwellers who

wanted to exclude themselves from the workers stayed away from social arenas such as the shopping bazaar, eateries, and recreational spaces created for and by FTZ workers. While both spatial and metaphorical boundaries were continuously being set and reshaped within the urban social space, the workers daily contested the institutional and private forces that sought to constrain and structure their lives. Through this struggle, the new gendered and classed subjects of the Katunayake FTZ were created and recreated within the social, cultural space of the city. The maneuverings of NGOs and the workers' responses were significant aspects of this struggle.

The Competition for Clientele

While there were five NGOs dedicated to working among FTZ workers, there were many others interested in helping FTZ workers or learning about them in order to later support them. These NGOs were foreign-funded, and their financial survival more or less depended on how convincingly they proved that FTZ workers were unwise and prone to get into trouble and therefore badly needed outside help. Contrary to Arjun Appadurai's rather romantic version of NGO alliances as international advocacy networks that created deep democracy and globalization from below,[11] I saw NGO politics and their international networks as another device that sought to create a particular subjectivity for the workers.[12] While FTZ work and living conditions and the resultant social conditions were certainly shocking, NGO representations all but covered workers' newfound sense of self, in which they celebrated relatively more freedom in the socioeconomic realm and the new forms of knowledge they acquired through FTZ employment and city living.

From the outset, however, NGOs seemed the only avenue that could generate a political space that respected the rights of the individual and strengthened community. Because they stood outside the government and appeared to be above economic interests, they seemed capable of providing the space for a public dialogue across divisions. However, NGOs formed around the FTZs competed with each other for foreign funds, study tours, and to attract more FTZ workers to their particular activities, which in turn legitimated their claims on foreign donor funds.[13] Ideological and class differences among the NGOs resulted in a visible hierarchy among the organizations and a tense competition for legitimacy and the right to speak for FTZ workers.

In 1999 I had the opportunity to attend a meeting of Labor Ministry officials, members of trade unions, and NGOs that worked among FTZ workers. This meeting, organized by Federic Ebert Stiftung (FES) Sri Lanka, a German funding agency, was held at a posh tourist hotel in Colombo. The seminar, titled "Achieving Social Partnership in the FTZ," focused on finding ways to create a dialogue between workers and employers on an equal footing. The seminar was conducted in English with some Sinhala translations. However, everyone struggled to continue the dialogue in English – perhaps out of respect for the German representatives of the FES. This resulted in shutting out members of some of the NGOs, including Dabindu, which has a grassroots base. Representatives from the American Organization for Labor Solidarity (AFLI) and the Shramashakthi (Strength of Labor) spoke with authority, and they seemed to have been unofficially chosen to present the NGO point of view at the seminar.[14] This distressed the members of Dabindu, who seemed to have somewhat different opinions but found it difficult to dissent due to their lack of English knowledge. They retaliated later at the lunch break by telling me secretly that those organizations considered workers as ignorant, low-class fools and treated them badly.[15] During their contributions at the seminar, it became clear that both AFLI and Shramashakthi considered NGO work to be akin to charity. This attitude was more pronounced in the Shramashakthi representative's contributions. An upper-middle-class female lawyer, she talked eloquently about the way her organization helped poor, hapless FTZ workers to adjust to city life.[16]

Traditional trade unions were also interested in roping the FTZ workers' votes for political parties with which they were affiliated. The United National Party had figured out by 1999 that forming a NGO was the best way to reach this valuable voting block. Three young women at the conference represented a NGO called Pragathi (Progress). They had two centers in the Katunayake FTZ and one at the Biyagama FTZ. In an interview with one of the representatives from the United National Party (UNP) trade union JSS (Jathika Sevaka Sangamaya, or National Workers' Union), it was revealed that the Pragathi centers were actually UNP-sponsored and established with the intention of garnering the workers' support during election campaigns. According to the interviewee, the centers were in the process of organizing cookery and sewing classes for FTZ workers since they believed the women would support UNP candidates in their villages during elections.[17]

An organization called the Association of Joint Council of Workers, also operated with foreign funds, was active among FTZ workers as well. This too was a male-dominated organization that sought to create and reproduce certain subjectivities for FTZ workers.[18] In 2000 this organization produced a video titled *Slaves of the Free Trade: Camp Sri Lanka*. This was an extension of another video produced in 1994, *Women of the Zone: Garment Workers of Sri Lanka*, and it included several new interviews. Both videos, produced with funding from a Labor Video Project in San Francisco, California, provided footage of women workers tearfully talking about their difficult and helpless conditions both at work and at boardinghouses. Neither video talked about the positive aspects of FTZ work, which workers themselves usually cited. Rather than calling for improvements in the conditions within which they negotiated city life, the videos seemed to reproduce the idea that city life was inherently bad and women preferred to stay at home if that was financially feasible. This was perhaps a genuine misinterpretation of the scene, but the overall tone and the focus on crying women prompted one to assume that the portrayal of women workers as a victimized and helpless constituency could well be designed to satisfy supposed donor concerns.

Creating Public Spaces and Expressing Public Identity

The particular social relations and cultural practices within a space define and label a space. The way the workers chose to use specific spaces around the FTZ contributed to a process that saw these spaces being reconceived as sites of gendered resistance through which women challenged hegemonic cultural norms. However, the practices that created gendered public spaces in and around the FTZ were constantly contested by male and middle-class elements. The stigma attached to the very characterization of their industrial employment, as women living away from their families, had a two-way relationship with the dynamic commercial, cultural, and public spaces they created. While these spaces became marked and degraded due to their association with the workers, the very nature of the newly created spaces added to the stigma of being away from one's home. However, FTZ workers enthusiastically consumed the public space created around their lives. On weekends they went to Aweriwatte junction to buy their food items, to shop, to get their horoscopes read, or merely to socialize. The area became full of women, with vendors catering to them and groups of young men following them. Women gathered in circles by the roadside, bus stops, and shop fronts to engage in loud conversations. The young men gathered near these groups of women and communicated via jokes exchanged from a short distance. This appropriation of public space for a group's activities had always been contested, and when the group was socially marginalized it generated fear and jealousy among middle-class people. According to Herbert Schiller,[19] "the uses of the public streets in the city has been a 'site' of social struggle as far back as the early nineteenth century." Middle classes always contested those who congregated on streets to socialize or participate in parades.

Dabindu maintained a street-drama group comprised of FTZ workers and regularly performed on the crowded streets near the bazaar on Sundays. Both women and men gathered around in a circle that took up more than half the street space. The police turned a blind eye to the obvious violation of rules, emphasizing how unique the FTZ area and FTZ Sundays are. However, FTZ workers' appropriation of the streets provided them only an ambiguous and contested space for social participation. While their presence was tolerated, the ways they used the space for assertive behavior and flirtation were similarly feared as a sign of moral degeneration and a challenge to the nation's purity.

Workers contested the prying eyes and eroticized language of male participants in the commercial sphere to continue consuming this public space as well as several other spaces, including the railway tracks.[20] There were boardinghouses attached to all the houses along the railway tracks for at least three miles. In the evenings, and especially on weekends, women got out of their crowded boarding rooms to sit on the railway tracks and socialize. They sat on the tracks in groups to comb each other's hair, sing, gossip, and quarrel. When family and friends visited, it was along the railway track that they sat and talked. Lovers walked hand in hand back and forth along the tracks, making visible that they were not up to anything funny. Petty traders, food vendors, palm readers, snake dancers, monkey dancers, and NGO music groups visited the railway tracks, providing women with cheap thrills. Every hour trains threateningly rushed toward them, continuously tooting their horns. Women waited till the last moment to get out of the tracks and then stood dangerously close to the tracks to reclaim their seats. This silent battle with the train extended to its passengers, and women stared back at suburban office workers who looked on disapprovingly.

Male neighbors and visitors to the area sometimes stopped to talk to women, but the tracks remained predominantly a women's gathering area, where they had relatively more room to freely express themselves. This more or less isolated gendered social space was significant in educating newcomers to the FTZ way of life. "Propriety" would seem an inappropriate term to describe FTZ workers' lives, but that was what they learned within this space – how to present an image that was understood, recognized, and approved by all who consumed the public space. Pierre Mayol writes, "Propriety is simultaneously the manner in which one is perceived and the means constraining one to remain submitted to it.... That is why it produces stereotyped behaviors, ready-to-wear social clothes, whose function is to make it possible to recognize anyone, anywhere."[21] Strangely, it seemed highly appropriate to use this very same term to analyze a space characterized by transgression to dominant culture.

Notes

1 Dabindu Collective, A Review of *Free Trade Zones in Sri Lanka* (Boralesgamuwa: CRC, 1997).
2 Malathie De Alwis, "The Production and Embodiment of Respectability: Gendered Demeanors in Colonial Ceylon," unpublished manuscript, 1997.
3 See Vijaya Samaraweera, "The 'Village Community' and Reform in Colonial Sri Lanka," *Ceylon Journal of Historical and Social Studies*, n.s., 8 (1978): 68–75; James Brow, "Utopia's New-Found Space: Images of the Village Community in the Early Writings of Ananda Kumaraswamy," *Modern Asian Studies* 33 (1999): 67–86; Mick Moore, *The State and Peasant Politics in Sri Lanka* (Cambridge: Cambridge University Press, 1985).
4 Caitrin Lynch quotes journalist Suresh's account of this speech in her article "The 'Good Girls' of Sri Lankan Modernity: Moral Orders of Nationalism and Capitalism," *Identities* 6 (1999): 55–89.
5 Lynch, " 'Good Girls' of Sri Lankan Modernity," 68.
6 Niluka Lakmini, "Little Sister," *Dabindu* (December 2003): 6.
7 Sally Engle Merry, "Spatial Governmentality and the New Urban Social Order: Controlling Gender Violence through Law," American Anthropologist 103 (2001): 16–17.
8 Sandya Hewamanne, *Stitching Identities in a Free Trade Zone: Gender and Politics in Sri Lanka* (Philadelphia: University of Pennsylvania Press, 2008); Sandya Hewamanne, "Performing Disrespectability: New Tastes, Cultural Practices, and Identity Performances by Sri Lanka's Free Trade Zone Garment Factory Workers," *Cultural Dynamics* 15 (2003): 71–101.
9 See Teresa Caldeira, "Fortified Enclaves: The New Urban Segregation," in *Theorizing the City: The New Anthropology Reader*, ed. Setha M. Low (New Brunswick, NJ: Rutgers University Press, 1999), 83–110; Setha M. Low, "The Edge and the Center: Gated Communities and the Discourse of Urban Fear," *American Anthropologist* 103 (2001): 45–58; Alan Smart, "Unruly Places: Urban Governance and the Persistence of Illegality in Hong Kong's Urban Squatter Areas," *American Anthropologist* 103 (2001): 30–44.
10 Hewamanne, *Stitching Identities*.
11 Arjun Appadurai, "Deep Democracy: Urban Governmentality and the Horizon of Politics," *Environment and Urbanization* 13, no. 2 (2001): 23–43.
12 All NGOs in the area claimed to be part of alliances involving international donor agencies, their Colombo offices, and the workers.
13 The same donor agencies funded several NGOs initiating competition. All NGOs strived to show that they had a grassroots base and tried to create a group of workers who attended their activities. The intense photographing and video recording that went on at NGO activities further evidenced their need to showcase the workers' participation. Taking a group photograph was given high priority, while the contents or the presentation style of lectures was not given much attention.
14 The American Organization for Labor Solidarity (AFLI) was funded by an American organization of the same name. As is with all other NGOs, Shramashakthi also received substantial foreign funding.
15 I was able to discern this attitude among the members of several NGOs. For example, several

NGO staff members spoke English, and there were a number of occasions when they talked to FTZ workers in Sinhala but quickly switched to English to explain their opinions to me. Thus while pacifying a worker in Sinhala, the staff member would turn to me and say in English, "It is her fault that she is in trouble" or "These people do not understand the simplest of instructions." Workers looked pained and humiliated whenever this happened. At another NGO, workers were asked to remove their shoes before entering the office while the staff strutted around in high heels.

16 These class divisions were conspicuously played out at the lunch table, where the "hi-fi NGO people," according to some other NGO members, ate efficiently with forks and knives while many others struggled with the cutlery. Several younger NGO members used their fingers to eat. The three groups sat at different tables. I wondered whether a dialogue on equal footing was feasible when class differences were so noticeably played out among the people who were supposed to work together to make workers' lives better.

17 When he was informed of my research among the FTZ workers he offered the services of one of the Pragathi staff members as an assistant and said I was welcome to interview the women who attended the cookery and sewing classes they planned to start soon.

18 Joint Council of Workers (JOC) is an organization that, according to the BOI manual, operated mostly as an intermediary between workers and FTZ management. The top official of the company chaired the council. The worker representatives were usually chosen by popular vote, but many women workers informed me that they had been informally discouraged to run.

19 Herbert I. Schiller, *Culture Inc.: The Corporate Takeover of Public Expression* (Oxford: Oxford University Press, 1989), 103.

20 Their enthusiastic participation in alternative religious spaces also allowed them to create and engage with urban religious spaces where they felt more at ease. Workers' enthusiastic consumption of an alternative religious space, called Pillawe Temple, contributed to this newly created religious place being labeled as a "garment girl temple."

21 Pierre Mayol, "Living," in *The Practice of Everyday Life*, vol. 2, *Living and Cooking*, ed. Michel de Certeau, Luce Giard, and Pierre Mayol (Minneapolis: University of Minnesota Press, 1998), 17.

25

Indo-Bhutan Relations Recent Trends

Tashi Choden

Introduction

The Kingdom of Bhutan is often described as being physically small with limited economic scope and military might. In spite of these limitations, Bhutan has earned the reputation of being a peaceful country where the development of threats from militancy, terrorism, and economic disparity within itself has virtually been absent. In this sense, Bhutan has thus far been more fortunate than many of its neighbours in the South Asian region.

This has been in part owing to its self-isolationist policy up until the second half of the 20th century, and the preservation and promotion of a strong sense of identity that has ensured social cohesion and unity. Having never been colonized, nor feeling any direct impact of two world wars and the cold war, Bhutan has been spared the conflicts and turmoil such as that of the legacy of hatred and mistrust generated by the partition of British India into present-day India and Pakistan.

Nevertheless, Bhutanese have historically been sensitive to issues of security with frequent disturbance occurring from internal warring factions prior to unification and establishment of the monarchy in 1907. External threat was present during the 17th and 18th centuries with several failed attempts at invasion from the Tibetans; 19th century Bhutan saw the loss of the Assam and Bengal Duars to British India.[1] As such, preserving its sovereign independence and territorial integrity has always been a matter of great importance for Bhutan.

By the early half of the 20th century, developments in the Himalayan region prompted Bhutan to re-evaluate the usefulness of its isolationist policy. Within this context, Bhutan began to develop political orientation towards its southern neighbour – nurturing a close relationship with India was one way of enhancing its own territorial security while at the same time enhancing the prospects for socioeconomic development. As for India with its contentious state of relations with China, Bhutan's strategic

Perspectives on Modern South Asia: A Reader in Culture, History, and Representation, First Edition.
Edited by Kamala Visweswaran.
© 2011 Blackwell Publishing Ltd. Published 2011 by Blackwell Publishing Ltd.

location between the two ensured the service of a buffer state that could enhance its own security.

The initiation of Indo-Bhutan friendship as it stands today, is credited to the efforts of Indian Prime Minister Pandit Jawahalal Nehru and His Majesty Jigme Dorji Wangchuck, the third King of Bhutan. Their meeting in the 1950s sparked the dialogue for development cooperation. Looking back over the decades since then, and under the continued guidance of the present king His Majesty Jigme Singye Wangchuck, Indian assistance has greatly expanded in every field of Bhutan's development and socioeconomic growth. To this day, India continues to provide the largest and most diverse assistance to Bhutan among all other donors. Often cited as a "shining" example of friendship and cooperation between a large country and a small neighbour, relations between the two continue to grow at all levels.

I. A Background on Indo-Bhutan Relations

Recorded historic relations between Bhutan and India date back to 747 AD, when the great Indian saint Padmasambhava introduced Buddhism in Bhutan, which has since then permeated all aspects of Bhutanese life. Aside from such shared cultural and religious heritage, other areas of interaction developed during the British rule in India, which include several Anglo-Bhutanese skirmishes and battles that were consequently followed by treaties and agreements. It was within this period of interaction with the British that trade between Bhutanese and Indians was also recorded to have taken place for the first time (1873).

China's invasion of Tibet (1910-12) and subsequent claims made on Bhutan resulted in the signing of the Treaty of Punakha in 1910 with British India. Although this treaty served to expel any claims that China might have tried to make, it did not define Bhutan's status technically or legally; for the Bhutanese, this was a source of uncertainty over its relations with India at the time that the British rule was nearing an end. After India's independence in 1947,

'standstill agreements' with Sikkim, Nepal and Tibet were signed to continue existing relations until new agreements were made; for Bhutan, its status became clearer following Nehru's invitation for a Bhutanese delegation to participate in the Asian Relations Conference in 1947. Following this, the negotiation for a fresh Indo-Bhutan Treaty started in the summer of 1949.

The basis for bilateral relations between India and Bhutan is formed by the Indo-Bhutan Treaty of 1949, which provides for, among others, "perpetual peace and friendship, free trade and commerce and equal justice to each other's citizens."[2] The much speculated Article 2 in the Treaty, in principle, calls for Bhutan to seek India's advice in external matters, while India pledges non-interference in Bhutan's internal affairs.

The geopolitical scene in the entire Himalayan region and Indian sub-continent underwent great change following the proclamation of the People's Republic of China in 1949 and the takeover of Tibet by the People's Liberation Army in 1950. These events, plus the presence of Chinese troops near Bhutan's border, the annexation of Bhutanese enclaves in Tibet and Chinese claims all led Bhutan to re-evaluate its traditional policy of isolation; the need to develop its lines of communications with India became an urgent necessity. Consequently, Bhutan was more inclined to develop relations with India, and the process of socioeconomic development began thereafter with Indian assistance. For India's own security too, the stability of Himalayan states falling within its strategic interest was a crucial factor to consider. With border tensions between India and China escalating into military conflict in 1962, India could not afford Bhutan to be a weak buffer state.

Based on this backdrop, Indo-Bhutan relations began to take on concrete form following state visits made by the third king, His Majesty Jigme Dorji Wangchuck to India, and by Prime Minister Jahawalal Nehru to Bhutan between 1954 to 1961. Besides emphasizing India's recognition of Bhutan's independence and sovereignty in his public statement in Paro, Nehru's visit in 1958 was also significant with discussions initiated for development cooperation between the two countries.

Formal bilateral relations between Bhutan and India were established in January 1968 with the appointment of a special officer of the Government of India to Bhutan. The India House (Embassy of India in Bhutan) was inaugurated on May 14, 1968 and Resident Representatives were exchanged in 1971. Ambassadorial level relations began with the upgrading of residents to embassies in 1978.

Beginning with India, Bhutan began to diversify its relations in the international community, thereby projecting its status as an independent and sovereign nation. With India sponsoring Bhutan's application for UN membership in 1971, the leaders of the two countries demonstrated that Article 2 of the Indo-Bhutan Treaty was not a restricting factor in the exercise of Bhutan's foreign policy.

II. Areas of Cooperation

Development assistance and economic relations
Planned development in Bhutan began in 1961, with the first two Five Year Plans (FYP) wholly financed by the Government of India (GOI). Over the years, Indian assistance has increased steadily from Rs. 107 million in the First FYP to Rs. 9,000 million in the Eighth FYP. Road construction by the Indian Border Roads Organization started in the first FYP (1962–66); the second FYP (1966–71) focused on public works, education, agriculture and health. While Bhutan's source of foreign aid has diversified significantly since it became a member of the United Nations, India continues to be the major donor of external aid to Bhutan – Indian assistance accounted for about 41 percent of total external outlay during the 8th FYP (1997–2002). Over the last four decades, India has provided assistance mainly in the social sectors such as education and human resource development, health, hydropower development, agriculture, and roads. In addition, India also provides partial or full grant assistance and gradually, economic relations have evolved with cooperation extending towards mutually

beneficial projects such as in hydropower development and industrial projects.

These projects are taken up outside of the FYP programmes with many major works awarded to Indian companies. Important projects invested in under Government of India–Royal Government of Bhutan (GOI–RGOB) cooperation include the Chhukha (336 MW), Kurichhu (60 MW), and Tala (1020 MW) Hydro Power Projects; the Penden and Dungsam Cement Projects; and the Paro Airport Project. A Memorandum of Understanding for preparing a detailed project report for the proposed 870 MW Puna Tsangchhu Hydropower Project was also signed between the two governments in September 2003. With the huge Indian market for electricity currently facing domestic supply difficulties, Bhutan has high potential to offer supply relief to India – presently, approximately ninety percent of electricity generated in Bhutan is exported to India, and this only translates to 0.5 of the total demand. Other mutual benefits generated by the Indian assisted and Bhutanese government owned projects include assured business opportunities in the manufacturing and other industries in both India and Bhutan.

Trade and investment
A new era in Bhutan's foreign trade commenced following the closure of trade routes between Bhutan and Tibet in 1960, and the construction of roads linking the Bengal–Assam plains to Phuentsholing, and Phuentsholing to Thimphu and Paro in 1962.

Over the period of 1981–2001, Bhutan's exports to India accounted for an average of 86.5 percent of its exports, and imports from India accounted for an average 79 percent of the total imports. Bhutan's main items for export to India are electricity, mineral products, products of chemical industries, base metals and products, and wood and wood products with hydropower generation being the most important area of comparative advantage. Imports from India include a wide range of items including machinery, mechanical appliances, base metals, electronic items, foodstuff and other basic necessities and consumer items.

Besides trade, Indian involvement extends into many other areas of Bhutan's private and public sector activities. In the area of Foreign Direct Investment, Bhutan has so far pursued a conservative policy, and the first and only foreign investor in Bhutan for almost two decades since 1971 was the State Bank of India (SBI). The SBI has worked in collaboration with the Bank of Bhutan (BOB) since its identification as partner in management and share holding in the capital of BOB, in addition to imparting banking expertise. BOB's collaboration with SBI was last renewed on January 1, 2002 for a period of up to December 31, 2006.

In addition, Indian nationals operate a range of small scale trading and service activities on licenses issued by the Ministry of Trade and Industry in Bhutan. Such ventures include small shops trading in a variety of products like grocery, auto parts and furniture, as well as scrap dealers, distribution and dealership agencies. Indians in Bhutan also run hotels/restaurants, saloons, tailoring and cobbler services. On a larger scale, Indian investment in Bhutan exists in the manufacturing and processing industries, construction, service, engineering, steel and electronic industries, and consultancy. Indian companies such as the Jaiprakash Industries and NHPC carry out major works for the Tala and Kurichhu Power Projects respectively. Similarly, many other Indian and Bhutanese companies (or joint ventures) benefit from the current requirements of massive power projects and manufacturing industries.

Although there is no in-depth study available on the level of informal trade between the two, it has been noted[3] that such activities are tolerated in practice partly because of the open and porous border between Bhutan and India. Another informal but common practice is the operation of a wide range of businesses by Indian persons using the licenses of Bhutanese nationals as indigenous fronts. These include anything from small shops trading in petty consumer items to large-scale investment businesses such as construction.

The prevalence of small-scale Indian investment as well as business fronting is understandably concentrated in southern Bhutan owing to

proximity of bordering Indian towns. The border town of Phuentsholing is the center of commercial hub in the country from where the exit and entry of goods as well as travelers largely takes place; the Indian town Jaigoan under Jaipalguri district is "just across the fence" where tailor-made foods suited to Bhutanese needs are especially stocked. Although statistics are not available, it is apparent that the business community in Jaigoan has prospered in large part owing to the level of trading activities with Bhutanese businessmen and other customers. (CBS et al: 2004, pp 79–189).

Labour relations
Beginning with the inception of development plans in the 1960s, Bhutan's requirement of semi-skilled and unskilled labour has been filled in by expatriates, particularly Indians, first in road construction and then in other sectors such as mining, agro-based industries and hydropower projects with the shift in development priorities. This dependence sprung from the lack of in-country experience and skills in road construction as well as technical skills and equipment. Indian personnel and labourers were recruited in large numbers, mainly from neighbouring Indian states. While Indian labourers found employment on Bhutanese roads, Bhutanese labourers (who were mostly farmers) were spared the sole brunt of undertaking the construction works. Currently, the public road maintenance is entrusted mainly to Project Dantak,[4] and at any given time it has an average 2000 Indian labourers working on roads in various parts of Bhutan.

Considering that the modern system of formal education in Bhutan was initiated only after 1955, and that it was a few decades before the first generation of qualified Bhutanese entered the civil service, many Indian personnel were recruited by the Bhutanese government to fill in administrative posts and others related to development programmes in the 1960s. While Bhutanese nationals have gradually replaced Indians in these posts, many continue to serve in both public corporations and the civil service to this day. However, a turning point has come where the successes of modern education have helped to gradually replace Indian expatriates in various professions such as teaching, health and medics, engineering, accounting and administration.

India's liberalization policies
Up until the 1990s, Bhutan has enjoyed more or less protected status in its trade relations with India. With economic liberalization on the rise in India, however, Bhutan is facing a gradual loss of this status, and unless Bhutanese industries

are able to remain competitive they could lose their market share in the increasingly open market in India. Bhutan has already felt the impact of the reform in India's subsidy policies that has resulted in a gradual phasing out of subsidies and a decrease in its budget for assistance to Bhutan. Bhutan will also have to face the effects that would be brought on by India gradually moving toward privatizing its power, petroleum and other traditional public sectors.

Notes

1   Ura, Karma. 2002. "Perceptions of Security" pp 59–79, in Dipankar Banerjee ed., *South Asian Security: Futures*. Colombo: Regional Centre for Strategic Studies, Sri Lanka.
2   As quoted on the website of the Indian Embassy in Bhutan at ⟨http:www.eoithimphu.org/indo.html⟩
3   The study on *Economic and Political Relations between Bhutan and the Neighbouring Countries*

(CBS et al: 2004) notes that much of the informal trade are not considered illegal economic activities, but more as 'extra-legal' trading; informal trade is described here as those that are unregistered, unlicensed, and not recorded by the government.
4   An organization of the Indian Border Roads Organization.

References

DADM (2001). *Development Towards Gross National Happiness* (Main Document, 7th RTM), Thimphu: Department of Debt and Aid Management, Royal Government of Bhutan.

Hasrat, B.J. (1980). *History of Bhutan: Land of Peaceful Dragon*, Thimphu: Education Department, Royal Government of Bhutan.

Kohli, Manorama (1993) From Dependency to Interdependence-A Study of Indo-Bhutan Relations, New Delhi: Vikas Publishing House.

Kuensel (2001). Editorial, 9 June, Thimphu.

Mathou, Thierry, "Bhutan-China Relations: Towards a New Step in Himalayan Politics", in *Papers Submitted for the International Seminar on Bhutanese Studies*, August 20-23, 2003, Thimphu: The Centre for Bhutan Studies, pp. 174-88.

CBS et al (2004). "Economic and Political Relations Between Bhutan and the Neighbouring Countries", in Sub-Regional Relations in the Eastern South Asia: With Special Focus on Bangladesh and Bhutan. Joint Research Program Series No. 132, Chiba, Japan: Institute of Developing Economies-Japan External Trade Organization (IDE-JETRO).

Parmanand (1998). *The Politics of Bhutan*, Delhi: Pragati Publications.

Planning Commission (1999). *Bhutan 2020: A Vision for Peace, Prosperity and Happiness*, Thimphu: Royal Government of Bhutan.

Planning Commission (2000). *National Accounts Statistics 1980-1999*, Thimphu: Central Statistical Organisation, Royal Government of Bhutan.

Planning Commission, Five Year Plan Documents (1st, 2nd, 3rd, 4th, 5th, 6th, 7th, 8th and 9th Plans), accessed at < http://www.pcs.gov.bt/ on 7-6-2003.

P.R. Chari ed. (1999). Perspectives on National Security in South Asia: In Search of a New Paradigm, Delhi: Manohar Publishers and Distributors.

Sonam Kinga (2002). Changes in Bhutanese Social Structure: Impacts of Fifty Years of Reforms (1952-2002), Chiba, Japan: Institute of Developing Economies.

Ura, Karma. 2002. "Perceptions of Security" pp 59-79, in Dipankar Banerjee ed., *South Asian Security: Futures*. Colombo: Regional Centre for Strategic Studies, Sri Lanka.

Yadav, Lal B. (1996). *Indo-Bhutan Relations and China Intervention*, New Delhi: Anmol Publications.

Part VI

Social Movements

Introduction

Jean Dréze and Amartya Sen remind us that assertion-based political activism and solidarity-based social movements are healthy for democracy.[1] In South Asia, the first strands of feminist thought and agitation for women's rights emerged in the context of anti-colonial nationalism. Muslim modernists and Hindu social reformers alike addressed issues of women's status, rights, and duties through a variety of media. In Afghanistan, which was never subject to British colonial rule, the late 19th and early 20th centuries saw a progressive monarchy undertake reforms designed to foster women's education, to limit the cost of weddings, and the tribal bride price system.

In British-ruled India, the debates about practices concerning Hindu women such as sati or widow immolation, female infanticide, and widow remarriage rarely involved women themselves, until the late 19th century. By then, women's magazines in Tamil, Marathi, Hindi, Bengali, Urdu, Bengali, and numerous other South Asian languages began to address women's own concerns about their condition. The Marathi writer, Tarabai Shinde, wrote a scathing critique of the treatment of women in her (1882) "A Comparison between Women and Men." Increasing literacy of the middle and elite classes also meant that educated women began writing in English. The Bengali Muslim social reformer Rokeya Hossein published in the *Madras Indian Ladies Magazine* the (1906) short story "Sultana's Dream," imagining a gracious, non-violent and utopic world where men, not women, were secluded at home and observed purdah.

The late 19th century emergence of Indian nationalism built upon women's involvement in the anti-caste politics of the Brahmo Samaj and Jyotirao Phule's Non-Brahmin movement, and expanded it to include women's mass-based participation in a variety of political movements: the Gandhian-led non-cooperation and civil disobedience campaigns

Perspectives on Modern South Asia: A Reader in Culture, History, and Representation, First Edition.
Edited by Kamala Visweswaran.
© 2011 Blackwell Publishing Ltd. Published 2011 by Blackwell Publishing Ltd.

of the 1920s and 1930s, their participation in communist organizations in the late 1930s, in the Indian National Army (under the Rani of Jhansi regiment led by Captain Lakshmi Saghal) in the early 1940s and in peasant struggles against landlords in the Telengana movement of the 1940s–1950s. Women from prominent families who had been active in anti-colonial struggles, such as Vijayalakshmi Pandit and Fatimah Jinnah found places in the governments of India and Pakistan. After Independence, women were admitted into Pakistan's navy while sex equality was enumerated in Article 14 of India's constitution. The legacy of women's participation in the anti-colonial movements of South Asia was to have far-reaching impact not only upon women's movements of the postcolonial period, but upon social movements in general. Today, a large number of social movements in South Asia are predominantly female; the last two convenors of India's National Association of People's Movements (NAPM) have also been women.[2]

While the women's movements described by Radha Kumar or Shahnaz Rouse, anti-caste movements described by Gopal Guru and Anuradha Chakravarty, and land rights movements have their roots in the anti-colonial nationalism of the 19th century, others are influenced by democratic movements in neighboring countries or by resource-based struggles for land and water; often seen in resistance to big dam and large-scale development projects (described by Chittaroopa Palit) which result in the massive displacement of poor and landless farmers, dalits, and adivasis. This has led to strong Naxalite and Maoist movements throughout eastern India,[3] and in Nepal, as Shobha Gautam, Amrita Banskota, and Rita Manchanda explain in their essay. The interview with Chitraroopa Palit describes the formation of the Narmada Bachao Andolan (NBA), a member of the NAPM, which has been protesting for more than twenty-five years the scale of displacement brought by the construction of large dams in the Narmada river valley, which neither produce enough electricity to justify their costs, nor bring water for irrigation or drinking to those who most need it.

When we look at the economic costs for other large-scale infrastructural projects, such as nuclear power generation, we also find that the amount of energy generated cannot recoup the initial cost outlay; thus many in the Indo-Pak peace movement regard nuclear power a thin justification for the nuclear weapons program. The recent (2008) India–United States nuclear deal will mean that India will spend many more millions of dollars to nuclearize its arsenal instead of investing in social programs. After the 1998 Indian nuclear tests by the BJP, Pakistan responded with its own tests. As Achin Vanaik explains, nuclearization also leads to increased insecurity between Pakistan and India. Zia Mian argues that if Pakistan were to demilitarize, India would have no justification for continuing to build its arsenal. And if India were to demilitarize, it would not only be able to free up money to attend to the needs of the poor and to reinvest in much needed social programs, but also radically transform the prospects for peace in South Asia.

Notes

1 Jean Dréze and Amartya Sen, *India: Development and Participation*, pp. 28–32. Delhi: Oxford, 2001.
2 The People's Rights Movement (PRM) also coordinates linked struggles among rural people in Pakistan, including that of farmers against the Pakistan military in Okara (Punjab).
3 The term "Naxal" or "Naxalite" is used to designate insurgent land struggles in India after the 1967 peasant uprising in the village of Naxalbari (West Bengal) resulted in splits from the Communist Party of India-Marxist (CPI-M) leading to the formation of the Communist Party of India (Marxist–Leninist). Maoist-influenced groups followed. These movements are now the strongest in eastern India (especially Andhra Pradesh, Orissa, Chhattisgarh, Jharkhand, Bihar, and West Bengal).

26

From Chipko to Sati: The Contemporary Indian Women's Movement

Radha Kumar

After India gained independence in 1947, the Congress (ruling party) government made partial attempts to fulfill the promises it had made to women by declaring in the constitution the equality of men and women, setting up various administrative bodies for the creation of opportunities for women, and inducting a number of feminists into the government. In the 1950s and 1960s, therefore, there was a lull in feminist campaigning. The movement that started in the 1970s was very different from its predecessors, for it grew out of a number of radical movements of the time.

In the early 1970s, the Indian Left fractured, and some factions began to question their earlier analysis of revolution. New leftist ideas and movements developed, albeit on a smaller scale. Among these the most interesting movements for feminists were the Shahada and anti-price rise agitations in Maharashtra and the Self-Employed Women's Association (SEWA) and Nav Nirman (New Light) in Gujarat. The Shahada movement, in Dhulia district of

Maharashtra, was a Bhil tribal landless laborers' movement against the exploitative practices of nontribal local landowners. Drought and famine in Maharashtra during this period exacerbated the poverty already created by invidious rates of sharecropping, land alienation, and extortionate moneylending charges, and these conditions contributed to rising militancy among the Bhils. The Shahada movement began as a folk protest (through radical devotional song clubs) in the late 1960s. It took on a more militant campaigning thrust when the New Left joined the movement in the early 1970s and helped the Bhils form an organization, the Sharmik Sangathana (Toilers' Organizations), in 1972. Accounts of the Shahada movement say that women were more active than men and that as their militancy grew, they began to take direct action on issues specific to them as women, such as the physical violence associated with alcoholism.[1] Groups of women began to go from village to village to storm liquor dens and destroy liquor pots. If any woman reported

Perspectives on Modern South Asia: A Reader in Culture, History, and Representation, First Edition.
Edited by Kamala Visweswaran.
© 2011 Blackwell Publishing Ltd. Published 2011 by Blackwell Publishing Ltd.

that her husband had beaten her, other women would assemble, beat him, and force him to apologize to his wife in public.

Meanwhile in Gujarat, what was probably the first attempt at forming a women's trade union was made in Ahmedabad by Gandhian socialists attached to the Textile Labour Association (TLA). Formed in 1972 at the initiative of Ela Bhatt, who worked in the women's wing of the TLA, the Self-Employed Women's Association was an organization of women who worked in different trades in the informal sector but shared a common experience of extremely low earnings, very poor working conditions (most of them either performed piecework in their homes or toiled on the streets as vendors or hawkers), harassment from those in authority (the contractor for homeworkers and the police for vendors), and lack of recognition of their work as socially useful labor. The aims of SEWA were to improve these working conditions through training, technical aid, and collective bargaining and to "introduce the members to the values of honesty, dignity and simplicity of lifegoals reflecting the Gandhian ideals to which TLA and SEWA leaders subscribe."[2]

Conditions of drought and famine in the rural areas of Maharashtra in the early 1970s led to a sharp rise in prices in the urban areas. In 1973, Mrinal Gore of the Socialist Party and Ahilya Ranganekar of the Communist Party of India–Marxist (CPI–M), together with many others, formed the United Women's Anti Price Rise Front, "to mobilize women of the city against inflation just as women . . . of the rural poor had been mobilized in the famine agitations."[3] The campaign rapidly became a mass women's movement for consumer protection and its members demanded that the government fix prices and distribute essential commodities. So many housewives were involved that a new form of protest was invented: At appointed times housebound women would express their support for demonstrators by beating *thalis* (metal plates) with *lathis* (rolling pins). The demonstrations themselves were huge, comprising between ten and twenty thousand women. Commonly, demonstrators would protest rising prices and

hoarding by going to the offices of government officials, members of Parliament (MPs), and merchants, surrounding them, and offering them bangles as a token of their emasculation or by going to warehouses where goods were being hoarded and raiding them.

Soon after, the movement spread to Gujarat, where it was known as the Nav Nirman movement of 1974. Nav Nirman, originally a students' movement against soaring prices, corruption, and black marketeering, became a massive middle-class movement joined by thousands of women. In its course the movement shifted from protesting these issues to mounting an all-out criticism of the Indian state. The methods of protest ranged from mass hunger strikes to mock courts passing judgment on corrupt state officials and politicians, mock funerals celebrating the death of those condemned by their courts, and *prabhat pheris*, or processions, to greet the dawn of a new era. Women also "rang the death knell of the Legislative Assembly with rolling pins and thalis." It took the police some three months to subdue the Nav Nirman movement, and between ninety and one hundred people were killed.[4]

In the same year as the Nav Nirman movement developed and was subdued, the first women's group associated with the contemporary feminist movement was formed in Hyderabad. Comprising women from the Maoist movement, the Progressive Organization of Women (POW) exemplified rethinking within the Left. As in the Shahada movement, Maoist women were beginning to stress the existence of gender oppression and to organize women against it; but whereas in the former the question came up through the single issue of wife beating, the POW attempted an overarching analysis of gender oppression in its manifesto, which was largely influenced by Friedrich Engels and Isaac Babel.[5]

The year 1975 saw the sudden development of a whole spate of feminist activities in Maharashtra. This has been seen by some feminists as the result of the United Nations' declaration of 1975 as International Women's Year. Perhaps the declaration did provide a focus for activities centering on women. But it seems likely that these activities would have taken place even without the declaration, for an interest in women's problems had been developing in Maharashtra since the early 1970s, as we have seen through the Shahada and anti-price rise agitations. Influenced by the POW, Maoist women in Pune formed the Purogami Stree Sangathana (Progressive Women's Organization), and Maoist women in Bombay formed the Stree Mukti Sangathana (Women's Liberation Organization). March 8, International Women's Day, was celebrated for the first time in India by both party-based and autonomous organizations in Maharashtra; the Lal Nishan (Red Flag) Party commemorated it with a special issue of the party paper. In August, the Marathi socialist magazine *Sadhana* (Contentment) brought out a special women's issue; in September *dalits* (untouchables) and socialists organized a conference of *devadasis* (literally, servants of the gods; or temple prostitutes); and in October a number of organizations that had developed out of the Maoist movement, such as the Lal Nishan Party and the Shramik Sangathana, organized a "United Women's Liberation Struggle" conference in Pune. It was attended by women from all over Maharashtra, including some from left-wing political parties such as the CPI–M, the Socialists, and the Republicans.[6]

Especially interesting was the connection now being made between the anticaste *dalit* movement and feminism. The *dalits*, classified as untouchable under the Hindu caste system for their association with such polluting tasks as curing leather or clearing excreta, had a long history of anticaste protest in Maharashtra. In the late nineteenth century, under the leadership of Jyotiba Phule, *dalits* had also espoused women's rights to education, against purdah, and for widow remarriage. *Janwedana* (Distress of the People), a *dalit* Marathi newspaper, brought out a special women's issue entitled "In the Third World Women Hold Up Half the Sky," a slogan borrowed from the Chinese Revolution to make clear its departure from First World feminism; some months later women from the *dalit* movement formed an intriguing new group called the Mahila Samta

Sainik Dal (League of Women Soldiers for Equality). The name itself, which stressed equality and conjured up images of a women's crusade, drew on the Black movement in the United States, and the Dal's manifesto claimed African-American activist Angela Davis as a sister. Both the Dal and POW emphasized women's oppression; the Dal additionally emphasized the oppressive character of religion and the caste system.[7]

The declaration of a state of emergency in 1975 by Prime Minister Indira Gandhi interrupted the development of the fledgling women's movement. Many political organizations were driven underground, thousands of activists were arrested, and most who remained at liberty focused on civil rights, such as freedom of speech and association, the right to protest, and the rights of political prisoners. The lifting of the emergency in 1977 and the formation of the Janata government in 1978 led to a renewal of some of the earlier movements. Women's groups were formed all over the country but mainly in the major cities.

Early Feminist Campaigns

The distinguishing features of the new women's groups were that they declared themselves to be "feminist" despite the fact that most of their members were drawn from the Left, which saw feminism as bourgeois and divisive; that they insisted on being autonomous even though most of their members were affiliated to other political groups, generally of the far Left; and that they rapidly built networks among one another, ideological differences notwithstanding. All three features were, however, defined and in certain ways limited by the history of these groups, whose first years were spent mainly in attempts at self-definition. The fact that most of their members were drawn from the far Left and belonged to the urban educated middle class influenced the feminist movement of the late 1970s and early 1980s in complex ways. For example, one of the main questions that feminists raised in the late 1970s was, How could women be organized and represented? While there was a general agreement that it was not the role of feminist groups to organize or represent women, there was considerable disagreement on why this was so. For some, feminist groups were in essence urban and middle class and so could neither represent Indian women as a whole nor organize them; others believed that, although autonomy was necessary for the development of feminist theory, in practice it would divide existing organizations and movements. The role of feminist groups, therefore, was to raise feminist issues in mass organizations such as trade unions or *kisan samitis* (peasant committees), which would then be in a position to organize and represent women as well as men. Yet others believed that once a women's movement began, it would naturally spread and grow in multiple ways, creating its own organizations and representatives, and so it was superfluous for feminist groups to debate whether they should organize and represent women.

Many groups opted for autonomy, which they defined as separate, women-only groups without any party affiliation or conventional organizational structure, for they considered this hierarchical, self-interested, and competitive. By contrast, the women's groups that were formed in the late 1970s were loosely organized and without formal structures or funds. The only party-based women's organization to be formed in the late 1970s was the Mahila Dakshata Samiti (MDS; Women's Self-Development Organisation), which was founded in 1977 by socialist women in the coalition Janata Party.

While there was therefore a feminist critique of party politics, the terms of criticism varied widely: Some feminists were critical of party practices but believed that parties could enact valuable reform and fulfill feminist aims; others were critical of entrenched political parties, and yet others argued that political parties, even of the Left, were so centralized that they would never fulfill feminist aims. Meanwhile, the influence of feminist ideas was growing. Though the feminist campaigns in the late 1970s and early 1980s were dominated by the new city-based groups, a similar growth of feminist consciousness had taken place in certain rural movements. The 1950s sharecroppers'

movement in the Telengana area of Andhra Pradesh was again renewed in the late 1970s, and the area was declared a "disturbed zone" by the government. In Telengana's Karimnagar district, where women had been especially active in the landless laborers' movement from the 1960s on, the new wave of agitation began with a campaign against the kidnapping of a woman called Devamma, and the murder of her husband, by a local landlord. According to the Stree Shakti Sanghatana (Women's Struggle Organization) formed in the late 1970s in Hyderabad (the capital of Andhra Pradesh), the demand for independent women's organizations came from the women themselves, who raised the issues of wife beating and landlord rape through the *mahila sanghams* (women's committees).[8]

At around the same time, in the Bodhgaya district of Bihar feminist issues were raised by women in the socialist students' organization, the Chhatra Yuva Sangharsh Vahini (Young Students' Struggle Organization), which was involved in an agricultural laborers' movement for land reclamation from the temple priest who owned most of the land in the area. As in the Shahada and Telengana movements, women were active in the struggle, and in 1979 a women's camp in Bodhgaya decided that Vahini campaigns to reclaim plots of land would demand that plots be registered in the names of men and women.

The Movement against dowry

The first campaigns of the contemporary Indian feminist movement were against dowry and rape. Protests against dowry were first organized by the Progressive Organization of Women in Hyderabad in 1975.[9] Although some of the demonstrations numbered as many as two thousand people, the protests did not grow into a full-fledged campaign because of the imposition of the emergency, which drove most activists underground. After the lifting of the emergency, a new movement against dowry started in Delhi. This time it was against violence inflicted upon women for dowries, especially against murder and abetment to suicide. There have since been protests against dowry harassment and murder in several parts of India, but Delhi has remained the site of sustained agitation against dowry and dowry-related crimes, largely because it seems to have the highest number of murders of women for dowry in the country.

Although the MDS was the first women's organization in Delhi's contemporary feminist movement to take up the issue of dowry and dowry harassment, it was Stri Sangharsh, a fledgling feminist group founded in 1979, that drew public attention to dowry-related crimes. On June 1, 1979, Stri Sangharsh organized a demonstration against the death of Tarvinder Karu, a young woman from Delhi who had left a deathbed statement saying that her in-laws had killed her because her parents could not fulfill the in-laws' ever-increasing demands. The demonstration was widely reported by the national press, and in the next few weeks there was a spate of demonstrations against dowry deaths, one of the biggest ones led by the Nari Raksha Samiti (Women's Rescue Committee) on June 12 through the alleys of old Delhi. Each demonstration was headline news, and a public debate on dowry and dowry-related crimes began.

Until this time women's deaths by fire (women doused with kerosene and set on fire, often by the in-laws and husband) had been termed suicide, and even these suicides were rarely seen as being due to dowry harassment. No one (including the police) had ever bothered to investigate them or even categorize them. And mostly they had been passed off as private affairs that took place within the family and were of no concern to the state. Within weeks, however, feminists reversed the indifference of decades, linking death by fire with dowry harassment and showing that many official suicides were in fact murders. Feminists recorded the last words of the dying woman, took family testimony, and encouraged friends and neighbors to come forward with their evidence. As a result, many families began to lodge complaints with the police against the harassment of their daughters by the in-laws for more dowry.

Campaigns against dowry deaths now began to be taken up by neighborhood groups, teachers' associations, and trade unions. Within feminist groups a series of strategies was devised to enhance public awareness of the problems associated with dowry: Stri Sangharsh produced a street play, *Om Swaha* (priests' incantation around the ritual wedding fire), that attracted large crowds all over the city and continues to be performed by different groups today; *Manushi*, a Delhi-based feminist magazine, organized a series of public meetings at which people pledged neither to take nor give dowry.

In 1980, a year after the antidowry agitation began, the government passed a law against dowry-related crimes that recognized abetment to suicide because of dowry demands as a special crime and made mandatory a police investigation into the death of any woman within five years of marriage. However, the law was a considerable disappointment to feminists. Although it acknowledged that dowry harassment could be construed as abetment, it did not specify the kinds of evidence that could be used to prove harassment, nor did it make abetment a cognizable offense. And though the law was passed in 1980, the first positive judgment under it did not occur until 1982, when a Delhi Sessions Court magistrate found two people guilty of dowry murder and sentenced them to death. The judgment was reversed by the Delhi High Court in early 1983. Women's groups from the party-affiliated Left and autonomous groups protested and were held for contempt of court. In 1985, the Supreme Court upheld the verdict but converted the sentence to life imprisonment. Moreover, the storm that women's groups raised in 1983 had some indirect effect: In December 1983 the Criminal Law (Second Amendment) Act was passed, which made cruelty to a wife a cognizable, nonbailable offense punishable by up to three years' imprisonment and a fine; the act also redefined cruelty to include mental as well as physical harassment. In addition, Section 113-A of the Evidence Act was amended so that the court could draw an inference of abetment to suicide. Technically this shifted the burden of proof and thus lessened the burden upon the complainant. Finally, the act amended Section 174 of the

Criminal Procedure Code, requiring a post-mortem examination of the body of a woman who died within seven years of marriage.

In practice most of these amendments do not make it much easier to secure convictions for dowry death. Hearsay evidence has to be overwhelming for an Indian court to convict, as people will say anything to gain a point, even before a court of law. Traditionally most women are raised with the belief that after marriage they have no source of support – including livelihood – other than their in-laws. So the women themselves are loath to bring charges of harassment. Similarly, postmortem examinations do not necessarily give evidence of murder. As most dowry deaths are the result of burns, generally with kerosene, it is difficult to prove that they resulted from murder, which is why so many dowry deaths were put down to stove accidents before women's groups began to argue otherwise.

Overall the agitation against dowry-related crimes led feminists to varying conclusions. On the one hand, they discovered they could get massive public support for campaigns against certain kinds of crimes against women, such as dowry-related murder. On the other hand, they found how difficult it was to work with the law against such crimes. This latter experience was repeated in regard to rape.

The agitation against rape
Beginning just a few months after the campaign against dowry-related crimes, the agitation against rape started with campaigns against police rape. The scale and frequency of police rape are quite startling in India: Police records themselves show that the number of rapes by government servants in rural and tribal areas exceeds one a day.[10] This figure vastly understates the actual number of such rapes, for it does not cover incidents of mass rape by the police (i.e., the rape of groups of women by groups of policemen, generally as a reprisal to underclass movements for redress in rural areas); even in the case of individual or gang rape, the figure cannot cover unreported incidents, which are likely to be at least as numerous as reported ones.

When the new feminist groups were formed in the late 1970s, they were already familiar with the categories of police and landlord rape, for both, especially the former, had been addressed by the Maoist movement. Moreover, the issue of police rape achieved new significance in 1978, just as feminist groups were in the process of formation, through an incident in Hyderabad where a woman called Rameeza Bee was raped by several policemen, and her husband, a rickshaw puller, was murdered when he protested his wife's rape. A popular uprising ensued: Twenty-two thousand people went to the police station, laid the man's dead body in the station veranda, set up roadblocks, cut the telephone wires, stoned the building, and set fire to some bicycles in the compound. The army had to be called in, and the uprising was quieted only after the state government had been dismissed and a commission of inquiry into the rape and the murder had been appointed.[11]

In 1979, there were women's demonstrations against incidents of police and landlord/employer rape in many parts of the country. Campaigns against these incidents, however, remained isolated from each other until 1980, when an open letter by four senior lawyers against a judgment in a case of police rape in Maharashtra sparked off a campaign by feminist groups. Known as the Mathura rape case, the incident had occurred several years earlier, when a sixteen- or seventeen-year-old girl, Mathura, was raped by local policemen. Under pressure from her family and the villagers, a case was registered against the policemen, who were acquitted at the Sessions Court, convicted on appeal at the High Court, and later acquitted by the Supreme Court. The defense argument for the policemen was that Mathura had a boyfriend and was thus a loose woman who could not by definition be raped. The open letter was in protest at the Supreme Court's acceptance of this argument.

The campaign against rape marked a new stage in the development of feminism in India. The networks that had begun to form in 1978–1979 were now consolidated and expanded and used to coordinate action.

Finding this letter in the left-wing journal *Mainstream*, the Bombay feminist group Forum Against Rape (FAR, which is now called the Forum Against Oppression of Women) decided in February 1980 to campaign for the reopening of the case and wrote to feminist groups across the country to propose that demonstrations be held on International Women's Day (March 8) to demand a retrial. In effect, this was the first time that feminist groups coordinated a national campaign. Groups in seven cities responded to the FAR letter and organized demonstrations on March 8 demanding a retrial of the Mathura case, the implementation of relevant sections of the Indian Penal Code, and changes in the rape law. In both Bombay and Delhi, joint action committees were formed of feminist groups and Socialist and Communist Party affiliates to coordinate the campaign.

Meanwhile, protests against police rape were reported from all over the country, only some of which were organized by feminists. As in the agitation against dowry, the first protests against police rape sparked off a series of protests by neighborhood and trade union-based groups in different parts of the country. The kind of press coverage that was now given to incidents of police rape and protests against them encouraged national parties to use the issue as a political lever against their rivals. When in June 1980 policemen arrested a woman called Maya Tyagi in the small town of Baghpat in Haryana state, stripped her naked, raped her, and paraded her through the streets, the incident aroused such furor from women's organizations and political parties that Home Minister Zail Singh went to Baghpat with ten women MPs and ordered a judicial inquiry into the incident. While they were in Baghpat, the Lok Dal, an opposition political party, staged a noisy demonstration (according to the newspapers) against the incident, claiming it underlined Congress misrule. Roughly a week later, Parliament debated the large-scale increase in the incidents of rape and atrocities against women, and several MPs used the issue to demand the resignation of the home minister and suggested that the death penalty be introduced to punish rapists.

Within months of the agitation, the government introduced a bill defining the categories of custodial rape and specifying a mandatory punishment of ten years' imprisonment, in camera trials, and a shift of the onus of proof onto the accused. The clause over which controversy raged was the burden of proof clause, which said that if the women could prove intercourse with the accused at the time and place she alleged, and if it had been forced upon her, then the accused would be presumed guilty until he could prove otherwise. Immediately there arose the cry that this violated the legal principle that a man was innocent until proved guilty, and the papers were full of articles vehemently protesting the clause, some of which exclaimed that this paved the way for every revengeful woman to frame innocent men.

The government had taken the wind out of feminists' sails by responding to their demands with such a radical piece of legislation. But this was only one of the reasons the agitation faded so rapidly. The highly publicized nature of the campaign and the speed with which rape was used by mainstream political parties in a welter of accusation and counteraccusation placed feminists in the invidious position of having to rescue the issue from political opportunists. Moreover, the nature of the issue, the kind of social sanction accorded to rape, and the problem of acquiring medical evidence to prove it in a country where only the big cities are technically equipped to provide such evidence constituted formidable obstacles.

These early years of the contemporary Indian women's movement taught women's groups a series of lessons, of which the foremost was that there was considerable public support – from men as well as women – for campaigns against gender oppression. In effect, a handful of feminists discovered that they could garner public support and influence policy even though their numbers were small and their groups weak. However, this discovery did not bring unmixed pleasure, for it also entailed having to deal with the political exploitation of feminist campaigns, as in the movement against rape.

Growth and Maturing of the Movement

The mixed experiences of the campaigns against rape and dowry led many feminists to question their methods and tactics. The discovery that there was little and faulty connection between the enactment and the implementation of laws left many feeling rather bitter that the government had easily sidetracked their demands by enacting legislation. This gave rise to further questions about the efficacy of basing campaigns around demands for changes in the law and, by extension, around demands for action from the state. On the one hand, this questioning strengthened decisions to take up individual cases and follow them through the intricacies of the courts, no matter how long it took. On the other hand, feminists began to move away from their earlier methods of agitation, such as public campaigns, demonstrations, and street theater, feeling that these had limited meaning unless accompanied by attempts to develop structures to aid and support individual women. In the early 1980s, women's centers were formed in several cities. These centers provided a mixture of legal aid, health care, and counseling; one or two of them also tried to provide employment, but they foundered for lack of sufficient resources.

Though centers to provide women with aid, counseling, health care, and employment had existed from the early twentieth century on, these new centers were different in several important ways. First, most of the earlier centers had concentrated on one or two issues, whereas the new ones attempted to provide help on a range of interrelated issues. Second, the earlier centers had had a social welfare ideology, whereas the new ones were explicitly feminist. For example, earlier centers providing health care had concentrated on maternity and child welfare alone. The new centers, in contrast, took a more holistic view, looking at how women treated their own bodies.

Third, the new centers represented an effort to put feminist concepts of sisterhood into practice as well as to redefine these concepts by basing them on traditionally accepted structures of friendship among women. In both Delhi and Kanpur, for example, the names of the centers symbolized moves to locate notions of sisterhood in a specifically Indian context. Both chose to focus on and thereby reinterpret the traditional concept of a girlfriend; in Delhi, the name chosen was Saheli (Female Friend) and in Kanpur, Sakhi Kendra (Center for Women Friends). Saheli, with its association of playfulness, was chosen by the Delhi feminists who set up the center to signify that they were concerned not only with helping women in distress but also with sharing moments of play and pleasure. The center's founders wished to give due to the positive aspects of women's lives, particularly their forms of celebration and creativity. This led Saheli to host a 1983 workshop for feminists from all over India at which there were sessions on song, dance, drama, and painting.

Attempts to appropriate symbols of women's power grew in the 1980s through reinterpreting myths, epics, and folktales and unearthing historical forms of women's resistance in India. To some extent an interest in tradition had been present in the Indian feminist movement since the 1970s. The street plays *Om Swaha* (against dowry deaths, first put together in Delhi in 1979 and performed all over the city and in several parts of northern India) and *Mulgi Zali Ho* (A Girl Is Born, performed in Bombay in 1979–1980) had both used traditional songs and dances; many exhibitions mounted by feminists had similarly used traditional images. At this stage, however, the main effort was to detail traditional forms of women's subordination in India, from birth to puberty, marriage, maternity, work, old age, and death. In the 1980s, the emphasis changed to looking for traditional sources of women's strength rather than simply suffering. For some, this consisted of identifying images of women warriors to be used as a battle cry for latter-day women and to appreciate and recast Kali, the all-powerful mother goddess, in a feminist mold.

If the interest in tradition led some feminists to reinterpret images, others were more interested in defining the ways in which ordinary women used the spaces traditionally accorded them to negotiate with their husbands, families, and communities. Special attention was now paid, for example, to the way in which women appropriated specific religious practices such as spirit possession, simulating possession by the *devi* (goddess), particularly during pregnancy, to wrest concessions from their husband or families that would otherwise have been impossible. Accounts now began to circulate of women who had simulated possession to reform alcoholic husbands or get money for household expenses, and this tactic began to be highlighted as a means of gaining power.

The search for historical examples of women's resistance led feminists to scrutinize the distant and immediate past, to look at the role women played in broader movements for social transformation, and to reclaim some of the movements predating contemporary feminism. One example was the Chipko movement against deforestation in the northern Indian mountain tracts. Beginning in the mid-1970s, Chipko (literally, cling to) was a movement to prevent forest destruction by timber contractors and was carried forward largely by women, who were traditionally responsible for fuel, food, and water in the family. There was little or no discussion of it as a women's movement until the early 1980s, when feminists began to celebrate it as a mass women's movement and theories of women's special relation to their environment began to be advanced.[12] A new awareness of women's role and problems developed within the movement, and the hitherto defunct government-sponsored village- and district-level *mahila mandals* were revitalized.

By the early 1980s, feminism had branched into a series of activities ranging from the production of literature and audiovisual material to slum-improvement work, employment-generating schemes, health education, and trade unions. New attempts to organize women workers' unions were made. Interestingly, these attempts focused largely on the unorganized sector, as SEWA had done; unlike SEWA, however, they grew out of campaigns for an improvement in living conditions. By this stage the feminist movement had diversified from issue-based groups into distinct

organizational identities. The first professions to feel the influence of feminism were journalism, academia, and medicine. Soon after the feminist movement began, most of the major English-language dailies had deputed one or more women journalists to write exclusively on feminist issues, and a network of women journalists evolved. In Bombay, this network was formalized into a women journalists' group in the mid-1980s, with the purpose of lobbying for better reporting on women's issues, such as dowry, rape, and widow immolation. Feminism thus had a much wider audience than before.

Women's studies took off in the 1980s, initially under the aegis of independent research institutes such as the Centre for Women's Development Studies (CWDS) in Delhi, though an attempt to fund research at the university level was made by the S.N. Damodar Thackersay (SNDT) Women's University in Bombay, which set up a women's research unit. The SNDT and CWDS began to jointly host annual national women's studies conferences, and interest in women's studies grew so rapidly that today the University Grants Commission, a central government body, plans to set up women's studies courses at the college level.

During the same period, the far Right began to organize its own bases among women. The Maharashtra-based Hindu chauvinist Shiv Sena (Shiva's Army) activated its women's wing to engage in anti-Muslim propaganda. Interestingly, its main argument was one advanced in the nineteenth century that had had enduring success in India: that the Muslim rate of reproduction is so prolific that it will outstrip that of Hindus. The time when it does so, of course, never comes.

An even more worrying development took place between 1982 and 1983 in Delhi, Rajasthan, and parts of Bengal, where attempts were made to revive sati, the practice of immolating widows on their husbands' funeral pyres. Under the aegis of the Rani Sati Sarva Sangh (an organization to promote sati), feminist discourse was used to propagate a cult of widow immolation. Women's demonstrations were organized in various parts of the country to demand women's "right" to commit sati.

In Delhi, feminists decided to hold a counterdemonstration along the route of a pro-sati procession. This was the first time that feminists were forced to confront a group of hostile women, which was in itself so distressing that it took the heart out of the counterdemonstration. Most distressing of all, however, was the way in which the processionists appropriated the language of rights, stating that they should have the right, as Hindus and as women, to commit, worship, and propagate sati. At the same time, they also appropriated feminist slogans on women's militancy, for example, "*Hum Bharat ki nari hain, phool nahin, chingari hain*" (We, the women of India, are not flowers but fiery sparks). The feminists who attended that demonstration experienced a humiliating sense of loss on discovering that their own words could be so readily used against them.[13]

The early 1980s witnessed a series of countermovements against feminist ideas by sections of traditionalist society. The rise of these countermovements was partly related to the spread of feminism and the influence it was beginning to have on women's attitudes, especially within the family. The kind of support that women's centers gave women who were being harassed for dowry or forced into arranged marriages, for example, provoked a considerable degree of public and private hostility, and feminists began to face attacks from irate families in person and through the police and the courts. However, where earlier such attacks would have led to a wave of sympathy for the feminists, from the mid-1980s on they were accompanied by a public, and increasingly sophisticated, critique of feminism. Much of this criticism took place in a context of growing communalism.

Challenges to the Movement

The issue of personal, or religion-based and -differentiated family, law became especially controversial for feminists in 1985 in what is now referred to as the Shah Bano case. In India, personal law falls under the purview of religion, though individuals can choose secular alternatives. This choice is, however, circumscribed: A woman married under Muslim or Hindu law,

for example, cannot seek divorce or alimony under secular law; she has to abide by what is offered by the religious laws by which she was married. Neither Muslim nor Hindu personal law entitles a woman to alimony. Under Muslim law she is entitled to the return of her engagement gift (*iddat*); under Hindu law she is theoretically entitled to the gifts that went with her at marriage (*stridhan*). Finding an abnormal number of destitute divorced women in India, the British colonial government passed a law under the Criminal Procedure Code (Section 125) entitling destitute divorced women to maintenance by their husbands. It was Section 125, which remains in Indian criminal law, that was at issue in the Shah Bano case.

Shah Bano was a seventy-five-year-old woman who had been abandoned by her husband and had filed for maintenance under Section 125. While her claim was being considered, her husband divorced her, using the triple *talaq*.[14] The Supreme Court, in its judgment, upheld Shah Bano's right to maintenance from her husband under both Section 125 and Muslim personal law.[15] It asserted that Section 125 transcended personal law. The court was critical of the way women had traditionally been subjected to unjust treatment, citing statements by both Manu, the Hindu lawmaker, and the Prophet as examples of traditional injustice. And the court urged the government to frame a common civil code because the constitutional promise of a common or uniform civil code would be realized only at the government's initiative.

The judgment was widely criticized by feminists,[16] liberals, and secularists as well as by Muslim religious leaders for what were held to be unduly weighted critical comments of Muslim personal law. The ulema (scholar-priests) issued a *fatwa* (proclamation) that the judgment violated the teachings of Islam. Wide publicity was given to the *fatwa*, and within a few months the whole issue took the form of a communal agitation claiming that Islam was in danger. One hundred thousand people demonstrated against the judgment in Bombay and at least as many in Bhopal, both cities with large Muslim populations. Supporters of the judgment were threatened, stoned, and beaten up.

Demands began for legislative action against Section 125. In August 1985, a Muslim League MP, G. M. Banatwala, offered a bill in Parliament seeking to exclude Muslim women from the purview of Section 125. Though the ruling Congress Party opposed the bill, as Muslim public protest against the Shah Bano judgment mounted, the party began to backtrack. To understand why the issue became so heated, one has to look at the context. In October 1984, the Vishwa Hindu Parishad (World Hindu Organization) launched an agitation demanding that a shrine in the precincts of Muslim mosque, the Babri Masjid, in the northern Indian town of Ayodhya be declared the birthplace of the god Ram and a temple be built on the spot. Parishad led demonstrations all over the country between 1984 and 1985, drawing as many as two hundred thousand people. The Babri Masjid issue and the Shah Bano case began to be linked as representing a Hindu communal onslaught on Muslims. The threat of Hindu communalism appeared especially strong in the wake of the November 1984 riots against Sikhs following the assassination of Indira Gandhi.[17]

In the 1985 state elections, the Congress lost in a number of Muslim constituencies. Alarmed by this, it announced that the government would consider a bill along the lines of Banatwala's bill, and in 1986 the Muslim Women's (Protection of Rights on Divorce) Bill was enacted. At the same time, they let a local magistrate's judgment that the shrine in the Babri Masjid be given over to Hindus go unchallenged.

For feminists, the agitation around Muslim women's rights to maintenance consisted of a series of bitter lessons. Discovering the ease with which a "community in danger" resorts to fundamentalist assertions, among which control over women is one of the first, feminists also confronted the ease with which the Indian state chose to accommodate communalism (by taking no action against the Vishwa Hindu Parishad agitation) and balance this by a concession to fundamentalism (allowing personal law to cut into the application of uniform laws such as Section 125).

At the same time, the agitation posed certain issues that were to become increasingly important for feminists in the years to follow. There were the questions of secularism; its definition and practice, particularly by the state; and its relation to religious freedom. By and large, opponents of the Muslim Women's Bill espoused a classic liberal democratic view of secularism as a system that separated religion from politics, that disallowed religious definition of the rights of the individual, and that allowed freedom of religious practice only insofar as it did not curb the rights of the individual. A 1986 petition against the bill jointly organized by feminists, social reformers, and Far Left groups, for example, argued that all personal laws "have meant inequality and subordinate status for women in relation to men" and that therefore religion "should only govern the relationship between a human being and god, and should not govern the relationship between man and man or man and woman."

As against this, the government definition of secularism appeared to be radically different. According to Prime Minister Rajiv Gandhi, "secularism is the right of every religion to co-exist with another religion. We acknowledge this by allowing every religion to have its own secular laws."[18] This statement seemed to imply that personal laws were defined as secular – presumably on the grounds that as religion in this instance defined the relationships between human beings rather than between humans and god, it was on "secular" terrain. Religion, then, could formulate secularism. Another implication of this statement was that all religions had the right to representation within the law and the right to make their own laws. While to a certain extent these rights were not new, the supremacy they accorded to personal law reaffirmed the colonial codification of religion-based family laws and ran counter to the constitutional promises of offering alternatives to personal laws and moving toward uniform rights.

So much pressure was put on Shah Bano that she gave up the right she had long fought for, abjuring the maintenance the court had accorded her. As in the agitation against rape, the problems and needs of women were soon submerged by the discourse of "community." Even worse, in this agitation, setting a trend for others to follow, the individual woman was smothered by a newly constructed symbol of woman, the "real woman" who followed men in demonstrations organized by Muslim religious leaders, who signed petitions against Shah Bano, who abhorred claims for maintenance because they were against her religion, and who saw feminists as unnatural creatures attempting to wrest her identity from her. This positing of the real woman in opposition to the feminist began to be widely made for the first time in the history of the contemporary women's movement in the mid-1980s, and it is revealing that this symbol arose in the course of communal–fundamentalist self-assertion. In the 1987–1988 agitation around sati that followed on the heels of the Muslim Women's Bill agitation, the issues of secularism, religious representation, the Indian nation-state, and the symbol of the real woman were expanded even further.

In September 1987, an incident of sati in the village of Deorala in Rajasthan sparked off a campaign that gave rise to a furious debate that spanned not only the rights and wrongs of Hindu women but also questions of religious identity, communal autonomy, and the role of the law and the state in a society as complex and as diverse as India. Within a couple of weeks of the incident of sati, several articles appeared that engaged in a polemic against Indian feminists, accusing them of being agents of modernity who were attempting to impose crass, selfish, market-dominated views on a society that had once given noble, spiritual women the respect they deserved.[19] These market-dominated views of equality and liberty were portrayed as being drawn from the West, so Indian feminists stood accused of being Westernists, colonialists, cultural imperialists, and, indirectly, supporters of capitalist ideology.

Given that there has been, on average, only one reported sati a year in postindependence India, the extraordinary debate that the 1987 sati incident aroused was puzzling. In a way it can be understood only as part of a process

of political reorganization in which the death of Roop Kanwar, the girl who was immolated, became the symbol of Rajput identity politics. In contrast to some of the other areas in which sati had been attempted, Deorala was a relatively highly developed village. The family was well off. Roop Kanwar's father-in-law was headmaster of a district school, while she herself was a graduate. A Rajput family, the Kanwars had links with influential Rajputs and mainstream state-level politicians.

Roop Kanwar had been married only a short while before her husband died. When her marital family decided that she would become a sati, the event was announced in advance because sati is always a public spectacle. Yet her natal family was not informed. Evidence pointed to murder: Some of her neighbors said that she had run away and tried to hide in a barn before the ceremony but was dragged out, drugged, dressed in her bridal finery, and put on the pyre, with logs and coconuts heaped upon her. The pyre itself was lit by her brother-in-law.[20] Reports indicated that the local authorities knew of the planned sati, yet their only action was to dispatch a police jeep, which was overturned on its way to the site. Following this debacle, three more days elapsed before a government representative visited Deorala.[21]

Immediately after the immolation, the site became a popular pilgrimage spot, and a number of stalls sprang up spelling auspicious offerings, mementos, and audiocassettes of devotional songs. Her father-in-law, prominent men from the village, and members of a newly formed organization, the Sati Dharm Raksha Samiti (Organization for the Defense of the Religious–Ethical Ideal of Sati), together formed a trust to run the site and collect donations. Within some three weeks the trust had collected around Rs 50 lakhs (close to $200,000).[22] The leaders of the Samiti were urban professionals or businessmen from landowning families whose sphere of influence extended over both rural and urban areas. Their propaganda was illuminating. Policymakers and the intelligentsia argued that a representative state should recognize and legitimate Rajputs' claim that sati was a fundamental part of their traditions; a refusal to legitimize sati, they said, was a deliberate attempt to marginalize the Rajputs. The women's groups, for example, were represented as using the issue as a means to attack Rajputs. In the 1990 state elections, several leaders of the Samiti won seats in the state legislature.

As the pro-sati campaign developed, the argument about Rajputs was extended to Hindu identity. The head priests of the major Hindu temples in such centers as Benares and Puri issued statements that sati represented one of the most noble elements not only of Rajput culture but also of Hinduism and claimed that issues such as sati should be placed under their purview as arbiters of Hindu personal law and not that of the state. At the same time, they also raised the bogey of "Hinduism in danger" from the opponents of sati.

The Hinduism in danger cry was echoed by far Right Hindu nationalists, spearheaded by the Shiv Sena, which organized a series of pro-sati demonstrations and argued that the Indian state was particularly biased against the Hindus, for it was willing to accede to the demands of minority communities for representation but was unwilling to do the same for the majority. The particular point of reference here was the Muslim Women's Bill, and, as in the Muslim Women's Bill agitation, the pro-sati agitation also posited real women against feminists.

The pro-sati agitators mobilized considerable numbers of women in their support. This allowed them to claim that they represented the "true" desires of Hindu women and to accuse the feminists of being unrepresentative. So the feminists were placed in the anomalous position of appearing to speak in the interest of women whom they could not claim to represent and who defined their interests differently.

The tradition versus modernity argument further isolated feminists. The bogey of modernism was so successful that it masked the fact that sati was being used to create a "tradition," despite feminist efforts to emphasize this. Tradition was defined so ahistorically and so self-righteously

that it obscured the fact that the pro-sati campaign was run on "modern" lines, with modern arguments, and for modern purposes, such as the reformation of electoral blocs and identity-based community representation within the state.

However, a closer look at the nature of women's support for the pro-sati agitation revealed that this was ambiguous and at many points consisted of firmly differentiating between the worship and the actual practice of sati. An examination of the women who were mobilized for the pro-sati demonstration made clear that they were not, in fact, the women who were most directly affected by the issue. Widows were conspicuously absent.

For most feminists, the campaign around sati revealed the growing opposition to feminism and spelled a considerable setback for the movement. Yet the challenges it posed to feminist self-definitions yielded some valuable insights: a more complex understanding of the ways in which different groups and communities saw themselves and a recognition that it is not helpful, especially at moments of crisis, to view the state as a monolithic entity, for it is important to assert that women have the right to a voice in the administration of their society. Representation consisted not merely of a show of numbers but also in the encouragement of a plethora of voices, which was to some extent taking place through the feminist and associated movements. Opposition to sati came from a variety of sources: Both the right-wing Hindu reformist tradition and maverick left-wing Hindu reformers such as Swami Agnivesh of the Arya Samaj (community of Aryans) opposed it. In fact, Swami Agnivesh challenged the head priests of the Puri and Benares temples to a debate on the scriptural "sanction" of sati. His challenge was declined. Opposition also came from sections of the Gandhians and from the anticaste movement. Within Rajasthan, considerable opposition to both sati and state inaction on Roop Kanwar's death was voiced by huge numbers of women, largely rural, who joined demonstrations to protest against the glorification of her death.

Notes

1   Maria Mies, "The Shahada Movement: A Peasant Movement in Maharshtra, Its Development, and Its Perspective," *Journal of Peasant Studies* 3, no. 4 (July 1976):478.

2   Devaki Jain, "The Self-Employed Women's Association, Ahmedabad," *How* 3, no. 2 (February 1980):14.

3   Gail Omvedt, "Women and Rural Revolt in India," *Journal of Peasant Studies*.

4   Vibhuti Patel, *Reaching for Half the Sky* (Bombay:Antar Rashtriya Prakashan Bawda, 1985), pp. 8–10.

5   Gail Omvedt, *We Will Smash This Prison* (London: Zed Books, 1980), Appendix II.

6   Omvedt, "Women and Rural Revolt."

7   Omvedt, *We Will Smash This Prison*, p. 174.

8   Stree Shakti Sangathana, "The War Against Rape," in Miranda Davies, ed., *Third World, Second Sex* (London: Zed Books, 1984), p. 201.

9   Dowry is the sum of money as well as other items (jewelry, furniture, car, other consumer durables) given by the bride's family to the groom's family at the time of marriage. Dowry is practiced mainly by Hindus of all classes but has increased most significantly in recent years among the urban middle classes. At the same time, the size of dowries has increased, and the groom's family has demanded additional dowry after the marriage.

10 Figures of reported rapes in India, year by year, are provided by the Bureau of Police Research and Development in Delhi. Evidence for the statements made here is in the bureau's report in the *Times of India, Statesman, Indian Express*, and *Patriot*, April 2–12, 1978.

11 This account compiled from reports in the *Times of India, Statesman, Indian Express*, and *Patriot*, April 2–12, 1978.

12 A classic example is Vandana Shiva, *Staying Alive: Women, Ecology, and Survival in India* (Delhi: Kali for Women, 1988).

13 This experience was recounted to me by Nandita Haksar and Sheba Chhachi, December 1983.

14 One of several methods of divorce permitted by Islam, the triple *talaq* is the easiest, requiring only that one party say "I divorce you" thrice.

15 In upholding her right to maintenance under Muslim personal law, the Supreme Court referred to two verses from the Koran that had been cited by Shah Bano's counsel, Daniel Latifi:

Ayat 241	*English Version*
Wali'l motallaqatay	*For divorced women*
Mata un	*Maintenance (should be provided)*
Bil maroofay	*On a reasonable (scale)*
Haqqhan	*This is a duty*
Alal muttaqeena	*On the righteous*
Ayat 242	
Kazaleki yuba Iyyanillaho	*Thus doth God*
Lakum ayatechee la Allakum	*Make clear His signs*
Taqeloon	*To you: in order that you may understand*

16 See, for example, Madhu Kishwar, "Pro-Women or Anti-Muslim?: The Shah Bano Controversy," *Manushi* 6, no. 2 (January-February 1986).

17 See "The Muslims: A Community in Turmoil," *India Today*, January 31, 1986.

18 Gandhi is quoted in a brochure for the film *In Secular India*, by Mediastorm.

19 These articles appeared first in the Delhi-based Hindi- and English-language national dailies *Jan Satta* ("Banwari, September 29, 1987), *Indian Express* (Ashis Nandy, May 10, 1987), and *Statesman* (Patrick D. Harrigan, May 22, 1987).

20 *Statesman*, September 18–20, 1987.

21 *Times of India*, September 17, 1987.

22 Ibid.

27

Women's Movement in Pakistan: State, Class, Gender

Shahnaz Rouse

Historical Overview of Women's Movement in Pakistan

Beginnings and evolution: 1940–1977
Any discussion of the historical development of a particular social movement must address the class structure of that movement. The origins of the women's movement in Pakistan can be traced back to the pre-independence period when bourgeois women constituted a vocal element in the anti-colonial struggle as well as in the Pakistan movement.[1] Their involvement led to a recognition of their contribution by Jinnah who made a strong plea for the removal of constraints against women. As early as 1944 he stated that: "No nation can rise to glory unless your women are side by side with you. We are victims of evil customs. It is a crime against humanity that our women are shut up within the four walls of the house as prisoners. There is no sanction anywhere for the deplorable condition in which our women have to live. You should take your women along with you as comrades in every sphere of life."[2]

Viewing the independent state of Pakistan as essentially a secular state, Jinnah asserted that women had claims to the same rights as did minorities, nationalities or other oppressed groups within the framework of a bourgeois democratic state. Even at this early stage the mullahs opposed the rights of women and were also vehemently opposed to the creation of Pakistan justified on the grounds that the Muslims of India had the right to a separate homeland. Voicing their total opposition to the creation of Pakistan, they called Jinnah 'kafir' or unbeliever because of his support for a secular state.[3]

Following the creation of Pakistan, women recognized some of their demands through the legal code. Women attained voting rights, and the Family Laws Ordinance was passed in 1961. Under this law, women were officially able to inherit agricultural property (in consonance with Islamic law), second marriages were made

Perspectives on Modern South Asia: A Reader in Culture, History, and Representation, First Edition.
Edited by Kamala Visweswaran.
© 2011 Blackwell Publishing Ltd. Published 2011 by Blackwell Publishing Ltd.

contingent upon agreement by the first wife, divorce was made more difficult for the male, women attained the right to initiate divorce for the first time, and a system of registration of marriages was also introduced.

By virtue of the family law coming into effect the rights of educated politically aware women were safe-guarded. However, this law did not penetrate very far. Working class women in the urban areas were only marginally able to benefit from it. The condition of rural women isolated as they were from the political scene and from the center of organizational activity, continued pretty much as before.

A few women's organizations existed at this time. They can be roughly divided into two categories: charitable women's organizations and organizations run by progressive women. The most well known among the former category was the All Pakistan Women's Association (APWA), among the latter Anjuman-e-Jamhooriat Pasand Khawateen. Although there existed a basic difference among the two in that APWA was an association of upper-class women providing services for women from less well-off socio-economic strata, whereas the Anjuman contained as its members women from more diverse class backgrounds, the latter was never really able to take off. My sense is that one of the contributing reasons for the failure of the Anjuman was that it failed to consciously separate women's issues from those of peace, social inequality, etc. Being closely linked in its leadership to the pro-Moscow Communist Party, they failed to develop an Independent position on women. The dominant pattern of work among publicly known women's organizations came to be social work–charitable organizations. By and large, these groups reflected their class position: altruism combined with reforms, reforms imposed from the top, changing the system to make it bearable but without fundamentally transforming reality or even directly confronting the inequities extant in it.

During the regime of Zulfiqar Ali Bhutto, the 1973 Constitution granted women rights including education to all rural and urban women.

This was also the period that saw the mushrooming of left wing political parties and a variety of women's groups in the professions, trade unions, and student's groups. Women did not feel threatened by Bhutto hence they chose to exploit the favorable environment to push for an extension of women's rights within the framework of the state.

An exception was the role played by women in the 1977 campaign against Bhutto. Bourgeois women led this movement, not protesting the abrogation of democratic rights by the regime (a criticism which many left groups and the national minorities levied against him), but mounting a right-wing opposition to his economic policies and the inflationary impact on their dwindling incomes.

In 1980 women emerged again on the political scene. This time, however, the organizations that moved to the forefront are qualitatively different in their emphasis, activities and approach. This change partially reflects the nature of the transformation of women's status and socio-economic involvement in the society and to the transformation of the Pakistani state.

Transformation of the women's movement
The transformation in the women's movement is directly connected with political processes in the country, as well as the transformation of the class structure. What this means is that two parallel developments have occurred. First, given economic trends in the country a middle class developed which has become dependent on women entering the work force. This was particularly critical in the urban areas, where traditionally middle class families had been loath to see their women step outside the house. Second, the increasing hold of the left which drew great numbers of men and women into the political process, led to the spontaneous mass movement that came into being towards the close of Ayub Khan's rule. Both these trends meant that women engaged in political processes in which they had not previously participated.

The late sixties and early seventies saw a blossoming of intellectual thought and grass-roots political organization, albeit in embryonic form. Women in large numbers joined the professions and though their numbers were relatively small they made significant progress. Television in particular broke the taboos generally connected in Pakistani society with music and the arts. College going women with artistic talents took advantage of this opportunity and became instrumental in portraying a different woman.

The mushrooming of left-wing political parties, mainly Maoist in character, tied as they were to the working class and the peasantry, drew into the political arena women who were previously totally dissociated from this process. Not only did this serve to politicize more women than ever before, but it also gave them badly needed organizational experience.

The first move against women and the political parties came shortly after Zia came to power. Attacks were mounted against two groups, bourgeois political parties, and the oppressed: workers, peasants and women. Women were faced with a two-pronged attack which threatened their active participation in civic society. This attack was partly ideological, an atmosphere of hate being created against them through state and religious proclamations; and second, a threat to their economic involvement in the work force. In response women realized that it was imperative that they organize and challenge the regime.

New organizational formations

September 1981 saw the birth of the Women's Action Forum (WAF), a mass-based popular front of many women's organizations and concerned individuals. The catalyst of WAF was a *Zina* case, where a fifteen year old woman was sentenced to flogging because of marrying a man of a lower class background contrary to her parent's wishes. This sentence triggered a response among women. Action was necessary as this case followed various other attacks on women including professors being molested, women being tortured for their political beliefs and affiliations, restrictions instituted against their professional activities and the imposition of a dress code for female public employees. It was also recognized that help could not

be expected from other quarters, either from the Movement for Restoration of Democracy (MRD) or the left since these groups were fighting for their survival, and had not taken an active part in fighting for women's rights in earlier periods. Women recognized that this was a fight they must lead themselves, that the need was to educate each other and fight for their rights to overcome previous inequalities.

Created initially by professional, middle class women, WAF received the endorsement of seven women's groups. These groups, while maintaining their independent existence, decided to rally under WAF's banner in a popular front dedicated to one common goal: the achievement of basic human rights for all Pakistani women. These rights include education, employment, physical security, choice of marital status, planned parenthood and non-discrimination.

Recognizing the enormity of the task confronting them, the organizers proceeded cautiously. Initially they devoted their attention to fighting to preserve rights under attack from the military. Given their limited numbers at this point a lobbying-cum-pressure group approach was used. The first action undertaken was a national signature campaign based on five issues affecting women. Over seven thousand signatures were collected between October and December 1981, and the document was presented to the Zia-ul-Haq.

Realizing that the state was likely to concede only token demands to them if they limited their activities to submitting petitions, WAF decided to broaden its base. Towards this end, in January 1982, the Karachi chapter of WAF organized a two day symposium on "Human Rights and Pakistani Women" while simultaneously running workshops on education, law, consciousness-raising and health. This was merely the first of a series of symposia and workshops held on a wide variety of topics of interest to women in English and Urdu as well as some of the regional languages.

WAF also began to reach out to minorities as well as to working class women. Their panels and workshops reflected their seriousness and included such topics as inflation, crimes against women, consume consciousness, and the nationality question. More recently there has been considerable discussion in the organization regarding organizing particularly in areas where working class women are concentrated.

While striving to deepen its base, WAF was at the same time extending it. October 1981 saw the creation of its second chapter in Lahore, the capital of the Punjab province. This was soon succeeded by one in Islamabad, and more modest beginnings in Peshawar Bahawalpur, Lyallpur, and Quetta. It was made clear that anybody who so wished could initiate a WAF chapter, provided that they were willing to adopt the charter drawn up by the Karachi chapter. The activities of each new chapter is subject to scrutiny by the two oldest chapters, i.e. Karachi and Lahore. If any discrepancy is noted between the activities of the local chapter and WAF's charter, the delinquent chapter is subject to expulsion.

WAF's chapters are also encouraged to incorporate as many women's organizations as possible in each area in order to expand the organization, facilitate coordination, avoid duplication of effort, and facilitate coalition building. WAF considers the gender question central to the formation of a united front for women. Their position is that women need to form a *mass* organization to fight for their rights. In their attempts to realize this goal, WAF constitutes a dynamic force. Its activities are constantly expanding, its membership growing, and the base expanding at an accelerated pace. By virtue of this dynamism WAF has shown that women *are* indeed a powerful force in the Pakistani politics scene.

WAF is also attempting to structure the organization in such a way that it remains democratically open. Each chapter is free to determine what its organizational structure should be. Within the organization representation and consent of members is given importance, as is work contribution, rather than official status. A working committee handling organizational matters connected with different chapters, and each chapter has a representative whenever all the chapters meet. In terms of its structure, membership and program, WAF represents a radical departure from previous women's groups.

WAF has served as a catalyst for other groups to become active in women's issues particularly groups connected with bourgeois political parties, e.g., the Tehrik-e-Istiklal, as well as women's groups with left wing sympathies, e.g., the Tehrik-e-Niswan, and Tehrik-e-Khawateen.

Shortly after WAF emerged, its successes became apparent to observers of the political scene. Bourgeois and middle class women were flocking to WAF's meetings, alarmed at the turn of events since the military take-over. Among WAF's membership were women with strong connections to bourgeois political parties, particularly the Tehrik-e-Istiklal, the protege of Asghar Khan, a retired armed forces officer. It is commonly felt by women within WAF that once bourgeois parties realized the political value of women's mobilization, they wished to capture the movement and utilize it for their own political advancement. WAF members with long-standing political experience recognized the danger of having women's issues again made subservient to a broader political agenda, or appropriated in a fashion not necessarily reflective of women's needs or demands.

Within the Lahore chapter where elements from the bourgeois political elements were most heavily represented, and the most politically developed membership existed, this resulted in conflict within the organization. The net result was that elements connected with bourgeois political parties split off from the main organization and created a separate chapter which they call WAF (democratic) as opposed to the original group which is called WAF (national). The lack of success of the splinter group is evident from the fact that they have not had much success in mobilizing more than a handful of women. This is not to suggest that the women involved in WAF (democratic) are not seriously committed to women's issues, but for many of them the issue is subservient to the dictates of their political party affiliations, or it is a part-time involvement. The possibilities for any serious advancement by this group appears to be extremely limited.

In contrast, other women's groups that have emerged or become more active since the creation of WAF constitute a left-wing alternative and are the Tehrik-e-Niswan in Karachi, and the Tehrik-e-Khawateen in Lahore. Each group places the women's question within the overall framework of the class question, and in consequence primarily focus on those sectors with whom the left has traditionally worked, i.e., working women, the peasantry, and students. They have shown varying degrees of success in mobilizing these sectors of the population. Around some events they have also shown a willingness to cooperate with WAF. Particularly in the case of Tehrik-e-Khawateen, they have had a positive effect in organizing rural women and in pulling WAF further to the left. The interaction of these groups with WAF has been principled in that they have not attempted to take over the organization. They continue to carry on their own activities, and whenever specific events warrant, cooperate with WAF to maximize the impact of their work and prevent a further deterioration in women's situation. Unlike the bourgeois groups which split off from WAF, these latter groups are engaged in independent work.

Class structure within the women's movement: Shifts and implications

In the early years of Pakistan few women were gainfully employed in the formal sector. This picture has been radically transformed largely as the consequence of a modernist developmental policy prior to the current regime where women entered schools and colleges and learned skilled trades. The extension of education and skills means that large numbers of middle class women are now gainfully employed. This has not necessarily resulted in an improvement of their position within the household, where they are still expected to perform domestic labor (unless they are privileged enough to hire others to take over this task). For the educated, skilled woman worker, however, it has meant a certain degree of heightened awareness. It is from this sector that the leadership of the women's movement comes, and it is also the sector from which most WAF recruits are coming.

There is, however, the informal sector of the economy in which women are also employed in large numbers such as domestics. Traditionally, there has been a fair degree of independence among these women from their menfolk, partly in consequence of the depressed conditions of their families. Like the Blacks in the United States, many of the males in these families have had to leave the household for extended periods to seek employment elsewhere. The women are left behind to manage and in the process learn and acquire a certain degree of militance and consciousness regarding their own situation, which is impossible to entirely eliminate upon the return of male family members.

There is a third category of women emerging, i.e., the wives of laborers who have gone to work in the Middle East. Like the women discussed above, one would expect to see radical changes occur in the demeanor of these women. To date very little work has been done examining what the nature of these changes are. One cannot automatically assume that they will acquire the same consciousness as their counterparts discussed above. This is partially mitigated by the material well-being of these families. Rural women vary dramatically from their urban counterparts. Even within this category, however, there is additional variation depending upon whether women come from settled agricultural areas or are located in the tribal economy. Further differentiation occurs depending upon their relation to property.

Rural women in settled agricultural settings have traditionally enjoyed greater mobility than their urban counterparts. This is primarily the consequence of their active and prolonged participation in the labor force. It is also a function of the lack of support for fundamentalists in the countryside. Government statistics totally overlook women's labor force participation, since data gatherers have traditionally relied on males to collect material. In terms of critical decisions of marriage, divorce and education, however, women remain the victims of male prejudice and control. Within the rural economy as in the urban, middle class women have been socially the most repressed. Affluence to a middle class rural family is often displayed by putting their womenfolk behind the 'veil'. In adhering to this custom, upwardly mobile families are merely duplicating the feudal forms still observable in Pakistani society whereby women of landed families were kept cloistered. Changes are occurring in all three categories and all are part and parcel of radical rural transformation that has been occurring since the late fifties.

Agrarian transformation has meant a steadily deteriorating life style for the vast majority of rural and urban dwellers including an increased dependence on the market. This in turn has meant an increased workload for women in the rural sector. With the introduction of new crops, women are productively employed in sectors which were previously unavailable to them. Agrarian change has also meant that certain types of jobs previously available to women are being eliminated because of the penetration of urban markets into the countryside. This contradictory dynamic has meant that women's lives have become harder. They have had to adjust to changes in productive employment, and often have had to bear the brunt of having households torn asunder because of migration by one or more household members to the city.

At the level of social relations, urban influences can be clearly seen in the villages. These are reflected not just in superficial changes, e.g. clothing, but also in attitudes towards education or travel by women. Traditional religious influences of Islamic orthodoxy mean very little to the vast bulk of the rural peasant populace. While spending time in rural areas of Pakistan, one is struck by the fact that, particularly among the landless, most families try to educate their woman if facilities are readily available. Taboos still exist prohibiting women from going away to school and economic realities make this an impossibility even when the will exists.

There exists in today's Pakistan then one general trend that unites the urban and rural areas. This is the overall deterioration in the economic well-being of large segments of its population. This is expressed by a concentration of economic resources in the rural areas and inflationary influences in the cities. Both these trends mean that women have to work for

wages and their menfolk, whether they like it or not, have to acknowledge the necessity of female participation in the labor force. The latter does not of course mean that these same individuals accept this as necessarily leading to the emancipation of women. On the contrary, it is precisely among segments of the population hardest hit by economic recession that Islamic ideology serves as an useful tool. As in the development of any fascist state elements of these classes especially in the urban areas prove the mostly likely recruits. It remains up to forces opposed to the development of fascist ideology, which in Pakistan's case fundamentalist Islamic Ideology serves to reinforce, to work to prevent that. And the women's movement has shown itself capable of taking on that challenge. Obviously, it still has a long way to go.

It is no coincidence that the women's movement has gone through an enormous transformation in the class basis of its members. This is certainly true of groups such as Tehrik-e-Khawateen, but it also applies to the Women's Action Forum. The shift in the class composition of the women's movement has important implications for the direction it takes. It means that altruism is no longer on the agenda and issues of equality, secularism, and democratic rights hold the center stage. There are various limitations that *do* still exist in the movement. For example, there is constant conflict among members representing different class interests and continued debates about direction and tactics. Often these debates tend to be resolved in ways looked askance at by women who belong to left parties, but the debates have the potential of moving the movement further to the left.

There is an attempt by the regime and its proponents in the media to portray the movement as the creation of a handful of western-educated women having no roots in their own culture. This charge has failed to take hold in popular perception both because the women's movement today is deeply embedded in our own reality, and also because most people view women as being actively engaged in struggle against the forces of repression. Whether this perception continues will depend on how fast and how deeply the movement is able to incorporate women of the most repressed economic classes and become what it purports to strive for – a mass movement.

Notes

1 Most of the Muslim women involved in this process did not work independently among women but more often than not alongside male family members.

2 Quaid-e-Azam, Mohammad Ali Jinnah, Aligarh University, 1944.

3 This term signifying "unbeliever" refers to Jinnah's opposition to a theocratic state of Pakistan as a homeland of Muslims, but not an Islamic state (itself a contradiction in terms). It had also in the post-partition period provided the basis for suppressing the rights of the nationalities, in particular, as well as of other sectors of the populace. All Muslim religious leaders in this period did not oppose the creation of Pakistan on the same grounds. There was a substantial segment among them, led by people like Maulana Azad, who saw the struggle as being primarily anti-British, anti-colonial, and nationalist (within the context of an united India). Similarly, the Khilafat movement leadership struggled in an anti-colonial effort, and refused to recognize the validity of an Islamic state claiming that the "nation" of Islam was not a geographically localized entity but rather the world. It is interesting to note that this position denies the rationale for a theocracy such as is now being supported and pushed by mullahs in Pakistan. It is also interesting to note that this history of religious opposition to Pakistan on these particular grounds is repressed in Pakistan as is the secular character and democratic program for an independent Pakistan envisaged by Jinnah. In government offices in today's Pakistan, Jinnah's picture (which one always saw present) is often conspicuous by its absence).

28

Monsoon Risings

Mega-Dam Resistance in the Narmada Valley

Chittaroopa Palit

Could you tell us about the Narmada Valley Development Project, and how the opposition to it started?

The Narmada River itself flows westwards across Central India over a course of some 800 miles, rising in the Maikal hills, near Amarkantak, and cutting down between the Vindhya and Satpura ranges to reach the Arabian Sea at Baruch, 200 miles or so north of Mumbai. It is regarded as a goddess by many of those who live along its banks – the mere sight of its waters is supposed to wash one clean of sins. The Valley dwellers are adjured, once in their lifetime, to perform a *parikrama* along its course – walking up one side of the river to its source, and back down the other. The Narmada runs through three different states – Madhya Pradesh, Maharashtra, Gujarat – and its social and physical geography is incredibly diverse. From the eastern hills it broadens out over wide alluvial plains between Jabalpur and Harda, where the villages are quite highly stratified

and occupied by farming communities and fishermen. Between Harda and Omkareshwar, and again between Badwani and Tanchala, steep, forested hills close in once more, mainly inhabited by tribal or *adivasi* peoples – the Kols, Gonds, Korkus, Bhils and Bhilalas. On the plains, there are Gujars, Patidars, Bharuds and Sirwis, as well as Dalits and boat people – the Kewats, Kahars, Dhimars and others.

Although over 3,300 big dams have been built in India since Independence, the Narmada Valley Development is one of the largest projects of all, involving two multipurpose mega-dams – Sardar Sarovar, in Gujarat, and the Narmada Sagar, in Madhya Pradesh – that combine irrigation, power and flood-control functions; plus another 30 big dams and 135 medium-sized ones. The four state governments involved – the non-riparian Rajasthan as well as the other three – have seen the Narmada's waters simply as loot, to be divided among themselves. In 1979, the Dispute Tribunal that had been adjudicating between them announced

Perspectives on Modern South Asia: A Reader in Culture, History, and Representation, First Edition.
Edited by Kamala Visweswaran.
© 2011 Blackwell Publishing Ltd. Published 2011 by Blackwell Publishing Ltd.

its Award – 18.25 million acre feet to Madhya Pradesh, 9 to Gujarat, 0.5 to Rajasthan and 0.25 to Maharashtra – and prescribed how high the dams must be to ensure this distribution. There was no question of discussing the matter with the communities that had lived along the river for centuries, let alone respecting their riparian rights.

Even before this, in the seventies, a Save the Soil campaign – *Mitti Bachao Abhiyan* – had arisen in the Hoshangabad district of Madhya Pradesh, in response to the large-scale water-logging and salinization of the rich black earth around the Tawa dam, part of the NVDP. The protest was Gandhian and environmentalist in character but rooted in the farming communities of the area. In 1979 a huge though short-lived popular movement arose against the Narmada Award, led by mainstream politicians, many from the Madhya Pradesh Congress Party – including Shankar Dayal Sharma, a future president of India, who was jailed for protesting against the height of the dam. But when they got into office, these leaders compromised completely, which led to much bitterness among the Valley communities and made it harder to start organizing from scratch again.

Nevertheless, by the mid-eighties there were several groups working in the Valley. In 1985, Medha Patkar and others formed the Narmada Ghati Dharangrast Samiti in Maharashtra, working with some thirty-three tribal villages at risk from the Sardar Sarovar dam. They demanded proper rehabilitation and the right to be informed about which areas were to be submerged. It was natural for them to link up with us in the KMCS, on the north bank of the river. There was also a Gandhian group called the Narmada Ghati Nav Nirman Samiti that worked in the villages of the Nimad plains in Madhya Pradesh. Their leader was a former state finance minister, Kashinath Trivedi. They undertook numerous 'long treks', or *padyatras*, to inform the villagers about the impact of the Sardar Sarovar dam, advocating an alternative 'small is beautiful' approach. The Jesuit fathers had also been doing ongoing work in the Gujarat area. The NBA – the Save Narmada Movement,

or *Narmada Bachao Andolan* – emerged from the confluence of all these protests, though the name was only officially adopted after 1989. Medha Patkar played a central role in uniting these initiatives, across the three different states.

But though the Narmada movement started with protests around rehabilitation for the villagers affected by the Sardar Sarovar project, within three years it had become plain that they were facing a much greater problem. The Narmada Tribunal Award had specified that those displaced by the dams should be recompensed with land of equal extent and quality, preferably in the newly irrigated area – the command zone – before any submergence took place. By 1988, the villagers had learnt from their own bitter experience that there was no such land available. As the mass mobilization spread eastwards from Maharashtra to the tribal and plains villages of Madhya Pradesh, it became clear that this was going to be an even worse problem further upstream. There was growing anger at the complete denial of the villagers' right to information by the state and central governments, combined with a deepening awareness of the environmental destruction that was being planned – and of the existence of viable alternatives. During the summer of 1988 there was a tremendous churning of resistance, with a series of meetings and mass consultations. In August 1988 the NBA called a series of simultaneous rallies in villages throughout the Valley, where the villagers proclaimed that they were no longer merely demanding proper rehabilitation – that they would fight the Sardar Sarovar dam itself.

Could you elaborate on the alternatives to the big-dam project, and the NBA's critique of the development paradigm?

We found that there were perfectly viable, decentralized methods of water-harvesting that could be used in the area. Tarun Bharat Sangh and Rajendra Singh of Rajasthan were able to revive long dried-up rivers in almost desert-like conditions by mobilizing local villagers' collective efforts to build tanks on a large scale. In Gujarat, remarkable pioneering work inspired by Prem Bhatia, Pandurang Athwale and Shyamji Antale has recharged thousands of wells and small water-harvesting structures using low-cost techniques. For a maximum cost of Rs. 10 million each – less than $220,000 – the problems of Gujarat's 9,000 water-scarce villages could largely be solved, with a total outlay of Rs. 90 billion, or $1.9 billion. Whereas the official figure for the Sardar Sarovar dam alone – almost certainly an underestimate – is at least Rs. 200 billion, over $4 billion.

Contrary to the Gujarat government's promises that Sardar Sarovar would provide for the state's two most drought-prone regions, Kutch and Saurashtra, we found that only 1.5 per cent of Kutch's total cultivable area was slated for the water, and only 7 per cent in Saurashtra. Most of it would go to the politically influential, water-rich areas of central Gujarat. Yet sugar mills were already being constructed in anticipation of water-guzzling sugarcane crops. Aqua parks and tourist resorts had also been planned; they and the urban centres would take the lion's share of the Narmada waters. The entire political economy of the dam project was beginning to unravel in front of us.

Huge multipurpose dams are full of contradictions. Their flood-control function demands that the reservoir be kept empty during the monsoon; yet irrigation requires stored water and, in turn, drains off the vast amounts required by hydroelectricity. Newly irrigated lands are often used to grow thirsty cash crops instead of traditional staples for direct consumption, leaving farming families at the mercy of the global market. There is also a huge ecological price to pay. In India, land irrigated by well water is twice as productive as that fed by canals – these raise the water table excessively, causing water-logging and salinization. Up to a fifth of the world's irrigated land is salt-affected. Dams have also eliminated or endangered a fifth of the world's freshwater fish. The Land Acquisition Act of 1894, originally passed by the British, allows for the confiscation of properties on grounds of 'public interest'. The NBA challenges the Narmada land expropriations on the basis that the public interest clearly isn't served.

If you look at the various Narmada projects it's obvious that these aren't based on any real assessment of needs, nor even on an integrated view of the river valley. I doubt that the government has a consolidated map of all the command and submergence zones that have been planned. The entire approach has been fragmentary, based on a concept of impoundment. This is true not only of the Narmada dams but of many other such developments, including the Linking of Rivers Project that the BJP government is now pushing – an insane proposal, both socially and ecologically. It represents an intensification of the neoliberal programme of enclosing the commons: appropriating the rivers from the common people as a precursor to their takeover by global corporations for large-scale trade in water and energy markets. The NBA has opposed this destruction of forests and rivers, and the communities who have lived along their banks for centuries, in the name of 'development'. At village meetings sometimes 30,000 strong we've highlighted the role of the Indian state and private capital, domestic and foreign, in this process of commodifying public goods – asking who pays and who benefits. This won us new friends but also new enemies, since the elites who stood to gain from the dam began to target the NBA as 'anti-development'.

The NBA campaign famously forced the World Bank to withdraw from the Sardar Sarovar project. Can you describe how this momentum was built?

In 1985, when the central bureaucracy in Delhi began to raise questions about Sardar Sarovar, the World Bank stepped in with a $450 million loan for the dam. The intervention made a nonsense of the Bank's customary defence for its funding of environmentally dubious projects – that these were matters upon which national governments must decide. The truth is that the Bank itself pushes for such projects and, in this instance, merely proposed 'better' rehabilitation policies. Though some NGOS worked with them to develop such practices for the oustees in Gujarat, the NBA refused to collaborate. The people of the Valley suffered terribly under the terms of the World Bank loan. Before each installment was disbursed, the Bank demanded that certain conditions be met – specific villages evacuated, surveys completed, data gathered – and the state governments of Madhya Pradesh, Maharashtra and Gujarat translated this timetable into a series of brutal assaults, with police opening fire on NBA protesters, making numerous arrests and even attacking pregnant women. Every time a World Bank deadline loomed, we knew repression in the Valley would intensify.

By the late eighties the Bank was facing growing criticism over its support for dam construction – from the southern-based International Rivers Network, Brazilian protest groups and northern NGOs such as Friends of the Earth. Northern environmentalists lobbied their governments, questioning what the public money going to the World Bank was being used for. As the international movement developed, our resistance strengthened too. In 1990, a huge rally in Manibeli, Maharashtra – the first village due to be inundated by the Sardar Sarovar project – passed an 'international declaration' against the World Bank. The turning point came in 1991, when we launched a mass 'struggle trek', or *sangharsh yatra*, to Gujarat, to protest against the dam. Nearly 7,000 people walked in the bitter cold of winter. We were stopped at the state border, a place called Ferkuwa. The trekkers set up camp there and seven people, including Medha, went on an indefinite fast. It was at this point that the World Bank gave way, and agreed to an independent review on the Sardar Sarovar project – the first in its history.

The Review's research team – led by Bradford Morse, a former UN Development Project head – spent a year and a half in India, travelling through the Valley and meeting everyone from bureaucrats to NGOs and villagers. Sometimes we resented their pointed questions, their whiteness, the fact that a team from the West could pass judgement on what was happening here. But the Morse Report, when it came out, was excellent. It argued that, given the lack of available agricultural land and political will, proper rehabilitation would be impossible; and that to push the project through in these circumstances would lead to an unmitigated disaster. Plans for Sardar Sarovar were fundamentally flawed on environmental and hydrological grounds, and its benefits had been greatly exaggerated. The World Bank was indicted for its self-deluding incrementalist approach – presuming that things would improve if it simply exerted more pressure. The Report's level of scholarship was outstanding, on a par with some of the treatises that early British scholars in India had written on forestry, tribes and so on.

The World Bank management responded by bringing out a document called 'The Next Steps'. This gave the Indian state six months to 'normalize' the situation, after which the Bank would take a final decision. We all knew this meant the repression would intensify. We were at a meeting in the tribal village of Kakrana, in Madhya Pradesh, when the news came through. The villagers laughed – they said that if they had been able to withstand the last ten years of brutality, the government was not going to succeed in the next six months. Sure enough, the officials and police we were supposed to be meeting with arrived within fifteen minutes of this discussion. They beat up and arrested several key activists from the area, myself included, and for the next four days subjected many of us to third-degree torture, with threats of electrocution. Over the next few months the repression escalated. There were mass arrests. Entire tribal villages, such as Anjanwada, were demolished. Homes and basic utensils were destroyed, seeds confiscated and so on. Their strategy failed. The villagers refused to relent and there were international protests against the treatment being meted out to the people of the Valley – which put even more pressure on the World Bank. In 1993 they announced they were withdrawing from the Sardar Sarovar project. The Morse Report had broken the back of the NVDP's legitimacy, though this did not stop the domestic repression. In reaction to the scrapping of the loan, the Maharashtra police opened fire on the protesters, killing a 16-year-old tribal boy, Rehmal Puniya.

A new phase began, with the NBA now face to face with the Indian state. In December 1994 we held yet another fast and month-long sit-in at Bhopal, the capital of Madhya Pradesh. The government there at last agreed to stop construction and, since all three states had to operate consensually, work came to a halt in Gujarat and Maharashtra as well. We had also submitted a comprehensive petition on the Narmada issue to the Indian Supreme Court earlier that year. In May 1995, the Court called for an interim stay on any further construction at Sardar Sarovar, pending its final judgement. When that came, in 2000, it was a bad blow to the movement, but there is no doubt that the temporary respite offered much-needed relief to the Narmada Valley people, who were facing enormous repression at that time.

The NBA has also succeeded in forcing foreign capital to withdraw from another dam project, at Maheshwar. How did you achieve this? What general lessons would you draw?

When construction stopped on the Sardar Sarovar site, people came to seek the NBA's help against other dam projects in the Narmada Valley. By June 1997, we were organizing people against six or seven dams – people began to connect up and share their experiences, on a pan-Valley basis. One key battle was over the Maheshwar dam in Madhya Pradesh. In 1992, this had been the first hydro-power project to be privatized – handed over to S. Kumars, an Indian textile company with no record in energy production. In line with the neoliberal policies introduced by the Indian government in the early nineties, the company was guaranteed payment by Madhya Pradesh of Rs. 600 crores, or nearly $130 million, over the next thirty-five years, whether any power was generated or not. Estimates for the project had increased five-fold by 1999, and the electricity it was set to produce had become prohibitively expensive – at least three times the cost of

existing power. Meanwhile, the dam was slated to submerge or adversely affect the livelihoods of over 50,000 people in sixty-one villages. Again, the NBA argued that the project was flatly against the public interest.

Construction on the dam began in earnest in November 1997. On 11 January 1998, 24,000 people took over the Maheshwar site; thousands squatted there for the next 21 days, demanding a comprehensive review of the project, and five people went on a fast. With state elections looming, the Madhya Pradesh government agreed to halt building work and set up a Task Force to report on the dam; but as soon as the elections were over, they restarted construction. Thousands of people then re-occupied the site on two consecutive days in April 1998. We were tear-gassed and badly beaten up. More than a thousand were jailed. As we got to know the terrain better, we managed to take over the dam and stop work there eleven times over the next three years. S. Kumars and the state government responded by drafting in some 2,000 police, including paramilitaries.

In May 1998, we started another form of agitation, setting up 24-hour human barricades on the roads leading to the dam site, to stop the trucks that were delivering construction materials. Of course, we let through those with food for the workers, mostly bonded labourers from Andhra Pradesh and Orissa and themselves brutally exploited. The government, initially non-plussed, responded by a cat-and-mouse strategy – every ten days they would send in a large police force to carry out mass arrests, often with a great deal of violence, and then push through a whole convoy of trucks while we were being held in custody. Though we could not stop all the material reaching the site, the barricades helped a lot to slow the pace of construction down. The protest also mobilized large numbers of people for months on end. The leading role of women in these actions – they braved hot summers and monsoons, kept vigil in the darkest of nights, suffered violent police beatings and brutal arrests – electrified the surrounding areas and put enormous pressure on the Madhya Pradesh government. But it was clear we were getting close to the limits of human endurance, so we shifted to another strategy: barricading the finances of the dam.

There were hugely lucrative opportunities for global capital when India's energy sector was thrown open for privatization in 1991. The initial plan for the Maheshwar dam project envisaged as much as 78 per cent of the finance coming from foreign sources. After failing to clinch deals with Bechtel and PacGen, S. Kumars found two German power utilities, VEW Energie and Bayernwerk, to take 49 per cent of the equity; they were supposed to bring in tied loans to purchase, among other things, $134.15 million's worth of electro-mechanical equipment from Siemens, with an export guarantee backed by the German government – underwritten, in other words, by public money. On the Indian side, again, this would be counter-guaranteed by more state funds. This is a weak point in the privatization strategies of global capital, the chink that leaves them open to popular intervention and interrogation – not only because the use of public money creates a potential space for democratic control, but because it exposes the contradictions of corporate globalization: the absence of the 'free-market competition' and 'risk-taking' that are supposed to be the virtues of private entrepreneurship.

In April 1999, the villagers affected by the Maheshwar dam set out on a month-long demonstration and indefinite fast at Bhopal. After twenty-one days of this, Bayernwerk and VEW withdrew from the project, with Bayernwerk citing the lack of land-based rehabilitation as a major concern. In March 2000, Ogden Energy – a us power company, part of the corporate entourage of President Clinton when he visited India that spring – agreed to take over the Germans' 49 per cent stake. Over the next few months, we mounted a struggle on all fronts, involving public actions in both Germany and the us. In Germany, the campaign was led by the NGO Urgewald, run by Heffa Schücking, who succeeded in making the export guarantee for Maheshwar a major issue for the SPD-Green government. In the US, protests were mounted by the Indian diaspora, particularly students, and by

groups like the International Rivers Network. We also held big demonstrations outside the German and American embassies in New Delhi. The result was that, after carrying out their own field survey, the German government refused an export guarantee for Siemens, who subsequently withdrew. In a parallel move, the Portuguese government vetoed a guarantee for Alstom – ABB's power equipment. The Maharashtra government, meanwhile, had reneged on an earlier agreement with Enron and, in light of all this, in 2001 Ogden Energy pulled out of the Maheshwar project too.

After the foreign corporations withdrew, S. Kumars tried to carry on with funds from state institutions – even though privatization had been justified in the first place on the grounds that insufficient public money was available. So in May 2002, the NBA took the struggle to the glass-fronted banks and financial corporations in Mumbai, combining dialogue with coordinated mass protests. We compiled a list of serious financial irregularities in S. Kumars' use of public money. The company got an ex-parte gagging order against the NBA, preventing us from organizing mass protests or putting out 'defamatory' press releases. But the publicity stopped the dribble of public funding that was keeping the Maheshwar project alive. All construction work came to a halt and, on 20 December 2002, the project's 'movable and immovable' properties were impounded by one of the state financial institutions that had been backing it.

We learnt a lot about the structures and processes of globalization through these struggles – and about the need for global alliances from below, to confront it. But though international political factors – the character of the governments involved, the existence of able support groups in the North – play an important part, they cannot supplant the role of a mass movement struggling on the ground. Soon after the SPD government in Berlin refused a guarantee to Siemens for Maheshwar, it agreed to underwrite the company's involvement in the Tehri dam in the Himalayas and the catastrophic Three Gorges Dam in

China – both just as destructive as the Narmada project; but in neither instance were there strong mass struggles on the ground. We never thought, when we began the struggle against the Maheshwar project, that it would become such a full-fledged battle against corporate globalization and privatization. One important outcome was that we found allies in other women's groups, trade unions and left parties, who had not participated as vigorously in our earlier protests.

What role have women played in the struggle?

On 8 March 1998 we set up a separate women's organization within the NBA – the Narmada Shakti Dal. Some two thirds of those on the dam barricades and occupations at Maheshwar were peasant women, and they also played an important role in the core decision-making group. In fact, we found that the choices that had to be made in order to sustain such a relentless struggle, in the face of growing exhaustion and terrible odds, could only be made because of the participation of women. They proved far more radical and militant than the men, and capable of more imaginative protests.

Peasant women were to the Maheshwar struggle what tribals were to Sardar Sarovar. They could give a moral leadership, firstly because their distance from the market meant that they never saw the land and the river – which they worshipped as a mother – as commodities that could be sold for cash. S. Kumars and the central government offered high levels of compensation when critical reports went against them, and that naturally attracted some of the families. But the majority refused to accept the compensation, basically because the women did not want to swap their lands for money and were prepared to fight for that position in their communities, and often in their own households. Villages like Behgaon saw the emergence of a strong women's leadership, and standoffs within families as women pitted themselves against the men's willingness to take the money. The women prevailed and the

unity of the village was preserved, at some small cost.

Secondly, the women's relative exclusion from the political system meant that their minds had not been colonized by mainstream party ideologies – they hadn't been deluded into construing their own destruction as 'development'. Nor did the power of the state leave them cynical or demoralized. Their imaginative approach kept opening up unexpected forms of struggle. For example, in January 2000, several thousand of us once again occupied the dam site. We were arrested and taken to Maheshwar jail. The authorities wanted to release us immediately but the women spontaneously refused to leave the prison until our questions had been answered. How much would the electricity from the new dam cost, compared to existing power sources? Where was the alternative agricultural land for the affected people? How much waterlogging would there be in the surrounding region? How could the state government justify its huge buy-back guarantees, which protected private promoters with public funds regardless of whether any power was produced? For the next three days we locked ourselves in, while the prison wardens fled. So although we had no illusions about negotiating with the Madhya Pradesh government, we were able to establish a much broader critical consciousness about the Maheshwar project through our repeated protests and pointed questions – even among those who were in favour of more electricity.

What lessons would you draw from the NBA's experience with the Indian Supreme Court? In retrospect, do you think it was a mistake to adopt a legal approach?

Firstly, the NBA never relied entirely on a legal strategy. We always kept up a process of direct action too. For example, every year since 1991 we've organized a monsoon *satyagraha* – 'urging the truth', in the Gandhian sense – in which people bodily confront the rising waters of the reservoirs, standing waist deep. Secondly, in answer to your question:

no, I don't believe we made a mistake in taking the issue to the courts in 1994. We can't completely dismiss the judiciary as a ruling-class institution – it represents a contested space and, like every other space in a democracy, people have to fight to retrieve it from the elites.

Nevertheless, when we submitted our petition on the Narmada Valley project in 1994, it was to a Supreme Court substantially different from the one that delivered the final verdict in 2000. Personnel apart, the shifting political climate of the nineties has been reflected in the higher echelons of the Indian legal system. The more activist judiciary of the previous decades – which allowed for a tradition of public-interest litigation that gave access to the poor and dispossessed – has reinvented itself, and produced a string of notorious judgements over the last two years. We have seriously underestimated the extent to which our democratic institutions – the judiciary included – have been reshaped, over the past two decades, by the processes of neoliberal globalization. If these have worked, at the micro-level, by a system of incentives and rewards, they have also succeeded in imposing a larger ideological framework in which any obstacle to capital's search for super-profits – whether popular movements, environmental considerations or concerns about people's livelihood – is seen as a constraint that has to be removed. What better way to do this than through the judiciary, whose verdicts are presumed to be just and impartial, and therefore beyond criticism?

Still, the final Supreme Court ruling on our petition in 2000 came as a shock. The majority judgement argued specifically that large dams served the public interest, at the expense of only a small minority; it completely dismissed the environmental issues. In a step back from the 1979 Narmada Award, it permitted construction to proceed before people had been rehabilitated. The judges made a few trivial recommendations for improvements to existing rehabilitation sites – more swings for the children, for instance – and then ruled that the height of the Sardar Sarovar dam wall could be raised first by two metres and then by five.

For the few of us who had stayed on in Delhi to hear the Supreme Court decision, those five metres were far more than an abstract figure. The reservoir would now engulf the *adivasi* area that had lain just above the submergence level for a number of years and whose people had not been rehabilitated. We were really shocked that the judiciary – that pillar of democracy – had betrayed us. The press called us repeatedly in the evening for our comments and all we could say was that the people of the Valley would meet to decide on what to do next. Then, almost immediately, there was a TV report saying that 4,000 people had already gathered in the Narmada Valley to condemn the judgement and to decide on its implications in a united manner, 'from Jalsindhi to Jalkothi'. We couldn't understand how they could have mobilized so quickly, but it turned out that the Maheshwar project villagers had occupied the dam site that afternoon anyway, in one of their many guerrilla actions. As soon as they heard about the Sardar Sarovar decision they sent out a press release, pledging their solidarity with the people there.

Two days later we had a meeting at Anjanwada, where the tribals of Alirajpur had assembled, as they were gathering elsewhere in the Valley. I was in such a deep depression I could hardly speak – it was like announcing a death sentence. Someone broke the ice by saying what we all already knew: that the Supreme Court had permitted a five-metre increase, on the basis of claims by the Gujarat, Madhya Pradesh and Central governments that adequate alternative land was available. Everyone began talking at once and within a few minutes the meeting had made its decision, without any disagreement: firstly, we would show those in power that we weren't mice, to be flooded out; and secondly, that we would expose the governments' land claims as false. Late that night, one of the tribal activists woke me up, one who had shared our faith in democratic structures. What happened, he asked, how could they give such a judgement? Was the

fact that there was no land for our rehabilitation not clear to them? But the *adivasis* were
up early the next morning, as always, laughing
their inexplicable early morning laughter, displaying their characteristic mixture of stoicism
and balance.

*How are decisions of this sort normally
taken within the NBA? How would you
describe the movement's internal
structures?*

In the Valley itself there are two independent
centres where decision-making takes place,
one in the Sardar Sarovar region and another
for the Maan and Maheshwar struggles; both
bring together the organic village leaderships
in those areas, plus a few urban activists.
Also, because the NBA is spread across three
different states, a loose network is necessary,
coordinated by meetings at several levels.
Resistance to the dams project is predicated as
a matter of survival – of life or death – for the
communities of the Narmada Valley. One of the
first slogans was 'Nobody will move, the dam
will not be built' – *koi nahi hatega, bandh nahi
banega*. When the waters began to rise, the
people came up with another chant, 'We will
drown, but we will not move' – *doobenge, par
hatenge nahi*. Such positions have to be based
on mass support and participation, rather than
minority activist structures.

The rhythm of activism is also dictated by the
pattern of the seasons. Every monsoon, as the
people of the Valley face the rising waters, we
hold a mass meeting. People from the various
villages affected will come together for a whole
day, sometimes two, to discuss the situation.
How much submergence will take place, and
how might it best be confronted? If the dam
wall has been increased over the last year, what
are the implications? What forms of resistance
are most appropriate for each *satyagraha*?
How should the logistics of wood, water, grain
and transport be managed, in the context of
the rising reservoir? Most of the time, we
are fighting with our backs against the wall
and we often have only a certain number

of options to choose from – state officials to
confront, buildings to occupy, sympathetic
supporters to call on, and so forth. So the range
of disagreement is limited and, in practice,
there is a great deal of consensus about these
decisions.

After each set of meetings we hold a collective consultation, in which representatives
from the different regions come together to
work out broader strategies for calling attention
to the distress and struggle of the Valley
people. Further discussion takes place on
the Coordination Committee, the *samanvaya
samiti*, comprised of intellectuals and activists
from outside the movement who contribute to
forging wider links. Ground-level resistance
needs to be supported by legal initiatives and
media campaigns, and by alliances at national
and international levels. The NBA's attempt
to question the development paradigm, for
example, has involved taking the debate to
the Indian middle classes, who are among the
strongest supporters of the Narmada Valley
project. We currently have some sixty urban
support centres, in cities all over India. There
have been periods over the last decade when
these structures have broken down or fallen
into disuse; but it is clear to us that, without
widespread consultation at many levels, both
inside and outside the movement, sustained
collective action would be impossible.

Often, as on the question of what general
course to take after the Supreme Court judgement, decisions are swift, consensual and to
the point – reactions in other tribal areas were
very similar, in that instance. But sometimes
we cannot reach a consensus. For example,
one senior activist wanted to respond to that
crushing final verdict by 'immersion', or *jal
samarpan* – where one remains motionless in
the face of the incoming waters, up to death.
This was hotly debated and opposed among the
Valley people and their supporters – a stance
that has so far prevented such a tactic from
being deployed. In good times, we don't require
formal structures, elected representatives, articulated organizational principles. But in times
of crisis or vacuum, when everything else has
collapsed, we see the need for them.

Can you describe some of your methods of struggle? How central is nonviolence to NBA philosophy – and how frustrating has this been, in the face of state repression?

The main forms of mass struggle in the Valley have been non-violent direct actions – marches, *satyagraha* and civil disobedience. In Sardar Sarovar, for example, in the aftermath of Ferkuwa, hundreds of villages refused to allow any government official to enter. In Maheshwar those affected by the dam have repeatedly occupied the site in the face of police repression. Other forms of *satyagraha* have involved people staying in their villages despite imminent submergence, or indefinite fasting to arouse the public conscience. State repression and indifference have often left us feeling frustrated and helpless, but I don't see that as a failure of our tactics. In an increasingly globalized world, we have to search for richer and more compelling strategies; but that does not mean compromising on the principle of non-violence, which remains fundamental for the NBA. If we fight for the inalienable right to life, and insist that such concerns should form the basis for assessing any development paradigm, how can we resort to violence? There have been a few unplanned incidents involving self-defence that cannot count as non-violent; situations where people have been pushed beyond the edge. But as a strategy, how could physical violence on our part ever match the armed might of the Indian state, or of imperialist globalization? Most importantly, only a non-violent struggle can provide the silence in which the questions we are asking can be heard. A strategy of violence results in a very different kind of political discourse.

But don't activists put their own lives at risk, through fasting and submergence?

The monsoon *satyagrahas* – where people in their hundreds stand ready to face the waters that enter their homes and fields – have to be distinguished from the practice of immersion, or *jal samarpan*. *Satyagraha* means more than putting pressure on the state – it is also a way of bearing witness to what the state is doing to the people. It affirms the existence of the Valley inhabitants and shows our solidarity. It makes a moral point, contrasting the violence of the development project with the determination of those who stand in its path. In most of the monsoon *satyagrahas* where the waters have actually flooded the houses – as in Domkhedi over the last two or three years – the police have physically dragged people out of the areas being inundated, in an attempt to rob the agitation of its symbolic power. As I have said, many of us are very critical of such methods as *jal samarpan*. We need to be alive to fight. We also need to assess whether the state can twist the issue to its own advantage by claiming that, since we are not willing to be rehabilitated, it is the protesters' own fault if we drown. Fasting is more gradual and allows us time to awaken the public conscience. But if you use the same weapons again and again they become blunt and ineffective.

Many in the Valley now advocate seizing federal land in Madhya Pradesh for self-settlement, and as a way to expose the government. Two and a half thousand acres belong to a state farm, which the Asian Development Bank has recommended should be hived off – it may go to one of India's biggest conglomerates. So there seems to be land for corporations but none for the millions whose homes have been taken away from them in the name of the 'public interest'. Not a single person in Madhya Pradesh has been given the legally required equivalent for his land. The record is also very poor in the other two states. They say 4,000 families are being rehabilitated in Gujarat and 6,000 in Maharashtra. But there are 25 million in the Valley whose lives will be adversely affected in some way and at least 500,000 displaced by direct submergence.

How does the NBA raise its money?

Almost 40 per cent of NBA funds come from the farmers of Nimad – the relatively wealthy plains area of the Narmada Valley. After the wheat harvest, each farmer contributes a kilogram per quintal produced and there are small cash donations after the cotton harvest, too; though their prosperity is now seriously threatened by the WTO. The other 60 per cent comes from our urban supporters. Several prominent Indian artists have contributed their works to the movement, and Arundhati Roy has consistently supported us through her writings; she donated her entire Booker Prize winnings to us, three years back, and has contributed generously every year since.

We decided very early on that we would take neither government grants – why should they pay for direct opposition to their policies? – nor foreign money, save for travel costs and local hospitality when we're invited to speak. Foreign donations would expose us to all kinds of questions about the autonomy of the movement; it would also allow the Indian government to exercise some control over us, since such finance has to be routed through the External Affairs Ministry. Of course, we defend our right to call for international solidarity; but we also believe that it is possible for the resources of Indian civil society to sustain popular struggles – and that to do so builds and affirms support for the movement.

Gujarat has been the most communally polarized of Indian states – the laboratory of Hindutva forces where, in the wake of the most brutal and deliberate anti-Muslim pogrom since Independence, the BJP has been returned to power with its greatest ever majority, over two-thirds of the vote. Is there a connexion between Gujarati communalization and the opposition of large sections of the population, especially its upper-caste, middle-class layers, to the NBA?

This is a real problem in Gujarat. A change took place in the political complexion of the state during the eighties. Middle and upper castes came to power after the break-up of the lower-caste alliance of KHAM, which had previously held sway in electoral politics – composed of *kshatriyas*, who are not upper castes in Gujarat, *harijans, adivasis* and Muslims. This new elite is far more communalized and lumpen than other sections of society. There is a lesson here for people's movements like the NBA. In spite of our work among tribals, we failed to take as seriously as we should have the issue of communalism, and the grassroots influence of the Right. The Sangh Parivar's continuous mobilization among tribals over the last two decades has yielded them a rich – for the others, a bitter – harvest of hate. This was happening all around us, but we never fully assessed the Sangh's destructive potential and failed to counter them. Why? I feel the problem lies in a seeming inability to offer our own holistic political philosophy as a consistent alternative.

At a certain point in the nineties, the NBA sought to move in the direction of developing such a holistic agenda, connecting issues of communalism, militarization, neoliberal globalization. Was there a gap between intentions and outcomes? Where does the NBA go from here?

I must confess that the NBA as a collective entity has not yet sat down and thrashed these matters out. We have taken some initiatives on these issues – international questions, anti-globalization struggles – but we urgently require a more concrete and coherent agenda, a collectively evolved action plan. In any case, there is no possibility of addressing these points on our own, without a wider alliance of movements. Since 1994, the NBA has been working with the National Alliance of People's Movements, of which Medha Patkar is the national convenor. The NAPM has three broad currents: Gandhians, Indian Social Democrats – to the left of Euro-socialism, but unsympathetic to the official Communist parties – and people's organizations from various backgrounds, including Marxist. In Madhya Pradesh, the NBA is also part of the broad front of the Jan Sangarsh

Morcha, which brings together numerous progressive organizations to challenge the World Bank and Asian Development Bank on issues such as energy, forestry and the dismantling of the public sector. But both the NAPM and JSM are at the embryonic stage – it remains to be seen whether they can combat the bankruptcy of the country's existing political structures or solve the social and ideological crisis it confronts.

Yet the real challenge is to begin from where we are, with our own constituencies. If we work only at the state or national levels, there is a real danger of losing the organic leaders who have emerged from the Narmada movement and form our real strength. There are hundreds of capable tribals, women, fisherfolk, with high levels of consciousness – the outcome of sixteen years of collective resistance. The real success of our struggle lies not only in stopping dams but in enabling such leaders to play a guiding role in broader struggles, not just against displacement, but against corporate globalization and communalism: to lead the defence of democracy in this country, and shape its economic and political future. It is the marginalized people of the Narmada Valley who know the system at its worst, and have some of the richest experiences in struggling against it. Their lives and tragedies have made them both sensitive to what is needed in the long term and courageous in their willingness to undergo whatever sacrifices prove necessary for prolonged resistance.

29

Where There Are No Men: Women in the Maoist Insurgency in Nepal

Shobha Gautam, Amrita Banskota and Rita Manchanda

Introduction

In whole villages in the western hill districts of Nepal, there are no men. This is the epicentre of the Maoist insurgency. From three districts in February 1996, the Peoples War has swept across two-thirds of the Himalayan kingdom of Nepal. Remote, backward hill districts have been transformed into guerrilla zones and 'base areas', provoking massive police repression on predominantly poor, peasant, minority ethnic groups of Nepal. To escape being picked up by the police or targeted by the Maoists, the men have become *farari* (absconders), who have fled into the surrounding jungles or melted into the cities of Nepal and across the open border into India. Left behind are the women, the stable element, who keep alive family and community in the midst of conflict. Traditionally, women form the backbone of the semi-feudal subsistence agrarian economy and even under normal conditions, a 45 per cent rate of underemployment drives the men to seasonally migrate in search of jobs to cities in Nepal and India. This time, the men have not come back.

In these villages without men, the women have been left to work with conflict, to negotiate with the police and the Maoists, the survival and security of their families. It is women who feed and shelter the Maoists who come at night. It is women who have become the heads of households, the providers for the children and the aged. It is women who have had to break tradition and take on the 'male' job of ploughing the land. It is women who in the space vacated by men, are challenging gender relations in both the private and public spheres with structural implications, difficult to reverse post-conflict.

Women, especially poor, peasant, illiterate and *jan jati* (tribal) women have achieved a political visibility never before imaginable in Nepal's politics. The majority of the women in the Maoist movement come from Nepal's disadvantaged Tibeto-Burman ethnic groups. Relatively speaking, they are culturally less oppressed than Hindu upper-caste Aryan women. Their identity is not constructed around a religious ideology. However, as in any community, women have the least rights

Perspectives on Modern South Asia: A Reader in Culture, History, and Representation, First Edition.
Edited by Kamala Visweswaran.
© 2011 Blackwell Publishing Ltd. Published 2011 by Blackwell Publishing Ltd.

and suffer on top of class, ethnic and regional oppression, gender oppression.

The ideological thrust of the Maoist movement is oriented towards expanding the rights base of the poor and the marginal, including women. In a predominantly rural society, the New Demo-cratic Revolution is essentially an agrarian revo-lution, where land reform is at the centre, both for women and for men. The movement has a strong appeal for women as its 40-point charter supports property rights for women.

This chapter focuses on the experience of poor peasant women as protagonists in the swirl of war, i.e., women negotiating survival and women joining the ranks of the guerrillas. Empirically, it is based on field interviews with peasant and rural women in two contrasting situations – (i) illiterate poor women in under-developed Rolpa and Rukum districts in the mid-western hills, and (ii) literate women in the more developed and prosperous Gorkha district in the central hills. Gorkha district stands out for the large number of girl students who have been drawn to the Peoples War.

Also interviewed were 'guerrillas' in prison, and top ranking woman leader, Hisila Yami. The interviews are oriented towards revealing through their life histories and memories of events, women negotiating conflict and their notion of violence and justice. The questions which arise, emerge from the lived experience of the women.

How do we understand women's transfor-mative experience from relative invisibility to visible protagonism? What does the shift in the roles of these women mean for the religiously sanctified sociocultural structures of feudal-patriarchal communities? The 'exclu-sions' which all Nepalese women face span right from the household level to the state level, i.e., political, economic and cultural domains. What does it mean for women socialised in conservative patriarchal cultures to become armed guerrillas or area commanders?

Is this one armed class struggle in which the women are not being told that the women's question has to wait till after the revolution? Evidently, the Peoples War ideology has created space for women to claim rights but the

women joining the movement have also helped shape that ideology. How have women defined the movement and how has the movement structured women's roles?

Leftist armed resistance movements tend to argue that the special conditions of revolutionary struggle make gender differences unimportant. That the liberation of the peasant/proletariat will in the process emancipate women from gender oppression. Is the Maoist movement in Nepal the exception? An analysis of the role of women in the Shining Path, the acknowledged model for Nepal's Peoples War, suggests that despite the fact that women achieved an important presence at all levels within the movement, Sendero was not capable of programmatically incorporating their gender interests. 'Shining Path established an instrumental relationship with its female members that re-produced patriarchal relations to benefit the party.'[1] Is the situation of the women in the Maoist movement in Nepal different?

In Nepal's Maoist movement, initially, among the top leadership, were women with accomplished political qualifications like Pampa Bushal, co-leader of the United Peoples Front, the political platform of the Maoists. Hisila Yami, as head of the Women's Front was also in the circle of the top leadership. But as the struggle has got more militarised and more hierarchically structured, the participation of women in the top policy making councils seems to have diminished. Women have become area commanders, party committee secretaries, but are the women in policy-making positions in the central leadership?

This chapter also dwells on the failure of Nepal's democratic political agenda to deal with the central issues of poverty, development and ethnic, caste and gender oppression. Its corol-lary is the weakness of the democratic forces in Nepal to forge solidarities on the humanitarian front of the war story and strengthen social capital needed to build a just peace.

Historical Prologue

Nepal's dominant historical narrative is struc-tured around the reunification of the petty principalities of the territory of Nepal nearly two-and-a-half centuries ago by the Shah dynasty which established a Hindu kingdom from the fiefdom of Gorkha. Nepal's palace history is presided over by the Shahs as conquerors, titular heads during the hereditary Rana prime ministers, as absolute rulers and as constitutional monarchs in a multi-party democracy. Power, however, remains monopolised by a minority governing elite of a few upper-caste Brahmins and Chettri families with the co-optation of some Buddhist Newar merchants and Sanskritised ethnic Magars. The system is feudal in nature and land remains the primary resource.

According to a Food and Agriculture Organisation (FAO) study, the rich peasants make up 10 per cent of the population and own 65 per cent of the land, poor peasants make up 65 per cent of the population and own 10 per cent of the land and 8 per cent of the peasants are landless.[2] The landholding structure in Nepal has not changed much. Nepal remains a semi-feudal, subsistence agriculture economy with low productivity and high underemployment. Seventy per cent of the population lives below the poverty line and the number of the absolute poor has doubled in two decades.[3]

Nepal's three distinct ecological regions, mountains, hills and plains accentuate inequalities and diversities. According to Nepal's Human Development Index the central hills which include Kathmandu and the Gorkha districts score the highest. The lowest scoring region is the mid-western hill area. The most backward and the most underdeveloped regions are also where the indigenous and ethnic groups are in a majority, so that there is a confluence of regional, cultural, linguistic and religious discrimination and regional deprivation. There are 60 ethnic groups and 60 living languages. The physical ruggedness of the region and the feudal structure of land relations have resulted in an enduring resilience of localised cultures and community life. The Maoists have tapped into this cultural tradition of tribal cooperation and the historical sense of deprivation and injustice. Rolpa, Rukum and Jajarkot, the flashpoints of the Maoist insurgency, are in the backward mid-western hills. Gorkha is in the central hills.

The restoration of democracy in 1990, the setting up of a constitutional monarchy and multi-party elections in 1991, found the ultra left parties joining parliamentary politics. Nepal has a long tradition of left activism and left factionalism. The historical roots of the Communists are entwined with those of the centrist Nepali Congress in the final days of the anti-Rana struggle in 1949. But many of the radical left groups owe their origins to the 1971 Jhapa rebellion, which paralleled the uprising across the border in Bihar and Naxalbari.

In the first multi-party elections, the Nepali Congress secured a comfortable majority with the Communist Party of Nepal–Unified Marxist Leninist (CPN–UML) establishing sway over a third of the seats. Its main electoral rival on the left was the United Peoples Front or UPF (Samyukta Jan Morcha), an umbrella organisation of avowedly Maoist parties who came together under the chairmanship of Dr Baburam Bhattrai. The UPF won nine seats. By the 1994 mid-term elections, the UPF was disenchanted. It split and the majority unit under Bhattrai pulled out of parliamentary politics along with the Communist Party of Nepal (Maoist) under Pushpa Kamal Dahal, alias Prachanda. Preparations began in earnest for a protracted armed struggle modelled on Peru's Shining Path.

In February 1996, barely six years after the restoration of democracy, the Communist Party of Nepal (CPN) (Maoist) launched the Peoples War to overthrow Nepal's constitutional monarchy and effect a socio-economic revolution – a New Democratic Revolution. Parliamentary politics had failed to make any difference to the people's grinding poverty and disempowerment. Nepal's tryst with multi-party democracy had produced in 10 years, eight governments comprising right and left coalitions of cynical convenience.

In the political vacuum, the Maoists have emerged as the voice of Nepal's poor and marginalised, the indigenous ethnic peoples, the lower castes, peasants, workers, students and women. Through their mass propaganda mobilisation, development activities and pro-people guerrilla actions against the symbols of rural oppression like the Agricultural Development Bank and local tyrants, the Peoples War has spread from three districts in 1996 to 45 of Nepal's 75 districts.

The district of Rolpa, the stronghold of the Maoists was in a sense a rehearsal of things to come. Two years before the launch of armed struggle, the UPF concentrated on political, cultural and developmental activities to strengthen the potential for class struggle. The state hit back with savage repression.[4] The UPF's supporters were targeted, false cases framed against them and more than 1,000 people arrested. The Maoists also hit back at political and class enemies. As the clashes between the two flared up, the government launched Operation Romeo in November 1995, a draconian police operation which drove 10,000 out of 200,000 able-bodied men into the jungle to escape police atrocities.

Three months later the Peoples War was launched with guerilla action, sabotage and propaganda. On 13 February 1996, there were lightning strikes on police outposts, state-owned Agricultural Development Bank offices and local feudal bosses in the districts of Gorkha in the central hills, Rolpa and Rukum in the mid-western and Sindhuli in the eastern hills. In the police repression which followed, thousands were arbitrarily arrested on charges of dacoity, arson and murder. Human rights organisations have documented the extrajudicial executions, rape and arbitrary arrests by the police and the killings, extortion and destruction of property by the Maoists.[5]

According to the home minister of Nepal, Purna Bahadur Khadka, in the last four years of the Peoples War, 1,128 people have been killed, 836 are Maoists, 115 police personnel and 177 are 'common men'.[6] The level of violence has been determinedly kept low. The weapons used by the Maoists are, largely, 303 rifles, *khukris* and farm implements. This is remarkable given that Nepal sits at the crest of South Asia, a region awash with AK-47s. Nepal has not deemed it necessary to call out the army. Moreover, its big neighbour, India appears to be not worried. The territory of Nepal abuts onto India's volatile state of Bihar

and it is highly unlikely that India will tolerate a successful social revolution in Nepal before one in India.

So far the Peoples War has not appreciably impacted upon life in the capital, Kathmandu or in the plains of Terai bordering India. Except for a few high profile executions of political leaders in the western hill districts during elections, the Peoples War is regarded as a sideshow in Kathmandu. The upper-caste Hindu Brahmin–Chettri power elite of Kathmandu treat it as essentially a law and order problem in the remote hills where largely, ethnic groups like Magars are killing other Magars. The Magars, the third largest ethnic group in Nepal, comprise 7 per cent of the population.

In its fourth year, the Peoples War has spread far beyond the Magar areas to two-thirds of Nepal's districts. The 40-point demand of the political front of the Peoples War, the UPF, calls for a new peoples' democracy based on a new constitution, seizure of monarchial privilege and protection of the rights of women, the oppressed nationalities, the downtrodden and the regionally disadvantaged. It calls for radical land reform, property rights for women, debt relief and guaranteed employment. Taking an anti-India stance, it calls for the repealing of unequal treaties with India and the regulation of the open border with India.

Women in Nepal: From Invisibility to Protagonism

The majority of the women directly involved in the conflict zone, either as negotiating survival or as party cadres and guerrillas are drawn from non-Aryan groups, especially the Kham Magars. However, many of the leading women in the Peoples War are upper-caste women like Pampa Bushal, or from the Buddhist merchant Newari community like Hisila Yami. In focusing on women's experience of the People War, through their life stories, inevitably, there is a misleading tendency to emphasise women's 'visibility' and 'protagonism' in the conflict situation and assume dormancy and invisibility before the crisis of the People War. As we shall explore below, there were also important continuities in the experience of the women. Notwithstanding this caveat, we argue that the conflict situation is producing a certain threshold of change or shift in gender relations for women directly involved in the conflict with implications for the disadvantaged status of women in Nepal, in general.

Gender discrimination in Nepal has actually increased, despite the kingdom's accession to the Convention on the Elimination of (all forms of) Discrimination Against Women (CEDAW) and other international instruments.[8] Women suffer from 23 discriminatory laws in Nepal. Nepal tops South Asia's gender inequality ratio at 1:6, a notch above India at 1:5 and way above Sri Lanka at 2:3. In Nepal, women's lifespan is shorter by two-and-a-half years. Women make up 49 per cent of the population. Nepal's maternity deaths are the highest in South Asia. Abortion is illegal. Work burden for women is four times that of the adult male. Literacy index is 54.3 per cent for males and 21.3 per cent for females. Gender disparity is similar for rural and urban areas. However, disaggregation across regions and social collectivities shows swings in the Human Development Index (HDI) and widening gender disparities in the mountainous regions. Gorkha stands out with 24.5 per cent adult literacy for women as against Rolpa with 8.7 per cent. The enrollment patterns for children aged 6 and above for the mid-western hills, the Maoist epicentre, is, for boys – 46.9 per cent, for girls – 17.6 per cent, i.e., an average of 31.8 per cent. The Nepal average is 40 per cent.

In Nepal's *mulki ain* (civil code), the daughter has no claim to parental property unless she remains unmarried till 35 years of age and then can claim her share, if it is still intact but forfeits it, if she marries. Women form the backbone of the subsistence economy, accounting for the bulk of agricultural work and animal husbandry, but have no legal rights over property. Currently, a bill on property rights for women is hanging in the fire in parliament, but the militant opposition to it demonstrates the difficulty of passing legislation guaranteeing property rights to women under the present system. Its opponents argue that property rights for women will destroy the very basis of the Hindu family. Officially, 98 per cent of the population of Nepal is Hindu. Given the geographic and economic isolation of the hill districts, acculturation to dominant Hindu beliefs and customs among communities like the Kham Magar, is limited but growing. Women's groups in Nepal blame women's lack of rights, especially property rights, for a social structure of exploitative practices, such as polygamy, *jari* (a man who takes away another's wife pays him compensation for the loss of his goods), wife beating and mass trafficking of girls to the brothels of India and the Gulf. Every year 5,000–7,000 Nepali women are trafficked across the border. The majority of them belong to the minority ethnic groups.

Religiously sanctified, 'exclusions' which Hindu women face span right from the household level to the state level and cover political, economic, and cultural domains. Citizenship is through the male line. Socio-cultural practices detailed in ancient Hindu codes like Manusmriti, have enshrined oppressive patriarchal structures, subjugating the Aryan upper-caste Hindu women, in particular. Women from the Tibeto-Burman communities like the Magars, Gurungs and Rais, have fewer religio-cultural restrictions. Widow remarriage is possible and divorce does not entail a loss of ritual status. The identity of the Magar women is articulated in a secular idiom.

As a result, the Kham Magar woman has access to a variety of economic options which gives her socio-economic independence. She is responsible for many important decisions concerning selection of seed, cropping, and disposal and sale of agriculture and household products. Informal entrepreneurial activity like the sale of *raski* (country liquor) is centred on women. Augusta Molnar in an anthropological study of the Kham Magar women of Thabang, before the Peoples War, demonstrated that although the women are denied legal right to land and family property, in the economic sphere they are accorded a position of complementary authority. It is a status they retain on divorce or widowhood. Women have primary responsibility for agriculture and animal husbandry. Ploughing is done by men but seed selection by women. Traditionally, men's work burden has been much lower than that of women.

Given that one in two households is involved in seasonal migration, women are obliged to take decisions in the absence of men. However, decisions on sale and purchase of land are rarely taken without consultation with a male but women determine how much of grain is to be consumed and how much set aside to make *raski*. Through the informal institutions of women's work groups women manage a wage-less labour exchange and small entrepreneurial activity. The household responsibilities of women channelled through the work groups provide women, more than men, with access to information and informal political power. Indeed the traditional esteem enjoyed by the Magar women in society has made socially acceptable for young educated Magar women to compete with males for posts as village officials.[9] However, after the Peoples War, it is illiterate peasant women who are emerging as protagonists.

Poor peasant women, and women from the oppressed nationalities have been the most active in joining the Peoples War. Nearly 70 per cent of the women in the Peoples War are from the Tibeto-Burman and non-Aryan communities, e.g., Magars, Tamangs, Kamis and Gurungs. The harsh conditions of life have made Tibeto-Burman and non-Aryan women tough. In a socio-economic power structure dominated by upper-caste Brahmin Chettri elite, the ethnic groups suffer from social, linguistic, cultural, economic and political discrimination. Their oppression is further reinforced by the backwardness of the regions where they are a majority. And, as in every community, the women are the most oppressed and the most marginalised.

In Nepal there is a tradition of armed political activism and struggle by women of ethnic and indigenous groups. Nepali history records the fight women and children gave the British at the battle of Nalapani in Dehradun in 1815. More recently, in the movement for democracy, the women of Lalitpur from the Brahmin, Chettri castes as well as the ethnic groups, were particularly active in their support, but behind the frontline.

Mobilising Women

The Maoist strategy is consciously oriented to drawing women into the Peoples War. In a woman-run subsistence economy, where one in every two men is involved in seasonal migration, women form the majority of the rural community. You cannot have an agrarian revolution without mobilising women and putting them in guerrilla fatigues. *The Worker*, in its 'Reports from the Battlefield', acknowledges that the 'fury of the women' has given a qualitative leap to the development of the Peoples War in the whole country.[10] In Maoist propaganda women guerrilla commanders have been projected as formidable fighters, more committed, disciplined, reliable and militant. It also exemplifies the limits of the space reserved for women in the movement.

The Maoists have championed the cause of autonomous governments for the oppressed nationalities; they have opposed discrimination against the downtrodden and the practice of untouchability. As for women, they are 'subjected to class, gender, national and regional oppression simultaneously', says *The Worker*. The participation of women is promoted through an active propaganda network. Anecdotes eulogise the exploits of women guerrilla leaders who are cast in a heroic, self-sacrificing and self-effacing mode like Shanti Shrestha or Kamla Bhatta. To instill grit, determination and revolutionary fervour among raw recruits, much play is given to the heroic defiances of comrades like Devi Khadka. Even after she was gang-raped by the police, her spirit was not broken. She vowed to fight on and take revenge.

Young girls from schools and colleges in Gorkha district are shown joining the long list of volunteers eager to enrol with the Maoists. Stories are spread of students becoming heroic guerrilla fighters. A schoolgirl had been arrested by the police. Her 'feudal' father bailed her out but she gave him the slip and went off to join the Maoists. In a reversal of the saga of widows of martyrs vowing to carry on their husband's work, *Janadesh*, a Maoist influenced paper spotlighted a report from Bardia district of widowers of martyred women vowing to join the movement.

How central the woman guerrilla is in the public construct of the Maoist movement is evidenced by the prominence given to women in the Peoples war in the propaganda windows of the Maoists. Their website carries the image of young women marching in battle fatigues carrying guns. Prachanda, the Commander of the Peoples War, in a recent interview with the organ of the Revolutionary Communist Party (RCP), USA, the *Revolutionary Worker*, celebrated the militant activism of the women in the movement.[11] Prachanda's comments also reveal the limits of the space reserved for women in the movement. He commented how initially it was difficult to find illiterate peasant women who could assume leadership positions but since then women are visible at all levels. In the politico-military leadership of the district committees there are 40 to 50 women. But has the presence of women at the level of area commanders and party secretaries influenced the programmatic content of the movement?

Programmatically Incorporating the Women's Question

Traditionally, socialist ideology has recognised gender oppression, but most left revolutionary struggles have dealt with it as a social problem to be resolved with the overthrow of capitalism. The women's question remains marginal, indeed, postponed till after the struggle is over. Within the revolutionary struggle the issue of gender discrimination is treated as something that dissolves when primary questions of feudal exploitation and class oppression are resolved. In short, gender oppression will melt away as more radical commitments are made by women and men.

In the Peoples War women make up a third of the movement. What impact has the massive presence of women in the Maoist movement had on redefining the women's question in the Peoples War ideology? Prachanda, the General Secretary of the Communist Party of Nepal (Maoist) admits that before the launch of the Peoples War, they had not taken the women's

question 'seriously' but afterwards with the dramatic importance of women's activism in the Peoples War, the women's question has been ideologically and programmatically incorporated. In programmatic content, the Maoist struggle at the ground level has given space to an anti-alcohol campaign, issues of sexual violence and women's exploitation. But on the issue of abortion, which is illegal in Nepal, Prachanda steers clear of the legal/illegal issue but engages with it at a gender-practical level, i.e., in the context of the Maoist women cadre who become pregnant and may be obliged to quit the movement. There is no inflection of a gendered discourse of women's rights.

With a third of the Maoist guerrillas being women in the areas where the Maoists are most active, practical considerations have obliged the party to put on the agenda the issue of maternity and child care of the women in the fighting ranks. Prachanda, in a wide ranging interview to *Revolutionary Worker*,[12] mentions the practical difficulties of women guerrillas becoming pregnant and the provision of foster care structures for children. Gender neutral discourses of revolutionary struggles often flounder on issues of sexual morality and when women guerrillas become pregnant. It is noticeable that in social–political revolutions, it is mothers who are expected to leave their children behind, not fathers. In Nepal's 'Peoples War', is there serious questioning of the feminisation of parenting or for that matter cooking?

At the ideological level, just before the launch of the Peoples War, the UPF had released a memorandum of 40 demands. Taking on board the women's question, No. 19 demanded: 'Patriarchal exploitation and discrimination against women should be stopped. The daughter should be allowed access to property.' The key phrase is the daughter's 'access to property'. In an agrarian revolution, women's 'access to property' means women's right to land.

The 'roots of women's oppression must be sought not only within the sphere of production but also reproduction, i.e., not only in the economic structure but also in the social and cultural structure,' asserts Hisila. The

CPN (Maoist) ideologically reaches out to women to join the Peoples War and smash the state, because the state treats them as 'second class citizens... [victim to] rape, trafficking and the process of commodification through advertisments'. Implicit is the recognition of a continuum in the structure of oppression for women which stretches from the family, society, the labour market and to the state in all its manifestations.

However, it is surprising, given the flood of women getting involved in the Peoples War, that the ideological patron of the Maoist movement, Dr Baburam Bhattrai does not engage with the women's question in his political writing on the New Democratic Revolution (NDR). Clearly, the importance of the presence of women in the movement is recognised, but Bhattrai, in a detailed analysis of the logic and structure of NDR and its core, land reform, finds no space to incorporate a gender analysis. In his article 'Politico-Economic Rationale of People's War in Nepal', gender oppression is subsumed in the overall struggle against feudal and imperialist oppression. With the shedding of the fetters of feudalism and imperialism, patriarchal oppression, automatically, will be cast off. The writings of the movement's ideologue, Bhattrai rarely make any serious mention of the women's question, in contrast to the focus on the question of oppressed nationalities.[13]

Hisila denies that the Peoples War subsumes gender oppression in class oppression. She maintains, that 'since the NDR is antifeudalism, it will at once remove feudal Brahminical Hindu rule which sees women in relationship to men. The anti-imperialist nature of NDR will discourage unequal trade relations with imperialist and expansionist forces, thus saving women from sweat shops where they are exploited sexually and economically. It will prepare the ground for removing prostitution, consumerisation and commoditisation of women in Nepal.' It is a rhetoric which echoes the dominant narrative of other revolutionary struggles, that gender oppression will dissolve when 'feudal exploitation and class oppression' is defeated.

But there is also the counter reality of how women in the movement have reshaped the ideology of the movement and ensured that at the ground level the women's question is not postponed. In the Maoist stronghold areas, most of the mass actions are related to getting women justice, punishing rapists, wresting back the usurped land of single women, punishing men for polygamy and mass action against liquor dealers. 'The women have more to gain than the men from the Peoples War', says Hisila Yami. 'That is why the women, especially the Tibeto-Burman and non-Aryan women constitute such an important part of the movement.'

In an incident narrated earlier, in Surkhet district, an all-women guerrilla squad punishes a wife beater, promotes anti-alcohol and adult literacy and creates political consciousness at the ground level of a structure in which oppression, poverty, wife beating, alcoholism and illiteracy, all coalesce. It is anecdotal, but reflects what is popularly spoken about as happening in thousands of villages where the Maoist women are active.

But this is essentially at the grassroots level. Have women been able to reshape the programmatic agenda at the ideological and policy determination level? Hisila maintains that women are given due representation in the political power being exercised in the 'embryonic new democratic state'. Women are party committee secretaries. Does it imply gaining policy responsibility? The experience of women in high party posts in the Shining Path counsels a cautious assessment of how empowering is the women's access to area commander or party committee secretary positions in Nepal's Maoist movement. However, it should be mentioned that there are armed struggles like Zapatista movement in Mexico, where women are once again highly visible as protagonists and commanders. Here the revolutionary project seems to have as its goal not only the transformation of relations with the state but also gender relations.[14]

As for the Peoples War in Nepal, four years after it was launched, women co-leaders of the movement like Pampa Bushal, are no longer prominent. Presumably she is one of the 'bourgeois intellectual women' denounced by

Prachanda. There are no women at the regional or central committee level. The majority of the women in the movement are illiterate or neo-literate. The exceptions are the students and teachers of Gorkha district who are joining the movement.

Notes

1   For a detailed analysis of the Women in the Shining Path, see Isabel Coral Cordero, 'Women in War: Impact and Responses', in Steve Stern, ed., *Shining and Other Paths: War and Society in Peru 1980–1995*, Duke University Press, Durham, 1998, pp. 345–74. The book as well as the cited article tends to emphasise people's resistance to the Shining Path.

2   See Dr Baburam Bhattrai's article 'Politico-Economic Rationale of Peoples War in Nepal' (1998) available on the website *http://www.maoism.org/misc/nepal*, Maoist Documentation Project. The landholding pattern of Thabang village, one of the 'liberated zone' villages in Rolpa district gives an insight into the relative deprivation of the peasants. Landholding of a third of the households was more than subsistence, a third was barely subsistence and a third was less than subsistence, with one member in active service and 10 per cent who drew pensions from the Nepal, Indian or British armies. See Augusta Molnar, *The Kham Magar Women of Thabang. Status of Women in Nepal*, vol. 2, Pt 2, CEDA, Tribhuvan University, Kathmandu, 1981.

3   According to official statistics 45 per cent of the population is below the poverty belt. However, *Nepal Human Development Report 1998*, Nepal South Asia Centre, Kathmandu, 1998, p. 295 (Study submitted to UNDP, Nepal), estimates it to be more likely 70 per cent. See also Dr Baburam Bhattrai, *Nepal: A Marxist View*, Jhilko Publication Pvt Ltd, Kathmandu, 1990.

4   *Nepal Human Rights Yearbook 1996: The Maoist Peoples War and Human Rights*, Informal Sector Service Centre (INSEC), Kathmandu, 1996, and South Asia Human Rights Documentation Centre, 'Midnight Killings in Rolpa', Human Rights Killing in the Maoist War, 1996.

5   *Nepal Human Rights Yearbook 1997: Criminalization of Politics*, INSEC, Kathmandu, 1997, and 'Red Salute to the Immortal Martyrs of the People's War,' *The Worker*, June 1996.

6   *The Kathmandu Post*, 28 January 2000.

7   David N. Gellner, Joanna Pfaff-Czarnecka and John Whelpton (eds), *Nationalism and Ethnicity in a Hindu Kingdom: The Politics of Culture in Contemporary Nepal*, Harwood Academic Publishers, Amsterdam, 1997, p. 53.

8   *Nepal Human Development Report 1998*, n. 3. 'Beyond Beijing Mid Decade Meet in South Asia: Nepal Monitoring Platform, Pledge and Performance', report presented by Beyond Beijing Committee, Lalitpur, Kathmandu, August 1999.

9   See Shree Khadka, 'Decision Making Role of Magar Women in Bukeni Village of Baglung District'. Ph.D. thesis, Tribhuvan University, Kathmandu, 1997.

10 *The Worker*, February 1999.

11 'Red Flag on the Roof of the World', interview with Comrade Prachanda, general secretary of Communist Party of Nepal (Maoist), *Revolutionary Worker*, 20 February 2000; website *http://www.mcs.net/rwor.org*.

12 'Red Flag on the Roof of the World', interview with Comrade Prachanda, n. 29.

13 Cordero claims that no official documents of the 1980s Shining Path nor Guzman's 'interview of the century' of 1988, contain any reference to the problem of gender. In a private Shining Path event, Guzman is quoted as saying 'We must see that we sidestepped the popular feminine movement, women being the half that holds up the sky: to fight the enemy that is transitorily strong with one arm tied behind one's back is foolish. The struggle for the emancipation of women is part of the liberation of the proletariat – this is the Communist way of understanding the problem – from which derives equality before law and equality in life.' Cordero, 'Women in War', n. 1, pp. 351–52.

14 Mariana Mora, 'Zapatismo: Gender, Power and Social Transformation', in Lorentzen and Turpin, *The Women and War Reader*, n. 1, pp. 164–74.

30

Developing the Anti-Nuclear Movement

Achin Vanaik

We now have a national network of various anti-nuclear groups who have come together to work on common objectives. This is the national Coalition for Nuclear Disarmament and Peace (CNDP) which emerged out of the National Convention in November 2000 in New Delhi. Groups and individuals have come together despite differences over the CTBT issue and over the issue of nuclear power or energy. If we are to progress then it is the view of this writer (and what follows in this text is purely the personal view of the writer put forward as a contribution to what one hopes can become a collective debate within the Indian anti-nuclear movement) that we have to find ways of working together which do not simply respect our differences but also institutionalise ways of discussing our differences so as to move towards overcoming them wherever possible. Where this is not possible we need to think of ways which can creatively advance our common positions. We have not done much of either so far, at least not since the establishment of our common platform of calling for basically three things.

First, we have demanded both a nuclear freeze plus a reversal of the step taken in May 1998 when India crossed the nuclear Rubicon and declared itself to be a nuclear weapons state even if not officially recognised as such by the rest of the world. Second, we have called for much greater transparency, the highest possible safety standards, full accountability of the atomic energy establishment of this country, and of course for proper recompense for radiation victims.

On the second aspect, the differences centre around one fundamental issue – whether we should have nuclear power plants or not. For those (like this writer) who are strongly opposed to the nuclear power programme, the way forward is to follow the examples of a number of countries from Italy to Germany to Sweden to Britain to many more in Europe, where the issue is not whether or not to have nuclear power, but how quickly and in what way are they to be shut down and replaced by the pursuit of other energy and civilian power sources. For countries like Japan, Russia and

Perspectives on Modern South Asia: A Reader in Culture, History, and Representation, First Edition.
Edited by Kamala Visweswaran.
© 2011 Blackwell Publishing Ltd. Published 2011 by Blackwell Publishing Ltd.

the US whose governments don't want to give up nuclear power, indeed want to expand them, the problem is that public opinion is so strongly against this and the economics of building such plants (when the costs of decommissioning are so great) are now seen as so forbidding, that they have great difficulty in going ahead to build new plants. Unless this situation is reversed, it means the unravelling, by default, of the existing power programme because there will be no new plants to replace older ones some of which will be closed down and others extended but obviously not indefinitely.

India, however, is a growing market for nuclear power plants. Incidentally, the five biggest markets for the export of materials–equipment related to nuclear power production are all in Asia. The main exporters are US, Russian, Japanese and European companies which for the most part cannot put up new plants in their own countries but are desperate to sell their stuff to any countries willing to buy what they can offer. Thus the Russians cannot put up any new VVER reactors in their own country but are selling two such full-scale projects to India. The main importers of such materials with ambitious nuclear power programmes/plans are Taiwan, China, South Korea, Indonesia and India. Since it is unlikely that there will be for a long time to come unanimity within the ranks of the Indian peace and disarmament movement on winding up the existing programme, or conversely on welcoming its continuation, is it possible to go beyond the simple unifying perspective of merely demanding the best levels of transparency, safety and accountability?

Nuclear Power Programme

I believe there could be. Would it be possible for all sections, both those opposed to the programme and those who in principle support nuclear power, to agree to a common demand that even before there is any question of setting up any proposed plant there must be the fullest democratic accountability and acceptability to the local residents of the district or area where the plant is supposed to be set up? What this must mean is that government spokespersons

must provide public and full information of its plants, including design, safety factors, operating procedures, output levels, etc. This must be done publicly, i e, the best fora for this are repeated Jansunwais (or public hearings) themselves preceded by dissemination of adequate information. There is no point in having such hearings without proper preparation including the time and freedom for local residents to obtain the help of outside experts if necessary who can properly assess and critique the processes and procedures involved.

The National Campaign for the Peoples Right to Information (NCPRI) through the leadership of Aruna Roy and others in Rajasthan has already shown how effective an instrument in institutionalising grass roots democracy Jansunwais can be. In Kalpakkam efforts are currently being made to have just such a Jansunwai on the issue of a power plant being set up there. Those who are against nuclear power have the opportunity to explain to a public that is going to be most directly affected by that plant or project why it should be opposed just as those who are pro-nuclear power, whether belonging to the government or outside of it, have the opportunity to do the opposite except that in making their case they must address adequately all fundamental concerns arising out of matters of efficiency, safety, transparency, accountability, elucidation of contingency plans in case of emergencies, crises and breakdowns, cost-benefit analyses, etc. What is more, the final decision whether or not to go ahead with the project must lie with the democratic wishes of the people concerned, i e, with a public referendum of the people of that district or area, itself suitably demarcated.

There is also another issue. Many people opposed to nuclear weaponisation have called for the scrapping of the 1962 Atomic Energy Act. This is a shamefully undemocratic act. It shields those who run the Department of Atomic Energy (DAE) in India from even the very minimal and very inadequate degree of public accountability that other government departments are subject to. The DAE is not answerable to parliament in any way nor to the cabinet but only to the PM. Behind this shield, the DAE could go ahead and carry out precisely this nuclear weaponisation-preparation which the anti-nuclear disarmament movement in India must oppose. The call for scrapping this act has been opposed by some sections of the peace movement on the grounds that what we should be demanding is its rectification or replacement since if we are to have a nuclear power programme (though not a programme) then there must be some form of legal regulation. Now that India has a military nuclear weapons programme, it has become even more imperative that we oppose the 1962 Act with its shameful opaqueness and lack of accountability and demand that the civilian and military parts must be separated.

Of course we oppose nuclear weapons and don't want an Act that regulates its operations or officially sanctions secrecy in the name of 'national interest' or 'national security'. We just want to get rid of nuclear weapons and have no such weapons programme. But there is now no justification for allowing the 1962 Act to persist with its inordinate levels of secrecy for the civilian programme. The earlier excuse that such secrecy was justified because of the 'military and security' dimension of the DAE no longer holds. Insofar as the government wants to continue with its civilian power programme there must now be a new Act that replaces the existing Act and provides full accountability and transparency for a civilian programme that the government now clearly and explicitly demarcates from its military programme. The Indian public has a right to know what the structures and institutions are that are concerned with the civilian programme and which are concerned with the military programme. Those who support nuclear power but oppose nuclear weapons should also have every interest in this rough demarcation (there will be dual-use facilities and crossovers which we must watch and oppose) so that they themselves can oppose the latter even as they support the former.

31

Pakistan's Fateful Nuclear Option

Zia Mian

Pakistan has thought and done the unthinkable. With its nuclear weapons tests it has demonstrated to itself, as much as to the world, that it is now a murderous state. It is willing and now able to commit nuclear mass murder. This was not done with universal consent. There were brave voices who spoke the language of right and wrong, and not that of power.

Nuclear Weapons Need Enemies

Despite the moral argument against nuclear weapons, in the states that have built these weapons there has been public support for them. This has not been because all these people woke up one day and wanted nuclear weapons. Public support for them is built by creating a sense of crisis and fear. They are told that there is an 'enemy' and the bomb is the only defence. And that is all. In this atmosphere of absolute conflict, peace is ruled out.

There is no doubt about the overwhelming elite support for nuclear weapons in Pakistan,

and that this is shared by large numbers of ordinary people. The nation-wide celebration of Pakistan's nuclear tests is sufficient to prove this. This level of support, according to opinion polls, has not changed for over a decade. This is remarkable. In one of the most tumultuous periods in Pakistan's history, where military dictatorship gave way to elected government, governments came and went, economic policies changed, the Cold War ended, the Soviet Union collapsed, and the United States imposed sanctions on Pakistan because of its nuclear weapons programme, nuclear weapons have remained beyond question.

There are two reasons behind this massive and enduring support for nuclear weapons. The first is that most people know little if anything about nuclear issues. This is an obvious inference from polling data showing that support for nuclear weapons in Pakistan is constant regardless of educational attainment. From the illiterate to those having only a basic education to those with degrees, about the same proportion of them support these weapons. There is rarely

Perspectives on Modern South Asia: A Reader in Culture, History, and Representation, First Edition.
Edited by Kamala Visweswaran.
© 2011 Blackwell Publishing Ltd. Published 2011 by Blackwell Publishing Ltd.

such unanimity except when based on a shared ignorance. In the absence of information, there is no incentive to change one's mind. There is indeed, no reason to even think about changing one's mind.

That the nuclear debate is starved of information is evident, one only has to look at newspapers, magazines and electronic media. There is never more than assertion that nuclear weapons are vital. This is the second reason for the strong and enduring support for nuclear weapons. For over a decade, Pakistan's people have had heard nothing but repeated public declarations by all of their Presidents, Prime Ministers and military leaders that Pakistan's nuclear weapons were vital for the 'national interest'. One former Chief of Army Staff, General Mirza Aslam Beg, went so far as to say that giving up Pakistan's nuclear capability' would amount to 'nuclear castration'. When things are presented in this way it is evident that many people will conclude nuclear weapons are Pakistan's last and only hope.

It is not just an abstract support for nuclear weapons that has been created. The weapons have been personified. They are now embodied in A.Q. Khan, who led the uranium enrichment project – to make the special nuclear material used in Pakistan's nuclear weapons and is now credited with having carried out the nuclear tests. He has for years been a national public figure, appearing on national television and making speeches at all kinds of public events. This is almost unprecedented, anywhere in the world, for the head of what is meant to be a secret military project.

But nuclear weapons need enemies to make them worthwhile. For decades, India has been projected as an absolute and unremittingly hostile enemy, without scruple, willing to exploit every opportunity. It is the source of everything that goes wrong in Pakistan. An Indian hand is identified behind every untoward event. Any challenge to the status quo is interpreted as an Indian conspiracy against national security. India cannot be talked to or reasoned with, it must be confronted. No one has summed this all up better than General Mirza Aslam Beg. He has declared that Pakistan faces an Indian threat 'emanating from the deeper recesses of the Hindu psyche.'

The final and darkest element in manufacturing a 'national consensus' in support of nuclear weapons is maintaining ignorance. That it is at work can be seen in the deliberate orchestration of hate by sections of the media against individuals and groups who argue against nuclear weapons. Debate that might inform people about alternative ways of thinking is not only discouraged, it is not tolerated.

Nuclear Weapons Are No Defence

Having laid out the immoral nuclear destructiveness that is now available to Pakistan's armed forces, and the ignorance and hate that are required to bring nuclear weapons into being and help keep them, it is time to turn to why Pakistan has nuclear weapons at all. At one level the answer is easy: Pakistan has nuclear weapons because India has nuclear weapons.

This justification for Pakistan's nuclear weapons has taken root in a wider public because it is simple, direct, to the point and has no reason behind it to argue with. It has been put most clearly by General K.M. Arif, former Vice-Chief of the Army Staff. He has argued that Pakistan needs its nuclear weapons because 'to counter a threat you must possess the same capability as the opponent enjoys. We must have a nuclear device against a nuclear device, a missile against a missile, and a plane against a plane, and a tank against a tank.'

What General Arif did not explain is why Pakistan should get nuclear weapons if India has them. A nuclear threat to Pakistan is simply assumed. It is believed that somehow India will use nuclear weapons to threaten Pakistan in peacetime, or in a war. Supporters of nuclear weapons often use this idea of 'nuclear blackmail'. It was used by Pakistan's Prime Minister in justifying the tests, when he said that 'Bowing and submitting to others is not our wont.' Having nuclear weapons, he said, would mean Pakistan would not be 'subservient'.

There is a long history of how 'nuclear blackmail' has been tried. During the Cold War, both the US and the Soviet Union made nuclear threats numerous times, with the United States making around twenty such threats and the Soviet Union making five or six. This suggests that nuclear weapons are no protection against nuclear threats. If a state with nuclear weapons is going to make a threat, it will make it regardless of whether the state being threatened has nuclear weapons of its own.

The facts of the last fifty years also tell another story. Nuclear weapons' states have elected to fight wars on many occasions. They have lost many of them. Britain fought and lost at Suez, even though it had already developed nuclear weapons. The United States suffered significant defeats during the Korean War and the war ended with stalemate. The French lost Algeria, even though they had their nuclear weapons. China's nuclear weapons did not help against Vietnam. The most famous examples are of course the defeat of the United States in Vietnam, and the Soviet Union in Afghanistan despite having enormous numbers of nuclear weapons. In all these cases, a non-nuclear state fought and won against a nuclear-armed state.

The only other argument made for nuclear weapons is that they are supposed to deter attacks by other nuclear weapons and so prevent war between nuclear-armed states. Pakistan's Prime Minister claimed in his speech announcing the nuclear tests that 'It is my opinion that had Japan possessed a nuclear bomb, Hiroshima and Nagasaki would never have been destroyed.' This is nuclear deterrence.

The proof of nuclear deterrence is supposed to be the absence of war between the superpowers during the Cold War. But this cannot be proven. All that can be said is that the absence of war coincided with both sides having nuclear weapons. It is not logical to deduce that nuclear weapons prevented a war that would otherwise have taken place. The absence of war between the United States and the Soviet Union may simply have been due to neither side wanting a war. The experience of total war in World War II was so terrible, more than 20 million Soviets were killed, that this may have been sufficient to prevent a major war. It should also be noted that

the US and USSR fought numerous proxy wars across the third world.

To understand nuclear deterrence one has to start with realising that it is fundamentally an American idea used to justify US nuclear weapons. While many supported it during the Cold War, especially academics and strategic thinkers, it is significant that General George Lee Butler, who actually had command over all of the United States' strategic nuclear weapons has said the world 'survived the Cuban missile crisis no thanks to deterrence, but only by the grace of God.'

The nuclear arsenals of the nuclear weapons states show what happens when a state searches for deterrence. None of them has stopped at a few simply atom bombs. Each nuclear weapons state has built hydrogen bombs – this is why India is said to have tested one on May 11. But having a hydrogen bomb is not enough. The nuclear weapons states have built hundreds if not thousands of them, along with nuclear submarines, specially hardened silos, or mobile missiles.

The nuclear tests by India and Pakistan are only a beginning. The next steps will demand to see nuclear weapons being assembled, tested and then deployed, ready for use. Realising that deterrence does not exist, both sides will try to create it. The consequences of such a move are all too obvious. The history of the superpower arms race is there for all to see. A recent study has estimated the United States spent at least $4 trillion ($4,000 billion) to develop, produce, deploy, operate, support and control the nuclear forces of the United States over the past 50 years. The cost of the nuclear weapons alone is estimated at $375 billion.

This is what the pursuit of deterrence costs. Incidentally, since Pakistan's military spending is now about $3 billion a year, it would take Pakistan a thousand years to pay for such a nuclear deterrent.

Nuclear Weapons Start Nuclear Wars

Pakistan's leaders have found one more use for nuclear weapons. It is as a deterrent against Indian conventional forces. Air Chief

Marshal (retired) Zulfikar Ali Khan has said that Pakistan's nuclear weapons would provide a deterrent against 'the overwhelming conventional military superiority that India has clearly achieved.' Nawaz Sharif reiterated this in his justification of the tests, saying 'These weapons are to deter aggression, be it nuclear or conventional.'

The use of nuclear weapons as a deterrent against conventional attack implies Pakistan is prepared to turn a conventional battle, like those fought by India and Pakistan in 1948, 1965 and 1971 into a nuclear war, a final war. Pakistan's refusal to agree to a no-first strike agreement with India, i.e. neither side will use nuclear weapons first, is suggestive that Pakistan's armed forces are prepared to do just this. What does it mean to even think of using nuclear weapons first in such a situation? It means that Pakistan is prepared to murder countless Indian civilians because of the failure of Pakistani politicians, diplomats and generals to prevent war.

Addressing the details of different nuclear war fighting scenarios may lead to some insight, but several factors will shape all these scenarios and suggest certain inescapable conclusions. According to Lt. General (retired) Mujib ur Rehman Khan, the first and obvious one is that Pakistan's first strike against India will bring the fury of India's atomic power on our heads and it will entail the devastation of Pakistan . . . . The world will pronounce Pakistan's doom.'

The reason, in part, is geography. Pakistan has a lack of 'strategic depth'. Everywhere is too close to India. This basically means that any Pakistani military offensive will only be able to reach at most a thousand kilometres or so into India. But everywhere in Pakistan lies within the reach of Indian military forces. If Pakistan uses nuclear weapons first, its choice of targets will be limited. With a few nuclear weapons it can wreck appalling devastation, but cannot hope to destroy India's ability to fight back. At the same time, by using nuclear weapons against India, it will have invited the complete nuclear destruction of Pakistan.

The second obvious and inescapable conclusion arises from asking when Pakistan would take a decision to use its nuclear weapons. Lt. General (retd.) Mujib ur Rehman Khan has asked 'will Pakistan resort to nuclear means at the fall of Lahore, or when a strategic area is about to be overrun? By the time we are in a position to take such a momentous decision, our present borders will have been pushed inwards towards the interior, putting us that much more at a disadvantage. At the same time, the Indians will have attained the necessary air superiority to have turned the scale of the conventional battle to their advantage. Under such adverse conditions, how do we launch this nuclear strike to stem India's military success?' He concludes there are no definite answers.

This presents a truly dreadful prospect. Under such 'adverse conditions' Pakistan's military leaders may use nuclear weapons because they feel their only alternative is to lose these weapons altogether. One way this could happen is that Indian conventional attacks on Pakistan's military airfields and troops, deliberately or accidentally, might undermine Pakistan's nuclear weapons arsenal. A hypothetical example is if India attacked the Sarghoda airfield, where Pakistan is supposed to keep its Chinese made M-11 missiles, or some place where the F-16s were waiting loaded with a nuclear weapon each. Pakistan's generals might be faced with the prospect of losing their nuclear weapons altogether, or having to use them even though the situation was not absolutely desperate.

Without anyone having planned it, there would be an instance of inadvertent escalation, conventional war would turn nuclear. The consequences would be devastating for India as well as for Pakistan.

It was just such fears that led both the United States and Soviet Union to rely on very large conventional armies facing each other in Europe, even though both had nuclear weapons. The fact is that amid all the talk of nuclear deterrence for much of the Cold War, in Europe where US and Soviet forces directly confronted each other, they relied on giant armies prepared for conventional battles. This is also why, even though it talks about its nuclear weapons deterring conventional attack, Pakistan keeps such a large army.

Even if there is no planned first strike with nuclear weapons that invites an even more terrible reply, and even if there is enough good luck that nuclear weapons are not used inadvertently, there is always the chance of their accidental use. This possibility has worried even former Pakistani Chief of Army Staff, General Beg. He has argued 'Pakistan and India may neither have the resources nor the capability to develop . . . a system for ensuring nuclear safeguards and security.' As a consequence, an attack, he says, could 'escalate to a nuclear level' where 'there can be a real danger of nuclear accident and unauthorised use of nuclear weapons due to the absence of a fail-safe system.' In other words, nuclear weapons could be used accidentally, or by someone who was not supposed to be able to make the decision.

The possibility of using nuclear weapons as a response to a conventional conflict is so immoral and dangerous that it must be rejected. It is clear that any first use of nuclear weapons by Pakistan, whether as a planned first strike, inadvertently or accidentally, would surely invite a nuclear response. The only way to ensure against all these risks is to remove nuclear weapons from Pakistan's military planning. It is only by not having them that there can be certainty that they will not be used. Renouncing nuclear weapons means Pakistan has the double benefit that it cannot use them and that these weapons will not be used against it. It will be neither a nuclear murderer nor a nuclear victim.

The Price of Nuclear Weapons

The cost of a nuclear weapons programme is far greater than simply the death of morality and the corruption of language and politics. The financial costs are great, this is why they are kept secret. In Pakistan even estimating the cost is hard. Part of the problem is that disentangling the money spent on the nuclear weapons programme from that of the money spent on the Pakistan Atomic Energy Commission (PAEC) is practically impossible. That they are tied together is indisputable. As he doled out the credit for the nuclear test, Prime Minister

Nawaz Sharif said 'The entire nation takes justifiable pride in the accomplishments of the Pakistan Atomic Energy Commission, the Dr A.Q. Khan Research Laboratories and all affiliated organisations.' Incidentally, for PAEC, this was illegal. It is bound by its charter to work only on the peaceful uses of nuclear energy.

At a more material level, many of the nuclear scientists and engineers who work on the bomb programme must have received their training by the PAEC, and some may be seconded from it; there are apparently 'seven thousand highly skilled and professional people, including more than two thousand PhDs, M Phils, MSs, MScs, BEs at Kahuta. Similarly, the uranium that is mined and processed at Dera Ghazi Khan is used by both to make fuel for the KANUPP nuclear reactor in Karachi and to make nuclear weapons material at Kahuta. Since the nuclear power plant at Karachi is so dangerous, old, and has produced a fraction of the electricity it was supposed to, it is possible to imagine that it is kept open as no more than a fig-leaf for the nuclear weapons project. In which case a large share of the greater than six billion rupees budget of PAEC over the last two decades, may have directly or indirectly subsidised the nuclear weapons programme.

To these costs must be added the military spending in Pakistan which has driven the nuclear programme. For years this military spending has meant a reduction in development spending. Military spending in the 1996 budget was twice the military budget in 1990. The significance of 1990 is that in that year military spending was equal to the budget allocation for development, i.e. for building schools, hospitals, roads, etc. Since then military spending has increasingly overtaken development spending and now far exceeds it.

The effects of persistently lower-than-necessary development spending are cumulative. Each generation that is deprived of decent healthcare and housing, education and employment, is less able to provide these for the generation that comes after. There is a spiral of underdevelopment. That this is at work in Pakistan is evident from the fact that on the United Nations Development Programme's aggregated measure of the quality of people's lives in different countries, the Human Development Index, Pakistan has slipped from number 120 in 1992 to 128th place in 1995, and in 1999 it had fallen to 138.

Making Nuclear Weapons Destroys People's Health and the Environment

The whole process of creating and maintaining even a nuclear weapons arsenal like Pakistan's exacts a terrible toll on people's health and on the environment. There is increasing evidence from around the world that from the moment uranium is dug out of the ground to the disposal of long lived radioactive waste that is dangerous for tens of thousands of years, the materials that form the essential ingredients for nuclear weapons bring with them the prospects of sickness and death.

The first public evidence of the human and environmental damage done by the nuclear programme has already emerged. It is to be found in Dera Ghazi Khan, the site of Pakistan's first, and for a long time its only, uranium mining and processing operation. Officially part of the Pakistan Atomic Energy Commission (PAEC), this is also where workers mined the uranium that went to Kahuta to make nuclear weapons. In 1996, the 500 or so workers at the plant went on strike, demanding 'payment of compensation to the heirs of the employees [who] died during their duty or became handicap[ped], provision of all necessary safety measures both at the plant and at the site, sacking of the doctor and lady doctor of the PAEC dispensary as due to their incompetence several employees lost their lives.' The government's response was draconian. Newspapers reported that 'Security guards of PAEC and other law enforcing agencies have besieged the colony and all installations. No one is being allowed to enter or come out of the area.'

That the first strike over health and safety issues in part of Pakistan's nuclear complex has broken out at Dera Ghazi Khan is not surprising at all. Uranium is both radioactive and poisonous, handling it in any form is fraught with risk. But, unlike in a laboratory where highly trained and careful scientists who know the risks may handle tiny amounts of such dangerous material with relative safety, the mining and processing of uranium ore is an industrial scale process. Its labour intensive character leads to large numbers of relatively unskilled workers, who know little about the short or long term risks that they are being subject to. The dangers to health are increased substantially in such a setting.

Briefly, the process of turning the tiny amounts of uranium found in some rocks into large amounts of pure uranium that can be used to make fuel for nuclear reactors or for nuclear weapons requires that huge amounts of rock need to be dug out of the earth, pulverised into dust and chemically processed. The uranium ore emits radiation and exposes anyone close to it even before it is taken out of the ground. Digging up the ore releases radioactive gases that were trapped inside the rock, adding to the risk. The ore has then to be crushed and the waste rock removed. The crushing produces a radioactive and poisonous dust that can be breathed in, that settles on clothes, in hair, and on the skin. Because it is so fine, it can be blown in the wind and settle in the surroundings, on grass, leaves, and water, contaminating everything.

Uranium mining, the first stage, leaves behind as waste over 99 per cent of the rock in which the uranium ore was located. This contains most of the radioactivity and many toxic heavy metals as well as the acids and alkalis used to extract the uranium. These can leach into the soil and groundwater. Because the processing is often done away from the site of the mining, the ore has to be transported to the processing plant. This is often done after the ore has been substantially crushed, and some of the waste rock removed, leaving less material that needs to be transported.

If the transport of the ore is done on open trucks, the uranium dust may well be blown around all along the route. Once at the processing plant, there is more crushing and grinding of the rock. But now even though the total amounts of material are smaller than at the mine, the risks of inhaling even small quantities of dust are larger. The impact on the uranium miners and the local environment of such waste is enormous.

The dangers do not end there, they just move to another site. The next step is transforming the uranium into a gaseous form that is suitable for enrichment at the Kahuta facility. This involves the use of highly corrosive and toxic chemicals that react violently with moisture in the air and are fatal if breathed in. Once the uranium has been enriched and can be used to make nuclear weapons, it leaves behind a radioactive, toxic and corrosive waste. This waste comprises almost all of the initial material, and needs to be disposed of safely. It is usually stored as cylinders of gas at the enrichment plant, but these will eventually degrade and lead to an environmental disaster.

There is no information about what has happened at the Kahuta plant with regard to health and safety issues or how the waste is dealt with. The US, which invented many of the processes and technologies used in making nuclear weapons, is still struggling to come to terms with this kind of waste from its nuclear weapons programme. A 1997 report claims the giant steel cylinders containing this waste gas are so radioactive that even the rust that forms and then falls off the outside is treated as 'dangerous waste'. The cylinders, despite being over one-third of an inch thick have corroded, and some leak, and 'every time one leaks, as some have, it releases puffs of toxic gas and uranium that can end up in the groundwater.'

Pakistan also has a new nuclear reactor, located on the banks of the Jhelum river, that uses uranium to produce plutonium, the other material used for making nuclear weapons. It is reported to have started operating. This adds new threats that the nuclear weapons programme poses to the environment. In particular, if this reactor has an accident it could pollute the river with radioactivity and thus poison irrigation and drinking water drawn from it. Further, the process of extracting plutonium produced by the reactor from the spent uranium fuel, known as reprocessing, generates the largest amounts and the most dangerous radioactive waste of a nuclear weapons programme. The US Department of Energy, responsible for making US nuclear weapons, has estimated that reprocessing accounts for 85 per cent of the radioactivity released in the nuclear weapons production process, 71 per cent of the contaminated water and 33 per cent of the contaminated solids. These wastes are so dangerous that they need to be stored safely for at least 1,000 years so that they do not get into the environment.

As long as Pakistan retains its nuclear weapons, it will need to keep at least some of these sites open. If, as seems possible, it starts to increase the size of its nuclear arsenal, more and more sites will become part of the nuclear weapons complex, and more communities exposed to the dangers of radioactive waste. These dangers and any accidents will most certainly be kept secret.

It is only by renouncing nuclear weapons that damage can be stopped. The sooner this is done, the less chance there is of more workers being exposed to radioactivity, and of further damaging the environment. Once this is done, there will be no need to keep these places secret, and the process of assessing the harm that has already been done, and cleaning up the mess can be started.

Index

Perspectives on Modern South Asia: A Reader in Culture, History, and Representation, First Edition.
Edited by Kamala Visweswaran.
© 2011 Blackwell Publishing Ltd. Published 2011 by Blackwell Publishing Ltd.